Ritual

ê RITUAL ê

Perspectives and Dimensions

CATHERINE BELL

New York   Oxford
Oxford University Press
1997

Oxford University Press

Oxford   New York

Athens   Auckland   Bangkok   Bogota   Bombay   Buenos Aires
Calcutta   Cape Town   Dar es Salaam   Delhi   Florence   Hong Kong
Istanbul   Karachi   Kuala Lumpur   Madras   Madrid   Melbourne
Mexico City   Nairobi   Paris   Singapore   Taipei   Tokyo   Toronto   Warsaw

and associated companies in
Berlin   Ibadan

Copyright © 1997 by Catherine Bell

Published by Oxford University Press, Inc.
198 Madison Avenue, New York, New York 10016

Oxford is a registered trademark of Oxford University Press

Library of Congress Cataloging-in-Publication Data
Bell, Catherine M., 1953–
Ritual : perspectives and dimensions / Catherine Bell.
p.   cm.
Includes bibliographical references and index.
ISBN 0-19-511051-X; ISBN 0-19-511052-8 (pbk)
1. Ritual. 2. Religion. I. Title.
BL600.B47   1997
291.3'8—dc20   96-23945

1 3 5 7 9 8 6 4 2
Printed in the United States of America
on acid-free paper

To my mother
and
in memory of
my father

The meaning of ritual is deep indeed.

He who tries to enter it with the kind of perception that
distinguishes hard and white, same and different, will
drown there.

The meaning of ritual is great indeed.

He who tries to enter it with the uncouth and inane
theories of the system-makers will perish there.

The meaning of ritual is lofty indeed.

He who tries to enter with the violent and arrogant ways of
those who despise common customs and consider
themselves to be above other men will meet his
downfall there.

Xunzi (third century B.C.E.)

Preface

While the activities we think of as "ritual" can be found in many periods and places, the formal study of ritual is a relatively recent and localized phenomenon. When made the subject of systematic historical and comparative cultural analysis, ritual has offered new insights into the dynamics of religion, culture, and personhood. At the same time, it has proven to be a particularly complicated phenomenon for scholars to probe—because of the variety of activities that one may consider ritual, the multiplicity of perspectives one may legitimately take in interpreting them, and the way in which defining and interpreting ritual enter into the very construction of scholarship itself.

In contrast to an earlier work, *Ritual Theory, Ritual Practice,* which addressed specific theoretical issues concerning the dichotomy of thought and action in ritual theory, this book is meant to be a more holistic and pragmatic orientation to multiple dimensions of the phenomenon of ritual.[1] It provides a fairly comprehensive depiction of the history of theories about ritual and religion (part I), the spectrum of both ritual and ritual-*like* activities (part II), and the fabric of social and cultural life that forms the context in which people turn to ritual practices—and even to ritual theories (part III). In continuity with the earlier book, however, this study brings a particular perspective to these discussions, namely, the position that "ritual" is not an intrinsic, universal category or feature of human behavior—not yet, anyway. It is a cultural and historical construction that has been heavily used to help differentiate various styles and degrees of religiosity, rationality, and cultural determinism. While ostensibly an attempt to identify a universal, cross-cultural phenomenon, our current concept of ritual is also, and inevitably, a rather particular way of looking at and organizing the world. The import of this particularity is one of the concerns of this book. While sections of part III extend some of the theoretical arguments raised in *Ritual Theory, Ritual Practice,* for the most part, this study is also a broad application of the methodological suggestions raised there.

To anyone interested in ritual in general, it becomes quickly evident that there is no clear and widely shared explanation of what constitutes ritual or how to understand it. There are only various theories, opinions, or customary notions, all of which reflect the time and place in which they are formulated. This complexity is portrayed in the organization of this book. Traditionally, comprehensive surveys of a topic lay out their subject in either of two ways: as a narrative telling of the "story" of the topic or as an analytic "inventory" of the topic's subtopics. This book attempts to take a third course by presenting the fluidity and confusion, as well as the consensus and commonsense, that have shaped so much of the way we have talked about ritual. Therefore, instead of approaching ritual as a clear-cut and timeless object of scrutiny, the following chapters focus on how a variety of definitions and constructed understandings of ritual have emerged and shaped our world. As such, this presentation recognizes that any discussion of ritual is essentially an exercise in reflective historical and comparative analysis.

While each of the major sections of this book plays a role in constructing the overall argument about ritual, they also organize the issues and data autonomously in terms of three distinct frameworks. Part I, Theories: The History of Interpretations, presents a roughly chronological ordering of the most influential approaches to defining and explaining ritual behavior. It begins with theories concerning the origins of religion and then depicts the emergence of various schools that have developed distinctive perspectives for analyzing ritual. While far from exhaustive, this account tries to highlight the significance of ritual to most of the important understandings of religion and culture. This account also suggests that the history of theories contains only limited instances of any progressive development and refinement of the idea of ritual. To a great extent, multiple and even mutually exclusive perspectives on ritual continue to coexist due to fundamental indeterminacies that attend the identification of ritual, on the one hand, and historical changes in the projects of scholarly analysis, on the other. Nonetheless, to provide as much clarity as possible, there are three special sections that present extended "profiles" of specific rituals that have been much studied by the preceding theoretical schools. These profiles give readers the opportunity to compare and contrast how different theoretical approaches have actually interpreted particular rites.

Part II, Rites: The Spectrum of Ritual Activities, opens by exploring those activities that most people consider to be good examples of ritual: birth and death ceremonies, healing and exchange rites, sacrifices and enthronements, and so on. In each case, the analysis attempts to uncover the particular logic and symbolic structures of these familiar genres of ritual practice. However, by shifting attention to various activities that are not ritual but are readily thought to have "ritual-like" qualities—such as etiquette, meditation, and certain sports or theatrical performances—it is possible to uncover some of the fundamental ways of acting that are intrinsic to ritualizing in European and American culture. These examples suggest that larger questions concerning the nature of ritual action may be very dependent upon the context in which certain qualities of action are elaborated or muted.

Part III, Contexts: The Fabric of Ritual Life, explores the broader relationships between ritual activities and social life, specifically addressing why some groups have more ritual than others, how rituals change, and the place of ritual in so-called traditional and modern settings. The vitality of much traditional ritual, experiments in new forms of ritualization, the influence of anthropological writings, and the development of a new paradigm for self-conscious ritualization—all indicate the variety of factors that influence both how we *view* ritual and how we *do* it. In this section, the instabilities of theory and data uncovered in parts I and II are recast in the context of the very emergence of "ritual" as a category for depicting a putatively universal phenomenon. Critiques of the function and operation of such universal categories necessitate a more systematic awareness of the way in which concepts like "ritual" construct a position of generally scholarly and objective analysis in contrast to the activities identified as data and as irredeemably locked within their cultural particularity.

These three frameworks contribute a number of perspectives to an overall analysis of the phenomenon of ritual. Let me highlight this analysis as succinctly as possible. Today we think of "ritual" as a complex sociocultural medium variously constructed of tradition, exigency, and self-expression; it is understood to play a wide variety of roles and to communicate a rich density of overdetermined messages and attitudes. For the most part, ritual is the medium chosen to invoke those ordered relationships that are thought to obtain between human beings in the here-and-now and non-immediate sources of power, authority, and value. Definitions of these relationships in terms of ritual's vocabulary of gesture and word, in contrast to theological speculation or doctrinal formulation, suggest that the fundamental efficacy of ritual activity lies in its ability to have people embody assumptions about their place in a larger order of things.

Despite the consensus surrounding this perspective on ritual, the emergence of the concept of "ritual" as a category for human action is not the result of any single or necessary progress in human development. Nor can the concept imply that all so-called ritual practices can be reduced to a uniform, archetypal, or universal set of acts, attitudes, structures, or functions. The definition, incidence, and significance of so-called ritual practices are matters of particular social situations and organizations of cultural knowledge. These have varied greatly even in European and American history. Critics of what we call ritual are found among the Old Testament prophets, Greek philosophers, Protestant reformers, and many secular participants in the current scene. Promoters of what we mean by ritual are just as varied. While 17th-century Quakers espoused a particularly radical antiritualism, the late-20th-century African-American writer and founder of the festival of Kwanzaa, Maulana Karenga, sees ritual as a primary means for self-transformation and cultural revolution.[2]

Ultimately, this book will argue that talk about ritual may reveal more about the speakers than about the bespoken. In this vein, analysis of the emergence of the concept of ritual and its various applications make clear the way in which the concept has mediated a series of relationships between "us" and some "other"—be they papist idolators, primitive magicians, or the ancient wise ones who have resisted the forces of modernity. The concluding arguments of part III attempt to demonstrate how the emergence and subsequent understandings of the category of ritual have been fundamental to the modernist enterprise of establishing objective, universal knowledge that, as the flip side of its explanative power, nostalgically rues the loss of enchantment. Overall, the organization of the book attempts to introduce the general but serious reader to the basics as well as the complexities of this area of discussion about religion. As part of that project, it includes familiar figures and ideas, and some of both that are not so familiar. I hope that the mix will stimulate fresh inquiry on the practices of religion.

The ancient Chinese sage Xunzi (pronounced Shyun'-dz), quoted in the epigraph, offers three pieces of practical advice for anyone attempting to talk about ritual.[3] In effect, he warns against the temptation to reduce this complex phenomenon to simplistic formulas or strict categories. He also suggests that elaborate theories constructed by means of labyrinthine methodological considerations will only lead one away from reality. Finally, he reminds us that we will never understand ritual if we are apt to look down on what other people do and view their actions from a position of intellectual or observational superiority. While recognizing the self-serving significance of this argument for a major proponent of Confucian teachings, this is still valuable advice that I have tried to take very seriously.

For historical clarity in part I and two chapters in part III, the dates for major theorists are provided in the first substantive discussion of their work but not for those born about 1940 or later. In general, foreign terms follow the spelling adopted in the *Encyclopedia of Religion*, edited by Mircea Eliade (New York: Macmillan, 1987), except for Chinese terms, which are given in the Pinyin system of Romanization. Various material in part III was previously published in *Studia Liturgica* (vol. 23, no. 1 [1993]) and *The Proceedings of the American Benedictine Academy* (Summer 1994), presented at Harvard University Divinity School in November 1995, and forthcoming in *Critical Terms in the Study of Religion*, edited by Mark C. Taylor (University of Chicago).

I want to acknowledge my debt to several diligent assistants: Victoria Waters, who helped edit the manuscript after Teresa Maria Romero and Jada Pogue assisted me in the research. I am also grateful for the assistance of colleagues who read sections of the manuscript, notably Frederick Denny, William Doty, Edmund Gilday, and Ninian Smart. I bear full responsibility, of course, for any errors of fact or interpretation. As usual, the most demanding critic and unflagging supporter has been my husband, Steven M. Gelber.

Santa Clara   C.B.
1997

Contents

❧··❧

PART 1

THEORIES

The History of Interpretation

It might seem logical to begin a book on the subject of ritual with an introduction to the data, namely, examples of rituals, and then proceed to examine the theories that have attempted to explain what rituals are and what they do. In actual fact, however, that apparently logical approach would probably prove to be more confusing for the simple reason that scholarship on ritual, as in many other areas, does not usually proceed so directly from data to theory. Most often, explicit theories or implicit assumptions lead scholars to find data that support or challenge these views. Hence, what counts as data will depend to a great extent on what one already has in mind, the problem that one is trying to solve. Human beings have been involved in ritual activities of some sort since the earliest hunting bands and tribal communities about which we have information. Yet it is only in the late nineteenth century that people began to perceive all such activities under the rubric of "ritual" and identify them as "data" against which to test theories concerning the origins of religion and civilization. In doing so, people were asking new types of questions about history and culture and beginning to look for new forms of evidence. Ultimately, of course, the priority of theory or data is a classic chicken-or-egg issue; we identify something as data when we have theories that require it, and we formulate theories more clearly, subjecting them to challenge or support, when we can elucidate them with data.

For these reasons, it is more instructive to begin an introduction to ritual with a survey of the major theoretical perspectives that have made people approach ritual as something identifiable and worthy of investigation. Although no introduction can be exhaustive, this survey attempts to do several things: first, to provide a fairly complete framework of major methods and figures so that the reader has a mental map that will facilitate further investigation; second, to provide background on the larger issues of religion, society, and culture so that the reader understands why scholars have asked the particular questions they have and why their answers were received the way they were; and third, to demonstrate how creative *and* how inconclusive scholarly investigation can be or, in other words, how attempts to understand our world do not yield simple answers so much as become part of the way we create our world.

This section is organized into three chapters, each addressing a major theoretical perspective. The first theoretical perspective is concerned with the origins and essential nature of ritual and religion; the second is more concerned with the role of ritual in the social organization and dynamics of human societies; the third perspective focuses on ritual as a form of cultural communication that transmits the cognitive categories and dispositions that provide people with important aspects of their sense of reality. All of these perspectives are represented by a variety of theorists, some of whom would no doubt balk at the company they are being asked to keep here. Naturally, the classifications are merely provisional and heuristic; they should not be taken as clear or fixed. Each major theoretical perspective, for example, is also represented by people who have challenged some of its core assumptions or combined them with the assumptions basic to other perspectives. Although some perspectives go further back in history, they are still repre-sented to some extent in current studies of ritual. Hence, while a loose historical thread runs through this section, many more theories are in use today than just those discussed at the very end of this section.

To illustrate as graphically as possible how different theoretical perspectives help shape our understanding of what constitutes data for the study of ritual, each of the three sections includes a "ritual profile," which is the presentation of a ritual that theorists of the preceding schools of thought tended to analyze. These profiles provide a brief illus-tration of how various theories of ritual have been applied. The ancient Babylonian new year ritual known as the Akitu festival is the first ritual presented in this way, followed by the African Mukanda ritual of male initiation, and then two traditional enthronement rites, the Swazi Ncwala rite and the coronation of Queen Elizabeth II of Great Britain.

❦ · ❧

ONE

Myth or Ritual

Questions of Origin and Essence

The study of ritual began with a prolonged and influential debate on the origins of religion that gave rise to several important styles of interpretation — evolutionary, sociological, and psychological — from which new fields of scholarship emerged. The simple question at the heart of this productive controversy was whether religion and culture were originally rooted in myth or in ritual. While the theoretical positions people adopted were more diverse and nuanced than any simple answer to this question would imply, their general emphases were nonetheless clear and decisive. This section will present this debate insofar as it influenced thinking about religion. There are four main lines of thought: several early theorists who raised the issues; the myth and ritual schools, which tended to see ritual as the source of religion and culture; a loose set of phenomenologists of religion who tended to emphasize myth; and, finally, the psychoanalytic approach, which borrowed heavily from all these areas. At various times in the last century, representatives of most of these groups have offered interpretations of the ancient Babylonian new year ritual known as the Akitu festival. Hence, a profile of these competing interpretations provides the opportunity to witness these theories at work.

Early Theories and Theorists

Friedrich Max Müller (1823–1900) pioneered one of the most influential early understandings of mythology in his comparative linguistic studies of the supposed Indo-European roots of Greek mythology.[1] Müller argued that what we know as myths were originally poetic statements about nature, especially the sun, made by the ancient Indo-Europeans, a nomadic people who migrated out in many directions from the central Asian steppe lands about 1500 B.C.E. However, their poetry was subsequently "misunderstood" by later generations of the cultural groups they conquered.

This view was soon challenged by many, notably the folklorist Andrew Lang (1844–1912) and the anthropologist Edward B. Tylor (1832–1917).[2] Tylor argued that myth should not be interpreted as a misunderstanding, but as a deliberate philosophical attempt to explain and understand the world. Although Tylor admitted that the results of mythological attempts at explanation were patently wrong, still myth cannot be dismissed "as mere error and folly." Rather, it should be studied "as an interesting product of the human mind" for insight into what Tylor and others saw as "primitive" ways of reasoning.[3] Tylor invoked an evolutionary view of human social development from childlike "savages" to "civilized man," in the course of which some primitive explanations lingered on as "survivals" in certain modern religious customs.[4] This approach to myth was linked to what Tylor saw as its role in the origin of religion. Religion, he suggested, originated in the experience of seeing the dead in dreams. "Primitive" people explained these experiences through a theory of souls and spirits, in effect, postulating that part of the deceased continued to live in some way after the corruption of the body. They also came to believe that similar spiritual or animistic forces inhabited nonhuman things like animals and plants. Tylor used the word *animism*, from the Greek *anima* (soul), to designate this earliest form of religion.

William Robertson Smith (1846–1894), a gifted linguist and Old Testament scholar, followed Tylor's evolutionary framework but argued for the primacy of ritual, over a notion of souls, in the origins of religion and society. Religion, he believed, did not arise in the explanations of animism but in activities that cemented the bonds of community. In other words, Robertson Smith saw religion as rooted not in speculative myths about the nature of things but in rituals that essentially worshiped divine representations of the social order itself: "religion was made up of a series of acts and observances . . . [it] did not exist for the sake of saving souls but for the preservation and welfare of society."[5]

Robertson Smith's most famous work reconstructed the early Semitic ritual practice of sacrificing and consuming a "totem" animal, an animal held to be a divine ancestor by a particular exogamic lineage group. The term itself comes from the expression "ototeman" in Ojibwa, the language of the Algonquins of Canada, and means "he is a relative of mine."[6] While Tylor's theory of ritual sacrifice implies a type of "gift" model, according to which human beings make offerings to ancestors and spirits in return for blessings, Robertson Smith boldly interpreted the Semitic sacrificial rite as a festive "communion" between humans and gods that has the effect of sacralizing the social unity and solidarity of the group. Hence, for Robertson Smith, ritual is the primary component of religion, and it fundamentally serves the basic social function of creating and maintaining community. He relegated myth to a secondary place, somewhat akin to its place in Müller's theory, by arguing that myth evolved as an explanation of what the rite was about when the original meaning was forgotten or confounded. In almost every case, he argued, "the myth was derived from the ritual, and not the ritual from the myth; for the ritual was fixed and the myth was variable, the ritual was obligatory and faith in the myth was at the discretion of the worshipper."[7]

Robertson Smith's investigations into ritual laid the groundwork for the basic tenets of three powerful schools of interpretation of religion.[8] The first was the "myth and ritual" school associated with Sir James Frazer's famous work, which argued that in order to understand a myth one must first determine the ritual that it accompanied. The second was the sociological approach to religion associated with Émile Durkheim, for whom religion was a social creation that exists, as Robertson Smith had noted, "not for the saving of souls but for the preservation and welfare of society."[9] A third interpretive approach, the psychoanalytical school founded by Sigmund Freud, adopted Robertson Smith's notions of totemism, primal sacrifice, and the social origins of religious authority, guilt, and morality. For the psychoanalysts, Robertson Smith's unequivocal emphasis on the importance of ritual pointed to modes of analysis and interpretation that look beyond what people themselves think about what they do or believe. In this way, Robertson Smith pioneered what has been called an "anti-intellectualist" understanding of human behavior, that is, behavior rooted in irrational impulses and not simply reasoning according to a primitive form of logic.

A student of Robertson Smith, Sir James George Frazer (1854–1941), was also concerned with the experiences and activities in which religion originated. While he was perhaps most interested in underlying beliefs, Frazer's research into ritual customs earned him the accolade of "the most illustrious ancestor in the pedigree of ritual."[10] Frazer began by appropriating Tylor's theory of myth as explanation but gradually came to see myth as a secondary remnant or survival of ritual activity. Hence, for Frazer, ritual is the original source of most of the expressive forms of cultural life.[11] Successive editions of Frazer's famous work, *The Golden Bough*, developed Robertson Smith's notion of the ritual sacrifice of the divine totem into a complex new theory, namely, that the universally diffused pattern underlying all ritual is an enactment of the death and resurrection of a god or divine king who symbolized and secured the fertility of the land and the well-being of the people. For Frazer and his followers, the theme of the ritually dying and reviving god became the basis of all myth and folklore, and Frazer indiscriminately cataloged customs of the "primitives" of his day (from the French peasantry to the more remote Pacific Islanders) that he thought evoked this theme. As a result, the third edition of *The Golden Bough* (1911–15) consisted of twelve volumes. Like Tylor and others before him, Frazer wanted to document the whole "evolution of human thought from savagery to civilisation," as well as the survivals of primitive magic and superstition within the "high religions" of Christianity, Judaism, and Islam.[12]

The Myth and Ritual Schools

Robertson Smith and Frazer were the two inspirational poles for what has been called the "myth and ritual school," an approach to the historical and cultural primacy of ritual that emerged in two interdependent branches: a group of biblical and ancient Near Eastern specialists on the one hand, and a group of Cambridge University classicists on the other.[13] Among the first group, the Old Testament scholar Samuel Henry Hooke (1874–1968) argued the thesis that myth and ritual—the thing said and the thing done—were inseparable in early civilizations. The religions of ancient Egypt,

Babylon, and Canaan were primarily ritual religions, centered on the dramatization of the death and resurrection of the king as a god in whom the well-being of the community rested. Essential to the ritual action was the recited story, which was deemed to have had equal "potency." Over the course of time, however, the actions and the story separated and gave rise to distinct religious and dramatic genres.[14]

Assembling the evidence to support this theory led the myth and ritual school to a number of ambitious analyses of the myths and rites of the Near Eastern cultures of the Nile, Euphrates, and Indus River valleys, including the new year activities of the king in ancient Israel. Hooke and his colleagues reconstructed a set of rites synchronized to the seasonal cycle of planting and harvesting in which the king was first humiliated and then symbolically killed, after which he descended into the underworld. He subsequently arose to reestablish order on earth through formal combat with the forces of chaos. Upon his victory over chaos, the king reclaimed the throne, celebrated a sacred marriage, and pronounced the laws of the land. According to Hooke, the symbolic enactments of these events were accompanied by the recitation of the story as an extended narrative account of creation itself. Although critics challenged the historical accuracy and scope of this interpretive reconstruction, it became a powerful model of sacred kingship that scholars attempted to use in other cultural areas as well.

The Cambridge school of classicists systematically developed this theory by arguing that folklore and literature derive from the ritual activities of ancient sacred kings, not from actual history or the folk imagination, as people had long believed. In particular, Gilbert Murray, Francis M. Cornford, and Arthur B. Cook tried to show how the model of the dying and rising Near Eastern god-king, also seen in the Dionysian fertility rites of ancient Greece, provides the structural models for Greek drama.[15] One of the most influential scholars among the Cambridge classicists was Jane Ellen Harrison, whose major studies, *Prolegomena to the Study of Greek Religion* (1903) and *Themis* (1912), attempted to root the origins of Greek myth, dramatic theater, and even the Olympic games (in a chapter of *Themis* contributed by Cornford) in the ancient rites described by Frazer.[16] Put most simply, Harrison saw ritual as the source of myth; myths arose as spoken and somewhat secondary correlates to the activities performed in the rite. Harrison's evolutionary framework also suggested that the original ritual activities tended to die out, while the accompanying myths continued independently in various forms. She argued that once the myth lost its original relationship to a ritual, it might try to account for its own existence and enhance its intellectual coherence. For example, even though a myth might have arisen to accompany a ritual, if and when the rite died out, the story could attach itself to specific historical figures and events, or it could even be adopted as a pseudoscientific explanation of particular phenomena.

This argument, presented in Harrison's *Themis*, crystallized the basic ideas of the Cambridge school; thereafter, many scholars began to apply them even more broadly. For example, Cornford's *From Religion to Philosophy* (1912) traced several philosophical ideas back to their supposed origins in ritual, Murray's *Euripides and His Age* (1913) applied the notion of ritual origins to the work of that great Greek dramatist, and Cook's *Zeus* (1914) analyzed Greek mythic heroes as "ritual concretizations."[17]

The work of the Cambridge school influenced scholars outside classical studies as well. Harrison's theory reappears, for example, in Jessie Weston's *From Ritual to Romance* (1920), which argued that the romance of the Arthurian Grail legend is nothing other than a "misinterpretation" of the fertility rite of the dying and rising god-king.[18] Weston's book had great influence, in turn, on the poetry of T. S. Eliot, especially *The Wasteland* (1922), as well as the literary studies of Northrop Frye.[19] Other scholars went on to scrutinize fairy tales, nursery rhymes, children's games, folk drama, law, language, and even experimental physics, seeking echoes of an original ritual pattern preserved in them.[20] A. M. Hocart's 1927 study, *Kingship*, found a basic royal initiatory ordeal to be at the root of a variety of historical survivals.[21] In 1937, F. R. R. S. Raglan published a study entitled *The Hero*, in which he argued that most myths and folktales, if they did not specifically originate in ritual, are at least associated with ritual activities and reflected ritual structures and patterns.[22] Raglan's work was one of the most ambitious studies of the myth and ritual school to that date and would be the focus of much later criticism. As with Otto Rank's earlier study, "The Myth of the Birth of the Hero" (1908), the model of the ritually dying and rising god-king was taken as a direct historical influence on the characteristic pattern of the hero in folklore, religion, and literature.[23] Raglan itemized some twenty-two elements that recur with great regularity in portrayals of heroes, arguing that they generally echo the ancient ritual activities of a king who is killed and then returns to life.[24] Throughout the 1930s and 1940s, further research continued to fuel the myth and ritual school's argument for the historical and cultural primacy of this ritual.

Theodore Gaster's (1906–1992) study *Thespis* (1950) converted the dying and reviving god motif into the more embracing thesis of a "seasonal pattern" in all ritual by which it regularly renews and revitalizes the total world order.[25] This seasonal pattern involves "emptying" (*kenosis*) rites of mortification and purgation and the "filling" (*plerosis*) rites of invigoration and jubilation—in other words, rites of death and resurrection. Ancient institutions of kingship in which the king personified the total world order epitomized the sequence and purpose of this ritual pattern. In Gaster's analysis, however, the place of myth shifts significantly. Myth is neither a mere outgrowth of ritual nor simply the spoken correlate of what is being done. Rather, myth is the "expression of a parallel aspect" that in effect translates the very real and specific ritual situation into an idealized and timeless model.[26] Yet like Hooke, Gaster also believed that this mythic aspect of the ritual eventually separates from the specific ritual acts to assume the form of literature, passing through stages of drama, poetry, and liturgical hymns. Although he argued that rite and myth should not be viewed as developing in a historical sequence, Gaster ultimately maintained that the survival of the seasonal pattern within the very structure of different works of literature constitutes nothing less than an argument both for the logical primacy of ritual and for the intrinsic ritual logic underlying all culture.

To substantiate these universal claims for the structure of ritual and culture itself, scholars continued to look everywhere for ritual patterns—in the music of American blues and in the work of Shakespeare, Thomas Mann, D. H. Lawrence, and F. Scott Fitzgerald.[27] As Stanley Hyman argued in 1955, with more admiration than caution, what had begun "as a modest genetic theory for the origin of a few myths thus eventually comes to make rather large claims on the essential forms of the whole culture."[28] Yet there was never a dearth of critics to challenge any of the theories discussed so far. From Müller to Gaster, the premises, methods, and conclusions of the myth and ritual school were frequently probed and disparaged. Frazer's legacy in this area came to be judged particularly harshly, even though its general popularity was not significantly dampened until the early 1960s. By that time, an impressive number of powerful critical analyses had accumulated.[29]

In a particularly important critique, Clyde Kluckhohn pointed out that although *some* myths are clearly related to ritual, it is silly to claim that *all* are. Not only is such a claim impossible to prove but also there is substantial evidence for a variety of relationships between myths and rites, including their complete independence from each other. "The whole question of the primacy of ceremony or mythology," Kluckhohn wrote, "is as meaningless as all questions of 'the hen or the egg' form." Based on his evidence, "neither myth nor ritual can be postulated as 'primary'."[30] In order to improve on the methods used by the myth and ritual school, Kluckhohn called for the testing of their generalities against real data and detailed studies of the actual relationships found between myth and ritual.[31] Joseph Fontenrose's critique, written nearly thirty years later, was more devastating than Kluckhohn's. While calling attention to all the inconsistencies and mistakes in the myth and ritual literature, particularly in the work of Frazer, Fontenrose effectively demonstrated that there are no historical or ethnographic data that can serve as evidence for the reconstructed pattern of the sacrifice in Near Eastern kingship. His critique, which was the culmination of the challenges raised by Kluckhohn and the others, effectively undermined the universalistic tendencies of this earlier generation of scholarship and their concern with origins.[32]

Despite the repudiation of Frazer's legacy, however, ritual has remained important in the study of religion and of society. For example, a focus on ritual has been central to the emergence of social functionalism in anthropology and to those approaches that have pursued the other side of the myth and ritual equation, namely, the historical and cultural primacy of myth. In this latter line of thinking, loosely known as the phenomenological approach, certain Frazerian ideas remain quite influential. Robert Segal, for one, also argues that the enduring value of the myth and ritual school's theoretical work on ritual is significant, even though many of their theories are wrong since they opened up questions concerning the relationship of practice and belief, and religion and science, that have been central to the study of religion in the 20th century.[33]

The Phenomenology of Religions

While the myth and ritual school was primarily rooted in a British intellectual tradition, another line of thinking developed on the continent that became known in German as *Religionswissenschaft*, or the "science of religion," a term first used by Müller to designate a nontheological and nonphilosophical approach to religion, even though he was not sure its time had yet come.[34] This term has also been translated as "phenomenology of religion," which I will use here; "comparative religions";

or, most officially, "history of religions."[35] While this line of thinking has been too informal and divergent to be considered a school as such, it can be identified on the basis of a few central premises and enduring emphases.[36] First, phenomenology of religions aligned itself with Müller's emphases on myth, as opposed to the later championing of ritual by the Cambridge ritualists, and on systematic comparison in understanding religion.

Second, this line of thinking tended to react negatively to what it saw as the reductionism of Tylor, Robertson Smith, and some later sociological or anthropological approaches to religion. For example, phenomenologists rejected Tylor's rationalistic approach to religion as a form of primitive explanation. They developed his notion that myths are a form of understanding, while rejecting his conclusion that such religious explanations, although interesting, are nothing more than subjective delusions and mistaken logical inferences.[37] The early phenomenologist Rudolf Otto (1869–1937), in his *The Idea of the Holy* (1917), explicitly approached religious experience as a real and irreducible phenomenon and urged scholars to explore the components of such experiences of "the holy" as something "wholly other."[38] Otto made several critical assumptions in characterizing this antireductionist phenomenology, such as the a priori existence of the holy (called "the sacred" by others), the universal nature of all religious experience, and its accessibility to a form of study that looked to structural similarities.

In the later development of a third emphasis, phenomenologists repudiated most attempts to determine the historical origins of religion and generally backed off from using an evolutionary framework to explain the differences among religions. Unless one recognized the transhistorical sacred, they argued, a purely historical approach is reductionism: "For the historian of religions the fact that a myth or a ritual is always historically conditioned does not explain away the very existence of such a myth or ritual. In other words, the historicity of a religious experience does not tell us what a religious experience ultimately *is*."[39] The phenomenologist's stress on the ahistorical aspects of religion accompanied the attempt to develop a sophisticated method of comparison by mapping religious phenomena in terms of essentially morphological categories, that is, in terms of what were assumed to be underlying patterns or structures.

Gerardus van der Leeuw (1890–1950) and Raffaele Pettazzoni (1883–1959), each in his own way, attempted to make this approach more systematic by identifying two formal components of religion: the phenomenological dimension, by which they meant the common structural elements underlying all religious experience; and the historical dimension, namely, the actual particular forms that these structures have in reality.[40] Comparative research among the various forms religion has taken in history—that is, the historical dimension—would disclose, they suggested, the phenomenological dimension of religion, namely, the structural commonalities underlying the multiple historical forms of religious experience.[41] At times, van der Leeuw seemed to assume that these common phenomenological structures had some sort of ontological status, that as pure universal forms they actually existed somewhere above and beyond their particular historical forms and, as such, were tantamount to "the sacred" itself. Elsewhere, he and others tended to identify these pure phenomenological forms as cognitive structures of the human mind, that which makes a human being *homo religiosus*. According to this latter view, therefore, "the 'sacred' is an element in the structure of consciousness," not a transcendent divine reality or a stage in the history of human consciousness.[42] While the ritualists of the myth and ritual schools were talking about a single evolutionary-historical pattern that diffused to become the underlying basis for all ritual, myth, and other cultural developments, the phenomenologists were trying to identify a more complex set of ahistorical universals (either the sacred out there somewhere or within the human consciousness) that manifest themselves in multiple historical forms. This search for ahistorical universals enabled the phenomenological argument to abandon the worst excesses of evolutionism but often at the cost of a truly historical framework.

A major effect of the phenomenological approach was to minimize the importance of ritual, although certainly not to dismiss it. Mircea Eliade (1907–1986), by far the most famous spokesperson for the phenomenological study of religion, gave a distinct primacy to religious myths and symbols. While Eliade argued this position on methodological grounds—that myths and symbols provide a clearer and more spontaneous view of the various forms in which humans experience and express the sacred than is afforded by ritual—he was also apt to attribute a greater primordiality to myths and symbols. Ritual is treated as a somewhat secondary reworking of mythic symbols: "A symbol and a rite . . . are on such different levels that the rite can never reveal what the symbol reveals."[43] Thus, in contrast to the myth and ritual school, which saw ritual as relatively stable and myth as more likely to change, phenomenologists have tended to hold the opposite view, seeing far more stability, even eternality, in the structures underlying myth.[44]

Eliade's position on myth embraced Tylor's idea that such primitive forms of reasoning should not be dismissed out of hand but analyzed for what they reveal about human perception and cognition. Eliade also enlarged upon the etiologic dimensions of myth formulated by the myth and ritual school, namely, how myth (often accompanying ritual) tells a sacred story about the actions of the gods and thereby explains how things came to be the way they are.[45] For Eliade,

> Myth narrates a sacred history; it relates an event that took place in primordial Time, the fabled time of the "beginnings." In other words, myth tells how, through the deeds of Supernatural Beings, a reality came into existence, be it the whole of reality, the Cosmos, or only a fragment of reality—an island, a species of plant, a particular kind of human behavior, an institution. Myth, then, is always an account of a "creation"; it related how something was produced, began to be. . . . Because myth relates the *gesta* of Supernatural Beings and the manifestations of their sacred powers, it becomes the exemplary model for all significant human activities."[46]

In this way, Eliade rejected Tylor's conclusion that myth is a misguided explanation and argued instead that myth explains only by reference to cosmic creation and symbols that express the awe and tremendum, as Otto would say, of an encounter with the sacred.

For Eliade, the identification of human acts with the divine models preserved in myth enables people to experience the ontologically real and meaningful, to regenerate cyclical notions of time, and to renew the prosperity and fecundity of the community. Ritual sets up the beginnings of this identification. Rites, he argued, are reenactments of the deeds performed by the gods in the primordial past and preserved in mythological accounts. By performing these deeds again in ritual, the participants identify the historical here and now with the sacred primodial period of the gods before time began. Through the ritual enactment of primordial events, according to Eliade, human beings come to consider themselves truly human, sanctify the world, and render meaningful the activities of their lives.[47] For example, when he looked at Frazer's data on agricultural rites, Eliade emphasized quite different points than Frazer had. For Eliade, the meaning of sacrificial offerings and practices that associate sexuality and fertility (e.g., nude women sowing seeds at night and carnivalesque festivals) lay not in primitive beliefs that the forces of the sacred must be seasonally regenerated but in the fact that these acts specifically repeat the mythical activities that created the cosmos: "A regeneration sacrifice is a ritual 'repetition' of the Creation. . . . *The ritual makes creation over again.*" Through the recitation of the creation myth, the animal being sacrificed is identified with "the body of the primeval being . . . which gave life to the grain by being itself divided ritually."[48] Nonetheless, just like Frazer, Eliade's focus on the relationship of ritual to the cosmogonic myth heavily evoked themes of death and rebirth, degenerative chaos and regenerative order.[49]

In sum, for Eliade, ritual is a reenactment of a cosmogonic event or story recounted in myth. The myth plays a critical role in establishing the system in which any activity has its meaning by ritually identifying the activities of the here and now with those of the gods in the period of creation. Thus, we might conclude that ritual is dependent on the myth, since it is the story that assures people that what they are doing in the ritual is what was done in that primordial age when the gods, heroes, or ancestors ordered the cosmos, created the world, and established divine models for all subsequent meaningful activity: "Thus the gods did; thus men do."[50] Yet Eliade acknowledges that in traditional societies the myth is never separated from the rite: telling the sacred story requires ritual, and intrinsic to the ritual reenactment of the events in the story is the recitation of the myth itself. Hence, in the final analysis, it would seem that Eliade did not think it possible to separate "living" myth from ritual; when such separation exists, myth is no longer myth; it becomes literature or art. At the same time, Eliade's approach also tends to place ritual on a secondary level, reserving a primary place for myth by virtue of its closer relationship to the underlying structures of all religious experience. Perhaps myth, as a matter of beliefs, symbols, and ideas, is deemed a manifestation of the sacred that is inherently closer to the cognitive patterns that define *homo religiosus*, while ritual, as action, is considered a secondary expression of these very beliefs, symbols, and ideas.[51]

The traditional emphases of the phenomenological approach have been simultaneously affirmed and significantly modified in the work of Jonathan Z. Smith (b. 1938). Smith is best known for his critical rereadings of classic studies of religious ritual and practice, where his close examination of historical detail puts the reputed structural (and universal) meaning of the ritual in a new light. Less concerned with how universal patterns underlie specific historical forms of religion, Smith has pointed instead to how historically specific rituals attempt to create broad patterns of order and meaning. This includes an emphasis on the situational as much as the substantive aspects of ritual.[52] Most simply, for Smith, ritual portrays the idealized way that things in this world should be organized, although participants are very aware that real life keeps threatening to collapse into chaos and meaninglessness. Ritual, he suggests, is an opportunity to reflect on the disjuncture between what is and what ought to be; it is a "focusing lens" through which people can attempt to see, or argue for, what is significant in real life.[53]

Through Smith's influence, phenomenology has come to see religion as central to the cognitive need to understand, explain, order, and adapt. This is an intellectualist approach that is very much in keeping with the orientation of most theorists who have pondered myth and ritual, with the possible exception of the social bent represented by Robertson Smith and the emotional bent represented by Otto. Whether it is a matter of so-called primitive peoples or so-called civilized ones, from this perspective, religion is essentially a human project to formulate stable and meaningful dimensions behind the accidental, chaotic, and shifting realities of human existence. Phenomenologists have described this project differently and chosen to locate "the sacred" in very different ways — in mystical confusion, in transhistorical commonalities, in cognitive structures, or in human interpretive endeavors. Yet the results are similar: myths and rituals are seen as attempting to present, model, and instill a coherent and systematic unity within all human experience. From the historical perspective of the myth-and-ritualists, the ritual pattern of seasonal dying and rising revealed a unity of human experience that hearkened back to the earliest stratum of civilization. From the cognitive or intellectualist perspective of the phenomenologists, myth and ritual are the means by which people keep forging some sense of this unity of human experience. For this reason, phenomenologists have stressed that such religious phenomena must be understood "in their own place of reference"; they cannot be reduced to "infantile trauma, glandular accident, or economic, social, or political situations."[54] Ultimately, phenomenologists conclude that the same principle of unification that lies behind the *practice* of religion must also underlie the *study* of religion: "the meaning of religious symbolism as an integrated, coherent unity and the interpretive work [of the historian of religions] as an integration of the various religious phenomena form a single and consistent correlation."[55]

Psychoanalytic Approaches to Ritual

Robertson Smith's researches into the social primacy of ritual suggested the presence of unconscious forces in shaping social behavior. Although he saw the primordial sacrifice and communal sharing of a totemic animal by the whole tribe to be the foremost means for cementing the social bonds of the group, the participants themselves would never have been conscious of this as the main purpose of the rite. Thus, underlying the more immediately obvious and rational reasons for performing a communal meal, Robertson Smith pointed to causes for social behavior about which the group itself knew nothing: "The 'real' purpose and significance of ritual were different at times even from what the actors themselves believed."[56] This insight was soon independently echoed in the work of Sigmund Freud (1856–1939), who developed theories of repression, the unconscious, and psychoanalysis as an interpretive approach to buried levels of meaning.[57] Yet it was Frazer's portrayal of totemism (*Totemism and Exogamy*, 1910) that influenced Freud most directly. Frazer—and Tylor before him—had advanced a theory of religion that relied heavily on psychological rather than social elements by suggesting that "primitive" peoples developed religion to explain and rationalize perplexing psychological experiences having to do with dreams, nature, and the effectiveness of magic.[58]

In a 1907 essay that predated his close reading of Frazer, Freud drew a provocative comparison between the obsessive activities of neurotics and those "religious observances by means of which the faithful give expression to their piety," such as prayers and invocations.[59] For Freud, the neurotic's innumerable round of little ceremonies, all of which must be done just so, as well as the anxiety and guilt that accompany these acts, imply a similarity between the causes of religion and the causes of obsessional neuroses. He suggested that both are rooted in the same psychological mechanisms of repression and displacement—specifically, the repression of sexual impulses in the case of neurosis and egotistical or antisocial impulses in the case of religion.[60] The parallelism led him to the conclusion that one might describe neurosis as individual religiosity and religion as a universal neurosis.[61] With this article, Freud took a step that proved to be fundamental to his subsequent studies of religion and ritual; that is, he moved smoothly from analysis of so-called individual neuroses (obsessive behavior) to analysis of so-called universal social neuroses (such as religion). Assuming a basic identity between individual psychic processes and social processes—"What is now the heritage of the individual was once, long ago, a newly acquired possession, handed on from one generation to another"—Freud began to reconstruct the psychological development of the human race on the basis of his clinical reconstructions of the psychic history of specific patients.[62]

After beginning to read Frazer, Robertson Smith, and other anthropological studies, Freud eagerly attempted to apply his earlier ideas to an analysis of totemism and its taboo against harming the totem animal.[63] In his 1913 study, *Totem and Taboo*, Freud first argued that the similarities between the repression that gives rise to obsessive neuroses and the repression that gives rise to religion are ultimately identical; in both phenomena, the repressed content was incestuous sexual desires. The evidence of this basis for religion could be seen with particular clarity in the ritual activities of primitive religion. Freud then focused on totemism's association with the practice of exogamy, whereby the members of one totem group could not marry or have sexual relations with each other, even though they were not blood relatives. He interpreted this totemic marriage rule as revealing "an unusually high grade of incest dread or incest sensitiveness." Drawing heavily on Frazer's less than reliable data, he also argued that it is one of the two oldest and most important taboos in primitive society, "namely not to kill the totem animal, and to avoid sexual intercourse with totem companions of the other sex." Things so strictly forbidden, Freud suggested with great simplicity, must have been greatly desired. Moreover, after noting how totems are frequently identified as father or ancestor, he concluded that both totemic prohibitions and their basis in underlying desires "agree in content with the crimes of Oedipus," that is, the killing of his father and sexual intercourse with his mother. Having elsewhere identified the "Oedipal complex" as a stage in adolescent psychological development when a young boy must overcome desire for his mother and murderous envy and fear of his father, Freud went on to argue that the totemic system itself results from the same conditions that give rise to the Oedipus complex.[64]

In the conclusion of his study, Freud combined Robertson Smith's depiction of a primal sacrificial meal, in which the totemic animal was slaughtered and eaten by its own clan, with Charles Darwin's notion of the primal horde, in which "there is only a violent, jealous father who keeps all the females for himself and drives away the growing sons."[65] Using these ideas, Freud developed a compelling scenario of the early history of the human race: "One day the expelled brothers joined forces, slew and ate the father, and thus put an end to the father horde. . . . The totemic feast, which is perhaps mankind's first celebration, would be the repetition and com-memoration of this memorable, criminal act with which so many things began, social organization, moral restrictions and religion."[66]

Freud theorized that the brothers, consumed by guilt, then attempted to undo their crime by renouncing the women for whom they had killed the father and pro-hibiting the killing of the totem, which was considered a father substitute. Hence, this primordial patricide resulted in the totemic cult with its taboos against killing the sacralized totem and against incest, though the latter taboo is extended to all sexual relations with nonkin women from the same totemic group. Although the totemic cult hides the reality of its own origins in desire and murder, it still promotes the repressed longings, ambivalence, and guilt of the original crime throughout its sub-sequent development into increasingly more complex forms of religion, forms that include the deification of the murdered father and a sacrificial rite of communion with him.

It became clear to Freud, therefore, that taboos are inseparable from ritual prac-tices since ritual is the acting out of the obsessional neurotic's mechanism of repres-sion. In other words, the taboo necessitates the ritual: "We cannot get away from the impression that patients are making, in an asocial manner, the same attempts at a solution of their conflicts and an appeasement of their urgent desires which, when carried out in a manner acceptable to a large number of persons, are called poetry, religion and philosophy."[67] This last statement summarizes the Freudian interpreta-tion of ritual: it is an obsessive mechanism that attempts to appease repressed and tabooed desires by trying to solve the internal psychic conflicts that these desires cause.

While Freud used religious ritual to help complete his psychological theory of "the whole mental content of human life," Theodor Reik (1888–1969) more narrowly applied Freud's early psychoanalytic principles to various forms of ritual. In a reveal-ing discussion, Reik suggested the appropriateness for psychoanalysis of a primary focus on the action of ritual, instead of myth, in the same way that Robertson Smith accorded primacy to ritual over myth. Reik was aware of the significance of the in-formation that could be gleaned from people's activities quite apart from their own verbal (mythic) account of why they do those activities. Yet he did not assume, as Robertson Smith did before him, that ritual is actually older than myth. On the con-trary, he appears to have believed that myth predates ritual and remains basic to any understanding of the first psychological conflicts in primitive societies. Indeed, myth, "in its original state, preserves in a far less disguised form the memory of those events which led to the institution of religion."[68] Yet for Reik and the psychoanalytic ap-proach, analysis of religious rituals paves the way for understanding myth, dogma, and cult, "just as an intensive study of the ceremonials of obsessional patients invariably leads us to the larger structures of their dreams, obsessional ideas, conscientious scruples and compulsive acts."[69] Methodologically, psychoanalytic ethnographers might begin with the ritual, but they must work backward, even past the etiologic myth, to uncover what is thought to be the "real" story of desire and repression, fear, and projection that is at the root. Unconscious motives are the profoundest and most explanative; the unconscious myth is the true one.[70] Explanation to uncover the true myth will uncover the meaning of the ritual in what Freud called the "return of the repressed."[71]

A few theorists have tried to pull a more positive interpretation of ritual from Freud's writings. Building on Freud's allusions to the therapeutic value of ritual, they tend to emphasize how ritual and religion are the means for a healthy accommodation of the repression of desire demanded by all culture and civilization, rather than the means used to create and then police this repression. Bruno Bettelheim (1903-1990), for example, argued that initiation rituals are an effective means to integrate asocial instinctual tendencies and adjust to prescribed social roles. He broke with Freud's view that Oedipal conflict and castration anxiety are the source and underlying logic of male initiation rituals, that such rites "result from the fathers' jealousy of his sons, and their purpose is to create sexual (castration) anxiety and to make secure the incest taboo." Bettelheim argued, instead, that these rites attempt to resolve, not instill, the ambivalence described in another Freudian psychoanalytic insight, envy of the sexual organs and functions of the other sex, especially male awe of female reproductive power: "I hope to show how likely it is that certain initiation rites originate in the adolescent's attempts to master his envy of the other sex, or to adjust to the social role prescribed for his sex and give up pregenital, childish pleasures."[72] Similarly, Volney Gay has also argued that Freud's theory of religious ritual can be interpreted in such a way that "ritual behavior is a product of the non pathological, often beneficial, mechanism of *suppression*" — not repression. As such, "rituals might, to the degree that they aid the ego's attempt to suppress disruptive or dangerous id impulses, further the cause of adaptation" or healthy maturation.[73]

Psychoanalysis and myth and ritual theory greatly influenced each other. While Harrison's argument in *Themis* was essentially an expansion of Frazer's work, it also enlisted the new psychological terminology concerning emotion and desire.[74] As a psychoanalyst, Rank's *The Myth of the Birth of the Hero* reduced various hero myths to several key episodes in which the hero enacts an Oedipal scenario. In Raglan's study *The Hero* (1936), the ritual pattern of the dying and reviving god is linked to an ancient regicide that echoes the murder of the father in Freud's *Totem and Taboo*.[75] Interpreters of religion from Geza Roheim to Georg Bataille have developed the use of psychoanalytic readings of themes drawn from the myth and ritual school, while the grand ambitions of Robertson Smith, Frazer, and Freud to determine the ultimate origins and universal meaning of religion and human culture itself still echo in the work of such recent mavericks as René Girard.[76]

René Girard (b. 1923) echoes these three early theoreticians in a series of studies depicting ritual, religion, society, and culture as all emerging from a foundation in primal violence.[77] He describes a process in which desire, channeled through the ritual of an original murder, is ultimately enshrined in every social institution, including language.[78] His notion of primal desire is not strictly Freudian, since he characterizes it as an asexual, "mimetic" desire to imitate an "other" and thereby create simultaneously both a model *and* a rival, which leads to indiscriminate violence that threatens all members of society—not desire for a mother or father that threatens to tear apart the family. To curb the destructiveness of asexual desire, Girard argues, and even repress consciousness of both the violence and desire, a human victim is seized as a scapegoat and ritually sacrificed. This ritual sacrifice is the means by which the community deflects or transfers its own desire and violence on to another, someone who has been made into an outsider, an "other."

For Girard, this act of scapegoating lies not only at the beginning of human history but also at the beginning of a sociocultural process that continually repeats and renews both the violence and the repression that renders the violence deceptively invisible: "Violence, in every cultural order, is always the true *subject* of every ritual or institutional structure."[79] As the sacrifice of a scapegoat, ritual lies at the heart of all social activity. As for Freud, this ritual process is the invention of society. In an interesting permutation of the traditional totemism argument, Girard argues that the group becomes conscious of itself as a group in relationship to the sacrificed totem victim not by means of identification with it but by contrast to it as "other." The danger that looms when an "other" has been identified and characterized with projected desire and violence gives rise to the ritualized killing of sacrifice. The solidarity of the group is ultimately the result of this ritualization, understood in Freudian terms as the repression of original impulses of desire and violence. In addition to Freud, there are Frazerian echoes of the dying and reviving god in Girard's description of the killing of the victim and its eventual deification when resurrected as a god, and even Eliadean themes of the ritual repetition of primal myths are pulled into Girard's larger theory.

The writings of Joseph Campbell (1904–1987), which became quite popular in the 1960s and again in the late 1980s, have offered another curious amalgamation of the myth and ritual school (especially Raglan), psychoanalysis (via the work of Carl Jung), and comparative mythological studies (primarily Eliade). Campbell's synthetic approach is obvious in the four functions he outlined for both myth and ritual: a metaphysical or mystical function that induces a sense of awe and reverence in human beings; a cosmological function that provides a coherent image of the cosmos; a sociological function that integrates and maintains individuals within a social community; and a psychological function that guides the individual's internal development.[80] Campbell is also known for his theory of a universal "monomyth," a type of Ur-myth underlying all myths and many other cultural developments, which is composed of basic stages like separation from the world, penetration to a source of great power, and then a life-enhancing return. This monomyth, he argued, is most readily perceived in the myth of the hero, which echoes the theme of the dying and rising god. Campbell's claims for the universality and modern relevance of the monomyth—that it is found everywhere and is the key to unlocking everything—captures something of the vision of ritual elaborated by both the early phenomenologists and the myth and ritual schools.[81] In the guise of Campbell's best known works—*Primitive Mythology, The Hero with a Thousand Faces, Myths to Live By, The Mythic Image,* and *The Power of Myth*—the theories of these schools continue not only to influence people's interpretations of the world of religion but also to shape that world.[82]

Profile: Interpreting the Akitu Festival

The Akitu or new year festival of ancient Mesopotamia and Babylon has been extensively interpreted by representatives of the two main theoretical perspectives examined this far, the myth and ritual schools and the phenomenologists. Indeed, this
festival, about which we have very little solid data, may be one of the most frequently
analyzed rituals in all scholarship, although almost exclusively by scholars from these
two camps.[83] As we shall see, other theoretical perspectives focus on rather different
types of rituals, those more appropriate to their particular concerns and theses. Hence,
the Akitu is a useful example of the way in which different theoretical orientations
ally themselves with different sets of data. It is also a useful example of how theorists
have wielded the preceding ideas in actually dealing with a specific ritual.

Little is known about the Babylonian Akitu, simply that it celebrated the agricultural cycle of sowing and harvesting the grain and that during the Ur III era (2100–
1900 B.C.E.) it involved a procession to an "Akitu house" built along a channel outside the city. Even less is known about an older Mesopotamian form of the festival to
which it is related. In its later Babylonian form (about 1000 B.C.E.), the Akitu was
nationally celebrated during the first twelve days of the first month of the year. It seems
to have involved the king, who at one point was slapped and humiliated, as well as
the god Marduk, the patron deity of Babylon, whose heroic role in the creation
of the cosmos is told in the *Enuma Elish*, an epic mythological poem recited during
the festival that has come down to us today nearly intact.

Frazer interpreted the Babylonian Akitu as evidence for his theory of the annual
sacrificial death and revivification of a divine king. He first focused on part of a later
version of the rite, known as the Sakaia festival, from the period when Babylon was
under Persian control, which he considered to be roughly identical to the Akitu. Using
a few extant descriptions of festival revelry, in which slaves and masters changed roles
and a common criminal was temporarily put on the throne, Frazer reconstructed a
scenario in which the substitute or mock king was first richly feted and indulged,
only to be stripped, beaten, and killed some days later. However, the evidence for
this interpretation of the meager details available to scholars has been seriously challenged on more than one occasion.[84] When he turned to Babylonian accounts of
the Akitu, Frazer interpreted the slapping and humiliation of the king before the image
of the god in the temple as a historical survival and evidence that once the king had
actually been put to death and a successor installed. Aside from the general weakness of Frazer's claim that the king was once killed, other evidence suggests that during
his humiliation the king was not considered divine, as Frazer's theory required.[85]

Gaster interpreted the twelve-day Akitu festival as displaying the full "seasonal
pattern" that was the centerpiece of his general theory of ritual.[86] Beginning on a
specific date of the new season, he argued, an initial series of rites of mortification
and purification expressed "the state of suspended animation" besetting the world
order at the expiration of the old season. This was a time of chaos in which the normal order of society was reversed, temporarily giving slaves authority over their masters and the throne itself to a substitute king. Hence, for Gaster, the Akitu was, in
part, an exercise in creative, chaotic reversals. However, another series of purification rituals, which used water and fire as well as human or animal scapegoats, was

performed to remove all evil influences. In this context, Gaster saw the slapping of the king as formal abasement and atonement for sin, followed by more positive rites of new life, including an orchestrated combat between life and death and other mimetic rites to promote fecundity. He pointed out that this mock combat reenacted the battle in which the god Marduk defeats the monster Tiamat, as narrated in the *Enuma Elish*. Various ceremonial races that seem to have been part of the festival may also reflect this "battle" symbolism. This stage of the ritual-seasonal pattern culminated, in Gaster's general theory and in his specific interpretation of the Akitu, with a "sacred marriage" in which the king as the bridegroom took the role of Marduk in marrying Sarpanitum, as described in the *Enuma Elish*. The climax of the festival as a whole, he argued, was a joyous celebration of life expressed in the formal rein-statement of the king and the descent of the gods to join in a great banquet or "feast of communion." Not only did the gods descend to the human world but also the dead returned in an ascent from the underworld. For Gaster, the festival involved an explicit pantomime of the myth in which the god Marduk sinks into the netherworld, is mourned by the people, but subsequently returns to earth to ensure its fertility and well-being. Yet the "durative" or immutable meaning of the Akitu, as Gaster put it, was not in its particular details but rather in its enactment of the passion and resur-rection of the god, most clearly seen in the rite's performative narration of the *Enuma Elish*.[87] Thus, Gaster's interpretation, like so many others from the myth and ritual school, emphasized how the historical details of the rite expressed an enduring, ahistorical structure or pattern—the one he had formulated.[88]

For Eliade, the Akitu festival served as a conclusive example of how a creation myth enacted in ritual effectively repeats the cosmogonic passage from chaos to cos-mos and thereby regenerates time and renews the creation of all things. Using the same textual sources as the others, Eliade stated that the *Enuma Elish* was recited several times during the festival and made all the ceremonial events into reactualiza-tions of the original cosmic events depicted in the epic, namely, the combat between Marduk and the monster Tiamat, Marduk's creation of the cosmos from the body of Tiamat, and the creation of humankind from the blood of the demon Kingu. Like Gaster, Eliade claimed to find evidence that the events of the mythic epic were spe-cifically mimed by actors. When the Babylonians repeated the mythical event in its ritual form, he suggested, "the combat, the victory, and the Creation took place *at that very moment*."[89] From this perspective, the intention behind the ritual enact-ment of the creation myth was not just performance to express worship, entertain, commemorate, or display political power; rather, the performance was instrumental in making the original creation symbolically happen again. The restoration of pri-mordial chaos and the repetition of the cosmogonic process effectively abolished past time and afforded a new, regenerative beginning. Eliade's interpretation of specific features, such as the humiliation of the king or the sacred marriage, are all subordi-nated to this main thesis. Hence, the slapping of the king becomes just another ex-pression of the primordial chaos of the period before creation, while the marriage, or *hierogamy*, is seen as a concrete realization of the rebirth of the cosmos.[90]

For yet another perspective on this still elusive festival, we turn to the work of Jonathan Z. Smith. True to his deemphasis of underlying universal structures in favor of close scrutiny of the historical details of particular situations, Smith's read-ing of the Akitu festival has focused on the "incongruity" of the rite.[91] In addressing the humiliation of the king, Smith explicitly rejects those interpretations that see it as evidence of a dying-rising motif, as a symbolic reversion into chaos, or as a purifying expiation of sin (i.e., the scapegoat pattern). Instead, he calls attention to the neglected "negative confession" made by the king in the course of the ritual, in which the king recites a litany of crimes against Babylon that he did *not* commit: "I did [not] sin, lord of the countries. I was not neglectful (of the requirements) of your godship. [I did not] destroy Babylon. I did not command its overthrow. . . . I watched out for Babylon. I did not smash its walls." Such actions, Smith points out, would not have been those of a native king but of the foreign kings who had conquered Babylon. The heart of Smith's argument is his contention that the ritual texts that describe the rite were written much later than scholars had assumed; scholars have taken these texts to be late copies of earlier ones faithfully depicting the early form of the ritual (from approximately the first millennium B.C.E.). For Smith, however, these late texts are not copies at all; they were written late and they describe the *late* form of the rite during a period when Babylon was under foreign domination. Although there clearly was an ancient Akitu festival constantly reinterpreted by subsequent generations, for Smith, the rite that scholars have been interpreting so cosmically was *not* ancient; he dates it from the 8th century through the 2d B.C.E., that is, from the first Assyrian conquerors through the Seleucid conquerors. The Akitu ritual preserved in these texts reflects a growing sense of apocalyptic crisis. As such, it was not a ritual repetition of ahistorical cosmogonic patterns, but a "ritual for the rectification of a foreign king"—that is, a ritual to try to make sense of the presence of a foreign king on the throne of Babylon. In this context, the slapping of the king at two distinct points in the rite suggests a different message, a very political one: "if the king does not comport himself as a proper, native Babylonian king (first slapping), the gods will be angry and 'the enemy will rise up and bring about his downfall' (second slapping)."[92]

Smith also challenges Eliade's assumptions concerning the supposed myth behind this ritual. Arguing that certain scholars have already demonstrated that the Akitu festival was not a reenactment of the creation myth, Smith points out that the *Enuma Elish* is not one specific myth or text.[93] The term "enuma elis" simply means some creation story, not a particular one. Based on the sources, only one late text connects the Akitu with any creation myth. Further, if the myth used then was a relative of the reconstructed *Enuma Elish* familiar to us today, it was not at all typical of Babylonian cosmology. Rather it was an "aberrant" composite, born of political crisis, which stressed the responsibilities of the king to the god Marduk, his city, and his temple.[94]

Hence, Smith's reinterpretation of the Akitu festival, a good example of his general theory of ritual, casts it as a way of dealing with the incongruities between people's ideals (native kingship that rules in cosmic harmony with the god) and their historical realities (foreign rulers on the throne and cosmic chaos portending). Moreover, the Akitu ritual known to us today is a particular reworking of older rites: on the one hand, it tried to force the foreign ruler into the role of a proper king; on the other hand, it also tried to rectify the historical anomaly of a foreign ruler by reintegrating the whole situation into some version of the ancient Babylonian cosmos.

While Freud never attempted an interpretation of the Akitu, it is not too difficult to imagine the details on which a generally Freudian interpretation might focus or the themes it might develop. First, giving a great deal of priority to the myth, a

Freudian would see in the *Enuma Elish* the story of how the god Marduk, in Oedipal fear of an assault by his ancestral father, was chosen by the other gods to battle and kill their ancient parents, Apsu and Tiamat, from whose slain bodies, Marduk fashioned the city of Babylon over which he proclaimed himself king. Taking the Akitu rites as historical and psychic evidence of this ancient crime, a Freudian interpretation would focus on how these festival activities appear both to replicate the crime and to attempt to atone for it at the same time. The sacrificed king might then be identified with both the victims and the agent of the crime, namely, the parental pair Apsu-Tiamat and their son Marduk. Hence, while the threatening father-god is vanquished in the son-king's ritual combat, the father is also contained or replicated in the son himself, who, as scapegoat for the community, must die for them in atonement for the original crime. However, he also rises again purified to wed and ensure the community's well-being. The repressed Oedipal desires and murderous deed are projected into the peculiar intensity of devotion to and identification with the city of Babylon that appears to have characterized the self-understanding of its ancient inhabitants. While this interpretation is a purely fanciful exercise, it is not unlike many accounts in popular publications that use myth and ritual or phenomenological themes to demonstrate enduring psychohistorical patterns that unify the ostensible diversity of human experience.

With just this selection of different readings of the Akitu in hand, it is certainly possible to conclude that the number of theories that can be generated to explain a single ritual is in inverse proportion to the number of ascertainable facts about the ritual. Less cynically, it is just as clear that each approach contributes fresh insights while also challenging theorists to find more reliable data and to reflect more critically on the dynamics of interpretation itself. Indeed, analysis of ancient rites such as the Akitu, which has been central to the project of exploring the "origins" of religious and cultural life, has led to specific reforms in the study of ritual. On the one hand, these analyses help demonstrate that attempts to understand ritual by focusing on its supposed "origins" can be highly misleading; on the other, they also suggest that a focus on underlying universal patterns common to cultures across space and time is likely to come undone by the details of history. Certainly, the history of interpretations of the Akitu festival demonstrates that definitions of ritual are also historical creations, and such historically determined definitions may or may not adequately describe what the annual festivities of ancient Mesopotamia and Babylon were all about.

Conclusion

Many of the earliest theories about ritual are primarily interesting to us today for what they reveal about the history of our thinking concerning religion and culture, primitive and modern societies, history, and universal structures. Much of the study of ritual recounted in this chapter was caught up in the quest to find both the historical origins and the ahistorical or eternal essence of religion. Note that for some theorists "primitive" did not apply to tribal peoples like the Australian aborigines but only to those groups regarded as "the fountainhead of culture," such as the Egyptians and

Mesopotamians.[95] Nonetheless, the study of ritual also pushed beyond these distinctions and helped construct a portrait of the so-called primitive psyche in terms of how it differed from modern ways of thinking and still survived in the very depths of modern consciousness. For the myth and ritualists, a single ritual pattern became the key to unlocking the meaning of a wide spectrum of ancient and modern cultural activities and artifacts. For phenomenologists, ritual patterns of thinking and acting were the only way to experience meaning in the face of the emptiness of history and the contradictions of human experience. Yet in all these theories, ritual is not a matter of clear-cut data to be recovered and analyzed. The idea of ritual is itself a construction, that is, a category or tool of analysis built up from a sampling of ethnographic descriptions and the elevation of many untested assumptions; it has been pressed into service in an attempt to explain the roots of religion in human behavior in ways that are meaningful to Europeans and Americans of this century.

Quite early in the study of religion the perspicacious scholar Andrew Lang wryly noted the tendency of scholars to find what they were looking for: "The theorist who believes in ancestor-worship as the key of all the creeds will see in Jehovah a developed ancestral ghost. . . . The exclusive admirer of the hypothesis of Totemism will find evidence for his belief in worship of the golden calf and the bulls. The partisan of nature-worship will insist on Jehovah's connection with storm, thunder, and the fire of Sinai."[96] Lang's concern is still a real one. We focus on explaining those things that constitute a problem of some sort *for us*. Hence, we are highly motivated to use our own assumptions and experiences to explain that problem in such a way as to make our world more coherent, ordered, and meaningful. The study of ritual arose in an age of unbounded confidence in its ability to explain everything fully and scientifically, and the construction of ritual as a category is part of this worldview. Nonetheless, as a constructed category, ritual is a rather liberal and enlightened one. It enabled these theorists to compare the activities of their own neighbors with those of the most remote and "primitive" societies—and find them to have fundamental similarities. Simultaneously, it was an age that was concerned to elaborate the depth of historical-cultural differences amid the persistence of striking continuities. These scholars wrestled to include both within a comprehensive intellectual system.

The views of the myth and ritual school, as well as their underlying model of primitive society, have remained popular long after the accumulation of a great deal of discrediting evidence.[97] Herbert Weisinger has suggested that the school represented by Frazer has been so popular because it created one of the great "myths" of the modern age! He argues that this myth, which is similar to the "myths" created by the other most influential thinkers of the 19th and 20th century—Darwin, Marx, and Freud—has significantly shaped the modern mind. In each case, the patterns that Darwin saw in nature, that Marx saw in history, and that Freud saw in the psychology of the individual are the same pattern of birth, struggle, defeat, and resurrection that Frazer projected as central to the religious lives of peoples everywhere since the beginning of time.[98]

A myth—like a ritual—simultaneously imposes an order, accounts for the origin and nature of that order, and shapes people's dispositions to experience that order in the world around them. The myths put forward by both the Frazerian ritualists and the myth-centered phenomenologists suggest that there is a coherent and meaningful unity to the diversity of religions, cultures, and histories that has become so apparent in the last two centuries. These myths suggest that all human beings share the powerful socialization imposed by the sacred, or by the seasons, or by the murder and resurrection of a divine king. Yet just as these mythic accounts of a common experience and universal logic appear to prove the unity within human diversity, they also attempt to delineate the broad outlines of what is meaningful human experience in general. In modern life, it is suggested, we may be removed from the more overt and primitive forms of these patterns and rhythms, but any such form of "estrangement" also testifies to the power of a potential return to meaning. This is the heart of the perennial philosophy of universal myth and ritual patterns that continues to speak to the imagination of new generations.

Whether these theories have been abandoned or still preside as the hoary ancestors of more current theories, their emphasis on ritual has a very positive legacy. While the study of religion as a sociocultural phenomenon has emerged only gradually from among long-entrenched and barely conscious theological assumptions, the focus on ritual has helped to elaborate theoretical models that could examine the dynamics of religion apart from questions concerning the truth or falsity of doctrinal beliefs.[99] First of all, ritual activity is tangible evidence that there is more to religion than a simple assent to belief; there are practices, institutions, changing customs, and explanative systems. R. R. Marrett, a contemporary of Frazer, concluded that "savage religion is something not so much thought out as danced out."[100] While debates developed over which was most primordial and essential to religion—conceptual beliefs, emotive experiences, social ceremonies, and so on—the appreciation of ritual formulated in these debates forced all theorists to account for the social dimensions of religion in some way. The evidence of ritual practices also pushed them to formulate a basis for comparison among religious cultures both modern and tribal that posited common structures beyond the obvious differences of basic beliefs. Hence, it is legitimate to credit these early studies of ritual with the articulation of basic methodologies still in use today: comparative studies, phenomenology, social functionalism, and cultural symbolism. The next generation of theoretical studies of ritual, presented in the following section, would continue to assert the sociocultural primacy of ritual activity but in the context of new data and arguments.

❧ · ❦

Ritual and Society

Questions of Social Function and Structure

The early work of Tylor and Robertson Smith, among others, while engaged in answering questions concerning the origin of religion, also bore the seeds of new questions. As formulated by those scholars who followed them, these questions were concerned less with the historical or psychological origins of ritual than with its role and purpose in society — in other words, ritual's social function. The theories grouped in this section are representative of this "functionalist" approach: they are all concerned with what ritual accomplishes as a social phenomenon, specifically, how it affects the organization and workings of the social group. This newly formulated issue did not lead theorists to ignore the insights and contributions of earlier scholars, or even to abandon the search for the most primitive forms of religion, but it did enable them to challenge the limits inherent in those earlier theories.

While functionalism as a style of scholarship did not fully materialize until the works of Bronislaw Malinowski and A. R. Radcliffe-Brown, a number of early scholars contributed to the formulation of this perspective by emphasizing the importance of ethnographic fieldwork, the pragmatic social uses of religion, and the structural links between religion and various forms of political and social organization. Among the most important of these precursors was N. D. Fustel de Coulanges (1830–1889). While Fustel argued the importance of studying a culture's earliest beliefs in order to understand its institutions, his theory of the role of the ancestor cult in maintaining the joint family lineage as the central social institution in the ancient cities of Greece and Rome made new sense of how a vast spectrum of classical rites and customs functioned socially, from marriage ceremonies to property and inheritance practices.[1] Fustel's work, with that of Robertson Smith, influenced the great French sociologist, Émile Durkheim.[2]

Early Theories of Social Solidarity

With his *Elementary Forms of the Religious Life*, first published in French in 1912, Émile Durkheim (1858–1917) effectively established religion as a social phenomenon, what in other writings he called a "social fact." He defined religion in such a way as to give priority to its social rather than its psychological dimensions: "Religion contains in itself from the very beginning, even in an indistinct state, all the elements which . . . have given rise to the various manifestations of collective life."[3] Indeed, what went on in a person's individual psyche is not the starting point of religion, Durkheim argued, since religion is first and foremost a way of socially organizing groups of individuals. While psychologists would continue to approach religion in terms of individual experience, Durkheim formulated a coherent sociological approach that focused on religion as a matter of social institutions.[4]

Basic to Durkheim's approach was a distinction he drew between the sacred and the profane, a distinction that he believed is at the root of all religion. "All known religious beliefs . . . present one common characteristic: they presuppose a classification of all the things, real and ideal, of which men think, into two classes or opposed groups, generally designated by . . . the words *profane* and *sacred*." He argued that religious beliefs are representations that express the nature of sacred things, while rituals are "rules of conduct" governing how people should act in the presence of sacred objects.[5] In his development of Robertson Smith's work on the social origins of religion, Durkheim concluded that such ideas of the sacred as God or the Ancestors, which are so central to religious worship, are none other than collectively projected representations of the social group itself. As a social phenomenon, he concluded, religion is a set of ideas and practices by which people sacralize the social structure and bonds of the community. In this way, religion functions to ensure the unconscious priority of communal identification.

Durkheim reasoned that rites and ceremonies play an important role in how religion does this. As periodic opportunities for the social group to assemble itself and project sacred images that actually represent the community, rituals are designed to arouse a passionate intensity, feelings of "effervescence," in which individuals experience something larger than themselves.[6] These emotional responses cause people to identify their innermost selves with this sense of a larger reality, what is, in effect, the collective community in a disguised form. Durkheim's development of a sociopsychic mechanism of projection by which God is a representation of the social group itself was echoed by Freud, who modified the argument to suggest that God is a projection of the familial role of father: "For Freud God is the father, for Durkheim God is society."[7]

Durkheim, like Robertson Smith, Frazer, Freud, and others, decided that the earliest form of religion was totemism, as exemplified by the aboriginal tribes of central Australia. In his analysis of Australian totemism, he attempted to demonstrate his social theory of religion and ritual by showing that the totemic animal is not as sacred as the totemic emblem. The emblem, carved on a piece of wood or stone called a *churinga*, symbolizes simultaneously sacred power, the tribal clan itself, and the essential identity shared by the clan and the totemic animal. While Australians do not eat their totemic animal in the manner reconstructed by Robertson Smith, neither do they worship the animal itself. Ceremonially, they worship the *churinga*, Durkheim argued, in order to instill a passionate reaction to this pictorial dimension of the totem as a sacral representation of the clan itself. Although more sophisticated ethnographic research has yielded evidence that seriously challenges Durkheim's analysis of Australian totemic rites, his insight into the social nature of religion and ritual has endured.

Durkheim's attempt to forge a truly sociological approach contrasts with the work of his contemporaries, such as Robert H. Lowie (1883–1957), Paul Radin (1883–1959), and Bronislaw Malinowski (1884–1942). Although these three placed great emphasis on ethnographic fieldwork, they were more traditional in locating religion in the psychological realm—personal feelings such as reverential awe, exhilaration, or fearful anxiety—not in any specific social actions. Indeed, despite his attempts to stay focused on "social" phenomenon, one of the critical problems in Durkheim's sociology is his own recourse to rather psychological descriptions of effervescence as the key experience at the heart of ritual. Nonetheless, he described religion as a matter of social images and behaviors that mold the dispositions of the individual. Unlike his contemporaries, he did not derive the data of religion from the mental or emotional state of individuals or derive ritual from the expressive overflow of such individual mental and emotional states. Durkheim clearly saw ritual as the means by which individuals are brought together as a collective group. Ritual functions to "strengthen the bonds attaching the individual to the society of which he is a member"; it does so not by means of a conscious act of affiliation but the *experience* of the collective representation as a simultaneously transcendent and immanent commonality—God above and the soul within.[8] The result for Durkheim is that the person is actually made up of "two beings facing in different and almost contrary directions, one of whom exercises a real pre-eminence over the other. Such is the profound meaning of the antithesis which all men have more or less clearly conceived between the body and the soul, the material and spiritual beings who coexist within us."[9] Periodic rituals reanimate people's experiences of these two selves, the sacred and the profane selves, shaping their perceptions of the nature of the divine and the human, and embedding these perceptions and experiences in their sense of community and self.

While Durkheim's study of the elementary forms of religion was still caught up in the quest for the origins of religion, he nonetheless opened up what would be an ahistorical, sociological approach to religion as a functioning system of social relations. His work suggested that religion is a universal and indispensable dimension of social life since it is the medium through which shared social life was experienced, expressed, and legitimated. Yet Durkheim also believed that in his day science was gradually asserting itself over religion as the dominant cognitive means by which people make sense of many aspects of life. He speculated that religion would continue to be important for purposes of social solidarity, but it would serve this function in ever more secular forms, such as civic rites in commemoration of national events.[10]

The strength of Durkheim's insight into the social function and determinisms of religion led to what has been called the flaw in his theory, its monolithic conclusion that society is "the unique and all-encompassing *fons et origo* [source and ori-

gin]" of religion, morality, and even knowledge.[11] Durkheim's definition of religion
in terms of society and of society in terms of religion implies a unity too often belied
by the dynamics of real social groups. Max Gluckman, for example, pointed out that
members of the congregation peaceably assembled in religious unity at a ritual are
readily enemies in other social situations.[12] Clearly, there are other social forces that
must be taken into account. Nonetheless, Durkheim's sociological approach would
stimulate many more insights in regard to both religion and ritual, as well as broader
issues such as the social construction of perception and knowledge.

Marcel Mauss (1873–1950), a student of Durkheim, also stressed the importance
of studying religion as a "total social phenomenon" but in using the word "total" he
meant something slightly less reductive than Durkheim's thesis. For Mauss, to study
religion as a total social phenomenon meant that religion must be analyzed in terms
of how it is linked to every aspect of society. Hence, he held that religion is eminently
social, but religion and society cannot be collapsed together as mutually defining.
Mauss explored the interrelationship of social life, religion, and cultural ideas in a
succession of studies of classification systems, sacrifice, and gift exchange, collabo-
rating with Durkheim, for example, in a 1903 study on how cultural categories of
classification and knowledge are "modelled on the closest and most fundamental
form of social organization."[13]

In an earlier study of the ancient Vedic tradition of ritual sacrifice in India, written in collaboration with Henri Hubert, Mauss addressed a number of issues concerning ritual sacrifice raised by Tylor, Robertson Smith, and Frazer.[14] In particular, Hubert and Mauss described how it is the very structure of the ritual, not simply
the experience of effervescence it generates, that is intrinsic to how the rite functions
socially. They also rejected any historical treatment (i.e., in terms of origins or evolution) in favor of a functional-structural analysis of the total Vedic sacrificial system.[15] Earlier, Robertson Smith had transformed Tylor's notion of sacrifice as a gift
or bribe addressed to the gods by emphasizing that the totemic rite was a "communion" in which the human and divine are identified through the sacrifice and consumption of the totemic animal. Hubert and Mauss, however, rejected Smith's
totemic model in favor of a more general description of how sacrifice works. They
pointed to two basic processes inherent in all forms of sacrifice, sacralization and
desacralization. An essentially profane offering is made sacred—consecrated, in effect—in order to act as the means of communication and communion between the
sacred and profane worlds. At the conclusion of the rite, however, a process of
desacralization reestablishes the necessary distinctions between these two worlds that
make up day-to-day reality.[16] In a modified Durkheimian fashion, they concluded
that sacrifice is "an act of abnegation" by which the individual recalls the presence
of collective forces even as those forces are channeled to work to the advantage of
the individuals involved in the sacrifice. Hubert and Mauss also suggested the idea,
soon developed by others, that this sacrificial process functions to reestablish social
equilibrium after it has been upset. Hence, while Vedic sacrifices are invoked by
individuals who hire the priests, supply the offerings, and make known specific concerns and requests to the gods, the activities and theological ideas of the ritual are
rooted in assumptions that ascribe a divine nature to essentially "social matters" and
"collective forces."[17]

Functionalism

The focus on the social purposes of ritual that characterized Durkheim's approach developed into a general school among British anthropologists, particularly under the guidance of Alfred Reginald Radcliffe-Brown (1881–1955). Radcliffe-Brown extended the sociological aspects of Durkheim's interpretation of ritual and religion in several specific ways.[18] For example, he sought a more systematic correlation between religious ideas and social structure, theorizing that if the image of God is a collective representation or projection of the social group, then different forms of social organization will have different self-reflective notions of God.[19] Although such a simple correlation of types of beliefs with types of social structure proved impossible to observe or show in practice, this general approach effectively ignored and eliminated the vestigial evolutionary framework of Durkheim's approach, as well as all the older questions concerning the origins of religion. In their place, Radcliffe-Brown delineated an ahistorical focus on social structure as the main determinant of religion. His approach to ritual deliberately eschewed any interest in how the religions of so-called primitive peoples, traditionally seen "as systems of erroneous beliefs and illusory practices," actually got started and evolved.[20] Indeed, Radcliffe-Brown's subordination of historical issues to questions of social organization and social function led to criticism that functionalism unduly dismissed history.[21] Yet, for Radcliffe-Brown, religion has to be approached as an "essential part of the social machinery" by which human beings live together in an orderly arrangement of social relations: "We deal not with the origins but with the social functions of religions, i.e., the contribution they make to the formation and maintenance of the social order."[22]

This emphasis on the immediate social determinants of religion was also a result of a growing firsthand involvement in fieldwork. While Durkheim had to rely on written accounts of such groups as the Australian Arunta, most of them written by missionaries, Radcliffe-Brown went to live in western Australia and later among the Andaman Islanders. Although his sojourn among these peoples was not as intense as later fieldwork guidelines would encourage, such immediate experience among contemporary tribal societies simultaneously helped to develop the sophistication of social anthropology and to diminish the importance of historical analysis, especially with regard to oral societies without formal historical records.

This more developed social perspective led Radcliffe-Brown to reject the Durkheimian view of ritual as the means for expressing collective representations in the guise of religious beliefs. In contrast, he was truer to Robertson Smith's emphasis on the priority of ritual and the importance of its social role in securing and maintaining the unity of the group. He argued that belief is the effect of rite, that action determines belief. Although Radcliffe-Brown acknowledged that cause-and-effect arguments (beliefs giving rise to rites or rites giving rise to beliefs) misrepresent how rites and beliefs are parts of a coherent whole, his formulation of social functionalism focused on what he took to be the more enduring activities of ritual life as opposed to less stable doctrines and beliefs.[23]

Radcliffe-Brown's position on ritual and belief made him critical of theories concerning ritual sentiment. Despite his insight into social life, Durkheim had ultimately described the social role of ritual in terms of the psychological states of individuals in groups. He saw orderly social life as dependent upon the presence in each member's mind of certain sentiments, such as solidarity, goodwill, love, and hate, which control each person's behavior. And he argued that rites are "regulated symbolic expressions" of these sentiments that "maintain and transmit from one generation to another sentiments on which the constitution of the society depends."[24] As such, religious ritual reestablishes a unified social order primarily by reaffirming the sentiments on which this social order is based. Malinowski, a contemporary of Radcliffe-Brown, put even more stress on individual emotional states by arguing that some rituals (magical as opposed to religious ones, he thought) have the practical function of alleviating anxiety, distress, fear, doubt, and sorrow.[25] Yet it was clear to Radcliffe-Brown that rites can also create anxiety, not simply relieve it, as when strict ritual injunctions to perform certain actions in very specific ways make people quite anxious that everything is done properly. He rejected the assumption that ritual is a means to express, affirm, or alleviate the intensity of prior mental states; instead, he saw ritual as creating mental states, not simply expressing them.[26] In particular, he argued, ritual simultaneously expresses and creates the sentiment of dependence on a type of moral or spiritual power that is thought to transcend the realm of the human. It is this sentiment at the heart of the unifying function of religious rituals that makes such rites essential to the constitution of society: "I suggest to you that what makes and keeps man a social animal is not some herd instinct, but the sense of dependence in the innumerable forms that it takes."[27] By focusing on experiences of social dependence, Radcliffe-Brown attempted to formulate a more purely "social" understanding than that afforded by Durkheim's notion of group effervescence or Malinowski's focus on individual anxiety.[28]

The functionalist approach is usually credited to both Radcliffe-Brown and Malinowski, with acknowledged debts to Durkheim and even the myth and ritual theorist Jane Harrison among others. Yet the positions of Malinowski and Radcliffe-Brown have been contrasted as thesis and antithesis.[29] While Radcliffe-Brown developed Durkheim's emphasis on the social group, Malinowski explicitly rejected this view of religion as a social phenomenon and promoted the idea that religion is rooted in individual experience, particularly the fear of death. Radcliffe-Brown emphasized the rules governing the structural organization of social relations, but Malinowski emphasized individual thinking processes, the flexibility of personal interactions, and the pragmatic activities of real people. Malinowski granted that some public rituals had social functions but others did not. In fact, he tended to define magical rituals as those that had the social function of alleviating anxiety, while religious rituals were those that had no such social purpose and were simply a form of communication with the gods.[30] Yet Malinowski was very aware of initiating a "functionalist revolution" by virtue of his abandonment of evolutionary and diffusionist paradigms in favor of analysis, based on intensive fieldwork, of how a society operates. For Malinowski, Radcliffe-Brown, and those they influenced, the functionalist approach tended to conceive of a culture as a closed system of social relations powered by an internal dynamism. This perspective contrasts with the more comparative approach of the myth-ritualists reviewed in the preceding section, for whom a culture tended to be a "patchwork" of transmitted or absorbed traits.[31] A functionalist interpretation of a social phenomenon made little if any appeal either to history or to ideas and practices borrowed from elsewhere; society was seen as a static, structured system of social relations. This view lent itself to two popular metaphors for social phenomena: the organic and the mechanical. Radcliffe-Brown invoked the former when he suggested that each custom and belief plays a particular role in the social life of a "primitive" community in the same way that "every organ of a living body plays some part in the general life of the organism." This integrated "mass of institutions, customs and beliefs forms a single whole or system that determines the life of the society," which is as real a thing as the life of an organism.[32] For social functionalists, therefore, ritual is a means to regulate and stabilize the life of this system, adjust its internal interactions, maintain its group ethos, and restore a state of harmony after any disturbance. As such, religion and ritual are social mechanisms with a particularly vital role to play in maintaining the system. While there was significant criticism of various aspects of this functional theory, many people readily accepted the view that functionalism provided at least a partial explanation of what ritual does and how society operates.

Neofunctional Systems Analyses

A variety of studies of ritual can be loosely grouped as "neofunctional" forms of "systems" analysis. They explore various ways that ritual activities serve to regulate the community or enhance the well-being of the individual. Yet, instead of limiting themselves to the parameters of the functionalist approach associated with Radcliffe-Brown and Malinowski, the neofunctionalists try to describe the interaction of multiple cultural systems. It should be noted, however, that few, if any, of the theorists grouped here would choose to characterize their work as "functional" in any way. This is due, in part, to the heavy criticism that has been heaped on functionalism over the years but also to the very real ways in which these theorists are working with complex models of social dynamics.[33] The theories of ritual included here—ecological, ethnological, biogenetic, and psychological—testify to the enduring value of a more nuanced functionalist concern with how ritual relates to social life.

In 1968, Roy Rappaport (b. 1926) introduced a radically new perspective on ritual in a series of studies of New Guinea tribes. These studies demonstrated how New Guinea ritual activities work to regulate the relationships between the people and their natural resources, thereby maintaining a delicate but essential environmental balance.[34] Ritual, Rappaport argued, not only regulates the interaction of one human community with another but also can regulate the interaction of humans with local materials, foodstuffs, and animals—especially pigs in the New Guinea case, since they are an important component of the diet and the economy. Sketching tribal life as a series of exchanges that include everything from genetic matter to stone axes, Rappaport cast social processes like ritual as an intrinsic part of a much larger and embracing cultural ecosystem.[35]

Rappaport described how the Maring-speaking peoples of New Guinea slaughtered domestic pigs only under special circumstances and within a ritual framework. For example, a ritual killing of pigs is organized if the number of pigs multiplies to the point that too much labor and food are needed to feed them. At such times, the pig becomes a parasite dependent on limited resources, rather than a resource for the community. During times of war, pigs may also be killed and eaten in a ritual meal but only by those warriors preparing to fight, although it is understood that the warriors' intake of protein and salt benefit all those whom the warriors defend. The ritual framework formalizes the killing of pigs and as such helps restrict such killing to particular circumstances. In addition, the major pig festival, the *kaiko*, is part of a complex series of interlocking ritual activities that link the land, plants, and interaction with enemy tribes. Rappaport's analysis concluded that this type of ritual helps "to maintain an undegraded environment, limits fighting to frequencies which do not endanger the existence of the regional population, adjusts man-land ratios, facilitates trade, distributes local surpluses of pig throughout the regional population in the form of pork, and assures people of high quality protein when they are most in need of it."[36] Rappaport's approach is, in many respects, a form of "systems analysis," in which ritual is shown to play a particularly key role in maintaining the system since it claims an authority rooted in the divine, as well as in tradition. In comparison, economic advisors or ecological managers would not be as effective in securing compliance with traditional methods of maintaining the ecological balance—indeed, quite the opposite: ritual is so important to maintaining this system because people believe that much more than physical resources are at stake.

Rappaport's suggestions concerning the role of ritual in mystification for the good of the community have been echoed much more explicitly in the work of Marvin Harris (b. 1927), an anthropologist who is often described as a "cultural materialist." Harris created a stir when he took a very extreme approach to other examples of the ritual regulation of resources, such as cow worship among Hindus in India and human sacrifice among the ancient Aztecs. In regard to the first example, Harris pointed out that the cow was an indispensable resource for Hindu farming families with small plots of land, not only enabling them to plow and plant but also supplying them with milk for food and dung for fuel.[37] If in times of severe crisis, such as an extended drought, people were to butcher and eat their cows, they would lose the one resource they needed most to get back on their feet later. Hindu cow worship, the religious obligation to show the greatest respect to cows, ensures that people do not eat their cows in times of crisis—at least not short of total desperation. Hence, the ritual attitude toward the cow guarantees the maintenance of a basic level of economic resources and does so more effectively than any economic argument would.

Harris similarly explains the human sacrifices ascribed to the Aztecs as a ritual means of regulating the limited dietary resources needed to maintain the community.[38] Arguing that the Mesoamerican ecosystem lacked adequate sources of animal protein to support the estimated population growth, Harris concludes that Aztec ritual slaughter was a "state-sponsored system geared to the production and redistribution of substantial amounts of animal protein in the form of human flesh."[39] Although critics have effectively challenged both the correctness of his raw data and the plausibility of his interpretations, Harris's approach to these ritual traditions has suggested new questions and possibilities about the variety of ways in which ritual might function.[40]

The field of ethology has another approach to ritual activities. Associated in its early forms with the work of Julian Huxley (1887–1975) and Konrad Lorenz

(1903–1989), ethology explores so-called ritualized patterns of behavior among animals that have raised many questions concerning the origins and social ramifications of human rituals.[41] Studies of the ritual-like behavior evinced in animal displays—such as courtship and mating routines, the elaborate signaling of territorial rights, the reciprocal etiquette involved in grooming, or the rules for fighting invoked in male tournaments—have led scholars to try to define such behavior in terms congruent with analogous patterns in human social life. Huxley defined these examples of "ritualization" as "the adaptive formalization or canalization of emotionally motivated behaviour, under the teleonomic pressure of natural selection." Such formalized patterns, he suggested, appear to promote clearer communication and stimulate more efficient actions in other animals which reduces damage or killing within the species and facilitates sexual or social bonding.[42] Hence, in exploring questions of function, ethologists developed an important early argument about the inherently communicative nature of ritual action and concluded that the ritual gestures of animals serve as codes or signals that transmit information useful to the well-being of the group. Some studies went on to suggest that much of human culture is probably rooted in these inherited patterns of early animal ritualization—not only mating and war but also play, dance, art, and education.[43]

In general, ethologists have held that ritualization among animals is a combination of genetically determined and socially acquired behavior. Likewise, they speculate, human ritual behavior may be shaped by genetic propensities that have accompanied the evolution of human beings as well as the highly symbolic activity humans acquire through cultural socialization. In this way, animal and human rituals can be considered akin biologically and evolutionarily, even though human ritual is understood to differ greatly in complexity, self-consciousness, and aesthetic.[44] On the basis of this presumed kinship, however, Huxley, among others, used the similarities between animal and human rituals to evaluate the state of ritual in modern society, specifically in light of the ills of twentieth-century civilization. He argued in 1966, for example, that people in the modern world are failing to ritualize effectively, and this is leading to a heightened propensity toward flawed communication, the escalation of conflict, needless killing of our own species, and weak personal and social bonding among our own kind. While rituals of breeding regulate procreation and population among animals, Huxley asked how, in the wake of readily available contraceptives, human beings would regulate their sexual contact so as to avoid promiscuity, overpopulation, and disease. He feared that older religious systems have fallen into irrelevance and that human communities have lost their ritual traditions of bonding just when new and larger social groups, such as the type of world community represented by the United Nations, need to be reinforced by the bonding that only ritual affords.[45]

More recently, ethological animal studies have been loosely synthesized with research in the area of sociobiology that focuses on genetics and evolution.[46] The combined field of inquiry could be called "neuroanthropology," but, in its application to the study of ritual, it has described itself as "biogenetic structuralism."[47] Like ethology, biogenetic approaches focus on the evolution of the capacity for ritual and on comparison of ritual activities between species, including humans. However, there have also been attempts to investigate the biopsychological roots of human ritual behavior and the effect of ritual behavior on both cognitive and more general neuro-physiological processes within the body. While it is widely assumed that ritual be-havior is deeply involved in the interaction of the brain's cognitive functions with the social-physical environment, some biogeneticists have also attempted to locate the specific brain sites responsible for ritual action.[48]

Ethology and biogenetics reflect strong concerns for the origins of ritual as well as the role of such formalized behavior patterns in human adaptation to physical and social environments. From this perspective, ritual is seen as a technology or mecha-nism deemed integral to how the brain works; biogeneticists surmise that it enables the individual, or the animal, to solve problems of adaptation that would otherwise be unyielding.[49] Although this form of functional explanation primarily views ritual in terms of how it aids physiological and social development, ethologists and biogeneticists have not been unsympathetic to its moral and religious dimensions, since these are indisputable aspects of how ritual has been and continues to be an important component in the evolutionary success of animals and humans.

Ethological and biogenetic approaches to ritual often invoke the psychological theories of Erik Erikson (1902–1990) and Jean Piaget (1896–1980) concerning physi-cal and social maturation.[50] Erikson, in particular, addressed the "ontogeny" or de-velopment of ritualization in stages of maturation within the human life cycle. He defined ritualization as a type of consensual interplay between two or more persons that is repeated in recurring contexts and has adaptive value for those involved.[51] His central example of such behavior is the peculiar greeting ceremony that unfolds between a mother and her baby in the morning. Their interaction is both highly individual and stereotypical, he argued; each does things that arouse predictable responses in the other and that are important for both physical and emotional rea-sons. Erikson concluded that human ritualization is grounded in such preverbal infantile experiences, although it culminates in the elaborate ceremonies of public life. As such, he saw ritualization as having a primarily adaptive function, the first concern of which is to help the infant overcome the sense of separation or abandon-ment it experiences when its mother is not there. While the experience of separation may be intrinsic to the formation of an individual ego, it must also be mediated or balanced by the ritual reassurances that pull one from an inhuman isolation into social relationships with others.

Erikson argued that various dimensions of ritual are elaborated and learned in eight successive stages of the life cycle necessary to a fully socialized and individu-ated human being. The preverbal rites between mother and child establish a numinous experience of the mutual recognition of separate selves, while the rites of early childhood establish the judicial ability to discriminate right from wrong. The child masters further aspects of dramatic elaboration and formal rules of performance at the age of play and thereafter in school. The conjunction of these dimensions of ritual in adolescence leads to the formation of a sense of ideological conviction that links one to a group. With the rituals of adulthood come the social sanctions that enable one to act responsibly and creatively in community. Ultimately, Erikson's theory makes ritualization an essential link between the development of the human individual (ontogeny) and the evolution of the human species (phylogeny).[52]

Other psychological approaches to ritual have also suggested neofunctional purposes for ritual. While many theorists attest to somewhat simplistic "cathartic" functions, others argue that ritual is a type of mechanism that channels the expansive and harmful tendencies of symbolic thought that could result in excessive individual anxiety or the disruption of social harmony.[53] Similarly, another proposes that ritual ceremonies, like the dreams studied by psychoanalysts, protect society from dangerous conflict by communicating, and therein releasing, harmful thoughts and emotions.[54] Most of these theorists, moreover, would not dispute the possibility that ritual activity is linked to particular dynamics in the brain and may well have had adaptive value in the development of social life. Some are "at least half convinced that there can be genuine dialogue between neurology and culturology."[55]

The foregoing neofunctional theories of ritual develop two underlying ideas. First, they hold that human behavior is determined by more than just social conditioning. At the very least, ecological, economic, genetic, or physiological conditions impose a set of parameters on the variation of social behavior. In other words, not all behavior is learned, and not all behaviors can be learned. This has been described as a matter of genetic chains that hold cultural patterns "on leash," though no one is sure how long the leash might extend.[56] Second, these theories are concerned with a particular location for what they see as universal qualities of ritual action. Instead of universal social structures or universal rules for how societies act and develop, some of these theories would suggest that what all ritual has in common has to do with human physiology; others would suggest that what all ritual has in common has to do with its ability to induce compliance with practices that maintain a balanced human ecology. Cultural variation in ritual is then ascribed to the interaction of human physiology with different physical environments. For this reason, Rappaport and Harris have been called cultural materialists, while the ethologists have been called scientific materialists. To their critics, these approaches seem to reduce religion and ritual to purely material matters. To their supporters, these theories contribute greatly to an understanding of some of the ways in which human activity is both conditioned and creatively responsive.

Structuralism

Implicit in the functionalism of Radcliffe-Brown was an appreciation of social structure as a system of relationships connecting people or their social roles. His focus on structure in social relations was modeled on the study of anatomical structures in paleontology, where constant comparison of differing species enabled scientists to reconstruct the logic of their anatomical development in adapting to particular physical environments. There has been some debate over whether the social structures isolated in this fashion actually exist in fact or whether they are merely abstract models useful to the ethnographer. Nonetheless, a simultaneous emphasis on invisible social structures and the fieldworker's immersion within the complexities of daily life were instrumental in generating two forms of explanation for ritual behavior. First, as noted before, one could analyze how ritual activities function—that is, how they facilitate the orderly cooperation of communal life. Second, one could also choose to analyze what ritual activities mean—that is, what cultural ideas and values are expressed in these symbols and patterns of activities. For Radcliffe-Brown, the structured relationships among symbols (meaning) had to be linked to the structured social relationships that comprised the society (function). As noted earlier, for example, he expected groups organized in particular ways to have corresponding images of god, spirits, death, fertility, and so on, all of which simultaneously functioned to express and maintain the social structure. Yet despite his predictions in this regard, Radcliffe-Brown failed to demonstrate any clear and direct links between social structures and patterns of symbols and beliefs. This raised a new question, which Malinowski among others began to ask: if such symbols, beliefs, and patterns of ritual activity do not serve simply to maintain the patterns of social relationships, then what do they mean to the people who use them? Analyses of the meaning of the structured relationships of ritual and religious symbols gradually emerged as a part of a more or less independent mode of analysis.

After prolonged field study of the ceremonial behavior of the Iatmul peoples of New Guinea, Gregory Bateson (1904–1980) produced a detailed and influential study of their *naven* ritual, a ceremony "in which men dress as women and women dress as men." He wanted to "relate this behavior, not only to the structure and pragmatic functioning of Iatmul culture, but also to its ethos."[57] It was an ambitious attempt at a synthetic explanation that would combine several levels of analysis: the social structures addressed by the rite; the emotional values of Iatmul life expressed in the rite, that is, the cultural structures; as well as the connection between individual feelings and activities on the one hand and shared cultural values and activities on the other. In the end, however, Bateson was not convinced that he had succeeded in explaining anything more than his own theoretical premises. As he worked out logical explanations for the *naven* ritual on each of these levels, he argued, it became apparent to him that all of the categories of analysis that he was using—structure, culture, the social, etc.—were not facts of New Guinea life but abstractions created and manipulated by social scientists like himself.[58]

E. E. Evans-Pritchard (1902–1973) undertook a similar project in his study of the Nuer of southern Sudan and emerged as an important figure in the modification of functionalism and the promotion of other forms of explanation, both structural (concerned with functions) and symbolic (concerned with meanings). While generally adhering to the functionalist position that religion can be understood only by relating it to social structure, Evans-Pritchard also explored how economic, historical, and environmental factors are part of the picture since they influenced social organization, and are reflected in Nuer concepts, values, and rituals.[59] In particular, he focused on the conceptual structure of Nuer religion, which he found to be highly complex and remarkably sensitive, refined, and intelligent; it reveals, he suggested, the inadequacy of most of the theories of religion we might apply to it.[60]

Evans-Pritchard basically agreed with Robertson Smith, Durkheim, Mauss, and others that religions are "products of social life," but he strongly disagreed with the idea that they are "nothing more than a symbolic representation of the social order." Indeed, he asserted, "it was Durkheim and not the savage who made society into a god." To correct what he saw as facile simplifications, Evans-Pritchard recommended that scholars conduct systematic studies of primitive philosophies. His explorations of both the collective and the individual aspects of religion reflect a refusal to reduce religion either to Radcliffe-Brown's social structure (the Nuer conception of God cannot be reduced to, or explained by, the social order) or to Malinowski's appeal to individual sensibilities (that Nuer religious thought and practices are influenced by their whole social life is evident from our study of them).[61]

These concerns led Evans-Pritchard to a new way of conceiving ritual. Ritual is where Nuer religious concepts, which are not concepts so much as "imaginative constructions," are externalized and could be observed. In contrast to those explanations of ritual that appeal to the arousal of communal emotions, he called attention to the great variety of feelings displayed at a ritual: far from displaying any collective emotional ethos, some people do not pay any attention, while others are serious or gay. "What is important in sacrifice is not how people feel, or even how they behaved," he asserted. "What is important is that the essential acts of sacrifice be carried out."[62] When these acts are mapped analytically, they indicate a system of ideas. In such a system, for example, humans and cattle are considered equivalent with regard to the higher order of god, so the sacrifice of an animal is a substitute for that of a human and acts as an offering to the god in exchange for aid. Evans-Pritchard's analysis of Nuer sacrifice depicts the system of ordered relationships of mutual dependency that links humans, animals, ancestors, and gods. As such, he argued in what amounts to an answer to Bateson's concerns, the rites of the Nuer can be understood only in terms of the Nuer's own conceptual oppositions, primarily the opposition between the realm of spirit and the realm of humans. In enacting this complex system of relationships, the rite underscores these opposing orders while simultaneously establishing contact between them. Therefore, the activities of the rite demonstrate and communicate the structural order of Nuer categories, which in turn both affects and reflects the structural order of social relations.

Evans-Pritchard went on to raise another question as well, namely, what do these rites and conceptions actually mean to the Nuer themselves? The full answer, he concluded, is to be found only in the interior experiences of the Nuer where the anthropologist cannot go.[63] In the end, Evans-Pritchard's analysis of ritual echoed functionalist concerns while also prefiguring the emergence of two new developments: Claude Lévi-Strauss's structural studies of kinship and mythological systems, on the one hand, and Clifford Geertz's symbolic studies of cultural meaning on the other.

A rather different concern with issues of function and structure shaped the work of Arnold van Gennep (1873–1957), who may have been less influenced by Radcliffe-Brown and his successors than by Frazer and his myth and ritual heirs. While not a member of the functionalist-structuralist lineage examined here—in fact, he was a strong critic of Durkheim, who appears to have ignored him—van Gennep came to exert significant influence on it.[64] His insights into the internal organization of ritual activities challenged many traditional ways of categorizing ritual and opened up new perspectives on the relationship of ritual to social organization.

While sharing the taxonomic concerns of Frazer and others, van Gennep deplored the Frazerian tendency to collect brief ritual descriptions and analyze them outside their real contexts. Rites can be understood, he argued, only in terms of how they are used in their original social setting; moreover, the most immediate context for any one rite is the sequence of rituals that immediately precede and follow it. For instance, he criticized Frazer's discussion of ritual circumambulation that used brief examples collected from around the world. For van Gennep, there can be no *intrinsic* meaning to circumambulation; its meaning depends on the whole sequence of rites in which it occurs and on the purpose of the sequence as a whole. This was the principle behind his "sequential method," which studies a ritual "only in relation to what precedes and what follows it."[65] Nonetheless, van Gennep was still very much concerned to demonstrate the universality of certain patterns, and his most famous work, *The Rites of Passage* (1909), clearly echoed Frazer's *Golden Bough* in its appeal to universal patterns within examples from many disparate traditions.

Van Gennep specifically focused on those rituals that accompany life crises, those critical moments in social life when individuals move from one status to another. In an echo of the three stages of the dying and rising god pattern—which he may have acknowledged when he noted that "man's life resembles nature"—van Gennep argued that these life-crisis rites display a three-stage sequence: separation, transition, and incorporation.[66] Through this sequence of activities, rituals effect the person's removal from one social grouping, dramatize the change by holding the person in a suspended "betwixt and between" state for a period of time, and then reincorporate him or her into a new identity and status within another social grouping. The first stage, separation, is often marked by rites of purification and symbolic allusions to the loss of the old identity (in effect, death to the old self): the person is bathed, hair is shaved, clothes are switched, marks are made on the body, and so on. In the second or transition stage, the person is kept for a time in a place that is symbolically outside the conventional sociocultural order (akin to a gestation period): normal routines are suspended while rules distinctive to this state are carefully followed (not touching the ground, no contact with other people). In the third stage, symbolic acts of incorporation focus on welcoming the person into a new status (in effect, birth of the new self): there is the conferral of a new name and symbolic insignia, usually some form of communal meal, and so on. Initiation rituals provide the clearest examples of this three-stage pattern, although they particularly elaborate the liminal aspects of the transition stage. Birth rites, marriages, and funerals also seem to follow this three-part sequence, but the emphasis of the sequence may shift to one of the other two stages. By means of this three-stage pattern, van Gennep attempted to demonstrate "a wide degree of general similarity among ceremonies of birth, childhood, social puberty, betrothal, marriage, pregnancy, fatherhood, initiation into religious societies and funerals."[67]

As part of his study of ritualized transitions through the social order, van Gennep collected many examples of rites in which changes in spatial location are used to designate changes in social identity. Moving people from one marked place to another, often passing through doors, arches, or gates, appears to be a common way both to signal and to effect a change in social status. A married couple passes through a festooned arbor or church door to signal their emergence into the new social state of marriage. A born-again Christian descends into a pool of water and emerges from the other side spiritually cleansed, committed, and "made new." His analysis of the logic of ritual movements in space remains one of the most useful explanations of both the internal structure of rituals and the way they work as symbolic orchestrations of socially real changes.

In this way, van Gennep pointed to a fresh interpretation of the symbolism of rebirth and regeneration so important to the myth and ritual school. While they had analyzed this pattern as the remnant of primordial events, van Gennep suggested its ahistorical, functional, and symbolic dimensions. His extension of the three-stage pattern beyond life-crisis rituals to rites demarcating seasonal and calendrical passages also established the pattern as a particularly effective formulation of a common structure apparently underlying all or almost all rituals, and influenced Eliade's treatment of new year rituals of cosmic regeneration. In addition, van Gennep presented a fresh analysis of the notion of the sacred, a concept common to a number of different scholarly orientations, notably those of Durkheim and Eliade. Van Gennep saw the sacred not as some sort of absolute entity or quality but as a relative one that readily shifts in different situations and at different ritual stages. What he designated as the "pivoting of the sacred" alerted scholars to the ways in which ritual can actually define what is sacred, not simply react to the sacred as something already and for always fixed.[68]

Van Gennep's functionalism, although implicit rather than explicit, was a powerful component of his analysis of ritual. He argued that rites of passage serve to order chaotic social changes that could threaten to disturb society. Such rites distinguish status groups with clearly marked boundaries, which contributes to the stability of social identities and roles. Rituals are the means for changing and reconstituting groups in an orderly and sanctioned manner that maintains the integrity of the system. These groups include religious associations, totem clans, phratries (exogamous kinship groups), castes, professional classes, age groups, families, the political and territorial community, the world of the living, the world before it, and the world of the dead after it. "Life itself," wrote van Gennep, "means to separate and to reunite, to change form and condition, to die and to be reborn."[69] These changes can occur smoothly and meaningfully as part of a larger, embracing, and reassuring pattern only by means of their orchestration as rites of passage.

In a related argument with important ramifications, van Gennep pointed out that the social changes of moving from childhood to adulthood, which are effected through formal initiation rituals, have little to do with the timing of the biological changes that accompany physical maturation. The sociocultural order of which ritual is a part is not there simply to legitimate the changes of the biological order, he concluded; the sociocultural world has its own order and purposes, and they can be exercised so as to try to dominate the imperatives of biology. Van Gennep also tried to suggest the importance of rites of passage to the psychological well-being of individuals, not just the structural-functional well-being of the community as a whole. "The critical problems of becoming male and female, of relations within the family, and of passing into old age," one commentator on van Gennep has written, "are directly related to the devices which the society offers the individual to help him achieve the new adjustment."[70] Indeed, van Gennep's theory contributed directly to the questions that have been raised about the relative lack in modern society of formal social rituals and the possible correlation of this lack with modern social ills.

In the spirit of the myth-and-ritualists, van Gennep pointed to an underlying pattern within all, or nearly all, rituals, although he argued that this three-stage pattern showed that ritual was intrinsically involved with marking and maintaining cultural notions of social order. In his demonstration of how ritual reflects "the structure of social relations and changes in these relations," van Gennep pointed both to functional dynamics and to the contextual dynamics of meaningful symbols.[71] Both sets of dynamics were developed more systematically and thoroughly by Max Gluckman and Victor Turner.

The British anthropologist Max Gluckman (1911–1975) brought two major insights to bear on the study of ritual; the first modified Durkheimian theory, while the second modified van Gennep's approach. Gluckman argued that Durkheim's model of ritual as the projected expression of social cohesion and the unity of the group does not do justice to the presence, degree, and role of conflict that is always built into any society. "Every social system," he wrote, "is a field of tension, full of ambivalence, of co-operation and contrasting struggle."[72] Stressing the difficulty of actually achieving social unity, Gluckman suggested that rituals are really the expression of complex social tensions rather than the affirmation of social unity; they exaggerate very real conflicts that exist in the organization of social relations and then affirm unity despite these structural conflicts. In particular, he pointed to what he called "rituals of rebellion," rites in which the normal rules of authority are temporarily overturned. In one example, he interpreted the famous opening scenario in Frazer's *The Golden Bough*, in which a candidate for the position of priest of the sacred grove of Nemi can succeed to the office only by slaying the current priest, as an instance of ritual rebellion. A better example, however, is seen in Zulu women's agricultural rites, which are occasions on which women boldly parade about in men's clothes, doing things normally forbidden to them. Although the traditional patriarchal order is completely, if temporarily, overturned by the women, the Zulus believe these rites are beneficial to society as a whole. Gluckman suggested that such ceremonies are ritualized rebellions that channel the structural conflict caused by men's social subordination of women. As such, they have the cathartic effect of releasing social tensions, thereby limiting discontent and diffusing the real threat contained in such discontent. At the same time, these rites also function to reinforce the social status quo, since temporary inversions or suspensions of the usual order of social relations dramatically acknowledge that order as normative. Hence, for Gluckman, instead of the simple expression of social cohesion suggested by Durkheim and Radcliffe-Brown, ritual is the occasion to exaggerate the tensions that exist in the society in order to provide a social catharsis that can simultaneously affirm unity and effect some semblance of it. The goal of ritual as such is to channel the expression of conflict in therapeutic ways so as to restore a functioning social equilibrium.[73]

In terms of van Gennep's concerns, Gluckman attempted to explain why some but not all social relationships required rituals of passage. He raised this issue by contrasting the greater ritualization of social transitions and relationships in tribal societies with their relative paucity in industrial ones. In a tribal society with a subsistence economy, he explained, each social relation tends to serve manifold and overlapping purposes or roles. In order to avoid conflicts of allegiance and competition, stylized and ceremonial techniques are used to differentiate roles and reduce tensions. Social relations in such societies are more highly ritualized than they need to be in groups where social roles are already differentiated more mechanically. For example, some of the most ritualized roles in tribal societies are positions of authority. In these cases, he argued, "the legitimation of authority takes on a mystical character because those in authority are involved in many other relationships with their followers." Ultimately, for Gluckman, ritual is "the symbolical enactment of social relations themselves" in all their ambiguity, tension, and strife. In this way, he tried to tie explanations of ritual to the specific context of dynamic social relations in a group.[74]

Significantly, Gluckman's work shifted the definition of ritual away from the Durkheimian notion that rite was primarily concerned with religion or "the sacred." Gluckman defined ritual as a more embracing category of social action, with religious activities at one extreme and social etiquette at the other.[75] With this approach, the term "ritual" could loosely refer to a wide spectrum of formalized but not necessarily religious activities. Henceforth, the study of ritual had to do with society and social relationships, not just religion or religious institutions. Moreover, ritualization came to be seen as a particular way of organizing social relationships: not simply a reflection of the structure of social relationships, ritual and its structure began to be recognized as a major means of working and reworking those social relationships.

Van Gennep's work on the structure of ritual and Gluckman's on the ritualization of social conflict were developed into a powerful analytical model by Victor Turner (1920–1983). Turner combined a functionalist's interest in mechanisms for maintaining social equilibrium with a more structural perspective on the organization of symbols. Like many of his colleagues, particularly Mary Douglas, Turner's work incorporated a variety of emphases, many of which helped to generate new questions about symbolic action that pushed his inquiry well beyond the explanative frameworks of functional and structural concerns. As a former student of Radcliffe-Brown and Gluckman, among others, Turner's first book, *Schism and Continuity in an African Society* (1957), extended the latter's analysis of structural conflict in social life.[76] He argued that many forms of ritual serve as "social dramas" through which the stresses and tensions built into the social structure could be expressed and worked out. Turner echoed Durkheim in reiterating the role that ritual, as opposed to other forms of social action, plays in maintaining the unity of the group as a whole, but he also echoed Gluckman in stressing how ritual is a mechanism for constantly re-creating, not just reaffirming, this unity. In subsequent studies, however, Turner went beyond the model of society as a closed and atemporal structured system that, when disturbed by conflict, could be returned to harmonious stasis through ritual catharsis. His notion of social dramas led him to envision social structure not as a static organization but as a dynamic process.[77] Rituals did not simply restore social equilibrium, they were part of the ongoing process by which the community was continually redefining and renewing itself.

During his fieldwork among the Ndembu of northwestern Zambia, Turner witnessed periodic public episodes of great tension and communal strife. Perceiving these events as far from random or chaotic, he approached them as social dramas with a temporal or processual structure that could be analyzed in terms of four main stages: a breach in normal relationships, followed by an escalating sense of crisis, which calls for redressive action, and eventually culminates in activities of reintegration of the alien-ated or social recognition of their separate status.[78] This appeal to an underlying tem-poral structure within social processes was developed in his later use of van Gennep's three-stage sequence of separation, transition, and reincorporation. Turner recast this sequence into a more fundamental dialectic between the social order (structure) and a period of social disorder and liminality (antistructure) that he termed *communitas*. Rituals, he argued, affirm the social order while facilitating disordered inversions of that order: through such inversions, the original order is simultaneously legitimated and modified—either in its basic structure or by moving people from one status to another.

In a number of studies, Turner focused on the transition stage, a period of liminality and communitas that is "betwixt and between" the structure of society at the beginning of the ritual and the structure of society that is affirmed at the end. In analyzing the elaborated transition stages found in initiation rites, Turner interpreted the symbolism as expressing ambiguity and paradox: the initiates are simultaneously treated as if they are neither dead nor alive, yet also as if they are both dead and alive. For example, young boys undergoing tribal initiation might be treated as polluted corpses or helpless fetuses in positions of burial not unlike those of gestation. Their names are taken from them and countless other details express "a confusion of all the customary categories" of the culture. For the duration of this stage of the ritual process, the initiates "have no status, property, insignia, secular clothing, rank, kin-ship position, nothing to demarcate them structurally from their fellows."[79] They are effectively outside the structure or organization of society, in a state of liminality or antistructure, which nonetheless fosters an intense experience of community among them. In fact, Turner compares the lifelong ties forged by this initiation experience to those established by fraternities and sororities on American college campuses or by graduates of the same class from naval or military academies in Europe.[80] At the conclusion of this stage, initiates are reborn into a new position in the social hierar-chy, given names or titles, and expected to assume the appropriate responsibilities and uphold the social structure of which they are now integral parts. From this, Turner inferred that "for individuals and groups, social life is a type of dialectical process that involves successive experience of high and low, communitas and structure, homogeneity and differentiation, equality and inequality . . . the opposites, as it were, constitute each other and are mutually indispensable."[81] Hence, not only does ritual involve orchestrated sequences of structural order and antistructural communitas, so does social life itself. The experience of order and structure in society must be balanced, he suggested, by the experiences of an underlying ethos of sacrality, egali-tarian unity, inversion, danger, and creative forces for renewal.

Turner saw ritual as the means for acting out social conflicts in a series of activi-ties through which people experience the authority and flexibility of the social order, the liminality and bonds of egalitarian communitas, and the passage from an old place in the social order to a new status in a reconstituted order. He went beyond some of the limits of Gluckman's model by arguing that as social dramas rituals do not simply release emotional tensions in a cathartic easing of social tensions. Rather, rites depict, act out, or otherwise give form to conflicts and the dominant values holding the group together. Ritual dramatizes the real situation, and it is through this dramatization that ritual does what it alone does.

Aside from this focus on social dramas, Turner also attempted to articulate what ritual does as precisely as possible through a close analysis of ritual symbols. In a series of studies of the complex symbols and symbol systems invoked in Ndembu rites, he called attention to the dynamic qualities of symbols, rejecting the more static approach represented by the structural studies of Lévi-Strauss.[82] Symbols are not timeless entities projected by society and reflecting the forms of social organization, he argued. Originating in and sustaining the dynamics of social relationships, they do not have a fixed meaning; they can condense many meanings together. Inherently "multivocal," symbols must be interpreted in terms of the variety of positions they can occupy in relation to each other in systems of symbols. When temporarily isolated, however, Turner found symbols to be structurally bipolar, referring to sensory experiences on the one hand and ideological or normative values on the other. A good example is the "milk tree" used in a Ndembu girl's initiation ceremony. When scratched, the tree exudes a milky white latex that explains why the Ndembu associate the tree with breast-feeding, with the mother who feeds, and with the swelling of a young girl's breasts. Yet these sensory aspects of the tree symbol are only part of its significance, Turner argues. By virtue of these properties, the tree also stands for the normative values of matriliny, which is the basic principle of Ndembu society structure, for tribal traditions, and ultimately "for the unity and continuity of Ndembu society." However, in other contexts or even in the same extended ritual, the milk tree can play other roles, such as signifying the tension between the initiate's mother (familial claims) and all the other women of the tribe (social claims).[83]

The mobilization of such symbols in ritual involves a dynamic exchange between their two poles: the orchestration of the sensory experiences associated with such symbols can effectively embed their allied ideological values into people's consciousnesses, endowing the ideological with sensory power and the sensory with moral power. Wrapped in a blanket at the base of the tree, the Ndembu girl is said to "swallow instruction" as a baby swallows milk. What she swallows, of course, is instruction in tribal matters, values, and images. In this way, Turner argued, the ritual provides tangible and compelling personal experiences of the rightness and naturalness of the group's moral values. It makes these values the stuff of one's own experience of the world. Ritual, for Turner, is a "mechanism that periodically converts the obligatory into the desirable." The symbol is the heart of this ritual mechanism; it is the irreducible unit of ritual activity.[84]

In Turner's analysis, symbols like the milk tree do not simply reflect Ndembu social values or express emotions of Ndembu communal solidarity. While the effects of ritual explored by the functionalists are not wrong, he argued, they do not give due weight to how symbols generate a system of meanings within which people act, think, and feel.[85] Turner eventually came to a very different position on the origins of symbols than did Durkheim and most functionalists. For example, Durkheim and Mauss had argued that the organization of the social group is the source of symbols and schemes of symbolic classifications, which are applied even to one's understanding of the body. Turner argued the opposite: that the human body is the source of symbols and systems of symbols, which are extended outward to organize and understand the social world. Among the most basic human symbols is the set of three colors composed of white, red, and black, representing the products of the human body: milk or semen, blood, and feces or decayed matter. Those situations in which these products are spilled from the body are ones of heightened emotion. Rooted in the body and associated with strong emotional experiences (in a way that spittle is not, for example), these colors (with their associated body products and experiences) are extended to organize other realms, such as physical drives (hunger, lust, aggression, excretion, etc.) or social relationships (children, spouses, enemies, ancestral dead, etc.). Through such networks of connections, the body becomes the basis for a cultural system for classifying the full gamut of social experience. "In contrast to Durkheim's notion that the social relations of mankind are not based on the logical relations of things but have served as the prototypes for the latter. . . . I would postulate that the human organism and its crucial experiences are the *fons et origo* of all classifications."[86] Rituals like the Ndembu girl's initiation ceremony exploit the depth, complexity and flexibility of these symbolic systems.

Turner's work is full of insights that were developed in a variety of interdependent directions. His rich ethnographic accounts of tribal personalities and political maneuvering prompted more attention to forms of network analysis, social strategies, and game theory. His emphasis on how ritual does what it does by means of a process of dramatization led him and other scholars to explore ritual as performance. In addition, his hermeneutical approach to symbols as an ambiguous and suggestive language for communicating complex ideas and attitudes about social structure led many to abandon some of the more rigid suppositions of functionalist-structuralist theory.[87]

Functionalism generated a number of concerns in the late 1950s and early 1960s about aspects of the structural organization of societies, ritual activities, and cultural symbols that functionalism itself was not able to answer. These concerns created a climate of receptivity to a rather different form of analysis, known as "structuralism," which was propounded by the French anthropologist Claude Lévi-Strauss (b.1908), a student of Mauss and, in his own words, an "inconstant disciple of Durkheim."[88] Lévi-Strauss produced a series of studies that began by analyzing the structure of kinship systems, paused to reinterpret totemism, and ultimately yielded a massive four-volume study of mythology entitled *Introduction to a Science of Mythology*.[89] In an earlier work, *The Elementary Structures of Kinship*, he argued that behind the great multitude of kinship practices there were a few principles or rules based on the reciprocal exchange of women between male lineages that were forbidden to marry their own women.[90] From these principles, he formulated a small number of models that underlie, he argued, the diversity of the kinship systems known to us. Ultimately Lévi-Strauss regarded all social phenomena like kinship, myth, or ritual as symbolic systems of communication, deriving from and shaped by structures of thought rooted in the human brain. Hence, in a clearly anti-Durkheimian position, Lévi-Strauss argued that the relationships of symbols orchestrated in these systems are not reflections of social structure. Rather, human beings impose these symbolic systems on social relations in order to structure and organize them. For Lévi-Strauss, social structure does not exist out there in the observable world of human interaction so much as it exists in the unconscious processes of human thought.

From this perspective, Lévi-Strauss offered a very different interpretation of the old problem of totemism, which had been central to the ritual theories of Robertson Smith, Durkheim, Freud, and many of their disciples. Instead of a mystical communion and confusion of humans and animals, Lévi-Strauss saw totemism as evidence for how cultural classification systems are rooted in a particular cognitive process. First, by virtue of structures of binary opposition within the brain, human beings oppose the cultural world to the natural world. Then, a natural taxonomy drawn from the world around them—specifically, the relationships among animals—is applied to the world of culture in order to organize, elucidate, and legitimate its sociocultural relationships. Lévi-Strauss argued that totemism is a matter of representing each human social grouping or clan by a distinct animal species, with the "natural" relationships among the animal species providing a way of thinking about the relationships among human social clans. In other words, the relationship between an animal and a particular social group is not one of mystical communion but one of logical analogy: "the term totemism covers relations, posed ideologically, between two series, one *natural*, the other *cultural*."[91] The contrast between nature and culture, he avowed, is the most fundamental of the binary oppositions that organize human thought. In this way, Lévi-Strauss analyzed conceptual systems like totemism as linguistic codes that communicated in the same way that a spoken language communicated, that is, by virtue of binary oppositions—a revolutionary view of language developed in the work of the linguist Ferdinand de Saussure (1857–1913).[92]

In analyzing ritual, Lévi-Strauss tended to oppose it to myth, casting the two as contrasting processes, one verbal, the other nonverbal, myth as a matter of content, ritual as a matter of form. He saw the mythical process as one that "turns away from the continuous to segment and break down the world by means of distinctions, contrasts and oppositions." The ritual process, however, attempts to take "the discrete units" created by mythical thinking and pull them back together as best it can into an experience of reality as continuous and seamless. For Lévi-Strauss, the experiential impossibility of fully reconstituting the seamless whole that myth had fractured and broken apart accounts for the "stubborness and ineffectiveness" seen in the "desperate, maniacal aspects of ritual."[93] Hence, he concluded, ritual is not a reaction to the world, emotional or otherwise, nor an enactment of the conceptual categories of the cultural group found in myth. Instead, it is a reaction to what thought and myth have done to the world, a rather doomed attempt to restore a mindless continuity to experience. Such a description hardly amounts to a real theory of ritual, and Lévi-Strauss was not especially concerned to develop one; he was content to see ritual primarily as a foil to myth. Nonetheless, his structural method for analyzing myth greatly influenced scholars who were very concerned with ritual, particularly Mary Douglas and Edmund Leach.

Like Turner, the British anthropologist Mary Douglas (b. 1921) also developed a special functional-structuralist approach that has had a major impact on ritual theory. Her 1970 study, *Natural Symbols*, presented a useful extension of Turner's notions of structure and antistructure in terms of contrasting degrees of "grid" and "group" in society. Grid refers to the strength of the rules governing the interrelationship of individual roles and formal positions in a society, while group refers to the strength of people's associations as a tightly knit or closed community: "[Grid] is order, classification, the symbolic system. [Group] is pressure, the experience of having no option but to consent to the overwhelming demands of other people."[94] Douglas used two intersecting axes to chart the degree of grid and group, generating four quadrants to correspond to four hypothetical types of societies: one with strong grid and strong group, one with strong grid but weak group, one with weak grid and strong group, and one with weak grid and weak group (see diagram).[95] She argued that societies with strong grid or strong group exert a great deal of control over individuals and are marked by a fair amount of ritual activity; societies with weak grid or weak group exert less control, have less ritual, and allow for more individualism.

Douglas's analysis tended to support Turner's idea that ritual provides a reinforcement of both gridlike structure and grouplike antistructural experiences of communitas. Indeed, her system is able to correlate, to an unprecedented extent, the degree of ritualization in a society, its general patterns of social organization and worldview, and a variety of other social attitudes toward such things as the body, god, sin, and sorcery.

Although she never departed from a fundamentally Durkheimian position on the origin of symbolic systems in the forms of social organization, Douglas also effectively replicated many aspects of Lévi-Strauss's work. "Ritual," she argued, "is preeminently a form of communication," and, like speech, it is generated from social relations and exercises in turn a "constraining effect on social behavior."[96] For Douglas, the symbolic communication of ritual activity always reproduces the real social relations among human beings, as seen in even her most "structural" interpretations of purity and pollution, food taboos in the biblical book of Leviticus, and the organization of a normal meal.[97] However, Douglas's British colleague Edmund Leach (1910–1989) went further in applying Lévi-Strauss's structural linguistics to anthropological issues, especially in a small book entitled *Culture and Communication: The Logic by Which Symbols Are Connected*.[98] Leach used a structural focus on binary oppositions to reanalyze rites of passage, such as those discussed by van Gennep and Turner, and ritual sacrifice, such as the animal offerings of the Nuer explored by Evans-Pritchard. Yet, in contrast to the binary oppositions isolated by Lévi-Strauss, Leach emphasized the role of mediating or liminal categories in keeping with the notion of a liminal stage in ritual described by van Gennep and Turner. This liminal state mediates old and new positions in the social order; in a similar way, the activities of the sacrifice mediate the realms of this human world and the other world of the gods. For Leach, rituals help sustain a neat, synchronic conceptual system by making it possible for distinct categories—like the sacred and the profane, the natural and the cultural—to impinge on each other in carefully circumscribed ways. Ritual is a form of nonverbal communication, but, like linguistic communication, its signs and symbols have meaning only by virtue of their place in systems of relationships with other symbols. Although ritual conveys information about the most basic conceptual categories and ordering systems of the social group, it is used primarily to transform one category into another while maintaining the integrity of the categories and the system as a whole. In other words, only ritual can transform a boy or girl into an adult, an animal into a gift to the gods, and the realm of the gods into a presence responsive to human needs while still maintaining all the boundaries that enable these categories to organize reality. In effect, Leach redescribed van Gennep's basic points in a Lévi-Straussian fashion.

In sum, structuralism grew out of a functional concern with the organization of social groups which tended to see ideas, values, theologies and symbols as direct or

Group

↑

STRONG GROUP, STRONG GRID

- Purity: strong concern for purity; well-defined purification rituals; purity rules define and maintain social structure
- Ritual: a ritualistic society; ritual expresses the internal classification system
- Magic: belief in the efficacy of symbolic behavior
- Personal Identity: a matter of internalizing clearly articulated social roles; individual subservient to but not in conflict with society
- Body: tightly controlled but a symbol of life
- Trance: dangerous; either not allowed or tightly controlled and limited to a group of experts
- Sin: the violation of formal rules; focus upon behavior instead of internal state of being; ritual (magic) efficacious in counteracting sin
- Cosmology: anthropomorphic; nondualistic; the universe is just and noncapricious
- Suffering and Misfortune: the result of automatic punishment for the violation of formal rules; part of the divine economy

STRONG GROUP, WEAK GRID

- Purity: strong concern for purity but the inside of the social and physical bodies are under attack; pollution present and purification ritual ineffective
- Ritual: ritualistic; ritual focused upon group boundaries, concerned with expelling pollutants (witches) from social body
- Magic: ineffective in protecting individual and social bodies; a source of danger and pollution
- Personal Identity: located in group membership, not in the internalization of roles, which are confused; distinction between appearance and internal state
- Body: social and physical bodies tightly controlled but under attack; invaders have broken through bodily boundaries; not symbol of life
- Trance: dangerous, a matter of demonic possession; evil
- Sin: a matter of pollution; evil lodged within person and society; sin much like a disease; internal state of being more important than adherence to formal rules, but the latter still valued
- Cosmology: anthropomorphic; dualistic; warring forces of good and evil; universe is not just and may be whimsical
- Suffering and Misfortune: unjust; not automatic punishment; attributed to malevolent forces

Grid ←————————————————————————→

WEAK GROUP, WEAK GRID

- Purity: pragmatic attitude; pollution not automatic; bodily waste not threatening, may be recycled
- Ritual: will be used for private ends if present; ego remains superior; condensed symbols do not delimit reality
- Magic: private; may be a strategy for success
- Personal Identity: pragmatic and adaptable
- Body: instrumental; self-controlled; pragmatic attitude
- Trance: not dangerous
- Sin: failure; loss of face; stupidity
- Cosmology: geared to individual success and initiative; cosmos is benignly amoral; God as junior partner
- Suffering and Misfortune: an intelligent person ought to be able to avoid them

WEAK GROUP, STRONG GRID

- Purity: rejected; antipurity
- Ritual: rejected; antiritual; effervescent; spontaneity valued
- Magic: none; magic rejected
- Personal Identity: no antagonism between society and self, but old society may be seen as oppressive; roles rejected, self-control and social control low
- Body: irrelevant; life is spiritual; purity concerns absent, but body may be rejected; may be used freely, or ascenticism may prevail
- Trance: approved, even welcomed; no fear of loss of self-control
- Sin: a matter of ethics and interiority
- Cosmology: likely to be impersonal; individual access, usually direct; no mediation; benign
- Suffering and Misfortune: love conquers all

↓

indirect projections of this social organization. However, this direct or indirection connection between social organization and cultural ideas became hard to demonstrate in a convincing fashion. Structuralism emerged as the attempt to pursue what increasingly appeared to be the autonomous order of cultural values, symbols, beliefs, and practices. No longer did theorists assume that a symbol was a projection of some social relationship. Rather, a symbol was seen to have no fixed meaning in itself or in relation to a fixed social reality; its meaning depended on how it was grouped with other symbols. The syntactical grouping of symbols in structured relationships, interconnecting systems, and elaborate classificatory taxonomies made it clear that this realm of symbols had a much more complicated relationship with social organization and action than functionalism had surmised. While Turner and Douglas began to expound more structural understandings of functionalism, Leach's work was particularly instrumental in demonstrating structuralism's potential for analyzing ritual. His contributions, as well as developments in the work of Turner and Douglas, are an important part of the next chapter. These new forms of structural analysis were also indebted to another contribution by social functionalists, namely, their repeated scrutiny of the categories of magic and religion. Indeed, speculations about magic rooted in the nineteenth century were a popular way of thinking about religious activities, especially those of other peoples.

Magic, Religion, and Science

Underlying the history of scholarly analysis of ritual just outlined is an important current of thinking about magic and magic's relation to religion and science that has been critical to shaping successive understandings of ritual. Traditionally, ritual has been distinguished from other modes of action by virtue of its supposed nonutilitarian and nonrational qualities. Due to this distinction, shaking hands is a ritual, but planting potatoes for food is not. Like nonutilitarian, nonrational denotes the lack of any practical relationship between the means one chooses to achieve certain ends. Hence, there is no intrinsic causal relationship between shaking hands and forming a nonthreatening acquaintance with someone; the handshake is an arbitrary cultural convention and could, in another culture, just as easily signify quite different intentions. Likewise, washing one's hands to clean them is not a ritual, since there is a necessary connection between the means and the end but the repeated hand washing irrespective of cleanliness that is seen in compulsive behavior is apt to be considered ritualistic, as Freud noted.[99] In brief, these distinctions have meant that if a cultural action serves no practical purpose, then it is ritual.

Just as this understanding of the nonrational and nonutilitarian has been a major criterion of what constitutes ritual and distinguishes it from ordinary, logical, or scientific modes of acting, it has also been invoked to express an underlying difference between modern and primitive societies, as well as between profane and sacred ways of looking at the world. A number of theorists have used these distinctions in even subtler extensions, such as distinguishing religious rituals from magical rituals. Rites deemed to be truly nonutilitarian, a matter of "pure worship" so to speak, were categorized as religious, while those nonrational acts that appeared to seek a very

practical result, such as healing or rainfall, were deemed to be magic. Some theorists explicitly contrasted both religious and magical practices to science, defined as
rational action in pusuit of a practical result. In this way the simple opposition of
utilitarian and nonutilitarian action generated the popular triad of magic, religion,
and science.[100]

Tylor and other early theorists were very concerned to distinguish clearly between the "higher" mode of religiosity seen in Christianity and the "lower" mode
seen in "primitive" religions. They saw the first as characterized by revelation, monotheism, morality, and intercessionary worship; the second was characterized as amoral,
polytheistic, and concerned only with the pursuit of personal advantage through
magical practices. From this perspective, Tylor considered magic totally distinct from
religion. Indeed, he saw it as more akin to science than religion, a pseudoscience, to
be precise, in the sense of an inherently faulty attempt to fathom the cause-and-
effect relationships in nature. In Tylor's evolutionary view, magic as such would eventually be replaced by both real religion and real science.[101]

Frazer followed Tylor in seeing magic as quite distinct from real religion, but
"never a science" and more a "bastard art" that does not worship and supplicate but
rather contrives to make things happen. He also linked magic, religion, and science
in an explicit evolutionary sequence. Yet, despite the relegation of magic to the more
primitive end of human experience, Frazer attempted to analyze the type of logical
reasoning used in magic as he understood it. He identified two principles of nonsci-
entific logic: first, "homeopathy," the law of similarity, or the principle that "like produces like" (pouring water encourages rain); and "contagion," the law of contact, or
the principle that "things which have once been in contact continue ever afterwards
to act on each other" (harm caused a piece of hair will be felt by the person who
owns the hair).[102] With these principles, Frazer attempted to make some sense of
the many odd rituals reported in ethnographic accounts. Of course, he was not alone
in trying to understand the so-called primitive mind. The very influential work of
Lucien Lévy-Bruhl, How Natives Think (1910), also attempted to unravel the irrational and mystical logic, or mentalité, behind the magical practices and worldviews of
native peoples.[103]

Durkheim took a more sociological approach to the question of magic, distinguishing magic and religion primarily on the basis of the social relationships involved
in each. His extended analysis developed the insight of Robertson Smith, who suggested that magic is opposed to religion as the individual is opposed to the social
group.[104] Religion differs from magic, for Smith and Durkheim, precisely because it
is not "an arbitrary relation of the individual man to a supernatural power" but the
relation of "all the members of a community to a power that has the good of the
community at heart."[105] Although beliefs and rites are found in both magic and religion, continued Durkheim, in religion they are shared by a defined group, and it is
the profession of them that unites the group into a single moral community or church.
Magical beliefs and rites, however, do not unite people no matter how popular they
may be, since such practices always involve individuals: "the magician has a clientel
and not a Church."[106] As an individual and not a communal practice, magic falls
outside the group dynamics that Durkheim believed gave rise to religion as a social
institution. In a basic way, therefore, he does not fully account for it.[107]

Malinowski explicitly rejected the evolutionary aspects of the theories of Frazer, Lévy-Bruhl, and Durkheim as typical of armchair anthropologists.[108] He knew from his firsthand fieldwork among the Trobriand Islanders, for example, that they were as rational as anybody and that magic, religion, and a body of scientific knowledge can simultaneously exist side-by-side: "There are no peoples however primitive without religion and magic. Nor are there, it must be added at once, any savage races lacking either in scientific attitude or in science."[109] Yet each type of reasoning is used for different purposes and in different contexts. Religious rituals, for example, are concerned with common traditions of communion with spirits, ancestors, or gods and tend to address emotional or psychological needs. By contrast, magic, for Malinowski, is essentially manipulative and thus contrasts with religion, which aspires to a more authentic relationship with divine beings. In his view, magic commands, while religion seeks. In magic, techniques are a means to an end; in religion, worship is an end in itself. Hence, while he saw both magic and religion as nonrational and the very opposite of scientific, technical, or causal activity, Malinowski also maintained the distinction drawn by Tylor and Frazer that magic is essentially manipulative — precisely because it is *not* a pseudoscience. It is a natural emotional reaction to situations in which technical knowledge or skills are unable to guarantee success. "Magic flourishes wherever man cannot control hazard by means of science. It flourishes in hunting and fishing, in times of war and in seasons of love, in the control of wind, rain and sun, in regulating all dangerous enterprises, above all, in disease and in the shadow of death."[110] He demonstrated, for example, that magical rituals were not used to sail canoes, at which the Trobrianders were very skilled, or to fish in shallow lagoons. However, magical rites were often used when fishing on the open sea, which could be both dangerous and unsuccessful. Malinowski gave a functionalist explanation by noting that in this type of context such rites made people adventurous and optimistic, enhancing the self-confidence that is necessary for effective cooperation. The logic of magical rituals lay in how they were used — primarily to alleviate anxiety. The function of magic, therefore, was "to ritualize man's optimism, and to enhance his faith in the victory of hope over fear."[111]

Evans-Pritchard's 1937 study of witchcraft among the Azande of the Sudan also stressed the intellectual rationality of their so-called magical beliefs: "Is Zande thought so different from ours that we can only describe their speech and actions without comprehending them, or is it essentially like our own though expressed in an idiom to which we are unaccustomed?" he asked.[112] Analyzing the categories of Zande thought, he found that magic and witchcraft are a coherent but flexible set of ideas. While so fully embedded in action that they are hard to formulate in the abstract, these practices explain what cannot be explained in other ways. Magic also proved to be part and parcel of Zande religious beliefs, not something separate either theoretically or practically. Yet the Azande distinguish clearly between witchcraft, sorcery, and good magic or bad magic. The fact that neighboring tribes like the Dinka and the Shilluk had few magical beliefs, while the Azande were completely preoccupied with them, suggested special aspects to Zande social life and worldview that Evans-Pritchard pursued.

Evans-Pritchard's most famous example is the Zande interpretation of the granary that collapsed, killing two people who happened to be sitting under it. The

Azande were perfectly well aware of the fact that termites had damaged the granary supports, leaving the edifice likely to fall over at any moment. Yet such "scientific" reasoning did not explain what was for them the most important and obvious question: why did the granary happen to fall just when it did, killing those particular people? To answer *this* question, the Azande turned to explanations of witchcraft.[113] Evans-Pritchard traced Zande witchcraft accusations and the use of magical medicines to their roles in social relationships and communal tensions. Ultimately, he argued, the purpose of magical beliefs and practices is not the Malinowskian notion of enhancing optimism and self-confidence but an attempt, simultaneously much more social and intellectual, both to relate unusual events to their systems of belief in larger forces and to seek to affect such events through these same forces. Hence, Zande witchcraft and magic form a comprehensive system of interpretations and ritual activities sufficiently flexible to deal with a wide variety of events and not be readily disproven by experience. Moreover, Evans-Pritchard made clear, magical rites may be performed in conjunction with technical or utilitarian actions, not in place of them. Without abandoning a distinction between empirical and ritual activities, he argued that each has to be understood in its own terms: rituals are not concerned with empirical ends, yet they are perfectly rational when understood in reference to the traditional beliefs about gods that accompany them.[114]

In an early study, Douglas raised two equally important questions concerning magic: why do some societies place more emphasis on witchcraft beliefs than others, and why have European scholars defined magic the way they have? After reviewing theories of magic from Tylor to Robertson Smith, Douglas wryly noted a curious parallelism, particularly clear in the work of Robertson Smith: namely, treatment of the "ethical" religion of the ancient Hebrews in contrast to the "magical" religion of their tribal neighbors paralleled Protestant views of the contrast between the ethical focus of the Reformed churches and the magical style of Catholicism so given to "mumbo jumbo" and "meaningless ritual." Douglas concluded that the study of comparative religion had unwittingly "inherited an ancient sectarian quarrel about the value of formal ritual" and that it was this sectarian quarrel that led scholars to define "magic" as a matter of primitive, manipulative rituals that expect to be automatically effective in contrast to the high ethical content and disinterested pure worship of "religion."[115] For Douglas, the solution was to treat both religion and magic as forms of symbolic action reflective of particular forms of social organization.

In a later discussion of the Bog Irish of London, Douglas contrasted these very traditional Catholics and their adherence to Friday abstinence from meat with Protestant religiosity, which has promoted the importance of good works and intentionality over such ritual practices that smack of totemic taboo. She argued that both types of religious ethos and their corresponding forms of ritual behavior, the magical-sacramental on the one hand and the ethical-commemorative on the other, are determined by social organization. It is certainly not the case that one involves magic, while the other involves real religion. Both forms of ritual and religiosity must be analyzed in terms of the expressive function of ritual and the different social values and structures that are being expressed in each case.[116] In this argument, Douglas dispensed with any intrinsic distinction between utilitarian and nonutilitarian forms of ritual behavior; both types of communities use ritual, but the *styles* of ritual differ in accordance with the different social organization and values of these communities. The Friday abstinence rituals of the Bog Irish are similar to the refusal to eat pork in traditional Jewish communities, and both practices can be explained in terms of social factors. For example, both communities are relatively closed groups intent upon maintaining their minority identity in the face of a powerful majority that has open rather than closed forms of organization and espouses universal values rather than particular customs. The so-called magical forms of symbolic action are simply the type of ritual practice found in such local and closed communities, while so-called religious forms of symbolic action are those types that derive from other social structures, particularly accompanying the emergence of translocal groupings. For Douglas, the basic principle of ritual action is the same in both cases: ritual is always a matter of symbolic actions that express sociological truths in cosmological terms.[117]

The nineteenth- and twentieth-century debate over magic, religion, and science has successively defined ritual activity as nonrational, then as rational given its premises, and finally as a fundamentally symbolic form of communication, which means that it is irrational with respect to science but rational in terms of its internal coherence and purpose![118] This last definition subsumes magical ritual and religious ritual, treating both in terms of the symbolic, expressive, and even linguistic nature of human activity. With this perspective, therefore, the distinction between magic and religion collapses and was soon retired; as a result a focus on "ritual" in general emerged more clearly. Nonetheless, lingering concerns and distinctions mean that ritual activity is still apt to be contrasted with utilitarian, technical, or scientific behavior. Stanley J. Tambiah (b. 1929) has straddled these transitions, on the one hand invoking Frazer and Malinowski's problematic formulations of magic and religion, while on the other hand beginning to apply a linguistic perspective on symbolic action that changes the nature of the original distinctions completely. In contrast, the work of Edmund Leach takes little cognizance of any significant differences among so-called magical rites and expressive political or technological actions—all are analyzed in terms of the logic of linguistics.

In an article entitled "The Magical Power of Words," Tambiah challenged a particular notion of magic rooted in the theories of Frazer and Malinowski, namely, that "primitive" peoples believe that words can accomplish things because of a mistaken belief in the intrinsic identity of the word and the thing. For example, the ritual casting of spells to exorcise demons, dispel pestilence, and so on has been considered magical because scholars presumed that the practitioners of such arts expected the power of the words themselves to accomplish the deeds. Tambiah attacked this scholarly presumption in several ways. First, he noted that despite a Frazerian contrast between spells and prayers, both can be readily found within a single ritual, and he used Sri Lankan rituals as examples. Second, he attempted to "explode the classical theory" by showing that so-called magic is not based on a belief in the "real identity between word and thing" but is based instead on an "ingenious" use of "the expressive and metaphorical properties of language."[119]

Tambiah used two terms from the linguistic studies of Roman Jacobson, whose influence was being widely felt in structural studies like those of Lévi-Strauss.[120] "Metaphor" and "metonymy" denote uses of language that are considered central to its expressive properties. A metaphoric relationship meant that A is treated as if it were B (a game of chess is compared to the game of life; pouring water is an analogy for rain), while a metonymic relationship treated A as if it were a part of B (a crown indicates royalty or the queen herself; the cross stands for Christ, and if it is a bit of the true cross, then it may be deemed to possess some degree of his holiness due to physical contact). These two principles echo Frazer's two laws of magic: he saw the law of similarity in the way that linguists see metaphorical relations, while the law of physical contact functions as a metonymical connection. In exploring how the metaphors and metonymies of ritual language actually work, Tambiah found only a heightened form of what constitutes ordinary language, not anything qualitatively different. Ritual language is not mumbo jumbo, he concluded; it is intelligible, rational, and logical in the way it exploits the properties of language in general. Ritual language works, he argued, by addressing participants, not gods, "using a technique which attempts to restructure and integrate the minds and emotions of the actors."[121] For example, from Malinowski's descriptions of Trobriand Island garden magic, a fertility-enhancing spell recited before turning the soil uses a formulaic invocation of metaphors to analogize planting and harvesting with larger concepts governing pregnancy, canoeing, and other realms organized by Trobriand cultural categories. For Tambiah, such formulas integrate the technical, aesthetic, and evaluative dimensions of human behavior.

In later studies, Tambiah continued to discuss "magical acts," by which he meant ritual modes of thought and action in contrast to scientific modes. While arguing that both science and ritual are based on analogical thought, he held that they differ in their objectives and criteria for validity. Ultimately, however, he also pointed to the notion of performance to explain how they differed: ritual acts are "performative" in nature and can be evaluated and understood only in terms of performative linguistic categories.[122] By "performative," Tambiah meant the particular way in which symbolic forms of expressions simultaneously make assumptions about the way things really are, create the sense of reality, and act upon the real world as it is culturally experienced. The performative dimension of ritual action has become a central idea in most current theories of ritual.

Leach also proposed a reinterpretation of magic in terms of its use of language. He took the example of a sorcerer who secures a piece of hair from the head of his intended victim; accompanied by spells and rites, the sorcerer destroys the hair and predicts that the victim will soon sustain injury. What is the logic underlying this activity, Leach asked. In answer, he argued that the so-called magical nature of the act is rooted in a logical fallacy, but it is a type of fallacy that we routinely use in our language due to the powerful symbolic effect that it can have. The sorcerer deliberately mistakes the relationship that obtains between a person and a piece of his or her hair: what is a disconnected and former piece of the person (a metonymical relation) is taken to be an analogous replica or stand-in (metaphorical relation) for the person. The actual relationship that results when a piece of hair is in the hands of the sorcerer is mistakenly understood as the same as having the head of the victim in the sorcerer's hands. For Leach, the logic of what has been traditionally dubbed magic is simply the juxtaposition of one set of relations for another. In terms of linguistic theory, a metonymical relation is taken to be metaphorical relation. The same type of operations also take place, he reasons, in the simple act of feeling for the familiar shape of a light switch in a dark room and expecting that a press of the switch will result in the illumination of the room by a light fixture somewhere. It is by virtue of convention and habit, not technical knowledge, that we take the pressing of a switch to signal the appearance of light. Leach makes clear that the logical fallacies by which the sorcerer could threaten his victim are commonplace in our various forms of cultural communication; there is nothing uniquely magical or ritualistic about these fallacies. "I am not suggesting," Leach writes, "that we *should* treat light switching as an act of magic, but only that, if Sir James Frazer had been consistent, *he* should have done so! The action is technical in intention and *may be* technical in its consequences, but the actual form of the action is expressive."[123]

The prominence of magic in early theories of ritual and religion has now given way to approaches to ritual that usually do not make these distinctions. Indeed, many of the scholars described in this chapter would now see the term as a hindrance to objective analysis and as closely tied to historical biases, such as Protestant-Catholic and modern-primitive prejudices. The recent tendency has been to see differences in forms of ritual activity as rooted first in different social structures, as when small local communities struggling to maintain their identities are compared to large, inclusive congregations attempting to create allegiances over and above local groups. A secondary recent tendency, rooted in linguistic analysis, also distinguishes forms of symbolic, expressive, or performative modes of communication. Nonetheless, witchcraft and sorcery are now nearly technical terms for describing specific forms of religious activity associated with particular social and doctrinal features.[124] In the end, they have all been subsumed as examples of ritual behavior, which now includes high mass in a Greek Orthodox church, the swearing in of the president, school graduation ceremonies, and the special talismanic actions taken by a pitcher as he gets ready to throw a baseball. This is not to say that scholars do not see any differences among these rites but simply that what they share has become of greater theoretical interest than what seems to distinguish them—at least for the time being.

Profile: Interpreting the Mukanda Initiation

Just the Babylonian Akitu festival attracted certain theories of ritual and became a much reworked example among those concerned with the origin or essence of ritual, the Ndembu Mukanda initiation for young boys is a good representative of the type of ritual that social functionalists and structuralists turn to interpret. Turner provided a very detailed description of the Mukanda as he observed it among the Ndembu in 1953, while also using other ethnographic accounts for comparison and amplification. His description makes explicit use of the theoretical views of other interpreters, notably van Gennep and Gluckman. After a very brief general sketch of the Mukanda itself, this section presents each level of Turner's analysis in artificially separate stages in order to demonstrate how each of these major theoreticians contributed to interpretation of this ritual. Van Gennep, Gluckman, and Turner are representative of the most influential approaches to ritual discussed in the foregoing section, even though they do not exhaust all the ways in which ritual has been defined and studied as a "social fact." Indeed, several theorists have addressed other initiations and developed rather contradictory interpretations. For example, Vincent Crapanzano explicitly challenges the notion of initiation ritual as a passage and, less directly, as a healthy medium for the definition of social identity and community.[125] Other challenges to a processual understanding of initiation—and to any theory of ritual that looks at only part of the evidence—also come from those working more closely with materials on women's experience, as in Bruce Lincoln's study of female initiation rites and Caroline Bynum's analysis of the dominant symbols in women's portrayal of the initiatory experience of conversion.[126]

The Mukanda initiation rite of the Ndembu of northwestern Zambia represents one version of the general pattern of male circumcision ceremonies found in the Bantu culture area.[127] It is also, as far as any particular ritual can be, a fairly representative example of a male initiation ceremony and typical of the many similar examples that have inspired and continue to support the theory of rites of passage. In the various myths explaining its origin, most relate how a boy was accidentally circumcised while playing among sharp grasses and the practice was thereafter adopted by all the males of the tribe. The word "Mukanda" means "to heal and make strong," and this emphasis in the ritual circumcision is borne out by the rite's symbols of purification, healing, and empowerment.

Like all male initiation ceremonies, the main purpose of the Mukanda rite is to turn boys into men. The critical mechanisms of this transformation are the removal of the boys from the care of their mothers, their circumcision by tribal elders who act as ritual experts, a period of healing and instruction in which the boys assume new duties and social identities that reinforce their relationships to their fathers, and finally a communal celebration that acknowledges the changed status of the young men as they return to places in the larger society. The full sequence of ritual activities has occasionally lasted for more than two months and involved a cluster of interdependent villages.[128] The themes stressed in the symbolism of these activities indicates that the uncircumcised boy is considered unclean, effeminate in his dependence on women, and outside the formal male governing structure of the tribe. The extended circumcision rites, therefore, act to purify him, break his connection to the world of women, and induct him into the male hierarchical power system.

The Ndembu appear to identify three main sequences within the overall Mukanda ritual, which neatly correspond to the tripartite structure van Gennep identified for rites of passage in general.[129] What van Gennep called the separation stage is known as *kwing'ija* ("causing to enter") and is marked by preliminary rites such as sanctifying certain spaces, ritual washing, and the removal of the boys from their ordinary routines into the bush, where activities culminate in the circumcision. The transitional or liminal state, identified as *kung'ula* ("at the circumcision lodge"), includes a variety of activities associated with the boys' seclusion in a specially constructed building that is off-limits to all but certain ritual officiants and male kin. There the boys are tended by their fathers and brothers as they recover from the circumcision. They receive instruction in esoteric Ndembu customs and undergo various trials and tests. The final ritual stage of incorporation, known to the Ndembu as *kwidisha* ("to take outside"), is a set of rites that return the young men to new positions within the community, including simulated intercourse to signify virility, burning the initiation lodge, dances, and a series of entries into the village. For van Gennep, the three-stage pattern reinforces the clarity or rigidity of the traditional Ndembu categories of boy and man, male and female, and circumcised and uncircumcised, while simultaneously moving people from one category to another. Hence, the ritual depicts the structure of the community as it reformulates who is who in the community; both processes are means for maintaining and enhancing the sense of community. The Mukanda also makes frequent use of the type of symbolic passage that van Gennep described so accurately, such as passing through gateways and crossing the boundaries of communal or sacral spaces, symbols of ritual killing and rebirth, secrecy and hiding, and changes in clothing and the revelation of new identities.

Max Gluckman's work on ritual pointed to the ways in which rites depict and resolve fundamental social tensions, and Turner presented ample data for applying Gluckman's theory to several levels of conflict and resolution in the Mukanda. On a structural level, Ndembu society is built upon the positive tension between two forms of organization: first, a matrilineal principle of descent that establishs one's primary identity in terms of the maternal lineage; and, second, a patrilocal principle of habitation and government according to which lineages and networks of men determine village residence and the political structure of interconnected villages. The Mukanda vividly demonstrates the conflicts that result from this dual mode of organization since the rite is orchestrated to weaken the first form of social bond, the mother-son relationship, in order to strengthen the second, the father-son relationship that is critical to the organizational harmony of clusters of villages.[130] On a symbolic level, Gluckman and Turner also find the tensions between these two forms of organization expressed in the rite. For example, the Ndembu compare a boy's uncircumcised penis to female genitals, which are considered wet and polluted. The act of circumcision is thought to correct this—it "makes manhood visible."[131] During the ritual, there is an analogous display of hostility between the mothers of the boys and the men who are ritually involved in breaking the dependence of the boys on their mothers. In keeping with this and the conflict of loyalties that needs to be resolved, a boy who cries out in pain for his mother will be deemed a coward, but no such judgment is made if he cries out for his father. On yet another more overtly political level of conflict, the Mukanda ritual is also a trial of strength for rival local leaders. Turner describes the complex and lengthy preliminary negotiations by which they compete and contend for the prestige of sponsoring it or performing important roles in the ceremonies.[132] While many of the specific activities involved in the Mukanda reflect complex power wrangling among the leaders, Turner argues that the ritual itself provisionally resolves these conflicts as people eventually play the parts they could secure for themselves and the ceremony unfolds as a living model of cooperation, tradition—and the reigning prestige order.

Besides incorporating the theories of van Gennep and Gluckman, Turner also developed specific interpretive themes of his own. In particular, he stressed how the liminal period of the initiation represents an inversion of the usual order of society. The equality of the boys is stressed when they are housed together in the bush, while other Ndembu conventions are consistently violated by means of obscene gestures, homosexuality, and taboos against touching the ground.[133] Turner saw this as a breakdown of the "natural" social hierarchy in order to facilitate an experience of communitas. It was in this vein that he also interpreted the appearance of the ancestors as masked dancers called *makishi*, whose presence collapsed distinctions between the living and the dead, the ancestral past and the present time—an interpretation that very much echoes aspects of the phenomenological theory of Eliade.[134] At critical moments in the course of the Mukanda, Turner argued, unrestrained festivities effectively asserted undifferentiated community in the face of the contending systems of structure, the matrilineal and the patrilocal. Hence, he concluded that the Mukanda is a ritual assertion of "the unity, exclusiveness, and constancy" of corporate groups and classes. In transforming "unclean" children into purified members of the male political community, the Mukanda "strengthens the wider and reduces the narrower loyalties."[135] When ritually portrayed in the Mukanda, even the mother-son and father-son relationships become symbols of more embracing and complex social relationships.

Turner echoed Gluckman when he concluded that the Mukanda is a "mechanism" for restoring a state of dynamic equilibrium among the component relationships of Ndembu society. In order to do this, the ritual mechanism must draw on time-honored practices of tradition as well as the current state of power relationships among members of the community. The goals of such a ritual are both to maintain traditional Ndembu society and to allow individuals to press for their own private interests. But Turner's analysis of the Mukanda also contrasts with how Gluckman would interpret it: the ritual does not really resolve social conflicts and result in social equilibrium; instead, the ritual dramatizes the tensions in a context in which the simultaneous expression of overarching social bonds and symbols of unity facilitates the ongoing dynamics that make up the processes of real social life.[136]

The Mukanda initiation of the Ndembu lends itself, of course, to the particular theoretical issues that concerned van Gennep, Gluckman, and Turner, and it is important that the last two developed and refined their theories among the Ndembu and peoples rather similar to them. In particular, their functional-structural theories appear particularly appropriate to groups whose social, economic and political organizations are sufficiently limited geographically that one can attempt to plot most of it and, in doing so, try to see the connections between symbolic actions and social life. Neither Gluckman nor Turner would have thought to analyze French or British ritual life with the same thoroughness, though they both regularly drew provocative comparisons. Likewise, they would not have jumped to analyze the historical records on the Babylonian Akitu festival, for which fieldwork was impossible and the information they would consider necessary to have was impossible to secure from limited records. In later works, Turner did address rituals that ranged beyond the grasp of the usual forms of fieldwork. In applying his theories of ritual to the practices of the followers of the 13th-century Francis of Assisi, medieval pilgrimage, and modern theater productions, Turner revealed an affinity with the myth-and-ritualists and the phenomenologists, namely, the concern to identify universal principles of ritual action.[137] The universality that Turner pursued was carefully couched in terms of science, that is, as a matter of regularities from which certain natural or social laws might be deduced, in contrast to the quest for a single original event, primordial pattern, or underlying essence. Nonetheless, these different orientations share the sense that ritual, if it is to be explained at all, must be interpreted in large part by reference to nonsituational principles.

In an analysis of women's initiation rituals, Bruce Lincoln suggests that van Gennep's spatial model for ritualized social passage does not work very well. There seems to be a different set of symbols used in women's initiations since the young girl is hardly ever really separated from village and family. She may be isolated but usually well within the orbit of her family. Instead of a symbolic logic of separation-liminality-reincorporation, Lincoln suggests that the symbols of enclosure-metamorphosis-emergence are more appropriate. He also finds that many women's initiations appear to rely on a logic of molding in order to transform an immature girl into culturally defined image of womanhood. While the symbolic activities used in this transformative process are varied, they tend to be more evocative of the cocoon metamorphosis of a caterpillar into a butterfly than of a boy passing through dangerous and purifying ordeals to return as a warrior.[138]

Using very different materials, the medieval historian Caroline Bynum finds a similar disjunction between the van Gennep–Turner theory of initiatory passage and women's experience. The experience of transition, liminality, and inversion so basic to Turner's model of initiation — and initiatory narratives — appears to fit accounts of male religious experience, such as the story of St. Francis, but not women's understandings of what they are experiencing. Male adoption of female dress or self-references at critical (liminal) turning points in their spiritual life clearly signifies loss of self and birth of a new self, but female recourse to male dress or symbols, if it happens at all, appears to be a pragmatic social decision while the woman's self-image remains stoutly female. Bynum could also find no structure of separation, transitional breach, and reincorporation or dramatic turning points and reversals. In the case of the 15th-century English mystic Margery Kempe, she "achieves spiritual growth not by reversing what she is but by being more fully herself." This may not be surprising since women in these centuries could hardly, like Francis, "take off all their clothes and walk away from their fathers or husbands."[139] Bynum suggests that while Turner accurately notes how liminal women are to men, thereby making female imagery a natural source of reference for dramatic changes in male status, the opposite was not true. Medieval women, at least, did not tend to see themselves as liminal or as liminal in relation to men. She concludes that Turner's theory may be truer for those who occupy a certain place in the structure, namely, elites, those who in effect *are* the structure. As such, van Gennep's and Turner's notions of a process of social transition marked by liminality may not be as universal as they supposed.[140]

Vincent Crapanzano also launched a frontal assault on van Gennep's theory of rites of passage and, by implication, those theories so indebted to van Gennep, such as Gluckman's and Turner's. On the basis of studies of Moroccan rites of circumcision, Crapanzano specifically argues that the alleged three-stage structure of rites of passage "may reflect less the reality of the ritual than the culture of the anthropologist."[141] Unlike most functionalists, who look to the structure of the rite to see how it works to reinforce the structural order of society, Crapanzano notes the perspectives of the individuals involved. These individual perspectives are not the same, of course, and any general theory of what ritual does would have to deal with this variety. However, to demonstrate the problems with van Gennep's reigning paradigm, Crapanzano focuses on the perspective of the young boy undergoing the ritual circumcision. This focus is sufficient, argues Crapanzano, to expose the "ritual illusion" to which scholars have succumbed, namely, the assumption that ritual actually does what it says it does. For example, if the ritual declares that the boy is now being made a man, scholars have believed that to be the case. Crapanzano suggests that what ritual is doing is much more complicated, and theories that emphasize ritual as a functional mechanism for legitimate passage and successful incorporation into social groups are misleading.

Based on his observations in Arab villages in Morocco, Crapanzano provides a rather different interpretation of circumcision as part of male initiation. The ritual, he argued, creates a fundamental disjunction, not passage:

> [The ritual] declares passage where there is in both ritual and everyday life no passage whatsoever—only the mark of passage, the mutilation that is itself an absence, a negation. . . . It is a precocious rite. The boy is declared a man before he is (emically as well as etically) physically a man—or is treated as a man. . . . [It is] a series of contradictory messages that remain unresolved, at least in the ritual immediate."[142]

In a Moroccan village, a boy is circumcised as soon as he is old enough to "remember" the event, usually between three and six years old, although economic factors and the presence of siblings can affect the timing. In contrast to the Ndembu Mukanda, the Moroccan ritual is a necessary prerequisite for both spiritual and sexual manhood; it does not confer manhood. The ritual involves only a temporary separation from the world of women, a brief and ambiguous excursion into manhood, after which the boy is returned to his mother. There is a public procession in which the father takes the boy, mounted on a horse or mule, to the central male domain, the local mosque, but while they say a few prayers, the father must carry his son to keep him from touching the ground. Prior to this procession, however, the womenfolk paint the boy's hands and feet with henna in the manner of a bride, and his head may be shaved. On returning from the mosque, the father disappears. The surgery is done by a male barber with other men to hold the boy still, but it is his mother who carries him into the room, stands by the door during the operation, and receives him in her arms, swaddled like an infant, when it is over. Then she dances for a short while with her bleeding son pressed against her bare back before taking him away to be tended by women until he is well again. Clearly, this is not a linear progression from boyhood to manhood. For Crapanzano, it is more of a circular return.[143]

With an ethnographically sophisticated reading of the psychosocial ramifications of Oedipal desires, Crapanzano implies that Moroccan circumcision is experienced by the boy as a sobering culmination of those taboo desires. It is, therefore, an event that thrusts a child out of the illusions of childhood into the cold, anxious world of reality. The child has no choice but to submit to the ritual, and it is the submission in pain and fear that he forever remembers. For Crapanzano, the rite is orchestrated to crystallize a particularly total and dramatic submission to the demands of civilization and the group; the repression of the individual's childish desires is made all the more complete by vivid and painful memories of the roles played in the ritual by his father, mother, and larger community. The ritual is meant to instill anxiety, not resolve identity, since the boy "in his 'manhood' is deprived of his manhood." For Crapanzano, the rite is meant to induce "profound feelings of inadequacy, inferiority and worthlessness that demand constant compensation." The ritual takes the great timeless Oedipal anxiety of separation from the mother and fear of the father and inscribes them into a single event that "grounds the individual in civilization and history."[144]

Crapanzano briefly reviews the history of explanations of ritual circumcision, noting the attempt to find rational and universal explanations. Some, for example, have explained circumcision rites as an attempt to imitate female defloration, to differentiate male and female more fully, as necessary to sexual virility and procreation, as a substitute for human sacrifice, as a mark of group membership, or as a practical solution to a host of medical problems. Psychoanalytic explanations usually explain circumcision in terms of envy of female fertility, the attempt to destroy a lingering femininity associated with the womb and dependence on the mother, or as a mock castration. Crapanzano's Freudian functionalism attempts to be more ethnographically grounded than these, and he is most convincing when he points to the importance of analyzing a ritual in terms of its own particular cultural setting. Ritual circumcision may not mean the same thing everywhere. Theorists who presuppose general patterns of ritual activity, such as van Gennep's three-stage process of initiatory passage, can fail to see the complexities of specific rituals—as well as their deep-rooted ambiguities. Ritual, Crapanzano suggests, is a cultural creation and, as such, involves all the neuroses that make us humans.[145] It is not some sort of pure technology that smoothly and neatly works to socialize human beings according to general laws. This tension between interpretations that appeal, explicitly or implicitly, to universalities and those that stress the highly particular and immediate situation is central to many current debates on ritual and is addressed further in the next section on questions of meaning.

Crapanzano's interpretation of a male initiation ritual, and its qualifications of a universal ritual process, has an echo in an independent analysis of Hopi initiation by Sam Gill, who addresses the part of the nine-day process in which the children are whipped rather harshly.[146] Hopis understand the whipping as connected to the great secrets that will be revealed to the initiates, either as payment for the new knowledge or as a warning never to divulge what they have learned. However, first-person accounts of the initiatory experience make it quite clear that the whipping is minor in comparison to the pain the children feel on learning the great secret—that the kachina dancers are not the gods come down to the village as the children have been taught, they are just men of the tribe dressed up and masked. One old man remembered his feelings on the last day of the ritual festival when the truth was made known to him:

When the Katcinas entered the kiva without masks, I had a great surprise. They were not spirits, but human beings. I recognized nearly every one of them and felt very unhappy, because I had been told all my life that the Katcinas were gods. I was especially shocked and angry when I saw all my uncles, fathers and clan brothers dancing as Katcinas. I felt even worse when I saw my own father—and whenever he glanced at me I turned my face away.[147]

A Hopi woman recounted a similar reaction: "I cried and cried into my sheepskin that night, feeling I had been made a fool of. How could I ever watch the Kachinas dance again? I hated my parents and thought I would never believe the old folks again.[148]

The rite ends "on this note of discord." In analyzing this ritual of "disenchantment," Gill suggests an attempt to shock Hopi children out of a naive realism and force them to "search out a new basis for perceiving a meaningful reality." The males are then brought into the kachina cult itself, and as dancers who don masks to impersonate the gods they now must work out a theology of divine presence in a world that has been experienced as painfully disjoined.[149]

Is the Ndembu Mukanda—as van Gennep, Turner, and Gluckman would argue—a smooth passage into a secure sense of Ndembu manhood and an orchestrated experience of liminal communitas that works to diffuse tensions between the matrilineal and patrilocal systems and renew the underlying sociocultural order of Ndembu society? Or—as Crapanzano and Gill suggest—is it a family- and society-induced trauma in which childhood desires and naiveté are cruelly exposed, socializing the child into adult roles by instilling anxiety, repression, and submission? While many aspects of these interpretations are not mutually exclusive, by themselves they generate very different models for the function of ritual. The examples of a rather different symbolic logic and imagery for women's initiation rites—specifically, metamorphosis rather than territorial passage—is an important clue that theories about universal ritual structures might fail to see important aspects of ritual action.

Conclusion

Questions about how ritual functions within society gave rise to useful and influential formulations of the social dimensions of ritual activity. Functionalists and early structuralists insisted on the practicality of ritual action—how it facilitates social life—in contrast to the theorists discussed in part I, who tended to emphasize its mysticism or emotionalism and how it facilitated individual psychic identity and coherence. The functional-structuralists explored what appeared to be the "social" work of ritual activities: the formation and maintenance of the social bonds that establish human community, the socialization of the individual through an unconscious appropriation of common values and common categories of knowledge and experience, the channeling and resolution of social conflict, and the periodic renewal or transformation of the social and conceptual structures underlying community life. These analyses, however, gradually began to raise questions that reached beyond concerns with ritual's social function.

New questions addressed two major issues. The first concerned history and raised questions about how ritual and social structures changed over time or under duress. Those asking these questions rejected the "ahistoricism" of the functionalists, who had been concerned in their turn, of course, to discard the antiquated evolutionism of the myth and ritualists. The second set of questions arose around the issue of communication and the emergence of interest in how symbolic and linguistic systems work. Religious symbols and the symbolic activity of ritual appeared too complex to be mere reflections of the social order; they were clearly embedded in elaborate systems that appeared to have their own logic, and the relationship of this logic to social organization was obviously not simple and direct. Scholars began to explore the communicative nature and linguistic logic of ritual activities. Instead of how ritual functions, therefore, they began to ask what ritual means.

❧ · ❧

THREE

Ritual Symbols, Syntax, and Praxis

Questions of Cultural Meaning and Interpretation

Theorists who began to go beyond the framework of functional structuralism have been called symbolists, culturalists, and, more awkwardly, symbolic-culturalists. In contrast to how functionalism closely links symbols to social organization, culturalists tend to see these links as weak and indirect and emphasize instead the autonomy and languagelike nature of a cultural system of symbols. In other words, culturalists interpret the symbols and symbolic action so important to ritual less in terms of their connection to the structures of social organization and more in terms of an independent system organized like a language for the primary purpose of communication. This has shifted interpretation from a focus on what social reality may be represented (and maintained) by a symbol to a focus on what the symbol means (communicates) within the context of the whole system of symbols in which it is embedded. This new focus, it is argued, illuminates something other than the social organization of human groups; it illuminates "culture" as a more primary level of meanings, values and attitudes that effectively acts to shape social organization. In this view, culture cannot be reduced to being the mere projection of social organization, and social organization is, theoretically, not primary but secondary. Defined as a primary system, culture has been deemed to have sufficient autonomy to be analyzed independently of social structure, although it is generally recognized that in actual fact cultural systems interact constantly with social organization in complex ways. Social and cultural systems clearly comprise a holism, and a fresh variety of methods have been proposed to analyze that holism without reducing the cultural to the social or the social to the cultural.[1] Indeed, many cultural theories of ritual implicitly or explicitly describe ritual as the means by which the cultural system and the social system are able to interact and harmonize with each other.

The emergence of a perspective more concerned with questions of meaning than with questions of function, with so-called cultural phenomena than with so-called social phenomena, was not a sudden one. Moreover, the difference in viewpoint is not simply a historical progression from one theory to another, since a British emphasis on social issues coexists with an American emphasis on cultural issues.[2] Nor can a clear line be drawn between functional-structuralists on the one hand and symbolic-culturalists on the other. Many theories incorporate aspects of both perspectives, and a number of theorists have emphasized one or the other at different stages of their careers. Some even attempt to synthesize the two perspectives within a single mode of analysis. Victor Turner, Mary Douglas, and Edmund Leach, for example, can be fitted into both groups. Therefore, the classifications of theories presented in this chapter simply reflect a rather provisional scholarly consensus as to the dominant emphasis of any theory or scholarly corpus.

Analogies with language had turned up in earlier theories of ritual, notably those of Radcliffe-Brown and Eliade. Both men noted the structural similarities between ritual and language when approached in terms of morphology, the study of form and structure. They suggested that linguistic morphemes, the smallest meaningful word units, were analogous to the smallest meaningful structural units of ritual, which they envisioned as either set routines of action (e.g., purification acts or offerings) or set units of symbolism (e.g., sun-fire-light symbols or water-birth-life symbols). Others scholars compared rites to texts, arguing that both needed to be "decoded" in order to determine their real meaning, which was a meaning other than the conscious intentions and interpretations given to those activities by the actors themselves. While some of this terminology evoked psychoanalytic notions of decoding an unconscious subtext, it also resonated with the emergence of a science of linguistics that focused on the unconscious processes and patterns underlying the spoken statement.

Symbolic Systems and Symbolic Action

The analytical power of the cultural approach derived from its distinction between (1) a cultural level frequently equated with the conscious and unconscious ideals and values of a group and (2) a social level frequently equated with the empirical realities of lived existence. This two-tiered model made it possible to analyze culture as a semiautonomous system, even though it provoked pressing questions concerning how such an autonomous cultural system related to the actual social conditions of a community.[3] When Lévi-Strauss introduced a particularly powerful method for analyzing cultural systems of symbols, many were simultaneously receptive to it and wary of the problems it raised.

Lévi-Strauss's method of structural anthropology used a linguistic model to explain cultural phenomena other than language. Language, he wrote, is "the cultural phenomenon par excellence . . . the most perfect of all those cultural manifestations which, in one respect or another, constitute systems, and if we want to understand art, religion or law, and perhaps even cooking or the rules of politeness, we must imagine them as being codes formed by articulated signs, following the pattern of linguistic communication."[4] His method drew on developments in structural linguistics pioneered by Roman Jakobson and Ferdinand de Saussure that revolutionized linguistics in several ways. Their work effectively shifted linguistics from study of conscious spoken speech to study of the unconscious infrastructure governing the production of speech. In addition, they focused attention on the relationships among terms and how terms formed a linguistic system, as opposed to an earlier focus on how each linguistic term, as an independent entity, related to some real object in the world. From this perspective, de Saussure and Jakobson were able to formulate what they saw as general and universal laws of language.[5] Lévi-Strauss did not consider language to be the origin of culture, nor did he regard cultural systems such as art or ritual to be anything more than "akin" to language. Yet he echoed a conviction held by many linguists when he suggested that the grammarlike rules that govern the production of cultural systems like art or myth or ritual exist neither in culture nor in social organization but in the biological organization of the human brain.

Lévi-Strauss attempted to uncover this underlying grammar by decoding two main types of cultural phenomena: kinship systems and myth systems. In both cases, his structural method attempted to go beyond the obvious meaning of kinship rules or mythic story plots to get at the unconscious grammar that regulates the structure of these kinship relations and story plots. In other words, he suggested that below the level of the manifest content of kinship patterns and myths, there is another level of meaning and message residing in the grammatical form or coded structure of the system. Human beings impose a meaningful pattern on raw experience, he argued, by classifying things in ways that are not so much logical as analogical, that is, based on common similarities and opposing differences. The resulting system of classes and binary oppositions acts as a framework with which to interpret and order what would otherwise be the chaotic randomness of human experience. For Lévi-Strauss, these underlying oppositions, the most basic of which is the opposition of nature and culture, are the fundamental grammar of symbols and symbolic action; they are the rules that enable such images and activities to effectively communicate and order experience.

Although the groundwork for this critical shift in the interpretive stance of the social sciences had also been laid by many nonlinguists, including the philosopher Ernst Cassirer and the anthropologists Lévy-Bruhl and Evans-Pritchard, Lévi-Strauss's model was an important turning point.[6] Prior to him, an anthropologist like Radcliffe-Brown approached a ritual by attempting to see how its religious ideas reflected a distinct form of social organization. It was expected, for example, that societies that ritually venerated a high god would have concomitant patterns of social organization and behavior. The interpretation of high-god rituals meant, therefore, demonstrating their rootedness in a particular form of social structure and their role in maintaining that structure. After Lévi-Strauss, however, religious ideas and symbols (high gods, ancestors, food offerings, etc.) were regarded as systems in themselves; the meaning of any one symbol depended on the logic of its relationships to other symbols. The theorist decoded these relationships to uncover the invisible and unconscious structures that determined the manifest interrelationships of symbols (father gods and son gods, types of food offerings, etc.). The real meaning of the system was thought to lie in the message communicated by the invisible structural patterns. Thus, the term "structure" in the "French structuralism" represented by Lévi-

Strauss does not refer to a functional isomorphism between the structure of ideas and the structure of human social relationships. For these new structural anthropologists, social organization does not determine ideas, nor does the symbolic system lay down rules for social organization. Rather, an underlying structuring process, located in the human brain, is thought to determine both the cultural and social dimensions of a society by providing the logical models with which to order experience and resolve intellectual and social problems.

Many anthropologists were not completely convinced that biology was the real explanation of the logic of symbolic systems. Some, like Edmund Leach, were fairly committed to some form of the Durkheimian emphasis on the effects of social organization on conceptual systems, and so they modified French structuralism to suit their purposes. Leach's 1976 study, *Culture and Communication*, mentioned earlier, was subtitled "An Introduction to the Use of Structuralist Analysis in Social Anthropology" to indicate his appropriation of Lévi-Strauss's work. While accepting the linguistic framework, Leach went on to use different assumptions and tools for decoding the messages transmitted by symbolic activities like ritual. He rejected the idea of universal mental functions, arguing that when the structuralist method was applied to the myths or rituals of a particular society, it did not arrive at universal structures, simply the cultural ideals of that particular society. Just as theorists generate abstract models of cultural ideals in order to impose order on the vagaries of social behavior, so each social group generates its own abstract models or cultural ideals; these are often expressed quite clearly in ritual, but may be seldom realized in actual practice. "We engage in rituals in order to transmit collective messages to ourselves," and these messages, Leach asserted, are always about the social order.[7] Although Lévi-Strauss argued for a single source for both cultural and social dimensions, Leach continued to maintain a clear distinction between them and, in a functionalist way, saw the social dimension as the source of a symbolic system that could nevertheless be analyzed independently of it.[8]

Leach used several linguistic terms to depict the possible relationships among symbols within a cultural system. The terms "metaphor" and "metonymy" were derived from Jakobson, while the analogous terms "paradigmatic" and "syntagmatic" were derived from de Saussure and Lévi-Strauss. He compared these sets of contrasting terms to other sets like harmony and melody or symbol and sign. Other scholars have added analogous pairs: synchronic and diachronic, signals and indices, and the set of relationships implied in the terms "sign," "symbol," "index," "signal," and "icon." As noted earlier, a metaphorical relationship is one of asserted similarity or resemblance between two things that are arbitrarily connected and otherwise quite unrelated. For example, a serpent is a symbol for evil in the book of Genesis, although the relationship between serpents and evil is metaphorical—that is, conventionally asserted but essentially arbitrary. In a metonymical relationship part of something is taken to stand for the whole of it, as a crown, which is a part of royal garb, is used to stand for sovereignty. Paradigmatic associations are based on a type of structural resemblance that can be transposed to different situations. For example, the relationship of a feudal lord to his vassal is paradigmatically replicated in the medieval notion of the relationship of God to the believer or a father to his son in the context of a family. Syntagmatic associations are chainlike relationships among elements in a type of series, such as the relationship among letters that make up a word, the musical notes that make up a melody, or the words that make up a poem. Leach compared both syntagmatic and metonymical relationships to a melody, understood as the sequence of musical tones; then he compared paradigmatic or metaphorical relationships to harmony, understood as the simultaneous replication of the same pattern of sounds by different instruments. The opposition between diachrony and synchrony, patterns of change in contrast to the unchanging structure of relationships, also roughly fits this comparison of melody (a matter of change) to harmony (a matter of simultaneity). Leach argued that all these terms help describe the difference between symbols and signs and thereby illuminate various forms of communication. A symbol evokes a metaphorical, paradigmatic, or synchronic relationship between itself and what it refers to. A sign, on the other hand, involves a metonymical, syntagmatic, or diachronic relationship between itself and its referent. Signs, as opposed to symbols, do not occur in isolation; they are always contiguous with other signs that together form part of a set; it is only as part of a set that a sign can communicate information. For example, a green light means "go" only as part of the set of juxtaposed colored lights, red, yellow, and green.[9]

Since mixtures of metaphor and metonymy characterize all human communication, Leach suggested that it should be possible to determine what mixture characterizes the distinctive communication style of ritual. For example, he pointed out that the significance of the veiled bride in white is dependent upon a metaphorical relationship with the veiled widow in black, even though the relationship is not consciously perceived. He also demonstrated the more complex metaphorical and metonymical associations underlying the sacrifice of an ox, which is replaced by a cucumber, in ritual offerings to the gods among the Nuer. While Lévi-Strauss pointed to how myth can transform one set of relationships into another, Leach suggested that ritual is primarily based on a logic by which metonymical relations are transformed into metaphorical ones. For example, in the sorcery example noted earlier, the metonymical relationship between a few strands of hair and the person is transformed into a metaphorical association between the sorcerer's action on the hair and action on the body of the person.[10]

For Leach, ritual is a medium for the expression of cultural ideals and models that, in turn, serves to orient, though not prescribe, other forms of social behavior. As a medium for cultural messages, ritual enables people to modify their social order at the same time that it reinforces basic categories of it. At times, Leach described ritual as a dimension present to some degree in all activity; at other times, he implied that ritual is a fairly distinctive medium, a language geared for intellectual operations of a particularly abstract and metaphysical kind.[11] Most specifically, he pioneered the idea of ritual as an intellectual operation in which the categories affirmed as the cultural order can be transgressed. Ritual can turn a young boy or girl into a recognized adult, a piece of stolen hair into the means to make someone ill, or bread and wine into the sacralizing presence of a transcendent god. In doing these things, ritual posits bounded categories — child/adult, action here/effect there, human/divine — and then formally transgresses them. The messages that are communicated by ritual use such systems of bounded and transcended categories to promote the continuity and the flexibility of the social order. In other words, for Leach, ritual keeps a system of cultural categories responsive to human needs; ritual keeps culture meaningful.

Clifford Geertz (b. 1926) made many of these ideas more explicit and concrete in his extensive treatment of ritual. He described religion as a cultural system, that is, a system of symbols that influences people's feelings and motivations by formulating coherent conceptions of the general order of existence.[12] The symbols of religious beliefs and the symbolic activities of religious ritual constitute a system of values that acts as both "a model of" the way things actually are and "a model for" how they should be. With this famous formulation, Geertz attempted to describe how the symbols and activities of ritual can project idealized images that reflect the actual social situation, on the one hand, yet also acts as a template for reshaping or redirecting the social situation on the other. Hence, for Geertz, the symbolic system that constitutes culture is neither a mere reflection of the social structure nor totally independent of it. It always exists in response to the problems of meaning that arise in real human experiences, such as the problems of evil and suffering. When lived out in ritual, such a symbolic system provides an embracing worldview (a coherent framework of general ideas) and induces an ethos (a set of moods and motivations). It is in ritual, he suggests, that images and attitudes about the nature of existence are fused with one's actual experiences of the realities of existence: "in a ritual, the world as lived and the world as imagined, fused under the agency of a single set of symbolic forms, turn out to be the same world."[13]

A similar formulation of the workings of ritual as a symbolic system is offered by the anthropologist Nancy Munn, who describes ritual as "a symbolic intercom between the level of cultural thought and complex cultural meanings, on the one hand, and that of social action and the immediate event, on the other."[14] How does such an intercom work? Munn contends that ritual symbolism and activities draw upon a cultural code or lexicon of categories that refer to various set areas of experience in a particular society, such as categories for types of persons, deities, and bodily experiences. As part of the cultural code, these categories are organized according to patterns of opposition (e.g., human versus divine, male versus female, hot versus cold, etc.) and associative clusters (e.g., water, fertility, female, nourishment in one cluster). Ritual manipulates parts of this cultural code, recombining categories and clusters in various ways in order to communicate convincing interpretations of real life situations (e.g., death as a passage, god as dangerous, or women as weak). In this way, ritual models connections of interrelated ideas that express values basic to social life but does so by objectifying those values in symbols that are emotionally experienced by participants in the ritual.

Culturalists not only broke with functionalists by analyzing culture as a relatively independent and languagelike system of symbols, they also attempted to talk about social and cultural change. Functionalists had treated the social system as more or less static in order to try to grasp its structural patterns of organization. They were only secondarily concerned with how those structural patterns changed over time. Yet the idea that ritual mediates the interaction of two levels, cultural ideas and social experience, gave theorists a means of depicting change as a constant process. Turner had been very concerned to explain how ritual facilitates both the continuity and the redressive transformation of social structures. Geertz gave ritual a similarly important place as a mechanism of sociocultural change, but a somewhat different description of how it works. In Geertz's description, ritual enables a group's ethos and worldview—that is, their attitudes and their general concepts of world order (their experiences and their ideals)—to temper and nuance each other.[15] It is a mechanism for the ongoing processes of adaptation and renewal that constitute communities, and plays a crucial role in the way in which the sociocultural holism of a living community works. Geertz implicitly contrasted his approach with functionalist analyses when he argued that religion is sociologically interesting not because it describes the social order but because it shapes it.[16] He demonstrates this point is a description of the Balinese rite of combat between the witch Rangda, who is the embodiment of fear and horror, and the foolish but lovable monster Barong, who expresses narcissistic playfulness. Geertz points out that these two characters are not representations but powerful presences that draw the crowd into dramatic experiences of participation in the struggle. In other words, Rangda and Barong do not simply reflect the audience's experiences of life, they effectively help fashion them.[17]

In another ethnographic example, Geertz described the ritual intricacies and significance of cockfighting in Bali, where, despite its illegality, it is as central to Balinese culture as baseball is to American culture. While cockfighting evokes concerns with status, money, virility, and pride, these rituals do not functionally affect anyone's actual social status or significantly redistribute income. What the emotion-laden contest does is "render ordinary, everyday experience comprehensible" by depicting it in terms of activities for which the practical consequences have been removed or minimized to matters of appearances. When represented in the ritual of cockfighting, the meaning of everyday experience is "more powerfully articulated and more exactly perceived."[18] It is, Geertz concludes, a Balinese interpretation of Balinese social experience, "a story they tell themselves about themselves."[19] Cockfights provide people with the imagery and cultural codes with which to conceptualize, order, and reinterpret their own experiences. With this approach, Geertz effectively argues not just for the importance of ritual to what cultural life is all about but also for the importance of a focus on ritual when interpreting culture. He concluded his analysis of the cockfight with two observations that went beyond his earlier formulations and suggested new directions in analyzing ritual. First, he observed that anthropological analysis parallels the interpretation of a text: "The culture of a people is an ensemble of texts" that the anthropologist is trying to read over their shoulders.[20] Second, he argued that the function, so to speak, of the rite is not to heighten or resolve social passions, as Gluckman or Turner might have avowed, but simply to "display" them.[21] These two images, that of textual analysis and that of display, have been developed further by other ritual theorists.

The idea of a languagelike system of symbols fueled various other forms of symbolic analysis. Studies of the "language" of the food offerings made to south Indian gods or the "message" of the spirit money offerings made to Chinese deities, ancestors, and ghosts are two examples.[22] In the latter case, Chinese gods are offered gold spirit money, of which there are various kinds that correspond to the three main classes of the celestial bureaucracy according to Chinese folk religion. The ancestors are offered silver money, and ghosts are given copper cash. The value of the offerings to any one group is a function of that group's place in the whole system of offerings.

Likewise, the system of offerings communicates messages about the relative status of the invisible recipient, effectively distinguishing among groups of spirits that have different relationships with the living. Within this ritualized semantic system of money offerings, alterations in what is offered to any particular type of spirit can affect that spirit's place in the hierarchy of gods, ancestors, and ghosts. An ancestor offered only copper cash is likely to become as problematic as any ghost, while a demonic spirit to whom gold "god" money is sacrificed is likely to grow in stature and power until he or she can confer godlike blessings on those who make the offerings.[23]

Linguistics

For Turner, Leach, and Geertz, ritual is a suggestive language for communicating statements about structural relationships, but each theorist developed this idea in a distinctive way. Turner and Geertz focused more on the interaction of social experience and cultural symbols, while Leach emphasized more purely linguistic features in an attempt to formulate the rules that govern the orchestration of a ritual sequence in the same way that rules of grammar govern a verbal sequence. The Turner-Geertz style of anthropological interpretation has been labeled "symbolic," "semantic," or "semiotic" because it is concerned with interpreting the meaning of statements, activities, and events. Geertz himself wrote that "the concept of culture I espouse . . . is essentially a semiotic one. Believing with Max Weber, that man is an animal suspended in webs of significance he himself has spun, I take culture to be those webs, and the analysis of it to be, therefore, not an experimental science in search of law but an interpretive one in search of meaning."[24] In contrast, Leach's direct appeal to the field of linguistics as a model, a direction developed more fully by others, has been labeled "syntactical" since its concerns are analogous to a focus on the pattern or structure of word order in a sentence. This type of linguistic approach has aimed at a more scientific and less "interpretive" methodology. That is, it has tended to eschew interpretation for explanation, meaning for efficacy, semantics and semiology for syntax. Such theorists do not ask what ritual expresses or means; instead, they ask what the grammatical rules are that generate and structure ritual as a form of communication.

Most of these syntactical theories of ritual reflect the influence of the idea of "performative utterances" developed by the analytical philosopher J. L. Austin (1911–1960).[25] Austin attempted to analyze the instrumentality of language, that is, how, in the case of some statements, to say something is to do something. For example, the "I do" voiced by the man and woman at the proper moment in a wedding ceremony, as well as the officiant's proclamation, "I now pronounce you husband and wife," actually render the two people married. These words do not *describe* the deed; they *are* the deed. Similarly, the meaning of the statements such as "I christen this ship the *Queen Elizabeth*" or "I declare this court adjourned" must take into account the deeds that these statements actually accomplish, not just the references for each individual word.

Austin's theory of performative utterances generated a larger analysis of "speech acts," which suggests that all acts of speaking have some performative dimension.

Austin theorized that the ability to generate effective speech acts is based on one's knowledge of rules that are really "conventions" to which one's speech must conform. John R. Searle (b. 1932) developed Austin's ideas into a more comprehensive analysis of the rules that govern effective speech acts. Most significantly, while Austin distinguished among the rules for speaking, the performative act of speaking, and the actual content of what is said, Searle demonstrated that these three dimensions are all inseparably constituted in the very act itself. The basic irreducible unit of linguistic communication, for Searle, is not the symbol, word, or sentence, but the illocutionary act of producing them.[26] Analysis of the rule-governed nature of this illocutionary act held out great potential for analogous treatment of the ritual act.

Although discussion of these theories could be quite complex, the simple insight that some words do things had a profound effect on studies of ritual. As a result, ritual as a symbolic language was said to communicate not by describing, expressing, or conveying ideas, as semantic theorists like Geertz had avowed. Rather, the symbolic language of ritual actually does something, although exactly what ritual speech acts do has been explained in different ways. The syntactical approach that was ushered in by those who read Austin and Searle even led some theorists to argue that semantic interpretations are insufficient since the most essential feature of ritual language is that they are acts that do things, not mere bearers of information. Frits Staal, for example, has argued that as "pure" performance, rituals do not have any meaning.[27]

The earliest uses of Austin's and Searle's work, however, still held on to something of a semantic concern with meaning as well as certain elements of the functionalist agenda. Ruth Finnegan's early application of the idea of performative utterances to both day-to-day and more formal ritual speech patterns of the Limba of Sierra Leone demonstrated how these verbal acts perform important social transactions involving personal and social commitments.[28] In a later and much more functional study, Benjamin Ray applied Austin's notion of performative utterances to the ritual speeches of the Dinka and Dogon tribes of eastern Africa. He ignored the symbolic meaning of these speeches, that is, what they expressed in values and attitudes, in favor of demonstrating their instrumentality or what the words accomplish, namely, the creation of certain social states.[29] However, both Finnegan and Ray only dealt with ritual speech. Other uses of the linguistic approach, building on the idea that ritual activity (including ritual speech) is a language or at least analogous to a language, attempted to treat ritual activities themselves on the model of performative speech acts. Tambiah, in particular, made an explicit appeal to extend Austin's ideas beyond just ritual speech to ritual action. This perspective enabled him to analyze the structure and performative efficacy of all magical-ritual activity, as he called it, as the key to its meaning and purpose.

Theorists like Turner or Geertz developed the semantic or semiotic side of the language analogy to stress what ritual communicates, that is, the ideas, values, and attitudes it expresses and transmits. Others, however, such as Leach and Tambiah, developed the syntactical side, stressing that ritual does not communicate concepts, it produces signs in structured patterns that trigger experiences that reproduce concepts in the minds of the participants. This last formulation, specifically developed by Valerio Valeri, suggests that ritual communicates only by producing model experiences that provide an implicit understanding of the cultural system. The communicative process is, in effect, subordinate to an experiential process distinctive to ritual.[30]

In his application of linguistic theory to ritual language, Maurice Bloch argued that semantics cannot be distinguished from syntax, that meaning is transmitted by the way in which lexical or symbolic units are grammatically combined.[31] What is distinctive about ritual, he suggested, are the particular constraints it places on syntax, which make the language of speech and song very stylized and formalized. Bloch demonstrated the "poverty" of expression in ritual, how *what* can be said is greatly restricted by the *way* it must be said in order to be recognized as authoritative and legitimate ritual. The formalization of speech in ritual is produced by restricting the syntactical structures that can be chosen for use, which leads to an archaic style of speech; form becomes more important than content, while content becomes very predicable and redundant. Bloch used Austin and Searle's terminology to describe how the minimal propositional force (content) and maximum performative force (form) of these restricted speech codes influenced people not by transmitting information but by catching them up in a situation of standardized statements and responses. "You cannot argue with a song," he points out.[32] Ultimately, for Bloch, the formalized language distinctive of ritual creates and maintains a type of religious and sociopolitical authority known as "traditional authority." In traditional authority, the power of an individual or an office is understood to come from sources beyond the control of the community, as the power of a king who rules by "divine right" differs from the power of an elected public official.[33] In contrast to the structuralism of Lévi-Strauss and the semantic symbolists, Bloch echoed a syntactical concern with what ritual does, not what it says. There is, he argued, no hidden code to crack. The obvious codes of formalized and restricted speech used in ritual are the very means by which it does what it does—namely, exercise considerable social control by creating situations that compel acceptance of traditional forms of authority.

Two major theoretical studies have followed up Leach's call for work on the grammatical rules that generate ritual language, the first by Frits Staal, noted earlier, and the second by E. Thomas Lawson and Robert N. McCauley.[34] Both projects rely heavily on the linguist Noam Chomsky's theory "generative grammar." Critical of the possibility of uncovering the structure of a language directly from the empirical data of human usage, Chomsky argued for a different method, a focus on the linguistic *competence* of an "ideal speaker-listener . . . in a completely homogeneous speech community," not the linguistic *performance* of the actually spoken language. Therefore, instead of analyzing behavior and its products, Chomsky attempted to analyze the system of tacit knowledge that goes into behavior, a shift, as Lawson and McCauley describe it, from the cultural dimension of language use to the cognitive dimension of linguistic ability.[35] In a second basic argument, Chomsky also suggested that all grammatical expressions have both a surface structure and a deep structure. Linguistic expressions are generated from the deep structure by applying rules, such as rules of transformation and recursivity. Like Lévi-Strauss, Chomsky's notion of deep structure suggests the existence of a universal grammar that constrains all particular natural languages; and his work on generative grammar has attempted to construct the syntax underlying all natural languages in terms of an abstract formal system.[36]

Chomsky's methods and model are implicit in Staal's theory of ritual, despite the fact that Staal's conclusions reflect different concerns. Staal first argues strongly for the inadequacy of semantic (meaning) interpretations of ritual. For example, he contrasts two types of activity: ordinary everyday acts and ritual acts. In ordinary activity, the results are what count, and, for that reason, ordinary activity is very open to spontaneous improvisation. In ritual, however, it is the rules that count: "What is essential in the ceremony is the precise and faultless execution, in accordance with rules, of numerous rites and recitations."[37] Staal also demonstrates that what makes an ordinary action into a ritual action is not primarily a change in its meaning but a rule-governed change in its form. Hence, he concludes, an ordinary action is turned into ritual action by being subjected to formal rules of transformation. For example, verses from the Indian Vedas are transformed into ritualized *mantras* by virtue of the application of rules that govern their meter and pronunciation. As a mantra, the verse is taken out of its textual context and turned into a series of highly stylized sounds, the meaning of which is of no consequence. Indeed, many Brahman ritual experts are quite ignorant of what the sounds actually mean, but they are highly skilled in rendering them precisely according to the rules.[38] Hence, for Staal, ritual is rule-governed activity that can be understood only as such. Its meaning, he continues, would be nothing more than the various rationales that may have accrued to it over time and as such of no use in analyzing ritual as ritual: "Like rocks or trees, ritual acts and sounds may be provided with meaning, but they do not require meanings and do not exist for meaning's sake."[39]

Staal argues that analysis of the syntactical rules of ritual holds out the promise of a real science of ritual in contrast to the descriptive hermeneutics generated by semantic approaches concerned with meaning. In other words, syntactical rules can explain ritual, not just posit another subjective interpretation. Staal does not actually deny a semantic dimension to language; he simply denies that ritual is a language. As a rule-governed activity, ritual is *like* a language but is not actually a language, and for this reason, and unlike other linguistic approaches, he goes on to analyze ritual activity, not with methods specific to linguistics, but with the mathematical and logical methods that, he argues, originally gave rise to linguistics in the first place.[40] Staal concludes, in effect, that ritual predates language, as animal ritualization predates human language, and linguistic syntax itself is derived from ritual syntax. He appeals to ethological evidence to uncover the origins of ritual activity but more immediately looks to prelinguistical principles, which are somewhat comparable to those used in Chomsky's generative grammar, to recover the rules that govern and comprise ritual activity. In keeping with the idea that ritual syntax was the root of linguistic syntax, Staal credits ancient Indian ritualists and grammarians with the first science of ritual and the first linguistic theory. Based on analysis of both performed rituals and the knowledge of ritual known to Vedic experts, he identifies several major syntactical rules that constitute the grammatical structure or patterned sequence of ritual activity: recursivity, embedding, and transformation.[41]

E. Thomas Lawson and Robert N. McCauley take a different tack by stressing the inherent complementarity of interpretation and explanation, culture and cognition, or semantics and syntax as the first of two "crucial metaphysical theses."[42] They go on to formulate an analysis of religious ritual that intends to appreciate how syntax (form) shapes semantics (meaning), on the one hand, while semantics (meaning) constrains ritual syntax (form), on the other. Like other linguistic theoreticians, they regard ritual as analogous to language in that both ritual and language are traditional cultural systems bound by rules. They also adopt aspects of Chomsky's linguistic competence model in order to analyze the rules by which people generate ritual action, not specific rituals. Stressing what they call a "cognitive" approach (in contrast to the intellectualist, symbolist, and structural approaches), they regard ritual as a formal system and attempt to deduce the small set of universal "grammatical" rules that govern the generation of all forms of ritual action and expression. Ritual participants, they suggest, would know these rules in the same implicit way that English speakers know that the sentence "Curious green ideas sleep furiously" is ill conceived but syntactically correct.[43] Their second crucial metaphysical thesis is that this "competence approach" to analyzing sociocultural systems integrates the individual and the cultural (the external inherited symbolic system) by focusing on the cognitive representations that constitute an idealized participant's implicit knowledge of the cultural system.[44]

Unlike almost every other contemporary treatment of ritual, Lawson and McCauley limit their analysis to specifically religious ritual, defined as rites influenced by a belief in supernatural agents. This is due in part to the fact that they see religious ritual as the paradigmatic focus of semantic approaches concerned to interpret meaning since these events "diverge less from their idealized cognitive representations than is the case with linguistic pehonomena" and thus appear to be particularly amenable to this form of analysis. In the end, they elicit two "universal principles" that govern their purely formal and abstract model of religious ritual systems. The first, the principle of superhuman agency, states that the most central rites are those in which the god is the main agent in contrast to those rites in which the god is passive. The second, the principle of superhuman immediacy, which can override that of agency, states that the fewer the number of "enabling actions" and superhuman agents involved in the rite, the more central the rite is. The most central rituals are presupposed in other rites, while disruptions or changes in the central rites will have more serious consequences for the rest of the ritual system. They conclude that the richness and complexity of a ritual system is directly proportional to the commitments to the existence and number of superhuman agents.[45]

Despite their concern to integrate semantic interpretation and syntactic explanation, Lawson and McCauley are committed to an approach that valorizes truly "scientific" analyses of religious phenomena in contrast to what they see as the overly descriptive and often undisciplined subjectivity of other approaches. Their cognitive method, they say, can formulate theories that are systematic and amenable to empirical testing and refinement.[46]

Performance

If concerns with syntax dominate linguistic and cognitive theories, concerns with both semantics and syntax are prominent in theories of ritual performance that began to gain currency in the 1970s. For a semantic theorist like Milton Singer, "cultural

performances" such as rituals, festivals, and theater are expressions of the more abstract and hidden structures of the comprehensive cultural system.[47] Others have
tended to see such activities less as expressions of an existing system and more as the
very form in which culture as a system actually exists and is reproduced. Some syntactically inclined theorists, particularly those building on Austin's model of
performative utterances rather than Chomsky's model of linguistic competence, have
used theories of performance to try to surmount the tendency to treat action like a
text to be decoded. Performance metaphors and analogies allow them to focus, they
say, on what ritual actually *does*, rather than on what it is supposed to mean.[48] While
performance theory can appear to be a welter of confusing emphases and agendas, it
does represent an important consensus on many aspects of ritual action.

Historically speaking, a number of ideas came together in the mid-1970s to yield
a "performance approach" to the study of ritual: Kenneth Burke's discussions of
dramatism, Victor Turner's descriptions of ritual as "social drama," Austin's theory
of performative utterances, Erving Goffman's work on the ritual units that structure
the performances of social interaction, and even Bloch's analysis of the effects of
formulaic speech and song.[49] Although myth and ritual theorists have long argued
that theater emerged from ritual, performance theorists tend to see more of a two-
way street.[50] And although the aesthetic connections among ritual, drama, music,
folklore, and dance had been studied, culturalists could see provocative suggestions
in the metaphors of drama and performance as to how the realm of cultural ideals
actually comes to be embodied in social attitudes and personal experiences.[51] In this
way, the old Durkheimian description of how ritual orchestrates experiences of collective enthusiasm so as to mold people's social identities continues to be recast in
less functionalist terms — by asking how symbolic activities like ritual enable people
to appropriate, modify, or reshape cultural values and ideals.

In particular, performance models suggest active rather than passive roles for
ritual participants who reinterpret value-laden symbols as they communicate them.
Cultural life has come to be seen as this dynamic generation and modification of
symbolic systems, as something constantly being created by the community. From
this perspective, change becomes a dynamic process integral to how people live and
reproduce culture, not something that happens to a passive and static social entity.
The active imagery of performance has also brought the possibility of a fuller analytical vocabulary with which to talk about the nonintellectual dimensions of what
ritual does, that is, the emotive, physical, and even sensual aspects of ritual participation. Hence, ritual as a performative medium for social change emphasizes
human creativity and physicality: ritual does not mold people; people fashion rituals
that mold their world.

While some performance theorists ally their work with ethology, most others
invoke semantic and syntactic understandings of meaning. James W. Fernandez, for
example, has used linguistic theories to generate a model of the "performative metaphors" that organize ritual action in contrast to the "persuasive metaphors" of
nonritual or rhetorical usage. He defines ritual as a strategy for applying metaphors
to people's sense of their situation in such a way as to move them emotionally and
therein provoke religious experiences of empowerment, energy, and euphoria.[52] For
those more semantically inclined, performance theory is a way to critique the syn-

tactical structuralism of Lévi-Strauss and his disciples, which tends to focus on the myths, rituals, and kinship systems of tribal nonliterate peoples and gives little attention to literate cultures, particularly the voices of poets, dramatists, novelists, and other artists concerned with feeling, imagery, and expression. Ronald Grimes, for example, in studies of contemporary American ritual, argues that ritual performances do not involve systems of opposing symbols. Rather, ritual performances appropriate symbols in so many different ways that, if they were all set out as a neat system, the result would be full of contradictions; performance allows such contradictions to be avoided.[53] Hence, performance theorists have tended to depict culture not as a fully articulated formal system or a set of symbolic codes, but as a changing, processual, dramatic, and indeterminate entity.

Several basic concepts are central to most performance approaches. First, ritual is an event, a set of activities that does not simply express cultural values or enact symbolic scripts but actually effects changes in people's perceptions and interpretations. Closely involved with this perspective on ritual events is an appreciation of the physical and sensual aspects of ritual activity. Some theorists appeal to kinesthesia, the sensations experienced by the body in movement, while others appeal to synesthesia, the evocation of a total, unified, and overwhelming sensory experience.[54] Grimes draws attention to these dimensions by cataloging some of the physical movements and sensibilities invoked in ritual activities.[55] Such theories attempt to grasp more of the distinctive physical reality of ritual so easily overlooked by more intellectual approaches.

Another important concept in performance theory is "framing." As first used by Gregory Bateson (1904–80), the term indicates the way in which some activities or messages set up an interpretive framework within which to understand other subsequent or simultaneous acts or messages. Frames, for Bateson, are a form of "metacommunication." For example, framing enables one monkey to hit another and have it understood as an invitation to play, not fight. In a similar example drawn from Radcliffe-Brown's study of the Andaman Islanders, Bateson points out that it is the frame placed on a ceremonial blow that makes it clear whether one is initiating war or making peace.[56] Many studies have explored the types of frames that ritual performances invoke and how they do so. There is some consensus that ritual performances are signaled, at least in part, by a way of speaking that contrasts everyday talk with more ceremonial styles of speech. This ceremonial style is "keyed," to use Goffman's word, by various means of metacommunication, such as the use of special codes of archaic speech, explicit statements announcing the beginning and end of the action, distinctive uses of metaphor and metonymy, stylized rhythms or distinctive vowel harmonies, and tempo or stress patterns.[57]

In addition to the principles of ritual as event and ritual framing, performance theorists are concerned with the peculiar efficacy of ritual activities, which distinguishes them from literal communication, on the one hand, or pure entertainment, on the other. Although there is not much agreement in this area, most performance theorists imply that an effective or successful ritual performance is one in which a type of transformation is achieved. Some have described it as a transformation of being and consciousness achieved through an intensity of "flow" or "concentration."[58] Others have debated whether the efficacy of ritual performance resides in the transformation of the meanings of symbols or in the nondiscursive, dramaturgical, and rhetorical levels of performance.[59] This issue is linked to the concern of performance theorists with what some have called the emergent quality of ritual, defined as a function of its performative dimensions, which refers to what ritual is uniquely able to create, effect, or bring about.[60] From this perspective, what emerges from ritual is, in one sense, the event of the performance itself. When analyzed further, this event is seen to have brought about certain shifts and changes, constructing a new situation and a new reality: a boy is now recognized as a man, prestige has accrued to some but not others, certain social relationships or alliances have been strengthened and others undermined. This emphasis on the efficacy of performance attempts to illustrate a major goal of performance theory, to show that ritual does what it does by virtue of its dynamic, diachronic, and physical characteristics, in contrast to those interpretations that cast ritual performances as the secondary realization or acting out of synchronic structures, tradition, or cognitive maps.[61]

In describing the construction of new cultural images, dispositions, and situations, performance theory has also focused creative attention on the importance of concomitant processes of self-reflection and interpretation termed "reflexivity." Many have seen the dramatic or performative dimension of social action as affording a public reflexivity or mirroring that enables the community to stand back and reflect upon their actions and identity.[62] As a distinctive quality of performance, one in which people can become an audience to themselves, reflexivity has invited further speculation in turn on the role of the theorist observing and studying ritual. It has been suggested that the study of ritual parallels the epistemological concerns of those who perform ritual, giving so-called theorists and so-called performers much to share.[63] Late in his career, Turner suggested that the ethnographic study of ritual should be supplemented with performances of it, by the theorists themselves, in order for them to grasp its meanings. His suggestions were picked up by others who have interwoven the study and the practice of ritual in various ways.[64] In a related development of these issues, Grimes has opened up the issue of ritual criticism, or "ritology," where the theorist helps ritual performers to reflect on the efficacy of their own ritual activities.[65]

Performance theory is apt to see a wide variety of activities—theater, sports, play, public spectacles—as similarly structured around cross-cultural qualities of performance, and performance approaches to the study of ritual have often drawn heavily from studies of these other genres.[66] Many have hailed these approaches for overcoming the misleading boundaries too often drawn between rituals, festivals, healings, dance, music, drama, and so on.[67] Indeed, the processes of creative socialization seen in cultural patterns of play may be particularly relevant to understanding ritual. Some analysts of the metacommunication patterns in play and ritual have stressed the similarity of "make believe" and "let us believe."[68] Rock concerts and football games have also been treated as cultural performances that can shed light on how ritual validates cultural values that cannot be proven real and correct in any other way.[69] John J. MacAloon's study of the Olympic games analyzes both the rituals that accompany the contests and the historical evolution of other genres of performance within this preeminent public spectacle of the twentieth century.[70] Similarly, theater and drama have been studied as forms of ritual in which performances serve as an effective medium for the reinterpretation of traditional images and concepts.[71]

As with most other theoretical approaches, the shortcomings of performance theory are probably the flip side of its strengths and insights. The comparison of ritual to all sorts of dramatic spectacles or structured improvisation effectively demonstrates shared features and similar processes. At the same time, such comparisons often result in simply describing one unknown in terms of another, and fail to account for the way in which most cultures see important distinctions between ritual and other types of activities. Yet performance theory has proven useful in its stress on the dramatic process, the significance of the physical and bodily expressiveness found in ritual, and its evocative attention to secular and new forms of ritual or ritual-like activity. Such research has made very clear, for example, that ritual is not simply a matter of the more formal and elaborate ceremonies familiar in the major religions. The use of the term "ritualization" by performance theorists, probably borrowed from ethological studies, undoubtedly helped to formulate a way of looking at ritual activity as activity that is picked up in recent theories of human activity as praxis.

Practice

In addition to performance theory, the 1970s also saw the emergence of several formulations of human action as *praxis*, or "practice," a term that has been heralded as a key idea in the last decade of anthropological theory, usurping, some have said, the place of "structure" as the dominant image for cultural analysis.[72] The term derives from Karl Marx's usage, which emphasized the inherent productive and political dimensions of human activity. Yet few of these theories can really be called Marxist, and most represent a highly synthetic convergence of several lines of thought. Indeed, practice theories share a number of concerns with performance theory, particularly the latter's critique of the inability of purely structural and semiotic approaches to account for historical change, action as action, and acting individuals as bodies and not just minds. In contrast to the static view of structuralism, which tends to see human activity as a matter of enacting cultural rules, practice theory claims to take seriously the ways in which human activities, as formal as a religious ritual or as casual as a midday stroll, are creative strategies by which human beings continually reproduce and reshape their social and cultural environments.

Practice theory also addresses several issues that differentiate it from performance theory. For example, it is less interested in specific types of acts, such as ritual or dance, and more interested in how cultural activity in general works. Yet some practice theoreticians do address ritual as such and cast it as "paradigmatic" activity, that is, as activity that particularly showcases cultural patterns. Many practice theorists are concerned with analyzing large processes of historical and cultural change, often developing more nuanced versions of Geertz's model of the interaction of human action, needs, and experiences, on the one hand, with traditional cultural structures, organizational patterns, and symbolic systems, on the other.[73] In addition, practice theorists are particularly attentive to the political dimensions of social relationships, especially with regard to how positions of domination and subordination are variously constituted, manipulated, or resisted. Not surprisingly, practice theory has emerged in conjunction with greater attention to the lingering effects of colonialism, the political ramifications of routine cross-cultural encounters, and the various social effects of economic and cultural domination.

In a number of highly theoretical ethnographic studies, the anthropologist Marshall Sahlins (b. 1930) developed a provocative model of the cultural practices involved in ritual activity.[74] Most simply, he argued that practice brings together structure and history, system and event, continuity and change. In other words, ritual enables enduring patterns of social organization and cultural symbolic systems to be brought to bear on real events; in the course of this process, real situations are assessed and negotiated in ways that can transform these traditional patterns or structures in turn. For Sahlins, human action is critical to the shaping of culture and history, and he has sought the theoretical tools that can display this. One of his most compelling ethnographic examples is a complex analysis of the death of the explorer Captain James Cook in 1778 at the hand of Hawaiians who, he suggests, mistook Cook for one of their more important gods. Cook's death has been the subject of a vigorous and ongoing interpretive effort by historians and anthropologists, in which most of the explanations proffered have been closely linked to the particular religious or methodological orientation of the interpreter.[75] Sahlins argues that Cook's death stemmed from the explorer's transgressions of the ritual status the Hawaiians had accorded him. Killing him was an active response to a cosmological crisis and not the mere reproduction of prescriptive rules or structures. As such it was an act of performative tradition, or practice, and thus the very creation of history.

For Sahlins, as for Turner and Geertz, the traditional formality and self-consciousness of ritual make it a type of human practice in which basic cultural processes are particularly accessible to observation and analysis. Moreover, in some societies, particularly those dominated by traditional forms of kingship, ritual activities appear central to cultural life in general. Hence, ritual can serve as a convenient example of the forces shaping all forms of social action. In his account of Cook and elsewhere, Sahlins tries to demonstrate how ritual creates a meaningful event out of a new and potentially incomprehensible situation, namely, by bringing traditional structures to bear on it. If done effectively, the ritual action enables those structures to embrace and subdue the new situation, rendering the situation meaningful and enabling the structures themselves to continue to thrive as legitimate, appropriate, and relatively unaltered. Should a situation resist the ritual formulas that are brought to interpret it—if someone is hailed as a king but does not act as one—then those structures must be reinterpreted and perhaps altered. For Sahlins, the application of cultural structures to new situations, most readily observed in ritual action, is the very process of history itself. With this view, he rejects those notions of history that see it as a descriptive account or consciousness of events unfolding throughout a neutral duration of time. Instead, he argues that history is the way in which a cultural traditions appropriate new situations. Like other practice theorists, he sees people as making their own history in their own cultural fashion and ritual as a frequently central instance of this activity.

A rather different tack has been taken by the French sociologist Pierre Bourdieu, who has proposed a formal "theory of practice."[76] While Sahlins looks to history to provide the dynamic missing in more static structural analyses and ends up redefining history in terms of anthropologically appreciable activities, Bourdieu attempts to go further by redefining both history and structure in terms of the dynamics of cultural action. In other words, ritual does not actually bring history and structure together since neither exists except insofar as they are embodied and reproduced in human activity as cultural values. For Bourdieu, these values are embodied and reproduced by means of strategies of human practice that are rarely conscious or explicit. Therefore, the theorist must focus on the acts themselves, not on abstractions like "structure" or "historical process." Bourdieu uses the term, "habitus," borrowed from Marcel Mauss and Max Weber among others, to designate human activity in its real and immediate context, that is, as the set of dispositions by which people give shape to social traditions or, in another formulation, as the structured and determined attitudes that produce structuring and determining practices.[77] In a key passage on myth, for example, Bourdieu argues that one should not approach a myth as some object complete in itself and lying open to analysis or as some sort of mythopoeic form of subjectivity. To "confront the act itself," in this case the act of mythmaking, one must address the principle underlying all practices, which is "the socially informed body."[78]

Although Bourdieu offers only brief analyses of specific ritual practices, he argues that ritual in general is not a matter of following rules, even in predominantly oral societies. In general, he characterizes rituals as strategic practices for transgressing and reshuffling cultural categories in order to meet the needs of real situations. The rites of plowing or marriage among the Kabyle of Algeria, he writes, "have the function of disguising and thereby sanctioning the inevitable collision of two contrary principles that the peasant brings about in forcing nature."[79] When that which nature has divided or united, according to the culture's taxonomy of categories of the natural, must be changed or reversed, it is ritual that can neutralize the dangers associated with such sacrilege. By means of its collective, public, and carefully delegated forms of authority, as well as its complex and "judiciously euphemized" symbolism, ritual can sanction—or even deny—the sacrilege in the very act of committing it.[80] Among the Kabyle, deflowering a bride, plowing the first furrow, cutting the last thread in weaving, or harvesting the last sheaf all presuppose an ordered set of cultural categories that both *should* not be violated and yet *must* be violated. Echoing Van Gennep, Bourdieu finds that ritual licenses these violations even as it reinforces the underlying sense of order that the violation transgresses. It affirms the differences and boundaries between the sacred and the profane, the divine and the human; but it is in ritual that these differences and boundaries are allowed, for a few careful minutes, to break down.

In another example, Bourdieu explores the rituals of gift giving in order to challenge explicitly structuralist models of ritual that have depicted gift exchange as an ordered system in which reciprocity establishes relatively egalitarian relationships and facilitates certain communicative functions. He demonstrates that the actual giving and receiving of gifts involve complex strategies of challenge, domination, and honor: "To reduce to the function of communication . . . phenomena such as the dialectic of challenge and riposte and, more generally, the exchange of gifts, words, or women, is to ignore the structural ambivalence which predisposes them to fulfill a political function of domination in and through performance of the communication function."[81] In other words, the ritual exchange of gifts or insults or women in marriage is not primarily the communication of messages about the social order. In actual practice, such ritualized exchanges are ways of establishing political dominance by means of what appear to be overtly fair exchange. Ritual is a tool for social and cultural jockeying; it is a performative medium for the negotiation of power in relationships.

Maurice Bloch has used both Marxist and Durkheimian ideas to explore how ritual goes about actually constructing authority, ideology, and power. As noted earlier, he has analyzed the restricted linguistic codes that are used in ritual to generate hierarchical structures of authority that appear to be sanctified by tradition. He emphasizes the contrast between ritual and other activities by arguing that ritual produces distinctly ideological forms of knowledge that are in tension with the more purely cognitive forms rooted in day-to-day behavior. Rather uniquely, Bloch concludes that ritual is not a necessary dimension of social life, as so many others have held; as a type of ideological mystification, it is "the exercise of a particular form of power," a form that makes "a power situation appear a fact in the nature of the world."[82]

Two other influential analyses of ritual as practice have also developed the connection between ritual practices and power, namely, Sherry B. Ortner's studies of Sherpa culture in Nepal, which address the rites of daily life as well as the political activities involved in the founding of Buddhist temples, and Jean Comaroff's study of changes and political tensions in the postcolonial ritual life of the Tshidi of South Africa.[83] In general, both studies understand ritual to be the means for mediating enduring cultural structures and the current situation. It is through ritual practice that culture molds consciousness in terms of underlying structures and patterns, while current realities simultaneously instigate transformations of those very structures and patterns as well. The ritual life of a people is the sphere where such accommodations take place. Beyond this basic similarity, both studies contribute fresh nuances to an understanding of ritual practices in a historical context. Ortner attempts to describe a dynamic cultural process by which human activities reproduce cultural structures in strategically reshaped ways. While her study of Sherpa Buddhist temple-building examines activities outside most formal definitions of ritual, it vividly illustrates the way in which human practices produce and negotiate relationships of power, providing a perspective quite useful for the analysis of discrete ritual activities.[84] Comaroff's study of precolonial and postcolonial rituals among the Zionist churches of the Tshidi of South Africa also attempts to uncover some of the complex negotiations of power involved in ritual activity. She argues that the Zionist synthesis of Tshidi tradition and Christian rites of healing is not a passive accommodation of colonialism but a set of highly coded efforts to control key symbols and defy the hegemonic order of colonialism. Ritual, she suggests, is "a struggle for the possession of the sign."[85]

The anthropologist Talal Asad, developing aspects of the work of Bourdieu and the historian Michel Foucault (1926–84), explicitly addresses the need to move from "reading symbols" to "analyzing practices." The former suggests that culture exists as some separate dimension, while the latter recognizes the fact that cultural values and meanings exist only insofar as they are embodied in what people do. Yet Asad distinguishes his approach from the preceding practice theories by virtue of a comprehensive perspective that addresses two fresh themes: the historicity of the concept of ritual and the involvement of this concept in practices that structure very wide-ranging power relationships. So, for example, he contrasts the medieval Christian concept of rites for developing virtue (an understanding of ritual in terms of discipline and morality) with the modern concept of rites as symbolic action (in societies where formal manners, not discipline, are deemed necessary to social morality). In a series of historical and ethnographic studies, Asad finds different "technologies of power" behind culturally distinctive constructions of the self, society, and the cosmos. Indeed, he argues that the whole modern perspective on "ritual" as symbolic activity is itself another historically shaped organization of power, one that is intimately linked to very modern Western assumptions about the self and the state. The "fundamental disparities" among various historical forms of so-called ritual activity lead Asad to conclude that the inadequacies of a single category like "ritual" to describe them all is further evidence of the politically and culturally hegemonic functions of the term. Hence, he warns against the normative application of concepts that are the historical products of a Christian history and Christian organizations of power.[86]

In an earlier work, *Ritual Theory, Ritual Practice* (1992), I also presented a critique of theoretical discourse on ritual and proposed a more systematic treatment of ritual as a form of cultural practice. The critique addressed two problems: the overdetermined circularity of theoretical discourse on ritual and the problems that attend the definition of ritual as either a distinct and autonomous set of activities or an aspect of all activity. With regard to first, the logic underlying most theoretical discussions of ritual depends on a dichotomization of thought and action. While this dichotomization facilitates a focus on action per se and on ritual as a type of action, it unwittingly structures the whole discussion of ritual around a series of oppositions, including an opposition between the theorist and the ritual actors. Ritual comes to be understood as that which mediates or integrates all these oppositions, as the sociocultural mechanism by which cultural ideas (thought) and social dispositions (action) are integrated on the one hand, and as the phenomenon that affords theorists (thought) special access to the dynamics of culture (action) on the other.[87] A clear example, although by no means the only one, is found in Geertz's analysis of ritual, which culminates in the statement that ritual performances are "not only the point at which the *dispositional* and *conceptual* aspects of religious life converge *for the believer*, but also the point at which the interaction between them can be most readily examined *by the detached observer*."[88] Ultimately, it is the theorist-observer's grasp of how ritual action synthesizes the conceptual and the behavioral that generates the theoretical meaning of the rite and, for Geertz, establishes a distinctly cultural level of analysis. While discourse on ritual need not be as closed and overdetermined as Geertz's argument suggests it is, the appeal of the category of ritual undoubtedly resides in part in how it appears to evoke and resolve, with great naturalness, some of the most subtle but compelling structures of modern thought, notably the dichotomy between thought and action. Using an argument that I will extend in part III of this book, *Ritual Theory, Ritual Practice* also suggested that this overstructured discourse on ritual have been vital to defining key aspects of the whole theoretical enterprise itself. A series of examples points to the way in which various conclusions about the nature of ritual and sociocultural life functioned to legitimate and even mandate the ethnographic and theoretical activities of scholars: "the theoretical construction of ritual becomes a reflection of the theorist's method and the motor of a discourse in which the concerns of the theorist take center stage."[89]

The second part of the critique addressed the dilemmas that attend two major ways of defining ritual, either as a distinctive and essentially different set of paradigmatic activities or as a set of qualities found to some degree in all activity. Both approaches can get bogged down in elaborate taxonomies and problematic distinctions between utilitarian and nonutilitarian action that end up with ritual action as expressive, noninstrumental, or irrational. These features are likely to have little to do with the categories relevant to ritual actors, and tend to invoke, moreover, methods of analysis that analyze action as the execution of a conceptual program. The very nature of activity and practice is lost.[90]

Ritual Theory, Ritual Practice proposed a more systematic framework for analyzing ritual as practice. First of all, human practice in general has some common features, namely, it is situational, strategic, apt to misrecognize the relationship between its ends and its means in ways that promote its efficacy, and it is motivated by what can be called "redemptive hegemony," a construal of reality as ordered in such a way as to allow the actor some advantageous ways of acting. Given these features, what sort of practice is ritual? Clearly, ritual is not the same thing everywhere; it can vary in every feature. As practice, the most we can say is that it is involves ritualization, that is, a way of acting that distinguishes itself from other ways of acting in the very way it does what it does; moreover, it makes this distinction for specific purposes. A practice approach to ritual will first address how a particular community or culture ritualizes (what characteristics of acting make strategic distinctions between these acts and others) and then address when and why ritualization is deemed to be the effective thing to do. Exploring some limited generalizations about how people ritualize, I focused on the series of oppositional schemes that are mobilized as the body moves through space and time; these schemes are generated by the gestures and sounds of the body and act to qualitatively structure the physical environment. In this process, some schemes come to dominate others in a seemingly natural chain of association. The structured environment provides those in it with an experience of the objective reality of the schemes. The agents of ritualization do not see how they project this schematically qualified environment or how they reembody those same schemes through the physical experience of moving about within its spatial and temporal dimensions. The goal of ritualization as such is completely circular: the creation of a ritualized agent, an actor with a form of ritual mastery, who embodies flexible sets of cultural schemes and can deploy them effectively in multiple situations so as to restructure those situations in practical ways. Among the most important strategies of ritualization is the inherent flexibility of the degree of ritualization invoked.

In this practice approach to ritual, therefore, the following points are most central.[91] First, ritual should be analyzed and understood in its real context, which is the full spectrum of ways of acting within any given culture, not as some a priori category of action totally independent of other forms of action. Only in this context can the theorist-observer attempt to understand how and why people choose to differentiate some activities from others. From this perspective, the focus is less a matter of clear and autonomous rites than the methods, traditions and strategies of "ritualization." Second, the most subtle and central quality of those actions we tend to call ritual is the primacy of the body moving about within a specially constructed space, simultaneously defining (imposing) and experiencing (receiving) the values ordering the environment. For example, the body movements of ritually knowledgeable agents actually define the special qualities of the environment, yet the agents understand themselves as reacting or responding to this environment. They do not see how they have created the environment that is impressing itself on them but assume, simply in how things are done, that forces from beyond the immediate situation are shaping the environment and its activities in fundamental ways.[92] For this reason, and as a third feature, ritualization is a way of acting that tends to promote the authority of forces deemed to derive from beyond the immediate situation. For example, participants may embody and deploy various schemes for molding an environment, and experiences within it, according to values that differentiate the sacred as autonomous and eternal and transcendent. The result is a ritualized agent who has acquired an instinctive knowledge of schemes that can be used to order his or her experience so as to render it more or less coherent with these ritual values concerning the sacred. In effect, the real principles of ritual practice are nothing other than the flexible sets of schemes and strategies acquired and deployed by an agent who has embodied them. This type of analysis of ritual practice affords the opportunity of analyzing more and less effective rituals, the various degrees of ritualization that are invoked, and the great diversity of cultural schemes and styles of ritualization. *Ritual Theory, Ritual Practice* closed with an analysis of how this approach to ritualization is less concerned with the issues of social control that most other theories of ritual address, and more concerned with mapping the orchestration of complex relationships of power—especially how the power at stake is deemed to be of nonhuman or nonimmediate (god, tradition, virtue, and so on) and is made amenable to some degree of individual and communal appropriation.

Practice theory makes it possible to focus more directly on what people do and how they do it; it involves less preliminary commitment to some overarching notion of ritual in general. It assumes that what is meant by ritual may not be a way of acting that is the same for all times and places. Ritual, or ritualization, may be best defined in culturally specific ways since cultures, and even subcultures, differentiate among their actions in distinctive ways. Hence, a universal definition of ritual can obscure how and why people produce ritualized actions; it certainly obscures one of the most decisive aspects of ritual as a strategic way of acting, the sheer degree of ritualization that is invoked. For these reasons, practice theory today seems to offer greater opportunity to formulate the more subtle ways in which power is recognized and diffused, interpretations are negotiated, and people struggle to make more embracing meanings personally effective.

In sum, the study of ritual as practice has meant a basic shift from looking at activity as the expression of cultural patterns to looking at it as that which makes and harbors such patterns. In this view, ritual is more complex than the mere communication of meanings and values; it is a set of activities that construct particular types of meanings and values in specific ways. Hence, rather than ritual as the vehicle for the *expression* of authority, practice theorists tend to explore how ritual is a vehicle for the *construction* of relationships of authority and submission. Most practice theories also share a number of assumptions that follow from this basic orientation. First, they attempt to see ritual as part of a historical process in which past patterns are reproduced but also reinterpreted or transformed.[93] In this sense, ritual is frequently depicted as a central arena for cultural mediation, the means by which various combinations of structure and history, past and present, meanings and needs, are brought together in terms of each other. As Comaroff notes, "ritual provides an appropriate medium through which the values and structures of a contradictory world may be addressed and manipulated."[94] The ability to address and manipulate them is the power to define what is real and to shape how people behave. In a second shared assumption that follows from the first, practice theories are explicitly concerned with what rituals do, not just what they mean, particularly the way they construct and inscribe power relationships.[95] A third assumption addresses the issue of individual agency, how persons "in their everyday production of goods and meanings, acquiesce yet protest, reproduce yet seek to transform their predicament."[96] Basic to this concern is a focus on the physical mind-body holism as the primary medium for the deployment and embodiment of everyday schemes of physical action and cultural values—as in the arrangement of a home or the orchestration of a game—that are the means by which culture is reproduced and individual categories of experience are forged. Finally, implicit or explicitly, many practice theories suggest the value of jettisoning the category of ritual as a necessary first step in opening up the particular logic and strategy of cultural practices.

Profile: Interpreting British
and Swazi Enthronement Rites

The complex and effective relationship between ritual and political power has probably been obvious to many since the first headdress was donned or crude scepter raised. Many of the earliest formal studies of ritual in general focused on kingship, and the issue of the divine king became central to the myth and ritual school. Social functionalists also analyzed a variety of political institutions, including kingship, in an attempt to explain how ritual maintains kingly authority and social order. From a different perspective, symbolic-culturalists have addressed political kingship in terms of how the symbolic action of ritual actually constructs royal power and authority. This section will trace two types of political rituals, the coronation of the queen of England and the Swazi Ncwala ritual, as they have been analyzed in a succession of functionalist followed by culturalist interpretations of the sort laid out in this chapter.

In a classic monograph, "The Meaning of the Coronation," Edward Shils and Michael Young set out to explain the intense emotional involvement of British citizens in the coronation of Queen Elizabeth II on June 2, 1952.[97] They concluded that the coronation was a "national communion," a ceremonial reaffirmation of the moral values that undergird the community. Durkheim had written that "there can be no society which does not feel the need of upholding and reaffirming at regular intervals the collective sentiments and the collective ideas which make its unity and its personality."[98] In this spirit, Shils and Young analyzed the coronation in terms of the ideals and sentiments that it seemed to depict. On one level, the queen herself acted out some basic values: by taking the oath, receiving the Bible, and being anointed by the archbishop, she demonstrated her human subservience to the laws of God and the moral standards of the society, even as she was given the right to rule that society in the eyes of God. On another level, by virtue of the presence of the people in the abbey as well as the power of the media, the coronation was a collective experience in which idealized social bonds were reaffirmed. Families celebrated together, congenial crowds assembled spontaneously, undisturbed by pickpockets who had taken the day off, and even feuding factions in one large housing complex settled their dispute and came together over a cup of tea to watch the event on television. For the authors, the monarch and her royal family were idealized models of the social relations that constitute the community; when acted out so explicitly in the coronation ceremonies, the values that underlie these relations are reexperienced and reaffirmed by the whole society.

The analysis by Shils and Young has been critiqued as an oversimplistic application of Durkheimian theory. In appealing to a more complex form of functionalism, the sociologist Steven Lukes challenged the basic assumption that values hold a society together and that a consensus on values must exist in any society.[99] What holds societies together, he suggested, is not consensus but compliance: people agree to go along with a particular way of seeing things. What ritual actually does is help "to define as authoritative certain ways of seeing society: it serves to specify what in society is of special significance, it draws people's attention to certain forms of relationships and activity—and at the same time, therefore, it deflects their attention from other forms, since every way of seeing it is also a way of not seeing." He saw this as a "cognitive dimension" of ritual, involved in "mobilizing bias" instead of consensus and encouraging the "internalization of particular political paradigms." In this way, ritual exercises a real form of social control; it "draws people's attention, and invokes their loyalties, towards a certain powerfully-evoked representation of the social and political order."[100]

Lukes's interpretation of the Shils and Young account modifies it in two ways: first, it recognizes multiple value systems within a society, not a single latent system; second, it attempts to demonstrate how ritual promotes one value system at the expense of another rather than forging any fresh experience of true consensus. If Lukes analyzed Queen Elizabeth's coronation itself, he would focus on situations in which symbols vied with each other until one effectively, if temporarily, came to dominate. Instead of seeing the main images of the coronation as invoking the ideals and latent values that hold society together, he would interpret how the orchestrated images of the queen and royal family silenced diverse opinions about government and England's postwar role under a deluge of symbols sure to invoke nationalist loyalties. For Lukes, the elaborately staged coronation was a political act that mobilized loyalty to some symbols at the cost of others. Insofar as it generated a dramatic experience of *communitas,* it successfully marginalized any and all who had less enthusiasm for the proceedings. In many ways, Lukes's appreciation of the role of ritual in addressing social conflict builds on Gluckman's analysis of ritual as a means for social integration but not necessarily value consensus.

The royal Ncwala ritual of the Swazi people of Swaziland in southeastern Africa is prodigiously complex; the best ethnographic description is a dense twenty-nine pages long, and any one summary appears to emphasize different aspects from other summaries.[101] Yet a brief outline of the ritual events is sufficient for our purposes. As a whole, the ritual is a firstfruits harvest type, composed of two structurally similar parts, the two-day "little" Ncwala, which begins on the new moon just prior to the December solstice, when the old year ends and the new one starts. It is followed by the four to six day "big" Ncwala, which starts a fortnight later on the full moon. The timing of the ritual is quite important, requiring the king to retire from the community when the moon is on the wane and "race the sun" to begin the ceremony before the solstice.[102] In the little Ncwala, priestly representatives of the king travel to the frontiers of Swazi-controlled lands in order to collect river water and seawater in special calabashes that will be used to invigorate the king. A black ox is also slain to secure medicines for the king. When all these things are assembled, the king enters a sacred enclosure and is "doctored" with these substances, eventually spitting through openings in the east and west, which is understood as consecrating or "stabbing" the new year. He enters the enclosure for treatment and spitting twice; the first time, the people sing the *Simemo*, a song that expresses hatred for the king, but the second time they sing praises. In the big Ncwala, the king again acquires special supernatural powers by being treated with waters and vegetation secured from all over the realm and with parts of an ox that has been driven wild and then killed. Again he spits to the east and west and this time bites into fruits from the first harvest (until the king eats of the harvest, it is taboo for anyone else to do so). Later, various groups in strict hierarchical order also bite into the crops. Warriors then enjoin a mock dance-battle against the king. At the height of these activities, the king appears in the guise of a legendary demonic spirit, dancing wildly, to signify the powers he has acquired. Through a series of activities, however, these powers are gradually controlled and sorted in ways that subordinate the powerful king to the well-being of social group. Punctuated by specific warrior dances, songs of praise, and a final feast, the king lights a purifying fire to burn the things of the old year and entreat rain. He then bathes, is treated with medicines, and finally takes the throne.

Gluckman's analysis of the annual Swazi Ncwala rite drew attention to how ritual actually displays "the powerful tensions which make up national life."[103] He argued that the Ncwala is "not a simple mass assertion of unity, but a stressing of conflict"— king against the people, people against the state, king and people against rival princes, queen and queen mother against the king, and so on. According to Gluckman, the Swazi believe that this symbolic acting out of conflicted and ambivalent social relations can bring about a cathartic unity and prosperity.[104] The prescribed behavior of the ceremony makes clear that even those caught up in these tense relationships with the king still supported his kingship. A concomitant message is also made clear: that the kingship is sacred, not the king himself. This idea underscores the virtue that is incumbent upon the ruler lest his behavior justify the eruption of a rebellion in order to protect the office from abuse. Despite the differences between the social, economic, and political circumstances of the Swazi and the British, and the stylistic differences in the way they ritually affirm their institution of kingship, Gluckman's conclusions still echo those Shils and Young: the ritual functioned to strengthen and unite the nation by displaying the values and dramatizing the ideal relationships that animate their social system.

Several theorists have challenged Gluckman's analysis of the Ncwala, notably T. O. Beidelman. Beidelman's more cultural approach led him to focus on the cosmological symbols and processes of the rite in terms of what they seemed to mean to the Swazi. He dismissed Gluckman's analysis of the rite's supposed sociopolitical dimensions as based on a flawed functionalism, an approach he saw as attempting to uncover "the latent functions and results" of a ritual without giving any consideration to its "culturally manifest purpose." Beidelman concluded that the Ncwala was not concerned with the expression of rebellious conflict or resentment, but rather with the systematic separation of the king from various groups within the Swazi nation in order to facilitate his unique and supernatural empowerment as "king-priest" of the whole nation.[105]

As these comparisons imply, political rituals have been a major focus for cultural as well as functional approaches. Geertz, for example, has echoed Gluckman's point that ritual puts social forces on display. Yet it does so, he argues, not to afford a cathartic experience of social solidarity, but to define what is cognitively real. In a study of the political world of premodern Bali, which he characterized as a "theatre state," Geertz attempted to demonstrate that royal rituals are neither simple displays of power nor displays that disguise real power.[106] Instead, these vast ceremonial displays of kingly ritual themselves constitute kingly power, just as performative utterances *do* things, not simply communicate things. He presents the traditional Balinese court as a microcosm of the supernatural order, the image of the universe, and the embodiment of the whole political order. In this political theater, state-sponsored rituals "were not the means to political ends; they were the ends themselves, they were what the state was for. Power served pomp, not pomp power."[107] From Geertz's perspective, Queen Elizabeth's coronation and the Swazi king's tasting of the firstfruits are "arguments made over and over again in the insistent vocabulary of ritual" that status in the human world is an approximate but legitimate reflection of the inherent hierarchical order of the cosmos itself. Such ritual arguments, communicated in the symbolic action of elaborate ceremony, he avowed, were the very workings of power in the Balinese state. Although the sociopolitical situations of England and Swaziland differ significantly from that of 19th-century Bali and each other, in each case, Geertz suggests, ritual creates the authority of the monarch, it does not simply display it. To think otherwise would be to radically misunderstand the nature of symbolic action.[108]

Maurice Bloch criticized Gluckman's interpretation of the Ncwala as reductionistic since it reduced a vast and complex ceremonial to just one social function, that of maintaining the social and political entity.[109] But Bloch also argued that Geertz's analysis of the ritual workings of power in Balinese kingly ritual is incomplete since it never explains how the symbolic construction of power is made persuasive or relevant to the people. Bloch himself argues for a dual understanding of royal rituals. First, such rituals use a variety of methods familiar to the people to construct a level of symbolic authority as the opposite of the contingent here and now. In this way, the ritual legitimates royal authority by showing how it is "an essential aspect of a cosmic social and emotional order."[110] Second, on another level, these rites create very specific cultural meanings by the way in which they adopt symbolic forms rooted in the culture's everyday life in order to make connections between the royal ceremony and the more humble ceremonies of daily life. It is this second dimension, he argues, that explains the emotional and ideological power the royal ritual has over its participants. For example, in terms of Bloch's first level, a series of symbolic actions link the coronation of the queen to the authority of God, his bishop, and the will of the people. On a second level, other symbolic activities link the young woman's accession to the throne to the succession of generations and the life of families, thereby associating the rather distant events in the abbey with symbols of great personal impact. Not only the divinely recognized mother of her people, Elizabeth II is also the daughter of the nation and the bride of the political power structure. While she is symbolically raised above all others, she is simultaneously made symbolically evocative of the emotional aspects of the daily life of all British families.

Despite their own sense of disagreement over differing methodological orientations, Bloch's dual analysis roughly coincides with two dimensions that Tambiah identifies in political ritual, namely, a symbolic dimension in which the structures of human authority are laid out as iconic with the nature of the cosmos, and an indexical dimension in which key features of the ritual relate to and legitimate the current social hierarchy.[111] In terms of the British coronation, Bloch and Tambiah might both point to the symbols that define the queen's human authority as subordinate to, but derivative of, the divine authority of God represented by the archbishop, the Bible, and the oath to uphold and abide by the laws of the land and of God. Moreover, these rites of submission to God's ultimate authority are followed by another sequence in which the "frail creature," divested of her regalia, is systematically transformed into a queen. First, she is anointed with consecrated oil in the same way that "Solomon was anointed king by Zadok the priest and Nathan the prophet"; then, she is presented with the sword of power and the orb of moral responsibility. The authority over others extended to the queen by God and the simultaneous demand for complete obedience to God replicate the hierarchical nature of God's divine presence and the condition of all humans subject to his ultimate authority. The structure of her authority defined by the ritual conforms, therefore, to a timeless picture of the order of the human and divine cosmos. However, all the ritual sequences that relate the queen to the human community also imply and validate a hierarchy, from the important eyewitness guests in the abbey itself to the most distant families gathered around a television set. The current social order, as well as the cosmic order, is defined from the highest to the lowest and all the tiers of social position in between. The effect of these iconic and indexical dimensions in the ritual is a series of emotive and political connections to a transcendent order, as well as a dynamic mechanism by which the universal and the particular each legitimate the other.[112]

In another reexamination of the Ncwala ritual, Bruce Lincoln undermines many previous interpretations, all of which relied heavily on the ethnographic description provided by Hilda Kuper, who observed performances in 1934, 1935, and 1936.[113] In keeping with the practice orientation of historical anthropologists like Sahlins, Comaroff, and Ortner, Lincoln points to the significance of the colonial context in which the recorded rite was performed, arguing that the observed performances were not the definitive Ncwala—if such a thing could be said to exist at all, since each and every Ncwala actually reflects a very distinct political agenda rooted in the historical events unfolding among the Swazi at the time. When Kuper returned to observe the Ncwala in 1966 on the eve of Swaziland's national independence, Lincoln notes, she found that it reflected a very different political ethos. Lincoln contrasts the Ncwala's symbolic construction of the political power of the king in three different periods: prior to colonialism, during colonial rule, which included the performances of the 1930s; and on the eve of independence. He argues that Gluckman's analysis of it as a ritual of rebellion was true for the precolonial period, but under colonialism the Ncwala also became a ritual of resistance to British domination. Hence, he concludes, Gluckman's emphasis on social unity in the Durkheimian tradition obscures the more complex power dynamics of domination and subordination between the British and the Swazi as well as the articulation of loyal and disloyal factions within the Swazi nation itself.[114]

As we saw with the Mukanda ritual and the Akitu festival, the various ways of interpreting royal ceremonies such as the Swazi Ncwala or the British coronation yield a plethora of interesting connections and nonexclusive insights. The most successful analyses appear to be those that can appreciate a multiplicity of purposes, strategies, and performances; that is, they may recognize structural components that are rooted both culturally (e.g., the queen's annointment by the archbishop indicates subordination to God) and more generally (the stages of separation, liminality, and reincorporation in the Swazi king's Ncwala), but the ritual is not reduced to some timeless repetition of enduring structures. Its historical context is vital and central. These interpretations share some recognition of the role of complex systems and how they mediate all action, reflection, and interpretation. These mediating systems are, in effect, what we mean by culture. For the most part, proponents of "cultural analysis" have found ritual an effective focus for tracking and formulating the dynamics that comprise culture—even if, as for the more practice-oriented approaches, the cultural exists nowhere else except in how it is constituted in action.

Conclusion

The three preceding chapters on theories of ritual cannot be read as a simple evolutionary sequence in which the earlier theories are deemed primitive and out of date, while the later ones are current and superior. In fact, the actual historical sequence is much more complicated than the abridged outline of this section can adequately portray. The sequence of major categories—that is, phenomenology, functionalism, structuralism, and so on—implies succession, when, in fact, all three approaches can still be found in studies of ritual today. Moreover, since these categories are not exclusive, many theorists can be legitimately placed in different ones at different points in their careers. In the end, few approaches are really autonomous. They appropriate insights from other methods but give them a new rationale; they layer older assumptions with new concerns; and they quietly synthesize opposing positions within more complex and dynamic models. Yet in the process of generation and self-presentation, each composite theory inevitably contrasts itself with all other theories.

Despite the importance of historical and ethnographic data, theories are always re-acting, or often overreacting, to other theories.

There are a number of other schools of thought concerned with analyzing ritual, particularly in relation to explicit political or confessional issues, that do not fit neatly into the history of major theoretical positions outlined in this section. One could argue that these schools, at least to date, have been more influenced by these major positions than they have exerted influence of their own on the direction of this his-tory of theory. Nonetheless, several examples of feminist analysis of ritual theory have justly attracted serious attention, notably Nancy Jay's study of the way in which gen-der issues are involved in the institutions of ritual sacrifice.[115] Her work reminds us that ritual practices and traditions have been critical to the establishment and natu-ralization of cultural hierarchies based on age and gender. Liturgical studies con-ducted from within religious traditions is another very vital area of reflection and scholarship—in part because it is one of the few areas studying ritual in highly liter-ate and heavily documented groups and societies, although theological issues readily shape much of this study. Many religious traditions developed various types of ex-perts in the practice of ritual and sometimes in the formal study of its history. For Christians and Jews in particular, study of their liturgical histories has been closely connected with movements for reform—either in terms of modernization or in a return to purer traditional models. Some of these dynamics within ritual communi-ties are addressed in the final section of this book. It is not common, however, for feminist or liturgical studies to concern themselves with the idea of ritual in general. For the most part, the perspective afforded by the general category of ritual has pro-vided them with more or less interesting and relevant views of their own specific tra-ditions of liturgical practices. Few have yet to suggest how their tradition's history and practices might, in turn, inform this general category. The most suggestive ex-ceptions to this tendency so far, however, are undoubtedly the work of feminist schol-ars: by virtue of their critical exploration of traditional gender roles, they stand some-what outside their religious tradition's ritual history *and* the history of formal scholarship on ritual in general. It is a perspective that can yield useful insights into the way in which our "science of ritual" remains historically and socially akin to the practice of particular liturgical traditions.

The lack of any definitive winner in the history of theory does not mean that scholarship on ritual has not forged useful tools for analysis and reflection. Ritual as the expression of paradigmatic values of death and rebirth; ritual as a mechanism for bringing the individual into the community and establishing a social entity; or ritual as a process for social transformation, for catharsis, for embodying symbolic values, for defining the nature of the real, or for struggling over control of the sign—these formulations are all tools that help us to analyze what may be going on in any par-ticular set of activities. They are also vivid reflections of the questions that concern us and indicate, therefore, something of the way in which we who are asking the questions tend to construe the world, human behavior, meaning, and the tasks of explanation.

❧ • ❧

PART II

RITES

The Spectrum of Ritual Activities

At one time or another, almost every human activity has been done ritually or made part of a ritual. In practice, however, neither ritualists nor scholars of ritual are ever tempted to consider everything to be ritual. The idea that some acts are intrinsically different from others appears to be basic to how people think of ritual, and the last section presented a number of attempts to provide a substantive definition of ritual that highlights this sort of intrinsic difference. Certainly the most obvious rituals are those activities that form part of a tradition or canon of rites, be it religious or secular. Yet other evidence suggests that ritual activities are also as situational as they are substantive, to use Jonathan Z. Smith's terms, a matter of what is selected to be done and how it is done in particular situations rather than fixed activities or even intrinsic principles that govern ritual everywhere. For example, we commonly describe many activities—from war games to cocktail parties—as "ritual-like" by virtue of specific features about the way they are done. Hence, in addition to designated ritual repetoires codified by tradition, often preserved in textual sources, and presided over by trained experts, there are multiple activities that people can ritualize to various degrees.

Since the earliest studies of ritual, scholars have imposed some order on this situation by setting up categories with which to distinguish among dissimilar types of ritual activities. While these taxonomies emerged from each theorist's particular perspective, resulting in a great deal of variety, it is not hard to find a fair amount of consensus on basic categories. Chapter 4 in this section explores six fairly standard ritual genres by presenting representative examples of each in some detail. The next chapter, however, explores activities that are harder to categorize, namely, those that can be ritual-like but are not quite ritual by cultural definition. The stylized behaviors demanded by conventions of social etiquette, sports, or political spectacles, to name just a few, are testimony to how a culture's notion of ritual is dependent upon a loose but total system of ways of acting. The degree of ritualization that one invokes and the degree to which one does so by appealing to tradition or formality, among other features, reveal some of the strategies by which such actions work in their world. By exploring the most generally accepted examples of ritual first and then turning to those activities that are often deemed ritual-like, we should be able to uncover some of the qualities that our culture associates with ritual and some of the strategies underlying how we ritualize.

❧·❧

Basic Genres of Ritual Action

Almost all of the theories of ritual examined in part I come with their own typologies or classification systems for analyzing the plethora of ritual activities. While often descriptively useful, these typologies are designed to support the particular theory being advanced and sometimes reinforce unconscious assumptions about ritual. For example, a simple system proposed by Èmile Durkheim divided "the confused multiplicity of all the ritual forms" into two fundamental types of ritual action: one negative, the other positive. Negative rites, he argued, attempt to separate the human realm from the realm of the sacred by imposing restrictions or taboos, while positive rites attempt to bring the human and sacred realms into contact or communion.[1] This classification system supports Durkheim's underlying distinction between the sacred and the profane as two separate categories of human experience. Another common classification system distinguishes instrumental rituals, which attempt to accomplish something, from expressive rituals, which voice feelings or communicate ideas. The distinction between instrumental and expressive tends to support the idea that so-called magical rites manipulate supernatural powers while so-called higher or devotional rites are a purer form of disinterested worship. For his part, Victor Turner ignored these systems and divided all rites into two basic genres, life-crisis rituals and rituals of affliction, two categories that stress the communal nature of ritual and Turner's view of its sociocultural functions. Yet Turner's categories are commonly used by other theorists who do not presume that these two types account for all ritual activity.[2]

Few systems are as simple as these. The more elaborate efforts have tried to account for the variety of ethnographic examples as well as the history of categories used by theorists. For instance, Ronald Grimes proposed a system of sixteen different categories: rites of passage, marriage rites, funerary rites, festivals, pilgrimage, purification, civil ceremonies, rituals of exchange, sacrifice, worship, magic, healing rites, interaction rites, meditation rites, rites of inversion, and ritual drama.[3] Others define ritual in such a way as to generate categories that include bird songs, conventional gestures like the handshake or driving signal, stock car racing, participation in a mass TV audience, and the educational curricula of American high schools. The more complete and nonreductive a system attempts to be, however, the more unwieldy it can be to use.

The following six categories of ritual action are a pragmatic compromise between completeness and simplicity. They are rites of passage, which are also called "life-cycle" rites; calendrical and commemorative rites; rites of exchange and communion; rites of affliction; rites of feasting, fasting, and festivals; and, finally, political rituals. This list of genres does not attempt to be definitive. There are many other recognizable rituals that could be usefully classified in other categories, and there are rituals that could logically be placed in more than one category. However, the examples described here are among those that have been taken as prototypes for most classification systems. They tend to be examples of rituals in which the action is primarily communal, traditional (that is, understood as carrying on ways of acting established in the past), and rooted in beliefs in divine beings of some sort. These types of rituals, usually associated with clearly defined religious traditions, have long been the dominant examples and primary data for ritual studies.

Rites of Passage

Rites of passage are ceremonies that accompany and dramatize such major events as birth, coming-of-age initiations for boys and girls, marriage, and death. Sometimes called "life-crisis" or "life-cycle" rites, they culturally mark a person's transition from one stage of social life to another. While these rites may be loosely linked to biological changes like parturition and puberty, they frequently depict a sociocultural order that overlays the natural biological order without being identical to it. Birth rites are not necessarily celebrated when a child emerges from the mother's body, and many initiation rites do not neatly coincide with the hormonal changes that usher in fertility and young adulthood. Marriage ceremonies may precede or follow adulthood or even first intercourse, while funeral rites may continue to be celebrated years after a family member has died—or, sometimes, before death. Indeed, life-cycle rituals seem to proclaim that the biological order is less determinative than the social. Physical birth is one thing; being properly identified and accepted as a member of the social group is another. Likewise, the appearance of facial hair or menses does not make someone an adult; only the community confers that recognition, and it does so in its own time. Some scholars have theorized that there is a deep human impulse to take the raw changes of the natural world and "cook" them, in the words of Lévi-Strauss, thereby transforming physical inevitabilities into cultural regularities. This impulse may be an attempt to exert some control over nature or to naturalize the cultural order by making physical events into elements of an embracing conceptual order of cognition and experience. In any case, the tension between the natural and cultural that is sometimes recognized and sometimes disguised in life-cycle rituals appears to be integral to the values and ideas that shape personal identity, social organization, and cultural tradition.

Arnold van Gennep interpreted all rituals as rites of passage with a three-stage process. In this ritual process, the person leaves behind one social group and its concomitant social identity and passes through a stage of no identity or affiliation before admission into another social group that confers a new identity. Such rites of passage from one stage of life to another, van Gennep went on to argue, provide the model for initiations into special groups whose membership is not closely tied to any formal stage of life.[4] For example, even though the practice of adult baptism is not necessarily linked to becoming an adult, it evokes the distinct framework of initiation into a new community and spiritual stage of life. Clubs, fraternities, and secret societies have traditionally put neophytes through ritual ordeals that culminate in acceptance into the new community—all independently of life-cycle transitions. The logic of these rites creates symbolic stages and passages that redefine social and personal identity. For this reason, it is not surprising to find symbolic and experiential similarities in the initiation of neophytes into the 19th-century Chinese secret society known as the Triads, basic training at a U.S. Marines Corps boot camp, and the three-year seminary program for new monks at a Zen monastery.[5] In these cases a series of ritual passages define a "before," a period of training that is "betwixt and between," and finally an "after" in which the transformation of the person is complete. They all orchestrate a physical removal from the rest of the world, physical changes of appearance (through shaved heads and identical, utilitarian clothing), and basic conceptual changes in one's sense of self (through physical challenges, lessons in submission, and new achievements). When this progression into a different framework for identity is thought to have established a new way of seeing and acting, the recruit is officially confirmed and socially recognized by others as having a new identity and community.

In most cultures, social life is a series of major and minor ritual events. While predominantly secular cultures may have just a few rites to mark birth, marriage, and death, more traditional or religious societies may envelop one in a nearly endless sequence of ritual obligations. Birth rituals, for example, are frequently an extended set of activities invoking fertility, the purification of birth pollution, the sexual identity of the fetus, the safety of mother and child, and the conferral of social status when the baby is named and introduced to the larger community. Whether one thinks in terms of van Gennep's pattern of passage (separation, liminality, reincorporation) or Lincoln's pattern of female transformation (enclosure, metamorphosis, emergence), birth and birth rituals appear to provide some of the most basic models and metaphors for all sorts of ritual processes, as well as religious experience in general.[6]

The traditional Chinese birth rituals still found in agricultural villages in Taiwan and mainland China are a complex orchestration of customs and concerns.[7] To begin with, marriage usually brings a young woman to live with her husband's family, where she is apt to be considered an outsider of little account until she gives birth to children, particularly sons to carry on the family line. The importance of childbearing is such that both the new wife and her mother-in-law might undertake the presentation of offerings in supplication for a son to special maternal deities, such as the Buddhist goddess Guanyin or other folk deities associated with children and childbirth. In Chinese culture as elsewhere, these fertility rites are part of a distinct female ritual culture focused on bearing and protecting children, which men tend to ignore or dismiss. One 1936 rural magazine urged young wives to visit older women in the village who had raised many sons to ask them for advice.[8] An earlier account of customs in Beijing at the turn of the century describes a "baby tying ceremony" passed on to a young wife by the experienced mothers of the neighborhood. In hopes of becoming pregnant, the young wife is told to undertake a pilgrimage to a temple renowned for its connections to childbearing. There, in the usual fashion, she should light a bundle of incense sticks and place them in a burner before the image of the main deity. However, on entering the Hall of the Goddess of Sons and Grandsons, she should select a paper image of an attractive baby boy from among an array of such figures, tie a red thread around its neck and pray that the "child" will come home with her to be born as her son. If she subsequently gives birth to a son, the new mother should return with offerings to thank the goddess.[9]

In Taiwanese reckoning, a child is created from the mother's blood and the father's semen.[10] The mother's blood requires the "seeds" in the father's semen in order to turn itself into flesh and bone. Once a child is conceived, menstrual blood collects in the mother's womb to form the child's body. Any excess is discharged at birth. Beliefs about this blood are related to the important god Taishen (or Thai Sin), whose name can be translated as either the God of the Placenta or the God of the Pregnant Womb. Taishen is thought to come into existence when a child is conceived and functions as a type of soul for the child. Not confined to the developing fetus or womb, however, the god is free to roam about the mother's bedroom and is particularly apt to do so about midway through the pregnancy. Taishen is treated like a temperamental guest who should not be disturbed. Even cleaning the room is thought to risk disturbing him, resulting in harm to the fetus or even a miscarriage. If disturbances do occur, especially any accompanied by unusual pain for the mother, a professional medium is summoned to try to appease the god. Since Taishen can reside in the birth fluids, they must be disposed of very carefully after birth in order to keep the child from falling ill.

Undisturbed, Taishen remains in the room until the mother and child formally end their seclusion some 30 to 40 days after birth, although in some areas Taishen may be "ushered" under the child's bed to reside there until the baby reaches young adulthood. In the secluded postpartum period, a woman is not supposed to wash her hair, body, clothes, or dishes. She must also avoid contact with drafts and "cold food," that is, foods associated with damp places and other yin qualities. The bedroom in which she stays during this time not only protects her from many such threats but also protects others from her, since she is considered polluted and dangerous throughout the pregnancy, birth, and recovery. Those who enter the room during or after the birth are affected by this pollution and may not attend weddings or enter temples, where they would offend the gods. Although her husband stays away throughout this period, the new mother is taken care of by a female companion, usually her mother-in-law.[11]

After giving birth, the process of postnatal recuperation is socially marked by a variety of small rites that gradually reincorporate mother and child into the family and then the larger village community. These include several purifying herbal baths and culminate in a ceremony known as the "full month ritual" that ends the thirty days of seclusion. In the case of a baby boy, he is bathed, his hair and eyebrows are shaved except for a tuft in the front and back of his head, his scalp is oiled, and he is dressed in a new, bright red outfit. He is formally shown off to guests at a luncheon celebration at which his name (*ming*), one of several conferred in his lifetime, is officially announced. The mother's room is thoroughly cleaned, and she is free to resume normal domestic life with her husband and family. However, she and the baby are still sufficiently polluted and vulnerable that they must stay quietly at home for another sixty days, altogether about one hundred days after the birth. By that time it is thought that Taishen, as the child's soul, will be sufficiently attached to the child that disturbances in the vicinity of the child no longer threaten to disturb it.

Traditionally, this rather standard ritual sequence has differed significantly in mood and elaborateness depending upon whether the baby is a boy or girl. If it is a girl, both mother and baby receive a great deal less attention. In fact, an old custom of disguising a boy baby with a girl's clothes or name in order to fool any gods or ghosts who might want to steal such a precious bundle clearly demonstrates the relative value of girls. The birth of a boy usually generates more excitement and festivities in patrilineal cultures, where social and personal identity is defined in terms of the father's family line. In these systems, women may have little social identity outside their roles as wives and mothers. While both boys and girls are given a name after thirty days, these names are rarely used, and family nicknames are preferred. Yet by middle age, a boy will usually have acquired four or five formal names, corresponding to a social and ritual process by which a man develops a progressively more individuated social identity. Women, in contrast, traditionally remained nearly nameless, losing their early name at marriage and thereafter known almost exclusively by kinship terms or impersonal labels like "auntie" or "old woman."[12]

Despite the male dominance seen in the importance of sons over daughters and in the concern for the pollution of pregnancy and childbirth, ceremonies like the full month ritual bring about an important change in the mother's domestic and social status. In giving birth and taking up the role of mother, a woman has made a dramatic and indispensable contribution to the prosperity of the family. This is true even for a baby daughter but fully appreciated most in regard to sons. The mother receives gifts, even from her own relatives, and the preparation of special foods to restore her strength testifies to the importance of her new maternal role. Her new responsibilities include continued recourse to rituals in order to safeguard her child, such as various offerings to ancestors and deities, bribes to ghosts, and protective devices, foods, and spells.

A fuller interpretation of the details of these childbirth rites would necessitate a long discussion of Chinese cosmology, customs and social organization. However, some general features of the Chinese example are echoed in birth rituals in many other cultures. Particularly widespread is the idea that pregnancy is a time of great vulnerability and the mother must not be disturbed in any way. Her activities, diet, and social contacts are often severely restricted. Equally common is the imposition of seclusion and greater restrictions during and after birth, since the blood, birth waters, placenta, and umbilical cord are considered highly polluting, dangerous to others, and a source of vulnerability for the child. In many cultures, these materials must be disposed of in careful accordance with traditional rules—usually by burial. Prior to this century, it was not uncommon for there to be a separate room or village hut used just for birth and nothing else. Scholars analyzing Chinese pregnancy and childbirth practices have pointed to different reasons for beliefs in the mother's pollution. Some stress how these ideas relate to an embracing cosmological and social system in which pollution ideas attend any major event that disturbs the boundaries of the family, especially the events of birth, death, and sex.[13] Others stress how such beliefs are used primarily to maintain a system of social relations that subordinate women in roles rendered as ambivalent as they are indispensable.[14] These themes also appear in analyses of childbirth procedures in American hospitals. R. E. Davis-Floyd argues that medical necessity cannot explain the highly symbolic ways in which childbirth is institutionally handled. She finds that values of family and mothering are ritually affirmed over and against those of individuality and sexuality in modern hospitals. Obstetrical procedures that include "preps, enemas, shaves, [and] episiotomies," she argues, are designed to be rites of passage that transform a woman as a sexual person into an asexual mother and custodian of the values of the culture.[15]

Many religious traditions go on to orchestrate the whole of human life as a series of ritual passages and obligations. Eastern Orthodox and Roman forms of Catholicism, for example, identify seven sacraments that span the course of a person's life. The rite of baptism removes the stain of the original sin of Adam and Eve and brings the child (or adult convert) into the community of those "reborn" both in the name of Jesus Christ and in the same manner that Christ himself was baptized by John. Baptism is followed by the rite of reconciliation (penance) at about seven years of age when the child confesses and makes restitution for his or her sins. Following closely is the rite of first communion (the eucharist, Lord's Supper) in which the child consumes a wafer of bread consecrated as the body and blood of Jesus Christ. The rite of confirmation (chrismation) takes place at about twelve years of age, signaling transition to a more adult stage marked by the indwelling of the Holy Spirit, the third person of the Christian godhead. Rites of marriage or holy orders may follow, while at death a priest performs the anointing of the sick (extreme unction), more commonly known as the "last rites," in which the dying person confesses his or her sins and is anointed with oil. While one performs some of these rites only once to make major transitions, others are repeated constantly throughout one's life.

Judaism lays out a series of ritual passages beginning with the *berit milah* or "covenant of circumcision" on the eighth day after the birth of a male child, which initiates him into the community governed by the covenant between God and Abraham. The bar and bat mitzvah, meaning son and daughter of the commandments, respectively, are celebrated at about thirteen years of age, initiating the young person into adult responsibilities for observing the laws binding on the Jewish community. A boy traditionally participates in the public reading of Torah in the synagogue, which is followed by a festive family celebration. Although the bat mitzvah for girls has been incorporated into most nonorthodox Jewish congregations (i.e., Conservative, Reform, and Reconstructionist) since the 1950s, its format still differs widely, although it can be an exact duplicate of the bar mitzvah for boys.

Marriage also marks a major life passage in Judaism, originally accompanied by separate rites of engagement, betrothal, and wedlock that have gradually merged. Jews ritualize death with communal activities and the observation of distinct mourning periods. Since embalming is eschewed, burial tends to take place as soon as possible, entailing a synagogue ceremony, a procession to the cemetery that stops seven times along the way to recite Psalm 91 ("O thou that dwellest in the covert of the Most High"), and graveside prayers that include the famous doxology known as the Kaddish, a prayer invoking the sanctity of God's name, the glory of his kingdom, and the coming of the Messiah.[16] During the initial seven-day period of mourning that follows, the family "sits shivah," that is, they stay at home; sit on low chairs or stools; refrain from sex, shaving, washing, or grooming; and eat special foods brought by family and friends, who are obliged to visit. Traditionally, a minyan, the group of ten men minimally needed to recite Jewish prayers, gathers twice a day during this week for prayer services in the home. The first-year anniversary of the death is observed with prayers and a memorial lamp.

Hindu life-passage rites known as *samskāras* (purifications) can number from ten to forty, varying with geographic, linguistic, or caste differences, although the system as a whole has traditionally been open only to males of the upper castes. The word "samskara" not only means to purify, but also to make over or transform, and ritually it denotes a series of actions that progressively refine and prepare the inner and outer person for the ultimate goals of Hinduism — better rebirth and final release from the cycle of life and death in this world.[17] A set of prenatal rites address fertility, physical well-being, and the goal of having a male child. Other samskaras are performed in early childhood and include rites for naming the child, leaving the birth room, first bites of solid food, first haircut for boys, ear piercing for girls, and so on. Rites during adolescence further prepare the maturing child for taking up his or her social role in the world. The most important of these is the *upanayana* initiation for upper-caste boys (eight to twelve years old) by which they are "reborn" into their caste identities through instruction in the ancient scriptures known as the Vedas. Prior to this critical rite, even upper-caste boys are seen as low caste (*Sudra*) and are not allowed to study the Vedas. The boy's transition is depicted in a series of actions that separate him from his former identity. After a night spent alone in silence, he eats a last meal at his mother's side, bathes, has his head shaved, and dons new clothes. Then he is formally presented to his new teacher, whom he takes as his guru. The teacher drapes a sacred thread (*yajnopavita*) over the boy's left shoulder and under his right arm. Then, laying a hand on the boy's heart, the teacher recites the sacred *Savitri* prayer, which is understood to give symbolic rebirth to the young man.[18]

Other samskaras mark the conclusion of the boy's period of studies and his return to the social community in readiness to marry. Marriage is considered to be the most important samskara since it is the basis of the family and the whole social order. It is also thought to effect a particularly extensive transformation of those involved. According to Bengali custom, writes Ralph W. Nicholas, marriage "completes the body of a male," bringing him into the formal status of a householder and therein able to make offerings to the gods. For the woman, the marriage rites are thought to transform her physical identity, remaking her into a member of her husband's family and, indeed, into his "half body." As the last samskara while one is alive, marriage joins "together into a single body what were previously two separate bodies.[19] Marriage rites differ from one locale to another in India, but they generally include a Brahman priest who guides the couple through the ceremony and builds a sacred fire to which offerings are made. The bridegroom takes the hand of the heavily veiled bride and leads her in circling the fire three times; in some places she is carried around him seven times. As each circle is completed, he has her step on a grinding stone and vow to be like a stone in firmness and resolve. In some places, their clothing may be knotted together; in other places, the bride may take seven steps in a northeast direction, each step symbolizing qualities sought in married life, such as fertility, wealth, and devotion. The groom paints on the bride's forehead the vermilion dot (*bindi*) that signifies a married woman.[20]

Traditionally, the fire from the wedding ceremony was taken back to the couple's home and kept burning for the duration of the marriage. At death, this fire could be used to light the funeral pyre on which the body is committed for yet another act of sacrificial purification (destruction of the corporal body) and rebirth into a further stage of existence (release of the subtle body). As in many religious traditions, smaller rites around the corpse and its cremation are followed by offerings of various sorts to appease the spirit of the dead, which is considered somewhat tentative and even dangerous until it has fully joined its ancestors. This latter transition is the object of the final samskara, the postmortem rites (*śrāddhā*) in which "pure" offerings of rice, water, and prayers are made to the deceased, usually every month for a year and then on the anniversary of the death.

There is another stage of life defined as a traditional ideal in Hinduism, that of the *sannyāsī*, one who renounces family, career, personal identity, and even standard ritual obligations in order to abandon all earthly attachments and seek salvation.[21] The sannyasi lives as a homeless wanderer, begging for food and seeking a total spiritual release from the cycle of death and rebirth. The ritual transition to this stage is marked by legal declarations in which the renouncer sheds all assets, debts, and obligations and then performs his own funeral ceremony. With the same purifying preparations used for a corpse, he shaves his head, clips his nails, and bathes. Then, performing his household ritual obligations for the last time, the renouncer burns all of the ritual implements, mentally internalizes the external fire, and finally lays his sacred thread in the flames. In effect, he renounces ritual itself.[22] With the words, "To me belongs no one, nor do I belong to anyone," the renouncer completes his death to the world. With this separation from the human community, the renouncer's subsequent life is lived in the most liminal fashion, awaiting the final incorporation into the great ultimate.[23]

In American society, as in other highly industrialized countries, rites of passage tend to be less highly organized and far from routine outside small communities or subcultures. While many people turn to familiar religious institutions to observe the traditional rites of birth, marriage, or death, others use more secular rituals, some of which are built into the legal and bureaucratic processes of the state, such as marriage by a justice of the peace. In small American subcultures, coming-of-age rites may still be quite formal, as seen in the debutante balls sponsored by the social elite of major cities or the high school graduations enthusiastically celebrated in midwestern farming towns. For less tightly knit communities, informal and ad hoc ritualizations tend to stand in as symbolic markers of the passage into adulthood. Owning a car, registering with the draft board, beginning to date, getting a first job, leaving home, or simply celebrating one's eighteenth birthday may all function as semiritualized markers of passage.

It is often suggested that the lack of clear life-passage rites in American culture has contributed to the loss of community and a growing sense of social alienation.[24] Some scholars and social critics have even argued that without formal testimony to their passage into adulthood, young people are pressured to prove themselves, both personally and publicly, in rash displays of daring or excess. Yet it is far from clear whether the loss of formal rites of passage is a cause or a symptom of the breakdown of small traditional communities, or that American life is so lacking in rituals. At particular times in history, however, such as the late 19th century until the Great Depression of the 1930s, American life clearly was much richer in ritual. In the Victorian period, for example, many of the domestic and public rituals we take for granted were devised and popularized, such as the elaborate domestic Christmas celebration with a decorated tree, stockings, gifts, and carolers. That period also saw an explosion of men's fraternal organizations dedicated primarily to elaborate series of secret initiations and ceremonies. The need to define and formally achieve gender identity, in this case masculine identity, in the rapidly changing social and economic conditions of the times appears to explain, in part, the "solace and psychological guidance" provided by fraternal rituals in a passage that Victorian America came to be see as fraught with problems.[25]

It is now generally recognized that cultures construct models of masculinity and femininity, subtly pressuring people to conform to them. To be a "real" man or a "real" woman, therefore, socially means much more than an anatomically correct body and mature sensibility. In fact, in most societies manhood and womanhood are not usually thought of as a natural or spontaneous process but a matter of socially orchestrated training that is learned and mastered despite difficult obstacles. As the profile of the Mukanda initiation demonstrated, this process can range from the fairly benign to the traumatic. Controversial initiatory practices—from forced drinking in fraternity hazings in America to female genital circumcision (clitoridectomy) in many parts of the world—suggest that fairly complex processes are involved in the way a society or subculture defines its men and women.[26] In a study of cultural constructions of masculinity, David Gilmore finds "a constantly recurring notion that real manhood is different from simple anatomical maleness." He compares a number of cultural models of manhood and asks "why people in so many places regard the state of being a 'real man' or 'true man' as uncertain or precarious, a prize to be won or wrested through struggle, and why so many societies build up an elusive or exclusionary image of manhood through cultural sanctions, ritual, or trials of skill and endurance."[27] Hazing rites that vary from the yucca whippings of the Tewa to the psychophysical rigors of the traditional British boarding school suggest that the purpose of cultural gender constructions and the rituals that reinforce them is to distinguish and polarize gender roles as the most fundamental form of cultural "ordering" that human beings attempt to impose on nature.[28] The more fundamental such constructions come to seem, the more natural and incontestable.

Psychologists and mythologists like Otto Rank, Carl Jung, and Joseph Campbell have used the model of Van Gennep's three-stage process of initiation, with its echoes of older myth and ritual theories of the dying and rising god, to analyze the structure of hero myths and, by extension, the process of human individuation that leads to the achievement of a mature sense of self.[29] These theories support the idea that rites of passage not only effect transitions in the social sphere but also concomitantly in the psychological sphere. Van Gennep's model has also been applied to the ritual-like, even initiatory, nature of pilgrimage and some of its more recent analogs. Setting out from home and a familiar world, the pilgrim endures the trials and tribulations of the journey, passes through strange lands to which he or she does not belong, and finally arrives at a place considered holier than others, a sacred center where wisdom or grace or gifts are dispensed. Securing a token of that dispensation, the pilgrim returns home bearing the transformed identity of one who has made the journey, touched the sacred objects, and received heavenly boons for the effort. These themes are visible in literary accounts of pilgrimage, from Chaucer's *Canterbury Tales* and John Bunyan's *Pilgrim's Progress* to the Chinese classic novel, *Journey to the West*, which recounts the journey of the 7th-century pilgrim Xuanzang to India to secure Buddhist scriptures, and to Malcolm X's decisive trip to Mecca as recounted in his autobiography.[30] Setting off on a journey has always evoked aspects of an initiatory ritual transition to a new identity, and in both fictional and historical versions the pilgrim is apt to find it hard to fit back into the old life afterward. Religious pilgrimage has continued to thrive amid the transportation developments of the 20th century, while its more secular counterpart, tourism, is apt to invoke very similar images of transformation and renewal, whether the destination is Paris, Gettysburg, or Disneyland.

Calendrical Rites

Beyond those ceremonies that mark social stages of life, an equally obvious and important corpus of rituals is calendrical in nature. Just as rites of passage give order and definition to the biocultural life cycle, so calendrical rites give socially meaningful definitions to the passage of time, creating an ever-renewing cycle of days, months, and years. Both types of rites make time appear to be "an ordered series of eternal re-beginnings and repetitions."[31] Calendrical rites occur periodically and predictably, accompanying seasonal changes in light, weather, agricultural work, and other social activities. Some occasions are reckoned according to the solar calendar and therefore occur on the same date every year, such as New Year's Day on the first of January or Christmas on the twenty-fifth day of December. Others are calculated according to the lunar calendar, causing their dates to vary every year, as seen in the holidays of Rosh Hashanah (Jewish New Year), Easter Sunday, or the Chinese lunar New Year. The use of various intercalary days to coordinate the lunar or solar calendars ensures a correspondence between the ritual occasion and a particular time of the year, often evoking a rich set of associations between the seasons of nature and the rhythm of social life.

The Islamic calendar presents a very interesting exception to these practices since it is designed to transcend the customary solar and lunar years, directly depicting the way that Allah is seen by Muslims to transcend the human and natural world. The Muslim calendar and annual cycle of ritual practices are tied to a critical point marking the beginning of Islamic time and history, Mohammed's emigration from

Mecca to Medina in 622 C.E., where he founded the Muslim community. This became year one in the Islamic era of the *Hijrah*, traditionally stated as 1 H. or latinized as 1 *anno hegira*.[32] Using a lunar year of true months, each month being 29 to 30 days or new moon to new moon, the Islamic year comes to approximately 354 days, 11 days short of the solar year. Most lunar systems add intercalary days or months to maintain the fit with the solar year, but the Qur'an forbids this adjusting of the natural order. Hence, many Muslim ritual days have no fixed relationship to the seasons; each year they are 11 days from where they were the year before. According to Frederick Denny, the Muslim religious calendar "slides slowly behind the 'seasons,'" untied to the usual calculations of the march of time and difficult to convert into other systems.[33]

Calendrical rituals can be roughly distinguished in terms of seasonal and commemorative celebrations. Seasonal celebrations are rooted in the activities of planting and harvesting for agriculturists or grazing and moving the herd for pastoralists. While these types of celebrations seem to appear in all communities directly or indirectly dependent on the fecundity of the land, the style of ritual varies with the type of cultivation. For example, the rites found in societies based on rice cultivation are similar to each other but differ from those found in societies based on the cultivation of wheat, corn, or yams or on animal husbandry. Despite these differences, however, rites of sowing-raising and harvesting-slaughtering often seem remarkably similar.

In brief, the sowing of seed is usually marked by offerings to ancestors or deities in order to secure protection for the fields. In return, harvest rites generally involve festivals in which the firstfruits are given back to the gods or ancestors, accompanied by a communal feast with abundant food, music, dance, and some degree of social license. Sometimes the gods or ancestors themselves are thought to arrive for the celebration and are escorted out of the village at the end of the festivities. In Japan, the traditional New Year celebration is calculated according to the lunar year and therefore celebrates the inception of spring and the planting of the rice. In the premodern period, Japanese New Year festivities included the erection of a pine tree, a symbol of both constancy and renewal, which served as a temporary shrine for the rice deities (*kami*) who come down from beyond the mountains. They are given offerings of rice, the "essence" of which was embodied in glutinous cakes called *mochi*.[34]

Like rites of passage, calendrical rites can be said to impose cultural schemes on the order of nature. These cultural schemes may attempt to influence or control nature, as when rites address the amount of rain or the fertility of the land, or they might simply try to harmonize the activities and attitudes of the human community with the seasonal rhythms of the environment and the larger cosmos. In both cases, they constitute working interpretations of the natural and social worlds. In some cultures, such as the Panare of South America, calendrical rites are literally seen as keeping the cosmos in motion; an eclipse of the sun could be blamed on a ritual poorly executed. Further, for a civilization like the ancient Inca, whose calendrical achievements were truly magnificent, the calendar operated in extensive and complex ways to integrate spatial positions, social hierarchies, genealogical histories, and dynastic power.[35] The attempt to coordinate human activity with the state of the cosmos underlies many of the techniques of divination and prognostication used to determine auspicious days to travel, marry, or sell grain. Ritual experts in China, India, and the Buddhist and Muslim worlds, among others, routinely consult elaborate astrological calendars before planning ritual events like a funeral, ordination, or the groundbreaking rites that precede construction of a building.

The second group of calendrical rites, commemorative ones, includes activities that explicitly recall important historical events, whether or not the date is accurate. For example, the Fourth of July in America commemorates the signing of the Declaration of Independence. Similarly, Bastille Day, celebrated in France on July 14, honors the launching of the French Revolution when a Parisian crowd stormed the infamous prison on that day in 1789. Significantly, with the formal founding of the French republic on September 22, 1792, the revolutionaries went on to set up a new, secular calendar in what one analyst has described as "undoubtedly the most radical attempt in modern history" to challenge the hegemony of the prevailing calendrical system.[36] The French republican calendar purged all the symbols and structures associated with the Catholicism of the Gregorian calendar, discarding not only long-cherished feast days but also Sunday and the seven-day week itself. A new ten-day week culminated in *Décadi* as the official day for rest. Moreover, the year no longer started on January 1 as established by the Catholic monarch Charles IX, but on September 22. Even history itself was recalculated independently of the birth of Christ. The republic replaced the Christian era with the republican era and September 22, 1792, retroactively became "day one" in the first year of the republic. Through these highly symbolic reforms, political history was started anew, and the break between the old and new orders was made total. Despite the dramatic symbolism of this radical tampering with time, however, popular support was far from widespread, so Napoleon did not hesitate to abolish the republican calendar in 1806.[37] The French effort to redefine the social polity by means of calendrical reorganization was echoed in the reforms initiated by Joseph Stalin in the 1920s and 1930s. He also experimented, ultimately unsuccessfully, with dissolving the seven-day week in favor of a five- and then a six-day version, in order to disrupt church attendance.[38]

The designation of December 25 as the birth date of Jesus of Nazareth in the Christian calendar is not, of course, historically accurate. That particular date is most likely a Christian appropriation of the day on which ancient Romans celebrated the winter solstice and birthday of *Sol Invictus*, the invincible sun, who was proclaimed the protector of the empire by Marcus Aurelius.[39] In the same way that the spread of Christianity in the 4th century led it to displace and appropriate the religious practices of the Roman Empire, so Buddhism appropriated practices associated with the indigenous folk religions of Southeast Asia as it spread into those areas from India. Hence, Buddha's Day in Southeast Asia, known as *Visakha Puja* since it occurs on the first full-moon day in the month of Visakha (April-May) at the beginning of the rice planting season, has little to do with reliable history and a great deal to do with a Buddhist rendering of an older calendrical festival. Nonetheless, Visakha Puja is the holiest day in the religious calendar, simultaneously commemorating the Buddha's birth, his enlightenment, and his entry into Nirvana at death, which are believed to have miraculously occurred on the same day of the year.[40] The appropriation of calendrical festivals already deeply engrained in the fabric of a community seems to be a very common and highly effective strategy in places where one set of religious practices encounters and tries to dominate another set. Jewish-American and African-American reactions to the powerful presence of Christmas in a predominantly white and Christian United States have also involved creative appropriations that will be analyzed in part III. Just as often, however, calendrical decisions have been used to segregate and sharply reidentify groups. For example, the Gregorian calendrical reforms of 1582 underscored the divide between Catholics and Protestants, while the French revolutionary reforms put the French out of step with the rest of monarchical Europe. The unique pace of the Islamic calendar has made appropriation of the solar or lunar rites of other groups very difficult. Even today the Islamic calendar provides a type of temporal segregation between those holidays rooted in Qur'anic tradition and those deriving from regional customs, no matter how Islamicized the latter may come to be. Such calendrical distinctions are effective in solidifying group identity, while the appropriation of local rites acts to extend that identity to new subgroupings.[41]

Many religious traditions define their whole calendar year through a series of rites that express the most basic beliefs of the community. The traditional Christian calendar is particularly elaborate in its annual chronicle of the birth, suffering, death, and resurrection of Jesus Christ. Additional saints' days and other holy days have traditionally created an ongoing round of rites in which the rhythms of the year are formed by religious devotions and responsibilities. The Islamic year also commemorates the birth and death of the prophet Mohammed (*Id-E-Milad* or *Mawlid al-Nabi*), his mysterious journey to heaven (*Mi'raj*), the first revelations of the sacred Qur'an on the "night of power" (*Laylat al-Qadr*) in the month of Ramadan, and his pilgrimage from Mecca to Medina (*Dhu Al-Hijjah*). In addition, there are important holidays such as the commemoration of the death of Mohammed's grandson, Husayn ibn 'Ali, which is of great historical and cultic significance to the identity of the Shī'ah, who see themselves as followers of Ali. In all these cases, calendrical ritual turns the events of a historical narrative into a type of cyclical sacred myth, repeated annually, generating powerful images and activities of corporate identity. In a study of Roman calendrical ritual, Mary Beard concludes that the calendar presented a majestic parade of images in "ritual time," whereby linear and historical features were collapsed into a series of overlapping stories. This ritual parade of images became the prime means of representing what it meant to be a Roman. For both the peasant and the sophisticated urbanite, participation in the sequence of calendrical rites was the discovery and rediscovery of "Roman-ness."[42]

The Jewish ritual meal known as the seder, literally the "order" of the service, which is held on the first night of the seven-day holiday of Passover, is a good example of an enduring rite rooted in both seasonal and commemorative traditions. Biblical evidence suggests that the holiday is a combination of two different ancient festivals. One was the pastoral festival of *Pesah* ("passed over"), probably associated with the new year in the southern tribes of Judah. With its sacrifice of a firstborn lamb or kid, it came to commemorate the exodus of the Jews from slavery in Egypt. The second ancient holiday was the seven-day spring agricultural festival of *matsah*, or unleavened bread, celebrated in the more northern areas. Not only did these two rituals eventually merge into one, bringing together images drawn from both animal husbandry and agriculture, but also the format and ethos of the resulting holiday continued to undergo subtle shifts that reflected the historical situation of the Jewish community.[43] In brief, these shifts corresponded to three main epochs in Jewish history.

During the first epoch, which closed with the reforms of King Josiah in 620 B.C.E., the feast of unleavened bread was held in the spring at the first harvest. It was distinct from the holiday of the paschal lamb, which was celebrated in the home, where the family placed the blood of a sacrificed lamb on their door posts and then dined on the meat, together with bitter herbs and unleavened bread known as *matsah*. King Josiah's reforms required every male head of a household to bring an animal offering for sacrifice at the Temple in Jerusalem at Passover. This requirement transformed the domestic Passover meal into a pilgrimage to Solomon's temple as the symbolic center of Judaism and a public cult supporting political centralization. In this context, the religionationalist dimensions of the Passover sacrifice took on much greater significance. Biblical and early postbiblical sources describe a holiday atmosphere as families traveled to Jerusalem, had their offerings ritually killed in the Temple compound, handed over part to the priests, and took most of the meat back for a family meal, accompanied by the traditional bitter herbs and unleavened bread. Those who could not make the trip to Jerusalem could observe the roughly simultaneous festival of unleavened bread, share a meal, and instruct their children in the story of the Exodus; they probably did not make an animal offering. Despite the destruction of the temple by the Persians in 586 B.C.E., this model for the Temple-centered Passover ritual endured throughout the period of the Babylonian captivity as Jews nurtured a sense of identity focused on the temple. With their subsequent return to Jerusalem and the rebuilding of the Temple, the Passover festival continued as a major holiday while gradually new features were added, such as the drinking of wine, more prayers and singing.[44]

The destruction of the second Temple by the Romans in 70 C.E. and the enforced exile of the Jewish community meant that the Passover rite could no longer be celebrated in the same way. In the subsequent third epoch, under the leadership of the emerging rabbinical movement, Passover was gradually reinterpreted once again as a ritual focused on the home and the newly organized synagogues. The new situation of the Jews, in exile from Jerusalem where the Temple was in ruins, accounts for a shift in the tone and the symbols in this revised Passover celebration. The animal sacrifice was no longer central. Instead, the leg bone of an animal was grouped with the unleavened bread (*matsah*) and bitter herbs to form a complex of sacrificial symbols linked less to the Temple than to the redemptive events of the Exodus itself. The paschal animal is eaten, it was said, because the Jews in slavery in Egypt sacrificed a lamb, put its blood on their door posts as a signal to the Angel of Death, and shared its meat in a family meal. The bitter herbs are eaten to recall the bitterness of their years in slavery, while the unleavened *matsah* recall how the escaping Jews did not have time to let their bread rise. As the feast of unleavened bread merged to become part of the weeklong observance of Passover, the unleavened bread itself became the more dominant symbol, evoking life, purity and humble recognition of God's hand in Jewish history. Changes gradually made in the narration of the Exodus account also emphasized a parallelism between the Exodus and the Diaspora, including expressions of trust in God's ongoing redemption of his people and the hope of eventual return to Jerusalem. This is the form in which the Passover seder comes down to us today.[45]

The historical events of the Exodus are retold in the Haggadah ("telling") that is formally recited during the family seder. The Haggadah is a collection of stories, songs, and prayers that assumed its current form in the medieval period, with different versions adding specific features. Available as a small booklet, it guides the family through the various stages of the meal and provides the prayers that they recite. For example, the oldest male present is the "master of the seder" and he opens the meal with a sanctification of the wine (*kiddush*), followed by the introductory prayer: "This is the bread of poverty which our forefathers ate in the land of Egypt. Let all who are hungry enter and eat; let all who are needy come to our Passover feast. This year we are here; next year may we be in the Land of Israel. This year we are slaves; next year may we be free men."[46]

The youngest male present then asks the first of four questions, "Why is this night different from all other nights?" The master and all present reply, together or taking turns, with the account of the delivery of the Jews from Egypt contained in the Haggadah. As the story unfolds, the significance of each symbol is explained. Three *matsot*, made at home or under the supervision of a rabbi are placed on the table under a cloth. After the sanctification of the wine, the middle one is broken in half, and one piece, called the *afikoman* ("dessert"), is traditionally hidden so that the children will later have the fun of trying to find it and bring it back to be eaten last. The master of the seder lifts the other *matsot* and asks:

> This matzah which we eat, what is the reason for it? Because the dough of our fathers had not yet leavened when the King over all kings, the Holy One, blessed be he, revealed himself to them and redeemed them.
>
> As it is said: "and they baked unleavened cakes of the dough which they brought forth out of Egypt, for it was not leavened; because they were thrust out of Egypt, and could not tarry, neither had they prepared for themselves any victual" [Exodus 12:39].[47]

Also present on the table is a concoction of bitter herbs, usually made with salad greens, called *maror:* "These bitter herbs we eat, what is the reason for them? Because the Egyptians made the lives of our forefathers bitter in Egypt."[48] Likewise, a paste made of nuts, fruit, and wine called *haroset* represents the mortar that the Jews labored to make into bricks for the Pharaoh. Salted or vinegared water in a bowl symbolizes the tears of suffering, into which a vegetable (*karpas*) like parsley or celery is dipped. A roasted shank bone and hard-boiled egg represent the paschal lamb and the part of it given in sacrifice in the days of the temple. Four cups of wine are drunk at specific places in the meal in celebration of God's deliverance of the Jews. After a closing set of prayers, the seder ends with hymns also included in the Haggadah booklet.

Like many commemorative rituals, the seder establishes a fundamental link between the past and the present, specifically, that every Jew has been delivered from Egypt by God. "In every generation let each man look on himself as if *he* came forth out of Egypt," reads the Haggadah.[49] All Jews are in exile and anxiously await their return to Jerusalem: "This year we are here; next year may we be in the Land of Israel. This year we are slaves; next year may we be free men."[50] This theme vividly demonstrates the power of a commemorative ritual to invoke the original events as ongoing acts of God. Even those rites that evoke secular events long past attempt to involve participants in experiencing and affirming a set of values seen as rooted in those events. Memorial Day, with its parades, wreaths, and prayers, began by commemorating Union soldiers killed in the Civil War. Developing into a day to honor the veterans of all American wars, it was one of the primary means by which different faiths, ethnicities, and social classes were integrated into a sacralized unity.[51] The Memorial Day rites so important in the small towns of America in the first half of this century testified to the values associated with those soldiers who sacrificed their individual lives for the good of the whole. Indeed, their sacrifices came to be seen as a type of death-conquering model or paradigm for what it meant to be a member of the national community.

As noted in chapter 1, Mircea Eliade drew attention to how the ritual reenactment of founding events is able to generate a meaningful, mythic, and cyclical sense of time, a temporal sense in which it is as if the original events are happening all over again. He thought this reenactment of sacred events released something of their original transformative power. Some theorists have argued that the more historical and secular a culture becomes, the more its calendrical rites give way to merely commemorative ones. In practice, however, many such rituals easily shift their emphasis back and forth, subtly evoking themes of cosmic renewal alongside themes of historical commemoration. Ultimately, it is the very rituals themselves that create the repetitions of seasonal and historical events that form the calendar.[52] Similarly, these calendrical systems exist only insofar as a rite evokes other rites to form a temporal series that molds time into a cycle of holy events and affords people the experience of some version of original events. As the complex product of a ritual understanding of time and space, the calendar and its attendant systems mold human life to the point that it can appear essentially calendrical in nature.[53]

Rites of Exchange and Communion

Among the best-known examples of religious rituals are those in which people make offerings to a god or gods with the practical and straightforward expectation of receiving something in return—whether it be as concrete as a good harvest and a long life or as abstract as grace and redemption. Edward Tylor described the logic of these human-divine transactions as "the gift theory"; one gives in order to receive in return (*do ut des*).[54] Direct offerings may be given to praise, please, and placate divine power, or they may involve an explicit exchange by which human beings provide sustenance to divine powers in return for divine contributions to human well-being. In less elaborate examples, one places flowers or incense before the image of a Hindu god until they are spent, while the rice and oranges one presents at a Chinese shrine can be removed for human consumption after the gods or ancestors have eaten their fill. More elaborate examples of these dynamics are found in the phenomenon of sacrifice. In the standard sacrificial scenario, an animal is killed, and part or all of it is presented as an offering to the gods in exchange for what the gods can give; leftover meat may be eaten in a type of communal meal.

Scholars have repeatedly attempted to organize these ritual activities in a logical way. Some have been concerned primarily to distinguish gifts, offerings, and sacrifice, each signifying a different form of human-divine interaction and social orga-nization.[55] Others have been more interested in a continuum of ritual practices that range from offerings that act as bribes to gifts that are said to have no purpose except the expression of pure devotion. Despite the tendency noted earlier to consider manipulative dynamics "magical" and disinterested devotion "religious," these dis-tinctions and their associated examples tend to break down when scrutinized more closely. In ritual, it is probably safe to say that no act is purely manipulative or purely disinterested. Ritual acts of offering, exchange and communion appear to invoke very complex relations of mutual interdependence between the human and the divine. In addition, these activities are likely to be important not simply to human-divine relations but also to a number of social and cultural processes by which the commu-nity organizes and understands itself.

Hindu devotional worship known as *puja* is a good example of a system of simple offerings that appears to have no purpose other than to please the deity. These offer-ings can range from the simple and private to the elaborate and public. Sometimes they are visualized rather than performed. Whether presented to the image of a deity in the home, at a temple, or at a religious festival, puja rites evoke the ceremonies of hospitality traditionally shown to honored guests, particularly in ancient court life. Indeed, it is fair to say that in the home or at a festival, such rites cast the deity as a lofty but temporary guest, while in a temple setting they acknowledge the deity as ensconced in the equivalent of his or her own palace.

Technically, puja involves sixteen different presentations called *upacāras* (at-tendances), although only a few might be used in any particular service. A devout family may have a small room just for worship in which there is an altar housing one or more images. Traditionally, the male head of the household performs a daily or twice-daily puja routine, although this job is frequently taken over by the woman of the house. The daily worship ceremony (*nitya puja*) in larger temples may be more elaborate, even repeating an upacara several times. When performing the main upacaras, the devotee first summons or awakens the god to be present at the ceremony. The god is offered a seat, and with a formal greeting, the devotee asks the god about its journey. The devotee then symbolically washes the god's feet and presents a small bowl of water so that the god might wash its face and rinse its mouth. Another bowl of water is presented for sipping, followed by a drink of water and honey. Next comes water for a bath, or, if the image is small, it may be submerged and dried with a towel. The devotee adorns the image with fresh garments, ornaments, perfumes, ointments, and flower garlands. Then the devotee steps back to offer incense to please the deity and a small burning lamp to give it light. Next come food offerings such as cooked rice, clarified butter, fruits, or betel leaf. At the end of the service, after the god has tasted the offerings, this food is distributed to those in attendance and eaten. Known as *prasada*, the return gift of food is thought to confer blessings from the deity. In a similar back and forth, all those present worship the image by prostrating themselves before it in an act known as *darśana* (seeing or auspicious sight), literally seeing the god and being seen by it in turn. Last, the god is dismissed, put to bed, or shrouded with a curtain.[56]

While flowers, lamps, incense, and prayers are offered to the images of deities in many traditions, Hindu puja fully plays out the underlying logic of human services rendered to anthropomorphized divine beings. The devotee who makes as if to fan the god's brow or brush its teeth may not expect that the god or image really requires such physical ministrations. Rather, they form a "grammar of devotion," according to Diana Eck, in which "gestures of humility . . . utilize the entire range of intimate and ordinary domestic acts."[57] Darshana, the exchange of sight, is central to this devotional grammar and has been called the most basic and sacramental act of worship in Hinduism. In the home, at the temple, amid a festival, or at any of the thousands of sacred pilgrimage places, the devout Hindu is said to "take" or "receive" *darsan*, while the deity or holy person (*sadhu*) is said to "give" it.[58] The moment of mutual seeing that passes between the sacred and the human is the culmination of the more tangible exchanges involved in these rites.

The reciprocity underlying Hindu puja is relatively low key. Devotional offerings to the deity are not meant to result in direct or immediate concrete benefits, although they are understood to nurture a positive human-divine relationship that will benefit the devotee spiritually and substantively. In contrast, rites involving Chinese spirit money are good examples of a system of offerings that often appears much less devotional and much more bureaucratic and pecuniary. Spirit money is coarse paper tied in bundles, on the top sheet of which there may be pasted a square of yellow or silver foil that identifies its currency and value. In Taiwan, gold spirit money, a wad of yellow paper topped with yellow foil, is given to the gods, while silver money is given to the ghosts and ancestors. Usually spirit money is burned to transfer it to the other world: the destruction of the material substance of the currency by fire is understood to release its essence in the other world.[59] By the same principle, paper versions of other objects—messengers, houses, televisions, or mahjong sets—are also burned to transfer them to the other world. Although Chinese stores now sell more realistic-looking "play money" for these sacrificial purposes, it is important to note that real money would be of no use in the other world, where it would become fake and constitute something of an insult to its intended recipient. According to the ancient classic on ritual, objects offered to the dead for their sole use must not be fit for actual use since it is not appropriate to treat the dead as if they were the same as the living.[60] Spirit money is usually burned in order to solicit favors from the gods, provide the dead with the cash they need to take care of business in the courts and hells of the underworld, bribe celestial bureaucrats, and placate offending demons or interfering ghosts. In Chinese cosmology, the bureaucracy of the human world continues into the invisible world. Both spheres operate on the same principles: virtue is rewarded, but cash is very effective in working out deals and cutting through red tape.

An ethos of economic exchange is particularly prominent in two Taiwanese rituals, the rite to "repay the debt" and the rite to "restore one's destiny."[61] In the first, life is assumed to be a type of monetary loan that must be repaid. At birth, one is given an advance from the celestial treasury; death, especially at an advanced age and after producing male descendants, is due to the exhaustion of these funds. At the funeral, relatives of the deceased burn a specially marked form of spirit money known as "treasury money" in order to pay off any remaining debt to the celestial treasury and in this way ensure the continuation of the deceased's soul in a future life. Similar rites conducted during one's lifetime can also replenish the funds in one's treasury account and stave off an early death. The ritual for "restoring one's destiny" shares these assumptions. It is usually performed on New Year's Day and at critical junctures in life—birth, the first month, one year, seven years, and so on—since such occasions are thought to drain one's life vitality. It may also be performed on the completion of a project or at the time of some professional success since such forms of good luck can also use up one's allotted vitality. If one's life vitality is sapped through too much success, one can become prey to demonic maladies of all kinds. Rites to restore this vitality may be simple or grand, performed by a Daoist priest, a folk medium, or the head of the house, each in their own distinctive way. The Daoist will call down deities that he alone has the power to summon, the medium will journey in trance into the invisible world, and the head of the household will burn a preprinted petition. In all three cases, a formal request is made that enumerates the blessings the family has received from the gods, and then specially designated "restoration of destiny" money is burned to deposit it in the celestial treasury.

The ritual grammar of human-divine interaction in these Chinese ceremonies is not the same as the humble hospitality seen in Hindu puja. It is a language of banking, bureaucratic hierarchy, and closed energy systems that enables human beings to influence the cosmos by extending the meaning and efficacy of those activities that seem to organize the human world most effectively. For the Chinese, the cosmos may be experienced as less capricious and intimate than what Hindus experience, but both use distinct cultural conventions to ritualize human-divine interaction and exchange. By contrast, Mexican culture uses yet another system for representing human and divine interactions, primarily a grammar of vows and thanksgiving. This system is most evident in the custom of hanging *retablos* to express thanks to Jesus or the Virgin Mother. These small votive paintings depict the troubled scene in which divine help was extended, usually including a written explanation and thank you—*doy gracias*—to acknowledge this divine intercession in a public way.[62]

It is hardly surprising that there should be great variety in the things offered to supernatural beings or in the symbolic grammar with which these offerings are made. More unexpected, perhaps, are the similarities, such as the widespread use of incense and smoke either as offerings themselves, as in Native American rites of the sacred pipe, or as a medium to bear offerings aloft to the gods, as seen in Chinese rites.[63] Equally common is the offering of dances, songs, and even theater productions to entertain the gods. Traditional performances of Chinese opera and folk theater, Japanese Noh theater, and the Javanese puppet theater known as *wayang*, all of which routinely begin with invocations to the gods, are often held in temple or templelike settings and show many strong associations with ritual. While some dances may reenact sacred events, such as the creation of the cosmos or the yearly return of the ancestors, others are narrative tales presented to entertain the gods—for whom special seats may be reserved. The performances of the female dancers (*devadasis*) traditionally offered to the god Siva in south Indian Saivite temples are rituals of offering and entertainment with powerful—and controversial—overtones of virility and fertility.[64]

The concept of "sacrifice" as a distinct form of human-divine interaction and exchange has been a major topic in ritual studies since the time of Tylor and Robertson

Smith.[65] More than any other form of ritual, sacrifice has been considered a type of universal or nearly universal "institution" that can be explained in terms of principles applicable to all cultural examples. Henri Hubert and Marcel Mauss made an important contribution by distinguishing sacrifice from other forms of ritual offerings through the principle of sanctification: in sacrifice the offerings are consecrated. Indeed, the word "sacrifice" derives from the Latin *sacer facere* (to make holy). As a logical corollary to this sanctification, the object offered in sacrifice is usually completely destroyed in the course of the rite, either burned to transfer the offering to the gods or consumed to share it with them. Inanimate or bloodless objects like vegetables, grains, and paper goods can be sacrificed, as in the Chinese examples, but the term usually implies blood offerings of animals, human beings, or their various substitutes. Distinctions drawn between offerings and sacrifices based on whether the object involved is inanimate or animate can be very hard to pursue systematically. For example, the ritual destruction of Chinese spirit money lies in a tradition of sacrifice that includes animal offerings and is quite distinct from simply leaving food on an altar. And according to Hubert and Mauss, the libations of milk offered in the Vedic sacrificial system prior to the development of puja offerings were "not something inanimate that is offered up, but the cow itself, in its liquid essence, its sap, its fertility."[66]

Theories of sacrifice have tended to focus on the "communion" it is thought to afford between humans and gods, although this terminology derives from the Judeo-Christian tradition and is not much used in many other cultures where sacrifice is important. The idea of communion with the supernatural recipients of the offerings is also used to distinguish sacrifice from ritualized killing. Communion implies that at a critical moment in the rite there is a union of the human and divine worlds: the offerer, the recipient, and the offering itself are understood to become together in some way, however briefly. The purpose of this form of cosmic union is usually explained as a matter of renewing the universe and reordering the human-divine relations that sustain it. However, other purposes are also given for the performance of sacrificial rites, including thanksgiving, the expiation of evils, and the placation of powerful deities, which are not incompatible with the notion of communion.

When defined in very general terms, some form of sacrifice can be found in almost all societies. The sacrifice of firstfruits in agricultural societies and of domesticated animals in herding societies demonstrates certain general correlations between the form of sacrifice and the type of socioeconomic structure. Cultural cosmology will also determine the format used. For example, the use of incineration and smoke to carry an offering aloft correlates with the belief that the gods reside somewhere beyond the human sphere; immersion is used to convey offerings to water deities, and abandonment of an offering in a ravine or on a hilltop is usually sufficient to convey it to gods thought to be abroad in the natural environment. The form of destruction can also reflect ideas about the type of human-divine interaction afforded by the rite: in some cases, total destruction of the offering appears to seal a contractual relationship; in others, communal consumption of the offering facilitates a sharing of substance.[67] Both forms of sacrifice are in the Hebrew Bible: the burnt offering or holocaust (*'olah*) in which the animal was completely incinerated, and the sacrifice of salvation or peace (*zevah shelamim*) in which part of the animal was burned, the blood poured out on the altar or earth, and the remainder consumed in a communal meal. While the latter is the form observed in the Passover rites described earlier, the former type of sacrifice is most familiar from the story of Abraham and Issac:

> After these things God tested Abraham, and said to him "Abraham!" And he said, "Here am I." He said, "Take your son, your only son Issac, whom you love, and go to the land of Moriah, and offer him there as a burnt offering upon the mountains of which I shall tell you." So Abraham rose early in the morning, saddled his ass, and took two of his young men with him, and his son Isaac; and he cut the wood for the burnt offering, and arose and went to the place of which God had told him. . . . Abraham built an altar there, and laid the wood in order, and bound Isaac his son, and laid him on the altar, upon the wood. Then Abraham put forth his hand and took the knife to slay his son. But the angel of the Lord called to him from heaven, and said, "Abraham, Abraham!" And he said, "Here am I." He said, "Do not lay your hand on the lad or do anything to him; for now I know that you fear God, seeing you have not withheld your son, your only son, from me." And Abraham lifted up his eyes and looked, and behold, behind him was a ram, caught in a thicket by his horns; and Abraham went and took the ram, and offered it up as a burnt offering instead of his son.[68]

For Judaism, this burnt offering established a close bond between God and the descendants of Abraham, which was later sealed in the covenant made between God and Moses when both forms of sacrifice were performed:

> And [Moses] rose early in the morning, and built an altar at the foot of the mountain . . . [where he] burnt offerings and sacrificed peace offerings of oxen to the Lord. And Moses took half of the blood and put it in basins, and half of the blood he threw against the altar. Then he took the book of the covenant, and read it in the hearing of the people; and they said, "All that the Lord has spoken we will do, and we will be obedient." And Moses took the blood and threw it upon the people, and said, "Behold the blood of the covenant which the Lord has made with you in accordance with all these words."[69]

As indicated earlier, most theorists stress the communionlike nature of sacrifice, which is clearest when the rites involve first the sacralization and then the killing of a living animal or person. Consecration or sacralization can make the offering participate in the divinity of the god to whom it is to be given, even to the point, in some cases, that the offering may be thought to become the god itself. This form of consecration is seen in diverse practices, such as Christian doctrine of the real presence of Jesus Christ in the sacralized bread and wine; the offering and ingestion of the intoxicating sacred drink *balché* to feed the gods of the Lacandon Maya of Chiapas; the ritual consumption of peyote among some Native American tribes; and the Aztec sacrifice of prisoners of war to their sun god.[70]

The peyote cult is a good example of a sacrificial ritual in which the symbolism of communion is very strong. The cult formally developed, particularly among Native Americans of the southern plains only about the turn of the century as an integral part of the Native American Church. Influenced by Christianity as well as pan-tribal religious beliefs and practices, the consumption of the sacred peyote button is thought to enable one to experience the closeness of the Great Spirit. The Great Spirit is said to have put his power into the sacred button so that when it is gathered by a shaman and eaten in the appropriate way that power can be absorbed by his people to help them. The hallucinatory effects that can be produced by the drug are considered quite secondary to the more powerful experience of the Great Spirit, who may reveal some truth or bestow some power.[71]

Sacralization of an offering in order to make it as divine as the god who will receive it appears to have been an important part of Aztec sacrifice.[72] As a principle of human-divine interaction, sacralization also sets up a type of economic exchange, according to Marshall Sahlins: "offered as food to the gods, the victim takes on the nature of the god. Consumed then by man, the offering transmits this divine power to man."[73] For the Aztecs, the offering clearly involved two identifications. First, the sacrifier, the one who sponsored the sacrifice and expected to benefit from it, was identified with the victim being offered and in some cases would declare that the victim "is as my beloved son." Second, a series of consecrations also identified the offering with the gods who were its ultimate recipients. Aztec mythology, in fact, describes an original self-sacrifice of the gods that enabled the sun to move across the sky. Evidence concerning the treatment of many victims after capture and prior to their death suggests that they were made to reenact this cosmogonic sacrifice of the gods: they were bathed, dressed, and painted to represent specific deities, feted, and taught special dances. When these victims were sacrificed on the altar at the top of the central pyramid of Tenochtitlán, the still-beating heart was offered to the sun, blood was splashed on the altar, and the body was rolled back down the steps to be dismembered by those waiting below. For the Aztecs, the victim going up and coming down the great steps of Tenochtitlán, not unlike the rising and setting of the sun in the sky, was the medium for a necessary exchange between the human and divine world that ensured the ordered continuance of the cosmos. In Sahlin's analysis, the victim closed a cycle between the sacrificers and the gods, linked the sacred and the profane, and facilitated the transmission of blessings and requests. Ultimately, he argues, "Victims, gods, and communicants become one. The consumption of human flesh was thus deifying"[74]

Human sacrifice has been found in many societies both ancient and modern.[75] There are some basic similarities among the types of victims and the forms of destruction used, as well as differences in the social and cosmic purposes ascribed to the ritual. Nonetheless, human sacrifice can be seen as a simple extension of the logic underlying other forms of offerings. Whether the purpose is to avert evil, placate gods, achieve communion, reconstruct idealized kinship relations, or establish the proper reciprocity of heaven and earth, the offering of something—firstfruits, paper money, or human beings—has been a common ritual mechanism for securing the well-being of the community and the larger cosmos.[76] Such offerings also redefine the culture's system of cosmological boundaries—the human sphere, the sphere of the gods, the sphere of the ancestral dead, the sphere of malevolent demons, and so on—while simultaneously allowing the crossing or transgression of those very same boundaries.

Rites of Affliction

Following Victor Turner, who frequently invoked this category of ritual, rites of affliction seek to mitigate the influence of spirits thought to be afflicting human beings with misfortune. Among the Ndembu, he found, if divination reveals that an individual has been "caught" by a spirit of the dead, an elaborate ritual is mounted to appease, and dismiss the troublesome spirit.[77] For the Ndembu, such spirits are usually identified as those of the dead, who are blamed for problems in hunting, women's reproductive disorders, and various forms of illness. Although rituals of affliction similar to those of the Ndembu are found in many cultures, the category can be broadened to include other understandings of affliction, such as those one brings on oneself, like sin or karma, as well as those recurring afflictions, such as the pollution of menstruation, childbearing, and death, that are morally neutral but still require purification.

In all of these cases, rituals of affliction attempt to rectify a state of affairs that has been disturbed or disordered; they heal, exorcise, protect, and purify. The type of ritual and ritual expert used will depend completely on the way in which a culture interprets the problematic state of affairs. One culture might diagnose some illness or bad luck as the result of an incomplete process of creation at the beginning of the world or as possession by spirits and prescribe a formal exorcism. Another culture might diagnose it as the ravages of sin and prescribe confession and rigorous penance, while a more secular society might diagnose the problem as a repressed childhood trauma and advocate three to six years of expensive ritual visits to the couch of a psychoanalyst. Within this broad genre, the dynamics of the ritual attempt to redress the development of anomalies or imbalances. Across the board, this takes the form of purging the body and mind of all impurities, which are nothing other than forces that have intruded upon the body-mind holism and disturbed its natural state. In some cases it may also involve the intercession of powerful beings to rectify intrusions and imbalances that go beyond the body of a single person.

Those affairs deemed out of order are often meteorological in nature. Numerous historical and contemporary accounts testify to a wide variety of rituals to bring rain in times of drought or protection in times of flood, pestilence, and other dangers. The logic of many rainmaking rites appears to follow what Frazer described as "sympathetic magic," whereby like produces like, so people squirt water on each other, imitate the calls of aquatic birds, or set out pots of water to draw down the rain. In other cases, people invoke the gods in control of these conditions, as the Greeks supplicated Zeus, who was thought to dispense rain. Citizens of the California town of Santa Barbara paraded a statue of the Virgin Mother during a drought in the late 1980s, perhaps to have her see for herself the dried-up lawns and threat of fire. If so, their approach was akin to the more aggressive methods used in ancient and medieval China, when statues of unresponsive gods would be taken from their cool temples and set out to roast in the sun so that they would know firsthand the suffering of the people and do something about it.[78] The great Chinese poet Bo Juyi (772–846) left an account of medieval Chinese divine-human interaction in a story about how a drought forced him to scold the Black Dragon of the north for near dereliction in his duties: "We are asking you for a favor, but you depend on us for your divinity. Creatures are not divine on their own account, it is their worshippers that make them so. If within three days there is a real downpour, we shall give your holy powers credit for it." However, the poet continued, if the Black Dragon allows the crops to dry up and the people to starve, then the "disgrace" will be his.[79] Other Chinese practices are recorded in which female shamans, secular officials, and even emperors would expose themselves to the heat of the sun or a ring of fire to demonstrate their willingness to assume personal blame for the drought and provoke the mercy of the gods.[80]

Healing rituals are particularly ubiquitous and express understandings of the nature of physical and mental infirmity that usually differ considerably from the rather recent scientific etiologies used in modern medicine in the 20th century. However, it is useful to keep in mind that these rites tend to address factors simply not dealt with by scientific medicine and for that reason often coexist alongside it even today. For example, supernatural forces that are ritually brought to bear on the situation are not only meant to affect the physical dimensions of a condition like small pox or infertility but also the psychological and social dimensions of the situation as well. While Western medicine is based on the idea that disease is a condition within the individual body system, many other healing therapies are based on the idea that disease takes root when key social relations—among the living or the living and dead—are disturbed. Rectification of these relationships are an important part of what traditional healing is all about. Indeed, even if someone recognizes that diseases like infant dysentery are caused by bacteria and treat it accordingly, bacteria do not explain why one child sickens and another does not. That type of explanation is sought elsewhere, usually in terms of social or cosmological factors. "Reality," writes one interpreter of traditional healing practices, "rests on the relations between one human being and another, and between all people and spirits."[81] This does not mean that physical and mental illnesses are simply attributed to invisible forces whose mere existence, aside from any responsibility for the problem, cannot be proven or disproven. Rather, it means that health and illness are understood as symptoms of a broadly conceived realm of order or disorder that draws no hard-and-fast boundaries between the individual and the community, the mind and the body, or the material and the spiritual.

In traditional Korean society, healing has been a central domain of the traditional shaman, the *mansin* or *mudang*.[82] While there are several types of shamans in Korea, the most common is a woman who experiences the descent of a spirit into her, frequently after a mysterious illness that may eventually be diagnosed as possession sickness (*sinbyong*).[83] When the woman accepts her new calling, the spirits allow her to recover. She then undergoes the training and initiation needed to acquire tutelary deities to aid her in her work. The healing powers of the mansin are exercised through two main rituals, a divinatory session (*chom*), where the problem is diagnosed, and an exorcistic ritual (*kut*), where the problem is rectified. A person, family, or even a whole village can consult a mansin and sponsor a kut, which is believed to have both curative and prophylactic powers. The kut may be a small affair held in the home, or a major public event held outdoors for three to seven nights, involving seven or eight mansin, numerous musicians, and tables laden with offerings to ancestors and deities.

At a typical divination session, the mansin questions her client closely, sometimes going into trance to determine the cause of the problem. For example, the performance of various divinatory techniques and skillful questioning of a client concerned about a sick daughter-in-law might yield the information that the client had quarreled with an uncle shortly before he was killed by a bomb during the Korean War. "That's it," the mansin announces. "That ancestor, your uncle is upset. His spirit is upset. Because you have not treated him well, he is angry. You must have forgotten to honor him with commemoration services. That's why there is sickness in your family. . . . You will have to honor him well. We can perform a kut."[84] Such a kut will usually last from dawn to late evening and includes a series of seances with a fixed pantheon of gods. Each seance has three stages. In the first stage, when the god is summoned, the mansin dances to slow music and goes into trance. In the second stage, the music is fast and loud. The god arrives by possessing the mansin, who assumes the distinctive manner and speech of the deity and issues a divine message (kongsu) explaining the illness and how to heal it. If an evil spirit is responsible, the god possessing the mansin dances around the patient to drive it out. A straw doll wearing a bit of the sick person's clothing may also be burned after the possessed mansin has driven off the intrusive evil spirit. In the third and final stage, the music and dancing gradually slow down and the god departs.[85]

Ritual responses to illness have proven quite capable of effecting psychotherapeutic cures. A number of psychological mechanisms appear to come into play, while the process itself provides an exhausting emotional catharsis in which clients must confront personal fears and social tensions temporarily embodied and demanding reconciliation. The ritual context assembles the full family of the afflicted one in addition to a useful number of ancestors and demons. The result can be seen as a particularly broad-based form of group or family therapy in which the values of traditional roles and responsibilities are reaffirmed as more important than the individual grudges, griefs, and fears cathartically released in the rite. Analysts also suggest that in those cultures in which possession and exorcism are both common events and metaphors, the self is defined vis-à-vis the rest of the social-spiritual world in ways that differ from European and American cultural tendencies. In particular, possession cultures identify powerful forces and influences outside the individual, while Euro-American culture often identifies them within the individual. Studies of various forms of spirit possession—especially in Morocco, Brazil, Sri Lanka, and Haiti—have generated much ethnographic speculation on the culturally diverse ways in which images of the self and the world are constructed and interrelated.[86] Similarly, studies of historical instances of possession, both as an acceptable phenomenon involving formally recognized expertise and as a highly undesirable phenomenon among the socially alienated, have also suggested important connections between the forms of religious expression and the larger sociopolitical milieu. In particular, rituals of trance and possession often occur in historical or structural opposition to other forms of ritual expertise. Analyses of female shamans in Korea, the infamous Salem witch trials, or modern ecstatic Hindu saints suggest that these phenomena involve elements of rebellion against social constraints; they may even institutionalize methods of inverting, reversing, or undermining other dimensions of the religious and social order.[87]

An interesting variation on the affliction ritual and its mode of sociopsychological restoration can be seen in the Ghost Dance that was desperately promoted and performed by the tribes across the Great Plains on the eve of their definitive defeat and loss of lands in the late 1800s. As the Plains Indians were subjugated and forced to retreat to smaller and more benighted tracts of land, the basis for any form of traditional life was destroyed. They began to starve as the number of buffalo plummeted and other game was eaten or driven off by settlers. Treaties were made and broken, and one tribe after another was gradually pushed into guarded camps and reservations. In this worsening milieu, the very brink of cultural anomie, various prophets began preaching how to reverse the annihilation of Plains culture by means of what came to be known as the Ghost Dance. Their message was a mix of prewhite beliefs of cataclysmic world regeneration held by the natives of the Pacific Northwest, Christian messianism, and traditional practices that included shamanism and "round dancing." The rites of the Ghost Dance, which spread from group to group across the plains, included trance, communication with spirits and the dead, purification, and the rectification of a cosmos gone awry. A Paiute prophet named Wovoka claimed to bring a message from the Great Father that this dance would renew the earth and restore the dead, the buffalo, and their stolen lands. In some prophecies, it was said that the dance would cause Indians and whites to become one people and live in peace; in others, the dance would summon armies of the dead to push the whites back into the ocean. Groups gathered together with scarce regard for traditional intertribal hostilities and danced for days, often going into trances, and communicating with the dead who came to them in visions. They sang songs taught to them by the prophets, and in their visions some saw magical designs that they painted on their shirts to repel bullets. Although in the tradition of round dance rituals, the Ghost Dance was a new communal rite, one that attempted to purify the dancers of the faults that had brought them to this historical impasse, to exorcise the evil in their midst, and to restore order to the world of spirits, humans, and animals. However, despite its social and psychological import, the dancing could not prevent the destruction that culminated in the massacre of 260 men, women, and children gathered for a Ghost Dance at Wounded Knee Creek, South Dakota, in 1890.[88]

Purification is a major theme within rites of affliction, although it can be understood in a variety of ways. It can involve freeing a person from demonic possession, disease, sin, or the karmic consequences of past lives. While some purification rites focus on personal problems and faults, others attempt to remove impersonal forms of contagion that generally afflict the human condition, such as the pollution acquired by being in a crowd, traveling to a foreign country, experiencing a death, or, as we have seen with regard to Chinese customs, a birth in the family. In each case, the pollution is defined differently, and so are the remedies to redress it. In Hindu culture, routine pollution from the inadvertent violation of caste rules can be dealt with by bathing. Likewise, the usual pollution that accrues to Chinese statues of gods in the course of their work as they preside over a temple is cleansed by an annual fire-walking ceremony in which young men of resolve and pure intent carry the statues over a bed of hot coals lightly dusted with rice.

The transgression of purity-pollution rules in Hinduism, Japanese Shinto, and orthodox Judaism, to mention just a few traditions, requires immediate purification in order to avert negative consequences. These rules may be dietary or govern bodily pollution. The traditional Hindu Brahman who has come into forbidden contact with untouchables or foreigners must immediately undertake physical and spiritual cleansing. In both traditional Hinduism and Japanese Shinto, as well as in medieval Europe and many other traditions, women polluted by menstruation or recent childbirth were forbidden to enter shrines and temples. In very orthodox forms of Judaism, the institution of the ritual bath, the *mikveh*, ensures the physical and spiritual cleansing of pollution for sexually active (i.e., married) menstruating women; it is also the way in which men cleanse themselves spiritually in preparation for the sabbath each week.[89] While fire and water are among the most common ritual agents of purification, other auspicious substances can act to purify, such as the five products of the cow in India: milk, curds, clarified butter (*ghi*), dung, and urine.[90] In some societies, possession and purification can be effected through music and dance, asceticism, or even drugs and intoxicants. For example, the powerful, home-brewed intoxicant balché, ritually consumed by the Lacandon Maya of Chiapas, Mexico, not only nourishes and placates the gods to whom it is offered but also is thought to purify spiritually and physically the worshipers who drink it. They readily credit the drink with healing properties, essentially purgative in nature, since it causes vomiting that leaves the worshipers feeling cleansed and cured.[91]

Spiritual purification is the purpose of one of the largest rituals in the world, the *Kumbha Mela* (pitcher festival) of India. According to legend, the gods and demons once fought for possession of a pitcher (*kumbh* in Sanskrit) that contained the nectar of eternal life, but in the struggle four drops were spilled upon the earth. This is the reason, it is said, that a *mela* or festival is held every twelve years in the four different sites, the most famous of which is the city of Allahabad where the sacred Ganges and Yamuna Rivers come together.[92] In Allahabad, however, it is not only these two great rivers that are the focus of pilgrims; they also believe that a third, purely mystical river known as the Saraswati joins the others at a particular spot. In 1989, 30 million pilgrims journeyed to the confluence or *sangam* formed by these three rivers in order to bathe away their sins and free themselves from the cycle of birth and death. While the Ganges itself, long worshiped as a mother goddess, is credited with the power to wash away sins, the samgam is thought to be thousands of times more powerful. Chanting "Bolo Ganga mai ki jai!" (All glory to mother Ganga), the pilgrims immerse themselves in the water and scoop some up in their hands to offer to heaven. More than 3,600 acres of land are covered with tents, where the pilgrims camp out for the 41 days of the festival—the affluent and the impoverished, middle-class matrons and naked holy men. Speaking different languages and even professing different religions and sectarian affiliations, the pilgrims arrive by oxcart, plane, bus, or camel—in effect, converging like another great river. The arrival of 6 million people in May 1992 for a mela on the holy Kshipra River in the central Indian city of Ujjain necessitated complex crowd-control measures to ensure that all had the opportunity to bathe at the most auspicious spot at the most astrologically propitious time.[93]

Rites of affliction demonstrate what has been called the "all too human" side of religion, namely, people's persistent efforts to redress wrongs, alleviate sufferings, and ensure well-being. Yet these rites also illustrate complex cultural interpretations of the human condition and its relation to a cosmos of benign and malevolent forces.

While early theorists tended to see this genre of ritual as particularly "magical" due to what they deemed to be its manipulative intent, more recent scholarship has usefully focused on other dimensions, in particular, the ways in which these rituals actually affect people and the larger community. Even aside from their psychotherapeutic effects, these rituals present an argument, to use Geertz's terms, for a cosmos of ordered and interdependent components. While human efforts at maintaining this order appear to pale in comparison to the power attributed to gods, ancestors, and demons, rituals of affliction hold all these powers to some degree of accountability and service. Indeed, even though this genre of rites may be particularly effective in maintaining the status quo of the traditional social order in a community, they demonstrate that the human realm is not completely subordinate to the realms of spiritual power; these rites open up opportunities for redefining the cosmological order in response to new challenges and new formulations of human needs.

Feasting, Fasting, and Festivals

While rites of affliction may draw large segments of the community into the action, it is useful to employ a separate category, however provisional, for those major communal fasts or feasts where the underlying ritual logic appears to differ from that of affliction and restoration. In fasting and feasting rites, there may be little overt testimony to the presence of deities but a great deal of emphasis on the public display of religiocultural sentiments. One might say that in these rituals people are particularly concerned to express publicly—to themselves, each other, and sometimes outsiders—their commitment and adherence to basic religious values. Such "cultural performances" may take the form of Muslim communal fasting during the month of Ramadan, huge feasts like that of the Kwakiutl potlatch or the New Guinea pig festival, the elaborate celebrations of carnival, or the sober suffering of penitential processions in Europe and Latin America. In addition to the notion of social and cultural performances, described in chapter 3, scholars have used other terms to explore the significance of these types of rituals. For some, they are "social dramas" by which the group enters into a dialogue with itself about itself; for others, they are delimited occasions of "licensed reversal" or "ritual inversion" by which the status quo is taken apart, relativized, and often reconstituted in changed ways.[94]

The potlatch, a type of competitive feast found among the native peoples of southern Alaska, British Columbia, and Washington state, is concerned with displaying and transferring social privileges that confer status and prestige; it is also about divine-human interaction and the interconnectedness of the cosmos as conceived by a primarily hunting and fishing society.[95] Traditionally, there were different grades of potlatch, from small feasts to mark the stages of childhood to elaborate festivals that accompanied chieftainship, marriage, or the erection of buildings and totem poles. On these more elaborate occasions, the invited guests are met by an enormous amount of food, an extravagant display of material wealth, and, in the form of dances and speeches, formal testimonials to the sponsor's wealth and status. The masked and costumed dances reenact sacred tales claimed to be part of a family's history, and social status is directly linked to possession of such dances and the pedigree that they imply. By eating generously of the provided food and accepting the gifts distributed by the host, the guests are formally witnessing and acceding to the host's claims to possess the rights to particular prestigious titles, dances, and masks.[96]

The Kwakiutl of Vancouver Island, once considered particularly incorrigible by Canadian authorities who tried to outlaw these ceremonies, have managed to preserve their potlatch tradition when it died out among other tribal groups. Prior to sustained contact with European and American traders, the Kwakiutl traded primarily in furs and skins, human slaves, handcrafted boxes and bowls. The most valuable traditional items, however, were large handcrafted copper shields ("coppers") that had elaborate pedigrees attached to them. Kwakiutl society was based on a hereditary ranking system composed of noble lineages, commoners, and slaves. Among the nobles were some seven hundred positions, each with a ceremonial name and particular privileges, such as the right to perform certain masked dances relating to mythological events, deities, and powers. By 1850, however, sustained contact with Europeans and Americans brought an influx of new trade items, like the Hudson's Bay blanket, which greatly affected traditional Kwakiutl wealth and social ranking. While not displacing the copper shields and other precious objects, the Hudson's Bay blanket emerged as a type of basic unit of currency for reckoning the value of these traditional objects. More intrusive, European diseases took an enormous toll on the population, while foreign governments outlawed the traditional tribal warfare that provided the larger context for potlatch. In this colonial-like situation, the potlatch actually became more widespread and elaborate, eventually emerging as the principal means to establish one's rights to a hereditary position, which were more available than ever before due to the great decline in population.

A Kwakiutl potlatch today requires an enormous amount of preliminary work. A 1921 potlatch took seventeen years of preparation, during which time the host amassed huge stores of materials by sending out goods as loans to his own people, then calling them back in just prior to the potlatch at nearly 100 percent interest. Nowadays it takes about a year to plan a potlatch, at which some seven hundred guests are feted and given gifts. Modern work schedules also make it necessary to cram the whole celebration, including travel, into a weekend instead of the traditional week. The women prepare by making afghans, pot holders, and shawls, but huge quantities of goods are also purchased at regular stores, including plastic goods, blankets, pillows, towels, clothes, fabric, flour, oil, rice, and sugar. Days before the potlatch begins, the women start to prepare the food, the big meeting house is readied, and the dances are rehearsed. When everyone has assembled inside the carved posts of the big house, there are brief mourning rites for those who have died, some ritual trading of valuable coppers, and possibly a marriage before the first of the food is served or any songs sung. At the right time, a series of masked dances begins, led by those masks that have been inherited by the host family or acquired through marriage. The beautifully costumed dancers tell the story of the family's origin myth, which relates how a particular ancestor made a special relationship with a divine being.

Many of the dancers impersonate important mythical beings and events in Kwakiutl cosmology, sometimes using elaborate props and sleight-of-hand tricks. The most dramatic dance is that of the *hamatsa*, in which the dancer is a wild man possessed by the cannibal spirit, known as Baxwbakwalanuxwsiwe. He is gradually sub-dued and domesticated through a series of ritual dances—reappearing garbed in hemlock boughs, then in cedar bark, and finally in a blanket—but not until he and the servants of the cannibal spirit have chased people around looking for flesh to eat.[97] Other dances follow until well after midnight, and eventually everyone participates. Finally, people help bring out the goods to be distributed and array them on the floor of the big house. The host begins to hand them out while visiting chiefs give speeches thanking him and praising him for his allegiance to the old ways. In return, each visiting chief is given money to thank him for his "breath" or speech. The main cer-emony concludes about two or three o'clock in the morning, when most people break up into smaller parties in private homes.[98]

Since the earliest ethnographic accounts, especially those emanating from the collaboration of Franz Boas, the American anthropologist, and George Hunt, the son of a Tlingit princess and a Scottish tradesman, the potlatch has usually been seen as an example of a primitive economic system of investment, a bellicose form of "fight-ing with property," as the Kwakiutl put it, or a crude materialism accompanied by an obsessive concern with social rank.[99] In exploring the religious ideas behind this ritu-alized distribution, however, others have tried to integrate the socioeconomic dimen-sions of the potlatch with the Kwakiutl understanding of the ritual's role in a "con-substantial" cosmos. Irving Goldman argues that the Kwakiutl cosmos is composed of four communities: human beings, animals, vegetable life, and supernatural be-ings. Each is "an incomplete segment" of the whole that must share with the others "or the entire system of nature would die." Kwakiutl religion, Goldman suggests, "represents the concern of the people to occupy their own proper place within the total system of life, and to act responsibly within it, so as to acquire and control the powers that sustain life."[100]

Among the many complex subsystems of cosmic exchange that are woven to-gether in the potlatch, one of the most central is human-animal reciprocity. The potlatch dancers perform the mythical events by which a lineage ancestor acquired special titles, powers, and favors from a supernatural animal donor, notably the abil-ity to hunt that animal species successfully. In return, the ancestor and the descen-dants who inherit the title and powers are obliged to perform the rituals in which the supernatural animal is continually reincarnated. The animal flesh eaten at the pot-latch and the skins that are distributed testify to the death of the "form" of the animal and hence the release of its soul for reincarnation. Thus the potlatch publicly wit-nesses to the fact that the sponsor has inherited key powers that have enabled him to acquire wealth but also oblige him to sacrifice it. Likewise, the animal spirit who sacrifices its animal flesh and skin so that the human lineage may live and prosper counts on the sponsored potlatch as a ritual death and funeral that facilitate its rein-carnation. The ritual reinvokes the mythic human-divine interdependence, trans-mits it to new generations, and fulfills the obligations inherent in it.[101]

The Kwakiutl potlatch can be contrasted with the Indonesian ritual feast known as the *slametan*, which Clifford Geertz has described as a "simple, formal, undra-matic, almost furtive, little ritual" at the very center of the Javanese religious system.[102] While it can be orchestrated for any number of special events—births, marriages, deaths, harvests, bad dreams, illness, political meetings, and so on—the basic structure of this communal meal does not change. Usually held in the evening, neighbors and local dignitaries are invited to a meal of traditional foods, each with a special meaning and blessed by a mosque official. With understated formality, incense is lit, Islamic prayers are chanted, and the host gives a ceremonial speech. Although men and women are segregated, men at the ritual meal, women in the kitchen, a key feature of the slametan, which makes it differ from the potlatch, is an emphasis on a general equality among the gathered guests, including the gathered spirits. It is, according to Geertz, a symbolic representation of the social and spiritual unity of the participants: "friends, neighbors, fellow workers, relatives, local spirits, dead ancestors, and near-forgotten gods all get bound, by virtue of their commensality, into a defined social group pledged to mutual support and cooperation." For the Javanese, "the food and not the prayer is the heart of the slametan," because it attracts all kinds of invisible beings who come to eat the aroma of the food.[103] The food shared among the human and divine guests is the central ritual means of reaffirming a Javanese sense of a consubstantial cosmos of human-human and human-divine interdependence.

Shared participation in a food feast is a common ritual means for defining and reaffirming the full extent of the human and cosmic community. Whether that community is conceived to be rigidly hierarchical or fundamentally egalitarian, the principle of sharing food marks it as a community. While almost all religiocultural traditions regard food and community in this way, some traditions affirm a universal community by exhorting people to feed anyone in need; others demarcate the boundaries of a particular community by specifying with whom one can share food. Most religiocultural traditions also recognize a value in periodic fasting, either privately by the individual or communally by the larger society. In contrast to communal feasting, however, the ritual logic of communal fasting points to some different purposes. While feasting seems to celebrate the consubstantial unity of creation, fasting seems to extol fundamental distinctions, lauding the power of the spiritual realm while acknowledging the subordination and sinfulness of the physical realm.

Private fasting was commonplace in early Christianity and the subsequent history of the churches, yet fasting as a duty imposed on the whole congregation also became a regular feature of the calendrical year. Fasting in the liturgical seasons of Advent and Lent were meant to prepare the Christian for the great holidays of Christmas and Easter, respectively. While the Advent fast might merely substitute fish for meat, as did the Friday fast kept by Roman Catholics until the mid 1960s, the Lenten fast was originally more severe—only one meal per day and only after the sun had gone down, a regimen echoed in later Muslim practices. By the ninth century, however, this single meal had been moved to noon, and a light snack was allowed at bedtime; meat was still forbidden and at various times animal products like milk, butter, and eggs were also avoided.[104] The Lenten period was the time in which the community publicly humiliated those guilty of grave sins; in places like Gaul, for example, they were formally initiated into the society of penitents by having ashes sprinkled on their heads, to be reinstated in the community on Easter Sunday. By the 11th century, all Christians were observing relaxed versions of this penitential practice, particularly the Ash Wednesday rite of marking the forehead with ashes. Penitence was certainly one of the main reasons for Christian fasting, but fasting was also an emulation of Christ's forty days in the desert without food or water and a method of disciplining one's physical desires. Nevertheless, fasting has played a relatively subordinate role in Christianity compared to its importance in other traditions, particularly Islam.

Fasting (*sawm*) during the ninth month of Ramadan is a central event in the Islamic year and one of the five pillars of Islamic practice enjoined in the Qur'an itself. Over and above its place in the prescribed tradition, however, the practice of fasting is integral to many people's sense of what it means to be a Muslim. Some describe it as the most central of Islamic rituals. During the month of Ramadan, Muslims fast throughout the daylight hours. From the first rays of dawn until the sun sets and the muezzin calls for evening prayers, they do not drink, eat, smoke, or engage in sexual activity. If necessary, a fast can be broken for serious reasons, including illness, pregnancy, and menstruation, as long as the days that are missed are made up by fasting at another time or by giving food to the poor. Among the particularly devout, however, some even shun medicine and others do not swallow their own saliva.[105] After darkness has fallen, Muslims first break the fast with a light snack, ideally some dates and water, before attending evening prayers. After prayers, there is a full meal and usually another light one before dawn.

Since the month of Ramadan commemorates the revelation of the holy Qur'an to Mohammed by the Angel Jabril (Gabriel), fasting is linked to the sacrality and centrality of the scripture. Jabril's revelations are particularly celebrated on the last ten nights of Ramadan, one of which is called the "night of power" (*Laylat al-Qadr*) when "angels and the Spirit descended." It is said that those who keep a prayer vigil until dawn will be forgiven all their sins.[106] The very devout may spend the last ten days of Ramadan in complete seclusion, then pray all night on the night of power, hoping for a vision of the light that is said to fill the world at this time. Although the nights of Ramadan require special long prayers and prostrations (*tarawih*) after the fast has been broken, there are also feasts celebrated with friends, lights, and entertainment. In some areas, these feasts can be quite elaborate and indulgent. Like the month of pilgrimage or hajj to Mecca, the month of fasting culminates in a feast, known as *'Id al-Fitr*, when neighborhoods and villages put up decorations and people don their best clothes to visit and congratulate each other. At this time of communal celebration, everyone who has the economic means must make a charitable donation to the poor (*Zakat Al-Fitr*).

While some Islamic theologians stress the way in which fasting disciplines human desires, to the point of enabling one to experience one of the divine attributes, freedom from want (*samadiyah*), others point to more communal functions. According to the modern conservative Islamic theologian, Sayyid Abû al-A'lâ Mawdûdî, fasting for a full month every year teaches piety and self-restraint to both the individual and community. Both rich and poor alike experience together the pangs of hunger and prepare themselves to endure any hardship in order to please God. Demonstrations of enthusiasm and empathy for the common corporate experience support this interpretation, as does the evidence that fasting sets Muslims off as a distinct community (*umma*) in contrast to their non-Muslim neighbors. Nonetheless, aside from the demonstration of corporate unity, the logic of fasting in Islam and other traditions also seems to be concerned with the importance of purity, asceticism, and merit in demonstrating the individual's submission (*islam*) to God.[107] From this perspective, the communal aspects of fasting are a powerful assertion and extension of doctrinal conformity in a manner that serves to differentiate the more devout from the more casual believer. The role of peer pressure in what has been called the quintessential act of individual submission also points to subtler ways in which a religious community socializes its members in physical practices that reproduce central doctrinal traditions and identities.[108]

In contrast to Christianity and Judaism in particular, Islamic festivals put more emphasis on prayer and charity, with relatively little on shared meals. For reasons that might derive from Islam's strict adherence to monotheism and the association of festivals with paganism and behavioral license, the development of this form of ritual appears to have been constrained and at times even opposed in the history of Islam. There are only two official festivals in the Islamic year, one concluding the month of fasting and the other marking the end of the month of pilgrimage — and the designation "festival" may be a bit strong for both of them. Then again, popular or unofficial forms of local Islamic practice have adopted many festivals from Persian, Egyptian, and other pre-Islamic cultures, often "islamicizing" them as birthdays of Islamic saints (*mawlids*) or of the prophet himself.[109]

In the month of Muharram, the first of the Islamic year, another period of privation is followed by a communal meal, although not a festival as such. The first ten days of Muharram are days of elaborate mourning in honor of Husayn ibn 'Ali (Al-Husayn), grandson of Mohammed, who was killed in 680 C.E. in a battle at Karbalā' (in modern Iraq) between his followers and the army of the Umayyad dynasty. Devotion to Husayn and his mother, Fāṭima, the daughter of Mohammed, is particularly important among the Shī'ah (partisans) minority who identify their sectarian origins with the murder of Husayn by the Sunni majority faction in order to thwart his rightful succession. Indeed, the martyrdom of Husayn sets the tone for Shiism as a minority religion of protest and suffering, while Karbalā' became for them an alternative to Mecca as the most sacred center of their religion.

Unlike the Sunni majority, festivals are very important among the Shī'ah, particularly those of Muharram that commemorate the death of Husayn. In Shī'ī communities in Iran, Iraq, Pakistan, and India, men and women observe this mourning period by wearing dark, unornamented clothing and attending services. Processions of devotees beat their breasts, weeping and wailing, to evoke the sufferings of Husayn and his mother, Fatimā. Passion plays (*taziya*) dramatically reenact the Karbalā' battle itself with unusual intensity. Indeed, for the Shī'ah such ceremonies of "remembrance and mourning" are thought to atone for one's sins, earn entry into paradise, and ultimately bring about the final rectification of history.[110] In large Shī'ī processions, some participants carry colorful standards and beautifully carved domed structures, said to be tombs of the saints; others flagellate themselves with chains and knives, walk across glowing coals, or recount poetic ballads of Husayn's sufferings and demise. At the end of the day, the saints' tombs are buried at a place designated as Karbalā', and a meal is prepared that is said to replicate one prepared by the ancient heroes from whatever food they could find on the battlefield. In some places, these rites continue for forty days, during which time no weddings are held, and sectarian violence is easily incited. The political confrontations of the 1970s that eventually brought down the government of the Shah of Iran have been depicted by devout followers of the late Ayatollah Khomeini as a modern-day version of the ancient battle between the evil Umayyad ruler and the righteous followers of Husayn.[111]

Emotional processions displaying a variety of physical mortifications were well known to medieval Christianity as well. Lay penitential associations, such as the Flagellants, often emerged at times of religious fervor and social unrest.[112] Similar groups are still active today in modern Spain and New Mexico.[113] In the medieval world, gruesome physical mortifications were a public display that bore witness to elite spiritualism. The penitents marched barefoot, singing hymns and swinging their whips, distinctively garbed in the hooded veil known as the *cagoule*, which dramatically separated them from the rest of society at the same time that it covered over and equalized all distinctions of rank among them. Although these penitential processions may appear to be an extreme form of ritual *fasting*, they also share many features with well-known examples of ritual *feasting*, such as carnival and Mardi Gras, which are occasions for excess and celebration before the season of Lenten asceticism begins. The masked costumes worn by carnival dancers, like the garb of the penitential associations, deny position and hierarchy; both carnivalers and penitents have been accused of challenging sumptuary laws concerned with demarcating clear levels of social rank. At certain times, these costumed festivals could act as a powerful rebuke to the spiritual legitimacy and political power of major institutions based on social rank.

Carnival, an occasion for maximum social chaos and licentious play, might at first seem the pure opposite of ritual, yet many observers have long appreciated the ritual nature of such bounded periods of orchestrated anarchy.[114] Carnival traditions are considered particularly ritualistic because they draw together many social groups that are normally kept separate and create specific times and places where social differences are either laid aside or reversed for a more embracing experience of community. Such traditions have also tended to follow customary rules, such as the appointment of a jester or king of fools to serve as a burlesque parody of institutional power and order. Other standard ritual inversions in Europe have parodies of the mass and the saint's day procession, such as the so-called Liturgy of the Drunkards, and wild parades of masked revelers who spray the crowds with dirty water and eggs. While the ruling classes ineffectively attempted to control such practices, they seem to have recognized the social usefulness of allowing the masses to let off steam. The mad rites of carnival also undoubtedly served to remind the ruling elites of the power of the poor and the contempt with which normal citizens were apt to characterize political and religious authorities. For these reasons, some scholars argue that rituals like carnival can help change the status quo, while others suggest that they actually worked to reinforce it.[115]

In Europe after the Reformation, the carnival began to die out as a public mass event while being reborn in the more formal and select world of the theater and masked ball. In the New World, however, it grew into a major national ritual in Brazil and assumed great importance in other parts of Latin America, the Caribbean, and the continental United States. In Rio, the dance procession that is the centerpiece of carnival is primarily the work of samba schools who spend all year preparing dances and costumes for the event. Drawing their members from the lowest classes in the hierarchy of Brazilian society, the samba schools usually turn out to dance as glittering kings and queens—although their places in the procession are determined by lottery. While the whole society participates in the event, the upper classes participate more vicariously.[116] The nearly opposite social situation prevails in the New Orleans carnival, where the whole ten-day celebration is called Mardi Gras, which traditionally refers to Shrove Tuesday (or Fat Tuesday), the day on which the festivities culminate before Lent begins on Ash Wednesday.

Since the mid-19th century, Mardi Gras festivities have been dominated by elite private clubs known as "krewes." Traditionally, most of the twenty-seven odd New Orleans krewes, particularly old established ones like Comus, Momus, Rex, and Endymion, have been segregated and refused membership to women, African-Americans, Jews, Italians, and all working-class people. Yet alternative krewes have also emerged, such as Zulu, a prestigious krewe founded in 1916 for black men that now includes some whites; Iris, a club for white women; the Virgilians for Italians; and Petronius for homosexuals. In the traditional krewes, members may be asked to contribute more than $2,000 a year for club activities, especially the Mardi Gras parades and balls. Their elaborately staging of masked balls and parades with fancy costumes and expensive floats effectively puts the highest levels of the social and economic hierarchy on display in the midst of the citywide festivities.[117] Archaic spelling, as in the "mystik krewe," and allusions to Greek heroes and the gods of debauchery, Bacchus and his son Comus, as well as the masked and regal Rex, who claims to be king of the carnival, all signal elite control of Mardi Gras symbols.[118]

The closed systems of social status and prestige that are put on public display in these particular carnival traditions do not simply illustrate the tensions between elitism and populism but also literally perform them, in a manner that Gluckman's and Turner's theories would recognize.[119] Some observers worry that newer and less traditional krewes, working with city tourist commissions and television stations, will begin to turn these city-focused rituals into interchangeable marching bands with pompom girls and fast food.[120] Others fear that a 1991 city council ruling demanding the integration of krewes that have traditionally enforced race, gender, and class segregation will destroy the New Orleans Mardi Gras completely. Many krewes threatened to withdraw from Mardi Gras if integration was forced on them. Others have been willing to accept men of other races, but both white and black clubs have reacted in horror to calls for the admission of women.[121] Hence, the ritual format here appears to put great priority on maintaining basic social distinctions of prestige and rank, even when the ritual itself is apt to play with these distinctions.

Carnival-like themes animate the popular Holī festival celebrated in northern India. Technically a calendrical rite marking the vernal equinox and the beginning of spring about March 31, Holī has been compared to the Roman celebrations of Saturnalia (December 17) and Hilaria (March 25), as well as the April Fool's Day (April 1) of Christian Europe. Holī involves a thorough disruption and inversion of the usual social order, as well as a celebration of symbols of sexual fecundity. The inversion is signaled by Holī's reputation as the festival of Śudras, the lowest group of the Hindu caste system, who go about this day disrupting the normal social order by dousing people, especially upper-class people, with colored powder or water. Women who are normally constrained to be quiet and submissive are apt to get drawn into the fun of dousing men or beating them with sticks. It is said that during Holī "the bully is bullied and the high are brought low." Lewd songs, the consumption of *bhang*, a milk-yogurt drink laced with hashish, and the general revelry on the streets, makes it risky to be out and about. Holī is a threat not only to one's clothes but also to quotidian morals, since Holī madness has been known to inspire sexual licentiousness and promiscuity. Not surprisingly, the counterpart to Holī in southern India is known as the "feast of love," dedicated to Kama, the god of love. In parts of north and central India where worship of the god Krishna is strong, Holī involves dramatic reenactments (*lilas*) of the god's amorous romping with boy and girl cowherds. The festivities end with an enormous bonfire, kindled at the rising of the full moon, that is personified as the female demon Holikā, who is destroyed as punishment for her evil and to renew the world.[122]

Like carnival and Holī, the festival or *matsuri* has been central to the social order—and antiorder—of traditional Japanese village life. Of Shinto origin and closely related to the seasonal cycles of rice cultivation in small agricultural communities, matsuri essentially propitiate the deities that influence human well-being and the fruitfulness of the harvest. Nonetheless, matsuri vary greatly in style, either serious or playful, traditional or modern and commercial. Recent evidence suggests that they remain important occasions of communal life even in suburban areas and among immigrant communities. One of the most central matsuri is *Obon*, a midsummer festival marking the temporary return of the spirits of the dead. Most Obon ceremonies involve bonfires, lamps to light the way of the dead, dancing and singing, food offerings, entertainment of the spirits of the dead, and their firm dismissal at the end of the three-day festival. Symbolically, the dead and the living are reconstituted as community, the effect of which is said to heighten fertility and facilitate the transformation of the recent dead into more remote ancestors.[123]

Practices of feasting, fasting, and social inversion have also been associated with the phenomenon of pilgrimage, although pilgrimage is more often seen as a classic rite of passage. Still, Victor Turner's theory of a period of communitas and cultural inversion at the heart of such rites of passage has been helpful in making sense of various festival-like pilgrimage customs.[124] It appears that ritual inversions can be meaningful on a much smaller scale as well, as seen in the group of antireligious Jews who have been known to gather publicly to eat pork on Yom Kippur, the holiest day of the Jewish calendar.[125] Like many inversions, however, such acts of defiance may simply help delineate the normative values of the community. Whether they contain explicit reversals of the social order or not, the communal feasts and fasts examined here all involve, simultaneously, the display of both the hierarchical prestige social system and the interdependence or unity of human and divine worlds.

Political Rites

As a particularly loose genre, political rituals can be said to comprise those ceremonial practices that specifically construct, display and promote the power of political institutions (such as king, state, the village elders) or the political interests of distinct constituencies and subgroups. Geertz, as noted earlier, argued that political rituals should not be thought of as simply giving form to power in the way that a bowl gives form to water or a light bulb and wires give form to electricity; instead, rituals actually construct power. The king's cult creates the king, defines kingliness, and orchestrates a cosmic framework within which the social hierarchy headed by the king is perceived as natural and right. Political rites, Geertz continued, are elaborate arguments about the very nature of power that make this power tangible and effective.[126] On the basis of this description, political rituals would certainly include the coronation of the Queen of England, the Swazi Ncwala rite, the Babylonian Akitu festival, Aztec sacrifice, and the Kwakiutl potlatch. In addition, however, we might also add national salutes like the American pledge of allegiance or the Nazi "Heil Hitler" salute, the public execution of a convict, the state funerals accorded John F. Kennedy or Mao Tse-tung, the cross-burnings of the Ku Klux Klan, the 1970 suicide by hara-kiri of the nationalist Japanese writer Yukio Mishima, or the oaths and initiations that were indispensable to the great Mau-Mau uprising against British colonialism in Kenya in the mid-1950s.[127]

In general, political rites define power in a two-dimensional way: first, they use symbols and symbolic action to depict a group of people as a coherent and ordered community based on shared values and goals; second, they demonstrate the legitimacy of these values and goals by establishing their iconicity with the perceived values and order of the cosmos. As such, political ritual is something very different from the use or threat of coercive physical force, although those who claim power can do so with both weapons and ritual, and ritual itself can include the display of weapons. It is through ritual, however, that those claiming power demonstrate how their interests are in the natural, real, or fruitful order of things. When effective, the symbolic imagery and structural processes of political ritual—what Roy Rappaport calls its "sanctity"—can transform "the arbitrary and conventional into what appears to be necessary and natural."[128]

One of the most prominent strategies by which political rituals define a community of ordered and legitimate power relationships is that of display. Excessive displays of wealth, material resources, mass approval, or record-high productivity all tangibly testify to the fruitful fit between the particular social leadership and the way things should be. When the former USSR paraded its military might through Red Square on May Day, the number of weapons, their intimidating proportions and alleged technological sophistication, and the size of the approving crowds certainly helped create much of the power of the premiers and party presidents watching from the balcony of the Kremlin. The system that could produce such products, leaders, approving crowds, and national pride was accorded either a "rightness" or at least some degree of acceptance.

When ritual is the principal medium by which power relationships are constructed, the power is usually perceived as coming from sources beyond the immediate control of the human community. For this reason, more ritual attended the coronation of Louis XVI, who claimed the "divine right of kings," than usually accompanies the inauguration of an American president or a British prime minister. As in the "theater-state" of ancient Java described by Geertz, traditional monarchs spend most of their time demonstrating that their court is "a microcosm of the supernatural order . . . and the material embodiment of political order."[129] The complex ritual life of the court creates a reflection of the solemn order of the universe and a model for the appropriate social order. Even with modern rulers who govern by consent of the governed, there are still overt ritual appeals to higher forces and designs, although the language of formal moral responsibility, rather than cosmological iconicity, is more apt to validate and control this type of authority. For example, after being sworn into office before God and the nation, an American president is at pains to demonstrate in his inauguration speech the moral leadership that transforms the electoral choice of this particular person into something other than an accident of history.

In its cosmological mode, this "dramaturgy of power" involves the creation of comprehensive ritual systems that raise the ruler above normal human interaction.[130] The restriction of admittance to the ruler's presence and the decorous regulation of behavior required of all those given admittance create relationships that actually empower the ruler. In this type of system, the distinctive status and power of the ruler are predicated in part on the distance separating him or her from other people. The institution of the Japanese emperor, involving what may be the oldest continuing state rituals in the world, is a good example.[131] The imperial system of Japan, much augmented by the "state Shinto" that was developed in the first part of the 20th century, created a cult in which the emperor was accorded an overt quasi-divine status. That status, in turn, mandated certain forms of loyalty and activities of respect. Since the end of World War II, when Emperor Hirohito made the radio speech in which he renounced all claims to divinity, and when a constitutional government was established, the Japanese people have expressed some ambivalence about how to treat their monarch. This ambivalence came to the fore in plans for the enthronement of Crown Prince Akihito a year after the death of Hirohito in January 1989.

Against a backdrop of imperial genealogies that identified Akihito as the 125th emperor of Japan, questions arose concerning the traditional enthronement ceremonies, which were not all as ancient as "tradition" implied, and the types of claims these ceremonies make about the emperor and Japan. Of particular interest to other nations was the question of whether the crown prince would perform the "great food tasting" ritual (daijōsai) associated with the conferral of divine status on the ruler.[132] Imperial claims to divinity—that is, to being a "living god" (akitsukami)—reach back into Japan's most ancient political history, although Japanese notions of "divinity" are not akin to Judeo-Christian-Islamic concepts of a single transcendent being. As heavenly sovereign (tennō), Japanese emperors routinely made offerings to the ancestress of the imperial clan, the sun goddess Amaterasu, and the numerous other gods (kami) of the Japanese islands. They would offer rice in the form of rice wine, which has been a central symbol of the links the Japanese see among humans, gods, the land, and purity. Traditionally, the emperor himself has cultivated a small plot of rice on the palace grounds, and the planting and harvesting of this rice for court ceremonies have been ritual events themselves.[133]

In the daijōsai, as recorded in the tenth century Engi-shiki, the emperor presents offerings of food and rice wine to the ten thousand gods of Japan in two identical but separate chambers, each containing a mat, a couch with a coverlet (shinza or "divine bed"), and a small table. He waits while the gods partake of the food and then sips sake in an act of communion. Layers of ancient mythology variously nuance these activities as a testing of the emperor, a sacred marriage in which he is the bridegroom, or the descent of the divine grandson of the sun goddess to be reborn in the human form of the emperor. Nonetheless, the historical evidence also suggests that the daijōsai has other connotations, such as filiality and connection to the land.[134] It had been performed by Hirohito in 1928, at a time when the government was run by militant nationalists and the imperial throne, which had regained real power only in the second half of the preceding century, was actively expanding its doctrine of the imperial divinity as the head of a state cult. There was little official explanation of the meaning of the 1928 daijōsai and, it turned out, no definitive historical account of even exactly how to do it. The vague and flexible mysticism that came to be attached to the ritual was probably the most politically effective interpretation.[135]

Japan's Asian neighbors were especially interested in how Akihito's 1990 enthronement would be conducted. Would he eschew all the ceremonial references and practices implying divinity that his father had performed? When it became clear that the enthronement would include the daijōsai, some were worried and others were critical. The government took sufficient cognizance of the concerns to issue a statement saying that the rite did not violate the constitution's separation of church and state. It was, they stressed, essentially a cultural harvest festival, and the government emphasized its traditionalism over any symbolic message. In addition, an imperial household official summoned to appear before a parliamentary committee prior to the enthronement clearly denied that the emperor engages in any mock sexual intercourse with the sun goddess. With these caveats, plans for the rite went ahead. On November 12, the first and public part of the enthronement ceremony was held with foreign guests in attendance. There were formal cries of "Banzai," which means "ten thousand years" or "long live the emperor." Ten days later, on the night of November 22, with some guests waiting in the dark outside, the emperor entered a specially built shrine accompanied by six attendants, then proceeded with just two attendants into the inner sanctum for the daijōsai. What exactly happened in that inner room is not known. Certainly the emperor offered prayers of thanksgiving and the first rice of the season to the sun goddess and the other deities, then consumed some of it himself. Whether he merely made the offerings to the bed on which Amaterasu was thought to be seated or wrapped himself in a cloth for a ritual rebirth, no one will say. As with the 1928 performance, the secrecy, mystery, and speculation probably heightened the effect.[136]

Although the ceremonies for Akihito included this powerful but obscure symbol of the imperial tradition, in many other ways the enthronement undermined traditional claims to divinity. For example, the rites left out all language that could be understood to imply an unconstitutional mixing of politics and religion, and Akihito specifically pledged to uphold the Japanese constitution. The prime minister did not wear the traditional court costume of a vassal; he delivered his congratulatory message in an elegant swallow-tailed coat, albeit from a podium placed below the level of the throne.[137] In effect, this modern enthronement appears to have tried to maintain the pageantry of the "heavenly sovereign" as an ancient ritual office but left out any formulations that conflated the emperor's ritual duties with claims to actual political authority. In this sense, the ceremonies for Akihito used the full ritual resources of Japanese tradition to make the emperor a more purely "ritual" symbol of

Japan. It seems that the same general ritual could be used to construct power relations of different kinds, including the integrated religious-political authority of Hirohito and the nonpolitical symbolic power of Akihito, which is still a formidable entity in the culture. In both cases, the ritual medium depicts the power of the emperor as the result of sacral forces that uniquely—if mysteriously—come to be embodied in these men. That power is not clearly defined, mapped, or interpreted. Indeed, ritual allows for the construction of power in terms that appeal to a sense of cosmological fit, *not* an explicit social contract.

In a study of historical and cultural changes in the treatment of prisoners and prisons, Michel Foucault described the 1757 execution of Robert-François Damiens, who attempted to assassinate the French monarch, Louis XV. When convicted of regicide, Damiens's sentence explicitly spelled out that he

> be taken and conveyed in a cart, wearing nothing but a shirt . . . to the Place de Grève, where, on a scaffold that will be erected there, the flesh will be torn from his breasts, arms, thighs and calves with red-hot pincers, his right hand, holding the knife with which he committed the said parricide, burnt with sulphur, and, on those places where the flesh will be torn away, poured molten lead, boiling oil, burning resin, wax and sulphur melted together and then his body drawn and quartered by four horses and his limbs and body consumed by fire, reduced to ashes and his ashes thrown to the winds.[138]

Clearly, the execution of Damiens was concerned with a great deal more than simply ending his life. Foucault suggested that this horribly drawn out public spectacle should be understood as a display of power—not only the power of the sovereign to impose impossible suffering but more important the power to judge Damiens's crime to be so ignominious that no degree of suffering could be sufficient punishment or atonement. A crime challenging the sovereignty of the ruler was answered with a display of power that overwhelmed the human offender, providing a "spectacle not of measure, but of imbalance and excess." In a similar case, when the prisoner died soon after the tortures had begun, the entire ritual of terror was still carried out precisely and publicly for all to see.[139] Such political rituals could make hideously clear to the gathered populace where real power lay, and its overwhelming abundance and ability to terrorize testified to its godlike nature and moral absolutism.

Yet, the display of power does not always proceed smoothly from the top down to the bottom. Foucault noted occasions when the cruelty of the sentence and the pious integrity of the convict's demeanor provoked sympathies in the crowd, occasionally prompting mobs to liberate the convict and subject the executioner, as a representative of the power of the ruler, to torture instead.[140] Hence, rituals meant to establish a particular power relationship are not invulnerable to being challenged, inverted, or completely thwarted by counteractions. One excellent account of the problems that can attend the interaction of different, perhaps competing ritual claims to power is the late-18th-century British diplomatic mission to the court of the Chinese emperor. The difficulties attending arrangements for the Qianlong emperor to receive the embassy led by George Lord Macartney in 1793, for example, illustrate the importance of ritual etiquette in organizing and displaying power. Lord Macartney refused to give the traditional kowtow—that is, to kneel three times touching one's head to the floor—to the equally stubborn emperor, who expected it as a matter of course from all visitors, so both parties had to negotiate an alternative set of physical exertions to act as the right formula of political deference from each side's perspective.[141]

A somewhat more current example, however, might be the arguments over political etiquette that ultimately led President Wilson to send American troops to invade Mexico at Vera Cruz in 1914. Due to mistakes and some suspicion, the American crew of a whaleboat on an errand to secure gasoline was arrested by Mexican officers, briefly questioned, and then returned to their ship. American reaction quickly escalated, however, and a rear admiral demanded more than an apologetic explanation from his Mexican counterpart.

> Responsibility for hostile acts cannot be avoided by a plea of ignorance. I must require that you send me, by suitable members of your staff, a formal disavowal of and an apology for the act, together with your assurance that the officer responsible for it will receive severe punishment. Also that you hoist the American flag in a prominent position on shore and salute it with 21 guns, which salute will be duly returned by this ship.

The Mexican president, Victoriano Huerta, was informed and promptly refused the Americans any such display of submission. Furious negotiations between Huerta and his friend, the American chargé d'affaires in Mexico City, Nelson O'Shaughnessy, led to an agreement on a simultaneous gun salute by the Americans and Mexicans. President Wilson, however, refused to accept anything less than a humiliating show of public deference from Huerta, and even then American forces that had mobilized in the area would stay on hand to prevent such incidents in the future. With Huerta's refusal to give in to Wilson's demand for the Mexicans to salute first, and Wilson's refusal to compromise with a simultaneous salute, the two nations could conceive of no alternative to military action. Trapped in the logic of their ritual definitions of political power, the Americans attacked Mexico several days later, landing troops in the town of Vera Cruz. Nineteen American sailors and at least two hundred Mexican soldiers and civilians were killed. The Americans occupied the port city for more than six months and left Mexicans with some bitter memories of Wilson's "moral imperialism."[142]

As this story makes clear, symbolic action is taken very seriously by those contending for power. Far from matters of "empty ritual," etiquette and ceremony can go to the heart of constructing relationships of political submission and dominance. In his study of political rituals, David Kertzer concludes that "rites create political reality." It is by participating in rituals that people identify "with larger political forces that can only be seen in symbolic form. And through political ritual, we are given a way to understand what is going on in the world, for we live in a world that must be drastically simplified if it is to be understood at all."[143] These sentiments are easy to see in the rituals that support the ruling order, such as the Japanese imperial enthronement ceremony, or even in the interaction of two powers, such as the Macartney mission or the Vera Cruz incident. There are more complex political examples, however, ranging from the rites of rebellion described by Gluckman to the symbolic activities of gangs and nativistic movements. These activities all attempt to create and display power, but by virtue of their challenge to a deeply entrenched power structure, they must negotiate the symbolic interaction quite differently.

Religiopolitical movements like the cargo cults of New Guinea and Melanesia or the Mau-Mau uprising against British colonialism in Kenya depended on ritual activity around key symbols in order to mobilize the population as a political force. Some analysts have even described these movements in terms of a single extended ritual process, taking the Mau-Mau as fairly typical.[144] Like other religiopolitical movements, the Mau-Mau tended to focus on two main themes: first, destroying their old way of life by demolishing what they owned and transgressing the traditional taboos that defined the old social and cosmic order; second, bringing on the new by performing ritual activities thought capable of producing the apocalyptic age they envisioned. When groups resort to violence to effect this new age, it was not uncommon for them to use ritual procedures to make themselves invincible. At this point, however, ritual reaches the limit of what it can do. The Papuans who attacked Japanese warships during World War II with nothing more than a few canoes and some wooden guns expected their holy water rituals to make them invulnerable to machine guns; they were wrong. In the same way, many Plains Indians believed that the "ghost shirts" revealed by the dead in the course of the Ghost Dance would render them invulnerable to all weapons.[145]

The Mau-Mau movement among the Kikuyu in Kenya (1952–56) evoked powerful symbols of the land as motherly nurturer of the living and the dead and as given to the Kikuyu by their original ancestors at the beginning of time. It was a just and holy cause, they argued, to reclaim their land from the British colonialists. Through the slogan "Uhuru" or "Freedom," they attempted to incorporate the aspirations of other tribes into a single nationalist cause. The central ritual, an oath of dedication to the cause, was a transformation of a traditional tribal initiation rite. While repeating many familiar features, such as passing through a ceremonial archway, donning wristbands of goat skin, lustral blessings, and the swearing of vows, the Mau-Mau changed the content of the vows and the accompanying ordeals. One critical ordeal, the simulation of sodomy with the carcass of a male goat, was an intentionally repulsive violation of traditional taboos; it would ensure that the ritual made the Kikuyu into a new kind of man, a warrior of the Mau-Mau. The emotional appeal of these oaths and rites made them a potent weapon for political liberation. Although the Mau-Mau movement was eventually crushed, it was directly instrumental in shaping the emergence of an organized national consensus that eventually led to independence in 1963.[146]

A very different set of rituals embodies the countercultural and antimodern spirituality of a grassroots religious group in Japan founded in the first half of this century. Ittōen is a utopian community founded by Nishida Tenkō (1872–1968), a mystic who embraced a wandering life of humble service, in particular, cleaning toilets. In the movement that developed around Tenkō, this toilet cleaning was called "communal prayer" (gyōgan) and defined as the main ritual act by which a devotee could conquer the self and contribute to world peace. Tenkō eventually became so well-known and respected that he was elected to the national Diet in 1947, where he sponsored legislation for moral reform and periodically cleaned the building's toilets. As Nishida and his followers established themselves as an organized community, the original teachings turned into institutionalized regimens that implicitly supported the social status quo instead of challenging it. Today, for example, most Japanese who go on retreat at Ittōen have been sent by their companies, which hope that the disciplined training in humble service will improve job performance. Members of the Ittōen community now go out to clean toilets only a few times a year, although modern flush toilets have also helped to make this ritual increasingly symbolic.[147]

Political rituals display symbols and organize symbolic action in ways that attempt to demonstrate that the values and forms of social organization to which the ritual testifies are neither arbitrary nor temporary but follow naturally from the way the world is organized. For this reason, ritual has long been considered more effective than coercive force in securing people's assent to a particular order. Reflecting on Chinese writings on ritual, the political scientist J. G. A. Pocock has mused that rites, since they are non-verbal, "have no contraries. They can therefore be used to produce harmony of wills and actions without provoking recalcitrance." When one is playing one's appointed role in a ritual, he continues, disturbing the harmony is nearly unthinkable, as unthinkable as a dancer suddenly deciding to move to a rhythm other than the one being played by the orchestra.[148] Of course, rituals do have contraries, as the Papuans and the Ghost Dancers found out, but contraries of brute destruction and blind weaponry are also what makes ritual appear to invoke quite different types of power.

Conclusion

Although these genres of ritual activity are not exhaustive, they illustrate some of the most prominent types of ritual situations and demonstrate some of the ways that ritual characterizes the social-cosmic order. The repetition of seasonal rites year after year creates a cyclical rhythm that may not exactly obliterate history, as Eliade has suggested, but can balance the unforgiving quality of historical change with tangible experiences of cyclical renewal and continuity. Even rituals that commemorate historical events subject those unique occurrences to a cyclical rhythm by returning each year to founding events and basic values. Naturally, the rituals that have marked the anniversary of Bastille Day have changed in conjunction with how the French have reinterpreted the significance of that day in their history. Yet the annual return to the Bastille—whether it be a matter of intellectual reconsideration, emotional identification, or just the hype of Independence Day advertising and consumerism—creates a steady rhythm of imagery that helps to define French national life.

Rites of passage have a similar effect on cultural understandings of human life. The biological processes of birth, maturation, reproduction, and death are rendered cultural events of great significance. By attaching cultural values to such natural phenomena—for example, in the way a son's role in continuing the family lineage is attached to experiences of procreation and childbirth—a society's worldview appears nonarbitrary and grounded in reality. The ritual observation of other life-cycle events, such as circumcision or marriage, makes them intrinsically natural parts of biological-cultural passage, as natural as greetings to the newborn and farewells to the dead.

Human life is given organization and direction when people participate in a cycle of passages that links generations and roots the value system with people's most intimate experiences of living and dying.

Rites of exchange and communion help articulate complex systems of relationships among human beings, gods, demons, ancestors, and animals. Such rites call attention to an order in these relationships that all depend upon for their well-being. Offerings to ancestors, gifts from the spirits, or sacrifices in which the object and the god become one all create a profound sense of cosmic interrelatedness and of human responsibility for more than one's own immediate needs. Similarly, rites of affliction that attempt to redress disorder in the cosmos explicitly demonstrate the rightness of the harmonious order underlying human affairs. A Korean widow grieving over the death of her spouse and frightened about how to manage alone in the world invites a ritual that demonstrates the continuation of relations after death, the subordination of her loss to an enduring value system, and a catharsis of her anger that enables her to reassume control of her life.[149] Fasting, feasts, and festivals are extended rituals that can overlay the religiosocial value system with nuanced experiences of relative holism and hierarchy. Whether the social order is overturned and inverted or paraded in strict visual ranks, such symbolic embodiments of the community suggest its powerful ability to reshape itself. Indeed, perhaps more than any other form of ritual, the alternative order implicit in such rites as the fast of Ramadan or the festival of Holī suggests that the most powerful forces of the cosmos cannot be reduced to and contained in the daily duties of cultural life, no matter how religiously and socially important these might be. By deconstructing the routines for a period of time, these rites appear to recognize sources of power outside the system. As Victor Turner tried to illustrate, such rites can facilitate and legitimate changes in the system. Religion and ritual do not just serve the status quo; they can also articulate major upheavals of it.

Political rituals, the last category explored in this section, indicate the way in which ritual as a medium of communication and interaction does not simply express or transmit values and messages but also actually creates situations. That is, rites of subordination to royal power, from bowing to the passing entourage of the Javanese king to watching the formal torture and execution of a convicted criminal, are not secondary reflections of the relationships of authority and deference that are structuring interactions between rulers and ruled. They create these relations; they create power in the very tangible exercise of it.

In most societies, rituals are multiple and redundant. They do not have just one message or purpose. They have many, and frequently some of these messages and purposes can modify or even contradict each other. Nonetheless, ritual practices seek to formulate a sense of the interrelated nature of things and to reinforce values that assume coherent interrelations, and they do so by virtue of their symbols, activities, organization, timing, and relationships to other activities. Yet rituals seem to be invoked more in some situations than others. What might these situations have in common? It appears that ritual is used in those situations in which certain values and ideas are more powerfully binding on people if they are deemed to derive from sources of power outside the immediate community. A young Hindu boy's rite of passage, for example, both assumes and reiterates a total social order in which there are hierarchies of children, adults, castes, females and males, students and teachers, clients and ritual experts; likewise, it assumes a cosmic order of spiritual substance, purity and pollution, human and divine relationships, and the direction of human exist-ence. When expressed in ritual, this sociocosmic order is implicitly understood as neither human nor arbitrary in its origins; rather, it is natural and the way things really are or ought to be. As a medium for expressing values in this way, participants see their ritual activities as simply the appropriate response to the existence of God, the presence of ancestors, the demands of tradition and history, status, and destiny. They do not see how acting ritually creates a sense of these entities, a type of sphere and power of the sacred. Since ritual acknowledges powers beyond the invention of the community and implies correct and incorrect relations with these powers, it is often more likely to generate a social consensus about things. A lecture about the power of the ancestors will not inculcate the type of assumptions about ancestral presence that the simple routine of offering incense at an altar can inculcate. Activities that are so physical, aesthetic, and established appear to play a particularly powerful role in shaping human sensibility and imagination.

❧ · ❧

Characteristics of
Ritual-like Activities

In modern Western society, we tend to think of ritual as a matter of special activities inherently different from daily routine action and closely linked to the sacralities of tradition and organized religion. Such connections encourage us to regard ritual as somewhat antiquated and, consequently, as somewhat at odds with modernity. Hence, ritual often seems to have more to do with other times and places than with daily life as we know it in postindustrial Europe and America. This view is borne out to a great extent by the examples in the previous section, which focused on those rituals that most people would tend to agree are good examples of what ritual is about. They are sufficiently distinctive and colorful that even a particularly dense foreigner dropped into the middle of things would not mistake a Shī'ī procession or a Korean *kut* for just another routine event in the daily life in those communities. With the examples that follow, however, the perspective is different. It will focus on a variety of common activities that are "ritualized" to greater or lesser degrees. Instead of ritual as a separate category or an essentially different type of activity, the examples described here illustrate general processes of ritualization as flexible and strategic ways of acting.[1]

As in the preceding section, the examples discussed here can be loosely organized into six general categories, each focusing on a major attribute of "ritual-like" action, such as formalism, the varying degrees to which activities may be formalized and thereby deemed akin to ritual.[2] The categories of formalism, traditionalism, disciplined invariance, rule-governance, sacral symbolism, and performance are, of course, neither exclusive nor definitive.[3] Many ritual-like activities evoke more than one of these features, and such activities span various continuums of action from the religious to the secular, the public to the private, the routine to the improvised, the formal to the casual, and the periodic to the irregular. Nonetheless, these attributes do provide an initial lexicon for analyzing how cultures ritualize or deritualize social activities. By exploring these attributes and how they are used, it is possible to see dimensions of the significance and efficacy of ritual activity that were not so obvious in the classic examples of the previous section.

In particular, these examples of ritual-like behavior demonstrate the importance of the body and its way of moving in space and time. The body acts within an environment that appears to require it to respond in certain ways, but this environment is actually created and organized precisely by means of how people move around it. The complex reciprocal interaction of the body and its environment is harder to see in those classic examples of ritual where the emphasis on tradition and the enactment of codified or standardized actions lead us to take so much for granted about the way people actually do things when they are acting ritually. If examples of ritual-like activity can throw light on what goes into the activities of ritualizing, they may also clarify the significance of the distinctions people draw between various types of activities, including ritual and non-ritual actions. However ritual-like heavyweight boxing may appear to be at times, for most people it is not the same thing as Sunday church service, and the differences are far from unimportant to them. In contrast to those in the previous section, the examples explored here will tend to be somewhat less established as public events, less codified by tradition, and less likely to appeal to divine beings. Yet they have all been deemed ritual or ritual-like on occasion, and their proximity to more conventional examples of ritual effectively informs our general cultural understanding of what ritual basically means to us.

Formalism

Formality is one of the most frequently cited characteristics of ritual, even though it is certainly not restricted to ritual per se. In fact, as a quality, formality is routinely understood in terms of contrast and degree. That is, formal activities set up an explicit contrast with informal or casual ones; and activities can be formalized to different extents. In general, the more formal a series of movements and activities, the more ritual-like they are apt to seem to us. When analyzed, formality appears to be, at least in part, the use of a more limited and rigidly organized set of expressions and gestures, a "restricted code" of communication or behavior in contrast to a more open or "elaborated code."[4] Formal speech, for example, tends to be more conventional and less idiosyncratic or personally expressive. Likewise, formal gestures are fewer in number than informal ones and are more prescribed, restrained, and impersonal. By limiting or curbing *how* something can be expressed, restricted codes of behavior simultaneously influence *what* can be expressed as well. The injunction to speak politely at formal events means that people tend to avoid frank discussions of topics about which they personally care a great deal; they tend to stick to more standard opinions on more impersonal subjects. And if personal political positions should become the topic on such an occasion, one is less likely to hear emotional or abusive characterizations of opposing positions, although sarcasm and wit can have the same effect without violating the formality of the situation. For the most part, high degrees of formality force people to state or affirm very generalized and rather impersonal sentiments about relatively abstract concerns.

Formalization, it has been argued, is very effective in promoting a loose social acquiescence to what is going on.[5] While people might challenge the expression of specific or concrete ideas, they tend not to challenge the routine expression of formulas or clichés. As we saw earlier, Maurice Bloch has made this argument most clearly in regard to the power of formal oratory in securing social control among the Merina of Madagascar. On ritual occasions, village elders adopt a mode of formalized oratory that differs from everyday speech in numerous ways, notably loudness, intonation, syntactic forms, limited vocabulary, and the fixity of the order and style.[6] Bloch found that what can be said in this formalized way is quite limited, and as a mode of communication that is stylistically very determined, oratory can appear to be all style and no content. Yet in that quality may lie its effectiveness: if people do not bother to challenge the style, they are effectively accepting the content. In other words, formalized speech appears to induce acceptance, compliance, or at least forbearance with regard to any overt challenge. For Bloch, "the formalisation of language is a way whereby one speaker can coerce the response of another. . . . It is really a type of communication where rebellion is impossible and only revolution could be feasible."[7] For example, if a person unconventionally addresses an accidentally assembled audience, in the manner that a street preacher might stake out a city corner and begin to preach hellfire and damnation, the informality of the preacher's position invites reactions to its content and its style. However, if an invited speaker addresses an intentionally assembled audience and proceeds according to the conventions of a formal lecture, one cannot informally break in to challenge the content without challenging the whole event; in such cases, most people will tolerate the talk by accepting the conventions of the event for the time being. Those who do attempt to challenge the content, and thus the whole event, are forced into the position of disruptive hecklers.

Generally, formalization forces the speaker and the audience into roles that are more difficult to disrupt. For this reason, Bloch finds that highly formalized ways of speaking and communicating tend to be closely connected with traditional forms of social hierarchy and authority, effectively maintaining the implicit assumptions on which such authority is based. In other words, formality most often reinforces the larger social status quo. It may be for this reason that many types of social, political, and artistic challenges to the content of the status quo have felt it necessary to challenge simultaneously the conventions of polite speech and conduct, no matter how minor such challenges might seem. Indeed, those making such challenges are apt to be dismissed as extremists or quacks because they challenge style as much as content, and such dismissals further insulate the community from taking such challenges seriously. For example, early feminist critiques of the social order pointed to how the male gesture of holding a door for a woman, while courteous and well-meaning, effectively promoted ideas that reinforced very constrained and traditional views of women as weak and in need of both protection and deference. Feminists began to refuse to enter doors held open by men, while men complained that they did not understand why women should be so touchy about such a small display of conventional civility. Yet gradually this little social ritual has been redefined as a more generalized courtesy: whoever reaches the door first, male or female, now tends to hold it open for the other, or the able-bodied adult holds it for children, the elderly and the infirm.

Formality, therefore, is not necessarily empty or trivial. As a restricted code of behavior, formalized activities can be aesthetically as well as politically compelling, invoking what one analyst describes as "a metaphoric range of considerable power, a simplicity and directness, a vitality and rhythm."[8] The restriction of gestures and phrases to a small number that are practiced, perfected, and soon quite evocatively familiar can endow these formalized activities with great beauty and grace. Indeed, mechanical or routinized action is not what we usually mean by formality because they lack just this aesthetic dimension. In addition, it appears that formalized activities can communicate complex sociocultural messages very economically, particularly messages about social classification, hierarchical relationships, and the negotiation of identity and position in the social nexus.[9] For the sociologist Erving Goffman, human interchange is a matter of ordered sequences of symbolic communication, which he calls "interaction rituals" or "ritual games." The limited and highly patterned nature of these interactions serves the purpose of creating a self that can be constructed only with the cooperative help of some and the contrasting foil provided by others. In effect, Goffman suggests, one constructs one's identity, or "face," as a type of sacred object constituted by the ritual of social exchange.[10] The social construction of self-images and their relations with other self-images generates a total "ritual order," he argues, that is, a system of communication that deals not with facts but with understandings and interpretations, as well as "blindnesses, half-truths, illusions, and rationalizations." The organization of social encounters into various formal acts and events trains people to be "self-regulating participants" who live by a set of moral and social rules that define what it means to be human in a particular culture.[11] In a related definition of ritual, Goffman suggests that perfunctory and conventional acts are the way in which individuals express respect for "some object of ultimate value," such as the personhood of another or the whole edifice of codified social relations.[12]

Gestures of greeting or parting are formal conventions for social interaction, often considered "patterned routines," miniature rituals, or systems of signs that convey symbolic information.[13] They are frequently described as ritual by virtue of an implicit contrast between their communication of symbolic information and more utilitarian modes of transmitting factual information. The person who answers the question "How do you do?" with a factual account, for example, has either misunderstood the situation or is deliberately breaking the rules of polite discourse. Symbolically, however, such rituals of greeting and parting can communicate a great deal.[14] Greetings express and affirm the existence of an acceptable social relationship rather than a mere physical proximity that can threaten aggression. Indeed, greetings identify both parties as social entities that have some form of social relationship and status vis-à-vis each other, either as equals or superior to inferior. In this way, very simple forms of greeting can invoke principles that underlie a whole system of social configurations, a system that can at times control the actors more than they control it.[15]

Most greetings and farewells, in fact, vividly illustrate some version of the dominant social hierarchy. The more elaborate and formalized the greeting or farewell, the more it calls attention to the relative social status of the parties. In this way, such conventions appear to function like complex rituals by clarifying the social order and, at times, effecting subtle manipulations in that order. The vassal who greeted his lord by falling to his knees, removing his hat, dropping his gaze, and pressing his hand against his breast left no ambiguity as to who was who in that social situation. Neither does the Brahman who leaves payment on the ground for a hired untouchable instead of handing it to him directly. In situations where social equality is stressed, however, everyone will be greeted in a similar fashion irrespective of rank, seniority, profession, or gender, as seen in the use of "citizen" to replace titles in postrevolutionary France or "comrade" after the revolutions in the former USSR, China, and Cuba.

Our sense of the ritual-like nature of gestures of greeting and farewell also derives from the way these involve bodily as well as verbal modes of expression. Sometimes a greeting or parting may be nothing more than a brief body movement, as in the wave of a hand or the mute *anjali* used in South Asia, in which the hands are clasped in a prayer position in front of the chest as one bows slightly. In these cases, the body is an especially expressive and communicative instrument. A Japanese language teacher tried to make this point for a class of American students when he demonstrated how to say "thank you" in Japanese. It is not enough to say the words correctly, he contended; to articulate "Domo arigato" without the correct bobbing of the head and torso would be to say it incorrectly, rudely, or even incomprehensibly. This lesson is further illustrated by watching some people talk on public telephones: in the case of a Japanese man talking to his boss, he still uses his whole body, bowing in deference, sagging and straightening while listening, then bobbing up and down in final agreement.[16]

Although greetings and farewells are themselves formalizations of social conversation and interaction, there can be great differences in the degree of formality. "Hi," "hello," and "how do you do" represent three different levels of formality that the socially trained English-speaker knows how to deploy in the appropriate situation. That is, despite the restrictions inherent in conventions of formality, such activities as handshakes, farewell speeches, and verbal greetings can all be performed with a great deal of personal expressiveness; one can personalize or nuance the conventional meanings attached to these actions. A handshake in which one person reluctantly offers just the fingertips, pumps the other's hand aggressively, or squeezes it with a playful wink all communicate important variations on the social message of "it is nice to meet you."

Table manners are another obvious area of activity formalized according to cultural conventions that bear only indirect links to the utilitarian purpose of getting nourishment into one's stomach.[17] As one commentator states, "We turn the consumption of food, a biological necessity, into a carefully cultured phenomenon."[18] For these reasons, table etiquette and most other forms of socially polite behavior are readily considered ritual-like in nature. While it is clear that table manners are rule-governed, a category considered separately in this chapter, a striking aspect of table rituals and many other forms of social etiquette is the variability of formality. There are rules for how to set a table, serve the food, and handle the implements, but the rules are not hard and fast. Despite a few constants, such as not eating and speaking at the same time and minimal use of one's fingers, the rules that apply in any one situation vary according to the desired degree of formality of the meal and its larger context. In some social systems, the rules of etiquette may be very elaborate, often acting to demarcate class boundaries and discourage transgression of them. In other societies, there may be attempts to relax and democratize such practices, which was the impulse behind Eleanor Roosevelt's *Book of Common Sense Etiquette* and other mid-twentieth-century American guides.[19]

Limiting acceptable behavior to a relatively few culturally standardized options can create distinctions among dining situations and, of course, among social groups.[20] The same group of people may eat hot dogs at the beach with very different rules of dining etiquette than they would use at an elaborate dinner banquet, but some groups who pride themselves on their intrinsic good manners or sense of style might well dine as formally at the beachfront as others would in the most exclusive dining room. As in many ritual situations, the more intimate the social relationships that are involved, the more casual the behavior. So a mother feeding a child on her lap is apt to ignore the usual table etiquette, but a group of relative strangers dining together tend to be more scrupulous. The greater the social distance experienced or desired between persons, the more their activities abide by those conventions that acknowledge social distance. Likewise, however, dropping some of these conventions can collapse some of the social distance and alter the relationships.

Like ritual, the formality of table etiquette conveys symbolic messages—about social class, the mannered person's place in and attitudes toward the hierarchy of social classes, and his or her understanding of the specific social situation. Table etiquette, for example, as the transfer of general principles of formal etiquette to the table, effectively demarcates the situation of dining from other forms of social activity, differentiating the table as a distinct ceremonial arena. In this way, table manners signal the social importance of eating and give social significance to how one eats. Thus, as many analysts have noted, the formalization of ingestion into a series of organized conventions governing every aspect of the physical process serves to blur distinctions between what is physical and what is social. Only under special duress, such as famine, war, or illness, is the mere consumption of food more important than sitting correctly at the table and eating a meal properly! Indeed, there is a long-standing cultural belief that table manners indicate not just the quality of one's upbringing but also one's moral or spiritual disposition as well.[21] This can become quite explicit in the social training of children, where the social codes they are taught to obey are seen not simply as "mere" conventions but also as intrinsically necessary social practices that civilize the wild brute lurking in all of us. In this way, the ritual-like qualities of table manners effectively disguise the basic arbitrariness of the cultural conventions of etiquette, and eating a meal properly reinforces the whole sociocultural edifice of the status, symbols, and ideologies. Yet, as in most ritual, formalization is not inflexible, and there are multiple ways in which the conventions of table etiquette are manipulated to create other highly nuanced messages, including ones that may fundamentally challenge the conventional social values expressed with knife and fork.

Table manners and dining rituals vary greatly from one culture to another and from one historical epoch to another. The feudal society of medieval Europe, which is generally understood to have had more religious and political ritual than the modern secular states in Europe and America, in fact contained far fewer rituals of etiquette than society today. The locus of most ritual activity in a society, whether it be the church or the dining room, is indicative of larger cultural forces. According to the classic study of Norbert Elias, the emergence of the concept of *civilité* and the social conventions of so-called civilized behavior specifically arose in the transition from the medieval world to early modern Europe. Elias correlated the emergence of centralized national states with the rearrangements of social relationships promoted by new rites of social etiquette. This was also a transition from forms of external social control, seen in the rites of church and state, to forms of internal self-control expressed in the ritual-like conventions of good manners.[22] In this process, the conventions of etiquette and good behavior, while culturally determined and socially acquired, became internalized as the compelling means by which individuals regulate themselves in order to participate in an ordered hierarchy of social classes. The social training and psychological development of the child are organized to effect this internalization of social norms as self-control.[23] As noted previously, more than a few scholars correlate the emergence of moral systems of values and ideas with the formulation and educational transmission of the proper use of table implements, although in some cultures the connection between etiquette and morality can be closer than in others.[24] Certainly the internalization of values of self-control that socialize the individual as a member of a group or class is one reason why formal modes of behavior are apt to strike us as ritual-like.

Any modern American guide to table manners and general social etiquette, such as *Emily Post's Etiquette* or *Amy Vanderbilt's New Complete Book of Etiquette*, makes an explicit distinction between informal and formal entertaining. They all carefully spell out the differences between an informal and formal dinner party, luncheon, tea, cocktail party, and so on—and the differences among them are basic to how each is defined.[25] That is, a formal occasion can be appreciated or "read" as such only if one understands what is formal about it, namely, how it contrasts with an informal occasion and what the contrasts are meant to communicate. In this way, formalization is a way of acting that actively heightens the specialness of a situation and its concomitant contrasts with less special events. The ease with which one simple gesture can heighten or diminish formality—such as the way in which one person greets another—parallels the way in which similar gestures can set a ritual situation off from daily routines or integrate it with those routines. Hence, the ritual-like nature of formality draws our attention to the way in which the contrasts with other activities—implicit and explicit, delicately signaled or dramatically marked—are intrinsic to the very construction of ritual activities. Further, formalization as the use of restricted codes of speech and movement also suggests some of the ways in which ritual can engage consent and promote the internalization of overarching social values by means of fairly discrete and specific acts. The type of formalization seen in gestures of politeness and table etiquette, however, reminds us that although codes for value-laden behavior exist as cultural conventions and expectations, they are eminently open to manipulation, appropriation, and nuance; in matters of etiquette and ritual, people do not just follow rules. Moreover, the processes for internalizing and deploying ritual knowledge and values are doubtless far from perfectly reliable, and most people's sense of ritual behavior is probably no more uniform than the spectrum of attitudes toward table manners.

Traditionalism

The attempt to make a set of activities appear to be identical to or thoroughly consistent with older cultural precedents can be called "traditionalization." As a powerful tool of legitimation, traditionalization may be a matter of near-perfect repetition of activities from an earlier period, the adaptation of such activities in a new setting, or even the creation of practices that simply evoke links with the past. The more obvious forms of traditionalization include the use of ancient costumes, the repetition of older social customs, and the preservation of archaic linguistic forms. For example, the Amish communities in Pennsylvania retain the dress, customs, and speech patterns of the late 17th and early 18th century, when Jacob Amman led them to break with the less conservative Mennonites in Europe. Likewise, the Hasidic communities concentrated in and near New York City and Jerusalem maintain the basic dress of Eastern European Jews from more than a century ago, often with the same fine-tuned distinctions in dress that marked important differences in social and religious status.[26] These methods of traditionalization tend to privilege an older historical model and make assimilation into the modern world both difficult and highly suspect. Such dramatically traditionalized patterns of dress establish a high-profile identity for those closely following the older ways, thereby helping to maintain the boundaries as well as the authority of the traditional community.

Most rituals appeal to tradition or custom in some way, and many are concerned to repeat historical precedents very closely. A ritual that evokes no connection with any tradition is apt to be found anomalous, inauthentic, or unsatisfying by most people. Thus, traditionalism is an important dimension of what we tend to mean and identify as ritual, while activities that are not explicitly called "rituals" may seem ritual-like if they invoke forms of traditionalism. Often formalism and traditionalism go together and underscore the nonutilitarian nature of activities, further heightening their ritual-like nature. Yet traditionalism can also be invoked without much concern for formality. For example, a Thanksgiving dinner may not be particularly formal if there is the usual chaos of cooking and company, but it makes a clear appeal both to a supposed historical precedent when the early Puritans and their friendly Indian neighbors shared a plentiful meal of turkeys and corn and to the particular domestic customs of the family itself. Such customs may be as simple as always using great grandmother's lace tablecloth, having rhubarb pie instead of the more common pumpkin or apple pie, or always delegating a particular person to say grace and carve the turkey. Indeed, most families are more likely to observe their own little traditions than simply to formalize the meal. Although Thanksgiving Day's "myth of origins" is far from solid historical fact, a clear national tradition of Thanksgiving has been institutionalized in American public life. Yet it is clearly an event that is traditionalized primarily in domestic ways.[27]

The British use of judicial regalia dating from the late 17th century is another example of an appeal to tradition that heightens the ritual-like nature of court proceedings in Great Britain. Judges and lawyers are required to don wigs, robes, buckled shoes, breeches, jabots (the lace neck ruff), and tippets (hood or cape) among other items of dress before appearing in court. Although the style of dress, roughly dated to the time of Charles II (1630–1685), was soon discarded by clergymen and courtiers, it was retained as mandatory dress in the court system except for the very lowest courts. Recently, when the British lord chancellor and lord chief justice suggested abandoning such archaic dress, those opposed to the change tried to convey some of the function and ethos of this traditionalism. A deputy administrator at Britain's main criminal court, the Old Bailey, argued that traditional garb added to the awe and mystery that is necessary to the authority of the courts. He said, "It is not unlike going into a high church where the priests are robed. There is a sense of respect."[28] While some defend the traditional dress in terms of the dignity it confers on court procedures, others argue that it reinforces elitism and intimidation. Even pragmatic arguments concerning the monetary costs and the physical discomfort of such garb in hot weather have been met by counterarguments, including the odd conclusion that "criminals expect a little bit of spectacle before they are sent away to prison. They would be terribly disappointed if they did not find the courtroom full of people in elaborate and rather ridiculous costumes."[29] Clearly, these elaborate costumes have long been thought to heighten the solemnity, authority, and prestige of court proceedings. Whether or not costumed judges are usually likened to priests, their gowns ensure that they are immediately taken to be the special bearers of a sacred tradition and a solemn set of duties.

A similar ethos is evoked by the use of academic robes.[30] In comparison to judicial attire, academic robes, hoods, and hats are related to what was once everyday dress for scholars and clerics in an even earlier period. Maintaining this garb on formal occasions despite centuries of radical sartorial change in society in general has served to heighten the contrast between the academic world and everybody else. Such distinctions foster the ethos that scholars are the custodians of timeless truths—or the useless minutiae of ages past—even though the adoption of ancient academic garb is fairly recent in most countries other than England.[31] People are visibly impressed by a long line of university professors filing past in full regalia, their long black robes setting off a colorful assortment of hoods and hats that denote different academic degrees, disciplines, and universities. This type of traditionalism evokes an authority rather different from that of institutions of uniformed military, medical, or postal workers; indeed, the ridiculous inefficiency of the outfits dramatizes an authority heavily dependent on its sheer endurance in time. The symbolic messages of such traditionalism do not stop at distinguishing the proud historicity of academia; they are also designed to distinguish the hierarchy of institutions, degree ranks, and organizational position. Indeed, two of the most ancient universities, Oxford and Cambridge, resolutely differentiated themselves from each other in the design of their gowns, hoods, and hats; although the Oxford and Cambridge gowns are the prototype for almost all university gowns in the world, institutions tend to adopt distinguishing features of their own.[32] Of course, it is such hollowed traditionalism that elicits symbolic counterstatements—either political protest or simply undergraduate antics. Decorating mortarboards with slogans or dispensing with any clothing under the gown are familiar ways to challenge the authority served by the traditionalism of academic ritual.[33]

Traditionalism in dress goes beyond the legal or ivy-covered walls of the court or classroom. The use of a Victorian-style bridal dress and the groom's tuxedo is a form of traditionalism that heightens the ritual nature of the ceremonial event, primarily by stressing a view of the bride and groom that appears to transcend current history and evoke eternal values. Traditionalism also goes well beyond mere dress, of course. Liberal recourse to Greek and Latin mottoes inscribed on university walls and letterheads attests to classical erudition and, it is hoped, enlightened morality. A dramatic form of traditionalism has been the use of Latin and Hebrew as liturgical languages when they were no longer spoken among the general population, although the Roman Catholic Church dropped the liturgical use of Latin in the mid-1960s and Hebrew was revived as a spoken language with the Zionist settlement of Israel in the late nineteenth century.

A particularly complex and diffused form of traditionalism can be seen in the social practice and significance in Chinese society of the teachings of Kongfuzi or Master Kong, otherwise known by the latinized name of Confucius (551– 479 B.C.E.). His teachings have been taken as the basis for a loose system of social order and morality that grounds Chinese life in a deep sense of respect for tradition and cultural continuity. *Li*, a term variously translated as ritual, ceremony, propriety, etiquette, moral conduct, or correctness, embodied for Confucius and subsequent forms of Confucian culture the proper ordering of all human relationships and, hence, the proper conduct of the moral person toward others. From a very early period on, this understanding of li made little appeal to gods and spirits, leading some analysts to suggest that it is primarily a philosophical idea rather than a religious one, although a philosophical reading does not do justice to the force of this notion.[34] For example, the writings attributed to Confucius state the following: "If (a ruler) could for one day 'himself submit to ritual,' everyone under Heaven would respond to his Goodness." [35] For Confucian philosopher Xunzi, rites put heaven and earth in harmony, make the sun and moon shine, and order the four seasons, the stars, and the constellations. They regulate people's "likes and dislikes, their joys and their hates." They are "the highest expression of the hierarchical order [of the cosmos]," and as such they are the basis for the strength, authority, and legitimacy of the state. In ritual, human action is brought into harmony with the principles that govern the cosmos itself.[36] As one modern interpreter notes, people "become truly human as their raw impulse is shaped by *li*. And *li* is the fulfillment of human impulse, the civilized expression of it."[37] This is the framework in which the presentation of simple offerings to one's ancestors can act as a linchpin for the whole social order.

For Confucius, these moral principles and the proper performance of li are laid out in the ancient classics, which contain the epitome of human wisdom, instructions for right conduct, and illustrations of the moral reasons behind the successes and failures of human affairs. To observe li, therefore, is to follow time-honored canons of ceremony and morality that equate such conduct with reverence for tradition itself. Hence, in teaching his ideas of moral behavior, Confucius denied that he was inventing anything new. The norms of traditional ceremony and virtue all come, he argued, from the example of the Duke of Zhou, who founded a dynasty one hundred years before the time of Confucius. Explicitly sidestepping the role of innovator, Confucius idealized the Zhou dynasty as a golden age of civilization that effectively provided models for how to live in the present, cultivate the self, control conduct, and perfect human virtue. He appealed to the idea of a preexisting tradition, embodied in Zhou, to which all Chinese are heir. Hence, for Confucian culture, li is not merely social etiquette or virtue but the observance of norms of behavior laid out in a pristine age of Chinese culture. To act properly is to close the gap between the past and the present. To observe li is to live the principles that unite Chinese history as a coherent cultural legacy and worldview. The traditionalism of Chinese culture, therefore, is a way of fostering consensus about moral and social values by establishing their authority in the distant past and demonstrating their efficacy in shaping history. While Chinese in the 20th century have criticized Confucian traditionalism from many different perspectives, it is still a vital force in Chinese culture.

Various theories argue that the power of traditionalism is rooted in the dominance of certain social classes, the symbolic power of cultural ideals, or even the need in modern life for the means to render contradictory experiences coherent. As such, traditionalism presupposes authoritative ideals embodied in an earlier time—even when such ideals, and even the image itself of an earlier time, are something of an innovation. This is aptly described as "the invention of tradition." Traditions can be invented by a "process of formalization and ritualization, characterized by reference to the past, if only by imposing repetition."[38] Indeed, many so-called traditions of contemporary life are quite recent in origin. The British monarchy, for example, is probably enveloped in more elaborate ceremonial than any other European institution with the possible exception of the Catholic papacy in Rome. And most educated people, especially journalists, routinely describe these ceremonies as a "thousand-year-old tradition," as having "gone on for hundreds of years," or as following "centuries of precedent." In truth, however, most of the royal ceremonial that attends the House of Windsor goes no further back than the very end of the 19th century and the beginning of the 20th, when a number of clumsy, older rites were extensively revised and elaborated, while many more new ceremonies were completely invented. This period of great creativity in British royal ritual coincided with a dramatic loss in real power for the monarchy; the elaborate ceremonial aggrandizement became a new way to exercise royal influence.[39] With the crowning of Queen Victoria as empress of India in 1877 and especially the celebration of her diamond jubilee in 1897, the scale and grandeur of royal events took on not only unprecedented pageantry but also frequent and quite unfounded appeals to "immemorial tradition." Some historians have argued that the unprecedented industrial and social changes of the period, as well as the effects of a burgeoning popular press, made it both "necessary and possible" to package the monarchy in a new way—as a ritualistic "symbol of consensus and continuity to which all might defer." The effort and planning needed to create ceremonies of sufficiently routinized grandeur as to imply centuries of tradition led to many small ironies, as when the bolting horses that disrupted Victoria's funeral were immediately made part of the tradition.[40]

It is ironic, therefore, that the early anthropologist Bronislav Malinowski contrasted the "invented" and "appropriated" traditions invoked in the pageantry of Hitler and Mussolini with what he saw as the more authentic traditionalism of the British monarch. The dictators, he argued, create

> In a hurry, from all kinds of ill-assorted odds and ends, their own symbolism and ritual, their own mythologies. . . . One of them becomes the Aryan godhead incarnate; the

other, blatantly, places the bays of the ancient Roman emperors on his own head. . . . Pomp and ritual, legend and magical ceremonies, are enacted round them with an *éclat* which outshines the time-honoured, historically-founded institutions of traditional monarchy."[41]

It appears that Malinowski's own sense of appropriate and time-honored institutions of leadership were molded by the very recent ritual reinventions of British royalty.

The establishment of special holidays, as seen in calendrical rituals, is a common means of traditionalization. For example, Bastille Day, which was described earlier, celebrates the storming of the prison that began the French Revolution, and multiple internal references throughout the holiday give the impression that the commemoration dates back to the years immediately following the revolution. However, it was not institutionally established until 1880, when the Third Republic very self-consciously invoked revolutionary imagery in order to assert its own political legitimacy and popular support. Organizing an official "Bastille Day" helped solidify a popular understanding of the revolution and its meaning. In fact, the French Revolution itself only gradually became a unified, coherent, and historically meaningful event—in response to very contemporary political needs and, at least in part, through the ritualizing strategy of traditionalization.[42]

The Pledge of Allegiance routinely taught to American schoolchildren is part of a daily patriotic ritual that gives the impression of great age and a scriptural solemnity that forbids tampering with the words. Yet the pledge is just one hundred years old. As written by Francis Bellamy, who modified an earlier version by James B. Upham, it was established in 1892 in conjunction with the Chicago World's Fair and a national school program to celebrate the 400th anniversary of Columbus's discovery of America. A 1954 congressional ruling further changed it by adding the words "under God."[43] Historical analysis suggests that the invention of this patriotic tradition around the turn of the century had a great deal to do with the enormous number of immigrants arriving in America and entering the school system. The 1954 addition occurred in the context of the cold war, when President Eisenhower heard a Presbyterian minister preach that the American Pledge of Allegiance "could be the pledge of any republic," something even "little Moscovites [*sic*]" could pledge to their flag. The Reverend George Docherty concluded that the pledge was missing "the characteristic and definitive factor in the American way of life" best expressed by the phrase "one nation under God."[44] A recent argument for change would replace the Docherty-Eisenhower addition with "one nation, united in our diversity, committed to liberty and justice for all," which conveys several new messages.[45]

Ultimately, it is hard to make any clear distinction between traditionalism and many other complex modes of ritualization. There is undoubtedly reason to debate whether traditionalizing is a way of ritualizing or an effect of ritualizing. Certainly, the conscious or unconscious creation of rituals often involves explicit appeals to some sense of tradition, even when that tradition is being created before one's eyes. As one analyst has put it, ritual is uniquely able "to make traditional that which is unexpected and new."[46] Indeed, there has been no attempt to hide evidence of the recent origins of British royal pageantry or the American Pledge of Allegiance; the ceremonies themselves just imply age, and few people would even think to challenge the allusions to tradition. To traditionalize in this way can be as simple as adding a few verbal references to the acts and words of "our ancestors" and as subtle as the mere act of teaching a new generation how to raise their hands to their hearts the way older people do it. Nothing more needs to be explained. The meaning and purpose are thought to be obvious, and the assumption that it has always been done this way slips in without official pronouncement. The anthropologist who inquires why the natives of an American small town or an Indonesian village perform certain gestures is likely to be told, "We have always done this." True or not, the direct appeal to traditionalism is often answer enough for those attempting to live within a coherent and enduring set of values and assumptions.

Invariance

One of the most common characteristics of ritual-like behavior is the quality of invariance, usually seen in a disciplined set of actions marked by precise repetition and physical control. For some theorists, this feature is the prime characteristic of ritual behavior.[47] The emphasis may be on the careful choreography of actions, the self-control required by the actor, or the rhythm of repetition in which the orchestrated activity is the most recent in an exact series that unites past and future. While traditionalism involves an appeal to the authority of the past that subordinates the present, invariance seems to be more concerned with ignoring the passage of time in general. It appears to suppress the significance of the personal and particular moment in favor of the timeless authority of the group, its doctrines, or its practices. The component of discipline certainly suggests that one effect of invariance is generally understood to be the molding or shaping of persons according to enduring guidelines and conditions.

Much human activity can be sufficiently repetitious to afford ready if trivial comparisons to ritual. A famous spoof on the elaborate daily routines of Americans obsessed with rigid codes of hygiene, grooming, and beauty describes them as the "body rites" of an exotic people called the "Nacirema." But it is not repetition alone that makes these acts ritualistic; more important is the punctiliousness with which the "natives" attend to the mouth, skin, and hair while standing in front of an altarlike box set into the wall above an ablution basis in the one or more shrine rooms found in every house. This is also true of Freud's characterization, examined earlier, of obsessive-compulsive disorders as ritual-like: repetition is part of this attribution, but the repetition is inseparable from a fixation on non-utilitarian thoroughness and exactitude. In a somewhat different example, the well-known format of the weekly meetings of Alcoholics Anonymous, often deemed ritual-like because of the unvarying program, suggests that in some contexts punctilious concern with repetition may have great utility.[48]

Activities that are merely routinized are not the best examples of the ritual-like nature of invariance unless they are also concerned with precision and control. The Nacirema routines of washing and brushing described by Miner are usually performed with care but not controlled precision. Yet the movements of factory workers on assembly lines have been described as ritualistic due to their robotlike precision. A more comprehensive example might be the routines of monastic life, which are governed by close attention to detail, discipline, and self-control. Indeed, traditional monastic life specifically encouraged the ritualization of all daily activities—dressing, eating, walking, working, and, in some places, even the humbler acts of defecation. In this environment, ritual is not meant to be separated from the rest of life; all of life is made as consistently ritual-like as possible in the service of a religious goal.[49]

One possible goal of the discipline of invariance comes across clearly in the daily routine of a typical Zen Buddhist seminarian. He rises at four or five in the morning, dresses in the uniform of the seminarian, and proceeds to the meditation room (*zendo*) to take up his particular place for the morning session of sitting meditation (*zazen*), the first of several throughout the day. While meditating, each monk sits cross-legged in silence in accord with traditional models. When the session is finished, breakfast is served in a precise order and without a sound. The monk must unpack his eating bowls in a specific way. He receives the food with particular gestures, eats slowly and completely, and rinses and dries the bowls before repacking them in their original order. The monk concentrates on the perfection of each act. His movements should be slow and smooth, deft and precise. The goal of Zen action—variously stated as "no self " or "mindfulness"—is thought to be served as much by the way one goes about eating as the way one meditates or interacts with others. As Grimes points out, the precise gestures used in this Zen meal do not refer to anything in particular, certainly not historical models, or symbolize any explicit doctrinal ideas. The precision is simply to make each gesture as "mindful" as possible, which is part of the general cultivation of a spontaneous mental and physical state of mindfulness.[50] Scholars remind us that this picture of Zen monastic practice is rather idealized.[51] In fact, few Zen priests meditate after leaving the seminary, when lay-oriented ritual duties take up much of their energy, time, and attention. Nonetheless, such monastic experiences do exist, and they revolve around the special type of training and cultivation afforded by disciplined invariance.

The invariant routines of Alcoholics Anonymous or Zen monasticism are understood to be necessary to the reshaping of the individual. For the first, the discipline of weekly attendance and public testimony encourages and supports the self-control needed to face the daily difficulties of avoiding alcohol. For the second, the control of one's physical self that is promoted by the monastic routine is designed to subordinate the demands, desires, and indulgences of the body and thereby encourage the greater discipline needed to control the mind. Many similar activities that have ritual-like tendencies toward routine and discipline are also concerned with more than molding or encoding certain dispositions within the body and mind. They specifically seek to foster holistic and integrated experiences that close the distance between the doer and the deed, and transform the precise and deliberate gesture into one of perfect spontaneity and efficacy. Some strategies of invariance envision, implicitly or explicitly, a process of training by which studied mindfulness molds the actor's basic disposition so as to foster action that is inherently anonymous, unattached to the particularities of the self.[52]

The practice of meditation, even more than the monastic lifestyle, is a better example of the way in which invariant practice is meant to evoke disciplined control for the purposes of self-cultivation, although some spokespersons for various traditions of meditation have attempted to distinguish meditation from ritual. Traditional Buddhist commentators and some modern scholars of Zen regard meditation as an explicit rejection of ritual. In this view, Zen is dedicated to eliminating the "mediation" of ritual (as well as images and scriptures) in favor of direct and personal experience. One commentator invokes this contrast by arguing, "The Buddha's teaching on this subject [meditation] was so wrongly, or so little understood, that in later times the way of 'meditation' deteriorated and degenerated into a kind of ritual or ceremony almost technical in its routine."[53] Other analysts have been more open to the ritual dimensions of meditation.

The ritual-like qualities of disciplined routines for molding individual dispositions have led many people to compare the whole educational process to ritual, quite apart from the many explicit rituals that are incorporated within the social world of the school. Educational institutions clearly attempt to do more than simply impart information through verbal and written instruction. They are concerned with fundamental forms of socialization that involve the internalization of cultural values. These values are promoted in the form, content, and very organization of the schooling experience.[54] Effective socialization attempts to transform what is ordained and permitted—that is, the "rules"—into what is taken for granted or even desired, a sense of right order in which one feels at home. Some school activities stress the school community as a unified whole and the concomitant values of group identification, consensus, and loyalty. Other activities stress the differentiation of persons and subgroups in terms of authority-seniority and ability-expertise. Aside from such explicit rites as convocation and commencement or even the total calendar of events that define a process of maturation from freshman hazing to the senior trip, there are multiple, redundant, and invariant routines that shape bodies and minds by repetition and disciplines of self-control. From the basic requirements of punctual attendance and alert responsiveness to bells, to the subordination of ego through uniformity of dress or submission to authority, it is clear that the most important things learned in school are not in textbooks. These ritual-like practices socialize young people to accept certain forms of authority (seniors, experts, and texts, for example), to interpret hard work in the classroom or the playing field as the source of rewards and prestige, and to associate personal well-being with the cooperative social order of the group.

Invariance can invoke both our admiration and dismay. The lock-step drill of a troop of soldiers or the synchronized precision of the Radio City Music Hall Rockettes effectively suppresses the chaos and creativity of more individual expressions. Both are the result of countless hours of training through which the corporate body is slowly constructed by reordering the instincts of each individual body. This does not mean simply the domination of the individual; it can also be his or her empowerment when allied to the group. In a discussion of the rise of nationalism, Benedict Anderson notes an analogous phenomenon of "unisonance" in the creation of a contemporaneous communal body.

> Take national anthems, for example, sung on national holidays. No matter how banal the words or how mediocre the tunes, the singing provides an experience of simultaneity. At precisely such moments, people wholly unknown to each other utter the

same verses to the same melody. The image: unisonance. Singing the Marsellaise, Waltzing Matilda, and Indonesian Raya provide occasions for unisonality, for the echoed physical realization of the imagined community. . . . How selfless this unisonance feels![55]

Although invariance is not always corporate, since the solo yogin or Zen practitioner also invokes it, its association with ritual lies in the simple means by which precise duplication of action subordinates the individual and the contingent to a sense of the encompassing and the enduring.

Rule-Governance

The novelist Joyce Carol Oates once introduced an essay on boxing and the career of Mohammed Ali with the following observation: "Though highly ritualized, and as rigidly bound by rules, traditions, and taboos as any religious ceremony, [boxing] survives as the most primitive and terrifying of contests . . . [it] is a stylized mimicry of a fight to the death . . . a Dionysian rite of cruelty, sacrifice and redemption . . . [a] romance of (expendable) maleness—in which The Fight is honored, and even great champions come, and go."[56] Aside from the appeals to repetition and traditionalism, these observations reflect another major characteristic accorded ritual-like activity, rule-governance. Rule-governed activity is often compared to ritual, particularly rule-governed contests in which violent chaos is barely held in check by complex codes of orchestration. This tendency has led some analysts to talk about driving a car as ritualistic, although others find such a comparison absurd. There is greater consensus around rule-governed activities that engage the rapt attention of an audience, as in the "ritualized combat" readily identified in sports, martial arts, traditional duels, feuds, or such cultural specialties as the bullfight. Yet both the scholar and the unschooled observer are apt to appreciate something ritual-like in many other games and forms of play, such as stylized displays of sexual sadomasochism, the controlled suicide of hara-kiri, or the chesslike lineup of traditional armies on both sides of a battlefield. Examples of controlled engagements of violence and disorder also include the highly coded forms of dress, speech, and gestures that identify rival teams, gangs, political parties, or armies. Should sheer brute force or the chaos of personal self-interest override the rules of controlled engagement, then the ritual-like nature of the event would certainly evaporate.[57]

People have long appreciated the similarities imposed by rule-governance across rather different classes of activity, such as sports and warfare. The highly stylized quip attributed to the Duke of Wellington, that "the battle of Waterloo was won on the playing fields of Eton" is echoed in the less elegant remarks of the Notre Dame football coach Frank Leahy, who said, "Ask yourself where our young men developed the qualities that go to make a good fighting man. . . . It is on the athletic fields."[58] While some people have always argued that greater emphasis on sports would channel aggression and eliminate war, others have countered that competitive sports reinforces the mind-set conducive to war.[59] For the most part, scholars tend to develop this second perspective by exploring how sports and games can strengthen basic cultural values and desirable forms of social behavior, such as the importance of male teamwork and the efficacy of aggressive competition.[60]

Much interest and conjecture attend the question of how sports may have originally emerged from religious ritual or been closely linked to it, as in the Mayan-Aztec ballcourt game or the Greek Olympic games.[61] Whether or not any such lineage is relevant to understanding modern sports, some observers are fascinated by the way in which sports attract various taboos, pollution beliefs, and "magical" practices. They point to the enormous number of patently nonutilitarian gestures used, such as pitchers who tug their caps in a particular way before each throw or the team taboo against crossing bats.[62] Such miniature rituals, defined as prescribed behavior that is scrupulously observed in order to affect an outcome, may not be part of the game in itself but on close examination seem nearly inseparable from real participation in sports.[63] For others, like Joyce Carol Oates, the ritualism of sports derives from the importance of the more encompassing sets of rules that define and regulate the activity. These rules constrain the contenders and force them to follow very controlled patterns of interaction. In the tension between the brute human energy being expended and the highly coded means of engagement, the sports event seems to evoke in highly symbolic ways a fundamental conflict or experience at the core of social life. While this perception about sports overlaps features discussed in the next sections, there is a real stress on how the rules create the event and hence its meaning and dramatic spectacle.

Similar considerations are behind the tendency to describe some forms of play as ritual. While the chess match is more like a sports contest than not and thus shares in some of the ways in which sports can appear ritual-like, most characterizations of play as ritual-like focus on examples that are communal, repetitive, and culturally patterned. These characterizations see in play a social license to manipulate, invert, or ridicule cultural symbols and patterns, even though such manipulations can effectively reinforce deeply embedded social assumptions about the way things are and should be.[64]

War is another social analog to the rule-governed expressive activities of sports and play that also appears ritualistic in many circumstances. Naturally, as with the previous examples, war usually involves many explicit rites and ceremonies, but observations concerning the ritual-like nature of war itself point to the role of rules in channeling, constraining, and simultaneously legitimating the violent interaction of opposed groups. Thus, the pageantry and costume of Roman or Napoleonic armies, as well as their rules of military engagement, often evidenced sufficient orchestration to appear heavily ritualized. Rules governed the formation of firing lines, charges by standard bearers, and battle cries but also prohibited indiscriminate barbarity, shooting someone in the back, killing civilians and prisoners, and looting and raping the defeated. Whether observed or merely given lip-service, such rules have helped to make the activities of killing appear civilized, humane, and expressive of important values such as loyalty, freedom or definitions of manhood. On more than a few occasions, scrupulous concern with ritual-like rules of engagement have helped to rationalize war as in the service of the greater glory of God.

The ritual-like dimensions of war are not hard to see in related practices like tribal feuds, where acts of aggression can include highly formalized exchanges of bullets or verbal insults. There is a long tradition in the Middle East, for example, of exchanging verbal abuse and indignities in verses strictly governed by classical canons of meter and rhyme. Many ancient Arabic poets specialized in this art of cursing enemies, a poetic genre known as *hija'*, or execration poetry. With the Iraqi invasion of Kuwait in 1990, there was a rather extraordinary revival of execration poetry in television broadcasts sent back and forth among Saudi Arabia, Kuwait, and Iraq. Using medieval Arabic, the literal meaning of which is barely understood by most Arabs, one Saudi poet sang out a variety of racist insults at Saddam Hussein:

> Saddam, O Saddam,
> Of our flesh not are you.
> Claim not to be a Muslim,
> For you are truly a Jew.
> Your deeds have proved ugly,
> Your face is darkest black.
> And we will yet set fire
> To your bottom and your back.[65]

The demand for such entertaining propaganda had both the Saudi and Iraqi governments holding contests with monetary rewards for the composers of particularly dazzling or damning verses. As propaganda goes, such medieval poetry would seem to be a bit esoteric, but the adherence to classical models seems to have evoked an effective framework of heroic imagery from the past with which to interpret the complexities of inter-Arab hostilities in the present.

Less aesthetically pleasing, perhaps, but often no less orchestrated and venomous, are the complex negotiations that attend formal bargaining between company management and labor unions.[66] Likewise, presidential debates, congressional hearings, debating societies, and even routine legal proceedings in which defense and prosecution contend in a court of law all follow an enormous number of prescribed rules that regulate and thereby facilitate conflicted forms of interaction. There is a general tendency toward ethological or functional explanations that see this kind of ritual and ritual-like practice as channeling aggression in order to create a fair and measured environment in which explosive differences can be safely aired. This suggests that ritualization by means of rule-governance can be deployed not only to control the engagement of powerful social forces, but also to create the impression that such powers exist. Rule-governance, as either a feature of many diverse activities or a strategy of ritualization itself, also suggests that we tend to think of ritual in terms of formulated norms imposed on the chaos of human action and interaction. These normative rules may define the outer limits of what is acceptable, or they may orchestrate every step. In either case, they hold individuals to communally approved patterns of behavior, they testify to the legitimacy and power of that form of communal authority, and perhaps they also encourage human interactions by constraining the possible outcomes.

Sacral Symbolism

Activities that explicitly appeal to supernatural beings are readily considered to be examples of ritual, even if the appeal is a bit indirect, as when the president of the

United States takes the oath of office by placing his left hand on the Bible and swearing to uphold the duties and responsibilities of the presidency. Although it is not part of the institutional life of a specific religious group, the oath of office clearly derives from Christian ritual and represents the Christian values in American civic religion.[67] Many other activities are not so overt in their appeal to a supernatural reality. More subtly, they simply assume and variously express a fundamental difference between sacred things on the one hand and profane things on the other. In doing so, these activities express generalized belief in the existence of a type of sacrality that demands a special human response. Aside from religious examples, such as the symbols of the Christian cross and the star of David, there are secular examples as well. National flags and monuments are routinely regarded as more than mere signs representing a country or an idea; they are symbols that embody values, feelings, and histories of national ideals and loyalty.[68] In the many public arguments over how the flag of the United States should be treated, no one argues that the flag itself is holy. Yet, many people seem to feel that this piece of cloth, when deliberately crafted as a flag, should be handled in very specific and respectful ways. It is thought to stand for something as large and diffuse as "the American way" and as specific as ideas about freedom, democracy, free enterprise, hard work, and national superiority. According to the anthropologist Sherry Ortner, the flag "does not encourage reflection on the logical relations among these ideas, nor on the logical consequences of them as they are played out in social actuality, over time and history. On the contrary, the flag encourages a sort of all-or-nothing allegiance to the whole package, best summed . . . [by] 'Our flag, love it or leave.'"[69] Symbols like the flag, which Ortner calls "summarizing" symbols, effectively merge many ideas and emotions under one image. This type of totalization generates a loose but encompassing set of ideas and emotions that readily evoke a collective sense of "we" — as in "our" flag.[70]

The complicated nature of such symbols becomes apparent when people attempt to define what it is that makes a piece of cloth into the flag as a sacral symbol: is it the specific red-white-and-blue arrangement of stars and stripes, the cloth itself, or would a paper flag merit as much respect? If so, what about a flag drawn in crayon on a white linen sheet? In other words, when is a flag "the" flag? In religious traditions, such questions have been answered through rituals of consecration: the Hindu statue of the god Siva is just a bit of clay until it is consecrated; then it must be treated with the respect one would have for the deity himself. The same is true in the Roman Catholic and Greek Orthodox traditions, where the ritual of consecration is thought to transform bread and wine into the body and blood of Jesus Christ himself. Such forms of consecration are not explicitly invoked in the secular or civic arena, although people tend to carry the concept over in various ways. Associations like the Boy Scouts and the armed forces teach "official" techniques for how to fold the flag, salute it, raise it each morning on a flagpole, and bring it down each evening. These rule-governed procedures underscore the ethos that a flag should never be treated as just another piece of colored cloth. Yet Supreme Court decisions that burning the flag is a protected form of First Amendment free speech are widely interpreted as retreating from the religious language of a sacred flag and all the legal complexities that would develop on how to define it.

Activities that generate and express the sacral significance of key symbols like the flag are often considered to be ritual-like. While ritual-like action is thought to be that type of action that best *responds* to the sacred nature of things, in actuality, ritual-like action effectively *creates* the sacred by explicitly differentiating such a realm from a profane one. If we were to try to pin down the exact nature of the sacrality evoked in such symbols, however, we would find a type of circularity by which sacredness, when not explicitly a religious claim to divinity, is a quality of specialness, not the same as other things, standing for something important and possessing an extra meaningfulness and the ability to evoke emotion-filled images and experiences. In other words, with regard to objects as sacred symbols, their sacrality is the way in which the object is more than the mere sum of its parts and points to something beyond itself, thereby evoking and expressing values and attitudes associated with larger, more abstract, and relatively transcendent ideas.[71] This quality of sacrality is attributed not only to objects, of course, but also to places, buildings, and even people.

As symbols, geographic places are thought to be more than mere arbitrary sites where something important happens or happened in the past. Somehow the distinctive landscape, interiors, or the events that transpired there serve to imbue the site with a significance that can evoke emotional associations for those who visit there. For example, one of the great symbols of America has traditionally been that unparalleled natural landmark, Niagara Falls. From the early nineteenth century to the middle of the twentieth, Niagara Falls was the primary objective of American travel. In his study of Niagara, John Sears argues that it was the place where ideas about God's power, nature's beauty, and America's destiny came together in experiences and attitudes that helped to define what it meant to be an American both corporately and individually. Many travel books from this period repeatedly use the analogy of pilgrimage to describe a visit to Niagara, no matter whether the visitors were among the swelling tide of tourists, honeymooners, or artists seeking an experience of transcendence. In an account entitled "My Visit to Niagara," Nathaniel Hawthorne (1804–64) evoked a "pilgrim's progress" by describing his gradual convergence on the sacred site and his culminating experience of a fundamentally moral lesson.[72] Even the heavy accretions of tourism and gross consumerism that quickly packaged the experience of the Falls could not diminish its symbolic significance. Indeed, the evocative power of Niagara actually endowed the extravagant commercialism with significance, providing a type of moral justification for tourism. It linked transcendental images of America with the robust energy of unbridled consumerism, mass society, and democratic kitsch; it even represented the convergence of aesthetics and religion with the sciences of geology and hydraulic engineering. For Sears, Niagara embodied "the values and the contradictions of the society for which it served as the principal shrine."[73] Clearly, ritual-like visits to Niagara Falls, like the ritual-like ways of treating the flag, point to the intrinsic circularity of rites and symbols, namely, how such activities create the powerful communal symbols that effectively induce and justify such ritual-like responses.

In a somewhat more remote example, the activities of the astronauts who first landed on the moon were distinctly ritual-like. Neil Armstrong's formal pronouncement, "One small step for [a] man, one great step for mankind," as well as the formal erection of the American flag in a manner so reminiscent of earlier rites of colonization, evoked a complex chain of symbolic associations with the moon. While some people declared that the mysterious moon of lovers and star gazers would never be the same, others voiced another set of symbolic associations: the moon as a distant point to conquer, a symbol of the triumph of American over Soviet science, and the manifest destiny of America to reach out into space. Very similar nationalist and universal associations also attended the "conquering" of Mount Everest by Edmund Hillary and Tenzing Norkay in 1953.

Historical sites can act as powerful symbols not simply because important events took place there but also because they embody contradictory and contested interpretations of those events. For example, American battlesites like the Little Big Horn, Gettysburg, and Pearl Harbor have long been considered a type of sacred ground because of the drama of their events as well as the sheer loss of life. Yet they are also the sites of a constant and concomitant struggle to define exactly what is most important about the place and what should be the proper response. Similarly complex sites, evoking both ritual-like acts of pilgrimage and contested interpretations, would include Lenin's tomb or the memorial museums at Auschwitz and Hiroshima. As with Niagara Falls, visits to these places readily take on the style of religious pilgrimages, even though these sites distinguish sacred and profane in very secular and historical terms. Their conjunctions of hope and horror, good and evil, chaos and order, heroism and despair evoke images and emotions so unlike those of daily life as to endow these places with a tangible spirituality. At the same time, it is possible that visitors seek some resolution of all these contradictions, some experience of holism that can pull together the fragmentation of personal and national life and grant a sense of the overall goodness or stability of the whole. Even if no resolution can be clearly formulated, sufficient demarcation of the acts of visiting, confronting, and feeling—via the use of boundaries, staged progression, and accompanying narrative—can often supply an overarching framework within which contradictory emotions and meanings can be embraced.

Symbolism can evoke ritual-like activities on a much smaller scale as well. A curious example is the highly formal miniature gardens traditionally cultivated in Vietnam, China, and Japan.[74] Called "miniature mountain" (*nui non bô*) in Vietnamese, "landscape in a container" (*penzai*) in Chinese, and "stones in a container" (*bonsai*) in Japanese, these gardens are usually constructed in a small basin of water, often filled with goldfish, in the middle of which rises a small mountain of rocks, dwarf trees, and sometimes diminutive pagodas and figures. It is a miniature universe, a microcosm that not only depicts the larger macrocosm but also evokes the forces and principles that animate it—the primary elements of earth, stone and water. Cultivation of the garden is a matter of tending the balance and harmony of these elements. The historian Rolf Stein describes this type of miniature garden as a ritually delimited work, a sacred place, and analogous to a holy city, temple, or magic circle.[75] In the Chinese tradition in particular, the gardens evoke both religious and artistic associations. Trees and rocks represent health and longevity, water is a mirror for reflection and the discernment of nondualistic reality, fish denote good luck and well-being, mountains reach to heaven while enclosing womblike caves for regeneration and transformation, and the diminutive distinctness of the closed garden evokes the spirituality of the hermit who has left the social world to return to the natural one. A well-known Daoist religious ceremony unfolds around an altar that recreates the four cardinal directions, the center, the heavens above, and the hells below; the Daoist master travels through this universe as he paces around the altar bringing the various levels of the cosmos into a synchronized harmony that allows an energizing renewal of his body, the community, and the universe.[76] By the same logic, the creation of a miniature garden is a ritual-like action that uses a vast system of correspondences to establish a bounded space that invokes the interrelationship of the microcosm and the macrocosm, enabling one either to ponder their intrinsic identity or to attempt to affect the balance of one by manipulating the balance of the other.

Such gardens make particularly clear the totalizing potential of powerful symbols, that is, the way they contain worlds of associations within a condensed image, in regard to which people can act out their sense of personal and corporate involvement. In Ortner's rubric, however, some symbols summarize or condense a wealth of human experiences, while other symbols elaborate these associations by helping to sort out experience, locate it in cultural categories, and enable people to understand "how it all hangs together." Summarizing symbols may discourage thought in favor of emotional reactions, but elaborating symbols seem to provide vehicles for thinking, imaging, and communicating.[77] If the American flag, or most any other national flag, is a good example of a summarizing symbol, the miniature garden is a good example of an elaborating symbol; it suggests how this mode of "totalization" provides a type of analysis of the cosmic order and enables people to participate in the creation and sustenance of that order. In contrast to national flags, the miniature garden does not have a pronounced communal dimension, even though it is a common public sight. It is not there to rally any group ethos. It is simply a highly aesthetic expression of the way in which the intimate and personal are linked to the cosmic and impersonal.

In all of the foregoing examples, ritual-like action is activity that gives form to the specialness of a site, distinguishing it from other places in a way that evokes highly symbolic meanings. Such activities differentiate a sacred world—however minute or magnificent—in the midst of a profane one, thus affording experiences of this sacrality that transcend the profane reality of day-to-day life. Where the flag is raised, the nation lives. It asserts a certain identity, history, and value system. But it does not do so because a piece of colored cloth is strung up a pole. The symbolness of the flag lies in the multiple activities that differentiate this cloth, handle it in special ways, and respond to it with particular emotions. In the same way, it was not the vast torrents of water that made Niagara the natural embodiment of America; it was the pilgrims, tourists, poets, and honeymooners who came to experience there a complex set of connections that linked American identity to this great work of God. Hence, what makes activities around certain symbols seem ritual-like is really twofold: the way they differentiate some places from others by means of distinctive acts and responses and the way they evoke experiences of a greater, higher, or more universalized reality— the group, the nation, humankind, the power of God, or the balance of the cosmos.[78]

Performance

In recent years, much attention has focused on what ritual has in common with theatrical performances, dramatic spectacles, and public events. Most of these comparisons rest on a recognition that the performative dimension per se—that is, the deliberate, self-conscious "doing" of highly symbolic actions in public—is key to what makes ritual, theater, and spectacle what they are. While a performative dimension often coexists with other characteristics of ritual-like behavior, especially in rule-governed sports contests or responses to sacral symbols, in many instances performance is clearly the more dominant or essential element. For example, a number of studies address the ritual-like aspects of clowns and clowning. They point out how clowns follow certain rules, usually rules of inversion, by which they upset and mock the status quo. By extension, clowns themselves function as powerful symbols of cultural inversion, ludic freedom, and social innocence. However, what is most essential to what clowning is all about is the elaborately dramatic "acting out" that it involves.[79]

The qualities of performance can be analyzed in terms of several overlapping features. First of all, performances communicate on multiple sensory levels, usually involving highly visual imagery, dramatic sounds, and sometimes even tactile, olfactory, and gustatory stimulation. By marching with a crowd, crying over a tragic drama, or applauding an unconvincing politician, even the less enthusiastic participants of the audience are cognitively and emotionally pulled into a complex sensory experience that can also communicate a variety of messages. Hence, the power of performance lies in great part in the effect of the heightened multisensory experience it affords: one is not being told or shown something so much as one is led to experience something. And according to the anthropologist Barbara Myerhoff, in ritual-like behavior "not only is seeing believing, doing is believing."[80]

Another feature of performance lies in the dynamics of framing. As noted with regard to sacral symbols, distinctions between sacred and profane, the special and the routine, transcendent ideals and concrete realities can all be evoked by how some activities, places, or people are set off from others. Intrinsic to performance is the communication of a type of frame that says, "This is different, deliberate, and significant—pay attention!" By virtue of this framing, performance is understood to be something other than routine reality; it is a specific type of demonstration.[81] It can also confer on the performance the ability to signify or denote larger truths under the guise of make-believe situations. Hence, since the person talking is framed by all the conventions of a theater production—stage, curtains, tickets, audience, familiar script—we know that he is not really Hamlet, Prince of Denmark. Although his overt identity is make-believe, by virtue of the way in which the theatrical framework sets his words and deeds off from day-to-day reality, the performance is credited with the ability to convey universal truths by means of an experience not readily accessible elsewhere.

Such frames not only distinguish performance as such, they also create a complete and condensed, if somewhat artificial world—like sacral symbols, a type of microcosmic portrayal of the macrocosm. Since the real world is rarely experienced as a coherently ordered totality, the microcosm constructed on stage purports to provide the experience of a mock-totality, an interpretive appropriation of some greater if elusive totality. For the sociologist Don Handelman, "all public events, in their creation of limited social worlds, are exercises in holism."[82] By virtue of this condensing or totalizing feature, Hamlet is generally understood to speak to the human condition itself, a set of issues much larger than the story of a Danish prince or even the real-life stories of the actors and members of the audience. As a three-dimensional representation of reality, public performances can provide powerful experiences of the coherence of cultural categories and attitudes — or their incoherence, as modern theater has demonstrated. Even when performances express complex ideas, tragic ambiguity, or competing demands of conscience, as in Shakespeare's story of Hamlet, Handelman argues, "Establishing visible external forms, [they] bring out of all the possible might-have-beens a firm social reality."[83]

Hence, the ritual-like nature of performative activities appears to lie in the multifaceted sensory experience, in the framing that creates a sense of condensed totality, and in the ability to shape people's experience and cognitive ordering of the world. In brief, performances seem ritual-like because they explicitly model the world.[84] They do not attempt to reflect the real world accurately but to reduce and simplify it so as to create more or less coherent systems of categories that can then be projected onto the full spectrum of human experience. When successfully projected over the chaos of human experience, these categories can render that experience coherently meaningful and are themselves validated in that process. Anthropologists who have explored a wide variety of cultural performances, from Balinese cockfighting to Hitler's Nuremberg rallies, look to how people use these events to formulate for themselves what their culture and their community mean. While such modeling events may invoke conflicting or incoherent categories, the processual structure as they unfold in time may still achieve a rough resolution of such conflicts. In this way, many public events claim an implicit power to transform: when experienced and embodied in these orchestrated events, the categories or attitudes that appear to be in conflict can be resolved and synthesized.

Some of these features of ritual-like performance are visible in the historical pageants that were particularly popular community events in the towns and cities of America from the end of the 19th century to the middle of the 20th. Indeed, there appears to have been a veritable explosion of commemorative pageants in which people used costumes and elaborate scenery to dramatize historical events associated with their community. The Morgantown municipal centennial celebration of 1885 had the usual historical oration, a display of historical relics, and the dedication of an imposing monument, but the centerpiece was a procession in which local citizens dressed up in historical costumes and rode old wagons and farm vehicles. By the turn of the century, such processions had given way to fully developed historical pageants depicting the adventures of the early Puritans or more local events. These pageants were the medium through which these communities created images of the past that gave form to a particular sense of history and tradition. They were highly public images — the results of an intense degree of community negotiation and heated disputes over interpretation and significance. They located a community in historical time and in the social fabric of the larger world, articulating the difference between timeless values and more contingent ones. For this reason, such events were a process that could both generate and integrate differences, with the final performance depicting a synthetic consensus in very visible and memorable images of the hard-won communal cooperation. Indeed, historical pageants were "rituals of social transformation" and the instruments for the very creation and dissemination of civic traditions.[85]

The more recent quincentennial commemorations of Christopher Columbus's arrival in the New World were comparable to these turn-of-the-century historical pageants, complete with exact replicas of his ships reenacting the crossing of the Atlantic, as well as ceremonies in Mexico City in honor of the Indians killed by the Europeans and their diseases. Even though the quincentennial was full of interpretive controversy, its various public celebrations and demonstrations were relatively good "mirrors" of who Americans are and how they see themselves. If the performances involved were simply a matter of entertainment, on the one hand, or political ideology, on the other, the significance of Columbus's "discovery" versus his "conquest and annihilation" of the New World would be trivial. But most participants in these events instinctively felt that the manner in which Columbus's adventures are represented today, some five hundred years after his landing in the Americas, will shape how this country defines itself in the future.

Scholars have studied many examples of ritual-like public events to explore the power of performance to shape values and perceptions. Hitler's Nuremberg rallies, painstakingly orchestrated to express power, adulation, German mythic motifs, and forceful symbols of national unity and purpose have been repeatedly analyzed as a particularly graphic example of the use of ritual-like politics. The sheer size of these spectacles, with hundreds of thousands marching, singing, and waving flags, guaranteed that the event overwhelmed and swept along the majority of those in attendance. Particular care was taken to choreograph an awesome spectacle that impressed people with the disciplined precision and near-spiritual unity of the marchers. It appears that Hitler was well aware of the effects of these rallies since he wrote that "the man who comes to such a meeting doubting and hesitating, leaves it confirmed in his mind: he has become a member of a community." Elsewhere he notes, "I personally could feel and understand how easily a man of the people succumbs to the suggestive charm of such a grand and impressive spectacle."[86]

In the case of Mohandas Gandhi, another master of political orchestration, different values but the same features of ritual-like performance animated his public spectacles of social protest. In his 1930 campaign against the salt tax, which was part of a larger effort to win India's independence from Great Britain, Gandhi and some of his followers, called *satyagrahis* (those who seize the truth), undertook a march to the sea coast some 240 miles away in order to collect their own salt and thereby challenge the British monopoly.[87] Thousands joined them along the way and when they came to the sea, they all deliberately broke the law by gathering up salt. As everyone expected, Gandhi and many others were arrested and brought to trial, where they could further voice their views on the injustice of the tax.

Another Gandhian salt campaign, led by followers while Gandhi himself was still in jail, created an even more powerful spectacle. About 2,500 satyagrahis planned to enter a salt factory to confiscate salt, and they notified the government of their plans in time for police and barbed wire to be set up to keep the protesters out. When the satyagrahis arrived, they waded through muddy ditches surrounding the factory and marched right up to the police patroling the barbed wire. As they approached, the police beat them on their heads with iron-tipped clubs, but not one of the protesters raised an arm to defend himself. A journalist described the scene as follows:

They went down like ten-pins. From where I stood I heard the sickening whack of the clubs on unprotected skulls. The waiting crowd of marchers groaned and sucked in their breath in sympathetic pain at every blow. Those struck down fell sprawling, unconscious or writhing with fractured skulls or broken shoulders. . . . The survivors, without breaking ranks, silently and doggedly marched on until struck down. Although everyone knew that within a few minutes he would be beaten down, perhaps killed, I could detect no signs of wavering or fear. They marched silently, with heads up, without the encouragement of music or cheering or any possibility that they might escape serious injury or death. The police rushed out and methodically and mechanically beat down the second column. There was no fight, no struggle; the marchers simply walked forward until struck down.[88]

This was political theater of a deadly earnest kind, a ritualized confrontation between two value systems in which one side deliberately and vividly demonstrated to everyone the moral superiority and, hence, the justice of its cause.

For Albert Bergesen, the periodic "witch-hunts" that have coursed through American national life from 17th century Salem to the "red scare" led by Senator Joseph McCarthy in the 1950s are also examples of sociopolitical spectacles that have functioned as "national rituals" and "ritual mechanisms" for the periodic renewal of communal values.[89] For some sociologists, such campaigns are comparable to the political means by which dictators or ruling elites attempt to rid themselves of real or imagined opposition—as with Stalin in the U.S.S.R., Mao Tse-tung in China, or Pol Pot in Cambodia. Such purges may also divert attention from failed policies, focus discontent on convenient scapegoats, or streamline and reinvigorate the vast bureaucracies upon which totalitarian regimes often depend. Yet there is also evidence that the hysteria, accusations, and public confessions of large-scale witch-hunts are more complex, indirect, symbolic, and ritual-like than these pragmatic explanations appreciate. For instance, the historical record suggests that dramatic purges occur in inverse ratio to the presence of real enemies or policy failures. When analyzed more symbolically, these political performances appear to divide up the world into two absolute camps, the good and innocent on the one hand and the deviant and reprehensible on the other. With these performances, the community itself simultaneously identifies images of political deviance and images of collective tradition and proper feelings. Evil is seen as infiltrating the good community from the outside in order to contaminate and undermine it: Bergeson argues that "just as purity requires dirt for its very existence, so do political ideas of national interest require those that would undermine them to periodically dramatize their very meaning."[90] Hence, the witch-hunt's orchestration of public accusations, trials, confessions, and punishments can be a powerful means for reaffirming the status quo of the larger group and forestalling the emergence of threatening attitudes or ideas.

What is particularly ritual-like about witch-hunts is the performative features by which an elaborate cast of people publicly dramatize a contest of values, compelling observers to align themselves with the larger community or risk identification as the enemy. The performative event helps to shape social attitudes by giving dramatic form to polarized positions; people must choose, and in doing so they are drawn into the event itself. From this perspective, it has been a logical step for some analysts to go on to describe the ritual-like nature of television and other forms of media in modern society. Some have called attention to how the television industry creates "media events" by defining special occasions and creating a "meta-narrative" about national life that is grounded in sharing dramatizations of these occasions.[91] Some analysts emphasize how the features of performance described here—multifaceted sensory experience, framing, and a totalizing objectification of values—enable television to transport a viewer into experiential situations of incredible diversity and intensity.[92] While one may not taste and smell the Serbian bombardment of the city of Sarajevo in the former Yugoslavia, or actually touch the children dying of starvation in Somalia, television provided an incredibly direct and emotionally compelling experience of these distant events. While the ability of ritual and television to shape social attitudes may sometimes be exaggerated, there is little doubt that this is a particularly widespread understanding of what the experiential aspects of ritual-like performance can do.

Conclusion

The spectrum of rituals and ritual-like activities in the preceding sections reveal basic ways in which people ritualize, that is, create, deploy, and reproduce rites. The most clear-cut examples of ritual, those depicting various genres of ritual, tend to be a matter of communal ceremonies closely connected to formally institutionalized religions or clearly invoking divine beings. However, the examples of ritual-like activity suggest that what goes on in ritual is not unique to religious institutions or traditions. There are many ways to act ritually and many situations in which people have recourse to these ways, and degrees, of ritualizing. The survey of genres and ways of acting demonstrates that there is no intrinsic or universal understandings of what constitutes ritual. Indeed, few cultures have a single word that means exactly what is meant by the English word "ritual"—and part I made clear that even the English term has meant a number of things. For historical and social reasons, many cultures do not make the same distinctions that lie behind the English term. For example, although European and American societies are apt to describe table etiquette, sports, theater productions, and political rallies as ritual-like, there is still a general consensus that they are not the best examples of what we usually mean by ritual. No matter how ritual-like sports and theater might appear to be at times, we are not apt to consider them the same thing as a church wedding ceremony. We have found it appropriate to see some basic distinctions among these ways of acting even if we occasionally note how blurred those distinctions can become. Other cultures also draw and blur various distinctions. What a culture distinguishes and with what degree of clarity can reveal interesting aspects of the ways in which people in that culture are likely to experience and interpret the world.

The anthropologist Barbara Ward argued, "There is no reason why anyone attempting an outsider's analysis of another culture—or his own as if from the outside—should not erect whatever categories seem to him to be the most useful." However, she continued, "if one is to interpret the native insiders' understanding of their own culture one must try to comprehend—and use—their categories, not impose one's own."[93] Ward demonstrates this principle in a close analysis of traditional Chinese theater and makes clear that Chinese categories do not distinguish ritual and theater in the same way that European and American cultures do. First of all, traditional Chinese theater, often called Peking opera, is quite different from any contemporary forms of Euro-American theater. More like the Italian Commedia dell' Arte tradition that was so popular throughout Europe from the 16th through the 18th centuries, Chinese theater has no realism. There are standardized roles with clear conventions for depicting heroes and villains. For example, in accordance with traditional Chinese color symbolism, red-faced characters are always good and brave, black-faced ones are honest and strong, but white-faced characters are understood to be evil, crafty, and cunning. Chinese theater also has little sense of interpreting a written script; performance itself remains the dominant medium. Ward finds that traditional staging is "not opera, not play, not ballet, but all three together with music-hall and acrobatics too" and it adds up to "a simultaneous assault upon nearly all the senses."[94] It may be this feature in particular that makes Chinese theater appeal to all social levels and classes, not just the cultured or affluent elite courted by most Euro-American theater productions.

There are several ways in which Chinese notions of theater and ritual appear to overlap. Like most traditional theater, Chinese opera performances are often part of a temple festival, usually held to honor the birthday of the temple deity. The stage is carefully placed where the deity can watch the show, and the most important performances during a festival are those that start late at night after the human audience has retired. From about two or three in the morning until dawn, the actors perform just for the god. Exacting rules for the orientation of the stage and the dressing rooms follow traditional geomantic and cosmological theories concerning *fengshui* (wind-water), yin and yang, and the five directions. The space demarcated by the temple and stage becomes "a kind of ritual precinct" for the duration of the festival: "the south-facing gods and the north-facing actors are each flanked by the Yang and Yin influences of east and west respectively and the audience sits, as it were, in the centre . . . of the cosmos under Heaven."[95] In addition to orienting the stage as an extension of the temple and offering the performances to the deity housed there, the whole acting troupe participates in the public offerings that accompany the temple festival. It is also customary for each actor to pay respects to a backstage shrine for the troupe's patron deity before he or she steps out on to the stage.

The ritual dimensions of traditional theater are also apparent in the "magical plays" and "shamanic roles" frequently performed. For example, whenever a theater is erected in a place for the first time, it is the actors who ritually exorcise any demonic forces in order to ensure the safety of the troupe and the audience. They do this by performing "The White Tiger," in which an actor dressed as a tiger is chased around the stage and dressing area by a black-faced deity who eventually subdues, chains, and rides the tiger away. Not only does this performance lack an audience—in fact, they are kept at a distance for their own protection—but it is also accompanied by various taboos, such as not speaking after the actor has donned the tiger mask. Both actors and local people take this exorcist performance very seriously. Many also believe that traditional theater performances can bring good fortune; that is, they are ritually effective at influencing deities and demons and delivering spiritual and material rewards to the community. Hence, the traditional Chinese view does not distinguish between ritual and technological acts, or even between the natural world and the supernatural world with a special corps of experts for each. Certainly some offerings and protective rites can be done by anyone; others are more complex and require the services of specialists, like actors or priests.[96] Whether the choice is a troupe of actors, an ordained Daoist priest, a Buddhist monk, or a local shaman depends on class, locale, and the type of ritual work to be accomplished.

If traditional Chinese theater is full of ritual, it is not surprising to find that traditional Chinese ritual is full of theater. One of the most striking aspects of Daoist rites for the dead in Taiwan and Hong Kong is the hiring, if finances permit, of an acrobatic troupe to aid the priest in his ritual work. In particular, the priest leads the acrobats in an elaborately orchestrated pantomine of an assault on the hells where the soul of the deceased is being held until officially rescued or pardoned. The acrobats repeatedly somersault off tiers of scaffolding to portray their descent to hell and dance with brandished swords in the ensuing battle to free the soul. Yet it is not quite correct to describe these activities in performative terms of "depicting" or "portraying." As ritual acts, they are understood to be actually effecting the release of the soul, not just symbolizing it. For a foreigner accustomed to associating ritual, especially funerals, with stern decorum, sober readings, and quiet hymns, the circuslike aspect of the Daoist funeral can be quite disconcerting. Certainly the European and American tendency to see ritual as an enactment of prescribed textual canons can attribute more instrumentality to the words than the actions that are performed. Yet this cultural assumption can obscure the ways in which ritualization is conceived in the traditional Chinese context, where actions are usually more instrumental than words.

Despite the potential for great cultural variations, however, it is still possible to point to some basic strategies that appear to underlie many ways of ritualizing. Certainly public assembly, the repetition of gestures already considered "ritual tradition" by a community, and the invocation of divine beings are widespread and familiar methods of ritualization. Yet Chinese theater and other examples of ritual-like action suggest that many essential qualities of ritual do not depend on the context of institutionalized religion. In particular, ritual-like activities reveal an even more fundamental dimension of ritualization—the simple imperative to *do* something in such a way that the doing itself gives the acts a special or privileged status. The style of doing creates a type of framework around the act that communicates the message "this has extra significance." People stand up and sit down, congregate and disperse, talk or sit quietly. *How* they do these things can set these activities off, both to the participants and to others, as bearing a nonroutine significance. Even if people simply sit and observe silence, as in the case of a Quaker meeting, the ritual framework is established by assembling according to practices that evoke a familiar Quaker tradition, express a meaningful ethos, and reflect a specific community structure. For Quakers these practices were laid out in the 17th century.

So Friends, when you come together to wait upon God, come orderly in the fear of God: the first that enters into the place of your meeting, be not careless, nor wander up and down, either in body or mind; but innocently sit down in some place, and turn in thy mind to the light, and wait upon God singly, as if none were present but the Lord; and *here* thou art strong. And the next that comes in, let them in simplicity of heart, sit down and turn in to the same light, and wait in the Spirit: and so all the rest coming in, in the fear of the Lord, sit down in pure stillness and silence of all flesh, and wait in the light."[97]

Hence, to ritualize silent sitting, whether one is a Quaker or a Zen monk, one first evokes a history of practices and beliefs as the context for this action. This is usually done simply by going to a place that, as defined by the tradition and current practice, is differentiated from other places and uses, either a meeting house or a meditation hall. One can, of course, ritualize quiet sitting alone in one's own home, and the techniques for doing so are versions of those used in the public gathering: one chooses a spot with some care and makes plans for remaining undisturbed; then one settles in with deliberate attention to body posture and mental discipline for a definite period of time. Both public and private rituals are usually performed according to a schedule, such as once every week on the same day at precisely ten o'clock in the morning or at the same time every day. Such scheduled periodicity not only facilitates the assembling of a community but also helps differentiate the activity as deliberate and meaningful in comparison to all other activities.

It is central to many practices and strategies of ritualization that people do not always see themselves as actually constructing such events. They are more apt to perceive themselves as simply responding to circumstances—whether the circumstances are a birthday party, a death in their midst, or the gathering of Friends at a Quaker meeting house. While the theories examined in part I formulate many different reasons for why people ritualize, these are not the explanations that most ritual participants themselves would give for their actions. For participants, the most common reasons given for joining in a ritual activity tend to be answers such as "we have always done this," "it's our tradition," or "we do it because it makes such-and-such positive thing happen." Although these explanations may not be particularly satisfying to the outsider, it would be wrong to conclude that most people do not know why they are involved in a ritual situation. Explaining why they do rites in terms an outsider would understand is not the same thing as a reflective self-awareness of ritual symbols, meanings, aesthetics, styles, rules, and oddities. Nonetheless, it has been suggested, and with good reason, that ritualized activities are ways of acting that do not particularly encourage a great deal of immediate and overt explaining. As these typical answers imply, ritualization gives people the sense that these activities do not need a lot of justification. They appear to address a very specific and obvious need, or have a sufficiently long history that in itself justifies them. Indeed, it is more common in most communities to need a good reason *not* to participate in ritual activities.

As with ritual action, people tend not to see how they construct tradition and meaning. They see the chanting of a medieval Latin litany, the recitation of the story of Exodus around the seder table at Passover, and the performance of a historical pageant celebrating the founding of their town. They do not usually see themselves selecting among practices, heightening their archaic prestige, and generally polishing a past that primarily acts to shape the significance of the present. In ritualization, people tend to see themselves as responding or transmitting—not creating. The highly orchestrated activities of ritualization appear to be the appropriate thing to do, if not the easiest.

This naturalization of ritual activity seems to be an effect of the performative and traditionalizing features of ritualization—as well as the strategic degree to which these and other features are developed. The performative dimension frames a particular environment—such as an altar, arena, or stage—usually as a type of totalizing microcosm. Given the construction of this specific environment, which is readily assumed and rarely noticed as such, the activities conducted within are perceived as natural and appropriate *responses* to that environment. At an altar created with steps, lamps, central table, offerings, and consecrating invocations, a priest naturally addresses God. In a purified arena precisely measured out with a circle of rice straw, the sumo wrestler from the team of the West faces off against the wrestler from the team of the East. On a stage telescoped by ever-widening rings of seats, a curtain is lifted, as if from a large window, and there in the circles of lights, framed tightly by false walls and horizons, we await a concentrated portrayal of distilled human experience. Ritualization quietly creates an environment within which quite distinctive symbolic behaviors can appear to be proper and effective responses.

The naturalness of ritualized activities is also promoted in part by traditionalism, the assumption that what is being done derives its legitimacy from precedents vaguely rooted in the past. Most theories of ritual have pointed out the nearly ubiquitous tendency of ritual action to invoke both the past and present, long-standing tradition as well as current concerns, or the larger cosmic order and the specific immediate situation. Roy Rappaport, for example, couches this observation in terms of the "canonical" elements of ritual, those more or less invariant messages already encoded that refer to things done before, in contrast to the "indexical" elements that transmit information concerning very immediate social, psychic, or physical states.[98] Similarly, A. L. Becker points out that the more spontaneous an action is, the more it is taken to express the present. In an absolute sense, no action can be completely spontaneous because we do not exist totally in the present; we carry categories and modes of expression acquired in our past and shared with others, and it is through these that we express ourselves in ways that others can understand. In contrast to the significance of spontaneity, Becker suggests that the least spontaneous activities, those dictated not by the current situation but by inherited or preshaped dispositions and concerns, tend to express the past.[99] While most effective action appeals to some balance of spontaneity and cultural repetition of the past, ritual action is especially characterized by such traditionalization and deliberate appeals to the past, even though it does not intend to ignore the current moment. Ritual repetition and redundancy, formal language and gestures, and direct and indirect references to an idealized tradition all effectively posit the existence of powerful forces understood as rooted in the past. These forces are invoked in ways that contextualize and subordinate the current moment, thereby ordering the relations of past and present and establishing a sense of continuity, security, and direction. Some methods of ritualizing even allow a participant to adjust understandings of the past in the light of new situations and a more promising sense of direction.

The naturalness of ritual action is also dependent on the coherence and degree of ritualization invoked. The greater the number of ritual features invoked, the more "set off," imposing, authoritative, and even traditional the event appears to be. The more spontaneity incorporated within the sequence and style of events, the more immediate, personal, and casual it seems. If the speeches are highly formal but the food and eating arrangements are very informal, the effect is quite different from the reverse situation. Greater formality in the speeches would attest to the authority and prestige of those talking, emphasizing hierarchical relationships and the power of their particular wisdom. Greater formality given to the shared meal would attest to the relative equality of the community, while casual speeches would further imply that power and wisdom are the collective possession of the immediate community and their traditions. If too elaborately ritualized, an event like a graduation ceremony might express an arrogant or even impersonal ethos. If, however, the occasion is too casually or haphazardly ritualized, it may not effectively evoke any sense of tradition or respect for the solemnity of the passage and the dignity of the community.

The degree to which activities are ritualized—for instance, how much communality, how much appeal to deities and other familiar rites, how much formality or attention to rules, and how much emphasis on performance or appeal to traditional precedents—is the degree to which the participants suggest that the authoritative values and forces shaping the occasion lie beyond the immediate control or inventiveness of those involved. It may be assumed that these values and forces are lodged in divine beings, in a historical models, or even in the natural superiority of some people over others. Fundamental to all the strategies of ritualization examined previously is the appeal to a more embracing authoritative order that lies beyond the immediate situation. Ritualization is generally a way of engaging some wide consensus that those acting are doing so as a type of natural response to a world conceived and interpreted as affected by forces that transcend it—transcend it in time, influence, and meaning, if not in ontological status. Ritualization tends to posit the existence of a type of authoritative reality that is seen to dictate to the immediate situation. In many sociological analyses, this is one of the most basic social acts in the construction of reality.[100]

❧ ⋅ ❧

PART III

CONTEXTS

The Fabric of Ritual Life

A ritual never exists alone. It is usually one ceremony among many in the larger ritual life of a person or community, one gesture among a multitude of gestures both sacred and profane, one embodiment among others of traditions of behavior down from one generation to another. In other words, for each and every ritual, there is a thick context of social customs, historical practices, and day-to-day routines that, in addition to the unique factors at work in any given moment in time and space, influence whether and how a ritual action is performed. The warp and weft of handed-down customs and real-life situations form the fabric from which specific rites are constructed and found meaningful. Hence, most of the activities surveyed in part II were presented quite unnaturally, removed from the general and specific contexts that would very much affect any particular performance and interpretation. The purpose of this section is to provide some discussion of the context of ritual action by introducing both the major analytic tools that have been used to define and characterize this context and the issues that have been central to debates on the place of ritual in sociocultural life.

Studies of ritual have addressed a number of the more obvious features of this ritual context, such as issues of density and style—why some societies have more or less ritual than others and why the general style of ritual can differ so clearly from one culture to another. Attempts to answer these questions have given rise to various analytic distinctions, such as typological schemes that differentiate primitive, classical, and modern styles of ritual, or contrasts between "orthodoxic" societies (where more emphasis is put on proper doctrinal beliefs) and "orthopraxic" ones (where more emphasis is placed on proper performance of ritual obligations). Deeply implicated in both types of schemes is yet a third one, the conventional if imprecise distinction between traditional societies and secular societies. In traditional societies, ritual tends to be regarded as a robust dimension of shared communal life, while in secular societies it is routinely described as constrained by the antireligious forces presumed to underlie modernity. Older distinctions between "church" and "sect" have also been used to explain aspects of ritual density, while more recent comparisons of the place of ritual in oral and literate societies have begun to track yet another set of significant factors.

These attempts to categorize and explain various types of ritual context, laid out in chapter 6, are closely connected to another major issue, ritual change, which is the focus of chapter 7. One's viewpoint on the usefulness of a number of the distinctions mentioned here will directly affect one's outlook on how and why ritual activity changes. Many religious, civic, and ethnic communities today are exploring various forms of deliberate change; they face anxious questions about the degree to which people can tamper with ritual traditions before the authority and dignity of these traditions are undermined. Other groups, in confronting either the creativity or the failure of newly invented rituals, wonder how a community goes about evaluating whether a ritual is working. The issue of ritual change also encompasses questions concerning the impact of tourism on the ritual life of traditional communities and the influence of televised rites and ritualized television on mass culture. As the context of ritual life in the twentieth century unfolds, it is providing unexpected evidence for new forms of ritualizing and new ways of thinking about ritual.

Many popular and scholarly books today address questions about ritual. In no small measure, questions about the place and nature of ritual are now the medium through which people are apt to talk about theological issues, religious institutions, the quality of modern spiritual life, and efforts for the future. Of course, there are no definitive judgments or answers. No one is even sure that the questions we are asking are the best ones. Yet the fact that these *are* our questions suggests a great deal about the role given to ritual in current understandings of religion and culture. Some people speak of an enduring human "need" for ritual, while others characterize human progress and social development as nothing less than a gradual escape from the social and ideological constraints of ritualism. Some see a historical rejection of ritual now being followed by a redemptive return to ritual; others, however, have heralded the definitive death of ritual while working heroically to stave off its total loss with archival film footage and recordings. Some have reidentified ritual in terms of a panhuman instinct for performance that is teetering on the edge of an unprecedented evolutionary leap into new modes of creative expression; others have begun to scavenger among any and all traditions to find novel bits and appealing pieces for dramatizing a new spiritual bricolage. Chapter 8 attempts to sort out these voices and perspectives. It traces the way in which the concept of ritual has functioned in our approaches to religion and to the ethnographic "other." It concludes with an analysis of the way in which the idea of a universal propensity for ritual has affected the way we both ritualize and theorize.

❧ · ❧

SIX

Ritual Density

The issue of ritual density—namely, why some societies or historical periods have more ritual than others—is rarely addressed directly. Usually some account of ritual density is the by-product of theories of the evolution of religion or the classification of types of religious cosmologies or institutions. For example, William Robertson Smith's early theory of ritual and religion, presented in chapter 2, contained an implicit explanation for why ancient Arabic tribal communities had more ritual, with a more compelling public nature, than the Free Church of Scotland did in his own day. More recently, Mary Douglas has explicitly addressed the issue by means of ahistorical sociological comparisons. Although this chapter can only review a handful of useful approaches, the issues they raise are arguably among the most interesting in the study of religion today. These approaches include formulations of the principles behind the systematic organization of rites, typological schemes (that is, sets of categories for different types of rituals), and contrasts between orthodoxy and orthopraxy, traditional and secular, oral and literate, and church and sect.

Systems

How rites relate to each other within a ritual system and how such systems differ from each other may be one of the most undeveloped areas in the study of ritual. Too often attention has focused on either one dominant ritual or a comprehensive cataloging of all ritual activity. There are only a few analytical tools or models for a systems analysis of ritual practices. One such tool is simply the identification of replicated symbols and gestures that create homologies among different ritual situations. The symbols of birth, for example, may not only dominate the rites to welcome a newborn but also turn up in rites to mark the transition to adulthood, the passage from the world of the living to the world of the dead, and even in the ancestral ceremonies that link the dead to the fertility of successive generations. In this case, the content or structure of the rites themselves create links that group them into a coherent set. While most of the rites presented in chapter 4 were removed from their actual context in a larger organzation of ritual practices, they were grouped in terms of identifiable classes of rites (such as rites of passage, calendrical rites, political rites). So Chinese birth rites were given as an example of the class of life crisis rites that also includes initiations, marriages, and death rites. For the most part, the classes identified in chapter 4 are analytical ones invented by scholars; in some cases, however, they also correspond to distinctions and connections among rites that are made by the ritual performers themselves by virtue of replicated symbols, gestures, and terminology.

Such systematic linkages can be terribly important for understanding the significance of a single ritual act. The Chinese "full month ritual" that ends the confinement of mother and newborn is echoed in the traditional capping ceremony to mark transition into adulthood and in the preparation of the corpse for burial. Likewise, the birth practices associated with the god Taishen and the restless soul of the newborn are echoed in the rites to settle the soul of the deceased in the extended sequence of funeral ceremonies. If the theme of rebirth is also replicated in the marriage ceremony, then marriage becomes a part of this extended sequence of interconnected rites, implying the intrinsic importance of a spouse to one's basic identity. In many cultures, however, marriage ceremonies are *not* symbolically linked to a birth-initiation-death ritual sequence. Instead, a rather different set of symbols links marriage to the rituals attending trade negotiations or the determination of the winner and the loser in contests of strength. The religious and cultural significance of marriage and marriage rituals could easily be misunderstood if the larger ritual context, created by symbolic echoes and duplications, is ignored.[1]

Generally, a society has more than just one ritual system; usually, multiple systems overlap, sometimes in tension with each other, sometimes in complementary harmony. At times, the Christians of China and Africa have felt caught between two ritual systems deemed incompatible—traditional rites to the ancestors on the one hand, and Christian rites that explicitly forbid the "idolatry" of worshiping other gods, on the other hand. Some groups, like the Chinese peasants who joined the 19th-century Christianized Great Peace (Taiping) Rebellion, burned their ancestral tablets so as to comply with the demands of the Christian system. Other groups tried to work out a compromise, frequently arguing that ancestral practices are not rituals of worship addressed to gods but simply customs signaling great respect. Most often, people tried to participate in both ritual systems without worrying too much about how they fit together.

Some cultures, such as traditional Hawaiian society, appear to have had a relatively neat ritual system that explicitly integrated, however loosely, multiple and sometimes competing subsystems by means of a loose hierarchization that simultaneously differentiated and integrated the pantheon, priestly specialists, sacred places and objects, ceremonial occasions, and even clientele.[2] The system behind the Mukanda initiation ritual of the Ndembu, described in Chapter 2, involved a temporal system of calendrical rites focusing on the village community that was complemented by a geographic system of regionally-defined rites, performed in response to particular events, which drew several villages together and underscored their mutual interdependence. The Mukanda, as a non-calendrical rite, was organized whenever enough boys came of age in the larger regional network. Some ritual systems have such complex histories and dynamics that any general principles of organization remain elusive or very provisional. Chinese religion, for example, has long demonstrated a complex interaction among any number of levels of ritual life, including the local level of village religion, which embraces but goes beyond domestic and lineage practices, the imperial government level of Confucian (or Communist) orthodoxy and bureaucratic control, and various regional levels defined by the practices of any number of Taoist, Buddhist, sectarian or lineage associations.[3]

The anthropologist Pierre Smith has tried to characterize the organization of rites in terms of a few structuralist principles. *Periodic* rites, such as those for life crises and calendrical holidays, are balanced by *occasional* rites that respond to specific situations, such as rites of affliction or political enthronements. In addition, rites organized around the *individual* are balanced by those organized around the *collective*. Periodic rites form a system "along an axis of the syntagmatic type; each rite in the series will necessarily be preceded and followed by another in a clearly determined order which will be repeated with each recurrence of the cycle." For Smith, therefore, any one ritual within a periodic system is incomplete and meaningless by itself; its significance depends upon its place in the complete sequence. The sequence of life crisis rites usually forms a periodic system for the individual, while a sequence of annual rites closely tied to the seasons forms a periodic system for the collective. Indeed, Smith suggests that all periodic systems attach themselves to the natural order, either the astronomical order of the seasons or the biological order of the human life span. As a result, an irreversible passage of time is experienced "as an ordered series of eternal re-beginnings and repetitions."[4] The close identification of the life of the collective with the eternal regeneration of the seasons can give rise to powerful symbols of the naturalness or rightness of the collective, even evoking a type of immortality accessible through identification with the continuity of this unending cycle. Such symbols are particularly prominent in nationalistic rites that emphasize the people's connection to the land or that attempt to inspire the "ultimate sacrifice" of laying down one's life for the sake of one's country.

In contrast to periodic rites, Smith sees occasional rites as primarily a reactive response to some form of disorder. They organize themselves into a loose system by virtue of a paradigmatic logic in which a basic ritual structure is replicated in a variety of quite independent situations. While most societies have some form of periodic *and* occasional ritual system, a society may emphasize one more than the other, possibly even differing as to which system is associated with the individual and the collective. Among the Bedik of Senegal, for example, Smith found that the collective rites are organized with seasonal periodicity but also closely integrated with a set of periodic life crisis rites. This organization suggests that the Bedik view of the relationship between nature and society differs significantly from the view Smith finds among the Rwandans. The Rwandans appear to have very little ritual recognition of the collective as an entity in need of periodic reaffirmation. In their view, society is an extension of nature and does not need any such effort. The bulk of their ritual focuses instead on occasional rites that intervene to correct a dangerous situation in the natural-political order, usually by repressing deviations that range from physical abnormalities to political uprisings. In contrast, the Bedik see their society as a cultural construction that needs to be regularly affirmed and legitimated, primarily by "naturalizing" it—that is, by working to make it correspond to the natural cycle of the seasons and to replicate the equally naturally cycle of biological life.[5]

There are other ways to perceive and analyze the organization of rites. One method that regularly turns up in discussions of ritual density concerns the historical development of a corpus of rituals guarded and maintained by a class of priests. In this case, an elite ritual system gradually grows quite distinct and removed from the more flexible ritual customs of the rest of the community; the latter may also develop their own ritual specialists, usually less formal, who offer their clientele ritual services not provided by the more elite priesthood. This is a simplistic description of the development of "high" and "low" ritual systems. The anthropologist Roy Rappaport has analyzed some properties of these types of systems by contrasting "rituals" and "liturgical orders." As such, rituals involve the performance of set sequences of formal physical and spoken acts not created by the performers themselves; they are primarily "self-referential," what Rappaport calls "indexical." That is, they express the current situation of the actors, pointing to immediate meanings and purposes. By contrast, liturgical orders, which also involve predetermined sequences of actions and speech, are best seen as predominantly "canonical"; that is, the messages encoded in them are invariant and impersonal, concerned with the universal and the eternal, and thereby invested with elaborate propriety. While liturgical orders may give some room to self-referential performances that communicate something immediate and individual about the activities or actors, they are, at best, minimally self-referential, and their authority, dignity and comprehensiveness rest on this canonicity.[6]

For Rappaport, individual "rites" are always part of a larger "liturgical order" that encodes a basic worldview that is simultaneously cosmic, cultural, physical, and biological. The more fully people are pressed to participate in a well-established liturgical order, the more they are being pressed to conform to the basic worldview encoded in the liturgical canon. The authority of this liturgical order is a result of the invariance of the canonical, non-self-referential encoding, and it gives rise to a particular notion of the sacred as that "quality of unquestionableness imputed . . . to postulates [that are] absolutely unfalsifiable and objectively unverifiable." In other words, the more participants in a ritual conform to the canonical structure of the liturgical order by minimizing any self-referentiality, the more authority is located within the liturgy itself. As a consequence, Rappaport concludes, in this type of system the "less than punctilious performance of a ritual" or any form of liturgical experimentation can undermine the authority of the liturgy and all that rests on it.[7]

The Christian sacramental system and the Indian Vedic ritual system have probably received the most attention by scholars interested in analyzing the overall logic, connecting symbols, and replicated structures of large ritual systems.[8] Smaller systems have also been studied, such as Chinese Taoist rites, the ritual life of the Sherpas of Nepal, and, as we will see, the modern system of Soviet rites established in the former U.S.S.R. in the late 1960s.[9] All of these studies provide convincing evidence that a ritual must be understood within the context of its larger system, whether this system is elaborate or minimal and the connections overt or latent. What is less clear is how the internal organization of multiple and overlapping ritual systems relates to the sociocultural roles and meanings of the rites. Some evidence suggests that the very practices that generate and maintain the systemization of ritual — processes of hierarchization, centralization, replication, marginalization, and the like — can be powerful forces in politics, regional identity and interregional relations, economics, social stratification, philosophical speculation, and theological abstraction.[10] As such, the systemization of ritual practice would not simply relate to other social and cultural phenomena as much as it would help constitute them.

Typologies

A variety of typological exercises represent the most comprehensive attempts to account for ritual density, although many of them no longer have broad support. Some of the principles built into these typological schemes, for example, echo the discredited assumptions behind the evolutionists and functionalists discussed in chapter 2. The evolutionists charted a developmental progression from the "primitiveness" of tribal magic to the higher or more civilized religions, such as Christianity. James Frazer, for example, echoed this point while adding that progress did not mean that all forms of magic are left behind, even in Christianity. Yet prior to Frazer's death, such evolutionary schemes for understanding different religions and ritual systems came to be seen as harboring a rich set of cultural biases. The functionalists, therefore, took a different tack by attempting to find a more or less direct relationship between the form of social organization in a community and the basic elements of its ritual and belief system. While direct relationships that prove particular social organizations to be the *cause* and particular types of religions to be the *effect* remained elusive, and direct functionalism in general was gradually discredited as simplistic, few scholars deny there is a relationship of some kind. The question remains of how best to conceive of what is related to what and how best to describe complex relationships that go well beyond any simple formulation of cause and effect. One way has been the use of typologies that provide a non-commital, non-causal correlation between forms of social organization and types of religious ideas, ritual behavior, and general worldview. Yet some typologies succeed better than others in laying out these correlations without recourse to undue emphasis on evolutionary developmentalism or cause-and-effect functionalism.

Most modern typological enterprises demonstrate the lingering influence of the great German sociologist, Max Weber (1864–1920), whose work explored both the historical and structural relationships between religion and society. In particular, Weber formulated the social constraints on religious experience and the influence of religious motives on social action and institutions. His best known study, *The Protestant Ethic and the Spirit of Capitalism*, for example, described the influence of ascetic Calvinism on the rise of capitalism in Europe.[11] His subsequent studies of the relation of religious ideas and socioeconomic attitudes in China, India, and ancient Israel attempted to support his thesis concerning the special interaction between Calvinism and capitalism. Weber's work was rooted in a vision of a relentless process of "rationalization" by which earlier, more unified religious and moral worlds gave way to the disenchanted ethos and secular institutions of the modern world. He did not intend a single, inevitable evolutionary process. Instead, he saw rationalization as a multidirectional process of increasing organizational differentiation and complexity; it enabled the social system to gain both greater autonomy and adaptability with regard to its environment. Hence, for Weber, magical (and futile) attempts to coerce the environment give way to more complex analyses of submission to fate, enabling a more efficient use of resources and more abstract processes of explanation. He described a complicated system of correlations whereby changes within the religious symbolic system (usually in the direction of greater differentiation) affect the whole sphere of social and religious life (theological concepts, religious experts, organizations, and the general place of religion).[12] The process of rationalization was the human effect of making distinctions, raising questions, and looking for intellectual coherence and economic efficiency by means of increasingly abstract levels of generalization.

Ultimately, Weber described these processes of rationalization by means of a set of ahistorical "ideal types" that illustrate different basic religious orientations, their social context, and their influence on history. In *Sociology of Religion*, he contrasted the magic, taboo, and emotionalism of so-called primitive religion with the more rational doctrines, practices, and ethics associated with world religions and the rise of modern society. Weber argued that as an "ideal type," or a model of one interwoven set of religious and socioeconomic forces, the supernatural order of primitive religion is experienced as immanent rather than transcendent, with the human and divine forming a single reality rather than two radically different ways of being. Spirits, which are associated with natural objects, artifacts, animals, or persons, are seen as impersonal yet willful and mobile. Concerned to secure aid and deflect mischief from these beings, primitive religion employs the magician, an ad hoc professional whose expertise rests on the ability to be possessed and mediate relations with these spirits. So-called magical rites that manipulate, cajole, or appease the spirits are rooted in the notion of *do ut des*, "I give (to you) so that you will give (to me)!"[13]

He went on to contrast the magician with the more rational-ethical religious system that emerges with the priest, who acts as a more formal mediator of a more stable form of cult. The magician's capricious world of spirits is also organized into a stable pantheon of deities that exists independently of human beings and, therefore, less open to human coercion. In this context, the ritual imagery used to address the spirits evokes selfless worship rather than exchange. Taboos to mandate communal values (do not swim in the month when the dead visit, do not speak to your father-in-law, do not mix dairy and meat products, and so on) give way to a more abstract system of ethical norms (love your neighbor as yourself, treat all people as your brothers and sisters, a noble man does not engage in pretense, and the like). A "rationalized" notion of the divine depicts a higher level of abstraction; it is a god that is more aloof, described in less anthropomorphic and more universal terms. The effect is to place more responsibility for the way things are on people, not on the activities of willful spirits and deities. Concomitantly, ritual activities shift from an emphasis on the importance of precise external actions to an emphasis on the importance of internal intentions.

Although he traced a developmental process from a primitive-magical worldview to a rational-religious one, Weber also acknowledged that all societies contain both orientations in varying proportions. The mind-set of *do ut des* clings, he wrote, "to the routine and the mass religious behavior of all peoples at all times and in all religions. The normal situation is that the burden of prayers . . . is the aversion of the external evils of this world and the inducement of the external advantages of this world."[14] Weber also went on to identify a third orientation, beyond both the magical and the rational models of religiosity and just as likely as either to be part of any particular religious tradition. It is characterized, he thought, by an ethic in which religious concerns are almost completely internalized and their purpose is to "bring about a meaningful total relationship" between the pattern of life and goals like salvation or enlightenment. In this model, ritual activities are replaced by ethical prescriptions, just as rituals of worship (e.g., chanted hymns of praise) replaced the magical practices of *do ut des* of exchange (e.g., gifts to ancestors to ensure a harvest).[15] The magician and priest are succeeded by the individual seeker of salvation through proper ethical intentions, a rather Calvinist figure, in fact.

Somewhat outside these ideal types and models of religiosity, Weber drew up another typological system based on what he identified as the two most critical principles shaping religious life. The first, the principle of religious action, imagines a spectrum in which the direction or purpose of religious action ranges from improvement of this world because it is considered redeemable, to abandoning this world in order to redeem one's innermost self. The second, the principle of religious experience, imagines a spectrum in which religious experience ranges from mystical perceptions of wholeness and identity to ascetic perceptions of unworthiness and alienation. Weber used these two principles to set up four logically contrasting positions: inner-worldly (world-improving) mysticism, otherworldly (world-abandoning) mysticism, inner-worldly asceticism, and otherworldly asceticism.[16] However, it is easier to describe them in a slightly different order. The otherworldly mystic tries to repress personal desires and worldly involvement since they obstruct the dissociation from this life that the mystic sees as necessary for salvation. The otherworldly ascetic, however, does not try to forsake the world so much as gain mastery and control over it, usually beginning with control over the bodily and then the mental self. The focus of the ascetic's disciplines of control are purely devotional goals, such as love of God; the rewards of this discipline will be reaped in another realm entirely. Inner-worldly mystics make no attempt to escape involvement in worldly affairs, but they often attempt to cultivate a type of indifference so as to experience an underlying unity with the whole. For inner-worldly ascetics, however, the focus is on attaining mastery and control over the worldliness (that is, the flaws or sins) within the human personality, with the expectation that the results of such mastery will be evidenced in this life in the human world.[17]

In applying this scheme, Weber characterized the inner-worldly asceticism of Protestantism, particularly Calvinism, as an extreme form of religious ethical-rationalism in which individual responsibility is of the greatest importance. God is very powerful but very remote; ritual is of limited use in fulfilling the ethical prescriptions on which salvation is seen to rest. Weber saw Buddhism as the other extreme, a pure form of otherworldly mysticism, promoted by contemplative monks who abandon their homes to wander and meditate in the hope of attaining complete deliverance from the bonds of human suffering. This extreme, he noted, also has relatively little use for communal, God-directed ritual.[18] One could deduce from the Weberian typology that ritual may be most prevalent and deemed most critical in the other two religious orientations, those he described as otherworldly asceticism or inner-worldly mysticism. This implies that ritual is closely associated with communal religiosity that sees the necessity of ritual experts to mediate its relationships to the spiritual world.

For the sociologist Robert Bellah, religious evolution is a matter of moving "from a situation in which world, self, and society are seen to involve the immediate expression of occult powers to one in which the exercise of religious influences is seen to be more direct and 'rational'" — a formulation that reflects both Weber's typological schema and late-19th-century evolutionary perspectives. Bellah identifies his own five "ideal types" of religiosity: primitive religion, archaic religion, historic religion, early modern religion, and modern religion, each a fundamental stage in a historical-evolutionary process in which religious, cultural, social, economic, and political forces interact.[19]

In Bellah's "primitive" stage, religious consciousness characteristically focuses on a single unified cosmos in which the order of the natural and social worlds is replicated in the order of the spirits. People are concerned to maintain the harmony of these orders and attain the basic human goods of bountiful harvests, health, and children. There is no sense of an alternative or transcendent reality, little formulation of a life after death, and ethical-moral-religious behavior (church and state are one and the same) is understood to be modeled on the activities of mythic ancestors. Ritually, primitive religion does not involve worship per se, but a type of mystical communion through sacrifice in which participants become identified with the mythical beings that they portray. Although Bellah describes this as "ritual par excellence," he notes that the distance between human and divine beings is too slight for propitiation, the mediation of priests, the formality of ceremony, or even the gathering of spectators. For Bellah, this is the religion of the Australian aborigines, described by Durkheim as the most elementary form of religion. In their ritual, the destruction of an offering transforms it into a divine substance itself and affords a communion in which this substance is shared by all. Such primitive ritual is mainly concerned with the solidarity of the community by socializing younger generations into the norms of behavior and the assumptions of the cosmology.[20]

Bellah characterizes "archaic religion" in terms of the emergence of a full cult organization with a pantheon of gods, priestly intermediaries, worship activities, and close links to some form of divine kingship. The archaic cosmology is still a monistic whole but much more hierarchically ordered. The religious and sociopolitical orders are still not differentiated from each other, and the priests do not have an autonomous clientele or congregation.[21] The ancient kingdoms of Babylon, Egypt, and China would be examples of this archaic form of religion.

"Historic religion" is the stage in which Bellah sees the development of the idea of a truly transcendent reality, the divine as totally different from human reality. This concept effectively breaks up the cosmic unity of primitive and archaic worldviews and generates ongoing speculation concerning the relationship of this world to the other one. Ideas about the fallen, sinful, or disobedient nature of humanity, the necessity of redemption, and the dualistic forces of good and evil all follow from this conceptual shift. For Bellah, this historic stage represents the beginnings of a "demythologization" of primitive and archaic religious traditions; that is, the highest deity comes to be conceived in more abstract, universal, and nonanthropomorphic terms. These developments, in turn, encourage a focus on the individual as an intrinsically autonomous unit, possessor of a highly individualized soul, and engaged in a personal struggle between good and evil for the sake of salvation. Such religious ideas begin to affirm individual identity as fundamentally independent of the group. While ritual activities of worship and sacrifice continue, their meaning changes. Instead of being acts of mystical communion and cosmological ordering, they are now thought to transform flawed human nature into something worthy of redemption. This devaluation of the world and the worldly self, in tandem with a deep-felt submission to obedience and discipline, leads to the cultivation of a sense of separation of oneself from others and, concomitantly, the separation of the whole sphere of religious activity from other forms of human behavior. Hence, historic religion starts the process of differentiating religious institutions from political or economic ones at the same time that it demands that people put religion first. The result is the rise of new tensions between religious ideals and social institutions, which will be the dynamic for changes of all kinds, from ritual innovation to political revolution.[22]

In Bellah's typology, the stage of "early modern religion" is characterized by a breakdown of the rigid hierarchical structuring of this world and the divine world established in the "historical" stage. Simultaneously, the struggle between good and evil and the attainment of salvation are reconceived in terms of commitment to this-worldly moral action. In terms of ritual, the breakdown of any fundamental distance between the human and the transcendent means that there is little need for the ritual intermediaries who once mediated these realms. The priestly role gives way to a new emphasis on the individual's own responsibility for a personal salvation built on a direct, unmediated relationship between the individual and the divine. Older practices involving sacrificial propitiation or beliefs in anthropomorphic deities are judged to be superstition and magic. In reinterpreting its own ritual traditions, early modern religion describes sacrificial activities like the medieval Eucharist as more commemorative than sacramental, denying any mystical communion of the human and divine. In this stage, ritual is no longer a matter of fixed and prescribed activities that are distinct from all other activities; instead, the notion of ritual activity is expanded to include all activities that seek to affirm a personal relationship with the divine. Older ritual practices are defined as magic, superstition or even "ritualism," ideas that would mean little to primitive, archaic, or historical religious communities.

The theological correlates of these changes in the meaning and style of ritual are doctrines in which human identity is reaffirmed as simultaneously good and evil, and salvation is possible despite the inevitable flaws of human nature. Voluntary forms of religious affiliation in which personal affirmations of faith and commitment are the main requirements gradually undermine traditional social and religious hierarchies and pave the way for a succession of sociopolitical changes, including democracy and revolution. These developments, in turn, help circumscribe the sphere of formal religious institutions. Churches and sects become separate organizations within the larger society, and the state no longer allies itself with a particular creed. As separate and distinct institutions with limited power, religious organizations tend to undertake projects to promote religious values in other institutions, like government and education, from which such values have been gradually eliminated.[23] Hence, the development of a public school system encourages the development of private sectarian schools and political lobbying for public school prayer.

For Bellah, "modern religion" is the hardest to characterize because we lack the benefit of hindsight. Nonetheless, some changes seem quite radical and may also prove to be characteristic of this stage. For example, there is the near collapse of any sense of the opposition between good and evil, heaven and earth, salvation and redemption, sacred and profane—ideas basic to the preceding two stages. Instead, in this stage religion comes to be grounded "in the structure of the human situation itself." Evil is no longer a force battling good in the universe or an intrinsic quality of soul; it is the result of negative social conditions, emotional experiences, and, sometimes, psychophysiological determinations. Likewise, a single yet multiplex cosmos replaces the older dual cosmos. Human life and personhood are thought to be constrained neither by a single internal defining essence nor by a clear set of external determining forces; they are characterized in terms of infinite potential. In this type of context, the liberal Protestant theologian Paul Tillich defined religion as that which is of "ultimate concern" to a person. In other words, religion does not define the nature of human beings, humanness defines the nature of religion. Concurrently, rituals and symbols are less clear-cut, more tentative, experimental, and open to individual appropriation—in part because any one symbol or set of symbols can command only limited consensus. While many people affiliate with religious institutions, they are less concerned with issues of doctrinal orthodoxy and more with issues of personal meaning and fulfillment. Although community-based forms of religion may be seen as affirming moral values and supporting one's personal search, the meaning people are looking for is ultimately understood as an intrinsically personal form of spirituality. This is *not* a religion in which rituals manipulate spirits, harmonize human affairs with the order of the seasons, seek to carry out the will of a demanding high god, or strive to inculcate universal norms of ethical behavior.[24]

Bellah offers a more critical characterization of this type of religious privatization and individualism in a later study. After noting the assertions by Thomas Jefferson and Thomas Paine, respectively, that "I am a sect myself" and "My mind is my church," Bellah describes the religiosity of a California nurse named Sheila Larson. Seeking her own spiritual path after an oppressive childhood, Larson described her faith as follows: "It's Sheilaism. Just my own little voice. . . . It's just try to love yourself and be gentle with yourself. You know, I guess, take care of each other. I think He would want us to take care of each other."[25] In an age of Sheilaism, Bellah argues, corporate and enduring forms of ritual life readily fragment. For those who leave the more traditional ritual communities in which they might have been raised, there is often a lingering desire for personally meaningful ritual and some experimentation to try to find it. Among those who stay in more traditional ritual communities, there is a common complaint that the ritual practices of the group often fail to speak to them. In this religious era, it seems, there is little fit between religious desires and religious resources.[26]

A more recent typology by Ronald Grimes uses a contrast between "modern" and "postmodern" eras of ritual sensibilities and worldviews, with the implication that they were preceded by "premodern" and "ancient" eras. According to this scheme, the worldview of the modern era is dominated by the understanding that "time is linear; spatial extension is the measure of the real; matter is inert; language is an arbitrary convention; persons are autonomous subjects; and truth is an agreement between propositions and the facts." Postmodernism is harder to characterize, Grimes finds, since "we seem to be in the middle of a transition of era," but he tentatively characterizes it as "the annulment of distance between life and art; writing about writing and reading [reflexivity]; emphasizing play and flow; a growing taste for ritual; the crossing of categories; a longing for intimate community; a critique of cause-and-effect reasoning; and a celebration of private and collective (as opposed to hierarchically structured) experience." In discussing the implications of this typology for ritual practice, Grimes contrasts the narrative emphasis of modern ritual with a postmodern emphasis on a deconstructive playfulness, indeterminacy, neotribal repetition, costumed performances, and a synthetic holism in which human beings are not "the measure of all things."[27] This typology reflects some of the new currents in ritual experimentation that have become prominent on the American scene, but it is probably too early to judge if there is a more general postmodern style of ritual.

Most of these typological schemes point to similar features, even though they derive from rather different analyses of religion. This redundancy may suggest something a bit too easy about these characterizations and perhaps typologizing in general, namely, the need to stress some sociocultural features at the expense of others so as to differentiate each type for maximum clarity. As a result, each of these types comes to imply a common model or essence, while appearing to ignore the variety of conflicting views and practices going on at any one time in any culture. Sometimes evolutionary assumptions linger in terminology of maturation and development, especially when stages of social history are implicitly correlated with stages of cognitive development in the individual life cycle. Yet despite much valid criticism, these typological schemes have made a useful contribution to the study of religion and ritual. Their correlations highlight specific features for closer comparison and analysis. Certainly the project of identifying relationships between density and styles of ritual action, on the one hand, and social organization, cultural worldview, and political-economic systems, on the other, continues.

Decrying the more evolutionary and functional premises behind most of the preceding typologies, the anthropologist Mary Douglas has forged a rather different system, one that has proven to be a provocative tool for further inquiry into the ways in which ritual form, substance, and density correlate with worldviews and social organizations. Douglas designed her system primarily to challenge the distinctions made between primitive and modern understandings of ritual. Whether a society is involved in those activities previously described as primitive-magical or rational-religious depends, Douglas maintains, on the design of their social system, not their stage of cognitive or historical development. As laid out in chapter 2, Douglas's system measures "grid" and "group," which are the degree of emphasis on hierarchical roles and formal positions in society and the degree of emphasis on being a member of a tight-knit group, respectively. Graphing degrees of grid and group along two axes generates a simple typology of four basic kinds of societies: a society with a high degree of both grid and group, a society with low grid but high group, one with high grid but low group, and one with both low grid and low group. (See diagram on p. 45.) This typological chart makes clear that the degree of ritual in a society can be correlated with an emphasis on either grid or group, but particularly group. In other words, societies with more group, and to some extent more grid, seemed to have more ritual as well.[28] Hence, ritual has some correlative relationship with social organizations that stress the interconnected solidarity of the whole, primarily through an undifferentiated but highly defined group identity, but also through an internal hierarchical ordering. Douglas sums up her main thesis that "the most important determinant of ritualism is the experience of closed groups" by noting that "when the social group grips its members in tight communal bonds, the religion is ritualist; when the grip is relaxed, ritualism declines."[29]

Douglas's typology also suggests that degrees of grid and group correlate with particular attitudes toward the body, individual identity, and the nature of the cosmos, which are all expressed in various forms of symbolic action. Indeed, for Douglas, the human body is the most important symbol for social and ritual purposes. How the body is handled, presented, decorated, or contorted is a fundamental indicator of more embracing social values. A culture with a high degree of hierarchical grid as well as a marked degree of groupism is apt to have very developed notions of bodily purity and impurity, which correlate in turn with a clear distinction between insiders and outsiders, a stress on loyalty, and a socialization process that sees personhood as a matter of internalizing social values so as to become an effective member of the whole. Its very controlled attitude toward the body is expressed in restrained body movements and modest clothing representative of one's place in society. The body is a routine ritual site for displays of deference or dominance through gesture and highly formalized speech. This type of social body seeks to suppress any public display of an organic loss of control as in crying, sneezing, spitting, or nursing a child; it accepts the appropriateness of a great deal of social control even in rather private activities and attitudes. As an example of this kind of high-grid, strong-group society, Douglas pointed to traditional Navajo society; other scholars have pointed to Japanese and, to a lesser extent, German society as well. Japan has a strong tradition of social hierarchy and position, as well as a strong sense of shared identity, a "Japaneseness" that can make the outsider despair of ever belonging. And few societies can rival the emphasis on ritual found in Japan.

Douglas's typology also predicts that in societies where there is little emphasis on either grid or group there will be very little ritual. Personal identity would not be particularly dependent on a sense of belonging, so there would be few rites that emphasized the whole; identity would not be dependent on one's position in society, so there would be few rituals to delineate position and rank. People would stress personal style (clothes, lifestyle, hobbies, etc.) in defining themselves since their group affiliations and formal positions would be understood as secondary to who they are. When rituals occurred, they would tend to reflect a cosmos where intermediaries are not needed: in an echo of one's personal experience of the social body, the divine might be understood as a diffused spiritual presence that can be found or evoked from within one's own interiority. Spontaneity rather than tradition would be trusted as more expressive and authentic, so whatever rituals there are would probably stress personal input, invention, and individual emotional fulfillment. Douglas cited several examples of this type of society, including the pygmies of the Ituri Forest who appear to have a striking lack of ritual. She found that theirs is a religion of "internal feeling, not external sign," of faith, not works; they are not concerned with cosmic order, purification, or transgressions of social or religious rules. The nomadic and independent Basseri, a group of Persian nomads who consider themselves "lapsed Muslims," also have little ritual. Although they are involved in complex migration cycles, a Basseri household displays a striking independence and self-sufficiency, which appears to enable the family to compete in the marketplace and live in virtual isolation from fellow nomads.[30]

Douglas's examples demonstrate that even tribal peoples, who would have been deemed primitive two generations ago, may have very little ritual; likewise, a modern industrial society may have a great deal of ritual. The degree and style of ritual, Douglas argues, cannot be linked to evolution or "rationalization" but simply to social organization. By implication, social organization is a matter of locale, resources, neighbors, and politics; it is not a stage in some historical trajectory of development. This has been a hard lesson to absorb. Douglas describes how difficult it has been to convince scholars that the Basseri, Nuer, Dinka, and Mbuti Pygmies contradict the stereotypes of primitive religion: they do not have much ritual, and their internalized spirituality and abstract notions of God are reminiscent of a style of religiosity that Weber might well have associated with modern, secular, and technologically "disenchanted" societies.[31]

Douglas's typological analysis ambitiously correlates cosmology, social structure, psychological attitudes, religious styles, forms and density of ritual, and notions of purity. Moreover, the grid-group organization system frees her to make more effective and accurate correlations than the lingering language of evolution and functionalism found in the preceding models. Yet Douglas's typology suggests that a society can be readily characterized as a whole with regard to grid, group, and all of their correlates. There is little or no flexibility for depicting the more common state of affairs, namely, the simultaneous presence of competing, complementary, or overlapping social and ritual subsystems.

For the purposes of this study, it is tempting to recast Douglas's typology so that it focuses primarily on ritual style in ways that allow for the flexible identification of interacting subsystems. The resulting four modes of ritual action would be extreme examples of the tendencies of particular forms of social organization. That is, they are heuristic models; they are neither universal nor exclusive. These four styles of ritual action can be designated as appeasement and appeal (or local religion), cosmic ordering, moral redemption, and personal spirituality.

In the first type, "appease and appeal," ritual life is a matter of frequent ceremonial actions to placate various gods, spirits, or ancestors so as to secure their protection or blessings and dispel their anger or mischief. While it is a ritual-social pattern closest to those ethnographic examples used by earlier scholars in illustrating or defending the label of magic, it often coexists with one or more of the other ritual styles. A good example of this ritual style is the Haitian religion of "Vodou," also called Voodoo, Voudou, Vodun and Hoodoo. For practitioners of Vodou, however, magic is what *other* people do since their Vodou traditions are deeply rooted in fundamental religious principles.[32]

Practiced by 80 to 90 percent of the people of Haiti, Vodou is a set of beliefs and rites that derives from the heritage of the enslaved men and women brought to the Americas in the 18th century from the west coast of Africa. The term probably comes from the word for "spirit," *vodou*, in the Fon language spoken in Benin, reflecting the influence of the Fon as well as the Yoruba and Kongo. While many Vodou spirits can be traced back to African deities, Haitian practice has also been heavily influenced by Roman Catholic symbols and images. Indeed, there is a remarkable number of distinct spirits to be propitiated, each with its own distinct disposition and particular rites. A person can incur responsibilities to spirits lodged in trees, wells, and more urban sites, or even inherit them. While simple ritual offerings may be left at cemeteries, crossroads, or temples, there are also elaborate rites of possession in which different drum rhythms and dances invoke the descent of different spirits. Equally prominent are rites of healing, rites to improve one's luck or to empower love potions, initiation rites, and pilgrimages.[33]

The practices and beliefs of Vodou bespeak a worldview in which everything that happens to people is the result of the often capricious actions of a vast pantheon of spirits. Since everything can be attributed to the spirits, the individual is considered relatively powerless, with only a limited and usually indirect ability to affect anything. The anthropologist Karen McCarthy Brown has described her own initiation into Vodou under the tutelage of a Haitian *mambo* who once complained in sardonic disbelief that "Karen say *she* the one responsible for her life, Ehh!" According to Brown, a ritual exchange of "gifts and countergifts" creates "webs of relationships" among humans and spirits that constitute Haitian personal identity and "ways of being in the world." When humans keep up their relationships with the spirits, properly feeding and honoring them, the spirits will respond, usually dispensing protection and good luck.[34]

From the perspective of current American and European culture, which has a worldview that often seems to overemphasize personal control and individual responsibility, on the one hand, and disinterested ethical action, on the other, the Haitian perspective can appear to be a very different way of understanding the world. Yet it is not surprising that Vodou coexists with traditional and modernizing forms of Catholicism, since historically Christianity has had many similar beliefs in spirits, devils, possession, glossolalia, and exorcism. Indeed, both the Roman Catholic Church and the Church of England still have officially appointed exorcists who routinely report their caseloads.[35] For many small Catholic communities around the world, ritual observances are still primarily based on appeals and appeasement. Rather similar patterns of entreating multiple spirits can be found in rural China or among the traditional Navajo in the United States. With the Navajo, for example, the courting of supernatural powers has little to do with a moral order or ethical concerns. Anthropologists point out that a man who commits murder is inviting ghost trouble, which could result just as readily from working in a hospital or burning wood from a hogan where someone recently died. Ghost trouble is a type of "ritual contamination" that has nothing to do with any sort of heavenly punishment for the immorality of murder, although it certainly discourages murder.[36] What would be called "ethical" considerations emerged in the later Navajo peyote cult, which Douglas correlates with the changes in clan structure following the impact of white culture.[37]

A similar form of "appease and appeal" religion coexists in Greek villages with the classical heritage of Eastern Orthodoxy and the urban secularism that increasingly turns belief in spirits into nostalgic elements of a quaint folklore. Yet for many villagers, the world is populated by legions of half-animal and half-human demons called *exotika*. Sometimes benevolent, more often not, they are deemed responsible for an enormous range of behaviors from theft and adultery to sunstroke and death. As in Haiti, these beliefs coexists with a form of Catholicism that makes room for the dynamic world of the exotika at the bottom of the hierarchical cosmology. One recent study demonstrates that spirit beliefs and the customary practices used to control them interact with church rites to create a unified and distinctive moral cosmos for the villagers.[38]

A second type of ritual style can be characterized as "cosmological ordering" since it focuses on the ritual re-creation of perfect harmony between the human and divine realms. It can also be thought of as a type of "theater" style of ritual, and several scholars have characterized particular cultures and political systems as "theater states" because of their reliance on the public performance of vast cosmos-ordering rites. This form of ritual practice tends to occur in societies or political systems in which a central monarchical figure is holding together a large and not totally homogeneous polity. The worldview, promoted by the central ruling class, despite incongruities with more local attitudes, envisions a single, vast, cosmologically rooted order in which all things, people, and spirits have their place. Needless to say, if everyone kept to their place, there would be harmony and well-being. Such ritual patterns stress elaborate pageantry at the center of the kingdom in which monarchs use colorful regalia and processions to synchronize themselves with this larger order and legitimate their position.

A good example of this type of worldview is the traditional Chinese state cult, rooted in the Confucian notion of *li* described in chapter 5. At various times in history, particularly when a monarch needed to pull together and exert control over a splintering polity, the Chinese state would overhaul its state ceremonial system. In the rise of the ancient Zhou Dynasty (1028–256 B.C.E.), the consolidation and expansion of the Han (202 B.C.E.–220 C.E.) and later the T'ang (618–906 C.E.), the imperial court developed elaborate ritual formulations to demonstrate the ceremonial place of the emperor as the legitimate "Son of Heaven," ruler over all the earth, and mediator between heaven and earth. The "Monthly Ordinances" section of one of the earliest ritual texts, the *Book of Rites* [*Liji*], used an elaborate system of correspondences to link the emperor's ceremonial life to the order of the universe. For harmony to reign in the realm, each month the emperor should wear a particular color, live in the corresponding section of the palace, perform a corresponding sacrifice to a particular god, and observe special prohibitions, all of which change for the following season. If the order is not observed, disaster results. Another section of the *Book of Rites* makes the same point: "If in the first month of spring, the ruler carries out proceedings proper to the summer, then the wind and rain will not come in season, the grass and trees will wither and dry up, and the nations will be in great fear."[39] Xunzi pushed the logic further when he wrote: "Rites are the highest expression of hierarchical order, the basis for strengthening the state, the way by which to create authority. . . . The fate of man lies with Heaven; the fate of the nation lies in ritual."[40] Yet the dominance of the cosmological ordering style of ritual eventually faltered in China, where it had long competed with other forms of ritual activity. Although aspects of cosmological ordering remained integral to much official ceremony, as well as other nonlocal ritual styles, different ritual postures became meaningful, particularly those concerned less with harmonizing the cosmic order and more with cultivating an internalized moral universe emphasizing personal intentionality and its expression in action. The inability of the imperial state cult to leave behind the outdated trappings of cosmic hegemony and effectively legitimate its rule in terms of this new moral style may well have contributed to the irrelevancy of the imperial institution in the 19th and 20th centuries.[41]

Traditional Chinese culture is also a good example of the complicated ways in which rites of appeasement and appeal may coexist with those of cosmological ordering. On the one hand, there has always been something of a continuum between local forms of folk religion and the more organized, national and official religion with its hierarchy of rites and ritualists reaching down from the emperor at the top to the village headman.[42] On the other hand, official religion shares many of the premises of the local practices from which it indeed emerged, while local religion also absorbed many aspects of official ritual. In practice, the official ritual system based on cosmological ordering could and would make room for local gods at the lower levels of its pantheon. At the same time, this official system was constantly attempting to control and at times eradicate those ritual practices that presumed a more "appease and appeal" worldview. One of the traditional criticisms of local cults involving mediums and regional deities or demons was that they violated the proper hierarchy of communication with the heavens. Such unregulated contact not only threatened to disorder the cosmological system but also involved a type of presumption of imperial prerogatives, a form of lèse majesté. [43] A full analysis of Chinese ritual life at the turn of the 19th century would probably find all four styles of ritual practice simultaneously taking up various corners of the social fabric, periodically overlapping or polarizing.

In a third type of ritual system, the "ethical-moral" style, ritual becomes less important than in the previous two since the major form of efficacious religious action is ethical and disciplinary in nature. In this system, basic ritual practices include admonishments to right action and right intention on an individual basis. It is understood that individuals are capable of sin or virtue, authenticity or inauthenticity, and that their behavior is scrutinized by a rather abstract divine principle possessing powers of judgment, salvation, and damnation. Despite the use of Christian terminology to describe this type, and the fact that Protestant Christianity is an excellent example, it is also found in other religions such as Buddhism and Islam. In these examples, the religious community is conceived in broad and inclusive terms; it is more than a local or national community. Indeed, it is possible to see this as the form religion can take when it attempts to extend beyond the local or national scene and thus requires a style that can overlay rather than directly challenge the local forms of religious practice it encounters.

Protestantism in the 16th century launched a particularly deep and sustained attack on traditional forms of ritual. Indeed, for the historian Peter Burke, "the Reformation was, among other things, a great debate, unparalleled in scale and intensity, about the meaning of ritual, its functions and its proper forms." In a variety of positions from Luther to the Anabaptists and Quakers, the reformers defined an ethical-moral position from which to challenge the "magical efficacy" of traditional ritual. Some went so far as to deny any power in ritual to make changes in the physical world, such as curing the sick, transmuting bread and wine, or even making a Christian of a person sprinkled with water. In cases like the last, they argued, such external gestures blind people to the necessity of internal action, especially the spiritual cleansing of the soul. For them, ritual had become a matter of outward, empty forms, disconnected from personal intention and sincerity.[44]

Presbyterianism developed this ethical-moral style most clearly. It was founded in the mid-16th century by John Knox, who was determined to bring the Reformed faith, primarily in its Calvinist form, to Scotland, despite the rule of the Catholic monarch, Mary Stuart. Seeking greater autonomy, Scotch-Irish and English Presbyterians immigrated to the American colonies, where the American Presbytery was formally established in 1706. Presbyterians tended to be highly educated and placed great emphasis on correct belief as formulated in creedal statements such as the famous 1648 Westminster Confession of Faith and its 1967 restatement known as the Presbyterians' Confession. Basic to these creeds is the conviction that the Bible is the "only infallible rule of faith and practice" and that God has absolute sovereignty over creation and salvation. Salvation is a matter of reconciliation with God and, as part of that, reconciliation with fellow human beings. Presbyterians have always distinguished their activities from those of the "liturgical" churches, such as the Lutherans and the Episcopalians, to say nothing of the Catholics, by seeing themselves as focused on simple gatherings where people come to preach and hear the word of God in all its directness, simplicity, and dignity. In keeping with the teachings of Calvin and Knox and their downplaying of ritual in general, Presbyterianism rejects the notion of any divine presence in the Christian sacraments. The sermon is the center of their ritual life, and it is primarily a teaching commentary on scripture. Sermons, songs, and prayers all appeal to an intellectual comprehension of the meaning of God's word, the necessity of conviction in articles of belief, and the renewal of a personal resolve to live a God-fearing life.[45]

The fourth type of ritual style, characterized by rites that focus on personal spirituality or the individual's spiritual potential, is usually associated with very recent forms of "privatized" spirituality. This is the style of religiosity that Bellah identifies with American individualism and the extreme of "Sheilaism." New Age religion and East-West hybrids like Transcendental Meditation—not unlike such predecessors as the Rosicrucians, Freemasons, Theosophists, or Swedenborgians—demonstrate this ethos of personal attainment of spiritual empowerment. Yet many new evangelical forms of Christianity also appeal to aspects of this style of spirituality. As a ritual system, it is a worldview in which private rites may be more emphasized than public ones, although public ceremonies stress the assembly of like-minded individual seekers pooling their strength. Doctrine and ethical teachings are downplayed in favor of language that stresses highly personal processes of transformation, realization, and commitment. Unlike the Presbyterian ethos, people are not seen as part of a divine plan but as individual seekers looking for meaning in a universe where no particular institution has the authority to speak "truth" for others. Indeed, it is a worldview that does not tend to think in terms of an overarching divine being; divinity or sacrality is more likely to be understood as an elusive quality, the opposite of ideology, behavioral codes, and belief, yet something that provides a tangible sense of self-empowerment. In this context, people need to find their own truths and their own ways of realizing sacrality.

This ethos of personal spirituality can be found in many forms, even certain parts of the conservative Christian right and Scientology. Conservative evangelical groups that give absolute authority to scripture as the direct word of God speak of the necessity of this word becoming a personal experience and a constant internal companion. In this type of theology, God is not a figure of towering transcendence to whom one owes allegiance and obedience. Instead, one owes allegiance to an experience of this God via the word in one's own heart. This emphasis on a spirituality of personal experience can coexist with other styles of religious and ritual behavior found in mainline churches and synagogues. Yet in such communities, people may observe the conventional ritual requirements and social outreach but look for and talk about the need for a dimension of personal fulfillment. They are less likely to see their customary rituals as traditional expressions of theological truths; they are more likely to look to them as a means of providing some experience of personal spirituality. For some, the customary rituals can do this; for others they fail to deliver enough personal nourishment. The relative unimportance of theological dogma leaves such communities open to experimentation and highly ecumenical borrowing, primarily of ritual elements. In other words, there is likely to be little theological resistance to including meditation in a Jewish seder or Christian mass since all ritual is seen as tools for the spiritual cultivation of the person.

What can we conclude from this extended exercise in ritual typologies? We should certainly conclude that the degree and style of ritual density can be correlated with different types of worldviews, forms of social organization, and notions of the self. We should also conclude that religious cultures are complex, often including more than one ritual style or system, sometimes in tension, sometimes coexisting in complementary harmony. It is also appropriate to infer that if a society passes through social and historical changes affecting its worldview, organization, economic activities, and exposure to competing ideas, for example, it will probably witness concomitant changes in its ritual system—even though ritual systems can be particularly resistant to change. Despite the reductive neatness of the preceding typologies, their correlations suggest that ritual practices are a type of sociocultural medium that is capable of grounding human attitudes, worldviews, and institutions in a vision of the nature of things in general. Hence, the elaborate ritualization of body etiquette in Japan or the many ritual services rendered to spirits in Haiti are ways of acting that ground a complex set of social and personal values within a person's conscious convictions and unconscious assumptions about how the universe is structured. One set of ritually expressed assumptions is not necessarily more primitive or advanced than the other, although each may have significant ramifications for personal, economic, and political activities. Whatever the commonalities among ritual in general, we must conclude that ritual practices can encode very different ways of being in the world.

Orthopraxy and Orthodoxy

In approaching issues of ritual density, it has been customary to distinguish the degree to which religious traditions put an emphasis either on correct belief in theological doctrines or on correct performance of behavioral responsibilities. The first style of religion is known as "orthodoxic," from the Greek words *orthos* (correct, right, straight) and *doxa* (belief, thought, opinion). The second style is called "orthopraxic," from the Greek *praxis*, meaning "correct action."[46] As a result of the dominance of Christianity in much of the West, which has tended to stress matters of doctrinal and theological orthodoxy, people may take it for granted that religion is primarily a matter of what one believes.[47] Yet in many religious traditions, concerns for what a person believes are often subsumed within more embracing concerns to live according to a code of behavior, a code that usually includes multiple ritual responsibilities. Whether a community is deemed orthodoxic or orthopraxic can only be a matter of emphasis, of course, since no religious tradition can promote belief or ritual at the total expense of the other, and many would never distinguish between them at all. Moreover, whatever the overall emphasis in a tradition as a whole, it is easy to find subcommunities stressing the opposite pole. As with the typologies discussed before, terms like "orthodoxy" or "orthopraxy" cannot be used effectively if accorded too much rigidity or exclusivity. Nor can they be used to suggest that one style is more truly religious than the other; the differences between orthodoxy and orthopraxy appear to emerge primarily from social organization and history, not the degree or purity of religiosity. Nonetheless, these can be useful terms for understanding aspects of the density, style, and domains of ritual in the life of a religious community.

Orthopraxy may well be the more common situation for religious communities, seeming to dominate wherever religion, culture, and national or ethnic identity are closely intertwined. Orthodoxy, by contrast, tends to be the emphasis of religions that are concerned, for various reasons, to break down or transcend such links, and keep religious orientation from being subsumed into a particular political-social identity. So-called world religions, religions that have grown beyond the regions where they originated, crossing a variety of cultural boundaries while seeking to maintain the sense of a coherent tradition and an embracing community of the faithful, are apt to evolve an emphasis on orthodoxic belief over orthopraxic action. The logic of this is not hard to see. In tribal or local societies, which tend to be relatively closed and homogeneous, religion is not something separate from community identity, ethnic customs, political institutions, and social traditions. Beliefs are rarely formulated and spelled out in these circumstances, and they do not need to be. It is the formal and informal customs and obligations—namely, ritual responsibilities like attending to the ancestors, arranging the marriage of one's children, and participating in communal festivities—that define one as a civilized member of this type of community. The historian of comparative religion Wilfred Cantwell Smith suggests that "what theology is to the Christian Church, a ritual dance may be to an African tribe," namely, their way of formulating how the human is linked to the divine. The way in which people are religious cannot be separated from the nature of their society and type of expressive media on which that society relies.[48]

Shinto, the indigenous religion of Japan, is an example of orthopraxic tradition. A highly diffused religion up until the late 19th century, Shinto did not have a name for itself until Buddhism arrived in Japan in the 6th century to provide a challenging contrast. It is primarily a religion of ritual observances, formal and informal acts of purification, exorcism, appeasement, and celebration. Shinto's understanding of the nature of the divine is closely intertwined with these observances, and there is little formulation of doctrine or theology as such. Despite some modern attempts at doctrinal codification, Shinto remains today primarily a means of ritual interaction with the cosmos.[49] Hinduism is a rather different type of example. Over the centuries what is called Hinduism has embodied a tremendous diversity of practice, including a rich and multifaceted tradition of theological and even *atheological* speculation. While on one level it is usually understood that the more embracing theological formulations point to something in common to all forms of Hinduism, it has remained fundamentally a religion of ritual observances with relatively less emphasis on doctrine or belief. So, while atheism is included as an acceptable position in Hinduism, what is *not* acceptable and effectively casts one outside the bounds of this loose and inclusive tradition is disrespect for the Vedas, the ancient and authoritative ritual texts that are understood to be the root of Indian civilization.[50]

Orthodoxic and orthopraxic traditions do not have an easy time understanding each other. Christians have traditionally criticized Judaism for what looked like an excessive concern with ritual with a perspective that sees the orthodoxic style as normative.[51] The terms "creed" or "faith" have long been very acceptable substitutes for the term "religion" in Europe and America, as in "people of all creeds and faiths," yet they clearly assume the priority of doctrine and belief. As a highly orthopraxic tradition, Judaism is said to lack any term for theology. In Hebrew, the word for religion is *dath*, originally meaning "law" and denoting adherence to prescribed and proscribed activities, which is essentially what religion has meant in Judaism until the modern period.[52] Although ancient Judaism distinguished itself from its neighbors by its avowal of monotheism, one God over and instead of many gods, this idea was not understood as a theological principle so much as a rule about who and what one could worship. Exclusive ritual practices came to define what it meant to be a Jew. Particularly after the destruction of the second Temple of Jerusalem and the subsequent exile of the Jews from the city that had been a locus of their ritual life, Jewish identity increasingly came to depend on a growing body of formulated laws known as Halakah. The laws were the means by which sacred scripture, Torah, could be applied to every aspect of daily life: marriage and sexuality, children, food, social relations, legal concerns, and so on. As a corpus of laws prescribing what and how things should be done, Halakah made no effort to theologize. According to the historian of Judaism Jacob Neusner, what Christians spelled out in theological writings, rabbinic scholars "wholly encapsulated in descriptions of ritual."[53]

Comparable in various ways to Christian monastic orders, rabbinic Judaism attempted to ritually prescribe or circumscribe almost every act. Nowadays, such intense ritualization of daily life is maintained only among those groups called the *haredim,* some of whom have actually increased their stringency in recent genera-tions.[54] Haredim is usually translated as "ultra-orthodox," but this is certainly some-thing of a misnomer, according to Samuel Heilman and Menachem Friedman: "strictly speaking, the term *Orthodox* is inappropriate because what distinguishes those Jews who have come to be called 'Orthodox' is not *doxa,* belief, but rather practices and a way of life punctiliously attached to ritual. It denotes a population that is gen-erally identifiable as championing tradition and ritual *orthopraxis* in the situation of modernity."[55] From the order in which to put on one's shoes in the morning to the days on which one can speak to one's spouse, ultra-orthodox obedience to the laws of Halakah, which often actually exceed the letter of these laws, is understood to be the way in which one worships God and proclaims a true embodiment of religious values. Such a life is known as "Torah-true," a model to those in the community and an accusation to those who have left for greater laxity.[56]

Such stringent ritualization has the powerful effect of tightly binding one to a small community of like-minded people. Indeed, one of the salient features of ex-treme ritualization appears to be a high-profile identity as a tight-knit group of *true* followers, a position that heightens the contrast and ill fit with other groups. On the one hand, this can result in a sharply differentiated sense of groupism that may lead to factional fighting among tiny sects competing in stringency; on the other hand, many of the more extreme forms of orthopraxy are, in fact, the very means by which a group heightens and maintains its internal group identity, often in the face of more diffused and complacent communities. When Jews were finally allowed to claim citizenship in late-19th-century Europe and could began to assimilate, tensions de-veloped between those staying faithful to the old food and dress codes that set them off and those who sought interpretations of traditional law that would legitimate more relaxed and pragmatic forms of adherence. Some scholars suggest that this historical situation generated a polarization in which both tendencies became more extreme in reaction to each other—one group going in the direction of increasing stringency in obeying the law, the other in the direction of increasingly flexible interpretation.[57]

A number of studies have attempted to chart degrees of adherence to traditional law in various ultraconservative Jewish communities. Solomon Poll's classic study of the Hasidic community of Williamsburg, Brooklyn, argued that the stratification of the Hasidic community is unlike any other American community, since it is based not on wealth, lineage, occupation, or education but on the frequency and intensity of ritual observance: "The greater the number of rituals and the more intensely they are observed, the greater the esteem accorded a person." These rites can be public or private. If private, they can start with one's first waking minutes: "A religious Jew upon awakening must rise immediately and be ready to serve his Creator before evil inclinations can prevail. He must wash his hands in a ritual manner, taking the ves-sel first in the right hand and then in the left; then he must spill the water with the left hand upon the right and then, in reverse, from his right hand upon the left, re-peating this performance three times."[58] Other ritual observances involve circumci-sion; stipulated forms of dress, including shorn hair and a head covering for married women, and covered heads in public for men, who also wear fringes (*tzitzit*) under their outer clothes; the degree or length of fasting on special days; the degree of obe-dience to the laws of kashrut concerning kosher food and its preparation; the degree of compliance with Sabbath laws that forbid all work, entertainment, and travel except by foot, but require attendance at services and the study of religious texts; and the regularity of observance of the ritual bath (*mikveh*) for married women after each menstrual period.[59]

Ritual in an orthopraxic tradition is an integral part of a holistic religiocultural way of life. Such orthopraxic traditions are experienced as cultural communities—often defined in ethnic or racial terms—to which one automatically belongs by birth. Hence, to be a Jew, one need only be born of a Jewish mother. But to be a *good* Jew, for some, one must observe local Jewish customs that signal one's alliance with this community and tradition. As an orthopraxic community, Judaism does not see itself as a world religion seeking to convert others but as a people maintaining a rich heritage in the face of pressures to assimilate and accommodate. In this context, ritual activities are a medium for sustaining that heritage. Although more conservative subgroups tend to stress preservation of the tradition as it is, while more liberal subgroups stress adaptation of the tradition to new concerns, both use ritual to perpetuate Jewishness as culture, spirituality, and peoplehood.[60]

The style of ritual found in orthodoxic traditions can differ dramatically from orthopraxic traditions. Since orthodoxic rituals are frequently concerned with avowing theological ideas and creedal statements, they often explicitly connect particular doctrines to what is being done in ritual. This can involve a formal restatement of key beliefs, as in the Christian creed ("I believe in God the Father Almighty" of the Apostles' Creed) or the Islamic duty to "witness" (the *shahada*, "There is no God but Allah and Mohammed is his prophet"). Ritual in orthodoxic communities may provoke theological speculation that can influence the future formulation of beliefs and even lead to changes in the ritual. Yet despite the importance, and perhaps even the historical priority, of central rituals, orthodoxic traditions tend to cast them as somewhat secondary, as *expressions* of things that should already be in the heart. While this secondary status does not automatically make all orthodox rites more flexible, the ritual corpus is not tied to a single, monolithic cultural tradition concerned to maintain its identity. As the expression of theological ideas, change may be rationalized more easily.

An understanding of ritual as a somewhat secondary complement to beliefs can be both a strength and a weakness: it is a strength in that the relative flexibility of the ritual tradition allows it to travel, adapt, and speak to other cultural groups, but it can be a weakness due to the vulnerability of such rites to challenges addressed to the central belief system. Hence, being a Christian has meant, for a good part of Christian history, that one believes in the divinity of Jesus Christ. Although there is a humorous acknowledgment of "cultural Christianity" and "cultural Catholicism," it is not sufficient simply to be born of Christian parents or raised in a Christian home. All Christian churches would hold that a personal commitment is required. Therefore, a person born and raised in a Christian environment who does not believe in the central ideas of Christianity is likely to feel that he or she has little reason to continue involvement in its ritual and communal life. It is interesting to speculate whether an orthodoxic emphasis is also not more likely to lead to criticism of ritual as empty and meaningless, a view that makes it particularly difficult to understand more orthopraxic communities.

As religious communities expand, sometimes coming to include cultural groups quite different from the one in which the religion originated, there is often a de-emphasizing of orthopraxic ritual customs in favor of more cross-culturally manageable orthodoxic beliefs. Christianity experienced something of this in its early development, as did Islam. However, Islam maintained a central and important tension between an Arabic revelation for an Arabic-speaking people, which is a tendency toward orthopraxy further evidenced in the development of Islamic law, and a universal mission to convert all people, which is a tendency toward orthodoxy further evidenced in the importance of personal submission to a radical monotheism. Indeed, the histories of Christianity, Islam, and Judaism are full of times when the tendency to be a highly prescriptive religion for the few and thereby maintain tradition and a clear identity has come into conflict with a tendency toward flexibility that could allow the religion to be embraced and appropriated by increasingly different communities.

In Judaism, the emergence of sectarian differences in how to be Jewish — Reform, Conservative, Reconstructionist, and Orthodox — has given rise to the heated religiojudicial issue of "who is a Jew." The issue of conversion has always been a particularly contentious one in Judaism, going back as far as the Roman occupation of Judea and the subsequent diaspora, even though conversions were rather frequent and sometimes plentiful. According to Shaye Cohen, the incorporation of converts into the Jewish community is still a "challenge," and the "major obstacle to their integration is the fact that we Jews see ourselves as members of an *ethnos* or nation or tribe, a people linked by descent from a common set of ancestors." At least, he continues, "we like to pretend that we are a single people."[61] If Cohen is right, this vision is a matter of constantly trying to create singleness in the face of the multiple forms of Judaism that emerged in the diaspora and even more dramatically in the last two hundred years. It is a vision that has raised difficult questions for the state of Israel, which wants to see itself as a national state among other states *and* as the primary representative of the larger world community of Jews.[62]

Yet Israeli national identity does not always fit easily with the tradition of Jews as a single, if scattered, people. In 1983 the Reform branch of American Judaism rescinded the ancient halakic rule that to be a Jew meant one had to be born of a Jewish mother. They decided that children of mixed marriages in which either parent was Jewish would be considered Jews "if they participated in appropriate and timely public and formal acts of identification with the Jewish faith and people."[63] So, while the ruling overturned a hallowed piece of tradition, it maintained an emphasis on an orthopraxic definition of the peoplehood of the Jews. Yet Jews recognized as such under this Reform ruling are not necessarily recognized by other Jewish sects. The issue became controversial for Israel when it adopted the Law of Return in 1950, which gave the right to immigrate to Israel to any halakic Jew (i.e., born of a Jewish mother) or any convert who does not profess another faith. In ruling on who is Jewish and eligible to immigrate to Israel, both the secular Israeli Supreme Court and the Israeli rabbinic courts have refused citizenship to halakic Jews (i.e., born of a Jewish mother) who converted to Catholicism or accepted aspects of Christianity. Some critics argue that this ruling not only weakens halakic identity and the orthopraxic bond of "public and formal acts of identification" but also threatens to adopt the type of orthodoxic criteria (i.e., belief) indicative of Christianity itself. For such critics, the traditional bonds of orthopraxy were also undermined when both courts ruled to recognize Ethiopian Jews, despite great differences in religious practice. This ruling led to Operation Solomon, a 1984 airlift of more than 14,000 Ethiopian Jews to Israel in order to escape war and famine. Yet after their warm reception, the assimilation of these culturally very different Jews has led to hard questions concerning long-standing Ethiopian customs that do not accord with Halakah, such as religious leaders whose roles and expertise do not fit traditional rabbinic requirements.

Islam, as noted previously, also presents an interesting tension between orthopraxy and orthodoxy. Basic to Islam is the practice of the five pillars: *shahada*, the witness that "there is no God but Allah and Mohammed is his prophet"; *salat*, prayers said five times daily facing Mecca; *zakat*, almsgiving as an act of worship and thanksgiving; *sawm*, fasting, which is particularly observed during the month of Ramadan; and *hajj*, pilgrimage to Mecca by all those who are physically and economically able to make the trip. Obligatory for all Muslims, the pillars establish the fundamental common denominator underlying a far-flung Islamic community. While all five are considered "acts of worship" and suggest an emphasis on orthopraxy, the first can also be seen as an act of faith, a declaration of right and true belief that certainly has been central to Islam.[64] In keeping with this dual emphasis, various Muslim scholars and writers through history, often described as philosopher-theologians, have decried the dangers of theology. According to Abu Hamid al-Ghazzali (1058–1111), "The Qur'an is like food, profitable for everyone, but theology (*kalam*) is like medicine, profitable for some but deleterious for most people."[65] Theological speculation should remain an activity of the scholarly elite, while teachings on correct practice should guide the masses. Of course, this view was shared by many leaders of the Roman church at that time.

The orthopraxic equivalent of heresy in Islam is the failure to adhere to religious and political norms of behavior prevailing within the community, making one a subversive dissident.[66] By this definition, the "blasphemy" for which the writer Salman Rushdie was accused by the mullahs of Iran in 1989 was rather atypical and something of a challenge to the traditional system. Some Iranian mullahs in exile did not hesitate to criticize as both illegitimate and specious the Ayatollah Khomeini's formal decree calling for the assassination of Rushdie. They argued that only a court of Islamic law can issue such a *fatwa*, and it would be issued after due process only to make "a general statement of opinion on a particular matter," not to "condemn a specific person."[67]

Although Christianity is generally considered a prime example of an orthodox tradition, it is by no means without orthopraxic subcultures. For groups like the Amish and Mennonites, a way of life that is largely at odds with the surrounding culture and even the rest of Christendom is a primary symbolic act of religiosity and identity. Mary Douglas fondly describes an Irish community in London as a similar type of orthopraxic community. As an island of Irish Catholics living in the midst of British Protestantism, the so-called Bog Irish are a highly ritualized community. Their prime defining act has been the Catholic taboo against eating meat on Friday, which establishes allegiance to what in London has been something of a despised culture. In this social context, the act of eating fish instead of meat on Fridays has come to be credited with nearly magical properties, shifting from a symbol of disciplinary penitence to a symbolic celebration of fish and of Christ as the fish and fisherman.[68] Douglas gives a spirited defense of the ritualism of the Bog Irish against well-meaning reformers, Catholic or otherwise, who are critical of such old-fashioned rites and would have the Bog Irish adopt a more sober or modern form of religious commitment, that is, something less ritualistic and more internal, intellectual, and ethical in style.

An equally exotic if still familiar example of a highly orthopraxic community is the neighborhood described in Robert Orsi's *The Madonna of 115th Street*, which portrays the ritual life of an Italian immigrant community in New York City through the first half of the 20th century. Every aspect of these people's lives was dominated by religion, particularly ritual observances. In the midst of these ritual activities, the larger Church as an institution and teacher of theological doctrine, was nearly marginal and held in some disdain. The community's religious and ritual lives were constituted by the set of established customs and values that celebrated and sustained the community as a distinct and autonomous subculture. Central to this culture was the annual *festa* of the Madonna of Mount Carmel, a complex religious drama that began with a procession that lasted for days. For several decades, it was customary for families to drag a female relative face-down the length of the main aisle of the Church of the Madonna so that she could lick the floor stones as she was hauled to the altar. As Orsi notes, such dramatic religiosity was considered quite peculiar by other groups of American Catholics, who remarked on the Italian tendency of devotion to rituals instead of "the great truths," which they considered more truly religious.[69]

Yet these outside observers had to question even the Italians' devotion to ritual: while everyone threw themselves into baptisms, marriages, funerals, and festas, there appeared to be little regard for Sunday mass. The men and women of Italian Harlem made no distinction between the religious and social aspects of such community events. The public and communal rites were, Orsi notes, "sacred theater," in which the denizens of the neighborhood disclosed their most basic social values, moral perceptions, and religious cosmology. Amid all the many meanings of the festa of the Madonna — simultaneously religious, communal, political, personal, and familial — it purged emotions, expressed frustrations, and defined the family as the dominant social world with women as the central guardians of its traditions.[70] Festa reestablished links to the old country, relegitimated the immigrant's overt severing of so many ties to past, kith, kin, and polity, while simultaneously recreating authoritative Italian tradition and Italian-American identity. As a study of a "theology of the streets," Orsi's analysis of the cultural and religious life of Italian Harlem illustrates the power of ritual activity to be the medium by which a people defines themselves and their tradition. These definitions were never a matter of belief in doctrines. Instead, they were shaped and preserved in the complex and layered modes of ritual orchestration.

Traditional and Secular

More common than the contrast between orthodoxic and orthopraxic styles of ritual life has been the distinction — variously drawn and amply debated — between "traditional" societies, in which religion has a strong central place, and "secular" societies, where religion seems weaker and marginal. With the development of sociology in the 20th century, "secular," "secularism," and "secularization" became technical terms for a social process by which religious worldviews and institutions give way to more scientific outlooks and this-worldly values—Weber's "disenchantment of the world." As the earlier discussion of typologies demonstrated, secularization is also correlated with the displacement of ritual, the dominance of moral-ethical values over intercession with divine powers, the emergence of lay authority over clerical authority, and the privatization of spirituality. Some specialized analyses, however, also suggest the reverse of privatization, that secularism brings new public and political personas for religious organizations which must compete in a context of religious pluralism.[71] Underlying many of the most nuanced discussions is the idea that secularism entails basic social processes in which major societal institutions are differentiated from each other and no longer represent the same values or work together to provide an overall coherence to social life.[72]

Secularization theories imply a contrast with so-called traditional societies, those societies in which a shared, religiously rooted cosmological and moral order maintains a strong congruence among the various dimensions of the social system—cultural, political, economic, and psychological.[73] According to this perspective, the social values, attitudes, customs, and conventions of behavior in a traditional society tend to fit together and reinforce each other. This reinforcement naturalizes basic units of social groupings, such as the family and regional leadership systems, and authenticates the more cognitive and psychological dimensions of the culture, such as the acceptability of certain emotions, characterizations of femininity and masculinity, and styles of spirituality. This view of traditionalism suggests a society characterized by a single dominant order of things that ensures a holistic sense of the basic fit among all aspects of social and personal life, although alternative orders may be latent or marginal. In a very fundamental way, therefore, there is no such thing as religion per se in a traditional society since religious beliefs and practices cannot be separated from how people organize their families, govern themselves, engage in hunting, agriculture, or trade, and so on. This description of traditionalism, which may be more imagination than reality, clearly includes an amalgamation of some of the notions of "primitive" societies deployed in the typologies discussed earlier.

By contrast, a secular society lacks this degree and type of coherence. By virtue of what some theorists have called "institutional differentiation," the religious system becomes independent of the political system (separation of church and state), and both are apt to separate from the educational system, the economic system, and maybe even the family and lineage system.[74] When each of these institutions achieves a relative autonomy, they will function differently and have different degrees of direct or indirect dependence on each other. Secular differentiation enables these institutions to develop value structures of their own, which may not always harmonize with each other. Hence, the competitive "dog-eat-dog" world of capitalist economics coexists, uneasily perhaps, with the value system of caring and mutual support extolled for family relationships; a political system might emphasize the freedom of democratic individualism, while the educational system may try to inculcate values of conformity and discipline.

In a secular society, people have many more choices about what to believe, how to act, and where to affiliate and devote their energies. The existence of these choices puts greater emphasis on the individual as the basic unit of the society and less on the family or clan or group as a whole. In a traditional society, by contrast, a person is more likely to locate his or her sense of personal identity within a set of inter-connected relationships. Like the point where the spokes of the wheel come together at the hub, individual identity is more likely to be experienced as the nodal point of a matrix of socializing and humanizing relationships. In secular societies, persons are also involved in relationships but are somewhat less likely to derive their sense of self from the sum total of those relations. Some analysts, like Robert Bellah, have argued that secularism gives rise to the type of excessive individualism in which a person defines him or her self only over and against other people, not through them or with them.[75] This is probably an exaggeration, but there does seem to be a ten-dency toward a more corporate sense of identity in traditional societies and a more isolated, individualistic sense of identity in secular societies.

Sociologists not only describe secularization differently but also attribute it to different causes.[76] Some see the loss of religious institutions and ways of acting pri-marily as a result of distinctive forms of social change. For others, the devaluation of traditional religion results from "the shrinking relevance of the values, institutional-ized in church religion, for the integration and legitimation of everyday life in mod-ern society."[77] Secularism is also formulated as the retreat of religion from the pub-lic and political sphere "to a private world where religions have authority only over their followers and not over any other section of the polity or society."[78] However, despite these different perspectives, it has become clear that secularization does not entail the progressive demise of religion in general but a transformation of its form. In a secularized or secularizing society, religious activities increasingly become a matter of personal choice and voluntary affiliation instead of an automatic cultural assumption or obligatory public duty. The content of religion tends to become less concerned with exact ritual performance and intercession with deities and more concerned with moral intentions, good works, and the social needs of the commu-nity here and now. Secularism has a positive connotation for many that is histori-cally associated with greater freedom of thought, practice, and personal belief but a negative meaning for those who experience this transformation as the marginalization and restriction of expressions of religious faith, such as school prayer.

While the causes of secularization are complex and much debated, a number of identifiable factors are clearly part of the picture: cultural pluralism, the legal sepa-ration of church and state, the concept of individual rights, industrialization and technological development, and the development of critical or scientific ways of thinking. Hence, many scholars and popular writers cast secularization as a specifi-cally modern phenomenon dependent on social and economic forces that began to be felt in post-Renaissance Europe. For Max Weber and Robert Bellah, underlying these forces was a more fundamental process of "rationalization," the beginnings of which can be found even in quite ancient societies. Yet others, like Mary Douglas, have eschewed any idea of a single, historical process; Douglas sees secularism as one type of worldview closely dependent upon particular modes of social organiza-tion. For that reason, it can turn up in any historical age and locale. Secularism,

Douglas writes, is not just a "modern trend, attributable to the growth of cities or to the prestige of science. . . . [Rather, it is] an age-old cosmological type, a product of a definable social experience, which need have nothing to do with urban life or modern science." Here secular means "this-worldly," unconcerned with transcendent explanations and powers, focused on inner experience instead of communal worship, having attitudes of antiritualism with little interest in developed religious institutions. Douglas finds these qualities in a variety of groups, including politically leftist movements rebelling against the current value system, tribal societies such as the Mbuti pygmies (and the Dinka and Nuer to a lesser extent), and Christian denominations gradually turning away from ritual and theological doctrines to more ethically sensitive and socially concerned styles of religiosity.[79]

If one sets aside all theories of "historical process," either long-term or short-term, as Douglas does, then the reason why one society is secular and another is not is reduced to the dynamics of social structure, which are not themselves explained in any way. Frustration with this impasse, perhaps, has led some scholars to take the more extreme position that there is no such thing as secularization, and our tendency to interpret things in this way is simply a function of our own cultural biases—particularly the tendency to assume the superiority of so-called modern technological society in contrast to the style of less technologically sophisticated cultures. The historian Peter Burke goes so far as to claim that "all societies are equally ritualised; they merely practice different rituals. If most people in industrial societies no longer go to church regularly or practice elaborate rituals of initiation, this does not mean that ritual has declined. All that has happened is the new types of rituals—political, sporting, musical, medical, academic and so on—have taken the place of the traditional ones."[80] Yet Burke's analysis does not try to explain why some societies attend church while others attend soccer games.

A more moderate position suggests that secularization is neither a linear developmental process that spells the demise of religion nor a mere interpretive bias on the part of Western scholars. Rather, it can be seen as a type of self-limiting process at work in all ongoing religious systems both ancient and modern. It is self-limiting because it can stimulate religious revival and innovation.[81] As such, secularism may result from some critical degree of contact with different cultures—afforded by travel, conquest, immigration, or competition with neighbors for access to limited resources. If the exposure to plurality—that is, to other value systems and alternative forms of social organization—is intense and sustained or occurs at times of internal social chaos, it can begin to undermine the coherent sense of a unifying order that underlies a traditional society. Some people opt for new and foreign ways of doing things, especially if they are not the ones benefiting from the old ways. People have choices they never had before, whether they want them or not. The mere existence of choices among ways of thinking and acting relativizes what was once deemed absolute, raises questions, necessitates decisions, and promotes experimentation. In this context, some groups become more defensive of tradition, attempting to shun all new options while preserving the old without any change whatsoever. They may even attempt to ignore or retreat from the world around them. Yet older customs strictly maintained in the face of change do not function the way they used to, when they never needed to be asserted and defended. As a society tries to hold together increasingly diverse points of view, one effect is the institutional differentiation that comes with secularism. For example, as Catholics and Jews moved into small, traditionally Protestant New England towns and claimed their rights as full citizens, the explicit and implicit role of Protestantism in the fabric of the town's social and economic activities was forced to retreat. What was a loss for some was a gain for others. As a result there is a shift of religion from the public and communal sphere to the private and personal, leaving some institutions shorn of all involvement in religion, while others become more explicitly the bastion of religious practice, values, and even public outreach and political lobbying.

As these perspectives demonstrate, there is great deal of controversy over the notion of a process of secularization, especially in regard to such associated features as modernization, increased rationalism, and decreased religion and ritualism. Yet a view of secularism as a theory of institutional differentiation precipitated by the force of pluralism has come to dominate, in part because it recognizes that religion does not die out in secular cultures. On the contrary, in the form of autonomous institutions, religion may have a much sharper profile, it may demand more personal commitment, and it may even exercise more single-minded influence on other institutions.

Ritual in traditional societies tends to be highly organized and communal, expressing collective concerns and establishing collective understandings of tradition, authority, and the community ethos. The festa of the Madonna of 115th Street, the Mukanda initiation among the Ndembu, and the potlatch among the Kwakiutl are examples of ritual in fairly traditional societies. In highly secular societies, however, ritual retreats from the most public arena to the relative privacy of particular religious subgroups. While there may be extensive rites of initiation into such a group, more general coming-of-age rites will probably fade away. The most widely shared rituals will be only vaguely religious, giving rise to the vast body of "civic" rituals that include pledging allegiance to the flag, swearing in political leaders, jurors and witnesses in courts of law, costumes on Halloween, and turkey on Thanksgiving.[82] As the typological theories suggested, this type of secular society is also likely to emphasize moral-ethical commands over ritual duties, even within the different religious subgroups, in part because moral-ethical injunctions are sufficiently abstract, universal, and embracive to enable religious people to have a sense of how to address, and live in, a nonreligious society. Undoubtedly some subgroups will use intense ritualization of their activities to foster a deep sense of community and separateness from the rest of the world; however, most churches do not want to abandon the secular world, but to address it and guide it.[83]

A final note of irony is particularly apt in any discussion of secularism. In 1982 Mary Douglas argued that scholars of religion, by clinging to theories that envisioned a relentless historical process of secularism at the expense of religion—theories she considered to be marked by "confusion, elitism, and bias interspersed with brilliance"—had turned out to be very poor predictors of the future of religion.[84] Most analyses projected the weakening of ritual and the total demise of religion in general. By the early 1980s, this was clearly wrong given the various forms of religious resurgence that had occurred around the world in the preceding decade, such as the Islamic revolution in Iran, Islamic resurgence in the Arabic and north African world, the radical Catholicism and Protestant evangelicalism of South America, the political influence of the Roman Catholic Church in Poland in the years before the dissolution of the Soviet empire, and the influence of the Christian Moral Majority in America, as well as the many civil wars (Ireland, Lebanon, the former Yugoslavia, and so on) ostensibly being fought in the name of religion. For Douglas, theories of modernization had gotten it all wrong. Since the 1980s, most scholars have absorbed the lesson, and recent analyses of secularism have been less sweeping and more self-reflective. Yet there is still a prominent tendency to depict the replacement of good, communal religion by an introverted, narcissistic spiritualism of the sort that Bellah identified as "Sheilaism."[85] If, in some fundamental way, we continue to see "modernity" as antithetical to religion and ritual, it may be due in part to how we have been defining religion.[86] For example, Gallup polls on declining church attendance have not asked about people's attendance at weddings and funerals or the civic or occupational rituals—such as weekly participation in Alcoholics Anonymous, Labor Day cookouts, ethnic festival activities, and Earth Day demonstrations—that have become important to the lives of many people and communities. Indeed, a greater percentage of Americans probably celebrate Halloween, Thanksgiving, and Christmas—in some fashion—than ever before.[87] While secular societies *do* experience a shift in traditional patterns of religious life, it is not at all obvious that religion or ritual declines.

Oral and Literate

Most theories of ritual have been rooted in ethnographic observations of oral societies. While such ethnography underscores the fact that there is nothing simple or primitive about such ritual systems, it can be convincingly argued that the ritual life of oral societies differs in significant ways from that of societies in which writing, literacy, the printing press, and, increasingly, computers have defined new forms of authority and community. Cultural change, for example, is thought to take different forms in these two types of societies. On one hand, the transmission of myth in stable oral societies tends to involve constant adaptation that keeps the myth in a "homeostatic" relationship with the concerns of the community. The presence of written texts, especially written records, on the other hand, introduces new dynamics: departures from the text as well as variation among texts are readily apparent, producing the sense of a breach between then and now, or here and there. Such ruptures can cause conflict, contradiction, a spirit of critical scrutiny of received knowledge, and the incentive to try to overcome historical time.[88]

In a study of the transmission of royal genealogies in premodern Tahiti, Van Baaren demonstrates the homeostatic relationship in oral societies between the myth-embodied value system and day-to-day life. Because the traditional Tahitian noble houses claimed direct descent from divine beings, genealogies were important to legitimate the reigning chief's claim to the throne. These genealogies were embedded in myths ceremonially recited at important festivals; it was understood that the recitation could not contain any errors or the priest who made the mistake could be executed. This severe prohibition appeared to guarantee to most people's satisfaction that the oral genealogical record was protected from mistakes and manipulations. However, when political events caused the dynasty to change, the traditional myth had to be brought into accord with the new political situation. To do so, the priests made small, unobtrusive errors every time they recited it until it was fully adapted. Officially nothing changed; in actuality, the genealogy was changing almost all the time.[89]

As this story suggests, change may be construed as a constant and relatively unproblematic occurrence in oral societies because the closest thing to an Ur-myth, Ur-genealogy, or Ur-ritual resides only in people's memories, as competing variants, always embodied in a particular situation. Changes can be routinely made in ritual since, without records that cast one version as original or true, such changes are easily ignored or rationalized. Van Baaren also cites the case of the Dayak of Borneo, who had the custom of making a foundation sacrifice when erecting important buildings like the community's longhouse. A slave was placed in the hole dug for the main pillar of the house and killed when the pillar was pounded into place. Dutch colonial administraters, however, prohibited this practice. Hence, the ritual had to be modified: a water buffalo was sacrificed in the pit instead of a slave, and the myth altered to explain that in the time of the ancestors a slave who was thrown into the pit had turned into a water buffalo.[90] Of course, this story does not mean that no one noticed or cared about the difference in the rites. It was undoubtedly a major problem at first requiring a great deal of discussion and negotiation, although a consensus was eventually reached on how to amend things. However, the issue of "truthfulness" as a matter of conforming to what exactly happened at some point in the past was probably not the issue that was most important for this oral community. Rather, the coherent and effective maintenance of tradition would have taken priority.

The role of myth and ritual in oral societies is to enhance, enforce, and codify cultural attitudes—something they can do best if they are continually brought into some sort of fit with the current circumstances of the community. How effective the ritual modifications will be depends on many other circumstances beyond the ritual arena per se. There is evidence that not all components of a rite can change equally well or easily.[91] Moreover, various units of the community can play an important role in maintaining adherence to remembered conventions or ratifying departures from custom. In this social context, the authority of the ritual expert and the authority of the ritual itself are rooted in tradition—yet tradition is something that exists nowhere but in its flexible embodiment in memory and in current cultural life. Ritual must have both a convincing continuity with remembered rites and a convincing coherence with community life. As one of the most visible and conservative embodiments of tradition in oral societies, ritual ratifies "the traditional" in general even as it recreates and revises it in the specifics of each performance.

Research on the effects of writing and literacy suggest that the emergence of literate social classes has important ramifications for ritual practice, the sense of tradition, and the locus of ritual authority. First of all, written records lead to what can be called a historical consciousness, the realization that today is different from yesterday, that practices, attitudes, and circumstances of today differ significantly from what they were in the past that is visible in unchanging records. Writing opens up a practical and metaphysical gap between then and now.[92] Second, writing down what people are doing or should be doing creates an account that is easily taken as normative and prescriptive. Ritual practice is deemed most correct and effective if it conforms to these normative guidelines. In this way, ritual can become a matter of *enacting* a canon of written guidelines. Indeed, with the emergence of authoritative texts and the sense of an historical gap, tradition itself comes to be understood differently: no longer directly embodied in custom and actual practice, tradition is now that which is described in and represented by texts; it is something to be reproduced as stipulated, to preserve, and protect from change. As the historical gap widens, the need to link immutable historical sources with very mutable living communities gives rise to complex institutions of interpretion and experts to mediate past and present. Authority tends to reside in written rules and, by extension, in those who know, elucidate, and apply them. Written religion, suggests anthropologist Jack Goody, heightens social stratification by differentiating the priest to whom the written word belongs from the rest of the people, who receive instruction.[93] As writing redefines a tradition's locus of socioreligious authority, ritual is no longer a matter of doing what it seems people have always done; it becomes the correct performance or enactment of the textual script. The audience has little right or opportunity to approve or disapprove, since only those who have access to the texts know whether it is being done correctly. In this framework, prayers are "recited" or "repeated," the liturgy is "followed" or "read," and aging linguistic forms can create a separate and professional liturgical language.

In an oral society, the embodiment of tradition can flexibly change to keep pace with the community and win people's assent as remaining true to tradition and appropriate to the current climate. Ritual can change without necessarily being very concerned with change as such. In literate societies with written models, however, change itself easily becomes a problem that is viewed as a threaten to tradition and authority. On the one hand, textually based ritual traditions can more readily forestall and control change because of the power of the authoritative text to act as a measure of deviance. On the other hand, the textual medium affords greater access to liturgical knowledge and more explicit challenges to its meaning, legitimacy, or originality; ultimately it helps to promote the rise of contending forms of expertise. In comparison to oral societies, therefore, change in literate societies is much more apt to be deliberate, debated, ridden with factions, explosive, and concerned with fundamentals. In other words, in literate societies change can be very untidy.

The textualization of ritual, that is, the emergence of authoritative textual guidelines, can be linked to a number of other developments as well, such as the ascendancy of increasingly universal formulations of values over more local and particularistic formulations; the organization of larger, more centralized, and bureaucratic institutions; and the formation of notions of orthodoxy versus heterodoxy in tandem with the codification of dogma. Hence, textually based ritual can lead to tensions between a centralized liturgical tradition that abides by written norms and local ritual life that maintains continuity with oral customs. Indeed, orality is never completely displaced by literacy, and many aspects of social life remain predominantly oral. This can create contending levels and types of ritual experts, such as literate experts with official positions and local folk experts with closer ties to localized subcommunities.[94]

Despite the abundance of ethnographic studies of ritual in predominantly oral societies, it is important to note that we do not know nearly as much as we should about ritual in literate, stratified, industrial, and postindustrial societies.[95] While some aspects of ritual in modern America and Europe appear similar to aspects of Ndembu ritual life as chronicled by Victor Turner, many other dimensions are clearly quite different—including the whole general place and style of ritual. While the far-ranging effects of literacy can explain some differences, the effects of very different economic and political structures are equally important and dramatic. Ethnographic models in which ritual is a central form of cultural production are probably poorly equipped to deal with the divisions of labor, class, knowledge, and ethnicity found in complex political economies.[96] Despite the fact that distinctions between oral and literate societies are necessarily provisional, and the fact that many literate societies are complex tapestries of both types of cultural transmission, the oral-literate contrast has helped to illuminate important dimensions of the data for the study of ritual and will continue to influence how such studies are constructed in the future.

Church, Sect, and Cult

After Max Weber raised the distinction between church and sect to the level of formal terminology, his colleague Ernst Troeltsch (1865–1923) developed it into a complete classification system that identifies the distinctive religious features for each. Many scholars have tinkered with the distinction since then, variously elaborating, modifying, criticizing, and simplifying it. In general, churches are understood to be open, inclusive, and often bureaucratic *institutions* into which one is usually born; they basically abide by and help promote the values of the larger society in which they exist. In contrast, sects are smaller, less stable, and more exclusive *movements* that either break away from churches or develop autonomously; in both cases they tend to reject or greatly qualify the values of the church and the society at large. One usually joins a sect voluntarily instead of being born into it, and its demand for a strong and exclusive commitment fosters both its rejection of the status quo and its sense of religious revitalization.[97]

Some scholars have argued that there is a dynamism to these types of religious organizations by which small unstable sects gradually become more churchlike until new discontent within spins off a fresh sectarian rebellion that will also in time take on the features of a church. Others have pointed to a possible continuum of tension between a religious organization and its social environment, ranging from the lack of tension with society seen in most churches to sects that operate in total critical disdain for social conventions and laws.[98] Rodney Stark and William Sims Bainbridge find it useful to distinguish between those groups that arise spontaneously using new or imported ideas, which they call *cults*, and those that develop through schism from a larger institution, which they call *sects*.[99]

Within the framework of these general distinctions, ritual life can differ markedly in churches, sects, and cults. Typically, a church has a fairly fixed and codified liturgical life claiming a long lineage rooted in tradition, divine models, canonical texts, or all of these things. Those churches that were originally schismatic sects often define themselves by critical differences in liturgy as well as theology. Hence, their founding liturgical formulations are central to what the group stands for and, as a result, may never be seriously questioned again. In a church, ritual experts are formally trained by means of accredited training that distinguishes various levels of competency and service. In tandem with the bureaucratic and worldly structure of the institution, therefore, the ethos of church-based ritual life tends to be hierarchical, with fixed roles for specially designated professionals, and some distance between these experts and the rest of the community. There are also fixed ritual events in the calendrical year with specially designated services and celebrations. Indeed, as an institution solidly identified with the social status quo, there is a tendency to emphasize calendrical and periodic ritual over rites that respond to unique or occasional situations. The content of the rituals is apt to address a somewhat hierarchical universe of religious power within which the ritual expert intercedes for the whole church, conceived as a nearly universal community, with somewhat less attention to the concerns of the local community or the immediate experiences of the individuals at the service. In this way, the local community sees itself as part of a much larger whole—a whole that is the church, the society, the rhythms of nature, and the order of the universe itself. Concomitantly, ritual life also affirms or ignores, rather than challenges, the values of the larger society, such as national loyalty, separation of church and state, and basic economic arrangements from valuing labor to tolerating the gap between the haves and the have-nots. Churches may sponsor missionary activities, giving a sense of dynamism and growth to the settled communities who raise money for such efforts, but in foreign locales the liturgical life of the church has more trouble being consonant with social values.

Sectarian movements often break with a church institution over the latter's worldliness and the concomitant corruption of its original ideals. Hence, the sect sees itself as inaugurating a "return" to a more original purity and simplicity of vision that by its nature constitutes a challenge to current society. In ritual terms, this often means a modification of liturgy in ways that favor less hierarchy and expertise. There may be a greater emphasis on individual experience and participation, instead of the passivity of an "audience." There is likely to be a valuation of spirit over the formality of rules and procedures. The rites may be emotional and spontaneous, or they may be reflective and meditative, but in either case their efficacy is seen as dependent on the active participation of the believers, even if they must simply open themselves to divine grace. In other words, sectarian ritual is not an autonomous apparatus, in contrast to church-based ritual, which can act to mediate human and divine by delivering sacraments, grace, or the Word of God to those who come to attend it. Sectarian rites also work to bind the immediate local community together by virtue of a heightened intimacy and a sense of being a distinct and spirit-filled community in opposition to so much around them. The ritual life of the group emphasizes the importance of personal decision and a commitment to break with the outer world for the sake of the community and movement. Hence, sectarian ritual activities are more likely to revolve around initiations and responses to immediate needs rather than predictable calendrical events.

The ritual life of cults can be quite idiosyncratic, the product of more individual syntheses, which might range from maintaining an audience for the teacher-leader to complex disciplinary regimens. In Stark and Bainbridge's usage, cults emerge independently of other religious groups; they are not schismatic like sects are. Hence, cults tend to see themselves not in opposition to a particular established group but more generally to society as a whole. This tension is often understood as a correlate of beliefs in an approaching Armageddon, a definitive point in time when the forces of good and evil will have their final confrontation. The cult may develop this millennial vision in various ways, both benign and ominous, assigning themselves the role of waiting it out, instigating it, or alerting humankind that the hour of truth is coming. Due to this vision and the underlying sense of an imminent end to the status quo, the ritual life of cults is not particularly developed or systematic. They are not interested in building structures but in discerning important revelations and making preparations for what is to come. Some initiatory activities, usually more ad hoc than traditional, emphasize loyalty to the leader, rejection of the world, and membership among the chosen. Corporate activities may heighten identification with the group, but often less so than in many sectarian settings. Here the group itself is temporary, a vehicle for "crossing over," although the leader as the source of revelation and instructions is indispensable.

Cults often involve communal living arrangements for some components of the core group. There are likely to be evening gatherings for teaching, revelation, and prophesy, for sharing, confessing, disciplining, or meditation and communal chanting. The idiom of being a "family" makes sense in this context and also legitimates the role played by a dominant leader, analogously understood to be the father or the mother of the group. Aspects of these features can be identified in the extremely antisocial activities of Charles Manson's "Family"; in the People's Temple founded by Jim Jones, who orchestrated the mass suicide of more than nine hundred followers in Guyana in 1978; and in the Branch Davidian movement led by David Koresh, who was killed with many of his followers when government agents attacked their compound in Waco, Texas, in 1993. However, rather peaceful groups also display this cult structure, including some subgroups of the Hare Krishnas, members of the Rajneesh International Foundation, and even the Unification Church under Sun Myung Moon.[100] In addition, the category of cult can legitimately include third-world "cargo cults" and UFO clubs in America. In most cases, such groups do not deserve the derogatory connotations the term can have in the popular press. Although some cults clearly become dangerous when their leaders have too much authority and power, Jonathan Z. Smith points out that the religious fanatic so vividly vilified in the newspapers is not always so different from the visionary hero we are apt to revere when safely lost in history.[101] Ultimately, according to Stark and Bainbridge, cults are important for their creative influence on more conventional forms of religion, even though few of them grow into "full-blown religious movements."[102] Usually occurring on the margins of society—although cults in successful middle-class communities have been documented—various analyses indebted to Victor Turner's terminology find they provide the liminal antistructural experiences of communitas, inversion, and experimentation that are needed to renew the structures of mainstream culture.[103]

The historical evidence suggests that cults may have always performed this function and as such have been indispensable to the richness of religious cultures.

No matter how flexibly it is used, the church-sect-cult typology does not seem to account for many features of the more significant changes of the last two decades in religious organizations and their rituals. For example, while American liberal mainline churches—namely, the Presbyterian Church (USA), the American Baptist Churches, the Evangelical Lutheran Church in America, the United Methodist Church, the Episcopal Church, the United Church of Christ, and the Christian Church (Disciples of Christ)—have lost membership since the mid-1960s, there has been great growth in interdenominational evangelical churches that do not readily fit any of these three categories, although one could try to press them into the sect category more easily than the other two. While these groups are often started by a religious entrepreneur and usually attract some of the disaffected from the mainline churches, there is no schismatic movement as such, and they have little concern with theological issues. The type of tension found between these new evangelical churches and the social status quo is not that generated by a systematic rejection of current social values—only a few flash points appear important. In general, these new church groups embody many of the features of traditional revivalism, a type of religiosity that has never been too far below the surface of American life. Their large services offer a fast-paced orchestration of singing, preaching, dramatic enactments, and personal witnessing that generate significant emotional responses from the audience. Indeed, these services see themselves as reaching out to "touch" each person and communicate spiritual sustenance and vision.[104]

American revivalism can be traced back to early New England, when a steep decline in the popularity of Puritanism in the early 1700s was soon followed by a series of religious revival movements, now known as the Great Awakening. The figure of Jonathan Edwards (1703–1758) is thought to embody the passion and style of this period, when the pulpit and sermon were used to move the audience both emotionally and intellectually to facilitate the experience of an abrupt "conversion," by which one passed into a new life and new commitment. A Second Awakening in the late 1700s and early 1800s took place predominantly on the expanding frontier, where the preaching style was more emotional and less intellectual. Traveling preachers pressed the audience for immediate conversions before moving on, while camp meetings that lasted a week would gather crowds and dozens of preachers. In the words of one observer of the time,

> Ten, twenty, and sometimes thirty ministers, of different denominations, would come together and preach night and day, four or five days together; and, indeed, I have known these camp meetings to last three or four weeks. . . . I have seen more than a hundred sinners fall like dead men under one powerful sermon, and I have seen and heard more than five hundred Christians all shouting aloud the high praises of God at once.[105]

The revival manner of emotional sermonizing—opening one's heart and then testifying to the power of the Lord in one's life—is clearly a style of public, communal ritual with deep roots in American culture. Christian evangelicalism draws on this tradition to assert the importance of being "born again" into a very personal relationship with God and then "sharing his Word" with others. As such, evangelical groups address the needs of the immediate community and encourage the emotional experience of an intimate relationship with God. They exhibit some features of sectarianism, especially by breaking with what are seen as dead, routinized forms of "comfortable" Christianity and being in tension with what they see as liberal values dominating the media and educational system. Yet the terminology of sectarianism may be more useful in characterizing a religious scene much less plural than that found in America today, where there are so many churches to rebel against, and they are all so divided within themselves. It may be more pertinent to note the undercurrent of revivalism. As a stratum of religious and ritual expression that emerges in times of experimentation, it ultimately appears to encourage the revitalization of ritual practices that seek a synthesis of public worship and private experience.

Conclusion

The density of ritual activity in a given culture is a fundamental aspect of the context within which any particular rite occurs. Yet there are only small islands of scholarly consensus on the factors affecting density, which can vary greatly even among neighboring communities. Certainly the degree to which rites have been organized and elaborated as parts of a system governs the meaning and significance of particular ceremonies. Aside from useful studies of the Indian Vedic system, traditional Hawaiian sacrifice, Chinese village religion, and a few other examples, there has been too little analysis of the historical and sociocultural dimensions of ritual systems to give much sense of the basic principles at work. More attention has been lavished on schematic typologies that analyze the type and degree of religious activity in a society in terms of long-term processes or correlations between social structure and worldview. Despite their usefulness in highlighting certain issues, the distinctions routinely deployed to characterize the patent differences in ritual in the world—distinctions between orthodoxy and orthopraxy, traditional and secular, oral and literate, or church, sect, and cult—often result in oversimplifications and static classifications. The specific conclusions associated with many of these analytical terms remain hotly debated, in good part because of the way these conclusions appeared tied to basic but unexamined assumptions about ritual, religion, and society. Nonetheless, questions concerning the density and style of ritual, however flawed they may be, appear to be a necessary means for reconnecting the individual rites examined in part II with the full human context in which they actually take place and have meaning.

SEVEN

Ritual Change

Questions of ritual density and style are not far removed from questions of ritual change, that is, the way in which rituals change over time. Yet the issue of ritual change has been much more central to study and analysis of ritual than the issue of density. Indeed, much controversy surrounds questions of ritual change among people involved firsthand in performing ritual. There are very few religious groups that are not concerned today with how best to adapt traditions of worship to shifting social and spiritual realities. At the same time, new religious organizations are also concerned with how to build ritual traditions and communities without replicating what they see as the problems of past traditionalism. A number of scholars, as either participants or observers, have been drawn to the issue of contemporary ritual change and, at times, drawn into the controversies surrounding it.

Part of the dilemma of ritual change lies in the simple fact that rituals tend to present themselves as the unchanging, time-honored customs of an enduring community. Even when no such claims are explicitly made within or outside the rite, a variety of cultural dynamics tend to make us take it for granted that rituals are old in some way; any suggestion that they may be rather recently minted can give rise to consternation and confusion. Indeed, as chapter 5 demonstrated, part of what makes behavior ritual-like is the way in which such practices imply the legitimacy of age and tradition. Yet there are also other reasons why we tend to think of ritual, especially effective or meaningful ritual, as relatively unchanging. Most theories of ritual have been rooted in ethnographic observations of oral societies, which afford less perception and evidence of historical change. These ritual traditions particularly give the impression—to both the indigenous peoples and foreign observers—that they are a matter of deep structures that do not change. Even though there is evidence that such rites are imperceptibly but homeostatically changing all the time, this constant modification is not usually interpreted as discrete instances of long-term processes known as change but simply as limited and commonsensical arrangements necessary in particular instances.

Foreign observers have tended to see unchanging rituals in oral societies unless they carefully record different performances and compare them, which was the case with the Ncwala kingship ritual discussed in chapter 3. A now discredited ethnographic contrast between societies "with history" and those "without history" express the perceptions of some Western scholars that oral societies have no real sense of the past.[1] While this idea is surely exaggerated, it is clearly possible that oral societies construct their past differently than literate societies do. Nonetheless, observers and theorists from literate societies with quite elaborate notions of historical change have tended to see ritual in general as fundamentally an unchanging thing that fares badly in societies where social change is marked and valued. Notions of function, structure, and even phenomenological essence, chronicled in chapters 1 and 2, also reinforce the tendency to think of paradigmatic or authentic ritual as a matter of relatively immutable sets of practices intent on preserving and promoting the unchanging structures of the sociocultural system.

In unstable circumstances, of course, the ritual life of oral societies can change with as much difficulty and drama as that of any literate society. Under the political control of a colonial government and the influence of Christian missionaries, for example, the ritual life of the Tshidi of South Africa–Botswana was dramatically transformed within the space of 150 years, as were major elements of their social organization and cultural life.[2] Long traditions of rituals and ritual experts were suddenly abandoned with the emergence of messianic and prophetic movements in Africa, cargo cults in New Guinea, the intertribal Ghost Dance of the American Plains Indians, or the religious reform movements of postcolonial Africa.[3] In his famous ethnographic account of the awkward funeral of a young Javanese boy, Geertz described the problems that occurred when the traditional Javanese beliefs and rituals began to break down in their new urban setting. This urban setting did not require the older, village-based assumptions and customs of interdependence, yet newer ritual and religious options were not sufficiently developed or satisfying to act as effective replacements for the old.[4]

Despite such evidence for change, it is nonetheless quite true that ritual activities generally tend to resist change and often do so more effectively than other forms of social custom. In fact, the ability of ritual to give the impression of being old and unchanging helps to protect it from alterations both frivolous and serious. Certainly, some rites have endured with very few concessions to the passing of centuries, such as the traditional annual rites to Confucius still performed in Taiwan, Hong Kong, and Singapore. The carefully preserved or reproduced robes, processions, texts, musical instruments, and melodies are taken out each year to be used according to time-honored customary and textual precedents. Yet it is pertinent to ask if a rite that is well over a thousand years old actually works today in the same way or means the same thing to people that it did when it was new, or only fifty or five hundred years old. Does the age of the rite, with its progressive distance from the rest of the social world, make it stand for something different today than centuries ago? Are meanings left behind or simply layered and relayered with new connotations and nuances? These are some of the questions that can shed light on ritual change and changelessness. The rest of this chapter attempts to address them in terms of the evidence presented by ritual practices themselves. The first section examines examples in which social circumstances cause ritual traditions to transmute; the second section focuses on some of the ways in which ritual is deliberately refashioned or invented; the final section examines the impact on modern ritual of new forms and forums of expressive media from tourism to video.

Tradition and Transformation

The history of the Christian ritual of baptism provides examples of both gradual and sudden ritual change and illustrates many of the issues concerning ritual density previously discussed. Indeed, a full descriptive history would vividly portray the dynamic role that context can play. The sociocultural context is not just the background for a ritual performance. By means of ritual action, people can simultaneously create a ground and foreground, to borrow Gestalt terminology, in which the foregrounded arena is both an expression of the ground and a way to act upon or affect that ground.

Scholars tend to divide Christian liturgical history into periods such as the early church, the medieval church, the Reformation, the Counter Reformation, the modern period, and the contemporary situation.[5] Despite the endurance throughout these historical periods of certain structural principles that have been intrinsic to the great stability and even rigidity of the ritual tradition, the emphasis, ethos, and theological meaning of Christian rites have changed significantly from one period to another.[6] Christianity began in Palestine as a Jewish sect, one among a number of movements concerned with the coming of a Jewish Messiah to liberate their people from Roman occupation. Only gradually did Christianity differentiate itself from Judaism, which was also undergoing radical changes in these centuries. The earliest Christian converts were mostly nonurban Jews who maintained their traditional practices, such as worshiping in the Temple of Jerusalem, while adding new ones that accorded a special status to Jesus of Nazareth. The practices of the subsequent generation of Christians also reflected the emergence of fresh trends in Judaism, namely, the Hellenistic and Rabbinic forms of Judaism developing in the synagogues of the Jewish diaspora after the Romans destroyed the second temple in 70 C.E.[7] Christians gradually superimposed a new set of doctrines centering on Jesus of Nazareth as the Son of God over the orthopraxy of their Jewish heritage, which in itself kept Jews from acknowledging the Roman gods, which all citizens of the empire were expected to do.

Meeting in homes, most often illegally, the Christians were a minority "sect" that had broken with the "church" of Temple Judaism. In keeping with Jewish ritual traditions, those present at these early gatherings would read portions of scripture, listen to expository preaching, invoke intercessory prayer, and close with the "amen" that Jews used to punctuate their petitions.[8] Recent study has strengthened the evidence that the last supper of Jesus with his disciples was probably a Passover seder.[9] Certainly the early Christian commemoration of that supper was directly based on Jewish table practices solemnized in the seder. As observed by these early Christian Jews, this Christianized seder was a commemorative memorial to Jesus as the "lamb" sacrificed to God, while also emphasizing the bread and wine that Jesus blessed in the traditional fashion and then shared. The 2d-century ritual manual known as the *Didache* contains many Christian versions of traditional Jewish table blessings, evidence of a nearly wholesale adoption of Jewish rites.[10]

In keeping with the Jewish tradition of orthopraxy, early Christian ritual emphasized doing the things that Jesus had done. The Eucharistic meal was a celebratory repeat of a historical event in time, an anamnesis or enactment of the deeds by which Jesus had signaled the ritual founding of his community of followers, his legacy to them, and how they should understand him when he was gone.[11] By the middle of the 2d century, the Eucharistic meal had acquired other meanings as well, as seen in the attempts of the early Christian apologist Justin Martyr to explain what Christian worship is all about to the citizens of Rome, who had heard wild stories of fanaticism, orgies, and cannibalistic feasts.[12] Although there is some debate among modern scholars, Justin's account suggests that Eucharistic prayers were also understood as a "thanksgiving," not just a remembrance. Recalling the story of Jesus, whose death had secured the salvation of his people, was a form of participation in those events that served to unite all of the baptized into one "communion-fellowship."[13]

The sectarian nature of early Christianity is also reflected in the comment of the 2d-century leader, Tertullian, who said that "Christians are made, not born."[14] As with most sects, in contrast to churches, people had to make a conscious decision to become Christians. One entered this community through baptismal initiation, a rite of passage originally derived from Jewish lustration rites of repentance for one's sins.[15] The earliest sources appear to expect that baptism would usually be accompanied by a sudden manifestation of the gifts of the Holy Spirit, such as the ability to teach, prophesy, or speak in tongues. Such religious experiences tend to be emphasized in relatively small, marginal, and unstratified religious communities that believe in direct relationships with the divine. However, as the Christian community became more stable and organized, the spontaneous outpouring of the spirit gave way to an increasingly elaborate initiation process that could take several years. As befits an alternative sectarian group outside mainstream Judaism and critical of Judaism's accommodations to a worldly ethos and political necessities, Christians made a sharp distinction between insiders and outsiders—the "way of life" and the "way of darkness"—and ritually guarded it with rites rich in the symbolism of death and rebirth. By the early 3d century in Rome, the initiate had to prepare for three years by taking religious instruction and concentrating on prayer, fasting, and almsgiving. During this time, the initiate, known as the "catechumen," was expected to change his or her life by withdrawing from all non-Christian relationships and abandoning certain professions abhorred by the Christian community. The baptismal rite was eventually held on Easter night in commemoration of Jesus' own passage from death to new life. The early-3d-century *Treatise on the Apostolic Tradition of Saint Hippolytus of Rome* describes the ritual.

> And when they are chosen who are set apart to receive baptism let their life be examined, whether they lived piously while catechumens, whether "they honoured the widows," whether they visited the sick, whether they have fulfilled every good work. If

those who bring them bear witness to them that they have done thus, let them hear the gospel.

Moreover, from the day they are chosen, let a hand be laid on them and let them be exorcised daily. And when the day draws near on which they are to be baptised, let the bishop exorcise each one of them, that he may be certain that he is purified. . . .

And let those who are to be baptised be instructed to wash and cleanse themselves on the fifth day of the week. And if any woman be menstruous she shall be put aside and be baptised another day.

Those who are to receive baptism shall fast on the Friday and on the Saturday. And on the Saturday the bishop shall assemble those who are to be baptised in one place, and shall bid them all to pray and bow the knee. And laying his hand on them he shall exorcise every evil spirit to flee away from them and never to return to them. And when he has finished exorcising, let him breathe on their faces and seal their foreheads and ears and noses and let him raise them up [sign of the cross].

And they shall spend all the night in vigil, reading the scriptures and instructing them. . . . And at the hour when the cock crows they shall first pray over the water . . . [which should be] be pure and flowing. And they shall put off their clothes.

And they shall baptise the little children first. . . . And next they shall baptise the grown men; and last the women, who shall have loosed their hair and laid aside [their] gold ornaments. Let no one go down to the water having any alien object with them.

And at the time determined for baptising the bishop shall give thanks over the oil and put it into a vessel and it is called the Oil of Thanksgiving. And he shall take other oil and exorcise over it, and it is called the Oil of Exorcism. And let a deacon carry the Oil of Exorcism and stand on the left. And another deacon shall take the Oil of Thanksgiving and stand on the right hand.

And when the presbyter takes hold of each one of those who are to be baptised, let him bid him renounce, saying: "I renounce thee, Satan, and all thy service and all thy works." And when he has said this let him anoint him with the Oil of Exorcism saying: "Let all evil spirits depart far from thee. [Turning to the East, saying] I consent to Thee, O Father and Son and Holy Ghost, before whom all creation trembleth and is moved. Grant me to do all Thy will without blame."

Then after these things let him give him over to the presbyter who stands at the water. And a presbyter takes his right hand and he turns his face to the East. Before he descends into the water, while he still turns his face to the East, standing above the water he says after receiving the Oil of Exorcism, thus: "I believe and bow me unto Thee and all Thy service, O Father, Son and Holy Ghost." And so he descends into the water.

And let them stand in the water naked. And let a deacon likewise go down with him into the water. And let him say to him and instruct him: "Dost thou believe in one God the Father Almighty and His only-begotten Son Jesus Christ our Lord and our Savior, and His Holy Spirit, Giver of life to all creatures, the Trinity of one Substance, one Godhead, one Lordship, one Kingdom, one faith, one Baptism in the Holy Catholic Apostolic Church for life eternal?" And he who is baptised shall say thus: "Verily, I believe."

And when he who is to be baptised goes down to the water, let him who baptises lay hand on him saying thus: "Dost thou believe in God the Father Almighty?" And he who is being baptised shall say: "I believe."

Let him forthwith baptise him once, having his hand laid upon his head. And after let him say: "Dost thou believe in Christ Jesus, the Son of God, who was born of Holy Spirit and the Virgin Mary, Who was crucified in the days of Pontius Pilate, and died and was buried. And rose the third day living from the dead and ascended into heaven, and sat down at the right hand of the Father, and will come to judge the living and the dead?"

And when he says: "I believe," let him baptise him the second time. And again let him say: "Dost thou believe in the Holy Spirit in the Holy Church, and the resurrection of the flesh?" And he who is being baptised shall say: "I believe." And so let him baptise him the third time.

And afterwards when he comes up from the water he shall be anointed by the presbyter with the Oil of Thanksgiving, saying: "I anoint thee with holy oil in the Name of Jesus Christ." And so each one drying himself with a towel they shall now put on their clothes, and after this let them be together in the assembly.[16]

The many successive phases of the catechumen's initiation into the Christian community described in this account emphasize the closed and sectarian nature of the organization. By the 3d century, the orthopraxy of the early phase of Jewish Christianity, already somewhat relativized by the importance of belief in Jesus Christ, began to give way to an emphasis on orthodoxy. In answer to a growing crisis in the Christian community about the middle of the 1st century, Paul decided that Gentiles (persons who were neither Romans nor Jews) who wanted to become Christians did not need to convert first to Judaism and obey all its laws; they simply needed to profess belief in Jesus. With this decision, Christianity took a decisive step toward distinguishing itself from Judaism and asserting more orthodoxic practices over orthopraxic ones. This step effectively made the message of belief in Christ independent of the cultural practices of a particular group, although Christianity continued to appropriate both Jewish and non-Jewish practices as its own and, as Hippolytus made clear, did not disregard rules and ritual. Indeed, there is evidence that many aspects of Jewish life, including food regulations and circumcision, were quite attractive to Gentiles at various times and places.[17] Nonetheless, what it meant to become a Christian was consciously streamlined and simplified; Christianity was deliberately distinguished as a new dispensation of personal faith in contrast to the old order, now depicted as involving excessive "empty" ritualism. The act of defining Christianity in terms of a few fundamental beliefs made it possible to spread the message by missionary efforts to all sorts of cultural groups within the loose grasp of the Roman Empire. In fact, the Roman Empire had done much the same thing by recognizing local legal and religious systems wherever it went, as long as they did not fundamentally oppose Roman interests and were ready to acknowledge the central Roman cult. While Judaism essentially remained an orthopraxic system committed to preserving a holistic religiocultural way of life threatened by the diaspora, the historical situation of Christianity encouraged this new synthetic religion to define itself in more belief-oriented terms.[18] This can be seen in the emergence of rules of faith (*regula fida*) that served as declarations of commitment to a developing creed and in a series of doctrinal controversies that were the vehicles for defining orthodox practice as well as heterodox practice, or heresy.

With the Edict of Milan in 313 and the conversion of Emperor Constantine, Christianity achieved legal status in the Roman Empire. Christianity was no longer outlawed; concomitantly, its adherents were no longer subject to intermittent persecution, forced to meet clandestinely in private homes or catacombs, or encouraged to define themselves in opposition to much of Greco-Roman culture. The result was a transition from the ethos of a sect to that of a church. Gradually, many Christians came to interpret its central message in ways that paralleled the Hellenistic mystery religions, as a matter of salvation *from* the world, not salvation *of* the world. Likewise, a "pagan" dichotomy between the heavenly sacred and the earthly profane began to shape Christian spirituality. More organizationally, new public church buildings followed the model of temples, as "the shrines of the deity" rather than as places primarily for the faithful to assemble. The rites held within them became more elaborate, performative, and hierarchical, with greater reliance on professional experts who acted on behalf of the larger group. As a church and public institution, Christianity began to take on new responsibilities for all aspects of life, fashioning rites for marriage and death and appropriating Roman festivals as Christian holy days. For example, the earliest certain evidence for the Christian celebration of Christmas comes from Rome in the middle of the 4th century, when it seems that Christians took over the Roman winter solstice holiday of Sol Invictus, the invincible sun. But Christians also adopted civil and court rituals to revise their Eucharistic meal. They transformed the humble communal meal of an outlawed sect into a public performance for a congregation of hundreds gathered in lofty basilicas. The scale of these basilicas demanded the orchestration of entrances and exits, lights, incense, music, and increasingly elaborate ceremonial robes donned just for the liturgy. In this context, the role of the clergy as an official priesthood became more focused, specialized, and exclusive.[19]

As a public church and the official religion of the empire, initiation into Christianity became a very different thing. With adult baptism increasingly formalized and standardized, one's prior entrance into the catechumenate was also marked by more ceremony and eventually advanced to infants. Yet the extended catechumenate gradually dissolved as child and even infant baptism became more common after Augustine's formulation of the doctrine of original sin. Meanwhile, the bishop's special touch and the invocation of the Spirit seen in Hippolytus's account became part of a rite of confirmation that concluded a period of instruction, when the baptized child was mature enough to make a truly personal commitment. Hence, the elaborate initiation of the adult catechumen ultimately divided into a rite of infant baptism, confirmation, and communion.[20] In this ethos, the Christian community was no longer a marginal schismatic Jewish-Gentile sect nursing millennial expectations of the end of the world. It was now in a position to be quite at home in the world, closely tied to the major political institutions of the early medieval period, with a growing understanding of its role in the world and in history. These contexts are invaluable in understanding what Christian ritual was about in any one period.[21]

The medieval period saw the development of yet another contextual ethos for the Eucharistic meal, with greater attention to the "real presence" of Jesus in the Eucharist and the special words uttered by the priest. The subsequent and continuing evolution of this ritual, its role in the Reformation and Counter Reformation, up through the decrees of the Vatican councils of the 19th and 20th centuries, reveals significant shifts in how Christians have understood their central beliefs and their place in the world. The notion of Jesus as sacrifice developed into an understanding of the mass itself as a sacrifice that redeemed the living and the dead, and eventually the service was conceived as a grand allegorical drama of the whole process of human redemption.[22] These ideas, developed as much in the practice of the rites as in the efforts of theologians, culminated in the ethos of the eternal universality of the church and the sacramental act of "transubstantiation" by which bread and wine became the body and blood of Jesus Christ. When performed by a properly ordained priest, this sacralization became the dramatic center of the ritual; communal sharing of the food became a secondary matter.

The liturgical scholar J. A. Jungmann argued that these developments divided the liturgical community by effectively institutionalizing an enormous distance between laity and priests.[23] This trend is seen in the erection of railings and screens to separate the laity from the altar, where several priests might go about the business of the mass. It was common for the laity to refrain from receiving communion and occupy themselves with more humble devotional activities. In fact, masses could be celebrated even if the church was empty, since it had become a cosmic act in the ongoing work of redeeming the human; it was no longer primarily a self-expression of a community of Christians. Indeed, within this ethos, concludes Geoffery Wainwright, "Mass was offered *for* the people (hence also private Masses), not celebrated *by* the people."[24] This new form of organization, emphasizing correct belief and godliness as obedience to the proper authorities, gradually dissolved the model of a smaller orthopraxic community. Not only was the church at home in the world; it was powerful enough to understand itself in terms of symbols of the transcendent identity of church and society.[25]

In the 16th century, the reformers attempted, in part, to restore the purity and simplicity of original Christianity. Hence, they were particularly concerned with the meaning of central sacraments like baptism and communion. While there were significant practical, theological, and ecclesiastical differences among the reformers and their followings, for the most part they attempted to prune the Mass of its sacramental implications and make it once again a commemorative, if participatory, imitation of the historical acts of the divine Jesus. Shifting to vernacular languages instead of Latin, to close reliance on the Bible instead of the papal institution, to a relatively egalitarian communalism in place of a hierarchy dividing clergy and laity, to graphic hymns from graphic images, and to didactic preaching over sacramental mystery— Reformation ritual life evolved a distinct ethos that stressed the ritual expression and communication of religious meanings over the ritual alteration of sacred and profane reality.[26]

The Counter Reformation focused on clarifying the medieval roots of its liturgical and theological positions, establishing an unprecedented uniformity of practice across the cultural domains of Catholicism and elaborating the "paraliturgical" activities (processions, rosaries, devotion to the saints, stations of the cross, etc.) that would tie local religiosity more closely to the church.[27] It was not until the 20th century, after some rumblings in the 19th, that Catholic ritual saw any further significant change. The Roman Catholic liturgical reform movement that began in European monasteries before the turn of the century encouraged new research into the textual and archaeological study of the history of Christian liturgy, as well as fresh pastoral concern for how people actually experience church liturgies.[28] When theological and historical justifications were marshaled, the case for change slowly gained credibility and support, culminating in the major revisions inaugurated by the second Vatican Council in 1963. The council's guidelines for "a general restoration of the liturgy" charted a new compromise between the traditional emphasis on the universal unity of practice and the need for cultural adaptation to local communities.[29] The changes that were initiated, often in a top-down, mandatory style, opened the door to liturgical innovations and wide-ranging discussions of ritual. For the most part, post-Conciliar ritual style places more emphasis on the communal aspects of the liturgy by enhancing the understanding and participation of the laity, although the sacramental focus is not abrogated. In this ethos, ritual is a means by which people "express" themselves, while the basis for spirituality and community are thought to reside within each the person, not in an external institution. In other words, the basis for a liturgical community is not ascribed to anything in the social, historical, or cultural environment, nor to simple obedience to traditional church hierarchical authority or customs. Rather, the liturgy implies that the basis for community can be evoked from within each person, both expressed and fully realized in the shared activities of the rite.[30] Hence, Catholic ritual today shares many of the characteristics of "modern religion" that were detailed in the typologies discussed earlier, although these features exist in some tension with older sacramental principles.[31]

Intrinsic to this history of ritual change has been the development within Christianity of its own practices of liturgical scholarship and interpretation. Like the literate traditions of Chinese Confucianism, Christianity has always reflected on its rites. And like the Vedic tradition in India, it developed methods of ritual analysis of its own, known since the middle of the 19th century as "liturgiology" or "liturgical studies."[32] The term "liturgy" comes from the Greek *leitourgia*, meaning an act of public service or ministry. It has been the preferred term for Christian scholars talking about their own rites and ritual tradition, although these scholars are increasingly comfortable with the neutral and more embracing term "ritual." That Christian scholars can situate their liturgies within the broad context of human ritual in general represents an important development in their liturgical tradition.

The liturgical writings of the Christian churches from the 1st through the 6th centuries were primarily descriptive and prescriptive. With the 6th century, however, the more elaborately symbolic rites of the Eastern churches gave rise to a new form of interpretation or exegesis, best represented by the figure Pseudo-Dionysius. His *De ecclesiastica hierarchia* attempted to expound what we would consider the purely mystical meanings behind ritual activities. This style of mystical interpretation was popular throughout the medieval period in the West and remained the main form of liturgical study in the Eastern Christian traditions until the 17th century. Yet there were also early attempts to pursue more systematic and historical forms of study. In the 8th century, the Frankish rulers Pepin (d. 768) and Charlemagne (d. 814) supported a school of liturgical study at court in order to facilitate the adaptation of the Roman rites for Gaul and to educate the clergy and the people. This school ultimately helped to popularize an allegorical style of interpretation that would be the dominant approach for centuries. The emergence of scholastic theology in the 13th century directed only minimal attention, and then mostly allegorical, to liturgical matters, but it did inspire a few influential works, such as the eight-volume encyclopedia *Rationale divinorum officiorum* by William Duranti the Elder.[33]

It was the Protestant Reformation in the 16th century that finally established the importance of a more historical study of Christian ritual, and this style began to displace allegorical interpretation. Protestant calls for greater participation by the people, the various liturgical revisions of the reformers, and the anti-Reformation codifications of the Council of Trent (1545–63) clearly initiated a new concern with historical authenticity and with simple explanations that the people could understand. Nonetheless, it was not until the 17th and 18th centuries that scholarly work on collections and critical editions gave way to more finely tuned historical studies, aided by the emergence of archaeological studies, university studies in the institutional history of the churches, and increasingly sophisticated scriptural studies.

The 19th and 20th centuries saw the continued development in all the major countries of Europe of a wide variety of formal liturgical studies—historical, pastoral, theological, and soon comparative—resulting in a number of classic works still consulted today.[34] Of particular interest is the birth of the modern Catholic liturgical reform movement, mentioned earlier, which was greatly indebted to the historical studies of three men: Prosper Guéranger (d. 1875), who founded a study center at the French monastery of Solesmes; Dom Odo Casel (d. 1948) of the German Benedictine abbey of Maria Laach; and Virgil Michael (d. 1938) of St. John's Abbey in Collegeville, Minnesota. The work of this movement led to the dramatic reforms in Catholic liturgy instituted by the Second Vatican Council in 1963.

In this century, the field of liturgical studies has attempted to explore all aspects of the Christian ritual tradition, the spiritual as well as the historical, the theological as well as the aesthetic, the pastoral as well as the comparative. While some see liturgical studies as a branch of theology, others see it as quite distinct by virtue of its comprehensive framework and its ultimately pastoral objectives. Its objectives have been to encourage appreciation, understanding, and participation in Christian worship, so it can be distinguished from the scholarship of those working in an exclusively academic context. Yet in practice the cross-fertilization among historical, theological, and pastoral approaches has been sufficient to ensure that the boundaries are very blurry.

Since the beginnings of the formal secular study of religion, often identified with the emergence of a "science" of religion associated with the work of Max Müller, Edward Tylor, and James Frazer among others, Christian scholars have not hesitated to use such scholarship to address a number of issues confronting Christian worship practices. On the heels of renewed interest in the historical roots of Catholic liturgy promoted by the early leaders of the liturgical reform movement, one question became particularly important. Since historical studies revealed great similarities between Christian rites and those of early Judaism, Hellenistic paganism, and even so-called primitive tribes in remote parts of the world, how was this evidence of historical dependence or cross-cultural universality to be reconciled with Christian belief in the unique and divine revelation of Jesus Christ, whose life was understood to furnish the models for the main sacramental rites of the church? Various answers emerged, but one of the more influential early ones was that of Odo Casel. Using the earliest studies of comparative religion promulgated by the myth and ritual school, Casel specifically addressed the surprising similarity between the Catholic mass and the pagan "mystery" rites of the Hellenistic world, in which one attained salvation by reenacting the death of a savior god. He argued that these pagan rites expressed a universal ritual pattern that was itself part of God's plan to prepare the world for the coming of the Christian mystery, the Eucharistic mass.[35] Casel's theory linked Catholic rites both to earlier stages of historical development and to the supposed universality of certain ritual forms, but it did so by seeing that history as designed by God to culminate in the special message of Christianity.[36]

Further scholarship on pagan and Christian ritual undermined this thesis from various angles even as the original underlying question itself changed. New formulations attempted to define the human, historical, or cultural dimensions of the Christian liturgical tradition as distinct from its unique, divine, and revelatory dimensions. This type of formulation was prompted not simply by more scholarship on the history of Christian liturgy and the cross-cultural nature of ritual in general but also by growing concern with issues of change. It was clear that ritual changed over time; therefore, some parts of the liturgy were historically "accidental," that is, more a matter of circumstance than revelation. It also seemed clear that rites needed to change to some extent in order to remain relevant to changing communities. To sanction such changes, however, it was necessary to know what parts of Christian liturgy were "accidental," human, and fallible—and therefore legitimately alterable—and what parts were divine, revelatory, and therefore beyond human tampering. The Constitution on the Sacred Liturgy issued by the Second Vatican Council made just this distinction and suggested guidelines for change.[37] In this way, the Catholic Church formulated the integration of two dimensions in ritual, the divine and the human, and the value of change for the sake of better understanding of the divine.[38] As a result, Latin was dropped in favor of vernacular languages, the altar was turned around so that the priest faced the people and they could see what he was doing, women no longer needed a head covering, singing was encouraged, and the laity increased their participation in the central sacramental activities.

With the changes ushered in since the 1960s, liturgical studies has also expanded and developed as a field of Christian scholarship that continues to emphasize pluralism. Most current liturgical approaches reflect a general consensus on a number of issues. They tend to identify some degree of "crisis" in the churches and in the culture, such as the antiritual attitudes encouraged by secular individualism, and they often find that the changes set in motion by the liturgical reforms of the Second Vatican Council have not always been successful. A sense of renewal and experimentation has been replaced by the conviction that ritual life needs to involve ongoing processes of change and reflection, not just sudden revisions that can quickly rigidify. While some liturgical scholars are primarily historians, the theological and pastoral concerns of others lead them to address controversial issues such as further adaptation of the liturgy to the needs of particular communities ("inculturation") and the evolving roles of laity in orchestrating the ritual life of the community (including the sacramental roles open to women).

Liturgical studies also addresses these issues by stressing aspects of ritual laid out in secular scholarship, such as the importance of ritual to community and the dynamics of ritual change.[39] These arguments invoke the work of a number of well-known ritual theorists: in psychology, Carl Jung and Erik Erikson in particular; in history of religions, Rudolf Otto and Mircea Eliade; and in anthropology, Margaret Mead, Victor Turner, Mary Douglas, Roy Rappaport, and Clifford Geertz.[40] In addition to close anthropological fieldwork and structural analysis of ritual symbols, liturgical scholars have also used performance theory and biogenetic structuralism to analyze Catholic ritual and its meaning.[41] Interest in these explicitly nonliturgical analyses of ritual has even led some church leaders to invite outside scholars to assess and discuss the quality of ritual life in Catholic parishes and monasteries.[42] In general, by invoking these other approaches to the nature of ritual activity, liturgical studies argue for continued ritual coherence *and* accommodation in the face of major debates on the ramifications of Catholic liturgical reform and the direction of the Christian churches in the 20th century.

Liturgical studies can appear at times to be in danger of overestimating the power of ritual. The more enthusiastic have gone beyond affirming the ability of ritual to renew faith and create community; they declare that ritual is what makes and keeps us human; it can prevent the inhuman destruction of warfare and orchestrate a transformation of the unjust social order that rational political methods alone cannot bring about.[43] The attempt to build church life on such an idealized understanding of ritual appears problematic to some secular scholars of religion, although others have lent their support to this direction. In any case, this concentrated focus on ritual is understandable at a time when issues of belief, theological doctrine, and organizational change appear to generate too little consensus to sustain serious discussion. In the end, it is likely that the formal study of ritual, in both its liturgical and secular modes, will continue to influence ritual practice by transmitting the very forces that gave rise to such studies in the first place — namely, a comparative and historical sensibility, the breakdown of tight-knit communities where social and religious orthopraxy are facts of life, and a growing emphasis on experiential individualism.

Liturgical changes in the Protestant churches, while less sudden, have also been historically significant and socially dramatic, particularly in the case of the 1980 revisions of the Anglican (Church of England) *Book of Common Prayer* and the Authorised Version of the Bible. The *Book of Common Prayer* (BCP) has maintained the essential shape of Anglican liturgy since its formulation in 1549 by Thomas Cranmer, the Archbishop of Canterbury, and the final revisions of 1662, even though the Anglican community has grown into a global fellowship of churches.[44] As such, the BCP is an excellent example of the powerful dynamics of textuality in a ritual tradition.

There have been additions and deletions in the BCP over the centuries, as well as various official alternatives, including the Scottish Prayer Book of 1637 and the American rite of 1794, among others. Yet by the 20th century, no one followed the BCP exactly for a variety of doctrinal, political, and practical reasons. Although some saw this state of affairs as belying the unity of worship that the book had always stood for, attempts to revise the book proved disagreeable to assorted constituencies. Revision efforts were more successful in America and South Africa, where the new BCP remains very much within the Anglican tradition; other revisions, such as the *Liturgy for India* and the *Ceylon Rite* are thought to go well beyond traditional Anglicanism.[45]

While Anglican liturgical scholarship in the 1960s and 1970s was less developed than in the Catholic tradition, similar pastoral concerns made the prospect of revision appear inevitable. The Anglican leadership introduced experimental services in 1969 with the understanding that by 1979 the results of these experiments would be brought to bear on revising the BCP. This was done and the *Alternative Service Book* (ASB) was published in 1980. In the end the ASB was not presented as an official replacement for the BCP but as a modernized supplement that would not be finalized until 1991, after another ten-year trial period.[46] Despite its 1,300 pages and heated debate over this form of ritual change, the ASB has sold very well since 1980. A new translation of the King James or Authorised Version of the Bible (now called the New English Bible) has added to the destabilization of tradition. Like the ASB, the new Bible expresses the idea that "worship is the work of the people," and for both theological and pastoral reasons the texts of worship should speak the same language the people speak, not an archaic parody.[47]

For those on both sides of the issue, the liturgical revisions expressed in the new *Alternative Service Book* are described as one of the most significant developments in contemporary Christianity.[48] Most of the negative reactions voice concern for maintaining the beauty of tradition in the face of a modern penchant for easy change and temporary relevance. The sentiments of one critic of change aptly illustrate the sense of tradition in a religious community: "To those of us who hold that tradition, in its essentials though not in every detail, is a priceless treasure which we hold in trust for the whole Church of Christ. . . . We can part with it only to our great loss." Appreciating the relationship between religious action and religious thought, critics also declared, "Change the liturgy and you automatically change the theology," echoing the old church debate on what comes first, *lex orandi* or *lex credendi*.[49] Others protested the watering down of symbols characteristic of British Anglicanism in favor of a bland universalism. All of these aspects of the British prayer book controversy support the theory of ritual change suggested by the anthropologist Roy Rappaport. As mentioned earlier, he argued that the unchanging "canonical" features of a liturgical order form the basis of a community's perception of its authority and majesty; if the liturgy is made more "indexical," that is, more immediately referential, the liturgy can lose that authority and majesty; hence, small changes can have enormous effects on the community's understanding of the nature of its religious experience.

When tradition becomes so embodied in a fixed text, the issue of change is likely to be a passionate one. The British debate, in particular, drew in anthropologists and sociologists on both sides of the issue—notably David Martin, Victor Turner, and Mary Douglas.[50] While the majority of them supported a rather conservative view of the proposed changes, it became clear that scholars had little ability to predict the outcome of changes made in traditional liturgies. When updated liturgies appear to be failures, it is hard to prove that the unrevised liturgy would have been more or less successful. On the one hand, scholars have evidence that rituals are always changing and do not necessarily need to be static to be effective; on the other hand, frivolous changes can undermine qualities that make ritual aesthetically moving or authoritatively reassuring. Theological agendas often pay insufficient regard to ritual aesthetics and mood, while attempts to democratize and modernize symbolism may fail to understand how symbols must resonate in one's experience, not simply catch the eye or echo common usage.

This extended discussion of changes in Christian liturgy demonstrates that even one of the most stable ritual traditions in the world has been subject to a constant diet of dramatic upheavals and gradual modifications. At times the structure of central rituals has changed, yet more often the meanings of those rituals have shifted as people looked to them with different concerns and questions. Aside from suggesting some of the historical dynamics of orthopraxy and orthodoxy, church and sect, literacy and orality, and the like, the preceding examples also offer an important counterweight to the tendency of ethnographic descriptions of ritual in oral societies to see the only effective or authentic forms of ritual as those that rise up spontaneously from the community by means of faceless social forces. The history of Christian ritual has numerous instances in which ritual was also reshaped from the top down or from the margin inward.[51] The assumption that authentic ritual must rise up spontaneously from the community not only denies the existence and validity of overt ritual change but also underestimates the role of ritualists, the people who take professional responsibility for organizing, performing, and even creating rites important to the religious life of a community.[52] A number of such ritual experts are familiar from well-known ethnographies, but primarily in their role as informants, such as the old, blinded hunter of the Dogon, Ogotemmeli, described by Marcel Griaule, or Muchona the Hornet, the Ndembu healer introduced by Victor Turner. For the most part, there has been little probing of the relationships among classes of ritual experts, ritual practices, and corresponding views of what ritual activity is all about.

One liturgical scholar, Mary Collins, has rightly drawn attention to this lacuna and questioned the assumptions on which it is based. "It is unheard of, say anthropologists, that rites expressing living belief should be devised and decreed by so-called ritual experts."[53] If they are right, Collins suggests, then the ranks of modern liturgists will have a very hard time understanding where they have come from and what they can do in shaping ritual practice. Yet it is far from clear that this ahistorical assumption is correct. The roles of ritual experts in devising and decreeing rites seems, in fact, to be much more widespread, dynamic, and complicated than most current models of ritual would lead us to suppose. Clearly, liturgical studies, which is so much closer to the realities of ritual practice, can contribute to secular ritual theory in this area, and perhaps in many other areas as well.

Ritual Invention

The tendency to think of ritual as essentially unchanging has gone hand in hand with the equally common assumption that effective rituals cannot be invented. Until very recently, most people's commonsense notion of ritual meant that someone could not simply dream up a rite that would work the way traditional ritual has worked. Such a phenomenon, if it could happen, would seem to undermine the important roles given to community, custom, and consensus in our understanding of religion and ritual. As Ronald Grimes notes, "Psychologists have treated private ritual as synonymous with neurosis. Theologians have regarded self-generated rites as lacking in moral character because they minimize social responsibility. And anthropologists have thought of ritual as traditional, collective representation, implying that the notion of individual or invented ritual was a contradiction in terms."[54]

For the anthropologist Barbara Myerhoff, the invisibility of ritual's origins and its inventors is intrinsic to what ritual is all about. "Underlying all rituals," she has written, "is an ultimate danger, lurking beneath the smallest and largest of them, the more banal and the more ambitious — [namely,] the possibility that we will encounter ourselves making up our conceptions of the world, society, our very selves. We may slip into that fatal perspective of recognizing culture as our construct, arbitrary, conventional, invented by mortals." We do not want to see our rituals, she continued, as "products of our imagination," but rather as reflections of "the underlying, unchanging nature of the world." If we should "catch ourselves making up rituals, we may recognize all our most precious understandings, the precepts we live by, as mere desperate wishes and dreams."[55]

Myerhoff elaborated this view in many different ways in her analyses of ritual: ritual as a collusive drama that all must be in on; as unique in its capacity to convince us of the unbelievable; by reaffirming the past and foreshadowing the future, ritual interprets change by linking it to grander, tidier totalities; or as shaping biological events to human purposes by encoding them as cultural dramas. Ultimately, she wrote that for one community, "Only regular, elaborate rituals could convince them that their way of life was real — a given and not a construct."[56] It would seem that for Myerhoff, and similar analyses, ritual is a unique mechanism for fooling ourselves — creatively, perhaps, and probably by necessity, but still the means by which people attempt to solidify meaningful illusions. This approach implies that as a performative medium, ritual teeters on the edge of revealing that the performance is not always an eternal, divinely mandated, communal response to the true nature of things. Therefore, in the performing, ritual must simultaneously disguise its techniques and purposes and improvisations and mistakes. It must make its own invention invisible.

This eloquent analysis of ritual is itself a remarkable piece of data; it is evidence of a particular worldview and probably linked to specific ritual and analytical traditions that deserve study in their own right. Yet its applicability to ritual activity does not seem to be very general or obvious. For a number of scholars, what Myerhoff described indicts the prevalent style of self-conscious ritual entrepreneurship in the modern world, an intrinsically chaotic state of affairs that is the result of losing authentic collective ritual and traditional forms of community. Whether Myerhoff attempted to describe all ritual or just modern ritual styles, it is an assessment that does not adequately portray what is going on in a number of contemporary — and some not so contemporary — ritual settings. Today there is a growing social legitimacy for many types of ritual improvisation as well as the unprecedented visibility of the very dynamics of ritual invention — from the highly idiosyncratic weddings that became popular in the late 1960s to a whole spectrum of new private and public rites, such as divorce ceremonies or rites to mourn the felling of the rain forest. Women gather for a "women's seder," families and friends devise funeral rites to recognize the particular horrors of the AIDS epidemic, and therapists use ritual to address dysfunctional family interactions. In all of these activities, people are quite aware that they are constructing their worlds, the moral precepts they should live by, and even the devotional images in which they decide to believe. They plan their rites step by step, watch themselves perform them, and are quite likely to sit down afterward and analyze what worked and what did not, both in terms of the ritual dynamics themselves and in terms of the effects the ritual was expected to produce.

Upon closer scrutiny, this self-conscious invention of ritual is not just a modern phenomenon, although the degree to which people now feel free to eschew any claims for ritual antiquity may be relatively unprecedented. Men's fraternal organizations in America in the 19th and early 20th centuries, such as the Freemasons and the Odd Fellows, offered elaborate rituals that were, in fact, their main attraction. Before most of these men's groups began to shrink dramatically in the mid-20th century, some actively solicited members to submit plans for rituals, awarding prizes of $50 to $100 for the "best and most perfect Ritual."[57] The history of the environmental movement in America is also the history of self-conscious devising of ceremonies, such as Arbor Day rites, to express changing perspectives on nature.[58] One Californian new age movement appointed a few members to sit down and design from scratch a complete set of communal rituals that would express the beliefs and ideals of the group. They devised a total package of rites, most of which were regularly and effectively performed for about twenty years, at which time the group changed in decisive ways for a host of external reasons.[59]

In some ritual situations, such as the development of American national rituals described earlier, it seems to have been important not to call undue attention to the facts of invention. In other cases, however, such as the development and introduction in the former Soviet Union of a full system of socialist rituals, this was less important since revolutionary socialist ideology explicitly expected Soviet citizens to remake the world. By the 1960s these freshly minted rites included public commemorations of political events, such as May Day and the anniversary of the Great October Socialist Revolution, initiations into various groups like the Young Pioneers or the army, life-cycle rites for the registration of newborns, marriages, funerals, and calendrical rituals associated with the agricultural cycle.[60] The story of Soviet ritual demonstrates that large-scale ritualization instigated and directed by a core of very self-conscious specialists could be effectively promoted and well received by the populace.[61] It was a ritual system designed and revised in government offices by various scholar-bureaucrats for the explicit purpose of social control and political indoctrination, a dimension that most citizens clearly understood. At the same time, many people could find or force into these occasions symbolic actions that had emotional significance for them.[62] While widespread public acceptance made the ideological intent of embedding communist values in every intimate aspect of Soviet life appear successful, the whole story suggests some important qualifications. It is far from clear, for example, that these rites were very effective in socializing anybody to embody particular ideological attitudes and dispositions. Researchers repeatedly point to the "stubborn selectivity" with which Soviet citizens accepted and participated in the civic activities of the state, and both Soviet and Western scholars have remarked in surprise at the degree to which people can differentiate what they do and what they believe.[63]

The leaders of the 1917 revolution had no interest, of course, in the development of an explicitly Soviet system of ritual. Politically and personally suspicious of ritual, the vanguard of revolutionary ideology saw itself as overthrowing a corrupt regime, setting up the rule of the people, and working to achieve the withering away of the state. Throughout the 1920s, Soviet leaders continued to believe that people could be persuaded to accept the "new blueprints" for a Marxist-Leninist society simply by using state education and "agitprop" (agitation and propaganda). The situation began to change, however, with the growing gap between socialist ideology and actual reality. In the end, industrialization and collectivization policies were established on orders from above, not by persuasion and education of the people. The issue of social support became more problematic as Stalin abandoned the posture of a Soviet revolutionary for that of a leader of a vast bureaucracy and entrenched political elite. As more social control became necessary, it was exercised in part through the promotion of emotional personality cults around both Stalin and Lenin. Khrushchev repudiated such cults along with the horrors of Stalin's regime, but a slowdown in economic development left the government casting about for new methods of political control and socialization. The Young Communist League put forward a number of suggestions for a system of socialist rituals that were eventually tried out and kept even after the ouster of Khrushchev and abandonment of most of his policies. Indeed, socialist rituals were one solution to the main problem facing Brezhnev and Kosygin, namely, how to perpetuate a 1930s-style political system with the minimum overt coercion among a population whose sympathies for Marxist-Leninism were increasingly remote.[64]

Adopting a perspective on ritual that echoed Marxist-Leninist analyses of religion, the government believed that ritual could be the ideal tool for effective socialization of an intellectually unsophisticated population. The corps of politically appointed ritual specialists were explicitly concerned with the ideological goals of the project, but their success was clearly aided by the fact that these ideologically cumbersome rites were addressing real human needs and there were no alternatives available. While critics of the system saw the socialist rituals as a strategy "to buy the people's souls" and party elites clearly saw them as "an ideological weapon," Christel Lane argues that many Soviet citizens actually managed to use them to add "colour, beauty, heightened significance and dignity" to their lives.[65]

Local organizations took the initiative in designing these rites, particularly in the city of Leningrad (now St. Petersburg) and the Baltic republics of Latvia and Estonia. By the early 1960s, many other places were also implementing socialist wedding services and birth rituals, with regional conferences organized to provide political support. The Central Committee took up the topic in 1963 and 1964 in tandem with controlling the appeal of religion and promoting atheistic education. Committee resolutions and then a ministerial decree called for new civic rituals to inundate the whole of Soviet life, establishing an "organic connection" between the new rites and the rhythm of people's lives that would systematically synthesize the logical, emotional, and aesthetic dimensions of experience. The new rites would replace older religious rites as communist morality and socialist internationalism would overpower bourgeois nationalism. Special commissions researched both general and local issues, devised systematic descriptions of particular rites, and gave practical assistance to those attempting to implement the rites on the local level.[66]

Designing a rite, according to Lane, involved activities analogous to the scripting and production of a new play on the one hand and the introduction of new political legislation on the other. A particular collective would rehearse the "script," invite critical comments from the creators and the performers, and revise it until it felt right. Then a commission would advertise and disseminate the rite on a regional scale. The first public performances were usually covered in the media, and gradually photographs and brochures were made available to interested parties. After the rite was established, there was a monitoring process that could introduce further changes as necessary and periodic seminars disseminated advice to the local officials. Of course, this process of development was not one of complete creation ex nihilo. Various familiar symbols and traditions were readily appropriated in bits and pieces to fashion something that was evocative while still espousing sentiments in keeping with official directives. Likewise, once the system was in place, specific parts of the new rites, such as the songs, could be put into the school curriculum to teach students a type of "ritual competence" and prepare them with associations that they could bring to their future participation in the ritual system.[67]

At the beginning, it was hard to achieve the right balance of structure and spontaneity, of the ideological and the emotional, or the collective and the personal. But the commitment to using ritual as a major tool of socialization made the designers learn from their mistakes and give more weight to the less ideological, more affective dimensions of ritual activity. The local officials who supervised the rites particularly observed the need for such changes. They saw that people were looking to these rituals for some form of emotional fulfillment, and they made it clear to the upper-level bureaucrats that strict ideology would not do. Local officials, for example, tried to explain to the towering chain of command over them that the 1920s birth ritual had to be changed or no one would use it. The original, unworkable wording had the new mother declare, "The child belongs to me only physically. For its spiritual education I hand it over to society."[68]

As an elite corps of ritual specialists emerged within the government, they defended their work by arguing that even Christian ritual was once new and had originated by means of conscious efforts on the part of the church leadership. Yet the Socialist ritual elite also set up various other levels of ritual experts. People were recruited on the local level and trained to act as officiants, usually a part-time job. Called "ritual elders" in the Ukraine and "leaders" in Russia, these officiants often requested more formal training for their demanding jobs; one local leader went so far as to compare their periodic seminars with the training of a priest. While the most active enthusiasm for the ritual system was probably concentrated in the party and its youth organizations, there was general cooperation from many sectors of the population with the notable exception of the intellectuals and artists. For calendrical holidays, most of the parades were organized by leaders of work collectives, who needed to resort to only mild pressure to get sufficient volunteers. Subtle forms of peer group pressure clearly pressed people to participate in workplace ceremonies, but not to the point of generating much resentment. However, the 1960s saw more overt pressure to discourage people who preferred religious alternatives to the sanctioned socialist rite. Yet as these socialist rituals became established and their performance more sophisticated, persuasion seems to have been limited to impersonal propaganda.[69]

In general, socialist life-cycle rites were concerned with strengthening the family as a unit while constraining its ability to socialize family members in ways that might deviate from the norms of socialist ideology. Towards this end a basic structure was promoted, but local variations were tolerated. Some places emphasized collective ideology, handing the new parents a bureaucratic certificate with the same solemnity as a receipt for a shipment of farm fodder or the payment of taxes. Other places tried to address the emotional situation of the people involved, even allowing people to continue using the Christian name of the birth rite, Christening. The Leningrad version of the Solemn Registration of the Newborn Child, celebrated in a specially built hall called "the baby palace," attempted to express both ideology and emotions and became a model for other districts.[70]

Weddings also had to try to balance these two dimensions. Special wedding palaces were in particularly high demand, and many local districts had long waiting lists even when wedding ceremonies were restricted to first marriages only. Government offices were the unpopular alternative. Usually the bride and groom and their guests rode in decorated limousines to the wedding palace, where they could buy flowers and the services of a photographer. The bride would slip away to a special side room for some last-minute touches to her dress, while the groom attended to the legal paperwork. The guests waited for the couple to lead them in a formal procession into the hall. Usually a small orchestra would play Mendelssohn or Tchaikovsky selections as the wedding party processed into a handsome room with a heavy wood table and a bust of Lenin. The master or mistress of ceremony, a local Soviet official, would give an opening speech that described the Soviet family as a loving unit that goes through life together *and* as "the most important cell of our State." The official then asked if the decision to marry was freely and sincerely made and if the couple was ready to take on the tasks of building a strong family and providing for the education of their future children ("A strong, good family is the might of our Motherland"). After an affirmative answer, the official formally declared the marriage "registered" and invited the couple to sign their names in the book of records. The orchestra began to play as the bride and groom put a ring on each other's finger. Finally, the official handed the couple their certificate of marriage and declared: "In accordance with the Law on Marriage and the Family . . . your marriage is registered. I pronounce you husband and wife." Congratulations followed, and all exited to the sound of a wedding march or waltz. There might be a champagne toast in an adjoining room before the wedding party headed off for less formal celebrations elsewhere.[71]

These rituals were either free or very inexpensive, usually underwritten by different local government agencies or, in the case of funerals, by collectives or trade unions. While a lack of available funds was a real constraint on the expansion of the system, it was not unusual for a local community to build their own ritual hall in order to have a special ceremonial place set apart from all other places. Most common were "Wedding Palaces" and "Palaces of Happiness," but there were also funeral pavilions and ritual spaces for non-life-cycle rituals, such as the ubiquitous initiations by which organizations took in new members. There were initiation rites for induction into the community of agricultural cultivators, grain collectors, students, and the three different communist youth organizations. While these initiations stressed the collective and ideological purposes of the rites at the expense of individual's emotional expectations, one should not underestimate people's emotional involvement in them.[72]

A typical example was the "initiation into the working class" sponsored by various groups of workers, such as factories like the Leningrad Kirov or the Kiev Arsenal. In the case of the Leningrad factory, the rite opened in the evening with veteran laborers lighting a great torch in the factory's open furnace, then parading it through the dark city streets in recognition of the city's and factory's "remarkable labour and revolutionary traditions." Workers decorated the factory's own "palace of culture" with slogans that hailed the new generation of workers. In the palace, veteran workers and leading members of the local communist party, youth organizations, and trade unions all took seats on a raised platform with the red flag as a dramatic backdrop, while an audience of parents and friends composed itself. Bugles sounded an opening fanfare, and the chandeliers suddenly lit up as the new workers paraded into the hall and took their seats to the applause of the crowd and the solemn music played by the orchestra. After a brief movie about the "heroes of labour and the Revolution," a drum roll signaled the arrival of the honor guard with the factory torch. One new worker would represent the rest in rising to face the torch and recite the labor oath: "We swear to follow always and in every way the traditions of the Petrograd proletarians. We swear. We swear to carry forward with honour the baton of our fathers. We swear." Then there were speeches, congratulations, more musical fanfare, and perhaps another brief documentary. Other factories used the same basic model, although they were free to add distinctive features from their own local or factory culture. Some might formally recount the history of the threshing machine and the surrounding town; others might have the new workers kneel to kiss the "scarlet cloth" of the flag. Some ceremonies put greater emphasis on the transition from an old status to a new, while others emphasized ideological themes. In either case, joining a work collective was considered a very important rite of passage for a young man or woman, both personally and in terms of the state's need to maintain a dedicated working class at a time when many young people tended to hope for very different careers.[73]

Some features of this history of socialist ritual invention readily turn up in situations more familiar to most people. Certainly the ritual dimensions of American national identity—the Pledge of Allegiance, Fourth of July parades, special ways to handle the flag, the national anthem, and so on—have also been formally created so as to socialize people into certain ways of thinking and feeling. People respond to these symbols and events in very personal ways, which can both support the original intentions and subvert them. Due to subtle strategies of traditionalization, most people take these activities to be old and authoritative, rarely questioning their origins. Yet, as we saw earlier, most of America's national rituals were rather recently established. The great influx of immigrants arriving in America beginning in the late 1800s led to the perception, according to the British historian Eric Hobsbawm, that "Americans had to be made." Immigrants were strongly urged to adopt those rites already in place, such as the Fourth of July commemoration of the overthrow of European colonialism and the Thanksgiving Day celebration of the Puritan (white Anglo-Saxon Protestant) values and mythology that had defined national culture up until this period. In return, of course, American life facilitated the emergence of a host of immigrant celebrations, such as Columbus Day and St. Patrick's Day. These helped various groups take up acceptable if somewhat constrained ethnic places within the fabric of American culture. Meanwhile, Hobsbawm argues, the school system self-consciously undertook a number of programs that made it "a machine for political socialization."[74] Led by the daily rite of pledging allegiance to the flag, which began to spread in the 1890s, these rites defined Americanism as an act of choice and a matter of specific practices and attitudes.[75] One predictable result of such a definition of what it meant to be an American was the simultaneous definition of "un-Americanism." Hobsbawm describes this un-Americanism as personified by the unassimilated immigrant, the foreigner "against whom the good American could assert his or her Americanism, not least by the punctilious performance of all the formal and informal rituals, the assertion of all the beliefs conventionally and institutionally established as characteristic of good Americans."[76]

The American national anthem, *The Star-Spangled Banner*, goes back to a poem written by the Baltimore lawyer Francis Scott Key in 1814, which was later set to the tune of a popular English song. By 1843 it was called "our national ballad," but it did not officially become the national anthem until 1931. The fact that it was formally adopted quite recently and, more aesthetically, that so few people can comfortably sing it has led some concerned citizens to suggest revisions or substitutions. Yet despite the obvious problems of the anthem and the obvious virtues of many of the suggested changes, the song appears to have entered the realm of tradition where it is accorded the respect of an aged symbol that cannot be tampered with.

In a 1992 plea to revise the Pledge of Allegiance, George P. Fletcher, a Columbia law professor, laid out the problem in terms that demand a ritual solution.

> If we once had a strong sense of American destiny, we now risk losing it. Forging a common national loyalty among immigrant children and the descendants of slaves is becoming ever more difficult. A new, inclusive form of patriotism is needed to underscore the unity in our diversity. . . . One way to realize the values of patriotism in our time is to rethink rituals like the Pledge of Allegiance and adapt them to the loyalties of a multicultural society."[77]

Fletcher calls attention to the fact that the pledge has been revised a number of times since it was proposed in 1892. "Under God," which was added by Congress in 1954, could be easily dropped, while the addition concerning diversity, he argues, evokes the ethos of *E pluribus unum* ("one out of many"), chosen by Benjamin Franklin, Thomas Jefferson, and John Adams in 1776 as a motto for the Great Seal of the United States. Fletcher would also revise the closing to express an aspiration to liberty and justice that would not encourage any complacency in this regard. "The point of the pledge," Fletcher declared, "is not to test the loyalty of the young but rather, by ritualized expressions of respect, instill an emotional attachment to their country." He acknowledges that such forms of ritual socialization cannot replace study of American history and the principles behind the Constitution and Bill of Rights, but concludes that "Ritual also has its place in opening the hearts of children to a greater commitment to the common ground of our history."[78]

Fletcher's concerns reflect a widespread understanding, shared with the corps of Soviet ritualists, that ritual is indispensable not only to nationalism but also to basic modes of communal socialization. In these roles, the process of ritual invention is neither completely self-conscious nor completely unconscious. For example, what was an explicit ritual invention from the perspective of Soviet officials was not nearly so clear-cut for the citizens who participated in them. They would find in these rites bits of folk custom remembered from childhood, songs sung in school, formalities that fit their expectations for proper etiquette, and tedious bits of government ideology. They could remain relatively unconcerned about the invention of the rites if the procedures were able to evoke and give form to an emotional response. Even if people disliked what was said during their wedding, resented the music, and deemed the official a pompous buffoon, they could find in the simple structure of the ritual a fitting marker with adequate emotional resonance. Is this part of the self-deception that Myerhoff described as intrinsic to ritual? Perhaps, but it not clear that such self-deception makes ritual more or less powerful as a tool for socialization for particular ideologies.

Many of the issues attending ritual invention surface in one of the most fascinating examples of modern ritualization, the international Olympic games. In 1896 Pierre de Coubertin revived the ancient games of the Greeks in Athens, explicitly envisioning them as "a festival of human unity" to foster mutual understanding among all nations.[79] They were to be a ritual by which people could affirm, celebrate, and promote a newly emerging world community. While the games today are more elaborate than those de Coubertin established a century ago, they undoubtedly reflect all the strengths, weaknesses, and ambiguities of modern global fellowship. From this perspective, it is interesting to explore how the ritual nature of the Olympics, like the socialist rites of the late Soviet Union, can act as a medium able to embody the contradictions, tensions, and ideals of a community trying to be born.

The ambiguity of the Olympics is one of its most striking features. Various scholars of ritual have examined, historically and sociologically, the way it simultaneously combines sports, games, warfare, and ritual. Mary and Max Gluckman, for example, pointed to the complex conjunction of these elements in the ancient Greek games when every four years all the participating city-states were bound to cease hostilities in order to engage each other in contests that honored the gods. Participants competed religiously as well as physically by playing under the patronage of different gods; the victors would make thanksgiving offerings to their divine patrons who, in effect, had demonstrated their power over the other gods. Nonetheless, for both the ancient Greek and modern international games, the competitions are not considered ritual per se.[80] John MacAloon, a historian and interpreter of the modern Olympics, suggests that the key to their importance is precisely the way they resist any simple categorization as ritual or sport or festival or spectacle. They are, he suggests, all of the above: "Olympic sports events are encased in a set of rituals surrounded by a huge festival and take on the magnitude of a spectacle."[81]

This complexity of format reflects the ambivalence of the community it profiles. The explosive growth that followed the small-scale Olympiad of 1896 testifies to a pressing interest—simultaneously political, economic, cultural, and spiritual—for an arena and medium in which the goals and contradictions of an emerging world community can be expressed. This tentative world community can only begin to attempt to acknowledge itself as such within the formality of ritual since ritual formality defines an identity symbolically, not empirically. Heavy on the rhetoric of common values while open to a great deal of variation in each participant's purposes, ritual makes few of the pragmatic or substantive political statements so vulnerable to disagreement and contention. Perhaps because of its ambiguity, therefore, the Olympics are, as MacAloon puts it, "the closest approximation to a truly global ritual symbol system that humankind has yet generated."[82] The United Nations is probably the only other symbol of world community (although Coca-Cola should not be underestimated), but the intrinsically political, military, and bureaucratic nature of its work makes it less emotionally effective and unifying. As a combination of ritual and sports, the Olympics are an apt way of expressing the ideal of a world community and its real-life contradictions and constraints. Indeed, the competitive open-endedness of the sports contests and the political concerns that are apt to disrupt the games are certainly more reflective of the way that modern nations experience the tension between global ideals and realities than a fully ritualized ceremony could express.

For de Coubertin, the ceremonies accompanying the competitions were not just aesthetic or entertaining additions. He argued that "it is primarily through the ceremonies that the Olympiad must distinguish itself from a mere series of world championships." In this vein, he sought to formulate a religious dimension to the games, gradually articulating a vision of the transcendent and "impassioned soaring" at the heart of the cult of athletics. As MacAloon points out, de Coubertin was designing a decidedly secular and rationalized form of religion that could still evoke the emotional appeal of religious symbols and rituals.[83] With these symbols and rites, de Coubertin explicitly wanted to give the world an idea of itself as a community, "a simple, clear and tangible idea can draw together not only people of all ages and all professions, but of all opinions and all situations."[84]

The effective ambiguity of the Olympics games is not simply the emergence of a new, blurred genre. The format of the event simultaneously affirms distinct national identities while superimposing a semblance of world unity. For both the Olympics and the United Nations, nationhood is a necessary form of political and social identity without which a people does not have the right or means to represent itself as an equal among others. Hence, somewhat contradictorily, the Olympics promotes nationhood as a requirement for participation in a world community that is attempting to transcend narrow national interests. Groups signal their adoption of this form of identity by means of the symbolic accouterments of a flag, government officials, passport regulations, stamps, embassies, and, of course, a team to send to the games. There its flag is hoisted alongside others, its representatives housed with the others, and its language aired among the ranks of interpreters and the banks of microphones. In this way, ritualized sports promote an organization of cultural identities, interests, directions, and patterns of behavior. Yet, as MacAloon and others have noted, the seeming universality of the language of organized sports still does not make it readily inclusive—a point demonstrated by the Tarahumara of Chihuahua, Mexico, perhaps the most superb distance runners in the world until they were brought to the games and lined up to run competitively at the blast of a gun in their ears.[85] Yet for all the cultural and political coercion involved in the demand for the trappings of a national identity, the effect is not without a leveling dimension that holds out the promise of a people being treated as one among equals, albeit in a very awkward and artificial arena.

The unified world community de Coubertin envisioned was intended to celebrate, not obliterate, cultural differences. The familiar Olympic symbols express this view of unity with diversity. For example, the lighting of the sacred flame at Archaia Olympic (Mount Olympus) and its relay to the site of the games does not collapse or deny geographic distance; it painstakingly traverses it. The flag of five linked rings that represent the five continents also expresses this idea, especially when it enters the arena as the culmination of the display of national flags.[86] The symbols of nationhood are not squashed for a vague oneness; they are paraded and then capped by Olympic symbols of commonality and cooperation. Likewise, when individual athletes contend and compete as persons and as national teams, their personal and national achievements are celebrated, as in the awards ceremony that plays the national anthem of the gold medal winner. Yet the gold, silver, and bronze medals depict Olympic insignia. In this way, de Coubertin orchestrated an extended ceremonial that accepted and built upon the realities of modern politics. A more idealistic view of human unity, without national or individual glory, would not have such great appeal. Nonetheless, he copied the ancient Greek "oath of honor and disinterest" taken by each athlete. This oath was central to de Coubertin's sense of the Olympics and more important to the religiosity of the games than any ceremony before the altar of Zeus. It was to be purifying ritual, "the secret of the ceremonies," sworn before the assembled flags of the competing nations before the opening of the games.[87] Still, in his major work, *The Olympic Idea: Discourses and Essays*, de Coubertin's pragmatism sees beyond oaths and ceremonies: "To ask the peoples of the world to love one another is merely a form of childishness. To ask them to respect one another is not in the least utopian, but in order to respect one another it is first necessary to know one another."[88] This emphasis on the individual and coming to know individuals, not just teams and nations, is one of the main dynamics by which the Olympics negotiate the tensions between national identities and global unities.

Several examples illustrate more explicitly the way in which the ritual nature of the Olympic games embodies the contradictions within the ideal of a world community. The closing rites of the 1988 games in Seoul followed the established practice of having each team enter the main stadium to the strains of its national anthem, garbed in its representative dress, and bearing its national flag. One team after another took their places to form a great parade that completed a full circuit around the field. That year, however, the American team members refused to stay in formation. In an attempt to share their exuberance, they broke ranks to wander into the center of the field and actively encouraged other teams and members of the audience to mingle with them. They felt, perhaps, the desire to express a deeper *communitas* than the rigid structure of the games allowed. However, their actions were not very effective. Most of the other teams ignored them and marched past in formation. The contrast made the Americans look somewhat disordered, undisciplined, and disrespectful. Clearly, for many of the participating teams, the order and structure of the final parade was more appropriate to how they wished to be viewed and to the national dignity they were commissioned to uphold. Perhaps it was only the Americans, confident of their competitive place in the games and the world at large, who could afford a looser hold on the structure of the event and temporarily allow unity to overwhelm identity.[89]

In another set of embodied tensions, the games bring national teams together to compete on relatively egalitarian terms, but no one can underestimate how disparities in training, numbers, and finances can give teams advantages and disadvantages irrespective of their physical skills. Yet Abebe Bikela, the barefoot runner from Ethiopia who won the marathon in the Roman games in 1960, upset the polished and disciplined performances of highly trained teams from Europe and the United States. He was an exotic and unthreatening underdog, and the crowd loved him for it.[90] Aspects of this tension between equal participation and unequal resources also affect the hosting of the games. In the cases of Japan and Korea—the first recovering from the destruction of World War II, the other recovering from the fragmentation of a more recent civil war—their successful hosting of the games in Tokyo and Seoul earned them a sense of prestige among the leading nations of the world. Indeed, hosting the Olympics has allowed the humbled, isolated, or reviled "nation" to try to change its image and show off its managerial skill, technological sophistication, and international poise. As a result, however, competition for the expensive honor of hosting the games has become very intense and often outrageously nationalistic and manipulative. The egalitarian aspects of the sports competition coexists with scrambling for a competitive edge in the international hierarchy. Barefoot runners and third-world hosts do not easily unseat the well-healed and well-connected, even though the possibility of doing so draws them into the attempt. In the end, the orchestration of these ritual games simultaneously affirms a hierarchical prestige order in which participants wish to secure a place at the same time that it also offers opportunities for that order to be reshuffled and restacked.

Most disturbing to de Coubertin's overt vision of the games have been the political events that have continuously intruded. It is said that the first 1896 games in Athens "helped topple two consecutive Greek governments."[91] Hitler's sponsorship of the lavish 1936 Berlin games, immortalized in Leni Riefenstahl's documentary film *Olympiad*, championed Nazi racial ideology, explicitly excluded German Jews, and left the Nazis visibly distressed by the record-breaking victory of the African-American runner, Jesse Owens. Hungarian and Soviet water polo players brawled at the 1956 Melbourne games held just three weeks after the Soviet invasion of Hungary. At the Mexico City games in 1968, the African-American athletes Tommie Smith and John Carlos raised black-gloved fists on the victory stand in a gesture of solidarity with the American Black Power movement.[92] By far the most serious political event was the murder in Munich in 1972 of eleven Israeli athletes and officials who had been taken hostage by Black September Palestinian terrorists in the Olympic Village, where lax security was meant to underscore international and racial harmony. African-American athletes protesting racial injustice in America boycotted the 1976 Montreal games. At President Carter's initiative, West Germany, Japan, and other nations joined the United States in boycotting the 1980 Moscow games to protest the Soviet invasion of Afghanistan. The Soviets, in turn, boycotted the 1984 Los Angeles games. New forces of a more commercial nature, however, marred the 1992 Barcelona games, particularly in the form of pro "dream teams" that did not want to join the other athletes in the spartan quarters of the Olympic village. Through all of these incidents, the International Olympic Committee has always argued that the "games must go on." For some of the athletes, however, the political events were reminders that, as one put it, "the underlying problems of all mankind . . . [are] reflected in the Olympics."[93]

As a ritual expression of an ambivalent world community, the Olympic games exemplify a number of themes discussed more theoretically in earlier sections. For example, rituals do not build community by simply expressing sentiments of collective harmony; they do it by channeling conflict, focusing grievances, socializing participants into more embracing codes of symbolic behavior, negotiating power relations, and, ultimately, forging images by which the participants can think of themselves as an embracing unity. In the real world of international politics and economics, ritual is not a magical solution: it cannot bring the world together in peaceful cooperation any more than the socialist rites of the USSR could ensure a transregional socialist citizenry or American rites of national loyalty can solve the tensions between assimilation and ethnic pride. Yet the physical and symbolic language of ritual is invoked, consciously or unconsciously, as a medium that can embrace real-life contradictions while still orienting people toward ideals, the mere articulation of which must be a first step in their embodiment and realization. This ritualization process, therefore, does not have to be hidden. In the case of the Olympics, its competitive and ceremonial dimensions are examples of very self-consciously invented rituals for very explicit purposes. At the same time, however, appeals to an ancient tradition, like the model of the Greek games, provide a more faceless, external, and neutral sort of authority. It suggests a type of canonicity, to return to Roy Rappaport's terms, that can downplay the indexical nature of the activities; in other words, the authority of "ancient tradition" can reassure potential but uneasy participants that their coming together is equally empowering.

A similar combination of invention and appeal to a neutral but authoritative tradition lies behind the modern ritual invention of Kwanzaa, the African-based new year ritual designed and promoted in 1966 by Maulana Karenga, a professor of black studies.[94] Karenga explicitly drew upon forms of symbolic action common to many different African rituals and festivities, while clearly disavowing any exact African model. Yet some people have continued to believe the rite is an authentic African tradition. The term comes from the Swahili phrase *matunda ya kwanza*, meaning the firstfruits of the harvest. Swahili terminology was adopted because it is a nontribal African language and, therefore, thought to be most generally representative of the shared heritage of African-Americans.[95] Kwanzaa begins on December 26, the day after Christmas, which may or may not be observed also, and ends on New Year's Day, January 1. The celebration period is marked by activities that promote and enjoy African-American cultural traditions and social bonds. In one sense it is a meaningful cultural substitute for the European-rooted customs associated with the Christmas season.[96] In another sense, however, it does what the European customs could never do: it symbolizes and promotes both personal and communal affirmations of a shared African-American heritage that can be embodied in all the usual forms of cultural expression—family relationships, values, cooking, dress, customs, and holidays.

The home is the main setting for the rituals of the week, although many communities also sponsor street fairs with vendors, musicians, and food stalls. In the home a table is arranged with a mat, on which are placed fruits, ears of corn, gifts, the unity cup, and a holder for seven candles. The fruits and vegetables symbolize a people's agricultural roots and the harvest themes of productivity, thanksgiving, and communal celebration. The cloth or straw mat symbolizes the traditions of Africa on which its descendants build. The ears of corn stand for the children of the household, one for each, as produce of the stalk who will become producers themselves. The gifts, preferably simple, traditional, and noncommercial, are for the children and symbolize sharing and mutual bonds. The unity cup is used to pour a libation to the ancestors. After reciting the libation statement, a verbal commitment to the heritage and the future, all the assembled family and friends drink from the cup. The seven candles symbolize seven principles, which form the value structure of seven-day holiday. Known as the *nguzo saba*, they are unity (*umoja*), self-determination (*kujichagulia*), collective work and responsibility (*ujima*), cooperative economics (*ujamaa*), purpose (*nia*), creativity (*kuumba*), and faith (*imani*).

As a candle is lit each evening of Kwanzaa, usually by a child, the text explaining the corresponding principle is recited. The center candle, symbolizing unity, is black, with red candles symbolizing blood to one side and green ones symbolizing hope to the other.[97] In recent years, some African-American communities have added the figure of the wise old man, Nia Umoja, the African equivalent of Santa Claus, who distributes gifts as well as advice and direction to the children. Annual workshops and publications for both children and adults add new ideas for orchestrating activities that can bring home the meaning of the Kwanzaa rituals.[98] At the same time, however, Kwanzaa has become involved in the debates that concern every other American holiday. As growing numbers of people celebrate Kwanzaa, over 13 million by one reckoning, more complain about the commercialization of the holiday and the difficulty of keeping the real meaning of the events in focus.[99]

In the light of other winter solstice rites, Kwanzaa suggests new levels of historical complexity involved in ritual change. As noted earlier, the Christians seem to have created Christmas by taking over the Roman holiday, Sol Invictus. Where Romans saw the rebirth of the sun in the dense center of winter, Christians appropriately saw the logical time to celebrate the birth of their god. In the end, the festival to Sol Invictus died out, and the Christmas interpretation became widespread and powerful. In the United States, the influence of Christmas is pervasive: the whole socioeconomic fabric of the culture gears up for this holiday: stores, schools, the media, and the moral and religious sentiments of public figures. Indeed, the mass media targeting of children makes it particularly difficult for non-Christians to avoid or ignore the holiday. In response, many American Jews have elaborated their winter solstice holiday of Hanukkah in order to avoid being swallowed up by the Christian and commercial culture of Christmas. Traditionally, Hanukkah has been relatively unimportant, and not very much is known about its origins. The most common story sees it as a commemoration of the victory of the Maccabees over the Syrian occupiers of Jerusalem in the 2d century B.C.E. Their liberation of the temple made it possible to celebrate the eight-day festival of Sukkot ("booths"), which was forbidden under Syrian occupation. According to later Talmudic legend, the Maccabee brothers found only enough oil in the temple to burn the candles of the traditional candelabrum, the menorah, for one night. Miraculously, however, the oil kept the candles burning for eight nights. Hence, Hanukkah commemorates this with the lighting of the eight-armed menorah (or *hanukkiyyah*) in the home and the synagogue—one candle the first night, two the second, and so on, each time reciting a declaration of God's "miracles, deliverances, and wonders." While unmentioned in the traditional sources, current custom dictates that presents are given to the children each night, most likely the influence of Christmas. In fact, it is quite probable that Hanukkah's association with lighting lamps derives less from the Maccabees and more from the same Roman winter solstice practices that inspired the Christians, whose continued influence on the Jewish holiday certainly predates the current impact of Christmas consumerism. As for the Kwanzaa practice of the lighting seven candles after Christmas, it has probably been influenced by the Hanukkah tradition as well as Christmas and, through them, by the Roman rites to Sol Invictus and a long history of solstice celebrations. Purity of lineage has never been an important principle of ritualization; evocative symbols and familiar practices are readily revised for new purposes or reinterpreted for new communities.

Hanukkah, Kwanzaa, the socialist rites of the former Soviet Union, and various American national rites all have invented features that adapt familiar images and patterns to new purposes, including the self-definition of communities. They are not that different from a growing number of ritual experiments in other areas, such as ecological rites. These rituals, celebrations, and even memorial ceremonies not only express a concern for respecting and safeguarding the earth but also attempt to redefine the human and natural worlds as one interrelated community for whom recognition of its interdependence is intrinsic to the health of the whole. *Liturgies of the Earth*, a manual of ritual directions composed by the Reverend Richard E. Kuykendall, testifies to "the inherent goodness and sacredness" of the earth. It speaks of the need to "re-establish our connection to it through rituals and liturgies which sing an ancient song of the cycle of life" and thereby lead people "into a new way of belonging" and a "new dance of interconnectedness, mutuality and interdependence."[100]

A similar ritual response to the need for new forms of relatedness can be seen in the spectrum of experiments with feminist and womanist rituals, as well as the more recent activities of the nascent men's movement. Spokespersons for women's rituals may describe themselves as reclaiming an ancient prepatriarchal heritage of goddess worship that venerated nature and the body, connectedness and process, holism and healing. Or they may describe their work as a matter of historically unprecedented religious experimentation in quest of a liberating religious and ethical breakthrough. With either position, it is clear to these ritualists that they are inventing rites for an age that has given women no other adequate form of ritual acknowledgment. Whether they use the terminology of reclamation or creation, they know they are involved in the construction of new traditions.[101] According to Layne Redmond, a recording artist and drumming teacher from New York City: "We truly have no meaningful ritual right now. People have a need to create their own."[102] The poet Marge Piercy writes: "Comprend, we sweat out our rituals together. We change them, we're all the time changing them! But they body our sense of good!"[103] For these feminists, in fact, women's ritual is the most "radical (proceeding from the root) affirmation of the revolutionary potential of the feminist movement."[104] In the last chapter, "Creating Religion: Toward the Future," of her early classic on goddess worship, *The Spiral Dance*, Starhawk analyzed goddess ritual as an attempt at re-creation and not revival. While drawing strength from the legitimacy and power of the benevolent Goddess, Starhawk wrote, "women are creating new myths, singing a new liturgy."[105] As the symbolic equivalent of the right to vote and receive equal pay, such writers see the "right to ritual" as an appropriation of the power to define, mobilize, and nuance the images that shape their lived reality.

In general, feminist rituals focus on several major themes such as bonding among women, embodied modes of shared symbolic communication, and personal empowerment. For example, feminist ritualization "reclaims" menstruation and childbirth, areas in which religion and ritual have tended to cast women as polluted or "cursed." New rites reinterpret these fundamental female experiences in ways that contribute to positive self-images and a sense of connectedness to nature and other women.[106] Most commonly, a "rite of passage" uses these themes to express personal transformation and communitas among cohorts. Another important mode of feminist ritual expression is to "rewrite" an older, male-focused ceremony using female language and images. For example, in the women's seder written by E. M. Broner and Naomi Nimrod, the four traditional questions asked by the youngest male child—"Why is this night different from all other nights?" and so on—are changed:

> "Why is this Haggadah different from traditional Haggadoth?"
> "Because this Haggadah deals with the exodus of women."
> "Why have our mothers on this night been bitter?"
> "Because they did the preparation but not the ritual. They did the serving but not the conducting. They read of their fathers but not of their mothers."
> "Why on this night do we recline?"
> "We recline on this night for the unhurried telling of the legacy of Miriam."[107]

A number of groups are exploring the theological and institutional ramifications of such revised liturgies. For example, the Catholic theologian Rosemary Radford Ruether writes on the organization of liturgical communities for women called "women-church."[108] Studies by Marjorie Procter-Smith and Sharon and Thomas Neufer Emswiler lay out careful critiques of the traditional participation of women in Christian liturgy and suggest changes that would make the tradition "true for us, for women living in these times."[109] While these new liturgies substitute inclusive language for terms that privilege the male, they also address the traditional exclusion of women from positions of ritual expertise and the general dismissal of women's experiences. For some, this demands a challenge to the lingering use of complex metaphors such as those of absolute monarchy readily found in many Anglican hymns: "The Son of God goes forth to war," "Eternal monarch, king most high," "Jesus shall reign," and even in the revised *Alternative Service Book*, "God of power and might."[110]

The new "men's movement" has also turned to ritual participation to reflect upon and facilitate changes in those cultural images of men that affect their sense of self and capacity for close relationships. Robert Bly, the guru of this movement, opens his book *Iron John* with the observation that "it is clear to men that the images of adult manhood given by the popular culture are worn out; a man can no longer depend upon them. By the time a man is thirty-five he knows that the images of the right man, the tough man, the true man which he received in high school do not work in life."[111] These images, Bly argues, have aided men's exploitation of the earth, their humiliation of women, and their obsession with warfare. They add up to a defective mythology of the hard man and the soft man, he asserts, and it is time that men move on.[112] Bly makes ample use of myth and the language of ritual initiation to talk about the personal-communal transformation process that men need: "The recovery of some form of initiation is essential to the culture."[113] Indeed, *Iron John* is essentially an eight-stage initiation process recapitulating the transformation of boy into man that is found in the classic formulations of the myth of the hero. At the same time, of course, Bly invokes a therapeutic understanding of ritual as a type of community process by which persons can find themselves. While the feminists invoke the same theme, they are likely to subordinate it to the task of creating new rituals that will have an impact on traditional social institutions. For the men's movement, institutional change is, at least for now, secondary to personal reorientation.

A similar quest to experience an essential inner nature that can defy the anemic roles forced on people by modern society underlies the popularity of such modern self-healing rites as fire walking. One analyst of the American firewalking movement suggests firewalking is a therapeutic ritual that empowers people by metaphorically moving participants from a culturally defined state of weakness to a culturally defined state of mental and physical healing.[114] Both scholarly and popular theories concerning the therapeutic properties of ritual have inspired many other attempts to employ ritual methods of building community, exploring identity, and evoking a sense of moral direction. For Joan Laird, who writes about the use of ritual in family systems therapy, ritual is "the most potent socialization mechanism" by which groups prepare individuals to perform the roles that the group considers essential, especially gender roles. She uses ritual to explore dysfunctional gender roles and reconstruct more effective ones. Her analyses of the ritual life of a typical family demonstrates that the ritual roles allotted to women are supportive and dependent positions that give the symbolic dominance to male authority. Laird does not propose to scrap these rites; rather, she advocates new family rituals to redefine the place of family members who have been overlooked or lost their voice in the collective life of the home. These may be patterned on rites of passage in which the whole family formally acknowledges the intellectual and sexual maturity of a daughter, the midlife transition of a fiftieth birthday, the significance of a young adult leaving home, or an overdue memorial service for a family that resisted the emotional complexities of mourning. In these cases, the ability of ritual to express multiple levels of the structural relationships that bind people into a domestic unit also means that ritual can help change relationships that have become problematic. Ritual therapy appears to suggest that it is one thing to talk and understand family problems in the context of a therapy session; it is quite another to begin to implement new understandings and ways of acting within the routines of domestic life.[115]

Other studies find similar applications for therapeutic ritual, from the scholarly study by Onno van der Hart, *Rituals in Psychotherapy*, to the recent popular work by

Evan Imber-Black and Janine Roberts, *Rituals for Our Times: Celebrating, Healing, and Changing Our Lives and Our Relationships*, an obvious spin-off of the self-help movement of the 1980s and 1990s.[116] Such works clearly extol both the need for ritual and the efficacy of invented ritual activity to organize, express, soothe, and define. However, their recourse to ritual solutions for certain types of problems also implies that the family or community already possesses all the resources it needs to deal with its problems; ritual is a means for tapping those resources without the intrusion of imposed outside expertise. The process of reflecting on ritual is thought to socialize family or community members into expressing and solving their own problems. Indeed, ritual solutions are advocated as effective ways to address alcoholism, sexual dysfunction, and even political trauma. The AIDS epidemic has led some therapists to develop new techniques to help those traumatized by multiple losses. Some have turned to workshops that employ ritualized dance and storytelling to bring some catharsis and control over feelings of despair. Terry Tafoya of the University of Washington and Leon McKusick of the University of California at San Francisco have used Native American mourning rituals to help those engulfed by AIDS, drawing on the historical parallels in which Western contact brought diseases to which Indians had no immunity. These rituals appear to help people who are afraid to mourn, fearing that the least expression of grief will drag them down into a never-ending chasm of heartbreak and emotional paralysis. Ritual seems to reassure people that they can release their grief in a safe and ordered context that will not allow them drown in horror and helplessness.[117]

Much ritual experimentation has naturally overlapped with experiments in performance that draw on traditions of circus shows, folk theater, and street actors, as well as the quasi-political and artistic events or "happenings" that appeared in the 1960s as "guerrilla theater." In addition, the new age ethos has often added its characteristic emphasis on ritual methods of healing, self-definition, and empowerment. One result has been the publication of sourcebooks such as *The Art of Ritual: A Guide to Creating and Performing Your Own Rituals for Growth and Change*, which offers guidelines and worksheets for designing effective rites.[118] Ronald Grimes has called attention to the various entrepreneurial groups providing ritual services, such as Rites of Passage, Inc., which offers high school seniors a two-month vision-quest course. He finds it problematic when grandiose claims are made for the effectiveness of ritual or when rites are deliberately disconnected from the communities in which they have traditionally been a part.[119] The latter issue has become a heated one as some Native Americans have begun to protest the use of their ritual tradition in the hands of new age, feminist, or ecological groups.[120] The ubiquitous dynamics of ritual appropriation are historically complex and politically charged, especially when socially or politically dominant groups appear to be mining the cultural traditions of the less powerful, taking the images they want and, by placing them in very new contexts, altering their meanings in ways that may sever these images from their own people. The freedom that many people feel to improvise rites that draw on a vast spectrum of cultural imagery is itself indicative of a particular understanding of ritual—as a type of psychosocial mechanism unbound and undetermined by any one religious or ritual tradition. This understanding conveys something of the "modern" ethos of pluralist and secular societies that the typologies described earlier attempted to formulate.

Most examples of ritual invention, as well as rituals variously reinterpreted in the contemporary context, suggest that a new paradigm of ritual has gradually replaced a set of more long-standing assumptions. In the newer model, ritual is primarily a medium of expression, a special type of language suited to what it is there to express, namely, internal spiritual-emotional resources tied to our true identities but frequently unknown and undeveloped. Ritual expression of these internal dimensions will unleash their healing power for the self and others. This is not ritual as time-honored or heavenly ordained worship by which the transcendent collapses the gulf between the human and the divine, on the one hand, and the human world dispenses its responsibilities to the heavenly one, on the other. The new paradigm is directed more inward than outward, apt to define community and society in terms of the self rather than the self in terms of the community. Metaphors of wholeness and attainment replace older ones of transcendence and deliverance.

There are probably many reasons why the new paradigm of ritual action has come to overlay and even marginalize the older one. Certainly the typologies presented in chapter 6 try to account for this shift in how people think of ritual. The inevitable relativism that comes with sustained interreligious and intercultural contact has promoted terms and practices that are less tied to particular religious or cultural traditions. The formal study of ritual itself may be a result, if not a cause, of this shift. Whatever the reasons for this new paradigm of ritual action, however, it is very much a historically shaped phenomenon with positive and negative dimensions. Positively, it allows for the formulation and expression of new identities and new ideals impossible to conceive within the rubric of older forms of ritual practice. Negatively, traditional arbiters of good sense and good taste have no authority in communities where the legitimacy of ritual experimentation indicates a fragmented social consensus.

This new ritual paradigm has more subtle ramifications as well. Traditionally, for example, the legitimate authority and efficacy of ritual were closely intertwined. For invented rites, which are not deeply rooted in a any shared sense of tradition, however, legitimacy and authority tend to be construed more lightly and on quite different grounds. For that reason, perhaps, much greater weight appears to fall on the dimension of efficacy. There is increased pressure for the invented rite to show that it "works"; this is what legitimates the rite since there is no tradition to do this. Of course, the expectations of what it means to work are also not the same as for traditional rituals, for which no one asked whether the rite worked, just whether it was done correctly. In some societies and cosmologies, correct performance of a ritual made it effective whether you wanted it to be or not. There is the story of the king who demonstrated his tribe's kingship ceremony tribe to a missionary, letting the missionary stand in for the king, only to find that many of his tribe thought he had effectively passed his power and title to the foreigner. Only after the elders conferred and decided that kingship was tied to a particular place could the hapless king move his tribe and be reinstalled.[121] In the ritual paradigm now becoming dominant in America and Europe, however, one expects the rite to work by affecting people's cognitive orientation and emotional sense of well-being—and one can judge quickly whether this has happened or not. As a result, people can now be generally disappointed in ritual. Other paradigms of ritual practice, as embodiments of a shared heritage and unquestioned fixtures of day-to-day life, for example, rarely have to bear the burden of such expectations.

Many of the controversies within modern ritual life, such as liturgical reform and the appropriation of Native American rituals, appear to involve a clash of basic perspectives on what ritual is all about. Indeed, Myerhoff's description of ritual's concern to obscure any signs of its own inventedness indicates a particular cultural paradigm of ritual, one that coexists today with rather different ways of ritualizing and understanding ritual. The emergence of alternative paradigms of ritual action and shifts in which ones are dominant need not reflect, as some of the typologists suggested, historical evolution; these paradigms may reflect types of social community and the cosmologies in which they understand themselves. Yet this perspective on the varieties of ritual practice is not well understood and hopefully will attract more research in the future.

Media and Message

Implicit in the foregoing discussions of ritual density and change is the fact that the contemporary world often presents a complicated context for ritual, even for the most traditional of rites. Several major forces have had a particular impact on the modern context for ritual, notably television, tourism, and multiculturalism.[122] In actual fact, of course, these forces are neither very new nor so distinct. Yet the modes of social interaction afforded by the ubiquity of television and video, by the unprecedented levels of tourist travel, and by increasingly multicultural societies are having an effect not only on why, what, and when people ritualize but also on how we conceive of ritual itself.

Television appears to affect ritual activities in two main ways. First, and most simply, televising a ritual for mass viewing alters both how the ritual is done and how it is experienced. A second and more complicated effect is the way in which television takes over some of the functions traditionally or typically provided by ritual. The interrelationship of these two dimensions of television's influence can be seen in the example given earlier of the 1952 enthronement of Queen Elizabeth. At the time observers noted the relatively unprecedented role of radio, television, and the press in making the ceremony into "a great nation-wide communion." Preliminary discussions over what to televise and what to keep "sacrosanct" were delicate ones that pitted tradition, good taste, and monarchical mystification against commercial exploitation, the public's right to know, and the vicarious participation of many more citizens. Yet the use of television and radio as a type of ritual medium also had less obvious results and raised unexpected issues. For example, people tended to participate in the televised coronation primarily as family units sitting together in their living rooms. Contrary to many traditional forms of ritual where affirmation of the solidarity of the family unit may be at the expense of the solidarity of the nation, or vice versa, the new form of media participation in the coronation explicitly affirmed the family unit as an integral aspect of the national unit. In addition, Shils and Young interpreted one family's invitation to a neighboring family to come watch the events with them on their TV as a newly simultaneous affirmation of local community, family and nation directly dependent on television. This type of affirmation is replicated and underscored in the new tradition of a Christmas broadcast in which the Queen talks about her family, the royals, to "millions of British families, and the nation as a whole, as though they are one," as Shils and Young put it.[123]

In addition, the semiofficial documentary of the coronation, now periodically broadcast on public television, makes the pageantry of June 1952 happen repeatedly.[124] Just as Walter Benjamin wondered about the meaning of art in an age of endless mechanical reproduction—an issue that Andy Warhol so vividly addressed—so we might also wonder how ritual affects its participants when the rite can be repeated endlessly or the participants multiplied without limit.[125] In their study of the royal wedding of Charles and Diana, Daniel Dayan and Elihu Katz point out the different effects of the ceremony on those participants who were "on location" in the streets and those watching it on television. For those physically present in the crowds surrounding St. Paul's Cathedral and Buckingham Palace, the wedding ritual was a theatrical spectacle and communal festival of shared enthusiasm and good feelings. For those participating through the television medium, there was little sense of shared participation in a communal festival, and the television "flattened" the event into pure spectacle. Nonetheless, television could compensate for this flattening by enabling a type of visual attendance at the whole thing. In contrast to those on the street struggling for a limited view of passing carriages, television viewers could vicariously enter St. Paul's Cathedral with Charles and Diana, just as they could enter Westminster Abbey with the young queen via television in 1952. Moreover, they could see the full length of the processions, hear interviews with the most colorful characters in the crowds, and peek into all the endless details concerning menus, dresses, guest lists, and party arrangements. In fact, many eyewitnesses to the physical events ran away to find a television in order to see what was going on.[126]

While television's ability to provide such total visual coverage may be able to compensate for its audience's physical distance from the event, this "totalism" can also be distancing unless the medium orchestrates some form of personal involvement. Dayan and Katz describe a number of strategies by which television attempts to break down some of the spectaclelike distance between the performers and audience in order to create those feelings of interaction and real participation necessary to a "nation-wide communion." In one strategy, television restores the aura of privileged access to special events by means of a hierarchical distancing of newspeople, from stars like Tom Fleming of the BBC and Walter Cronkite and Barbara Walters of CBS to the lowly reporter trying to see over the crowds and be heard over the noise. The important newspeople sit in the studio, just as the audience sits at home, but can talk to the lowly reporters on the scene, who are either being bumped around or forced to fill time when nothing is happening. In effect, the audience is handed over from one spokesperson to another and thereby brought in stages from the home to the scene and back again in a manner that keeps collapsing distance. Using another common strategy, television narrators resisted interjecting their voices between the event and TV audience; at times they stepped aside as much as possible to let the audience "flow" with the unmediated symbolic communication that comprises such ritual events. In an additional television tactic for contravening any sense of discontinuity between the event and the audience, the cameras appealed to an epidemic of celebrations, covering one party after another and merging them into each other until it seemed the whole country was having one vast party. Although television does not often succeed in realizing its intentions, Dayan and Katz suggest that it has been gradually creating a new form of public event, replacing a more theatrical style based on real contact between the performers and the audience with a more narrative style, filled out with simulations and based on an assumption of no real contact.[127]

Their conclusions are echoed in analyses of a succession of major public ceremonies in Japan in recent years, namely, the funeral of the emperor Hirohito, the enthronement of his son Akihito, and the marriage of the Crown Prince Naruhito to Masako Owada. These were historic public ceremonies not just covered by the media but mediated by it. The effect, some would argue, has been to interpret and nuance the events in such a way as to redefine the Japanese emperor system (*tennosei*) in terms of the very forces shaping a mass culture inundated with television. Takashi Fujitani concludes, for example, that media coverage of these national rites creates a "hyper-reality" that acts as the context for national processes of self-reflection and the construction of a national identity.[128] His analysis is based in part on the funeral for Hirohito, which he witnessed first-hand. In February 1989, elderly and middle-aged men and women gathered at dawn in the rain outside the Imperial Palace to wait for the emperor's funeral procession to pass through the high-walled gates. Hours later, when the procession of limousines finally appeared, it whizzed past the crowds in a matter of seconds. Shocked and disappointed, the crowds awkwardly cast about and then broke up. The event, argues Fujitani, was not designed for live spectators, but for television audiences: "We who had gone out into the streets were much like the 'live studio audiences' put together for television shows. While we thought and acted as if we were spectators, we were, in fact, part of the spectacle, live props for a television-viewing audience."[129]

Tokyo, like most large cities and seats of government, was essentially laid out in a period in which public ceremonial involved enormous theatrical displays and the physical presence of thousands of people. The Imperial Plaza was constructed in the last century for large ritualized celebrations and nationalistic pageants. The same sort of space is found in Westminister Abbey, where British monarchs have been crowned for centuries, Hitler's monumental stage for his mass rallies in Nuremberg, Mao's creation of Tiananmen as a symbol of "popular sovereignty" just outside the Forbidden City of the imperial sovereigns, or the Washington Monument with its view of the White House to the north and the Capitol to the east. These are all traditional theaters for the national rituals of an era before television. In the age of televised ritual, however, ceremonial style is much less theatrical and public. National rituals can afford to be more muted and private since television makes it possible for great numbers of people to participate visually in the smallest details over and over again. In fact, the audience's sense of participation is heightened by stressing the personal or domestic nature of the events that they are being allowed to share.

The media coverage of John F. Kennedy's assassination on November 22, 1963, and all the ritual events that subsequently followed have been repeatedly analyzed by scholars concerned with the way in which the media shape both cultural and personal experience.[130] Yet these media-mediated ceremonies are also provocative examples of the way in which ritual has been reshaped. Part and parcel of the extended experience of the Kennedy events was, of course, the immediacy with which the media could pull people into situations that were still unfolding. Within one hour of the Dallas shooting, 90 percent of Americans had learned the news—most from friends and family who had heard it from radio or television. [131] Closing the gap between the personal and the distant tragedy with countless interviews asking people, "What were you doing when you heard Kennedy was shot?" television portrayed the national event on a most intimate scale, repeatedly focusing on the blood on Mrs. Kennedy's pink suit as the vice president was sworn into office and on John Jr.'s prompted salute to the caisson that carried the casket. These film sequences were reproduced endlessly even as new footage on unfolding events was added each day.

In this way, television's coverage of the assassination became increasingly narrative. On the one hand, the ability of television to totalize its coverage meant that equal attention was given to a variety of smaller rites, creating a series of ritually discrete but linked events that formed a process and told a story: the Friday afternoon shooting, the hospital announcement, the swearing in of Vice President Lyndon Baines Johnson, the flight back to Washington, D.C., the public viewing of the casket in the Capitol rotunda, and so on, until the final visit of Jacqueline Kennedy to the grave with a bouquet of flowers at midnight on Monday night. On the other hand, television filled in the time with footage that recounted the story of Kennedy's family and background, gradually weaving a tale of how he came to be the youngest elected president and a hero cut down in his youth. The mythologizing ability of the media—its ability to suggest cultural themes, simplicities, and stereotypes in organizing a story and orchestrating an experience—is familiar to most people. The effect on ritual is less familiar. Because of its ready use of a narrative structure, the focus of media-mediated ritual shifts. Instead of a theatrical ethos of a staged performance highlighting a single and exemplary moment in time, televised rites tend to create an emotional process that viewers feel compelled to see through to the end. As a packaged story, the sequence of rituals can be replayed interminably, in pieces or in its entirety. In the case of the Kennedy coverage, one might even speculate that one reason for the vitality of the conspiracy theory movement is the emotional necessity for a more novelistic ending to the vivid narrative constructed by the media.

Aside from the narrative structuring encouraged by the totalizing, private, and repeatable nature of television coverage, the Kennedy coverage points to another way in which the ritual medium interacts with the television medium—namely, television's adoption of some of the strategies and functions of ritual. In other words, television has not only affected and modified those rituals that consciously or unconsciously anticipate extensive media coverage but also taken over some dimensions of traditional ritual to become the source of much of the symbolic imagery and shared values in our culture. From this perspective, television can be at times both highly ritualistic and a type of ritual medium itself for the culture. By transposing reality into a spectacle, according to the analyst Jean Cazeneuve, the mass media perform the functional equivalent of what traditional myth and ritual used to do when they imbued reality with a sense of the sacred. In fact, he argues, television is particularly equipped to take over many of the functions of traditional ritual because its emphasis on audiovisual stimuli and communication enables it to express the complexities and nuances of symbolic thinking. There is some speculation even that the soap opera is structurally analogous to the myths expressed in the rituals of tribal societies.[132]

Drawing on psychological studies of children's understandings of television, Cazeneuve analyzes the ways in which television orchestrates the intersection of fiction and reality to fulfill the human need for sustaining symbols. Television mediates the interaction of reality and the symbolic order to create a working synthesis, he suggests, a spectacle in which symbols are capable of appropriating reality — what Fujitani calls "hyper-reality" — and dulling the anxiety of the human condition. For Cazeneuve, this modern method of "sacralization" reflects the need for both transcendence and security. For many viewers, he explains, the television is an instrument that can give them "the illusion of staying integrated in a secure society and of being linked to the world of the marvelous."[133]

In a more extensive analysis of television as ritual, Gregor Goethals argues that television has taken over two of the prime functions of traditional ritual, namely, social integration and communion with transcendent beings. In terms of the first, television in the main medium by which most people today have a sense of shared participation and personal involvement in central events, whether it is a case of the less overtly ritualized reporting of the CNN broadcasts on the Persian Gulf War or the more ritualized pace of the Senate Confirmation Hearings involving Clarence Thomas and Anita Hill. In terms of the second function, television affords communion with transcendent beings through its intimate coverage of events like Pope John Paul II's inaugural mass, the funerals of leaders like Hubert Humphrey as well as John F. Kennedy, and Martin Luther King's prayers at the 1976 Democratic Convention. In addition to television's role in providing these experiences, Goethals also points to how television uses ritualization in its own format, particularly in regard to the nightly news. The use of uniform patterns, timing, and symbols on a daily evening news program creates, she argues, "a shared perception of order" that is indispensable to both a successful program and human psychological well-being. While disclosing the many "truths" of national or international importance creates a confidence in Truth itself, the juxtaposition of these truths with laxative and detergent commercials also reassures audiences that the immediate and minor problems of daily life are just as important and even more easily solved. Taken together, the alternation of news and commercials provides a tightly packaged symbolic perspective on reality. While viewers know that news programs can give incomplete or misleading information, there is a visual sense that the camera does not lie. The images woven together by a figure like Walter Cronkite ("and that's the way it is") can give people a sense of coherence and manageable order.[134]

For some media analysts, television takes up much of the work done by traditional ritual in confirming and maintaining idealized cultural patterns of thought and action. Television icons like *The Waltons* communicated a traditional system of values and a domestic model that intertwined the history of the country and a particular family. Alternative icons like *All in the Family, Dallas,* or *One Day at a Time* may have incorporated more irony and realism, but the domestic framework also ordered and organized their complex tapestries into an affirmation of basic values that could facilitate, perhaps, greater flexibility concerning other values. In the end, the result is the distilling and modeling of a cultural ethos, a "modeling of" and "modeling for," in Geertz's formulation. While this process confirms many symbols and values, its also allows for change, although it tends to be controlled change that is rendered consistent with visions of past and future. In this regard, television's appropriation of ritual strategies and functions may be part of an ongoing and many-faceted cultural instinct by which any popular medium must afford the construction of meaningful "realities" that support community, continuity, adaptive change, and confidence.[135]

The use of video to preserve and inform also has a direct bearing on understandings and modes of ritual. Videotaped ritual instructions are becoming more commonplace, and an early spoof on the practice by the Japanese film maker Juzo Itami captures all the obvious ironies of the situation. In his 1984 film, *The Funeral (Ososhiki)*, a middle-aged Tokyo couple who make television commercials for a living attempt to follow the video instructions for how to play their parts in the funeral ceremony for a parent. In Itami's hands, the couple finds it hard to sort out the role-playing from the reality and to find any room for sincerity, spontaneity, and directness.[136] A more complicated example of video ritual is the 1975 international project in which a team led by the linguist Frits Staal arranged to film a performance of the magnificent twelve-day Vedic fire ritual, the Agnicayana. Until that time, the Agnicayana had not been performed by the Nambudiri Brahmans of Kerala in southern India for nearly twenty years. And according to the conservative customs by which this small group has maintained the ancient Vedic tradition, it should be performed for Nambudiris only. With a century of Western scholarly interest in this ancient ritual to prompt him, and substantial international funding to make it possible, Staal went to India to talk the Nambudiris into giving another performance, one that would allow the historic ritual to be recorded in its full richness. At first the Nambudiris were reluctant to do the rite at all; even when they were convinced to go ahead, Staal feared it might well be for the last time.

In the end, Staal assembled what may be the most comprehensive study to date of a major ritual: twenty hours of film, eighty hours of recordings, and hundreds of pages of ritual text, description, and scholarly analysis.[137] From his perspective, the project was a documentary recording of an authentic ritual performance, not the artificial staging or scholarly reconstruction of a lost tradition. Indeed, Staal described the filming as literally "continuing" the tradition, and the book project, he wrote, was "a unique opportunity, indeed a responsibility, to continue the oral tradition by means of a book." Yet these hopes raise some unsettling questions. Aside from the obvious merits of documenting a rare instance of an ancient ritual, one is forced to wonder if the Nambudiris would agree with Staal that his book continued their tradition. The Nambudiris have carefully maintained a tradition of oral transmission of Vedic rituals that even differs from the indigenous Vedic textual tradition. Early in the project, Staal showed them the Sanskrit texts for the rite that they were planning to perform, and pointed out the differences and discrepancies. The Nambudiris' response was simply one of polite interest, and they continued to plan the ritual the way they knew it should be done, that is, the way their own teachers had taught them.[138]

Other discrepancies arose in the performance that also affected the Indian and Western parties quite differently. For example, the traditional sponsor of the ritual, the person who puts up the money and has an important role to play in the performance (*yajamana*), nearly backed out, although a substitute was kept in the wings. For this performance, however, the money was all put up by foreigners, so the sponsor was actually a type of hired substitute.[139] More central to the ritual tradition was the prohibition that no non-Brahmans could enter the altar area, which ruled out the presence of a film crew. Unusual viewing arrangements had to be made so that they could use a tower constructed to look down on the action. A conflict arose between Nambudiri tradition and current Indian sentiments when widespread objections developed to the killing and disemboweling of fourteen goats, the central sacrificial action of the Agnicayana. This crisis nearly caused the whole project to collapse. Ultimately, the Nambudiri pundits found some pertinent ritual precedents and at the eleventh hour agreed to a compromise: rice cakes wrapped in banana leaves were used as ritual substitutes for the goats while the correct mantras were used. Of course, as one critic rightly noted, this train of problems is hardly unique; this is how all ritual works and evolves.[140] Staal himself points out that the historical precedents for substitution make clear that the more inflexible and critical part of the rite were the mantras: goats could be replaced by rice cakes, but the mantras must be correct.[141]

Ultimately, however, the video documentation of this Vedic ritual became an oddly ambiguous project. On the one hand, the project created a definitive documentary record of a ritual tradition about to be lost to time. On the other hand, this particular Agnicayana was a highly untraditional performance, perhaps not even "Vedic." Of course, it *had* to be somewhat untraditional to be recorded at all. And the various preparations, arrangements, and crises involved in this Agnicayana simply illustrate how all performances are creative improvisations on a tradition. There is never an exact repetition of some pristine, age-old model. Instead, there are living embodiments and expressions of tradition in constantly changing circumstances. In this case, the circumstances included unprecedented involvement of foreigners and foreign funds. Still, how far can a ritual tradition be stretched before it is no longer what it has always been? Insofar as Staal's documentation does not admit the full scope of the unusual setup of the performance, it can give the appearance of a stable, unchanging tradition captured in pure form on film. In truth, the documentary cannot be a neutral and passive recording of the tradition. It is a constructed view of a new ritual hybrid, a conjunction of foreign interests and funding with Indian tradition and resources.[142] For most people interested in ritual, even Vedic ritual, these concerns may be taken for a scholarly splitting of hairs. Nonetheless, the story of this project illustrates some of the complexities that arise in laudable ethnographic efforts to use other media to preserve ritual traditions that are dying out in the world. It alerts us to the ways in which the very media for appropriating some understanding of ritual—videos and books, filming, foreign investment, special staging—cast their own shadows over the particular event.

Modern tourism is another force shaping the context for ritual today. Of course, many studies argue that tourism is closely related to the ritual activities traditionally involved in religious pilgrimage.[143] For some, this kinship is a matter of modern secular substitutes for traditional religious experiences; for others, it is a matter of underlying structural similarities, that is, a fundamental ritual pattern of transformation by means of a spatial, temporal, and psychological transition. That sacred places still command an enormous if not unprecedented draw is readily observed in numerous locales, from the Sacred Mosque in Mecca to the Basilica of the Virgin of Guadalupe in Mexico City, from the banks of the sacred Ganges river in Allahabad, India, at the time of the Hindu Kumbha Mela, to the shrine of St. James the Greater at Compostella in Spain, which is still the destination for a very active system of European pilgrimage routes dating back to the medieval period. It is not hard to see how the ritual nature of such journeying underlies aspects of the history and methods of tourism. Certainly the creation of hierarchies of sacred places has delineated the history and boundaries of religious and national communities. The Muslims who leave their homes to travel to Mecca, the Catholics who visit Rome, or Pueblo Indian accounts of ancient travels from the sacred hole (*sipapuni*) from which they emerged into this world—all locate their particular homes and identities in relation to the sacred centers of their communities. In the case of Niagara Falls, Auschwitz, or a Caribbean island paradise, people today still journey to places where historical or spiritual significance is thought to be concentrated. As Lincoln implied at Gettysburg, a place can be sacralized by the events that unfolded there or by the formal words and acts of dedication that have defined some place as special. In either case, it may become a spatial point for an ordered encounter with forces variously conceived of as dangerous, compelling, revitalizing, or powerfully "authentic."

For the anthropologist Erik Cohen, however, traditional and modern societies have very different styles of journeying. In a traditional society, one could journey in either of two directions: toward the sacred center that orders the known cosmos or in the opposite direction, toward the "other," beyond the periphery of the ordered world, where chaos both threatens and beckons. The first sort of journey was legitimate and laudable; the second was suspect and heretical. By contrast, the modern world has no *single* compelling sacred center since centers of all sorts have multiplied. This "geographical denouement of the world" can turn multiple places into "attractions" whose mere difference from one's own appears to hold out the possibility of experiencing a fresh "authenticity."[144] Certainly market factors and the money to be made from tourism have prompted the packaging of all sorts of traditional sacred places as international attractions. The Hawaiian volcano Kilauea, sacred to the goddess Pele, is an important tourist destination. The small New Mexico chapel of Santuario de Chimayo, reputed to have healing mud, was long an ancient stop on a pilgrimage circuit for devout Mexicans but is now visited by non-Christian tourists sincerely interested in the religious qualities of these places. In some places, tourism can threaten to destroy the local economy and the cultural legacy itself.[145] In other places, tourism has prompted a type of cultural reinvestment to preserve dying traditions and architecture. The envisioned economic benefits of tourism have prompted communities to revive rituals, customs, and dress that had been derelict for a long time. Too often, all these situations lead to museumlike "displays" instead of a living culture, although some argue that this form of "museumization" at least preserves some aspects of traditions otherwise completely lost to memory. A few places have resisted what James Clifford calls "the restless desire and power of the modern West to collect the world," sometimes by restraining tourism, more often by redefining its cultural heritage in ways that attempt to meet external demands and respect internal traditions and their reformulation.[146]

While dynamic ritual traditions are more popular with tourists than static objects and buildings, they are much harder to organize in conjunction with a tourist schedule. When the Balinese stage special ritual performances just for tourists, the tourists complain that they prefer more "authentic" performances. An alternative approach, of course, is to bring one's own rituals, which is the focus of one company that sets up bar and bas mitzvah family tours to Israel. The ceremony can be held at beautiful and solemn Masada, with a special service added at Yad Vashem or other religious and historical sites.[147] Usually, however, the marketing of indigenous ritual performances for foreign visitors is quite complicated. A growing number of ethnographic studies describe the cultural complexities behind ritual performances that attempt to mediate external demands and internal developments. In the case of the Toraja of Indonesia chronicled by the anthropologist Toby Volkman, tourism has influenced the way rituals, sponsored by individuals, compete for social prestige, as in the case of an elaborate double funeral arranged by a nouveau riche family.[148] The introduction of tourism and a cash economy among the peoples of the eastern highlands of Papua New Guinea has commercialized the famous pig distribution ceremonies mentioned in chapter 2. They are now competitive and commercial dance festivals known locally as "singsing bisnis," which significantly reorganize traditional forms of exchange in ways more congruent with a profit- and wage-based economy and the social complexities of contemporary New Guinea.[149]

Observers of traditional festivals in Taiwan suggest that the combination of television and tourism has had a dramatic effect. Most recently, temples have begun to court media coverage in order to attract tourist revenue. In 1971 the ceremonies at the temple to the goddess Matsu in the town of Tachia were a regional attraction, involving 53 hamlets and about 2,000 people. In 1992, after years of expanding media coverage, the processions were televised live. Nearly 100,000 pilgrims and tourists showed up, accompanied by more than 100 reporters. While other temple communities envy this type of success, especially the good fortune of the temple chosen for the site of a television serial drama, traditional customs concerning purity and pollution are being lost or expediently discarded. One Taiwanese temple decided to forgo its usual "harbor cleansing" ritual in order to try to preserve images that were too old to be assailed by any more seawater, but they changed those plans when it was learned that a television company had counted on using the ritual in a television program.[150]

In 1994 the Imperial Palace in Beijing performed an elaborately reconstructed imperial ritual to kick off a new overseas tourism program, China Heritage '94, which featured trips to many historical and cultural sites recently restored for this purpose.[151] Likewise, the 1988 renovation and expansion of a temple-mausoleum complex in Hunan dedicated to the mythical emperor Yan was followed by the revival of public memorial ceremonies featuring colorful costumes and traditional musical instruments. While it is said that nearly half a million foreigners have visited the site in recent years, the temple is particularly popular with Chinese travelers from Taiwan, Hong Kong, and Singapore, where there are local temples to Emperor Yan. Indeed, there are plans to expand the mausoleum further, creating a recreation park and an Emperor Yan Cultural Village among other things.[152] While cultural analysts talk about "restored" rituals and behaviors, these examples probably involve a fair degree of creative innovation, not just restoration.[153]

A few Native American communities have made strict rules about tourists attending their performances. While some dances and ceremonies are orchestrated as public events for all, others are secret and closed. This is especially true among the Pueblo peoples of the Southwest, who have guarded their ceremonial traditions with particular zeal and conservatism through centuries of Spanish colonization, Catholic missionizing, and, until 1928, the tendency of Bureau of Indian Affairs to outlaw traditional ritual.[154] Most of the rites that attend the annual coming of the kachinas, the masked and costumed figures that are seen as manifestations of spiritual beings in the Hopi tradition, are performed in private in kivas, underground ceremonial chambers entered through an opening in the roof. Yet dances and performances in the Pueblo plaza are open to all, and those marking the "going home" or close of the kachina season, when the spirits are sent off to their mountain homes, can draw large crowds of neighbors and tourists.[155]

Tourists are apt to bring home elements of exotic ritual performances, and the symbols of an increasingly international and interreligious ritual repertoire are becoming familiar to many. Much current ritual invention actively searches for multicultural forms of symbolic expression as a way to identify communities that see themselves straddling traditional ethnic, racial, or cultural boundaries. This situation is akin to the meeting of east and west seen in the 1975 Nambudiri Agnicayana mentioned earlier. It also shares some aspects of the ritual life of the Italian-American community centered on the Madonna of 115th Street, where ritual forms of religio-cultural expression were used to negotiate the maintenance of an ethnic heritage. On the one hand, ritual is vital to the construction of community, cultural identity, or ethnicity; it can preserve a tradition by mediating its essential features with new external demands. On the other hand, ritual is also invoked to reorganize communities around less traditional identities, in effect, to constitute new ones based not on cultural, ethnic, or racial solidarity but more on shared spiritual, political, or even class concerns. The media and tourist industry are just two of the more prominent forces helping to shape the context for ritual today, particularly the way in which ritual traditions are reproduced and invented in contemporary society.

Conclusion

The examples in this section demonstrate how the relationships between ritual and its context can generate a variety of changes in the structures, symbols, and interpretations of ritual activities. Despite many popular preconceptions and a number of anthropological models of ritual, ritual is not primarily a matter of unchanging tradition. On the contrary, some analysts now see ritual as a particularly effective means of mediating tradition and change, that is, as a medium for appropriating some changes while maintaining a sense of cultural continuity. It is necessary to remember, however, that if ritual plays such a role, it does not do it as some type of external mechanism that acts on a culture from the outside. Ritual can play such a role only from within the system, that is, as a component of the system that is defined and deployed in ways that interlock with how tradition and change are viewed. Hence, we should not be surprised to find that ritual itself is understood a bit differently from one culture or historical period to another, particularly in regard to what is considered ritual, how it is thought to differ from other activities, the origins and reasons for ritual, its relation to tradition and change, and the type of authority it is accorded.

More specifically, we have seen that ritual can change as the conditions of the community change. In addition, all sorts of formally designated or self-styled ritual experts have at times devised and shaped ritual activities. Ritualized activities can be taken as traditional within a very short time; they can also be very flexibly appropriated; they may be practiced more or less faithfully despite strong reservations about every aspect of them. New rites, even the awkward ambivalence of those embodied in the Olympic games, are integral to the construction of many forms of communal identity. At the same time, ritual alone cannot create a community when no other relationships exist among the participants. The same rituals performed over the course of a thousand years can simultaneously affirm long-standing communal values of continuity and authoritative tradition while also allowing people to experience these values with different expectations and needs. Finally, effective ritual need not be uncontested or invulnerable to political manipulation and trendy commercialization.

Many of the examples discussed in this section suggest the ideological power of ritual. Soviet bureaucrats launched their socialist rites in an explicit attempt to socialize people to communist values. In a different ethos, African-Americans celebrate Kwanzaa and Jewish feminists perform the women's seder in order to counter the dominant value system and build communities based on another vision. If such examples were multiplied, one might conclude that the ritual medium is able to serve many ideological masters—from staid institutions to preachers announcing the apocalypse. Nonetheless, it is not really clear how effective ritual actually is in socializing, resocializing, or desocializing. No one can say how much people internalize, appropriate, and ignore what goes on in a ritual or even what parts of the ritual are likely to be the most or least affective. The socializing—or ideologizing—effects of ritual appear to depend on many factors, such as the degree of people's involvement in the rites, the amount of ritual repetition, and the degree to which the values espoused in the deep structure of the ritual are reinforced in other areas of social life. While some people have defined ritual as the foremost social tool for inculcating social values, that remains a questionable claim. When brought to bear on the question of how ritual defines and negotiates competing ideologies and power relationships in general, the historical and ethnographic records suggest a very complex spectrum of possibilities.

As stated earlier, no ritual stands by itself. It is always embedded in a thick context of traditions, changes, tensions, and unquestioned assumptions and practices. Ritual is a way that people can act in the world, and all those factors that influence how any person and group acts will influence the performance and understanding of ritual. A community's attitudes and styles of ritualizing are inseparable from their worldview, and it is not hard today to find a great variety of communities, worldviews, and styles of ritualizing living in close proximity to each other.

❧ · ☙

EIGHT

Ritual Reification

Discussions of ritual density and change inevitably imply that there is something essential and stable that undergoes variations according to time and place. These discussions and each of the theories of ritual outlined in part I reify ritual, that is, assume there is a substantive phenomenon at stake, not simply an abstract analytical category. The spectrum of ritual and ritual-like activities explored in part II appears to give little cause for inferring the substantive existence of some universal form of action best known as ritual. Nonetheless, the reification of ritual has become an important factor in our understanding of the rites around us today and even in the way we are apt to go about doing them. For this reason, the *study* of ritual as a universal mode of action has become an influential part of the context of ritual practice in contemporary Europe and America.

As part I demonstrated, the study of ritual has gone through several historical perspectives that, in hindsight, seem to have had less to do with how people ritualize and more with how Western culture has sorted out relationships between science and religion, on the one hand, and relationships between more technologically developed cultures and more localized tribal cultures, on the other. A number of the formal theories invoked in that section were also vitally concerned with relationships between tradition and modernity, between cultural continuity and social change, between authentic and inauthentic modes of orchestrating cultural communication, and, of course, between engaging in a series of religious activities and analyzing this engagement as ritual. Such scholarship purports to identify "ritual" underlying all the permutations of form, variations of place, and changes of time that it documents and organizes. This chapter explores the ways in which scholarly study of certain types of religious and cultural practices has generated the notion of "ritual" and how, in turn, this notion has affected these religious and cultural practices.

Repudiating, Returning, Romancing

The emergence of the concept of "ritual" as an universal phenomenon that is substantively manifest in human nature, biology, or culture appears to be the result of a successive layering of scholarly and popular attitudes. These attitudes range from an early modern "repudiation" of ritual at home while finding it prevalent in so-called primitive societies, a subsequent "return" to ritual that recognized it as an important social and cross-cultural phenomenon, followed by a tendency to "romanticize" ritual by both practitioners and theorists as a key mechanism for personal and cultural transformation. The following analysis suggests that these attitudes toward ritual are intrinsic to concerted intellectual efforts to deal with the "other" in the various religious and cultural guises in which this "other" has been perceived.

People talk about the decline and repudiation of ritual in two ways: either in terms of a general stage in an embracing process of social evolution or in terms of particular historical-political situations, such as the 16th-century Protestant Reformation. While the latter situation is usually characterized by specific social circumstances, the first is depicted in terms of more abstract forces of rationalism, secularism, or modernization by which traditional religious communities are dramatically remade by science, pluralism, and individualism. The popular contention that ritual and religion decline in proportion to modernization has been something of a sociological truism since the mid-19th century. The British philosopher Herbert Spencer (1820–1903) was probably among the first to formulate an evolutionary opposition between industrialization of modern culture and the rituals of tribal or feudal cultures, but Max Weber followed up a generation later by contrasting ritual and magic with the rationalism and "disenchantment" of modern life. For the historian Peter Burke, the 19th-century tendency to oppose ritual and reason was itself the product of an earlier opposition, rooted in the ethos of the Reformation, in which ritual came to be seen as artifice and mystification in contrast to the virtues of sincerity, simplicity, and directness. In this ethos, Burke argues, ritual was associated "with the shadow rather than the substance, the letter rather than the spirit, the outer husk rather than the inner kernel."[1] Emerging fields of study focused on ritual as an ideal representation of what was different from reason, what reason needed to explain and, ultimately, enlighten and transform.[2] According to Mary Douglas, among others, these attitudes led comparative studies of religion to elevate ethical Protestant-like religions in contrast to the magical ritualism of primitive, Catholic-like religions.[3]

In the second half of the 20th century, the trend in scholarship began to swing the other way. Burke notes that people began to assume that "that all societies are equally ritualised; they merely practice different rituals. If most people in industrial societies no longer go to church regularly or practice elaborate rituals of initiation, this does not mean that ritual has declined. Instead, new types of ritual—political, sporting, musical, medical, academic, and so on—have taken the place of the traditional ones."[4] From this perspective, ritual is deemed good and healthy, humanly important, universal, and constantly concerned with what Weber, and Geertz after him, called "the Problem of Meaning."[5] Yet this more recent attitude, embodied in the work of both Victor Turner and Clifford Geertz, continues to rely on the opposition between ritual and modernization assumed by Spencer and Weber. This time, however, the opposition casts ritual as a natural mitigator of the harsh and unwanted aspects of modern life. It is possible that 16th- and 19th-century formulations of a modern, secular repudiation of ritual may have contributed to cultural attitudes associated with a decline in ritual participation. There is certainly evidence that the more recent and positive view of ritual promoted by Turner and Geertz has been influential in people's return to ritual. In any case, it is pertinent to ask if the widespread repudiations and returns identified by the theorists have really existed.

There are many sociohistorical situations in which people reject ritual, either their own ritual traditions or those imposed on them by others. In addition to the rejection by 16th-century Protestant reformers of what they saw as papist idolatry and vain superstition, there are many other historical examples, including the rejection of ritual (*li*) by the ancient Taoists, the criticisms of outer ritual form in favor of inner intention by Greek and Roman philosophers, as well as Saint Paul; and a series of movements in Hinduism from the ancient Upanishadic teachers to the early-19th-century Hindu reformer, Ram Mohun Roy. In most cases such criticisms were not attacks on all forms of ritual, just on certain features of pomp, mystery, rigidity, or claims for material efficacy. In the complex milieu of the Reformation, Burke points out, many different understandings of ritual were formulated and challenged. The result was not so much a general repudiation of ritual as a widespread and pluralist debate over different styles and understandings of ritual. As a consequence, he concludes, western Europeans may have become "unusually self-conscious and articulate on the subject."[6]

Typological systems as different as those of Bellah and Douglas, presented earlier, suggest that different types of social order and cultural worldview can be correlated with different styles of ritual. Yet rarely does a society have only one style or one worldview. Usually there are several different cosmological orders more or less integrated with each other but capable of tense differentiation and mutual opposition. Different parts of a society—social classes, economic strata, or ethnic groups—may hold different perspectives on ritual, or the same subgroup may have different attitudes on different occasions. Hence, any repudiation of ritual, like all ritual practice, must be seen as a very contextual thing. For example, when the most radical of the Protestant reformers, the 17th-century Quakers, went so far as to reject even conventional greetings as artificial "bundles of fopperies, fond ceremonies, foolish windings, turnings and crouchings with their bodies," it was in the context of a particular group distinguishing itself from others by taking ideas of inner versus outer spirituality to a new logical extreme.[7]

From this perspective, the evidence for a general, long-term historical process of repudiating ritual begun in 16th-century Europe becomes rather slim. It seems more likely that the century saw the emergence of alternative understandings of ritual that had close links to issues concerning the constitution of personhood, national community, and religious authority. While these clashes would not forbid the future emergence of a general consensus about ritual, the cultural pluralism amplifying the debate can make it difficult to imagine. Certainly there has been no single, smooth process of ritual atrophy in European and American culture since then. However, there has been a process in which the emerging disciplines studying religion and culture associated ritual with the primitive, tribal, and nonrational. And despite the variety of other modes of ritual surrounding them in their own societies, such theorists could convince many of a loss of ritual in modern life.

If a general repudiation of ritual in modern industrial society has been somewhat exaggerated, therefore, it is possible that the evidence for a return to ritual has also been overstated. For example, a great deal of attention has been given to the "return" of secular Jews to more demanding forms of orthodoxy. In this context, of course, the word "return" should be examined. In most cases, the people involved had never left orthodoxy; they were born and raised in secular Jewish families and communities. The fact that they are called "those who return" (baalei teshuvah in Hebrew) reflects the perspective of the orthodox segment of the Jewish tradition (as well as Zionist interpretations), the view from within the fold, as it were, for whom a secular Jew is a sinner and all Jews who "return" must repent for transgressing correct observance of Jewish law.[8]

The notion of return is also problematic because it rarely means simply picking up the tradition as it has been practiced in the past. Indeed, it is argued that some forms of Jewish orthodoxy to which people are said to return constitute a modern phenomenon, not a traditional one.[9] What is seized upon as tradition is usually a rather new synthesis of custom and accommodation. Many of the secular Jews who have adopted orthodoxy, for example, have no automatic place in the traditional social fabric. Institutional innovations have been necessary, including special yeshivas, synagogue programs, and the quite untraditional Manhattan outreach program for returning singles that has enrolled some 1,200 men and women. In addition, those who convert tend to embrace some aspects of tradition more than others and bring with them new needs to which the tradition must respond. This type of "return" to tradition, therefore, is clearly a force that opens the tradition to many changes. Nonetheless, Jews are embracing orthodoxy in significant numbers; although some research suggests that they do not appear to offset Jews who drift away from orthodox communities.[10]

A variety of reasons have been proposed to explain this type of return to ritual. In most general terms, it is usually analyzed as a form of resistance to secularization, modernization, and, in the case of Judaism in particular, to assimilation.[11] Yet the decision to embrace orthodoxy is itself possible only in a secular society where there are various options for religious affiliation and where the whole issue is considered a matter of individual choice. Hence, if the choice of a return to orthodoxy is a form of resistance to secularism, it also reinforces some of the more central values of secularism, namely, individual choice and a plurality of options. In addition, the most statistically dominant reason for returning to orthodoxy, marriage to an orthodox spouse (by either a secular Jew or a non-Jew), suggests some ambivalence since it indicates that significant numbers of orthodox Jews are marrying outside their communities.[12] The effect of a visit to Israel is another reason commonly given for orthodox conversion, and it is testimony to the emotional impact of experiencing Judaism as a living ethnic culture. Comparably, in America and Europe today, the decision to join a highly ritualized community is often based on an interest in ethnicity as a framework for community, identity, and a sense of tradition and belonging. The sociologist Herbert Danzger finds that the formal belief system is usually less important to the newly orthodox than what Peter Berger called the "plausibility system," that is, the network of people who share the beliefs and make them appear to be a credible understanding of the true nature of things. The family is the most important component of this plausibility system, but the local community or peer group plays a decisive role as well. Identifying with this community by means of dress, residence, and lifestyle — particularly the style of interaction between men and women — can secure one a place in a high-profile, clearly demarcated community.[13]

The decision of women to embrace orthodox Judaism merits particular attention since it is a choice that would seem to fly in the face of the larger movements for women's social and personal emancipation in this century. In exploring the appeal of orthodoxy to young, middle-class, educated women, Lynn Davidman finds the "characteristic dilemmas of modern life, such as feelings of isolation, rootlessness, and confusion about gender." As a possible solution to these dilemmas, different women looked to different types of orthodox community — some that took complete control over their lives, others that encouraged them to continue living independently. Yet all of these communities honored women's roles as wives and mothers and held out to their female converts the promise of a religion that gives pride of place to a fulfilling domestic life. The primacy accorded women's domestic roles is understood in terms of the importance of a series of rituals governing food preparation and consumption, marital relations, and the observance of the Sabbath and other holidays. Orthodox women say they find in these rituals a deep recognition of their womanhood and their role in the well-being of the family.[14]

Often what is called a return to ritual may be as simple as a heightened interest in symbolism. For example, two Protestant denominations, the United Methodist Church and the Presbyterian Church (U.S.A.), recently "reclaimed," in their words, the Catholic and pre-Reformation practice of receiving a smudge of ashes in the shape of a cross on their foreheads on Ash Wednesday, the beginning of Lent, the forty-day period of preparation for Easter. The use of ashes was originally a Jewish practice, reinterpreted by Christians but rejected by Protestant reformers who looked to biblical teachings over external marks of piety. Most of the reasons given for the return to ashes appeal to an emotional resonance with this symbolic reminder of mortality and sin — and a new appreciation of the evocative power of ritual. In the words of Reverend Deborah A. McKinley, spokesperson for the Presbyterian Church (U.S.A.), people "are discovering the importance of ritual action and its ability to draw us beyond the cerebral."[15]

Reverend McKinley's comment reflects the attitude, popular since the early 1970s, that ritual is basically good for you. This is certainly the conviction of much recent scholarship, which has helped to promote and legitimate this perspective among the wider public. The post-Reformation opposition of external form and internal feeling, appears displaced by a somewhat different understanding. The same is true for the early modern opposition of rational-industrial to the mystical-tribal. Ritual is now more likely to be seen as a medium of emotional, intuitive expression that is able to express the spiritual states, alternative realities, and the incipient connectedness in which individuals and communities are embedded. While ritual once stood for the status quo and the authority of the dominant social institutions, for many it has become antistructural, revolutionary, and capable of deconstructing inhuman institutions and generating alternative structures. A long-standing concern with the falsity of ritual, conveyed in the negativity of such words as "ritualistic" and "ritualism," has been replaced in many quarters with a desire for ritual as a healing experience. The older conviction that increasing modernization, rational utilitarianism, and individualism would inevitably do away with most forms of traditional ritual life has given way to a heroic championing of ritual as the way to remain human in an increasingly dehumanized world.

In 1982, Douglas argued that most scholars of religion in the postwar period were apt to overemphasize the positive and integrative aspects of religion, implicitly opposing it to modernity in the same way that theology has opposed salvation to worldliness or, in a different debate, scientific rationalism opposed the delusions of traditional religion to the progress of reason.[16] Indeed, the positive and integrative aspects of ritual action are so taken for granted that no effort is made to substantiate them. Vincent Crapanzano's conclusion that Moroccan male initiation rites cruelly traumatize a child in ways that benefit the conservatism of the social group is a rare example of a critical analysis.[17] It is dramatically outweighed by the number of studies attempting to show how initiations are good and healthy social experiences, the lack of which in modern society has resulted in profound sociocultural impoverishment. The assumptions behind this type of statement are never laid out and tested against any empirical evidence.

Since Douglas's criticism of these tendencies toward an indiscriminate affirmation of religion, the opposition of ritual and modernity has actually gone a step further and overly romanticized ritual. It is characterized by testimonies to its creative solutions to the anomie of modern society, which promise among other things, that initiation rites can solve adolescent delinquency and that communing with the earth can rectify our ecological relationships with the environment. A variety of of analyses have pushed ritual as a curative for the ills of modernity to the point where ritual appears to act independently of any sociocultural determinism. Indeed, it is set up to act almost salvifically. Aside from all the nonscholarly appeals to the roots of ritual in the "eternal wisdom of ancient peoples," there are theorists who locate ritual in pre-linguistic grammars, in the biogenetic foundation of the "reptilian brain," and in basic, cross-cultural gestures of the human body.[18] All of these views cast ritual as independent of any sociocultural context. They never implicate ritual in the emergence of modernity. Instead, ritual remains a pure, inadequately tapped human resource for ameliorating the evils of modernity—specifically, the personal and communal wholeness fractured by ethnicity, religious ideology, and areligious passivity. Tom Driver writes that "the human longing for ritual is deep," although often frustrated; he extols ritual as essentially liberating and the means of salvation for the modern world. Unable to ignore completely some of the latent contradictions in the position, however, Driver notes that Mohandas Gandhi, the spiritual leader of the Indian independence movement, and Joseph Goebbels, the director of the Nazi's "final solution" for the Jews, were both "consummate ritualist[s]."[19] Yet Driver never analyzes why ritual in the hands of Gandhi was good and in the hands of Goebbels was horrific, or how ritual in general can be so liberating if it can support both men's visions of human aspirations.

The roots of this most recent romanticization of ritual are many and complex, as are its effects. One clear result, however, is a blindness to how contemporary ritual practices are part and parcel of the modern world, often effectively promoting the very forces of modernity that such perspectives implicitly condemn.

The Emergence of "Ritual"

The twists and turns of repudiating, returning, and romancing ritual have been closely intertwined with the emergence of the very concept of ritual as a universal phenomenon accessible to formal identification and analysis. The anthropologist Talal Asad argues that modern use of the term has very specific dates attached to it. The earliest editions of the *Encyclopedia Britannica*, put out between 1771 and 1852, defined ritual as a "book directing the order and manner to be observed in performing divine service in a particular church, diocese, or the like." Even with the addition of references to the rituals of "heathens" like the ancient Romans, it is clear that ritual meant a type of prescriptive liturgical book. Similarly, the entries for "rite" indicated "the particular manner of celebrating divine service, in this or that country," for example, the Roman rite or the Eastern rite. After 1852, there were no entries for either term until 1910, by which time the meaning had clearly shifted. The brief paragraphs of the earlier editions were replaced by a long article with sections on magical elements, interpretation, change, and classification, as well as a bibliography noting the works of the early theorists discussed in part I. For Asad, this shift is "something quite new." Ritual is "no longer a script for regulating practice, but a type of practice" found in all religions and even outside religion, involving expressive symbols intrinsic to the sense of self and workings of society.[20]

To conceive of ritual as a panhuman phenomenon rather than simply to point and gawk at the strange activities of another culture must constitute some form of progress. Yet it is also the result of a drawn-out, complex, and intrinsically political process of negotiating cultural differences and similarities. The observation of ritual commonalities between "our worship" and "their customs" was facilitated by a term, a noun, which asserted a common denominator. At the same time, however, this new commonality effectively relocated "difference." No longer the difference between "our worship" and "their customs," it became the difference between those who sufficiently transcend culture and history to perceive the universal (and scientific) in contrast to those who remain trapped in cultural and historical particularity and are therein so naturally amenable to being the object of study.

Some of the intricacies of this process of negotiating new forms of commonality and difference are preserved in the real-life vignettes of those scholars who literally mapped a frontier, marking out the borders between the newly similar and dissimilar "other." While they emerged as scholars of ritual practices, the people they studied emerged as practitioners of ritual. At one end of the spectrum of experiences and scholars that created this border, there is the story of the Third Cavalry Captain John G. Bourke's reaction to the rites of a secret Zuñi society, the Ne'wekwe (or Nehue-Cue).[21] His initial encounter with them in 1881 provoked intense nausea, which, in turn, inspired him to undertake a ten-year study of Zuñi ritual. According to the literary historian Stephen Greenblatt, who has dramatically chronicled some of the themes implicit in Bourke's work, this experience of disgust served to define what was of ethnographic interest, what was "other" (in this case, not Hebrew or Christian) and thus in need of explanation.[22]

At the other end of the "us-them" spectrum, there is the story of Frank Cushing's romantic identification with the Zuñi. An ethnologist sent by the Smithsonian in 1879 to study the Southwest Indians, he acted as Bourke's host. But in contrast to Bourke, Cushing became uncomfortable as an outside observer-scientist putting these people under a type of microscope; he wanted to learn about being Zuñi from the inside. Living with them for many years, he became fluent in their language and so comfortable with their customs that they eventually adopted him into the tribe and initiated him as a priest and war chief. Cushing claimed to think like a Zuñi. It is said that in "going native" he stopped writing about secret Zuñi myths and rituals, unwilling to publish sacred information that had been transmitted to him in confidence. There is some question, however, whether this was the real reason Cushing did not complete several of his ethnographic projects; some suggest that his reticence had less to do with idealism and more to do with sloppy work habits.[23] It is also possible that he was not as well integrated into the tribe as he thought, and his claims to think like a Zuñi may not have been perfectly echoed by the Zuñi themselves. Indeed, they appear to have been very aware of significant peculiarities about Cushing, as shown in the song they composed about him, related by Sam Gill:

> Once they made a White man into a Priest of the Bow
> he was out there with the other Bow priests
> he had black stripes on his body
> the others said their prayers from their hearts
> but he read his from a piece of paper.[24]

Aside from the contrast between prayers said from the heart and those read from the paper, the song also refers to Cushing's striped body paint. According to Gill, the Zuñi refer to paper with writing as something "striped." So it seems that Cushing's reliance on texts and writing—the instruments for the objectification of ritual and of Zuñi culture—was so distinctive that they made it his emblematic sign. In other words, as Gill tells it, they painted him up as a walking piece of writing.[25]

In the annals of ethnographic history and interpretation, many instinctive reactions of disgust or romantic attraction have been used as markers of the differences that make another culture "other," suspect, barbaric, and exotic. Such reactions, moreover, never go in just one direction. Many peoples greeted Europeans and European customs with equal reactions of disgust. Greenblatt notes the reaction of a Native American to the European practice of "collecting and carrying around mucus in handkerchiefs."[26] Early Chinese accounts of Westerners also record many formulations of the "us-them" differences. One early Chinese visitor to the United States graphically described "the red-haired, green-eyed foreign devils with hairy faces" for his audience back home. They were, he continued, "wild and wicked, and paid no regard to the moral precepts of Confucius and the Sages; neither did they worship their ancestors, but pretended to be wiser than their fathers and grandfathers." Worse yet, men and women "were shameless enough to walk the streets arm in arm in daylight." A later Chinese visitor, more accustomed to these differences, carefully instructed his readers back home in the intricacies and repellent immodesties of that most foreign of rituals, the dinner party, where a man must be prepared to shake a strange woman's hand, offer her his arm, and even engage her in polite conversation.[27] Chinese routinely concluded that Americans had no *li*, that is, no sense of proper behavior.

Somewhere in between the extremes of Bourke's and Cushing's defining encounters with the "other" lies the well-known story of the early sociologist and ordained minister, William Robertson Smith, whose theories were discussed in chapter 1. His career represents a more complex stage in the emergence of the notion and study of ritual. Smith's work on "totemic sacrifice" among the ancient Semitic tribes of the Sinai Desert established the role of ritual in unifying the social group. Using what he presumed was a firsthand account of "the oldest known form of Arabian sacrifice" written by a hermit named Nilus, Smith described how a tribe would tie up a camel and place it on an altar of piled stones. The head of the group would lead them in chanting around the altar three times before inflicting the first wound. Everyone rushed to drink the blood that gushed forth, after which they would all "fall on the victim with their swords, hacking off pieces of the quivering flesh and devouring them raw with such wild haste, that in the short interval between the rise of the day star . . . and the disappearance of its rays before the rising sun, the entire camel, body and bones, skin, blood and entrails is wholly devoured."[28] Not unlike Bourke's experience of nausea, the brutality of this communal sacrificial meal proved its distance from modern religion; in other words, it testified to the primitiveness of the rite and hence its potential for indicating the origin and essential meaning of all communal rites. Yet even this degree of distance was threatening since it presumed some historical relationship between primitive carnage and modern worship. When Smith brought some of his critical methods of ethnographic analysis to bear on the Bible, even quite indirectly, it provoked a major conflict within the Free Church, a branch of the Church of Scotland, in which he was an ordained minister. In 1881 he was dismissed from his professorship at the Free Church Divinity College of the University of Aberdeen and put on trial in a protracted libel case known in its day as the "Robertson Smith affair."[29] The trial was essentially an accusation of heresy by conservatives reacting to the implications of his work, particularly the implication that common social forces underlie primitive *and* revealed religions.[30]

It is interesting to note that Robertson Smith himself never aired any doubts about the revealed nature of Christianity. On the contrary, he appears to have been convinced that careful and critical scholarship would only help to unfold the central revelations of the Christian scripture. His interpretation of the typical distinction of his day saw all the "lower" religions mired in the social forces that he was among the first to describe, while Christianity as the revealed truth was able to transcend such determinisms.[31] Smith's attempts to negotiate the relationship between the Bible of belief and the demands of objective scholarship were integral to the emergence of another aspect of the "us-them" boundary, the boundary distinguishing the *practice* of religion from the *study* of it. In Smith's work, this particular boundary followed from how he nearly transgressed the first one: while affirming the distinction between Christianity as revealed religion and all other religions, he also appeared to transgress it with hints of some sort of commonality—the suggestion that perhaps all acts of ritual communion shared a common origin. While such hints were too much for Smith's church, many of his colleagues and students continued to look for the origins and commonalties underlying grossly different forms of religious practice. The splits between church and academy would widen, of course, as scholars distinguished between their practices as a Christian believers and their objective studies, and as the term "ritual" began to be used to talk about common forms of religious practice underlying our liturgies and their barbaric sacrifices.

Although Robertson Smith's tendency to see the ancient rite of totemic sacrifice in as primitive a light as possible did not prevent him from suggesting some modern connections, it seriously misled him in another, rather ironic way. The ancient text on which he relied for a description of this totemic sacrifice was not an authentic account of an ancient tribal ritual at all. It was, in fact, a highly dubious source, a fifth-century Christian text, *The Story of Nilus*, and a type of fictional travelogue in which a witty and sophisticated urban traveler details his hair-raising—and completely fabricated and exaggerated—adventures among stereotypically ferocious desert tribes.[32] Smith mistook this farcical tale for an objective, detached, and reliable account akin to what he himself wished to produce. Since his book laid out the first sociological theory of ritual and was the basis for much subsequent scholarship on ritual, we can wonder what it means that the study of ritual was founded on a pulp tale of primitive barbarism!

The adventures of scholars like Bourke, Cushing, and Robertson Smith along the emerging border between us and them, scholar and practitioner, and theory and data established the basis on which the term "ritual" came to denote group-oriented religious activities that are common, in fundamental ways, to all cultures and peoples.[33] At the same time, as part I demonstrated, the concept of ritual became important to scholarly debates over how to distinguish the magical, the religious, and the rational. The effects of this simultaneous universalization and differentiation are complex. On the one hand, as the foregoing makes very clear, a focus on ritual has enabled scholars to determine the basic similarities among very different ritual practices and traditions. At the same time, however, on a more suble level, the deployment of "ritual" as a universal has also established new distinctions and borderlands, especially between those who wield such universal categories and thereby transcend their culture and those who, locked in their cultural perspectives, are the recipients of categorizations that may seem meaningless or threatening.[34]

In the end, the history of the concept of ritual suggests that the term has been primarily used to define and mediate plurality and relationships between "us and them," with the practices of "them" ranging from primitive magic to papist idolatry to the affirmation of traditional wisdom in the face of brutal modernity. Yet there is another important dimension to the emergence of these perspectives on ritual. Approaching ritual as a universal medium of symbolic expression has had significant consequences for the very practice of ritual in Europe and America. In other words, the concept of ritual has influenced how many people in these cultures go about ritualizing today. As parts of the public have come to share an awareness of the cross-cultural similarities among rituals within very different doctrinal systems, social organizations, and cosmological worldviews, "ritual" has emerged for them as a more important focus of attention than the doctrines that appear so tied to particular cultures and histories. Indeed, scholarly studies of "ritual" that demonstrate the evolution and variation of ritual practices over time have been used by components of the larger public as authoritative justifications for making fresh changes in their traditional practices. As a result, the scholarly perspectives on ritual described previously have come to undermine some forms of traditional ritual authority—the authority of having been divinely mandated by God or the ancestors, the authority of seeming to be the way things have been done since time immemorial, and the authority of being the sole possession of this particular community and thus intrinsic to its particular worldview. Hence, the study of ritual practices and the emergence of "ritual" as an abstract universal have the effect of subordinating, relativizing, and ultimately undermining many aspects of ritual practice, even as they point to ritual as a powerful medium of transcultural experience.

While some observers of the current scene see social expressions of a new freedom to ritualize, others see chaotic and idiosyncratic performances that lack all authority. In actual fact, recent forms of ritualization locate their authority in rather nontraditional ways. Most common, perhaps, is an implicit appeal to the authority lodged in the abstract notion of ritual itself. Scholars, ritual inventors, and ritual participants do not usually see how scholarship has constructed this notion of ritual or the type of authority it has acquired. They think of "ritual in general" as something that has been there all along and only now discovered—no matter whether it is thought to be a social constant, a psychological necessity, or a biological determinism. As an abstraction that determines all particular rites and ceremonies, ritual itself becomes a reified construct with the authority to sanction new forms of ritualization that appeal to it as a quintessential human and social dynamic.

There are few ritual leaders and inventors these days who have not read something of the theories of Frazer, van Gennep, Eliade, Turner, or Geertz, either in an original or popularized form. Turner, in particular, by identifying a "ritual process" weaving its way through micro and macro social relations and symbol systems, has been the authority behind much American ritual invention. His books, even when only half-read, legitimize the appeal to ritual as a universal process that authenticates changes in traditional rites or empowers people to invent new ones. The ever increasing corpus of studies on ritual also functions as further testimony to the solidity of ritual as a universal phenomenon and to the legitimacy of activities done in its name. In a typical introduction to a general-audience book on the need for ritual in the modern era, the editor states:

> We take Turner's view that the "betwixt and between" times, the threshold transition times, deserve special attention as constructive "building blocks" for change, or possibly transformation and initiation to another level of consciousness. These liminal or threshold times have a power of their own for both the individual and the culture at large. . . . Our book is essentially practical, applying basic ideas and patterns of initiation for several age groups.[35]

Here, the abstract patterns "identified" by Turner as common to all initiations—something that has never been proven, and strongly contested by some—are taken as intrinsically human.[36] This view of ritual gives legitimacy to the rites invented by the authors; it also interprets many different personal and cultural experiences as reflecting, and thereby further authenticating, these patterns.

Another book offering advice for creating one's own rituals uses the same logic. It states that "all cultures recognize the need to ritualize major life transitions. In 1929, anthropologist Arnold Van Gennep coined the term 'rite of passage' to describe the universal practice of ceremonializing life's major events."[37] Here the universality of the phenomenon pointed out by van Gennep is the authority behind the rites presented in the book. In a more scholarly study, the author suggests that Turner's model of pilgrimage as a transforming ritual transition should be adopted by the Roman Catholic Church as a central strategy for the pre-Cana activities meant to prepare non-Catholics for marriage in the church.[38] The authority for using this particular ritual structure is not rooted in Catholic doctrine or revelation, although the author does refer to a minor historical precedent for pilgrimage metaphors. Rather, the effective authority for using this ritual pattern is the universality accorded the ritual process described by Turner. The explicit authority vouchsafed to scholars of rituals is certainly significant and perhaps unprecedented. At various times in church deliberations over liturgial matters, the recent tendency has been to consult outside secular scholars. For modern ritualists devising ecological liturgies, crafting new age harmonies, or drumming up a fire in the belly, the taken-for-granted authority to do these things and the accompanying conviction about their efficacy lie in the abstraction "ritual" that scholars have done so much to construct.[39]

We are seeing a new "paradigm" for ritualization. Belief in ritual as a central dynamic in human affairs—as opposed to belief in a particular Christian liturgical tradition or the historical practice of Jewish law—gives ritualists the authority to ritualize creatively and even idiosyncratically. Ritual is approached as a means to create and renew community, transform human identity, and remake our most existential sense of being in the cosmos.[40] Popularized versions of the Turner-Geertz model of "the ritual process" make people expect that these rites can work as a type of social alchemy to transform good intentions into new instincts or weave the threads of raw and broken experiences into a textured fabric of connectedness to other people and things. Ritual practitioners of all kinds in Europe and America now share the sense that their rites participate in something universal. They consider what they do as fundamentally symbolic and having much in common with the equally symbolic practices of Chinese ancestral offerings, Trobriand garden magic, or Turner's accounts of Ndembu healing. And these modern practitioners can reconcile this commonality with personal commitment to the practices of a particular, if newly flexible tradition. This is a fascinating development in the West and one that needs to be examined more closely. There is nothing inherently wrong with it, except that it is clearly not the last word on either ritualization or the concept of ritual. It is a set of attitudes that are as historically determined as the definitions laid out in the earliest editions of the *Encyclopedia Britannica*.[41] Yet in a pragmatic sense, these recent developments may also imply that only now do we have "ritual" as such in European

and American cultural life. Only now do people do various rites with a consciousness of participating in a universal phenomenon.

Just as modern theories of ritual have had a powerful effect on how people ritualize, how people ritualize profoundly affects what theorists set about to describe and
explain. There is no "scientific" detachment here: ritual theorists, experts, and participants are pulled into a complex circle of interdependence. Recognition of this
interdependence makes it easier to consider how our use of the notion of ritual can
influence our understanding of people who do not abstract the same experiences in
the same way. In other words, our theories of ritual may do a lot to translate Confucian ancestor practices or Trobriand gardening practices into more abstract terms
and models that make sense to us. But these analyses do not necessarily help us understand how these activities figure in the worldview of the Chinese or Trobrianders;
they may even distort Chinese and Trobriand cultural experiences. If only now do
we have "ritual" as such in European and American cultural life, then it may not be
inappropriate to contend that what many Chinese and Trobrianders are doing is not
"ritual."

With this historical perspective, we can be sympathetic to the critique of the
anthropologist Talal Asad, who suggests that the category of ritual may not be appropriate to other, non-Christian cultural milieus, such as Islam, which involves very
different "technologies of power" and "moral economies of the self." If our historically determined notion of ritual should appear to explain Islamic ritual to our satisfaction, Asad proposes, then perhaps we need to reexamine whether we have constructed categories that inadvertently tell us only what we want to know. Asad fears
that Western scholarship is so powerful that it is impossible for Trobriand garden
magic to survive in any form but as data for the great mills of scholarly theory. More
specifically, he fears that the categories of ritual and religion will influence and even
be adopted by those who would not traditionally have defined their lives in these
ways.[42] While such developments may foster easier communication and shared values, they may do so by means of political subordination and substantive diminution
of the diversity of human experience.

Western scholarship *is* very powerful. Its explanatory power rests not only on tools
of abstraction that make some things into concepts and other things in data but also
on many other social activities, simultaneously economic and political, that construct
a plausibility system of global proportions. Hence, it is quite possible that categories
of ritual and nonritual will influence people who would define their activities differently. If scholarship on ritual as a universal construct has succeeded in creating the
beginnings of a shared sense of ritual in many religious and civic practices of Euro-
American culture, then we cannot dismiss the concern that such a construct can reach
out to restructure practice elsewhere. We may well be in the very process of actually
creating ritual as the universal phenomenon we have long taken it to be. Yet creating it has not been our intention, and does not appear to further our more self-
conscious goals of understanding.

Richard Schechner concludes his study, *The Future of Ritual*, with a vision in
which ritual's pairing of restraint and creativity is the best means by which human
beings can avoid complete self-extinction.[43] While his romantic evocation of ritual

as a force for global good is not likely to garner the support of empiricists, this sort of vision is tied to practices that could construct as concrete a phenomenon as any empiricist might wish, by encouraging people everywhere to begin to understand their practices as cultural variations on an underlying, universal phenomenon. Certainly the construction of interpretive categories and the propensity to reify them are among the ways by which people have always shaped their world. Abstractions like freedom, human dignity, evil, or true love have had powerful and concrete effects on human affairs. A global discourse on ritual, understood as a transcultural language of the human spirit, is more likely to promote a sense of common humanity and cross-cultural respect than the view that one set of religious rites are the revealed truth itself and the idols worshiped by all other peoples must be destroyed. Yet it is clear that this discourse is being constructed not without violence, loss, and deeply rooted assumptions of cultural hegemony.

In a purely methodological vein, such concerns suggest the need for revised methodologies. The practice theories examined at the close of chapter 3 attempt to focus on activities in such a way as to minimize the amount of preliminary selecting and framing of the data in terms of such powerful categories as ritual, religion, technology, ideology, and so on. There are also attempts to formulate elements basic to "reflexive" and "self-critical" forms of scholarly analysis.[44] There may be other alternatives as well, perhaps even a reconstructed phenomenology—a phenomenology for the post-postmodern era, so to speak—in which the scholar and the conditions of the scholarly project itself are systematically included as part of the total phenomenon under scrutiny. In any case, the links between the emergence of ritual as a category of analysis and the shifts in how people in European and American society ritualize make very clear that ritual cannot be approached as some transparent phenomenon out there in the world waiting to be analyzed and explained. It exists only in sets of complex interactions that we are just beginning to try to map.

Conclusion

The contexts in which ritual practices unfold are not like the props of painted scenery on a theatrical stage. Ritual action involves an inextricable interaction with its immediate world, often drawing it into the very activity of the rite in multiple ways. Exactly how this is done, how often, and with what stylistic features will depend on the specific cultural and social situation with its traditions, conventions, and innovations. Why some societies have more ritual than others, why ritual traditions change or do not change, and why some groups abstract and study "ritual" as some kind of universal phenomenon when others do not—these are questions of context that are at the heart of the dynamics understood as religion and culture.

The way that European and American scholars generate questions about ritual reflects and promotes basic elements of their cultural worldview. The notion of ritual has become one of the ways in which these cultures experience and understand the world. So what does this interest in ritual tell us about ourselves? Most readily, it tells us that we do not live with a seamless worldview; what we do and what we think or believe are routinely distinguished, separated out, and differently weighted. It suggests a certain drive toward transcending the particularities of place, time, and culture by means of the "higher learning" embodied in scientific, artistic, historical, and hermeneutical forms of analysis. This interest in transcending the particular suggests a fundamental drive toward world transformation and self-determination. It suggests an eagerness to find or forge spiritual-cultural commonalities among the heterogeneity of beliefs and styles in the world, but primarily in terms that extend our historical experiences as nearly universal. The hubris is not unconstructive, but it now comes face to face with a fresh set of challenges. Whether it can address and solve them is not clear, but these are the issues that ritual and the study of ritual will struggle with in the near future.

The central concern of this study has been to introduce systematically all of the issues, debates, and areas of inquiry that comprise the modern study of ritual. In most cases, this has meant raising open-ended issues, rather than presenting an authoritative consensus. Of course, the topic of ritual is not unique in this regard. Without sacrificing any of the complexity and convolutions involved in these issues, this study has also tried to impose some minimal order on them for the purpose, at least, of suggesting other orderings and contexts. If it was not clear at the beginning, it should be clear by now that "theories," "activities" and "contexts" can be only provisional frameworks. Theories and contexts affect what is seen as ritual and by whom, while those activities deemed to be ritual in turn have theoretical and contextual consequences.

In the end, "ritual" is a relatively new term that we have pressed into service to negotiate a variety of social and cultural differences, including the differentiation of scholarly objectivity and generalization as distinct from cultural particularism and parochialism. The work and hopes of many theorists and practitioners today are pinned to it, and there is no doubt that ritual has become one of the ways in which we structure and interpret our world. As an interpretive tool, it inevitably corrects a bit here and distorts a bit there, or, in terms of practice theory, it addresses problems by shifting the very terrain on which they appeared. In the future, we may have better tools with which to understand what people are doing when they bow their heads, offer incense to a deity, dance in masks in the plaza, or give a lecture on the meaning of ritual. Yet all these acts are ways of dealing with the world and its perceived forces and sources of power. The form and scope of interpretation differ, and that should not be lightly dismissed, but it cannot be amiss to see in all of these instances practices that illuminate our shared humanity.

Notes

Preface

   1. Catherine Bell, *Ritual Theory, Ritual Practice* (New York: Oxford University Press, 1992).

   2. Peter Burke, "The Repudiation of Ritual in Early Modern Europe," in *The Historical Anthropology of Early Modern Italy: Essays on Perception and Communication* (Cambridge: Cambridge University Press, 1987), p. 233; Maulana Karenga, *Kwanzaa: Origin, Concepts, Practice* (Los Angeles: Kawaida Publications, 1977), p. 18: "The first act of a self-conscious, self-determining people is to redefine and reshape reality in its own image and according to its own needs."

   3. Burton Watson, trans., *Hsün Tzu: Basic Writings* (New York: Columbia University Press, 1963), pp. 94–95.

Chapter 1

   1. See F. Max Müller, *Lectures on the Science of Language* [1861] (New York: Scribner, Armstrong and Co., 1967).

   2. Andrew Lang, *The Making of Religion* [1898] (New York: AMS Press, 1968).

   3. Robert Ackerman, "Frazer on Myth and Ritual," *Journal of the History of Ideas* 36 (1975): 117, using the revised 1924 edition of E. B. Tylor's *Anthropology* (London: Macmillan, 1881).

   4. Edward B. Tylor, *Primitive Culture* [1871] (New York: Harper, 1958).

   5. William Robertson Smith, *Lectures on the Religion of the Semites: The Fundamental Institutions* [1889] (New York: KTAV Publishing House, 1969), pp. 28–29.

   6. For a fuller discussion, see Brian Morris, *Anthropological Studies of Religion* (Cambridge: Cambridge University Press, 1987), pp. 270–74.

   7. Robertson Smith, *Lectures on the Religion of the Semites*, p. 18. Also cited in full in Robert Ackerman, "Frazer on Myth and Ritual," p. 120.

8. T. O. Beidelman, *W. Robertson Smith and the Sociological Study of Religion* (Chicago: University of Chicago Press, 1974), pp. 57–61.

9. Robertson Smith, *Lectures on the Religion of the Semites*, p. 29. For further discussion of Robertson Smith's role in pioneering a social-anthropological approach, see Ackerman, "Frazer on Myth and Ritual," pp. 118–20; Mary Douglas, *Purity and Danger: An Analysis of Concepts of Pollution and Taboo* (New York: Praeger, 1966), pp. 13–19; and E. E. Evans-Pritchard, *Theories of Primitive Religion* (Oxford: Clarendon Press, 1965), pp. 51–53.

10. Ackerman, "Frazer on Myth and Ritual," pp. 115, 122.

11. This statement is something of a simplification. On the many complex shifts in Frazer's thinking, see Ackerman, "Frazer of Myth and Ritual," pp. 123, 132.

12. James George Frazer, *The Golden Bough: A Study in Magic and Religion*, 3d ed. [1911] (London: Macmillan, 1955), vol. 10, p. vi. Also cited in Jonathan Z. Smith, "When the Bough Breaks," *History of Religions* 12, no. 4 (1973): 345.

13. For further discussion of these schools, see William G. Doty, *Mythography: The Study of Myths and Rituals* (Tuscaloosa: University of Alabama Press, 1986), pp. 73–78; and Robert A. Segal, "The Myth-Ritualist Theory of Religion," *Journal for the Scientific Study of Religion* 19, no. 2 (1980): 173–85.

14. S. H. Hooke, ed., *The Labyrinth: Further Studies in the Relation between Myth and Ritual in the Ancient World* (London: Society for Promoting Christian Knowledge, 1935), pp. v–vi. Also see S. H. Hooke, ed., *Myth and Ritual* (London: Oxford University Press, 1933).

15. Shelley Arlen, *The Cambridge Ritualists: An Annotated Bibliography of the Works by and about Jane Ellen Harrison, Gilbert Murray, Francis M. Cornford, and Arthur Bernard Cook* (Metuchen, N.J.: Scarecrow, 1990); and William M. Calder, ed., *The Cambridge Ritualists Reconsidered* (Atlanta: Scholars Press, 1991).

16. Jane Ellen Harrison, *Prolegomena to the Study of Greek Religion*, 3d ed. (Cleveland: Meridian, 1966); Jane Ellen Harrison, *Themis: A Study of the Social Origins of Greek Religion*, 2d ed. (Cleveland: Meridian, 1962).

17. Stanley Edgar Hyman, "The Ritual View of Myth and the Mythic," *Journal of American Folklore* 68 (1955), pp. 463–65, reprinted in Thomas A. Sebeok, ed., *Myth: A Symposium* (Bloomington: Indiana University Press, 1965), pp. 136–53.

18. Jessie L. Weston, *From Ritual to Romance* (Garden City, N.Y.: Doubleday, 1957).

19. Doty, *Mythography*, p. 77.

20. Hyman, "The Ritual View of Myth and the Mythic," pp. 465, 472.

21. In addition, Hocart's *The Life-Giving Myth and Other Essays* [1952] (ed. F. R. R. S. Raglan [London: Tavistock, 1970]), addressed the process by which myth goes beyond its ritual origins to develop an etiological function. See Hyman, "The Ritual View of Myth and the Mythic," p. 469.

22. F. R. R. S. (Lord) Raglan, *The Hero: A Study in Tradition, Myth, and Drama* (New York: Oxford University Press, 1937), reprinted in Otto Rank, Lord Raglan, and Alan Dundes, *In Quest of the Hero*, compiled by Robert A. Segal (Princeton: Princeton University Press, 1990), pp. 89–164.

23. Otto Rank, "The Myth of the Birth of the Hero," reprinted in Rank, Raglan, and Dundes, *In Quest of the Hero*, pp. 3–86.

24. Rank, Raglan, and Dundes, *In Quest of the Hero*, p. 138.

25. Theodor H. Gaster, *Thespis: Ritual, Myth and Drama in the Ancient Near East* [1950], rev. ed. (Garden City, N.Y.: Doubleday, 1961; New York: Harper and Row, 1966).

26. Gaster, *Thespis*, pp. 3–5.

27. Hyman, "The Ritual View of Myth and the Mythic," pp. 465, 470–71. For a summary of the myth-ritual pattern in literary criticism, see Doty, *Mythography*, pp. 167–91.

28. Hyman, "The Ritual View of Myth and the Mythic," p. 472.

29. Andrew Lang, *Magic and Religion* (London: Longmans, 1901); Robert H. Lowie, *Primitive Religion* (New York: Liveright Publishing, 1952); and *The History of Ethnological Theory* [1937] (New York: Holt, Rinehart and Winston, 1966); Wilhelm Schmidt, *Origin and Growth of Religion* [1931] (New York: Cooper Square Publishers, 1972); A. A. Goldenweiser, "Sir James Frazer's Theories," in *History, Psychology and Culture* (London: Kegan Paul, 1933) and in *Anthropology* [1937] (New York: Johnson Reprint Co., 1972); Clyde Kluckhohn, "Myths and Rituals: A General Theory," *Harvard Theological Review* 35 (1942): 42–79; Henri Frankfort, *Kingship of the Gods* (Chicago: University of Chicago, 1948) (see Hooke's refutation of Frankfort in his "Myth and Ritual: Past and Present," in S. J. Hooke, ed., *Myth, Ritual and Kingship* [Oxford: Clarendon Press, 1958], pp. 1–21); William Bascom, "The Myth-Ritual Theory," *Journal of American Folklore* 70 (1957): 103–14; S. G. F. Brandon, "The Myth and Ritual Position Critically Considered," in S. H. Hooke, ed., *Myth, Ritual and Kingship* (Oxford: Clarendon Press, 1958), pp. 261–91; Mircea Eliade (trans. Rosemary Sheed) *Patterns in Comparative Religion* (New York: New American Library, 1958), pp. 362–65; Edmund Leach, "Golden Bough or Gilded Twig," *Daedalus* 90, no. 2 (Spring 1961): 371–87 and "Frazer and Malinowski," *Current Anthropology* 7 (1966): 560–75; Jonathan Z. Smith, "When the Bough Breaks"; Hans H. Penner, "Myth and Ritual: A Wasteland or a Forest of Symbols," *History and Theory* 8 (1968): 46–57; and Joseph Fontenrose, *The Ritual Theory of Myth* (Berkeley: University of California Press, 1971).

30. Kluckhohn, "Myths and Rituals: A General Theory," pp. 54, 55.

31. Kluckhohn, "Myths and Rituals: A General Theory," p. 59.

32. Fontenrose, *The Ritual Theory of Myth*, especially pp. 56–59, goes on to applaud a functional type of approach using, for example, Malinowski's formulation of myth.

33. Robert A. Segal, "The Myth-Ritualist Theory of Religion." pp. 173–74.

34. Max Müller, *Chips from a German Workshop* [1869] (Chico, Calif.: Scholars Press, 1985), pp. xi, xx. Müller was not yet sure that "the time had come for attempting to trace, after the model of the Science of Language, the definite outlines of the Science of Religion" (p. ix), though, a few pages later, he was very sure that the results of such a science of religion would be to "assign to Christianity its right place" and "restore to the whole history of the world" the knowledge of its "unconscious progress towards Christianity, its true and sacred character" (pp. xix–xx). On this term and the emergence of *Religionswissenschaft* as a field of study, see Mircea Eliade, *The Sacred and the Profane: The Nature of Religion*, trans. Willard R. Trask (New York: Harcourt Brace Jovanovich, 1959), pp. 216–32; and Jean Jacques Waardenburg, *Classical Approaches to the Study of Religion*, 2 vols. (The Hague: Mouton, 1973).

35. "History of religions" was adopted as the official English title of the international association for *Religionswissenschaft*, known as the "International Association for the Study of the History of Religions." See Joseph M. Kitagawa, "The History of Religions in America," in *The History of Religions: Essays in Methodology*, ed. Mircea Eliade and Joseph M. Kitagawa (Chicago: University of Chicago Press, 1959), p. 15.

36. Phenomenologists of religion have tended to depict the emergence of *Religionswissenschaft* very inclusively; see Mircea Eliade, "The Quest for the 'Origins' of Religion," in *The Quest: History and Meaning in Religion* (Chicago: University of Chicago Press, 1969), pp. 37–53; Jan de Vries, *Perspectives in the History of Religions* [1961], trans. Kees W. Bölle (Berkeley: University of California Press, 1977); and Douglas Allen, *Structure and Creativity in Religion: Hermenuetics in Mircea Eliade's Phenomenology and New Directions* (The Hague: Mouton, 1978), pp. 4–5. I will restrict use of the label to just those theorists generally identified with phenomenology of religions as represented by Eliade.

37. See Allen, *Structure and Creativity in Religion*, pp. 15–17.

38. Rudolf Otto, *The Idea of the Holy* [1917], trans. John W. Harvey, rev. ed. (New York: Oxford University Press, 1929).

39. Mircea Eliade, "The Quest for the 'Origins' of Religion," p. 53.

40. Gerardus van der Leeuw, *Religion in Essence and Manifestation*, 2 vols. [1933] (New York: Harper and Row, 1963); Raffaele Pettazzoni, *Essays on the History of Religions* (Leiden: Brill, 1954). Van der Leeuw tended to emphasize the phenomenological dimension, while Pettazzoni emphasized the historical (Allen, *Structure and Creativity in Religion*, pp. 65–67).

41. For a fuller discussion of these structures, see Geo Widengren, "An Introduction to Phenomenology of Religion," in Walter H. Capps, ed., *Ways of Understanding Religion* (New York: Macmillan, 1972), pp. 142–51.

42. Mircea Eliade, *History of Religious Ideas I: From the Stone Age to the Eleusinian Mysteries*, trans. Willard R. Trask (Chicago: University of Chicago Press, 1978), p. xiii.

43. Mircea Eliade, *Patterns in Comparative Religion*, p. 9. For a useful collection of Eliade's writings in this area, see Wendell C. Beane and William G. Doty, eds., *Myths, Rites, Symbols: A Mircea Eliade Reader*, 2 vols. (New York: Harper and Row, 1975).

44. Hans H. Penner, "Myth and Ritual," p. 54. It could be argued that Eliade's description of the otiose god implies historical changes in myth (see Mircea Eliade, "Cosmogonic Myth and 'Sacred History'," in *The Quest*, pp. 72–87; also reprinted in Alan Dundes, ed., *Sacred Narrative: Readings in the Theory of Myth* [Berkeley: University of California Press, 1984], pp. 137–51). Eliade has also differentiated such mythic structures in terms of primitive (elsewhere, archaic) societies as distinct from modern, historical, or literate societies, a distinction that is exemplified by a contrast between the "living" myth apt to be found among tribal peoples and the literary forms (*mythos* turned into *logos*) found in Greek and Greek-derived cultures. See Mircea Eliade, *Myth and Reality*, trans. Willard R. Trask (New York: Harper and Row, 1963), pp. 1–20.

45. Doty, *Mythography*, p. 141.

46. Eliade, *Myth and Reality*, pp. 5–6.

47. Eliade, *Sacred and Profane*, pp. 99–100.

48. Eliade, *Patterns*, p. 346. Emphasis in the original.

49. Also see Mircea Eliade, *The Myth of the Eternal Return or, Cosmos and History*, trans. Willard R. Trask (Princeton: Princeton University Press, 1954), pp. 17–27, 51–62.

50. Eliade, quoting the Taittirīya Brāhmana, *The Myth of the Eternal Return*, p. 21.

51. For an analysis and critique of the thought-action dichotomy in the study of ritual, see Bell, *Ritual Theory, Ritual Practice*, pp. 19–54.

52. Jonathan Z. Smith, *To Take Place: Toward Theory in Ritual* (Chicago: University of Chicago, 1987), p. 104.

53. Jonathan Z. Smith, *Imagining Religion: From Babylon to Jonestown* (Chicago: University of Chicago, 1982), pp. 64–65. Also see the perceptive analysis of Smith in Burton Mack, "Introduction: Religion and Ritual," in Robert G. Hamerton-Kelly, ed., *Violent Origins: Walter Burkert, Rene Girard, and Jonathan Z. Smith on Ritual Killing and Cultural Formation* (Stanford, Calif.: Stanford University Press, 1987), pp. 32–51.

54. Eliade, *The Quest*, pp. 4–5.

55. Penner, "Myth and Ritual," p. 55.

56. Beidelman, *W. Robertson Smith*, p. 65.

57. See Doty, *Mythography*, pp. 132–43.

58. Evans-Pritchard has categorized all of the myth and ritual theorists as representative of a psychological rather than social approach to religion (*Theories of Primitive Religion*, pp. 20–47).

59. Sigmund Freud, "Obsessive Acts and Religious Practices," in *Character and Culture* (New York: Collier Books, 1963), pp. 17, 23.

60. Freud, "Obsessive Acts," pp. 24–25.

61. Freud, "Obsessive Acts," p. 126.

62. Freud completed his statement as follows: "The Oedipus complex itself must therefore have its own process of development, and the study of prehistory can help us to find out something about it" (see his 1946 introduction to Theodor Reik, *Ritual: Psycho-analytic Studies* [Westport, Conn.: Greenwood, 1975], p. 11); also see Sigmund Freud, *Totem and Taboo* (New York: Vintage Books, 1946), pp. xi, 3.

63. For a defense of this chronology of Freud's reading, see Volney P. Gay, *Freud on Ritual: Reconstruction and Critique* (Missoula, Mont.: Scholars Press, 1979), p. 25.

64. Freud, *Totem and Taboo*, pp. 9, 44, 160, 171.

65. Freud, *Totem and Taboo*, p. 182. The notion of primitive society as "a corporate family group ruled by a despotic patriarch" actually goes back to Henry Maine's *Ancient Law* (1861), a work that has been deemed pivotal in the emergence of anthropological concerns with so-called primitive society (Adam Kuper, *The Invention of Primitive Society: Transformations of an Illusion* [London: Routledge, 1988]), p. 5.

66. Freud, *Totem and Taboo*, p. 183.

67. Freud's Introduction to Reik, *Ritual*, p. 10.

68. Reik, *Ritual*, pp. 16–18.

69. Reik, *Ritual*, p. 19.

70. Reik, *Ritual*, p. 49.

71. Sigmund Freud, *Moses and Monotheism*, trans. Katherine Jones (New York: Vintage Books, 1955), pp. 160, 164.

72. Bruno Bettelheim, *Symbolic Wounds: Puberty Rites and the Envious Male* [1954], rev. ed. (New York: Collier Books, 1971), pp. 19–22.

73. Gay, *Freud on Ritual*, pp. 1–2, 185; also Volney P. Gay, *Reading Freud: Psychology, Neurosis and Religion* (Chico, Calif.: Scholars Press, 1983). Using Freud's own admission that his theory does not exhaust the essence of religion, S. H. Posinsky, for one, has argued for a more balanced psychoanalytic view of ritual in "Ritual, Neurotic and Social," *American Imago* 19 (1962): 375–90.

74. For a fuller discussion, see Penner, "Myth and Ritual," pp. 49–50.

75. For a fuller discussion of the Oedipal motif in Rank and Raglan, see William Bascom, "The Myth-Ritual Theory," 109–11.

76. One critic has described Girard's work as "a daring nostalgic return to a criticism of ultimate explanations unlocked by a simple theory as irresistible as a *passe-partout*" (see Vincent Farenga, review of Girard's *Violence and the Sacred*, in *Comparative Literature* 32 [1980]: 420).

77. René Girard, *Violence and the Sacred* [1972], trans. Patrick Gregory (Baltimore: Johns Hopkins University Press, 1977); with Jean-Michel Oughourlian and Guy Lefort, *Things Hidden since the Foundation of the World* [1978], trans. by Stephen Bann and Michael Metteer (Stanford, Calif.: Stanford University Press, 1987); *The Scapegoat* [1982], trans. by Yvonne Freccero (Baltimore: Johns Hopkins University Press, 1986); and Robert G. Hamerton-Kelly, ed., *Violent Origins.*

78. There is some ambiguity as to whether Girard is suggesting a single murder at the dawn of history or whether many such murders are abstractly understood as a single, mythical, and "original" one—the same ambiguity that attends Freud's patricidal scenario in *Totem and Taboo*. For a fuller discussion of this, see James G. Williams, "The Innocent Victim: René Girard on Violence, Sacrifice, and the Sacred," *Religious Studies Review* 14, no. 4 (October 1988): 323; Tomoko Masuzawa, *In Search of Dreamtime: The Quest for the Origin of Religion* (Chicago: University of Chicago Press, 1994), pp. 80–84.

79. Girard, *Things Hidden since the Foundation of the World*, p. 210.

80. Joseph Campbell, *Myths to Live By* (New York: Viking, 1972), pp. 214–25. For a fuller discussion of Campbell, see Doty, pp. 52–55, 108–12, 176–78. For other discussions of

Campbell—both the man and the work—see Robert A. Segal, *Joseph Campbell: An Intro-duction*, rev. ed. (New York: New American Library, 1990); also Segal's introduction to Rank, Raglan, and Dundes, eds., *In Quest of the Hero*, pp. xvi–xxviii and p. xxxviii, note 54 for fur-ther bibliography; and Segal, "Joseph Campbell on Jews and Judaism," *Religion* 22, no. 2 (April 1992): 151–70, where other sources are given as well.

81. On Campbell's debt to Arnold van Gennep, who will be discussed in the next sec-tion of this chapter, see Stanley Edgar Hyman, "The Ritual View of Myth and the Mythic," p. 467.

82. Joseph Campbell, *The Mythic Image* (Princeton, N.J.: Princeton University Press, 1975); *Myths to Live By* (New York: Viking, 1972); *The Hero with a Thousand Faces*, 2d ed. (Princeton, N.J.: Princeton University Press, 1972); *Masks of God*, 4 vols. (New York: Viking, 1959).

83. For a useful overview of what is known about the Akitu festival, see Mircea Eliade et al., eds., *The Encyclopedia of Religion*, vol. 1 (New York: Macmillan, 1987), pp. 170–72. For a selective bibliography on the Akitu, see Ivan Engnell, *Studies in Divine Kingship in the Ancient Near East*, 2d ed. (Oxford: Basil Blackwell, 1967), pp. 201–2.

84. Most notably by Fontenrose, *The Ritual Theory of Myth*, p. 6.

85. Fontenrose, *The Ritual Theory of Myth*, p. 7.

86. Gaster, *Thespis*, pp. 34–37.

87. Gaster, *Thespis*, p. 51.

88. For another permutation of the myth and ritual interpretation of the Akitu, see Henri Frankfort, *Kingship of the Gods*, pp. 315–28, who argued that "ritual observances and the actuality of nature were felt to interlock" (p. 327).

89. Eliade, *The Myth of the Eternal Return*, pp. 54–56, parentheses in the original.

90. Eliade, *The Myth of the Eternal Return*, pp. 57–58.

91. Jonathan Z. Smith, "A Pearl of Great Price and a Cargo of Yams: A Study in Situ-ational Incongruity," in *Imagining Religion*, pp. 90–101.

92. Smith, *Imagining Religion*, pp. 91 (parentheses and brackets are in the original), 92, 94, 93, respectively. For another historical critique of the myth and ritual interpretation explicitly and the phenomenologists more implicitly, see J. A. Black, "The New Year Cer-emonies in Ancient Babylon: 'Taking Bel by the Hand' and a Cultic Picnic," *Religion* 11 (1981): 39–59. Black uses a wide variety of textual evidence to demonstrate "that the [New Year ceremonies at Babylon] had nothing to do with a dying and resurrected vegetation god or with an act of atonement by or on behalf of the people" (p. 56).

93. Also see Fontenrose, *The Ritual Theory of Myth*, pp. 24, 50.

94. Smith, *Imagining Religion*, pp. 93–94.

95. S. J. Hooke, ed., *Myth and Ritual*, pp. 1–2. On the notion of a "primitive mental-ity" among 20th-century tribal peoples, see Lucien Lévy-Bruhl, *How Natives Think* [1926] (New York: Washington Square Press, 1966).

96. Cited by Evans-Pritchard, *Theories of Primitive Religion*, p. 16.

97. On the persistence of the notion of "primitive" societies, see Adam Kuper, *The Invention of Primitive Society*. The continuing popularity of many of Frazer's ideas caused the anthropologist Edmund Leach to suggest that people remain fascinated with descrip-tions of the brute sadism of primitive sacrifice when depicted "so elegantly that even clergymen's daughters could read them with equanimity" (Edmund R. Leach, "Golden Bough or Gilded Twig?" *Daedalus* 90, no. 2 [Spring 1961]: 383.

98. Herbert Weisinger, "The Branch That Grew Full Straight," *Daedalus* 90, no. 2 (Spring 1961): 388–89.

99. On the emergence of the category and study of religion, see J. Samuel Preuss, *Explaining Religion: Criticism and Theory from Bodin to Freud* (New Haven: Yale Univer-

sity Press, 1987); and Talal Asad, *Genealogies of Religion: Discipline and Reasons of Power in Christianity* (Baltimore: Johns Hopkins University, 1993), pp. 27–54.

100. W. Richard Comstock, ed., *Religion and Man: An Introduction* (New York: Harper and Row, 1971), p. 35.

Chapter 2

1. Numa Denis Fustel de Coulanges, *The Ancient City* [1864], trans. Willard Small (New York: Doubleday, 1963); also see Evans-Pritchard, *Theories of Primitive Religion*, pp. 50–51.

2. On Durkheim's debt to Robertson Smith, see Steven Lukes, *Émile Durkheim: His Life and Work: A Historical and Critical Study* (New York: Penguin, 1977), p. 237.

3. Lukes, *Émile Durkheim*, pp. 9–11, 237, note 1, respectively.

4. Durkheim wrote that "it was not until 1895 that I achieved a clear view of the essential role played by religion in social life. It was in that year that, for the first time, I found the means of tackling the study of religion sociologically. This was a revelation to me" (Lukes, *Émile Durkheim*, p. 237).

5. Durkheim, *The Elementary Forms*, pp. 52, 56, 461.

6. Durkheim, *The Elementary Forms*, p. 258; and Lukes, *Émile Durkheim*, p. 463.

7. Evans-Pritchard, *Theories of Primitive Religion*, p. 63.

8. Cited in Lukes, *Émile Durkheim*, p. 471.

9. Durkheim, *The Elementary Forms*, p. 298.

10. For a fuller discussion, see Lukes, *Émile Durkheim*, pp. 475–76.

11. Lukes, *Émile Durkheim*, p. 481.

12. Max Gluckman, *Essays on the Ritual of Social Relations* (Manchester: Manchester University Press, 1962), pp. 40–41; also cited by Lukes, *Émile Durkheim*, p. 483, note 45.

13. Émile Durkheim and Marcel Mauss, *Primitive Classification*, trans. Rodney Needham (Chicago: University of Chicago, 1963), p. 82.

14. Henri Hubert and Marcel Mauss, *Sacrifice: Its Nature and Functions* [1898], trans. W. D. Hall (Chicago: University of Chicago, 1964).

15. Hubert and Mauss, *Sacrifice*, pp. 8, 9.

16. Hubert and Mauss, *Sacrifice*, p. 98.

17. Hubert and Mauss, *Sacrifice*, pp. 102–3.

18. For a fuller discussion of Radcliffe-Brown's use of Durkheim, see Adam Kuper, *Anthropology and Anthropologists: The Modern British School* (London: Routledge & Kegan Paul, 1983), pp. 38, 42–43, 49–51, 168.

19. For a fuller discussion, see Evans-Pritchard, *Theories*, pp. 74–76.

20. Jacques Waardenburg, ed., *Classical Approaches*, vol. 1, p. 589, citing Alfred R. Radcliffe-Brown, "Religion and Society," *Journal of the Royal Anthropological Institute of Great Britain and Ireland* 75 (1945): 33–43.

21. For a fuller discussion of this critique, see Brian Morris, *Anthropological Studies of Religion*, pp. 186–203 and, more secondarily, pp. 122–31.

22. Waardenburg, *Classical Approaches*, vol. 1, pp. 589–90.

23. Waardenburg, *Classical Approaches*, vol. 1, p. 591.

24. Waardenburg, *Classical Approaches*, vol. 1, p. 591; also see Kuper, *Anthropology and Anthropologists*, p. 43.

25. For a fuller discussion, see Robert A. Segal, "The Myth-Ritualist Theory of Religion," 179.

26. A more recent version of the argument that ritual both expresses and creates emotions is developed in Bruce Kapferer, "Emotion and Feeling in Sinhalese Healing Rituals," *Social Analysis* 1 (February 1979): 153–76.

27. Waardenburg, *Classical Approaches*, vol. 1, p. 604.

28. For a fuller discussion of the differences among these three, see George C. Homans, "Anxiety and Ritual: The Theories of Malinowski and Radcliffe-Brown," *American Anthropologist* 43 (1941): 164–72.

29. See Kuper, *Anthropology and Anthropologists*, p. 166.

30. Bronislaw Malinowski, *Magic, Science and Religion, and Other Essays* [1925] (Boston: Beacon Press, 1948). For a fuller discussion, see Morris, *Anthropological Studies of Religion*, pp. 148–51.

31. Kuper, *Anthropology and Anthropologists*, p. 3.

32. A. R. Radcliffe-Brown, *The Andaman Islanders* [1922] (New York: Free Press, 1964), pp. 229–30. According to Kuper, Radcliffe-Brown knew the limits of the analogy and that it should not be taken literally, once stating, "Societies are not organisms; they do not experience parturition nor death" (*Anthropology and Anthropologists*, p. 50).

33. For example, see Roy A. Rappaport, "Ecology, Adaptation, and the Ills of Functionalism," in *Ecology, Meaning, and Religion* (Richmond, Calif.: North Atlantic Books, 1979), pp. 43–95, where Rappaport challenges characterization of his work as a functionalist, either the old or the new style.

34. This approach is most clear in Rappaport's earlier work, *Pigs for the Ancestors* [1968], 2d ed. (New Haven: Yale University Press, 1980).

35. Rappaport, "Ritual Regulation of Environmental Relations among a New Guinea People" [1967], in *Ecology, Meaning and Religion*, p. 29.

36. Rappaport, "Ritual Regulation," in *Ecology, Meaning and Religion*, p. 41.

37. Marvin Harris, "The Cultural Ecology of India's Sacred Cattle," *Current Anthropology* 7, no. 1 (February 1966): 51–66, and a revised version entitled "The Origin of the Sacred Cow," in *Cannibals and Kings: The Origins of Cultures* (New York: Random House, 1977), pp. 211–29.

38. Marvin Harris, "The Cannibal Kingdom," in *Cannibals and Kings*, pp. 147–66.

39. Harris, "The Cannibal Kingdom," p. 164.

40. Among the best challenges to Harris's Aztec study are the following: Bernard R. Ortiz de Montellano, "Aztec Cannibalism: An Ecological Necessity?" *Science* 200, no. 4342 (May 12, 1978): 611–17; and "Counting Skulls: Comment on the Aztec Cannibalism Theory of Harner-Harris," *American Anthropologist* 85, no. 2 (1983): 403–6; and Marshall Sahlins, "Culture as Protein and Profit," *New York Review of Books* (November 23, 1978): 45–53. For a recent version of this type of argument, see J. Stephen Lansing, *Priests and Programmers: Technologies of Power in the Engineered Landscape of Bali* (Princeton: Princeton University Press, 1991).

41. See Sir Julian Huxley, ed., "A Discussion on Ritualization of Behavior in Animals and Man," *Philosophical Transactions of the Royal Society*, series B, vol. 251 (1966), which includes Huxley's "Introduction" (pp. 249–71) and Konrad Z. Lorenz's "Evolution of Ritualization in the Biological and Cultural Spheres" (pp. 273–84).

42. Huxley, "Introduction," p. 250.

43. See Huxley, "A Discussion on Ritualization," for articles on these topics; also Ellen Dissanayake, "An Ethological View of Ritual and Art in Human Evolutionary History," *Leonardo* 12, no. 1 (1979): 27–31. This is also the bent of the recent work by Walter Burkert, *Creation of the Sacred: Tracks of Biology in Early Religion* (Cambridge, Mass.: Harvard University Press, 1996).

44. For a critique of this position, see Edmund R. Leach, "Ritualization in Man in Relation to Conceptual and Social Developments," in Julian Huxley, ed., "A Discussion on Ritualization," pp. 403–8.

45. Huxley, "Introduction," pp. 266–67.

46. See Edward O. Wilson, *Sociobiology: The New Synthesis* (Cambridge: Harvard University Press, 1975). Another study by Wilson, *On Human Nature* (Cambridge: Harvard University Press, 1978), has a chapter that discusses religion and ritual, specifically exploring how religious practices confer biological advantages. Sociobiology attempts to account for the origin of religion "by the principle of natural selection acting on the genetically evolving material structure of the brain" (*On Human Nature*, p. 192).

47. See Charles D. Laughlin and Eugene G. d'Aquili, *Biogenetic Structuralism* (New York: Columbia University Press, 1974); Eugene G. d'Aquili, Charles D. Laughlin, and John McManus, eds., *The Spectrum of Ritual: A Biogenetic Structural Analysis* (New York: Columbia University Press, 1979); Robert L. Moore, Ralph Wendell Burhoe, and Philip J. Hefner, eds., "Ritual in Human Adaptation," *Zygon* 18, no. 3 (September 1983): 209–326; and, more recently, Charles D. Laughlin, "Ritual and the Symbolic Function: A Summary of Biogenetic Structural Theory," *Journal of Ritual Studies* 4, no. 1 (Winter 1990): 15–39.

48. Eugene G. d'Aquili and Andrew B. Newberg, "Liminality, Trance and Unitary States in Ritual and Meditation," *Studia Liturgica* 23, no. 1 (1993): 2–34.

49. Laughlin, "Ritual and the Symbolic Function," pp. 15–16.

50. For example, see John McManus, "Ritual and Ontogenetic Development" in d'Aquili et al, eds., *The Spectrum of Ritual*, pp. 183–215, who extensively cites Piaget.

51. E. H. Erikson, "Ontogeny of Ritualization in Man" in Huxley, ed., "A Discussion on Ritualization," pp. 337–50, reprinted in Rudolph Loewenstein et al., eds., *Psychoanalysis—A General Psychology* (New York: International Universities Press, 1966): 601–21; also Erik H. Erikson, "The Development of Ritualization" in Donald R. Cutler, ed., *The Religious Situation 1968* (Boston: Beacon, 1968), pp. 711–33.

52. See his "Eight Ages of Man" in Erik H. Erikson, *Childhood and Society*, 2d rev. ed. (New York: W. W. Norton, 1963), pp. 247–74. In later works specifically on ritual, however, he identified six stages; compare the tables entitled "Epigenesis of Ritualization" and "Ontogeny of Ritualization," respectively, in Erikson, "Ontogeny of Ritualization," in Loewenstein et al., eds., *Psychoanalysis*, p. 615, and in "The Development of Ritualization" in Cutler, ed., *The Religious Situation 1968*, p. 731. Erik H. Erikson, *Toys and Reasons: Stages in the Ritualization of Experience* (New York: W. W. Norton, 1977), p. 12.

53. Jay Meddin, "Symbols, Anxiety, and Ritual: A Functional Interpretation," *Quantitative Sociology* 3, no. 4 (Winter 1980): 251–71.

54. Elizabeth Bott, "Psychoanalysis and Ceremony," in J. S. La Fontaine, ed., *The Interpretation of Ritual: Essays in Honour of A. I. Richards* (London: Tavistock Publications, 1972), pp. 205–6.

55. Victor Turner, "Body, Brain, and Culture," *Zygon* 18, no. 3 (September 1983): 243. Turner was impressed by advances in neuroanatomy and theories that link the functions of particular brain sections to various forms of social behavior. He hypothesized that the two polar properties of symbols that he had identified as the sensual (orectic) pole of meaning and the normative or ideological pole of meaning might well correspond to two sections discovered in the brain: first, the limbic system or visceral brain, identified by Paul MacLean in 1949 as the old mammalian brain, which controls drives and emotions; and second, the upper brain activities of both the right and left hemispheres. Turner marveled that a strong symbol like the Ndembu "milk tree" appears to "replicate in its structural and semantic make-up what are coming to be seen as key neurological features of the brain and the central nervous system" (p. 242).

56. Victor Turner, "Body, Brain, and Culture," p. 224.

57. Gregory Bateson, *Naven* [1936], 2d ed. (Stanford, Calif.: Stanford University Press, 1986).

58. For a fuller discussion of these points, see Kuper, *Anthropology and Anthropologists*, pp. 75–77.

59. For a fuller discussion of his approach, see Morris, *Anthropological Studies of Religion*, pp. 188–203. Evans-Pritchard recognized the dilemma of constructed categories pointed out by Bateson, but defended their validity for the project of interpretive analysis by an outsider: "[The underlying structure of a society] cannot be seen. It is a set of abstractions, each of which, though derived, it is true, from analysis of observed behavior is fundamentally an imaginative construct of the anthropologist himself. By relating these abstractions to one another logically so that they present a pattern he can see the society in its essentials and as a single whole" (cited in Morris, p. 189, quoting *Essays in Social Anthropology* [London: Faber and Faber, 1962], p. 23).

60. E. E. Evans-Pritchard, *Nuer Religion* [1956] (New York: Oxford University Press, 1974), p. 311.

61. Evans-Pritchard, *Nuer Religion*, pp. 313, 315, 320.

62. Evans-Pritchard, *Nuer Religion*, pp. 207–8.

63. Evans-Pritchard, *Nuer Religion*, pp. 321–22.

64. For a fuller discussion, see Evans-Pritchard, *Theories of Primitive Religion*, p. 67; and Solon T. Kimball's introduction to Arnold van Gennep, *The Rites of Passage*, translated by M. B. Vizedom and G. L. Caffee (Chicago: University of Chicago Press, 1960), p. vii.

65. Van Gennep, "On the Method to Be Followed in the Study of Rites and Myths" [1910], in Waardenburg, *Classical Approaches*, vol. 1, pp. 298–99.

66. Van Gennep, *The Rites of Passage*, p. 3.

67. Van Gennep, *The Rites of Passage*, p. 3.

68. Van Gennep, *The Rites of Passage*, p. 12. This view of the sacred is closer to that of Mauss and Hubert, who recognized processes of "sacralization" and "desacralization" at work in ritual action (*Sacrifice*, pp. 98).

69. Van Gennep, *The Rites of Passage*, p. 189.

70. Solon T. Kimball, "Introduction" in van Gennep, *The Rites of Passage*, p. xvii.

71. Gluckman, *Essays on the Ritual of Social Relations*, p. 6.

72. Max Gluckman, *Order and Rebellion in Tribal Africa* (New York: Free Press, 1963), p. 127.

73. Gluckman, *Order and Rebellion in Tribal Africa*, pp. 110–36. Gluckman also analyzed the *ncwala*, the Swazi rite of kingship, described in the third Profile in this part, as a rite of rebellion because it included songs of contempt for the king and required the king to walk naked in front of his people (pp. 126–31). His example could serve as a model for reinterpreting the humiliation of the king in the ancient Babylonian Akitu festival discussed in the previous Profile. Such a reinterpretation would be in keeping with Jonathan Z. Smith's analysis of the Akitu. For a fuller discussion of Gluckman, see Kuper, *Anthropology and Anthropologists*, pp. 146–47. Gluckman's approach is also seen in the conclusion of Raymond Firth, who argued that ritual provides for "the routinization and canalization" of personal and social tensions (*The Work of the Gods in Tikopia* [1940; New York: Athlone Press, 1967], p. 23).

74. Gluckman, *Essays on the Ritual of Social Relations*, pp. 2, 15, 26, 49–50.

75. Gluckman, *Essays on the Ritual of Social Relations*, pp. 20–24.

76. Victor Turner, *Schism and Continuity in an African Society* (Manchester, England: Manchester University Press, 1957).

77. Victor Turner, *Dramas, Fields, and Metaphors: Symbolic Action in Human Society* (Ithaca, N.Y.: Cornell University Press, 1974), pp. 23–35; Kuper, *Anthropology and Anthropoplogists*, pp. 156–57.

78. Turner, *Dramas, Fields, and Metaphors*, pp. 38–41.

79. Victor Turner, *The Forest of Symbols: Aspects of Ndembu Ritual* (Ithaca, N.Y.: Cornell University Press, 1967), pp. 96–97, 98–99.

80. Turner, *The Forest of Symbols*, p. 101.

81. Turner, *The Ritual Process: Structure and Anti-Structure* (Ithaca, N.Y.: Cornell University Press, 1969), p. 97.

82. Turner advocated a triadic system instead of the binary system associated with Lévi-Strauss; see *Forest of Symbols*, pp. 59–92.

83. Turner, *Forest of Symbols*, pp. 20–21, 24.

84. Turner, *Forest of Symbols*, pp. 30 and 19: "the smallest unit of ritual which still retains the specific properties of ritual behavior."

85. Turner, *Forest of Symbols*, p. 46.

86. Turner, *Forest of Symbols*, p. 90.

87. Kuper, *Anthropology and Anthropologists*, pp. 153, 166.

88. Cited in Morris, *Anthropological Studies*, p. 265.

89. Claude Lévi-Strauss, *Introduction to a Science of Mythology (Mythologiques)*: vol. 1 is *The Raw and The Cooked* (New York: Harper and Row, 1969); vol. 2, *From Honey to Ashes* (New York: Harper and Row, 1973); vol. 3, *The Origin of Table Manners* (New York: Harper and Row, 1978); vol. 4, *The Naked Man* (New York: Harper and Row, 1981).

90. Claude Lévi-Strauss, *The Elementary Structures of Kinship*, trans. James Harle Bell, John Richard von Sturmer, and Rodney Needham (Boston: Beacon Press, 1969).

91. Claude Lévi-Strauss, *Totemism*, trans. Rodney Needham (Boston: Beacon Press, 1963), p. 16.

92. Ferdinand de Saussure, *Course in General Linguistics* [1913], ed. C. Bally, A. Sechehaye, and A. Riedlinger; trans. Wade Baskin (New York: McGraw-Hill, 1966).

93. Lévi-Strauss, *The Naked Man*, p. 679. There is a clear echo of Freud in this perspective.

94. Mary Douglas, *Natural Symbols: Explorations in Cosmology* (New York: Random House, 1970), p. 81.

95. See Douglas, *Natural Symbols*, pp. 49–50, 84, 177. The text in the diagram is from Sheldon R. Isenberg and Dennis E. Owen, "Bodies, Natural and Contrived: The Work of Mary Douglas," *Religious Studies Review* 3, no. 1 (January 1977): 7–8, revised by Owens, 1997.

96. Douglas, *Natural Symbols*, pp. 41–42.

97. See Douglas, *Purity and Danger*, pp. 41–57; also "Deciphering a Meal," in *Implicit Meanings: Essays in Anthropology* (London: Routledge & Kegan Paul, 1975), pp. 249–75.

98. Edmund Leach, *Culture and Communication: The Logic by Which Symbols Are Connected: An Introduction to the Use of Structuralist Analysis in Social Anthropology* (Cambridge: Cambridge University Press, 1976).

99. Edmund Leach, "Ritual," in David L. Sills, ed., *International Encyclopedia of the Social Sciences*, vol. 13 (New York: Macmillan, 1968), p. 521.

100. For a fuller discussion of this 19th-century triad, see Stanley Jeyaraja Tambiah, *Magic, Science, Religion, and The Scope of Rationality* (Cambridge: Cambridge University Press, 1990).

101. See Tambiah, *Magic, Science, Religion*, p. 50.

102. Frazer, *The Golden Bough*, vol. 1, pp. 52–54.

103. Lucien Lévy-Bruhl, *How Natives Think*.

104. Durkheim notes this debt, *The Elementary Forms*, p. 61, n. 62. However, he also draws heavily on the earlier work of Mauss, "Esquisse d'une théorie générale de la magie," *Année sociologique* 7 (1902–03), reprinted as *A General Theory of Magic* (London: Routledge and Kegan Paul, 1972).

105. Robertson Smith, *Lectures on the Religion of the Semites*, p. 55.

106. Durkheim, *The Elementary Forms*, p. 60.

107. For a critique of this position, see Douglas, *Purity and Danger*, p. 21.

108. Kuper, *Anthropology and Anthropologists*, p. 27.

109. Bronislaw Malinowski, *Magic, Science and Religion*, p. 1. Also cited in Morris, *Anthropological Studies*, p. 147.

110. Bronislaw Malinowski, *Sex, Culture, and Myth* (New York: Harcourt, Brace and World, 1962), p. 261. Also cited by Morris, *Anthropological Studies*, p. 150.

111. Morris, *Anthropological Studies*, p. 150.

112. E. E. Evans-Pritchard, *Witchcraft, Oracles and Magic among the Azande* (Oxford: Clarendon Press, 1965), p. 4.

113. Evans-Pritchard, *Witchcraft, Oracles and Magic among the Azande*, pp. 63–70.

114. Evans-Pritchard, *Witchcraft, Oracles and Magic among the Azande*, p. 12.

115. Douglas, *Purity and Danger*, pp. 18–19. Old Testament studies, she suggests, may be in even worse shape because of this fallacy (pp. 25–27). Jonathan Z. Smith identifies the same sort of problem in his analysis of the effect of "Protestant anti-Catholic apologetics" on scholarship in *Drudgery Divine: On the Comparison of Early Christianities and the Religions of Late Antiquity* (Chicago: University of Chicago Press, 1990), p. 34.

116. Douglas, *Natural Symbols*, pp. 59–76, 26.

117. The philosopher Susanne Langer reached similar conclusions concerning magic and ritual as symbolic languages but without Douglas's concern for social organization (see *Philosophy in a New Key* [New York: Mentor Books, 1964], p. 52).

118. For a fuller discussion, see Morris, *Anthropological Studies*, pp. 301–3.

119. S. J. Tambiah, "The Magical Power of Words," *Man* n.s. 3, no. 2 (1968): 188, 202.

120. Roman Jakobson and M. Halle, *The Fundamentals of Language* (The Hague: Mouton, 1956). Lévi-Strauss, following the work of the linguist Saussure, primarily wrote of syntagmatic and paradigmatic relations. See Leach, *Culture and Communication*, pp. 9–16.

121. Tambiah, "The Magical Power of Words," p. 202.

122. See Stanley Jeyaraja Tambiah, "The Magical Power of Words" (pp. 17–59) and "A Performative Approach to Ritual," (pp. 123–66) in *Culture, Thought, and Social Action: An Anthropological Perspective* (Cambridge, Mass.: Harvard University Press, 1985).

123. Leach, *Culture and Communication*, pp. 31–32.

124. See Mary Douglas, ed., *Witchcraft, Confessions and Accusations* (London: Tavistock, 1970).

125. Vincent Crapanzano, "Rite of Return: Circumcision in Morocco," in Werner Muensterberger and L. Bryce Boyer, eds., *The Psychoanalytic Study of Society* 9 (1981): 16.

126. Bruce Lincoln, *Emerging from the Chrysalis: Rituals of Women's Initiations*, rev. ed. (New York: Oxford University Press, 1991); Caroline Walker Bynum, "Women's Stories, Women's Symbols: A Critique of Victor Turner's Theory of Liminality," in Robert L. Moore and Frank E. Reynolds, eds., *Anthropology and the Study of Religion* (Chicago: Center for the Scientific Study of Religion, 1984), pp. 105–25.

127. Most of the data in this section is drawn from Victor Turner, "*Mukanda*: The Rite of Circumcision," in *Forest of Symbols*, pp. 151–279.

128. The duration appears to be dependent on the time it takes for the wound to heal. Turner states (*Forest of Symbols*, p. 223) that the seclusion he witnessed lasted from June 14 to August 8 but notes that this was a rather short time due to use of Western medicines to spur the healing process.

129. Turner, *Forest of Symbols*, pp. 185, 187.

130. Turner, *Forest of Symbols*, p. 155.

131. Turner, *Forest of Symbols*, p. 192.

132. Turner, *Forest of Symbols*, pp. 155–59.

133. Turner, *Forest of Symbols*, p. 192.

134. Turner, *Forest of Symbols*, pp. 239–40.

135. Turner, *Forest of Symbols*, p. 66.

136. Turner, *Forest of Symbols*, pp. 270, 278.

137. Also see Bynum's critique of Turner's handling of European history, particularly St. Francis, in "Women's Stories, Women's Symbols," pp. 105–10.

138. Lincoln, *Emerging from the Chrysalis*, pp. 1–3, 94, 100–101. Lincoln also cites evidence that women's initation rites are practiced by more societies than men's initiations (p. 3).

139. Bynum, "Women's Stories, Women's Symbols," pp. 113–14.

140. Bynum, "Women's Stories, Women's Symbols," pp. 118–19.

141. Crapanzano, "Rite of Return: Circumcision in Morocco," p. 16.

142. Crapanzano, "Rite of Return: Circumcision in Morocco," p. 32 (parentheses in the original).

143. Crapanzano, "Rite of Return: Circumcision in Morocco," p. 31.

144. Crapanzano, "Rite of Return: Circumcision in Morocco," pp. 32–34.

145. Lincoln also calls attention to the social brutality of initiatory molding (*Emerging from the Chrysalis*, pp. 111–14). Maurice Freedman described how Chinese marriage rites, and all the socialization that attends them, inculcate in the young husband the sort of fears and anxieties that will make him instinctively defend his family against the machinations of his new wife. See *The Study of Chinese Society*, ed. G. William Skinner (Stanford: Stanford University Press, 1979), p. 272.

146. Sam D. Gill, "Hopi Kachina Cult Initiation: The Shocking Beginning to the Hopi's Religious Life," *Journal of the American Academy of Religion* 45, no. 2 supplement (June 1977): 447–64.

147. Gill, "Hopi Kachina Cult Initiation," p. 451.

148. Gill, "Hopi Kachina Cult Initiation," p. 452.

149. Gill, "Hopi Kachina Cult Initiation," pp. 454, 456.

Chapter 3

1. See Geertz, *The Interpretation of Culture* (New York: Basic Books, 1973), pp. 142–46.

2. Edmund Leach, "A Poetics of Power [review of Geertz's *Negara*], *The New Republic* 184 (April 4, 1981): 30–33.

3. See Kuper, *Anthropology and Anthropologists*, pp. 156–82.

4. Cited in Bob Scholte, "The Structural Anthropology of Claude Lévi-Strauss," in John J. Honigmann, ed., *Handbook of Social and Cultural Anthropology* (Chicago: Rand McNally, 1973), p. 658.

5. Scholte, "The Structural Anthropology of Claude Lévi-Strauss," pp. 658–59.

6. Morris, *Anthropological Studies*, p. 182.

7. Leach, *Culture and Communication*.

8. Leach, *Culture and Communication*, p. 45

9. Leach, *Culture and Communication*, pp. 9–16.

10. Leach, *Culture and Communication*, pp. 27, 31.

11. Edmund R. Leach, "Ritual," in David L. Sills, ed., *International Encyclopedia of the Social Sciences*, p. 524.

12. Geertz, *The Interpretation of Culture*, p. 90.

13. Geertz, *The Interpretation of Culture*, p. 112.

14. Nancy D. Munn, "Symbolism in a Ritual Context" in John J. Honigmann, ed., *Handbook of Social and Cultural Anthropology* (Chicago: Rand McNally, 1973), p. 579.

15. See Geertz, *The Interpretation of Culture*, pp. 142–46.

16. Geertz, *The Interpretation of Culture*, p. 119.

17. Geertz, *The Interpretation of Culture*, pp. 114–19.

18. Geertz, *The Interpretation of Culture*, p. 443.

19. Geertz, *The Interpretation of Culture*, p. 448.

20. Geertz, *The Interpretation of Culture*, p. 448.

21. Geertz, *The Interpretation of Culture*, p. 444.

22. See Gabriella Eichinger Ferro-Luzzi, "Ritual as Language: The Case of South Indian Food Offerings," *Current Anthropology* 18, no. 3 (1977): 507–14; Arthur P. Wolf, "Gods, Ghosts and Ancestors," in Arthur P. Wolf, ed., *Religion and Ritual in Chinese Society* (Stanford, Calif.: Stanford University Press, 1974), pp. 131–182, esp. p. 180.

23. In addition to Wolf, "Gods, Ghosts and Ancestors," also see Ching-lang Hou, *Monnaies d'offrande et la notion de trésorerie dans la religion chinoise*, vol. 1 (Paris: Mémoires de l'Institut des Hautes Études Chinoises, 1975).

24. Geertz, *The Interpretation of Culture*, p. 5. For a comparison of semiotic and functional approaches to ritual, see F. Allan Hanson, "The Semiotics of Ritual," *Semiotica* 33, 1/2 (1981): 169–78, especially pp. 175–78.

25. J. L. Austin, *How to Do Things with Words*, 2d ed. (Cambridge, Mass.: Harvard University Press, 1975).

26. John R. Searle, *Speech Acts* (Cambridge: Cambridge University Press, 1969), especially pp. 59–61.

27. Frits Staal, *Rules without Meaning: Ritual, Mantras and the Human Sciences* (Bern: Peter Lang, 1989), p. 239. Also see, "The Meaninglessness of Ritual," *Numen* 26, no. 1 (1975): 2–22. For similar positions, see Stanley J. Tambiah, "The Magical Power of Words"; and Wade Wheelock, "The Problem of Ritual Language: From Information to Situation," *Journal of the American Academy of Religion* 50, no. 1 (1982): 49–71, especially pp. 51, 58.

28. Ruth Finnegan, "How to Do Things with Words: Performative Utterances Among the Limba of Sierra Leone," *Man*, n.s. 4, no. 4 (1969): 537–52, especially pp. 548–550. Finnegan also pointed out that the notion of performative utterance solves the difficulties posed by a polarization of utilitarian-functionalist versus expressive-symbolic styles of speech and action, which was, of course, the type of distinction that kept differentiating magic, science, and religion, as well as drawing distinctions between primitive versus modern.

29. Benjamin C. Ray, "'Performative Utterances' in African Rituals," *History of Religions* 13, no. 1 (1973): 16–35. It is interesting to note that both Tambiah and Ray refer to the old theory that magic is a mistaken belief in the power of words, yet they show that the so-called magical point of view is correct: words do accomplish things, although what they accomplish is interpreted as inherently social or cultural in nature (e.g., the reaffirmation of community bonds), not physical (e.g., the banishment of possessing demons or guarantees of a good harvest).

30. Valerio Valeri, *Kingship and Sacrifice: Ritual and Society in Ancient Hawaii* (Chicago: University of Chicago Press, 1985), pp. 344–45.

31. Maurice Bloch, "Symbols, Song, Dance and Features of Articulation" in *Archives europeénes de sociologie* 15 (1974): 55–81; see pp. 55–56.

32. Bloch, "Symbols, Song, Dance and Features of Articulation," p. 71.

33. Bloch, "Symbols, Song, Dance and Features of Articulation," p. 64.

34. Leach, "Ritual," in Sills, ed., *International Encyclopedia of the Social Sciences*, p. 524.

35. E. Thomas Lawson and Robert N. McCauley, *Rethinking Religion: Connecting Cognition and Culture* (Cambridge: Cambridge University Press, 1990), p. 67.

36. For a very accessible introduction to Chomsky's work, see Steven Pinker, *The Language Instinct* (New York: William Morrow, 1994).

37. Staal, "The Meaninglessness of Ritual," p. 9. He developed this argument more fully in *Rules Without Meaning: Mantras and the Human Sciences* (Bern: Peter Lang, 1989).

38. Frits Staal, "The Sound of Religion: Parts I-III," *Numen* 33, no. 1 (1968): 55–59, 63.

39. Frits Staal, "The Sound of Religion: Parts IV-V," *Numen* 33, no. 2 (1968): 218.

40. Staal, "The Sound of Religion: Parts I-III," pp. 42–43.

41. Staal, "The Meaninglessness of Ritual," p. 19.

42. E. Thomas Lawson and Robert N. McCauley, *Rethinking Religion*; E. Thomas Lawson, "Ritual as Language," *Religion* 6 (1976): 123–39; and E. Thomas Lawson and Robert N. McCauley, "Crisis of Conscience, Riddle of Identity: Making Space for a Cognitive Approach to Religious Phenomena," *Journal of the American Academy of Religion* 61, no. 2 (Summer 1993): 201–23.

43. Lawson and McCauley, *Rethinking Religion*, p. 105. The sentence derives from Chomsky's "Colorless green ideas sleep furiously," which makes the same point.

44. Lawson and McCauley, *Rethinking Religion*, pp. 3, 59, 77, 83, 170–71.

45. Lawson and McCauley, *Rethinking Religion*, pp. 83, 124–27.

46. For a fuller critique of Lawson and McCauley's argument about the study of religion, see Catherine Bell, "Modernism and Postmodernism in the Study of Religion," *Religious Studies Review* 22, no. 3 (July 1996): 181–83.

47. Milton Singer, *When a Great Tradition Modernizes* (New York: Praeger, 1972), pp. 64–65, 67.

48. Richard Bauman ("Verbal Art as Performance," *American Anthropologist* 77 no. 1 (1975): 290–311) takes a performance approach rooted in sociolinguistics and anthropology.

49. Kenneth Burke, *The Philosophy of Literary Form*, 3d ed. (Berkeley: University of California Press, 1973); Erving Goffman, *The Presentation of Self in Everyday Life* (Garden City, N.Y.: Doubleday, 1959) and *Interaction Ritual* (Chicago: Aldine, 1967), among others.

50. Richard Schechner, *Essays in Performance Theory 1970–1976*, (New York: Drama Book Specialists, 1977), p. 68.

51. See Dan Ben-Amos and Kenneth S. Goldstein, eds., *Folklore: Performance and Communication* (The Hague: Mouton, 1975), especially Dell Hymes, "Breakthrough into Performance," pp. 11–74, who distinguishes the significance of performance in folklore studies from its role in linguistics, especially Chomsky's generative grammar (p. 13).

52. James W. Fernandez, "Persuasion and Performances: On the Beast in Every Body ... And the Metaphors of Everyman," *Daedalus* 101, no. 1 (Winter 1972): 39–60, especially 54–56.

53. Ronald L. Grimes, *Symbol and Conquest: Public Ritual and Drama in Santa Fe, New Mexico* (Ithaca, N.Y.: Cornell University Press, 1976), esp. pp. 45–46.

54. Schechner, *Essays on Performance Theory*, pp. 99–107; Lawrence E. Sullivan, "Sound and Senses: Toward a Hermeneutics of Performance," *History of Religions* 26, no. 1 (1986): 6–8.

55. Ronald L. Grimes, *Beginnings in Ritual Studies* [1982], rev. ed. (Columbia, S.C.: University of South Carolina Press, 1995).

56. Gregory Bateson, *Steps to an Ecology of Mind* [1955] (N.Y.: Ballantine, 1978), pp. 179–89.

57. Bauman, "Verbal Art as Performance," p. 295, and Erving Goffman, *Frame Analysis: An Essay on the Organization of Experience* (New York: Harper and Row, 1974).

58. Richard Schechner and Willa Appel, eds, *By Means of Performance: Intercultural Studies of Theater and Ritual* (Cambridge: Cambridge University Press, 1989), p. 4, citing the concept of "flow" developed by Mihaly Csikszentmihalyi.

59. Edward L. Schieffelin, "Performance and the Cultural Construction of Reality," *American Ethnologist* 12 (1985): 707–10.

60. Bauman, "Verbal Art as Performance," pp. 302–5; Schiefflin, "Performance and the Cultural Construction of Reality," p. 721. In a slightly different usage, Grimes speaks of nascent ritual to mean new "genres of action," that is, rituals that are new (nontraditional) and experimental (improvised) explorations in expressive possibilities of body language. These experimental forms of ritual action are usually understood to demonstrate how the particular efficacy of ritual lies in its performative dimensions. See Grimes, *Beginnings in Ritual Studies*, pp. 58–74.

61. Hymes, "Breakthrough into Performance," p. 13.

62. See Victor Turner, "Are There Universals of Performance in Myth, Ritual, and Drama?" in Richard Schechner and Willa Appel, eds., *By Means of Performance* (Cambridge: Cambridge University Press 1989), p. 8; Sullivan, "Sound and Senses," p. 13; and Bruce Kapferer, "The Ritual Process and the Problem of Reflexivity in Sinhalese Demon Exorcisms," in John J. MacAloon, *Rite, Drama, Festival, Spectacle* (Philadelphia: Institute for the Study of Human Issues, 1984), pp. 179–207.

63. Theodore Jennings, "On Ritual Knowledge," *Journal of Religion* 62, no. 2 (1982): 111–27. For a critique of this position, see Catherine Bell, *Ritual Theory, Ritual Practice*, pp. 47–54.

64. Victor Turner, *From Ritual to Theater: The Human Seriousness of Play* (New York: Performing Arts Journal Publications, 1982), pp. 89–101.

65. Ronald L. Grimes, *Ritual Criticism: Case Studies in Its Practice, Essays on Its Theory* (Columbia: University of South Carolina Press, 1990). Also see Richard Schechner and Willa Appel, *By Means of Performance*, p. 6.

66. Schechner and Appel, *By Means of Performance*, p. 3.

67. One interesting example is Michael A. Salter, "Play in Ritual: An Ethnohistorical Overview of Native North America," *Stadion* 3, no. 2 (1977): 230–43. Also see Edward Norbeck, "The Anthropological Study of Play," *Rice University Studies* 60, no. 3 (1974): 1–8; Victor Turner, *From Ritual to Theater: The Human Seriousness of Play* (New York: Performing Arts Journal Publications, 1982); Clifford Geertz, "Deep Play: Notes on the Balinese Cockfight," in *The Interpretation of Culture*, pp. 412–53; and Helen B. Schwartzman, ed., *Play and Culture: 1978 Proceedings of the Association for the Anthropological Study of Play* (West Point, N.Y.: Leisure Press, 1980), pp. 49–103.

68. Don Handelman, "Play and Ritual: Complementary Frames of Meta-Communication," in Anthony J. Chapman and Hugh C. Foot, eds., *It's a Funny Thing Humor* (Oxford: Pergamon Press, 1977), p. 187.

69. Susan P. Montague and Robert Morais, "Football Games and Rock Concerts: The Ritual Enactment of American Success Models," and W. Arens, "Professional Football: An American Symbol and Ritual," in W. Arens and Susan P. Montague, eds., *The American Dimension: Cultural Myths and Social Realities* (Port Washington, N.Y.: Alfred Publishing, 1976).

70. John J. MacAloon, "Olympic Games and the Theory of Spectacle in Modern Societies," in MacAloon, ed., *Rite, Drama, Festival, Spectacle* (Philadelphia: Institute for the Study of Human Issues, 1984), pp. 241–80.

71. James L. Peacock, *Rites of Modernization: Symbolic and Social Aspects of Indonesian Proletarian Drama* (Chicago: University of Chicago Press, 1968).

72. Sherry B. Ortner, "Theory in Anthropology since the Sixties," *Comparative Study of Society and History* 26 (1984): 158, 114–57; John D. Kelly and Martha Kaplan, "History, Structure and Ritual," *Annual Review of Anthropology* 19 (1990): 141.

73. Ornter asks, for example, how human action modifies the underlying structures of cultural life in the very process of reproducing them, and, at the same time, how do these underlying structures shape and restrict human action. See Sherry B. Ortner, *High Religion:*

A Cultural and Political History of Sherpa Buddhism (Princeton: Princeton University Press, 1989), pp. 11–18.

74. See Marshall Sahlins, *Culture and Practice Reason* (Chicago: University of Chicago Press, 1976); *Historical Metaphors and Mythical Realities* (Ann Arbor: University of Michigan Press, 1981); and *Islands of History* (Chicago: University of Chicago Press, 1985).

75. See the bibliography provided by Annette Weiner, "Dominant Kings and Forgotten Queens," *Oceania* 58 (1987): 157–60; and, more recently, Gananath Obeyesekere, *The Apotheosis of Captain Cook: European Mythmaking in the Pacific* (Chicago: University of Chicago, 1992).

76. Pierre Bourdieu, *Outline of a Theory of Practice*, trans. Richard Nice (Cambridge: Cambridge University Press, 1977); *The Logic of Practice*, trans. Richard Nice (Stanford, Calif.: Stanford University Press, 1990); *In Other Words: Essays toward a Reflexive Sociology*, trans. Matthew Adamson (Stanford, Calif.: Stanford University Press, 1990); and, with Loïc J. D. Wacquant, *An Invitation to Reflexive Sociology* (Chicago: University of Chicago, 1992).

77. See Marcel Mauss, "Techniques of the Body" [1935], *Economy and Society* 2, no. 1 (1973): 73; Max Weber, *The Sociology of Religion*, pp. 158–59. Also see Roger Chartier, *Cultural History: Between Practices and Representations* (Ithaca, N.Y.: Cornell University Press, 1988), pp. 24–27, 32, and 85–88, who discusses the use of *habitus* by Erwin Panofsky and Norbert Elias.

78. Bourdieu, *Outline of a Theory of Practice*, pp. 72–95, 124.

79. Bourdieu, *Outline of a Theory of Practice*, p. 133.

80. Bourdieu, *Outline of a Theory of Practice*, pp. 136–37.

81. Bourdieu, *Outline of a Theory of Practice*, p. 14.

82. Maurice Bloch, *Ritual, History and Power: Selected Papers in Anthropology* (London: Athlone, 1989), p. 45.

83. Sherry B. Ortner, *Sherpas through Their Rituals* (Cambridge: Cambridge University Press, 1978); and *High Religion*; Jean Comaroff, *Body of Power, Spirit of Resistance* (Chicago: University of Chicago Press, 1985).

84. Ortner, *High Religion*, pp. 11–18.

85. Comaroff, *Body of Power*, p. 196, echoing Dick Hebdige, *Subculture: The Meaning of Style* (London: Methuen, 1979), who leans heavily on the work of V. N. Volosinov (*Marxism and the Philosophy of Language* [1929] [Cambridge, Mass.: Harvard University Press, 1986]).

86. Talal Asad, *Genealogies of Religion*, pp. 55–79.

87. Catherine Bell, *Ritual Theory, Ritual Practice*, p. 47.

88. Geertz, *The Interpretation of Culture*, p. 113. Emphasis added.

89. Bell, *Ritual Theory, Ritual Practice*, p. 54.

90. Bell, *Ritual Theory, Ritual Practice*, p. 72.

91. Bell, *Ritual Theory, Ritual Practice*, pp. 88–93.

92. For two good formulations of this point, see Valerio Valeri, *Kingship and Sacrifice*, pp. 341–42 and John D. Kelly, "From Holi to Diwali in Fuji: An Essay on Ritual and History," *Man* (n.s.) 23 (1988): 53–54.

93. M. E. Combs-Schilling states: "Rituals propel novel cultural inventions onto the historical stage, creating pristine popular experiences of history in the culture's own image" (*Sacred Performances: Islam, Sexuality, and Sacrifice* [New York: Columbia University Press, 1989], p. 31).

94. Comaroff, *Body of Power*, p. 196.

95. Kelly and Kaplan, "History, Structure and Ritual," p. 139.

96. Comaroff, *Body of Power*, p. 1.

97. Edward Shils and Michael Young, "The Meaning of the Coronation," *The Sociological Review* 1 (1953): 63–81.

98. Cited in Shils and Young, "The Meaning of the Coronation," p. 67.

99. Steven Lukes, "Political Ritual and Social Integration," *Sociology: Journal of the British Sociological Association* 9, no. 2 (1975): 289–308.

100. Lukes, "Political Ritual," p. 302.

101. Hilda Kuper, *An African Aristocracy: Rank Among the Swazi* [1947] (London: Oxford University Press, 1961), pp. 197–225; Max Gluckman, "Rituals of Rebellion in Southeast Africa," in *Order and Rebellion*, pp. 119–26; Pierre Smith, "Aspects of the Organization of Rites," in Michel Izard and Pierre Smith, eds., *Between Belief and Transgression: Structuralist Essays in Religion, History and Myth* (Chicago: University of Chicago Press, 1982), pp. 103–281; T. O. Beidelman, "Swazi Royal Ritual," *Africa* 36 (1966): 373–405; Bruce Lincoln, *Discourse and the Construction of Society* (New York: Oxford University Press, 1989), pp. 53–74.

102. Gluckman, "Rituals of Rebellion in South-east Africa," in *Order and Rebellion*, p. 119.

103. Gluckman, "Rituals of Rebellion in South-east Africa," p. 125. Also see Pierre Smith, "Aspects of the Organization of Rites," pp. 103–281.

104. Gluckman, "Rituals of Rebellion in South-east Africa," p. 126.

105. T. O. Beidelman, "Swazi Royal Ritual," p. 401.

106. Clifford Geertz, *Negara: The Theater State in Nineteenth Century Bali* (Princeton, N.J.: Princeton University Press, 1980).

107. Geertz, *Negara*, pp. 110–11.

108. Maurice Bloch, "The Ritual of the Royal Bath in Madagascar," in *Ritual, History and Power*, p. 294.

109. Bloch, "The Ritual of the Royal Bath," p. 187.

110. Bloch, "The Ritual of the Royal Bath," p. 208.

111. Stanley J. Tambiah, ed., *Culture, Thought and Social Action*, pp. 155. Also Tambiah, *World Conqueror and World Renouncer* (Cambridge: Cambridge University Press, 1976).

112. See Kelly and Kaplan, "History, Structure and Ritual," pp. 126–27. Bloch's suggestion that the power of a central ritual lies in the way it adopts shared symbolic forms rooted in everyday life is elaborated further in a study of kingship in Morocco by M. E. Combs-Schilling, *Sacred Performances*.

113. Bruce Lincoln, *Discourse and the Construction of Society*, pp. 53–74.

114. Lincoln, *Discourse and the Construction of Society*, pp. 58, 71–72.

115. See Nancy Jay, *Throughout Your Generations Forever: Sacrifice, Religion, and Paternity* (Chicago: University of Chicago Press, 1992).

Chapter 4

1. Durkheim, *The Elementary Forms*, pp. 339–40.

2. Turner, *Forest of Symbols*, p. 6.

3. Ronald L. Grimes, *Research in Ritual Studies* [1982] (Metuchen, N.J.: Scarecrow Press, 1985), pp. v–vi, 68–116. For descriptions of other classification systems, see Mircea Eliade et al., eds., *The Encyclopedia of Religion*, vol. 12, pp. 412–14, 418.

4. Van Gennep, *The Rites of Passage*, p. 65.

5. For more examples and details, see J. S. Fontaine, *Initiation* (Manchester: Manchester University Press, 1985).

6. This belief, of course, was central to the myth and ritual school discussed in Chapter 1.

7. Unless noted otherwise, descriptions are based primarily on the following studies: Emily M. Ahern, "The Power and Pollution of Chinese Women," in *Women in Chinese Society*, ed. Margery Wolf and Roxane Witke (Stanford, Calif.: Stanford University Press,

1975), pp. 169–90; and Martha Nemes Fried and Morton H. Fried, *Transitions: Four Rituals in Eight Cultures* (New York: W. W. Norton, 1980), pp. 51–57.

8. "Birth Customs," trans. Nancy Gibbs, in Patricia Buckley Ebrey, ed., *Chinese Civilization and Society: A Sourcebook* (New York: Free Press, 1981), pp. 302–3, provides materials from 1936 rural Guangdong.

9. H. Y. Lowe, *The Adventures of Wu: The Life Cycle of a Peking Man*, vols. 1 and 2 (Princeton, N.J.: Princeton University Press, 1983), pp. 6–40.

10. Ahern, "The Power and Pollution," p. 172.

11. For other pollution restrictions during pregnancy, see Gibbs, "Birth Customs," p. 302.

12. Rubie S. Watson, "The Named and the Nameless: Gender and Person in Chinese Society," *American Ethnologist* 13 (1986): 619–31.

13. Ahern, "Power and Pollution," especially pp. 188–90.

14. See Gary Seaman, "The Sexual Politics of Karmic Retribution," in Emily M. Ahern and Hill Gates, eds., *The Anthropology of Taiwanese Society* (Stanford, Calif.: Stanford University Press, 1981), pp. 381–96.

15. Robbie E. Davis-Floyd, "Birth as an American Rite of Passage," in Karen L. Michaelson, ed., *Childbirth in America: Anthropological Perspectives* (South Hadley, Mass.: Bergin and Garvey, 1988), p. 171.

16. See *The Encyclopedia of the Jewish Religion*, ed. by R J. Werblowsky and Geoffrey Wigoder (New York: Holt, Rinehart and Winston, 1966), pp. 221–22.

17. See Ronald B. Inden and Ralph W. Nicholas, *Kinship in Bengali Culture* (Chicago: University of Chicago Press, 1977), pp. 35–52, especially 37–38.

18. See Brian K. Smith, "Ritual, Knowledge, and Being: Initiation and Vedic Study in Ancient India," *Numen* 33, fasc. 1 (1986): 65–89.

19. Ralph W. Nicholas, "The Effectiveness of the Hindu Sacrament (*Samskara*): Caste, Marriage, and Divorce in Bengali Culture," in Lindsey Harlan and Paul B. Courtright, eds., *From the Margins of Hindu Marriage: Essays on Gender, Religion, and Culture* (New York: Oxford University Press, 1995), p. 140.

20. For a full inventory, see Inden and Nicols, *Kinship in Bengali Culture*, pp. 39–51.

21. The rite of renunciation is not formally a samskara per se, but a *diksa* or preparatory rite of purification that often marks transition into a fourth stage of life, or *āśrama*. See Louis Dumont, "World Renunciation in Indian Religions," *Contributions to Indian Sociology* 4 (1960): 33–62.

22. See Patrick Olivelle, *The Aśrama System: The History and Hermeneutics of a Religious Institution* (New York: Oxford University Press, 1993), pp. 122–23.

23. David R. Kinsley, *Hinduism: A Cultural Perspective* (Englewood Cliffs, NJ: Prentice-Hall, 1982), pp. 7, 35, 92, 110; Thomas J. Hopkins, *The Hindu Religious Tradition* (Encino, Calif.: Dickenson, 1971), p. 83.

24. See, for example, Louise Carus Mahdi, Steven Foster, and Meredith Little, eds., *Betwixt and Between: Patterns of Masculine and Feminine Initiation* (LaSalle, Ill.: Open Court, 1987), especially the Introduction and chapters 8–11.

25. Mark C. Carnes, *Secret Ritual and Manhood in Victorian America* (New Haven: Yale University Press, 1989), p. 14. On Victorian ritual, also see John R. Gillis, *A World of Their Own Making: Myth, Ritual, and the Quest for Family Values* (New York: Basic Books, 1996).

26. Hussein Aziza, *Facts about Female Circumcision* (Cairo: Cairo Family Planning Association, 1983); Hanny Lightfoot-Klein, *Prisoners of Ritual: An Odyssey into Female Genital Circumcision in Africa* (Binghampton, N.Y.: Haworth Medical Press, 1989).

27. David D. Gilmore, *Manhood in the Making: Cultural Concepts of Masculinity* (New Haven: Yale University Press, 1990), pp. 1, 11.

28. Gilmore, *Manhood in the Making*, pp. 15–23.

29. See Otto Rank, et al., *In Quest of the Hero*; Carl Jung, *Symbols of Transformation* (Princeton, N.J.: Princeton University Press, 1967); Joseph Campbell, *The Hero with a Thousand Faces*.

30. See Victor Turner, *Dramas, Fields and Metaphors*, pp. 166–230.

31. Pierre Smith, "Aspects of the Organization of Rites" in Michael Izard and Pierre Smith, eds., *Between Belief and Transgression: Structuralist Essays in Religion, History, and Myth*, trans. John Levitt (Chicago: University of Chicago Press, 1982), p. 109.

32. David Pinault, *The Shiites: Ritual and Popular Piety in a Muslim Community* (New York: St. Martin's Press, 1992), p. 4.

33. Frederick M. Denny, "Islamic Ritual: Perspectives and Theories," in Richard C. Martin, ed., *Approaches to Islam in Religious Studies* (Tucson: University of Arizona Press, 1985), pp. 71–72, 75. For more on this topic, see Marshall G. S. Hodgson, *The Venture of Islam*, vol. 1 (Chicago: University of Chicago Press, 1974), pp. 20–22.

34. U. A. Casal, *The Five Sacred Festivals of Ancient Japan: Their Symbolism and Historical Development* (Rutland, Vt.: Charles E. Tuttle Co., 1967), pp. 1–4, 8, 13–14.

35. Lawrence E. Sullivan, *Icanchu's Drum: An Orientation To Meaning in South American Religions* (New York: Macmillan, 1988), pp. 167, 172.

36. Eviatar Zerubavel, *Hidden Rhythms: Schedules and Calendars in Social Life* (Berkeley: University of California Press, 1981), p. 83.

37. For a fuller and quite fascinating account, see Zerubavel, *Hidden Rhythms*, pp. 73, 82–95.

38. Zerubavel, *Hidden Rhythms*, pp. 73, 94.

39. Frank C. Senn, *Christian Worship and Its Cultural Setting* (Philadelphia: Fortress Press, 1983), p. 41; and Joseph A. Jungmann, *The Early Liturgy to the Time of Gregory the Great*, trans. Francis A. Brunner (Notre Dame, Ind.: University of Notre Dame Press, 1959), pp. 145–48.

40. Donald K. Swearer, *Wat Haripunjaya: A Study of the Royal Temple of the Buddha's Relic, Lamphun, Thailand* (Missoula, Mont.: Scholars Press, 1976), pp. 43–46.

41. Eviatar Zerubavel, "Easter and Passover: On Calendars and Group Identity," *American Sociological Review* 47 (April 1982): 284, 288; also *Hidden Rhythms*, pp. 70–81.

42. Mary Beard, "Rituel, Texts, Temps: Les *Parilia* Romains," in Blondeau and Schipper, eds., *Essais sur le rituel* (Louvain: Peeters, 1988), pp. 15, 28–29.

43. On images from animal husbandry and agriculture in Jewish ritual life, and the reasons for the ultimate dominance of animal metaphors, see Howard Eilberg-Schwartz, "Israel in the Mirror of Nature: Animal Metaphors in the Ritual and Narratives of Ancient Israel," *Journal of Ritual Studies* 2, no. 1 (1988): 1–30.

44. See Gerald L. Bruns, "Canon and Power in the Hebrew Scriptures," in Robert von Hallberg, ed., *Canons* (Chicago: University of Chicago Press, 1983), pp. 65–83, especially 68–71.

45. See Baruch M. Bokser, "Was the Last Supper a Passover Seder," *Bible Review* 3, no. 2 (Summer 1987): 24–33; and *The Origins of the Seder: The Passover Rite and Early Rabbinic Judaism* (Berkeley: University of California Press, 1984).

46. Nahum N. Glatzer, ed., *The Passover Haggadah* (New York: Schocken Books, 1953), p. 25.

47. Glatzer, *The Passover Haggadah*, p. 59.

48. Glatzer, *The Passover Haggadah*, p. 59.

49. Glatzer, *The Passover Haggadah*, pp. 59, 61.

50. Glatzer, *The Passover Haggadah*, p. 25.

51. W. Lloyd Warner, "An American Sacred Ceremony," in *American Life* (Chicago: University of Chicago Press, 1956), p. 8.

52. Sullivan, *Icanchu's Drum*, p. 177; Pierre Smith, "Aspects of the Organization of Rites," pp. 108–9.

53. Sullivan, *Icanchu's Drum*, p. 190.

54. Edward B. Tylor, *Primitive Culture*, vol. 2, pp. 461–62, 483.

55. See Raymond Firth, "Offering and Sacrifice: Problems of Organization," *Journal of the Royal Anthropological Institute*, 93 (1963): 12–24.

56. For a detailed description of temple puja, see Jan Gonda, *Viṣṇuism and Śivaism: A Comparison* (London: Athlone Press, 1970), pp. 76–86.

57. Diana L. Eck, *Darsan: Seeing the Divine Image in India* (Chambersburg, Pa.: Anima Books, 1981), pp. 35, 37.

58. Eck, *Darsan*, pp. 3, 5.

59. See Arthur P. Wolf, "Gods, Ghosts and Ancestors," pp. 131–82.

60. James Legge, trans., *Li chi: Book of Rites*, vol. 1 (New Hyde Park, N.Y.: University Books, 1967), p. 148.

61. Ching-lang Hou, *Monnaies d'offrande et la notion de trésorerie dans la religion chinoise*, pp. 49–81. Also see Anna Seidel, "Buying One's Way to Heaven: The Celestial Treasury in Chinese Religions," *History of Religions* 17, nos. 3, 4 (February–May 1978): 419–31.

62. For one genre of retablos, see Jorge Durand and Douglas S. Massey, *Doy Gracias: Iconografía de la Emigración México–Estados Unidos* (Guadalajara: Programa de Estudios Jaliescienses, 1990).

63. See Jordan Paper, *Offering Smoke: The Sacred Pipe and Native American Religion* (Moscow: University of Idaho Press, 1988).

64. See Amrit Srinivasan, "Reform or Conformity? Temple 'Prostitution' and the Community in the Madras Presidency," in Bina Agarwal, ed., *Structures of Patriarchy: State, Community and Household in Modernising Asia* (London: Zed Press, 1988), pp. 175–98.

65. The literature on sacrifice is enormous. For overviews, see Eliade et al., eds., *The Encyclopedia of Religion*, vol. 12, pp. 544–57; Richart D. Hecht, "Studies on Sacrifice: 1970–80," *Religious Studies Review* 8, no. 3 (July 1982): 253–58; and Ivan Strenski, "Between Theory and Speciality: Sacrifice in the 90s," *Religious Studies Review* 22, no. 1 (January 1996): 10–20.

66. Hubert and Mauss, *Sacrifice*, p. 13.

67. Hubert and Mauss, *Sacrifice*, pp. 2–3.

68. *The Holy Bible: Revised Standard Version* (New York: New American Library, 1962), Genesis 22:1–14. Also see the account of Cain and Abel's offerings (Genesis 4:1–5).

69. Exodus 24:4–8.

70. On *balché*, see R. Jon McGee, *Life, Ritual and Religion among the Lacandon Maya* (Belmont, Calif.: Wadsworth, 1990).

71. Weston La Barre, *The Peyote Cult* [1964] (Norman: University of Oklahoma Press, 1989); Barbara G. Myerhoff, *Peyote Hunt: The Sacred Journey of the Huichol Indians* (Ithaca, N.Y.: Cornell University Press, 1974).

72. For an overview of human sacrifice in Mesoamerica, see Jacques Soustelle, "Ritual Human Sacrifice in Mesoamerica: An Introduction," in Elizabeth P. Benson and Elizabeth H. Boone, eds., *Ritual Human Sacrifice in Mesoamerica* (Washington D.C.: Dumbarton Oaks Research Library and Collection, 1984), pp. 1–5.

73. Marshall Sahlins, "Culture as Protein and Profit," p. 46.

74. Sahlins, "Culture as Protein and Profit," p. 47.

75. See Nigel Davies, "Human Sacrifice in the Old World and the New," in Benson and Boone, eds., *Ritual Human Sacrifice in Mesoamerica* pp. 211–24. Capital punishment has been repeatedly analyzed as a modern ritual of human sacrifice—see the discussion

entitled "political rituals" in this volume—but for an overview, consult Elizabeth D. Purdum and J. Anthony Paredes, "Rituals of Death: Capital Punishment and Human Sacrifice," in Michael Radelet, ed., *Facing the Death Penalty: Essays on Cruel and Unusual Punishment* (Philadelphia: Temple University Press, 1989): pp. 139–55.

76. For a provocative analysis of the significance of sacrifice in establishing patriarchal relationships, see Nancy Jay, *Throughout Your Generations Forever: Sacrifice, Religion, and Paternity* (Chicago: University of Chicago, 1992).

77. Turner, *Forest of Symbols*, p. 9.

78. Alvin P. Cohen, "Coercing the Rain Deities in Ancient China," *History of Religions* 17, nos. 3, 4 (February–May 1978): 249–50.

79. Cited in Peter N. Gregory and Patricia Buckley Ebrey, "The Religious and Historical Landscape," in Patricia Buckley Ebrey and Peter N. Gregory, eds., *Religion and Society in T'ang and Sung China* (Honolulu: University of Hawaii Press, 1993), pp. 7–8.

80. Edward H. Schafer, "Ritual Exposure in Ancient China," *Harvard Journal of Asiatic Studies* 14 (1951): 130–84; Alvin P. Cohen, "Coercing the Rain Deities," 244–65.

81. Thomas Adeoye Lambo, "Psychotherapy in Africa," *Human Nature* 1 (March 1978): pp. 32–39, citation from p. 35. See also Robin Horton on the social side of healing, "African Traditional Thought and Western Science," in *Patterns of Thought in Africa and the West* (Cambridge: Cambridge University Press, 1993), pp. 197–258.

82. For a discussion of the significance of these terms, see Laurel Kendall, *Shamans, Housewives and Other Restless Spirits: Women in Korean Ritual Life* (Honolulu: University of Hawaii Press, 1985), pp. x–xi.

83. Youngsook Kim Harvey, "Possession Sickness and Women Shamans in Korea," in *Unspoken Worlds: Women's Religious Lives in Non-Western Cultures*, ed. Nancy A. Falk and Rita M. Gross (San Francisco: Harper and Row, 1980), pp. 41–52; also, Richard W. I. Guisso and Chai-shin Yu, *Shamanism: The Spirit World of Korea* (Berkeley, Calif.: Asian Humanities Press, 1988).

84. This generic reconstruction of a dialogue is from Guisso and Yu, *Shamanism*, p. 134.

85. Guisso and Yu, *Shamanism*, pp. 139–40.

86. See Claude Lévi-Strauss, *Structural Anthropology* (Garden City, N.Y.: Anchor Books, 1967), pp. 181–201; Robin Horton, "African Traditional Thought and Western Science"; Bruce Kapferer, "Mind, Self, and Other in Demonic Illness: The Negation and Reconstruction of Self," *American Ethnologist* 6, no. 1 (February 1979): 110–33.

87. See David Holmberg, "Review Article: The Shamanic Illusion," *Journal of Ritual Studies* 7, no. 1 (Winter 1993): 163–75. For an interesting discussion of the circumstances surrounding a Chinese woman whose strangeness was *not* deemed to constitute a true possession, see Margery Wolf, "The Woman Who Didn't Become A Shaman," *American Ethnologist* 17 (August 1990): 419–30.

88. The basic account of the Ghost Dance is that of James Mooney, *The Ghost Dance Religion and the Sioux Outbreak of 1890* [1896], abridged with an introductory by Anthony F. C. Wallace (Chicago: University of Chicago Press, 1965); for a challenge to Mooney's basic understanding of the movement, also see Omer C. Stewart, "The Ghost Dance," in W. Raymond Wood and Margot Liberty, eds., *Anthropology on the Great Plains* (Lincoln: University of Nebraska Press, 1980), pp. 179–87.

89. See *The Encyclopedia of Judaism*, ed. Geoffrey Wigoder (New York: Macmillan, 1989), pp. 490–91; Judith Baskin, "The Separation of Women in Rabbinic Judaism," in *Women, Religion and Social Change*, ed. Yvonne Yazbeck Haddad and Ellison Banks Findley (Albany: State University of New York, 1985), pp. 3–18; Rachel Biale, *Women and Jewish Law*

(New York: Schocken Books, 1989), chapter 5; Jacob Neusner, *Method and Meaning in Ancient Judaism* (Atlanta: Scholars Press, 1979), pp. 79–100.

90. Stephen A. Tyler, *India: An Anthropological Perspective* (Prospect Heights, Ill.: Waveland Press, 1986), pp. 79–80.

91. Mc Gee, *Life, Ritual and Religion*, pp. 48–49, 71–73.

92. See Jack Hebner and David Osborn, *Kumbha Mela: The World's Largest Act of Faith* (La Jolla, Calif.: Entourage Publications, 1990).

93. Dev Varam, "Ascetics Lead Millions to Holy Dip at Kumbha Mela," *India-West* (May 22, 1992), p. 27.

94. See Kelly and Kaplan, "History, Structure, and Ritual," pp. 136–39.

95. Irving Goldman, *The Mouth of Heaven: An Introduction to Kwakiutl Religious Thought* (New York: John Wiley, 1975); Aldona Jonaitis, ed., *Chiefly Feasts: The Enduring Kwakiutl Potlatch* (Seattle: University of Washington Press, 1991).

96. Jonaitis, *Chiefly Feasts*, p. 11.

97. The complex *hamatsa* dance is controversial due to reputed traces of cannibalism. For example, the dancer can take serious bites out of people who are paid for their cooperation, and there are allusions to the eating of corpses. The hamatsa initiate is said to be taken away by the cannibal spirit during the winter, when he in effect goes through an extended period of "training," reappearing to run around wild during the time of the Winter Dances. See Jonaitis, *Chiefly Feasts*, pp. 97–100.

98. Jonaitis, *Chiefly Feasts*, pp. 227–48.

99. Goldman, *The Mouth of Heaven*, pp. 170–73, 176.

100. Goldman, *The Mouth of Heaven*, pp. 22, 177.

101. Goldman, *The Mouth of Heaven*, pp. 86–90, 98–120, 122–24, 177–79.

102. Clifford Geertz, *The Religion of Java* (Chicago: University of Chicago Press, 1976), p. 11.

103. Geertz, *The Religion of Java*, pp. 11–15.

104. Bridget Ann Henisch, *Fast and Feast: Food in Medieval Society* (University Park: Pennsylvania State University, 1976), pp. 31–33.

105. Glen Yocum, "Notes on an Easter Ramadan," *Journal of the American Academy of Religion* 60, no 2 (Summer 1992): 206.

106. Marjo Buitelaar, *Fasting and Feasting in Morocco: Women's Participation in Ramadan* (Oxford: Berg Publishers, 1993), p. 17, citing Surah 97:1–5.

107. Buitelaar, *Fasting and Feasting in Morocco*, pp. 3–4.

108. Yocum, "Notes on an Easter Ramadan," p. 223.

109. Hava Lazarus-Yafeh, *Some Religious Aspects of Islam* (Leiden: E. J. Brill, 1981) pp. 38–39, 41–42.

110. John L. Esposito, *Islam: The Straight Path* (New York: Oxford University Press, 1991), pp. 112–13.

111. See Esposito, *Islam*, p. 177.

112. Robert A. Schneider, "Mortification on Parade: Penitential Processions in Sixteenth- and Seventeenth-Century France," *Renaissance and Reformation* 10, no. 1 (1986): 123–45; also William Christian Jr., *Local Religion in 16th Century Spain* (Princeton, N.J.: Princeton University Press, 1981), pp. 190–91.

113. Marta Weigle, *Brothers of Light, Brothers of Blood* (Albuquerque: University of New Mexico Press, 1976).

114. Most notably, see Victor Turner, *The Ritual Process*; Mikhail Bakhtin, *Rabelias and His World* (Bloomington: University of Indiana Press, 1984); and Roger D. Abrahams and Richard Bauman, "Ranges of Festival Behavior," in Barbara A. Babcock, ed., *The Reversible World: Symbolic Inversion in Art and Society* (Ithaca, N.Y.: Cornell University Press, 1978).

115. See Natalie Z. Davis on the theories of Victor Turner and Mikhail Bakhtin in *Society and Culture in Early Modern France: Eight Essays* (Stanford, Calif.: Stanford University Press, 1975), pp. 97–123, especially p. 103.

116. Roberto Da Matta, "Constraint and License: A Preliminary Study of Two Brazilian National Rituals," in Sally F. Moore and Barbara G. Myerhoff, eds., *Secular Ritual* (Amsterdam: Van Gorcum, 1977), pp. 244–64, esp. pp. 247–48.

117. See Roberto Da Matta, *Carnivals, Rogues and Heroes: An Interpretation of the Brazilian Dilemma,* trans. by John Drury (Notre Dame, Ind.: Notre Dame University Press, 1979), pp. 122–23.

118. On the term "krewe," see Samuel Kinser, *Carnival, American Style: Mardi Gras at New Orleans and Mobile* (Chicago: University of Chicago Press, 1990), pp. 115–17.

119. Kinser, *Carnival, American Style,* p. 282.

120. Kinser, *Carnival, American Style,* p. 259.

121. The New Orleans ruling was eventually revised so as to encourage, not demand, integration. See Frances Frank Marcus, "New Orleans Weights Anti-Bias Law on Carnival," *New York Times,* December 7, 1991, p. 7; and "New Orleans Outlaws Bias by Mardi Gras Parade Clubs," *New York Times,* Dec 21, 1991, p. 7; Larry Rohter, "Bias Law Casts Pall over New Orleans Mardi Gras," *New York Times,* February 2, 1992, pp. 1, 18; and "New Orleans Weakens Mardi Gras Bias Law," *New York Times,* February 7, 1992, p. 17; Frances Frank Marcus, "Law Is Softened to Quell Furor over Mardi Gras," *New York Times,* February 8, 1992, p. 6; "Behind the Fears, Mardi Gras as Usual," *New York Times,* February 25, 1992, p. 12; "Council Eases Anti-Bias Law on Mardi Gras," *New York Times,* May 10, 1992, p. 24; and "Mardi Gras Group Quits to Protest New Law," *New York Times,* August 19, 1992, p. A18.

122. McKim Marriott, "The Feast of Love," in Milton Singer, ed., *Krishna: Myths, Rites, and Attitudes* (Chicago: University of Chicago Press, 1966), pp. 200–12.

123. Kokugakuin University, *Matsuri: Festival and Rite in Japanese Life* (Tokyo: Kokugakuin University, 1988). Also see Michael Ashkenazi, *Matsuri: Festivals of a Japanese Town* (Honolulu: University of Hawaii Press, 1993).

124. See Juan Eduardo Campo, "Authority, Ritual, and Spatial in Islam: The Pilgrimage to Mecca," *Journal of Ritual Studies* 5, no. 1 (Winter 1991): 65–91; William R. Roff, "Pilgrimage and the History of Religions: Theoretical Approaches to the Hajj," in Richard C. Martin, ed., *Approaches to Islam in Religious Studies* (Tucson: University of Arizona Press, 1985), pp. 78–86.

125. Ari L. Goldman, "Culture and Religion Unite in a Day of Fasting by Jews," *New York Times,* July 31, 1990, p. B2.

126. Geertz, *Negara,* pp. 102, 124, 131.

127. For fine discussions of some of these examples, see David I. Kertzer, *Ritual, Politics, and Power* (New Haven: Yale University Press, 1988), pp. 15–21, 57–61, 88, 98. Also see Frederic Wakeman Jr., "Mao's Remains," in James L. Watson and Evelyn S. Rawski, eds., *Death Ritual in Late Imperial and Modern China* (Berkeley: University of California Press, 1988), pp. 254–88.

128. Roy A. Rappaport, "Liturgies and Lies," *International Yearbook for Sociology of Knowledge and Religion* 10 (1976): 81.

129. Geertz, *Negara,* p. 13.

130. On this term, see Abner Cohen, *The Politics of Elite Cultures: Explorations in the Dramaturgy of Power in a Modern African Culture* (Berkeley: University of California Press, 1981), p. 14.

131. Jerrold M. Packard, *Sons of Heaven: A Portrait of the Japanese Monarchy* (New York: Macmillan, 1987), p. 5.

132. See Steven R. Weisman in the *New York Times*: "Tokyo Journal: Emperor's Ritual Bed Keeps Secret," (October 9, 1990); "Japan Enthrones Emperor Today in Old Rite with New Twist," (November 12, 1990); and "Akihito Performs Solitary Rite as Some Question Its Meaning" (November 23, 1990). Also see Edmund T. Gilday, "Imperial Ritual in the Heisei Era: A Report on Research in Progress," *Pacific World*, n.s. 10 (Fall 1994): 205–18.

133. See Emiko Ohnuki-Tierney, *Rice as Self: Japanese Identities through Time* (Princeton, N.J.: Princeton University Press, 1993), especially pp. 44–50, 58–62.

134. On aspects of the history of the imperial rites, see Robert S. Ellwood, *The Feast of Kingship: Accession Ceremonies in Ancient Japan* (Tokyo: Sophia University, 1973); Daniel C. Holtom, *The Japanese Enthronement Ceremonies*, 2d ed. (Tokyo: Sophia University, 1972); Helen Hardacre, *Shinto and the State 1868–1988* (Princeton, N.J.: Princeton University Press, 1989); Edmund Gilday, "Processing Tradition: The Making of an Emperor, 1989–91," unpublished manuscript (on filial connotations, Gilday, private communication).

135. For a description of the 1928 *daijōsai*, see Packard, *Sons of Heaven*, pp. 8–9, 18–21. For an excellent overview of ways to interpret the *daijōsai*, see Carmen Blacker, "The *Shinza* or God-seat in the *Daijōsai*—Throne, Bed, or Incubation Couch?" *Japanese Journal of Religious Studies* 17, nos. 2, 3 (1990): 179–97.

136. Edmund T. Gilday, private communication.

137. Gilday, private communication.

138. See Dale K. Van Kley, *The Damiens Affair and the Unraveling of the Ancien Régime* (Princeton, N.J.: Princeton University Press, 1984).

139. Michel Foucault, *Discipline and Punish: The Birth of the Prison*, trans. Alan Sheridan (New York: Vintage Books, 1977), pp. 3, 49–51. Also see Louis P. Masur, *Rites of Execution: Capital Punishment and the Transformation of American Culture, 1776–1865* (New York: Oxford University Press, 1989).

140. Foucault, *Discipline and Punish*, pp. 59–65.

141. See James L. Hevia, "A Multitude of Lords: Qing Court Ritual and the Macartney Embassy of 1793," *Late Imperial China* 10, no. 2 (December 1989): 72–105, as well as Robert A. Bickers, ed., *Ritual and Diplomacy: The Macartney Mission to China 1792–1794* (London: British Association for Chinese Studies/Wellsweep, 1993).

142. See Robert E. Quirk, *An Affair of Honor: Woodrow Wilson and the Occupation of Vera Cruz* (New York: McGraw-Hill, 1964).

143. Kertzer, *Ritual, Politics, and Power*, pp. 1–2.

144. Kenelm Burridge, *New Heaven, New Earth: A Study of Millenarian Activity* (New York: Schocken Books, 1969).

145. On the Papuans, see Peter Worsley, *The Trumpet Shall Sound: A Study of "Cargo" Cults in Melanesia*, 2d ed. (New York: Schocken, 1968), pp. 141–42. On the "ghost shirts," see James Mooney, *The Ghost Dance Religion and the Sioux Outbreak*, ed. Anthony Wallace (Chicago: University of Chicago Press, 1965), pp. 30, 42, 76, 118.

146. See Benjamin C. Ray, *African Religions: Symbol, Ritual, and Community* (Englewoord Cliffs, N.J.: Prentice-Hall, 1976), pp. 165–73.

147. Winston Davis, "Ittōen: The Myths and Rituals of Liminality," *History of Religions* 14, no. 4 (May 1975): 282–321; and 15, no. 1 (August 1975): 1–33, reprinted in Winston Davis, *Japanese Religion and Society: Paradigms of Structure and Change* (Albany: State University of New York, 1992), pp. 189–225, especially pp. 304, 319.

148. J. G. A. Pocock, "Ritual, Language, Power: An Essay on the Apparent Meanings of Ancient Chinese Philosophy," *Political Science* 16 (1964): 6; also cited by Kertzer, *Ritual, Politics, and Power*, pp. 13–14. See B. Watson, *Hsün Tzu*, p. 118.

149. See Du-Hyun Lee, "Korean Shamans: Role Playing through Trance Possession," in Richard Schechner and Willa Appel, eds., *By Means of Performance: Intercultural Studies of Theatre and Ritual* (Cambridge: Cambridge University Press, 1990), pp. 150–56.

Chapter 5

1. For analogous discussions, see Ronald Grimes, *Ritual Criticism*, pp. 13–14; and Onno van der Hart, *Rituals in Psychotherapy: Transition and Continuity* (New York: Irvington Publishers, 1978), pp. 3–16.

2. With a different perspective, Grimes has also formulated "six modes of ritual sensibility: ritualization, decorum, ceremony, liturgy, magic and celebration" (*Beginnings in Ritual Studies*, p. 35).

3. Compare Rappaport's list of the "obvious aspects of ritual," which include formality, performance, and instrumentality, in *Ecology, Meaning, and Religion*, pp. 175–77.

4. These terms are used by Basil Bernstein and Mary Douglas; see Douglas, *Natural Symbols*, pp. 42–49, esp. 44.

5. Maurice Bloch, "Symbols, Song, Dance and Features of Articulation: Is Religion an Extreme Form of Traditional Authority?" *Archives Europeénes de Sociologie* 15 (1974): 55–81. Also see Roy Rappaport's "The Obvious Aspects of Ritual," in *Ecology, Meaning and Religion*, pp. 173–222.

6. Bloch, "Symbols, Song," p. 6.

7. Bloch, "Symbols, Song," p. 64.

8. Douglas, *Natural Symbols*, p. 55, quoting Basil Bernstein.

9. Douglas, *Natural Symbols*, p. 79.

10. Erving Goffman, *Interaction Rituals*, pp. 19, 22–23, 31–33.

11. Goffman, *Interaction Rituals*, pp. 42–45.

12. Goffman, "Supportive Interchanges," in *Relations in Public* (New York: Basic Books, 1971), pp. 62–74, cited in Deborah Schiffrin, "Handwork as Ceremony: The Case of the Handshake," *Semiotica* 12 (1974): 189–202, esp. 189. Also see Dean MacCannell, "A Note on Hat Tipping," *Semiotica* 7, no. 4 (1973): 300–312.

13. Raymond Firth, "Verbal and Bodily Rituals of Greeting and Parting," in J. S. La Fontaine, ed., *The Interpretation of Ritual* (London: Tavistock Publications, 1972), p. 29.

14. There is a fair amount of literature, both scholarly and popular, on gestures and the cultural conventions that govern their use as communication, notably Desmond Morris, *Gestures* (New York: Stein and Day, 1979) and Roger E. Axtell, *Gestures: The Do's and Taboos of Body Language around the World* (New York: John Wiley, 1991). On polite speech, see Penelope Brown and Stephen C. Levinson, *Politeness: Some Universals in Language Usage* (Cambridge: Cambridge University Press, 1987); and Richard J. Watts, Sachiko Ide, and Konrad Ehlich, eds., *Politeness in Language: Studies in Its History, Theory, and Practice* (Berlin: Mouton de Gruyter, 1992).

15. Edmund Leach asserts that ritual is no more than a symbolic expression of status (*The Political Systems of Highland Burma*, 2d ed. [London: Athlone Press, 1945], pp. 10–11, 16).

16. For more on conversational rituals and strategies, see Haruo Aoki and Shigeko Okamoto, *Rules for Conversational Rituals in Japanese* (Tokyo: Taishukan, 1988) and Kaidi Zhan, *The Strategies of Politeness in the Chinese Language* (Berkeley: Institute of East Asian Studies, University of California, 1992).

17. Two good studies that illustrate various aspects of dining rituals are Mary Douglas, "Deciphering a Meal"; and Robert Jameson, "Purity and Power at the Victorian Dinner Party," in Ian Hodder, ed., *The Archeology of Contextual Meanings* (London: Cambridge University Press, 1987), pp. 55–65.

18. Margaret Visser, *The Rituals of Dinner: The Origins, Evolution, Eccentricities, and Meaning of Table Manners* (New York: Grove Weidenfeld, 1991), p. ix.

19. Eleanor Roosevelt, *Book of Common Sense Etiquette* (New York: Macmillan, 1962).

20. On the significance of formalization in academic lecturing, see Jean La Fontaine, "Invisible Custom: Public Lectures as Ceremonials," *Anthropology Today* 2, no. 5 (1986): 3–9.

21. Bridget Ann Henisch, *Fast and Feast*, p. 190.

22. Norbert Elias, *The Civilizing Process: The History of Manners*, 2 vols., trans. Edmund Jephcott (New York: Urizen Books, 1978). See his discussion of Erasmus's influence on the way "outward bodily propriety proceeds from a well-composed mind" (vol. 1, p. 56).

23. Elias, *The Civilizing Process*, vol. 1, p. xiii, and vol. 2, pp. 229–47.

24. See Claude Lévi-Strauss, *The Origin of Table Manners*, p. 20, who also refers to Erasmus's work on civility (498–99); also Henisch, *Fast and Feast*, esp. chapters 6 and 7. On the different connections between etiquette and morality, see Edward Norbeck, *Religion in Human Life: Anthropological Views* (Prospect Heights, Ill.: Waveland Press, 1974), pp. 28–29.

25. Amy Vanderbilt, *Amy Vanderbilt's New Complete Book of Etiquette: The Guide to Gracious Living* [1952] (Garden City, N.Y.: Doubleday, 1967), pp. xx–xxi. Vanderbilt's book of etiquette starts out with "the ceremonies of life," otherwise known as rites of passage. Elizabeth L. Post's *Emily Post's Etiquette*, 14th ed. (New York: Harper and Row, 1984) was first published in 1922 as *Etiquette in Society, in Business, in Politics and at Home*.

26. Solomon Poll, *The Hasidic Community of Williamsburg: A Study in the Sociology of Religion* (New York: Schocken, 1969), pp. 16–17, 59–69.

27. See Samuel M. Wilson, "Pilgrims' Paradox: Thanksgiving Is in the Eye of the Beholder," *Natural History* 100, no. 11 (November 1991): 22–25.

28. William E. Schmidt, "British Courts to Doff Wig? Verdict Asked," *New York Times*, August 23, 1992, p. 4.

29. Schmidt, "British Courts to Doff Wig? Verdict Asked," p. 4.

30. See Kevin Sheard, *Academic Heraldry in America* (Marquette: Northern Michigan College Press, 1962); Hugh Smith, *Academic Dress and Insignia of the World: Gowns, Hats, Chains of Office, Hoods, Rings, Medals and Other Degree Insignia of Universities and Other Institutions of Learning* (Cape Town: A. A. Balkema, 1970).

31. On America's adoption of a uniform "Intercollegiate Code" governing academic attire in 1895, see Hugh Smith, *Academic Dress*, vol. 2, pp. 1527–28.

32. See G. W. Shaw, *Academical Dress of British Universities* (Cambridge: W. Heffer and Sons, 1966); Hugh Smith, *Academic Dress*, vol. 1, p. 1.

33. Vernon Silver, "Mortarboards Become Billboards for Protests," *New York Times*, June 7, 1993, p. B5.

34. Frederick W. Mote, *The Intellectual Foundations of China* (New York: Alfred Knopf, 1971), p. 31.

35. Arthur Waley, trans., *The Analects of Confucius* (New York: Vintage Books, 1938), p. 162 (12:1).

36. Burton Watson, trans., *Hsün Tzu*, pp. 71, 94, 89–111 passim.

37. Herbert Fingarette, *Confucius: The Secular as Sacred* (San Francisco: Harper and Row, 1972), p. 7. The following discussion is also based on Fingarette's thesis.

38. Eric Hobsbawm, "Introduction: Inventing Traditions," in Eric Hobsbawm and Terence Ranger, eds., *The Invention of Tradition* (Cambridge: Cambridge University Press, 1983), pp. 1–4.

39. David Cannadine, "The Context, Performance and Meaning of Ritual: The British Monarchy and the 'Invention of Tradition,'" in Hobsbawm and Ranger, *The Invention of Tradition*, p. 108.

40. Cannadine, "The Context, Performance and Meaning of Ritual," pp. 120–21, 125, 133.

41. Cited in Cannadine, "The Context, Performance and Meaning of Ritual," p. 148.

42. Eric Hobsbawm, "Mass-Producing Traditions: Europe, 1870–1914," in Hobsbawm and Ranger, *The Invention of Tradition*, p. 271. While focusing on the importance of language to the emergence and definition of nations, Benedict Anderson also points to numerous examples of highly ritualized language. See his *Imagined Communities: Reflections on the Origin and Spread of Nationalism*, rev. ed. (London: Verso, 1991), pp. 144–45.

43. George P. Fletcher, "Update the Pledge," *New York Times*, December 6, 1992, op-ed page. Fletcher wanted to change it again, adding: "one nation, united in our diversity, committed to liberty and justice for all."

44. Stephen J. Whitfield, *The Culture of the Cold War* (Baltimore: Johns Hopkins University Press, 1990), p. 89.

45. Fletcher, "Update the Pledge."

46. Barbara Myerhoff, "A Death in Due Time," in John J. MacAloon, ed., *Rite, Drama, Festival, Spectacle* (Philadelphia: Institute for the Study of Human Issues, 1984), p. 151.

47. Eugene d'Aquili, "Human Ceremonial Ritual and the Modulation of Aggression," *Zygon* 20, no. 1 (1985): 22; Terrence Deal and Allan Kennedy, *Corporate Cultures: The Rites and Ceremonials of Corporate Life* (Reading, Mass.: Addison-Wesley, 1982).

48. Horace Miner, "Body Ritual among the Nacirema," *American Anthropologist* 58 (1956): 503–7; reprinted in James P. Spradley and Michael A. Rynkiewich, eds., *The Nacirema: Readings on American Culture* (Boston: Little, Brown, 1975), pp. 10–13.

49. See Ilana Friedrich Silber, "'Opting Out' in Theravada Buddhism and Medieval Christianity," *Religion* 15 (1985): 251–77, especially endnotes 1 and 2, p. 268.

50. On Zen practice as "ritual," see Ronald L. Grimes, *Beginnings in Ritual Studies*, pp. 158–178, especially pp. 161–62.

51. On the ideals and realities of Zen training, see Bernard Faure, *The Rhetoric of Immediacy: A Cultural Critique of Chan/Zen Buddhism* (Princeton, N.J.: Princeton University Press, 1991); Robert E. Buswell Jr., *The Zen Monastic Experience* (Princeton, N.J.: Princeton University Press, 1992); and Mohan Wijayaratna, *Buddhist Monastic Life according to the Texts of the Theravada Tradition*, trans. Claude Grangier and Steven Collins (Cambridge: Cambridge University Press, 1990); Chen-Hua, *In Search of the Dharma: Memoirs of a Modern Chinese Buddhist Pilgrimage*, ed. Chün-fang Yü and trans. Denis C. Mair (Albany: State University of New York, 1992).

52. See David L. Preston, *The Social Organization of Zen Practice: Constructing Transcultural Reality* (Cambridge: Cambridge University Press, 1988), especially pp. 78, 97, 103, 108.

53. Walpola Sri Rahula, *What the Buddha Taught*, 2nd rev. ed. (New York: Grove, 1974), p. 67.

54. See Judith L. Kapferer, "Socialization and the Symbolic Order of the School," *Anthropology and Education Quarterly* 12, no. 4 (1981): 258–74; Peter McClaren, *Schooling as a Ritual Performance* (London: Routlege & Kegan Paul, 1986; and B. Bernstein, H. L. Elvin, and R. S. Peters, "Ritual in Education," *Philosophical Transactions of the Royal Society of London*, series B, 251 (1966):429–36; Jacquetta Hill Burnett, "Ceremony, Rites, and Economy in the Student System of an American High School," *Human Organization* 28 (1969): 1–10; David F. Lancy, "The Social Organization of Learning: Initiation Rituals and Public Schools," in *Human Organization* 34, no. 4 (Winter 1975): 371–80. On a different note, Carol Gilligan's groundbreaking study of gender and ethics suggest that boys' greater involvement in organized games correlates with a distinctively masculine ethical viewpoint, in contrast to the less competitive views expressed by girls; see *In a Different Voice: Psycho-*

logical Theory and Women's Development (Cambridge, Mass.: Harvard University Press, 1982), pp. 9–11, 16–17.

55. Anderson, *Imagined Communities*, p. 145.

56. Joyce Carol Oates, "The Cruelest Sport," *New York Review of Books*, February 19, 1992, p. 3 (3–6).

57. Mary Gluckman and Max Gluckman, "On Drama, and Games and Athletic Contexts," in Sally F. Moore and Barbara G. Myerhoff, eds., *Secular Ritual* (Amsterdam: Van Gorcum, 1977), pp. 227–43, esp. pp. 239–40.

58. W. Arens, "Professional Football," p. 7.

59. Richard G. Sipes, "War, Sports, and Aggression: An Empirical Test of Two Rival Theories," *American Anthropologist* 75 (January 1973): 64–86.

60. See Allen Guttman, *From Ritual to Record: The Nature of Modern Sports* (New York: Columbia University Press, 1978); Scott Kilmer, "Sport as Ritual: A Theoretical Approach," in *The Study of Play: Problems and Prospects*, ed. David F. Lancy and B. Allan Tindall (Cornwall, N.Y.: Leisure Press, 1977), pp. 44–49; Susan P. Montague and Robert Morais, "Football Games and Rock Concerts"; Steven M. Gelber, "Working at Playing: The Culture of the Workplace and the Rise of Baseball," *Journal of Social History* 16, no. 4 (June 1983): 3–22.

61. Gluckman and Gluckman, "On Drama," pp. 237–8; Guttman, *From Ritual to Record*, pp. 19–20.

62. George Gmelch, "Baseball Magic," in James P. Spradley and David W. McCurdy, eds., *Conformity and Conflict: Readings in Cultural Anthropology* (Boston: Little, Brown, 1990), pp. 350, 352.

63. Gmelch, "Baseball Magic," p. 348; Kendall Blanchard,"Sport and Ritual in Choctaw Society," in Helen B. Schwartzman, ed., *Play and Culture* (West Point, N.Y.: Leisure Press, 1980), pp. 83–90.

64. Kendall Blanchard, "The Ritual Dimensions of Play: Structure and Perspective — Introduction," in Schwartzman, *Play and Culture*, pp. 49–50, 54–55, 57, 68.

65. Ehud Ya'ari and Ina Friedman, "Curses in Verses," *Atlantic Monthly* (February 1991): 22–26.

66. Murray Edelman, *Politics as Symbolic Action: Mass Arousal and Quiescence* (Chicago: Markham Publishing, 1971).

67. For an inventory of the ritual patterns in American public life, see John F. Wilson, *Public Religion in American Culture* (Philadelphia: Temple University Press, 1979), pp. 74–88.

68. See the following studies: Gershom Scholem, "The Star of David: History of a Symbol" in *The Messianic Idea in Judaism* (New York: Schocken, 1971), pp. 257–81; Eric R. Wolf, "The Virgin of Guadalupe: A Mexican National Symbol," *Journal of American Folklore* 71 (1958) 34–39; and Carolyn Marvin, "Theorizing the Flagbody: Symbolic Dimensions of the Flag Desecration Debate, or, Why the Bill of Rights Does Not Fly in the Ballpark," *Critical Studies in Mass Communication* 8, no. 2 (1991): 119–38.

69. Sherry B. Ortner, "On Key Symbols," *American Anthropologist* 75 (1973): 1338–46, especially p. 1340.

70. On "totalization," see Richard P. Werbner (*Ritual Passage, Sacred Journey: The Process and Organization of Religious Movement* [Washington D.C.: Smithsonian Institution Press, 1989], p. 13), who defines it somewhat differently.

71. For a theory of symbols, see Don Handelman, *Models and Mirrors: Towards an Anthropology of Public Events* (Cambridge: Cambridge University Press, 1990), pp. 12–13; for his notion of a structural "holism" in ritual-like events, see p. 21.

72. John F. Sears, *Sacred Places: American Tourist Attractions in the Nineteenth Century* (New York: Oxford University Press, 1989), pp. 3–30, especially pp. 6–7, 13–14, 23–24, 29–30.

73. Sears, *Sacred Places*, pp. 8–11, 18–19, 29.

74. See Rolf A. Stein, *The World in Miniature: Container Gardens and Dwellings in Far Eastern Religious Thought*, trans. Phyllis Brooks (Stanford, Calif.: Stanford University Press, 1990).

75. Stein, *The World in Miniature*, p. 3.

76. On the Daoist *jiao* ritual, see Michael R. Saso, *Taoism and the Rite of Cosmic Renewal* (Pullman: Washington State University Press, 1972) and Kristofer M. Schipper, *The Taoist Body*, trans. Karen C. Duval (Berkeley: University of California Press, 1993).

77. Ortner, "On Key Symbols," pp. 1340.

78. Compare David Chaney, "A Symbolic Mirror of Ourselves: Civic Ritual in Mass Society," *Media, Culture and Society* 5 (1983): 119–35, especially p. 120.

79. See Handelman, *Models and Mirrors*, pp. 236–65; Paul Bouissac, "The Profanation of the Sacred in Circus Clown Performances," in Schechner and Appel, eds., *By Means of Performance*, pp. 194–207; and Barbara Babcock, "Arrange Me into Disorder: Fragments and Reflections on Ritual Clowning," in MacAloon, ed., *Rite, Drama, Festival, Spectacle*, pp. 102–28.

80. Barbara G. Myerhoff, "We Don't Wrap Herring in a Printed Page: Fusion, Fictions and Continuity in Secular Ritual," in Moore and Myerhoff, eds., *Secular Ritual*, p. 223.

81. See Richard Bauman, "Verbal Art as Performance," *American Anthropologist* 77, no. 1 (1975): 290–311, especially p. 293.

82. Handelman, *Models and Mirrors*, p. 81.

83. Handelman, *Models and Mirrors*, p. 12, citing Mary Douglas.

84. Handelman, *Models and Mirrors*, p. 23.

85. David Glassberg, *American Historical Pageantry: The Uses of Tradition in the Early Twentieth Century* (Chapel Hill: University of North Carolina, 1990), pp. xv, 9–16.

86. Kertzer, *Ritual, Politics and Power*, pp. 163–67, especially 164–65; Handelman, *Models and Mirrors*, pp. 41–42, 276, note 12.

87. Cited in David R. Kinsley, *Hinduism: A Cultural Perspective*, 2d ed. (Englewood Cliffs, N.J.: Prentice-Hall, 1993), pp. 107–08.

88. Louis Fischer, *The Life of Mahatma Gandhi* (New York: Harper and Row, 1950), pp. 273–74, cited in Kinsley, *Hinduism*, p. 108.

89. Albert Bergesen, *The Sacred and the Subversive: Political Witch-Hunts as National Rituals* (Storrs, Conn.: Society for the Study of Religion, 1984), p. viii.

90. Bergesen, *The Sacred and the Subversive*, p. 12.

91. Handelman, *Models and Mirrors*, pp. 266–69, especially p. 268.

92. See Gregor Goethals, *The TV Affair: Worship at the Video Altar* (Boston: Beacon, 1981).

93. Barbara E. Ward, "Not Merely Players: Drama, Art and Ritual in Traditional China," *Man* (n.s.) 14, no. 1 (March 1979): 18–39, p. 36. For other aspects of the Chinese interrelationship of theater and ritual see: Kristofer Schipper, *The Taoist Body*, trans. Karen C. Duval (Berkeley: University of California Press, 1993), pp. 44–55, 77–78; and Stephan Feuchtwang, *The Imperial Metaphor: Popular Religion in China* (London: Routledge, 1992), pp. 180–98; and David Johnson, ed., *Ritual Opera, Operatic Ritual* (Berkeley: Chinese Popular Culture Project, 1989).

94. Ward, "Not Merely Players," p. 21.

95. Ward, "Not Merely Players," p. 28.

96. Ward, "Not Merely Players," p. 35.

97. Richard Bauman, *Let Your Words Be Few: Symbolism of Speaking and Silence among Seventeenth-Century Quakers* (Cambridge: Cambridge University Press, 1983), p. 121, citing guidelines found in an epistle of Alexander Parker (1660).

98. Rappaport, *Ecology, Meaning and Religion*, p. 179.

99. A. L. Becker, "Text-Building, Epistemology, and Aesthetics in Javanese Shadow Theatre," in A. L. Becker and Aram A. Yengoyan, eds., *The Imagination of Reality: Essays in Southeast Asian Coherence Systems* (Norwood, N.J.: Ablex Publishing, 1979) pp. 214–15.

100. Rappaport, *Ecology, Meaning and Religion*, p. 174; also see Peter L. Berger and Thomas Luckmann, *The Social Construction of Reality: A Treatise in the Sociology of Knowledge* (Garden City, N.Y.: Doubleday-Anchor, 1967).

Chapter 6

1. For an example of this type of marriage symbolism, see Judith Romney Wegner, *Chattel or Person? The Status of Women in the Mishnah* (New York: Oxford University Press, 1988).

2. Valerio Valeri, *Kingship and Sacrifice*, pp. 135–39; also see Bell, *Ritual Theory, Ritual Practice*, pp. 124–40.

3. For two recent and fully compatible views, see Kenneth Dean, *Taoist Ritual and the Popular Cults of South-East China* (Princeton: Princeton University Press, 1993), especially pp. 173–86; and Stephan Feuchtwang, *The Imperial Metaphor*, especially pp. 150–79.

4. Pierre Smith, "Aspects of the Organizations of Rites," pp. 108–9.

5. Smith, "Aspects of the Organizations of Rites," pp. 110–16.

6. Roy A. Rappaport, "Veracity, Verity, and *Verum* in Liturgy," *Studia Liturgica* 23, no. 1 (1993): 35–38.

7. Rappaport, "Veracity, Verity, and *Verum* in Liturgy," pp. 39, 40, 44.

8. See Monica K. Hellwig, *The Meaning of the Sacraments* (Dayton, Ohio: Pflaum/Standard, 1981); and Joseph Martos, *Doors to the Sacred: A Historical Introduction to Sacraments in the Catholic Church* (Garden City, N.Y.: Doubleday, 1981). On the Vedic system, see Frits Staal, *Agni: The Vedic Ritual of the Fire Altar* (Berkeley, Calif.: Asian Humanities Press, 1983), vol. 1; B. K. Smith, *Reflections on Resemblance, Ritual and Religion* (New York: Oxford University Press, 1989); and Richard Davis, *Ritual in an Oscillating Universe* (Princeton, N.J.: Princeton University Press, 1991).

9. See John Lagerwey, *Taoist Ritual in Chinese Society and History* (New York: Macmillan, 1987); Sherry B. Ortner, *Sherpas Through Their Rituals*; Christel Lane, *The Rites of Rulers: Ritual In Industrial Society — The Soviet Case* (Cambridge: Cambridge University Press, 1981).

10. Bell, *Ritual Theory, Ritual Practice*, p. 130.

11. Max Weber, *The Protestant Ethic and the Spirit of Capitalism*, trans. Talcott Parsons (New York: Charles Scribner's Sons, 1958).

12. Robert N. Bellah, *Beyond Belief: Essays on Religion in a Post-Traditional World* (New York: Harper and Row, 1970), pp. 21, 24.

13. Max Weber, *The Sociology of Religion*, pp. 3, 27.

14. Weber, *Sociology of Religion*, pp. 26–27, 82.

15. Weber, *Sociology of Religion*, pp. 209, 254.

16. H. H. Gerth and C. Wright Mills, trans. and eds., *From Max Weber: Essays in Sociology* (New York: Oxford University Press, 1946), p. 325. Emphasis in the original.

17. Weber, *Sociology of Religion*, pp. l–liii.

18. Gerth and Mills, *From Max Weber*, p. 269, and Weber, *Sociology of Religion*, p. lii.

19. Bellah, *Beyond Belief*, pp, 16, 24.

20. Bellah, *Beyond Belief*, pp. 8, 28.

21. Bellah, *Beyond Belief*, pp. 29–32.

22. Bellah, *Beyond Belief*, pp. 32–36.

23. Bellah, *Beyond Belief*, pp. 36–39.

24. Bellah, *Beyond Belief*, pp. 40, 43.

25. Robert N. Bellah et al., *Habits of the Heart: Individualism and Commitment in American Life* (New York: Harper and Row, 1986), pp. 221, 233.

26. Joseph M. Kitagawa proposed a more economical version of the same sort of typology; see his "Primitive, Classical and Modern Religions: A Perspective on Understanding the History of Religions," in Joseph M. Kitagawa, ed., *The History of Religions: Essays on the Problem of Understanding* (Chicago: University of Chicago Press, 1967), pp. 39–65.

27. Grimes, *Ritual Criticism*, pp. 23–26.

28. For other applications of Douglas's categories, see Sheldon R. Isenberg and Dennis E. Own, "Bodies, Natural and Contrived: The Work of Mary Douglas," *Religious Studies Review* 3, no. 1 (January 1977): 1–16; and Jerome H. Neyrey, "Body Language in 1 Corinthians: The Use of Anthropological Models for Understanding Pual and His Opponents," *Semeia* 35 (1986): 129–70.

29. Douglas, *Natural Symbols*, pp. 32–3.

30. Douglas, *Natural Symbols*, pp. 33–34, 37–38.

31. Douglas, *Natural Symbols*, p. 35.

32. Serge Larose, "The Meaning of Africa in Haitian Vodu," in *Symbols and Sentiments: Cross-Cultural Studies in Symbolism*, ed. Ioan Lewis (New York: Academic Press, 1977), p. 85.

33. See Alfred Métraux, *Voodoo in Haiti* (New York: Schocken Books, 1972); and Karen McCarthy Brown, *Mama Lola: A Vodou Priestess in Brooklyn* (Berkeley: University of California Press, 1991).

34. Karen McCarthy Brown, "'Plenty Confidence in Myself,' The Initiation of a White Woman Scholar into Haitian Vodou," *Journal of Feminist Studies in Religion* 3, no. 1 (1987): 68–70, 74–75.

35. Felicitas D. Goodman, *How about Demons? Possession and Exorcism in the Modern World* (Bloomington: Indiana University Press, 1988), pp. xiii (forward by Linda Dégh) and xv.

36. David Aberle, *The Peyote Religion among the Navaho* (Chicago: Aldine, 1966), p. 196.

37. Mary Douglas, "The Contempt of Ritual I," *New Blackfriars* 49 (1968): 478. Larose, however, points to the moral values found in Haitian vodou; see "The Meaning of Africa," pp. 85–116.

38. Charles Stewart, *Demons and the Devil: Moral Imagination in Modern Greek Culture* (Princeton, N.J.: Princeton University Press, 1991).

39. See W. Theodore de Bary, Wing-tsit Chan, and Burton Waton, eds., *Sources of Chinese Tradition*, vol. 1 (New York: Columbia University Press, 1960), p. 210 ("Spring and Autumn Annals"), for the most readable translation of this section.

40. Watson, trans., *Hsün Tzu: Basic Writings*, pp. 71, 86.

41. John B. Henderson, *The Development and Decline of Chinese Cosmology* (New York: Columbia University Press, 1984).

42. David McMullen, "Bureaucrats and Cosmology: The Ritual Code of T'ang China," in *Rituals of Royalty: Power and Ceremonial in Traditional Societies*, ed. David Cannadine and Simon Price (Cambridge: Cambridge University Press, 1987), pp. 181–236.

43. Catherine Bell, "Ritualization of Texts and the Textualization of Ritual in the Codification of Taoist Liturgy," *History of Religions* 27, no. 4 (May 1988): 366–92.

44. Peter Burke, "The Repudiation of Ritual," pp. 226, 228, 233, 237.

45. Julia Mitchell Corbett, *Religion in America* (Englewood Cliffs, N.Y.: Prentice-Hall, 1990), pp. 67–68.

46. There are few formal discussions of these categories; see Shelia McDonough, "Orthodoxy and Heterodoxy," and Judith A. Berling, "Orthopraxy," in Mircea Eliade, ed., *The Encyclopedia of Religion*, vol. 11, pp. 124–29 and pp. 129–32.

47. For a fuller discussion, see Wilfred Cantwell Smith, *Faith and Belief* (Princeton, N.J.: Princeton University Press, 1979), pp. 13–14.

48. W. C. Smith, *Faith and Belief*, p. 15.

49. For the political circumstances of this codification project, see Hardacre, *Shinto and the State*.

50. W. C. Smith, *Faith and Belief*, pp. 14, 56–57.

51. Burke, "The Repudication of Ritual," p. 226.

52. W. C. Smith, *Faith and Belief*, pp. 14–15.

53. Jacob Neusner, "Ritual without Myth: The Use of Legal Materials for the Study of Religions," *Religion: Journal of Religion and Religions* 5 (Autumn 1975): 91, 100.

54. Menachem Friedman, "Life Tradition and Book Tradition in the Development of Ultraorthodox Judaism," in *Judaism Viewed from Within and from Without: Anthropological Studies*, ed. Harvey E. Goldberg (Albany: State University of New York, 1987), p. 235.

55. Samuel C. Heilman and Menachem Friedman, "Religious Fundamentalism and Religious Jews: The Case of the Haredim," in Martin E. Marty and R. Scott Appleby, eds., *Fundamentalisms Observed* (Chicago: University of Chicago Press, 1991), p. 199.

56. Samuel C. Heilman and Steven M. Cohen, "Ritual Variation among Modern Orthodox Jews in the United States," in *Studies in Contemporary Jewry* 2 (1986): 164. Also see Samuel Heilman, *Defenders of the Faith: Inside Ultra-Orthodox Jewry* (New York: Schocken, 1992), pp. 17–18.

57. Friedman, "Life Tradition and Book Tradition," pp. 239–40; Heilman and Friedman, "Religious Fundamentalism and Religious Jews," pp. 199–201.

58. Poll, *The Hasidic Community of Williamsburg*, pp. 59, 60.

59. Heilman and Cohen, "Ritual Variation," pp. 174–77.

60. Heilman and Cohen, "Ritual Variation," pp. 171, 175–76.

61. Shaye J. D. Cohen, "Can Converts to Judaism Say 'God of Our Fathers,'" *Judaism* 40, no. 4 (Fall 1991): 428.

62. Ephraim Tabory, "Jewish Identity, Israeli Nationalism, and Soviet Jewish Migration," *Journal of Church and State* 33, no. 2 (Spring 1991): 288.

63. Peter Steinfels, "Beliefs: Who Is Jewish," *New York Times*, August 7, 1993, p. 6A.

64. Richard C. Martin, *Islam: A Cultural Perspective* (Englewood Cliffs, N.J.: Prentice-Hall, 1982), p. 14.

65. W. C. Smith, *Faith and Belief*, pp. 183, 14.

66. Martin, *Islam*, p. 54.

67. Letter to the editor, "Islam Doesn't Sanction Rushdie Decree," by Ayatollah Jalal Ganjei (Paris), *New York Times* (March 11, 1993). Also see Leonard W. Levy, *Blasphemy: Verbal Offense against the Sacred from Moses to Salmon Rushdie* (New York: Knopf, 1993).

68. Douglas, *Natural Symbols*, pp. 64–65.

69. Robert Anthony Orsi, *The Madonna of 115th Street: Faith and Community in Italian Harlem, 1880–1950* (New Haven: Yale University Press, 1985), pp. xiii–xiv, xv.

70. Orsi, *The Madonna of 115th Street*, p. 131.

71. Notably, José Casanova, *Public Religions in the Modern World* (Chicago: University of Chicago Press, 1994); also see Jan Platvoet and Karel van der Toorn, eds., *Pluralism and Identity: Studies in Ritual Behavior* (Leiden: Brill, 1995).

72. For a readable analysis of secularization theories, see David Martin, "Sociology, Religion and Secularization: An Orientation," *Religion* 25, no. 4 (October 1995): 295–303.

73. Richard K. Fenn in "The Process of Secularization: A Post-Parsonian View," *Scientific Study of Religion* 9, no. 2 (Summer 1970): 117.

74. Fenn, "The Process of Secularization," p. 126.

75. Bellah et al., *Habits of the Heart*.

76. See the comprehensive overview in Karel Dobblaere, "Secularization: A Multi-Dimensional Concept," *Current Sociology* 29, no. 2 (Summer 1981): 1–213.

77. Thomas Luckmann, *The Invisible Religion: The Problem of Religion in Modern Society* (New York: Macmillan, 1967), p. 39.

78. Daniel Bell, "The Return of the Sacred? An Argument on the Future of Religion," in *The Winding Passage: Essays and Sociological Journeys 1960–1980* (Cambridge, Mass.: Abt Books, 1980), pp. 332–33.

79. Douglas, *Natural Symbols*, pp. 36, 40–41.

80. Burke, "The Repudiation of Ritual," p. 223.

81. Rodney Stark and William Sims Bainbridge, *The Future of Religion: Secularization, Revival, and Cult Formation* (Berkeley: University of California, 1985), pp. 1–2.

82. See Robert N. Bellah, "Civil Religion in America," *Daedalus* 96, no. 1 (1967): 1–21.

83. For a vivid, novelistic description of the dynamics of "secularization," see Chinua Achebe's story of the effect of missionaries on an Ibo village in *Things Fall Apart* ([1959] London: Heinemann, 1989); also, Cheikh Hamidou Kane, *Ambiguous Adventure* (New York: Macmillan, 1969).

84. Mary Douglas, "The Effects of Modernization on Religious Change," *Daedalus* 111, no. 1 (Winter 1982): 1.

85. Bellah et al., *Habits of the Heart*, p. 235.

86. See Martin, "Sociology, Religion and Secularization," especially p. 295.

87. See Richard K. Fenn, "Recent Studies of Church Decline: The Eclipse of Ritual," *Religious Studies Review* 8, no. 2 (April 1982): 124–28.

88. See Jack Goody and Ian Watt, "The Consequences of Literacy," in *Literacy in Traditional Societies*, ed. Jack R. Goody (Cambridge: Cambridge University Press, 1968), pp. 27–68. Also discussed in Catherine Bell, "The Authority of Ritual Experts," *Studia Liturgica* 23, no. 1 (1993): 104–09.

89. Th. P. van Baaren, "The Flexibility of Myth," in *Sacred Narrative: Readings in the Theory of Myth*, ed. Alan Dundes (Berkeley: University of California, 1984), p. 218. For other genealogical practices that support van Baaren's point, see Douglas L. Oliver, *Ancient Tahitian Society*, 3 vols. (Honolulu: University of Hawaii Press, 1974), pp. 624–25, 1117, 1179–81.

90. Van Baaren, "The Flexibility of Myth," p. 219.

91. On "canonical" and "indexical" dimensions of ritual practice and change, see Roy A. Rappaport, "The Obvious Aspects of Ritual," p. 179.

92. Goody and Watt, "The Consequences of Literacy," pp. 27–68.

93. Jack Goody, *The Interface between the Written and the Oral* (Cambridge: Cambridge University Press, 1987), p. 161.

94. According to Goody, it is a mistake to divide societies into oral and literate, since literacy never completely replaces orality, but he makes the distinction nonetheless (*The Interface between the Written and the Oral*, p. xii). For an excellent study of some of these dynamics in Chinese history, an exemplary instance of the interaction of ritual, literacy and texts, see Patricia Buckley Ebrey, *Confucianism and Family Rituals in Imperial China: A Social History of Writing about Rites* (Princeton, N.J.: Princeton University Press, 1991).

95. See, for example, Jeremy Boissevain, ed., *Revitalizing European Rituals* (London: Routledge, 1992).

96. See Ulf Hannerz, "Theory in Anthropology: Small Is Beautiful? The Problem of Complex Cultures," *Comparative Studies in Society and History* 28, no. 2 (1986): 362–67.

97. Stark and Bainbridge, *The Future of Religion*, pp. 21–23; Bryan R. Wilson, "An Analysis of Sect Development," in *Patterns of Sectarianism* (London: Heinemann, 1967), pp. 23–25.

98. Stark and Bainbridge, *The Future of Religion*, pp. 22–23.

99. While Bryan Wilson offers a descriptive classification of various types of sects ("An Analysis of Sect Development," pp. 25–29), Stark and Bainbridge describe and classify cults (Stark and Bainbridge, *The Future of Religion*, pp. 25, 26–30).

100. Robert S. Ellwood and Harry B. Partin, *Religious and Spiritual Groups in Modern America*, 2d ed. (Englewood Cliffs, N.J.: Prentice Hall, 1988).

101. J. Z. Smith, *Imagining Religion*, pp. 102–20.

102. Stark and Bainbridge, *The Future of Religion*, pp. 26, 529–30.

103. For a discussion of cult activity among well-to-do suburbanites, see Steven M. Gelber and Martin L. Cook, *Saving the Earth: A History of a Middle-Class Millenarian Movement* (Berkeley: University of California Press, 1990).

104. For an economic analysis of these forces, see Laurence R. Iannaccone, "A Formal Model of Church and Sect," *American Journal of Sociology* 94, supplement (1988): S241–S268.

105. Cited in Corbett, *Religion in America*, p. 198; on evangelism, see pp. 196–98.

Chapter 7

1. Eric R. Wolf, *Europe and the People without History* (Berkeley: University of California Press, 1982).

2. Jean Comaroff, *Body of Power*.

3. On the Bwiti cult among the Fang, see James Fernandez, "Symbolic Consensus in a Fang Reformative Cult," *American Anthropologist* 67 (1965): 902–29, especially pp. 914–15; and Bell, *Ritual Theory, Ritual Practice*, pp. 183, 213.

4. Clifford Geertz, "Ritual and Social Change: A Javanese Example," in *The Interpretation of Culture*, pp. 142–69; also see Bell, *Ritual Theory, Ritual Practice*, pp. 33–34.

5. Compare Cheslyn Jones, Geoffrey Wainwright, Edward Yarnold, S.J., and Paul Bradshaw, eds., *The Study of the Liturgy*, rev. ed. (New York: Oxford University Press, 1992), p. 61.

6. Also Jones et al., eds., *The Study of the Liturgy*, p. 61. Among the best studies of Christian liturgical change is the work of John Bossy, especially *Christianity in the West, 1400–1700* (New York: Oxford University Press, 1985). For a complete bibliography, see Paul Post, "John Bossy and the Study of Liturgy," in Charles Caspers and Marc Schneiders, eds., *Omnes Circumadstantes: Contributions Towards a History of the Role of the People in the Liturgy* (Kampen: Uitgeversmaatschappij J. H. Kok, 1990), pp. 31–50.

7. John G. Gager, *Kingdom and Community: The Social World of Early Christianity* (Englewood Cliffs, N.J.: Prentice-Hall, 1975), pp. 122, 139.

8. Senn, *Christian Worship*, p. 21.

9. Baruch M. Bokser, *The Origins of the Seder*.

10. Senn, *Christian Worship*, p. 22.

11. For a fuller discussion, see Catherine Bell, "Ritual, Change and Changing Rituals," *Worship* 63, no. 1 (January 1989): 37; and Gregory Dix, *The Shape of the Liturgy*, rev. ed. (New York: Seabury, 1983), pp. 12–15.

12. Bard Thompson, *Liturgies of the Western Church* (Philadelphia: Fortress Press, 1961), pp. 3–4.

13. Thompson, *Liturgies of the Western Church*, pp. 6–7.

14. Mark Searle, "The Rites of Christian Initiation," in *Betwixt and Between: Patterns of Masculine and Feminine Initiation*, ed. by Louise Carus Mahdi, Steven Foster, and Meredith Little (LaSalle, Ill.: Open Court, 1987), p. 457.

15. Senn, *Christian Worship*, p. 30; Jones et al., eds., *The Study of the Liturgy*, pp. 68–80.

16. *The Treatise on the Apostolic Tradition of Saint Hippolytus of Rome*, ed. and trans. Gregory Dix (London: SPCK, 1968), pp. 30–38; also see Jones et al., eds., *The Study of Liturgy*, pp. 87–89.

17. Gager, *Kingdom and Community*, pp. 137–38.

18. Gager, *Kingdom and Community*, pp. 123, 125–26, 128.

19. Senn, *Christian Worship*, pp. 41–42; Jones et al., eds., *The Study of Liturgy*, pp. 486–87, 499–500, 528–35.

20. Senn, *Christian Worship*, pp. 32–34; J. A. Jungmann, S.J., "The State of Liturgical Life on the Eve of the Reformation," in *Pastoral Liturgy* (New York: Herder and Herder, 1962), pp. 64–80.

21. Jones et al., eds., *The Study of Liturgy*, p. 64; Dix, *The Shape of the Liturgy*, pp. 303–305.

22. Thompson, *Liturgies of the Western Church*, p. 48.

23. J. A. Jungmann, "The State of Liturgical Life," pp. 66–72.

24. Jones et al., eds., *The Study of Liturgy*, p. 64.

25. See Keith Thomas, *Religion and the Decline of Magic* (New York: Scribner's, 1971), pp. 151–53.

26. See Michael Aune, *"To Move the Heart": Rhetoric and Ritual in the Theology of Philip Melanchthon* (San Francisco: Christian Universities Press, 1994).

27. Jones et al., eds., *The Study of Liturgy*, p. 65.

28. J. Lamberts, "Active Participation as the Gateway towards an Ecclesial Liturgy," in Charles Caspers and Marc Schneiders, eds., *Omnes Circumadstantes*, pp. 234–61.

29. Vatican Council, *Constitution on the Sacred Liturgy* (Collegeville, Minn.: Liturgical Press, 1963), section III, article 21. See A. Bugnini and C. Braga, eds., *The Commentary on the Constitution and on the Instruction of the Sacred Liturgy*, trans. by V. P. Mallon (New York: Benziger Brothers, 1965), pp. 13, 84, 100.

30. See Bell, "Ritual, Change and Changing Ritual," pp. 38–40; R. Grainger, *The Language of the Rite* (London: Darton, Longman and Todd, 1974); Mark Searle, ed., *Liturgy and Social Justice* (Collegeville, Minn.: Liturgical Press, 1980); A. J. Chupungco, *Cultural Adaptation of the Liturgy* (New York: Paulist, 1982); and *Liturgies of the Future: The Process and Methods of Inculturation* (New York: Paulist, 1989).

31. For excellent statement of this, see Helen Rose Ebaugh, "The Revitalization Movement in the Catholic Church: The Institutional Dilemma of Power," *Sociological Analysis* 52 (1991): 1–12.

32. On the Vedic tradition of ritual study, see Frits Staal, *Agni*.

33. W. J. O'Shea, "Liturgiology," *New Catholic Encyclopedia*, vol. 8 (Washington, D.C.: Catholic University of America, 1967), pp. 919–27.

34. For example, Joseph A. Jungmann, *The Mass of the Roman Rite*, 2 vols., trans. F. A. Brunner (New York: Benziger, 1951); Dix, *The Shape of the Liturgy*; Louis Bouyer, *Rite and Man: Natural Sacredness and Christian Sacraments* (Notre Dame, Ind.: University of Notre Dame Press, 1963); Jean Daniélou (1905–1974), *The Bible and the Liturgy* (Notre Dame, Ind.: University of Notre Dame Press, 1956); Anton Baumstark (1872–1948), *Comparative Liturgy* (Westminister, Md.: Newman Press, 1958).

35. Odo Casel, *The Mystery of Christian Worship and Other Writings* [1932], ed. by Burkhard Neunheuser, O.S.B. (Westminister, Md.: Newman Press, 1962), pp. 6, 33–34.

36. See Louis Bouyer, *Rite and Man*, pp. 34–35; also *Liturgical Piety* (Notre Dame, Ind.: University of Notre Dame Press, 1955), pp. 86–98.

37. *The Constitution of the Sacred Liturgy*, #21–40, in *Commentary on the Constitution and on the Institution on the Sacred Liturgy*, ed. A. Bugnini and C. Braga.

38. See Chupungco, *Cultural Adaptation of the Liturgy*, p. 434; and *Liturgies of the Future*. It is interesting to note that Zhu Xi, the Chinese medieval reformer of the classical canon of rites, made the same distinction by arguing that ritual has both "fundamental elements" and "elaborations"; the first must never be changed, while the second must be kept in their place, not crowding out the fundamental elements and adapted as needed to make the essential parts relevant to the people. See Patricia Buckley Ebrey, *Chu Hsi's Family Rituals* (Princeton, N.J.: Princeton University Press, 1991), p. 3.

39. For example, see Janet Walton and Marjorie Procter-Smith, eds. *Women at Worship: Interpretations of North American Diversity* (Louisville, Ky.: Westminister/John Knox Press, 1993); Charlotte Canon, *To Make and Make Again: Feminist Ritual Thealogy* (New York: Crossroad, 1993).

40. Examples include: Robert Taft, S.J., *Beyond East and West: Problems in Liturgical Understanding* (Washington, D.C.: Pastoral Press, 1984); Mary Collins, "Critical Ritual Studies: Examining an Intersection of Theology and Culture," in *The Bent World: Essays on Religion and Culture*, ed. John R. May (Missoula, Mt.: Scholars Press, 1981).

41. Margaret Mary Kelleher, OSU., "The Communion Rite: A Study of Roman Catholic Liturgical Performance," *Journal of Ritual Studies* 5, no. 2 (Summer 1991): 99–122; G. Ronald Murphy, S.J., "A Ceremonial Ritual: The Mass," in Eugene G. d'Aquili, Charles D. Laughlin, Jr., and John McManus, eds., *The Spectrum of Ritual: A Biogenetic Approach* (New York: Columbia University Press, 1979), pp. 318–41.

42. See Ronald L. Grimes, *Ritual Criticism*, pp. 28–62 for his evaluation of a report, *Liturgical Renewal, 1963–1988: A Study of English Speaking Parishes in the United States*, commissioned by American bishops.

43. Tom F. Driver, *The Magic of Ritual* (New York: Harper Collins, 1991).

44. R. T. Beckwith, "Thomas Cranmer and the Prayer Book," in Jones et al., eds., *The Study of Liturgy*, pp. 101–5. Although Cranmer worked with an edition of the first prayer book of Edward VI, which had been preceded by various vernacular texts, Cranmer is credited with the special beauty of the language found in the BCP.

45. Stephen Neill, "Liturgical Continuity and Change in the Anglican Churches," in David Martin and Peter Mullen, eds., *No Alternative: The Prayer Book Controversy* (Oxford: Basil Blackwell, 1981), pp. 1–11; Beckwith, "The Prayer Book after Cranmer," pp. 106–10.

46. Parliament relinquished any responsibility for the Church of England in 1974, *except* for the power to authorize "forms of service other than those prescibed in the BCP of 1662"; see Martin and Mullen, eds., *No Alternative*, p. 203.

47. Jones et al., eds., *The Study of the Liturgy*, p. 66. Needless to say, the revisions introduced more gender-neutral language in place of the male-centered language of earlier translators.

48. Brian Morris, "Introduction," in *Ritual Murder: Essays on Liturgical Reform*, ed. by Brian Morris (Manchester: Carcanet Press, 1980), p. 7.

49. Neill, "Liturgical Continuity and Change," pp. 9, 10; and David Martin, "Personal Identity and a Changed Church," in Martin and Mullen, eds., *No Alternative*, p. 10.

50. See Bell, "Ritual, Change, and Changing Rituals," pp. 31–33; David Martin, *The Breaking of the Image* (New York: St. Martin's Press, 1979); Victor Turner, "Ritual, Tribal and Catholic," *Worship* 50 (November 1976): 504–26; Mary Douglas, "The Contempt of Ritual," and *Natural Symbols*, pp. 59–76.

51. For a dramatic example, see Eamon Duffy, *The Stripping of the Altars: Traditional Religion in England, c. 1400–c.1580* (New Haven: Yale University Press, 1992).

52. Lane, *The Rites of Rulers*, p. 45.

53. Mary Collins, "Liturgical Methodology and the Cultural Evolution of Worship in the United States," *Worship* 49, no. 2 (1975): 87; also "Critical Ritual Studies," p. 132. Also see Bell, "The Authority of Ritual Experts," p. 100.

54. Grimes, *Ritual Criticism*, p. 109; also "Reinventing Rites," *Soundings* 75, no. 1 (Spring 1992): 21–41.

55. Barbara Myerhoff, "A Death in Due Time," p. 152.

56. Myerhoff, "A Death in Due Time," p. 158.

57. Mark C. Carnes, *Secret Ritual*, pp. 5–11, especially p. 9.

58. See Leigh Eric Schmidt, "From Arbor Day to the Environmental Sabbath: Nature, Liturgy, and American Protestantism," *Harvard Theological Review* 84, no. 3 (1991): 299–323.

59. Gelber and Cook, *Saving the Earth*.

60. Lane, *The Rites of Rulers*; Jennifer McDowell, "Soviet Civil Ceremonies," *Journal for the Scientific Study of Religion* 13 (1974): 265–79; Ethel Dunn and Stephen P. Dunn, "Religious Behavior and Socio-cultural Change in the Soviet Union," in Bohdan R. Bociurkiw and John W. Strong, eds., *Religion and Atheism in the USSR and Eastern Europe* (Toronto: University of Toronto Press, 1975); Christopher A. P. Binns, "The Changing Face of Power: Revolution and Accommodation in the Development of the Soviet Ceremonial System: Part I," *Man* 14, no. 4 (1979): 585–606.

61. Lane, *The Rites of Rulers*, pp. 4, 27, 45.

62. For a notable exception, see McDowell, "Soviet Civil Ceremonies," pp. 276–77.

63. See Dunn and Dunn, "Religious Behavior and Socio-cultural Change," p. 143.

64. Lane, *The Rites of Rulers*, pp. 28–31.

65. Lane, *The Rites of Rulers*, pp. 33–34, 49.

66. Lane, *The Rites of Rulers*, pp. 46–48.

67. Lane, *The Rites of Rulers*, pp. 50–52.

68. Lane, *The Rites of Rulers*, pp. 58, 61–64.

69. Lane, *The Rites of Rulers*, pp. 54–57.

70. Lane, *The Rites of Rulers*, pp. 67–69.

71. Lane, *The Rites of Rulers*, pp. 76–77.

72. Lane, *The Rites of Rulers*, p. 64.

73. Lane, *The Rites of Rulers*, pp. 110–13.

74. Hobsbawm, "Mass-Producing Traditions," pp. 279–80.

75. Stuart Berg Flexner, *I Hear America Talking* (New York: Van Nostrand Reinhold, 1976), p. 337.

76. Hobsbawm, "Mass-Producing Traditions," p. 280.

77. George P. Fletcher, "Update the Pledge," p. 19.

78. Fletcher, "Update the Pledge," p. 19.

79. Pierre de Coubertin, *The Olympic Idea: Discourses and Essays*. ed. Carl-Diem-Institut (Stuttgart: Hofmann, 1967), pp. 86–87. Also see John J. MacAloon, "Olympic Games," pp. 248–50.

80. Mary Gluckman and Max Gluckman, "On Drama," pp. 237–38.

81. John J. MacAloon, "Double Visions: Olympic Games and American Culture," *Kenyon Review*, n.s. 4 (1982): 104; MacAloon, "Olympic Games," pp. 241–42; de Coubertin, *The Olympic Idea*, p. vii.

82. John J. MacAloon, "*La Pintada Olímpica*: Puerto Rico, International Sport, and the Constitution of Politics," in *Text, Play, and Story: The Construction and Reconstruction*

of Self and Society, ed. Edward M. Bruner (Washington, D.C.: American Ethnological Society, 1984), pp. 315–16.

83. MacAloon, "Olympic Games," pp. 250–51.

84. De Coubertin, *The Olympic Idea*, p. 56.

85. MacAloon, "Double Visions," p. 100; Alex Markels, "A Run to Moonlight for Food and More," *New York Times*, August 21, 1994, p. 24.

86. MacAloon, "Olympic Games," p. 252.

87. De Coubertin, *The Olympic Idea*, pp. 15, 34–35, 118.

88. Cited in MacAloon, "Olympic Games," p. 257.

89. American athletes have certainly not been immune to nationalism, even when they have some ambivalence about the experience. Dick Fosbury of Oregon, inventor of the "Fosbury flop" in the high jump, entered the Olympics as an individual, seeing himself as one person competing against other individuals. Yet he became unexpectedly emotional and patriotic when, in the context of the games, he heard the American national anthem. "Being a college student at that time, I was against everything the government was doing as far as Viet Nam . . . I really was kind of unpatriotic. And then I go to the Olympic Games and they play the anthem and I get this overwhelming feeling and it was pretty confusing. I couldn't believe it was happening. I guess it didn't make any sense to me. Maybe I did feel proud to be an American and proud to be from Oregon and proud to be representing my friends and different people from my hometown, but at the same time I didn't respect the government." See MacAloon, "Double Visions" pp. 108–10.

90. MacAloon, *This Great Symbol*, p. 219.

91. MacAloon, "Double Visions," p. 98.

92. As a result of this planned act of defiant politics, both men were suspended from the U.S. team, evicted from the Olympic Village, and forced to leave Mexico.

93. Neil Amdur, "Munich 1972: Tragic Blot on Olympic Family Memory," *New York Times*, September 6, 1992, p. 25 (sports section).

94. Maulana Karenga, *Kwanzaa*; and *The African-American Holiday of Kwanzaa: A Celebration of Family, Community and Culture* (Los Angeles: University of Sankore Press, 1988).

95. Karenga, *Kwanzaa*, pp.12–14, 16, 53–54.

96. On American Christmas practices not so rooted in European history, see Penne L. Restand, *Christmas in America: A History* (New York: Oxford University Press, 1995).

97. Haki R. Madhubuti, *Kwanzaa: An African-American Holiday That Is Progressive and Uplifting* (Chicago: Third World Press, 1972), p. 13.

98. See David A. Anderson, *Kwanzaa: An Everyday Resource and Instructional Guide* (New York: Gumbs and Thomas, 1992); Eric V. Copage, *Kwanzaa: An African-American Celebration of Culture and Cooking* (New York: Morrow, 1991); and Cedric McClester, *Kwanzaa: Everything You Always Wanted to Know But Didn't Know Where to Ask* (Gumbs and Thomas, 1990).

99. Michel Marriott, "New Side of Kwanzaa: Marketing," *New York Times*, December 25, 1991.

100. Richard E. Kuykendall, *Liturgies of the Earth* (Brea, Calif.: Educational Ministries, 1992), p. 5.

101. Also see Hallie Iglehard, *Womanspirit: A Guide to Women's Wisdom* (San Francisco: Harper and Row, 1983); and Barbara G. Walker, *Women's Rituals: A Sourcebook* (San Francisco: Harper and Row, 1990).

102. "Women Explore Drums as Means of Expression," *New York Times*, January 2, 1993, pp. 21, 27.

103. Cited in Kay Turner, "Contemporary Feminist Rituals," in *The Politics of Women's Spirituality: Essays on the Rise of Spiritual Power within the Feminist Movement*, ed. Charlene Spretnak (Garden City, N.Y.: Doubleday Anchor, 1982), pp. 219.

104. Turner, "Contemporary Feminist Rituals," pp. 222.

105. Starhawk [Miriam Simos], *The Spiral Dance: A Rebirth of the Ancient Religion of the Great Goddess*, 10th anniversary edition (San Francisco: HarperCollins, 1989), pp. 200, 201–3.

106. See Judy Grahn, "From Sacred Blood to the Curse and Beyond," in Spretnak, ed., *The Politics of Women's Spirituality*, pp. 265–79; also Karen Ericksen Paige and Jeffery M. Paige, *The Politics of Reproductive Ritual* (Berkeley: University of California Press, 1981).

107. E. M. Broner, "Honor and Ceremony in Women's Rituals," in Spretnak, ed., *The Politics of Women's Spirituality*, pp. 237–38.

108. Rosemary Radford Ruether, *Women-Church: Theology and Practice of Feminist Liturgical Communities* (San Francisco: Harper and Row, 1985).

109. Marjorie Procter-Smith, *In Her Own Rite: Constructing Feminist Liturgical Tradition* (Nashville: Abingdon, 1990), p. 13; Sharon Neufer Emswiler and Thomas Neufer Emswiler, *Women and Worship: A Guide to Nonsexist Hymns, Prayers, and Liturgies*, rev. ed. (San Francisco: Harper and Row, 1984); also see Marjorie Procter-Smith and Janet R. Walton, eds. *Women at Worship: Interpretations of North American Diversity* (Louisville, Ky: Westminister/John Knox Press, 1993).

110. Cited in Douglas Brown, "Our Mother, Which Art in Heaven?" *History Today*, 42 (November 1992): 8–9.

111. Robert Bly, *Iron John: A Book about Men* (New York: Random House, 1990), p. ix.

112. Bly, *Iron John*, pp. x–xi.

113. Bly, *Iron John*, p. 35.

114. See Loring M. Danforth, *Firewalking and Religious Healing: The Anastenaria of Greece and the American Firewalking Movement* (Princeton, N.J.: Princeton University Press, 1989).

115. Joan Laird, "Women and Ritual in Family Therapy," in Evan Imber-Black, Janine Roberts, and Richard A. Whiting, eds., *Rituals in Families and Family Therapy* (New York: W. W. Norton, 1988), pp. 331–62.

116. Onno van der Hart, *Rituals in Psychotherapy: Transition and Continuity* (New York: Irvington Publishers, 1978); Evan Imber-Black and Janine Roberts, *Rituals for Our Times: Celebrating, Healing, and Changing Our Lives and Our Relationships* (San Francisco: HarperCollins, 1992).

117. Elisabeth Rosenthal, "Struggling to Handle Bereavement As AIDS Rips Relationships Apart," *New York Times*, December 6, 1992, pp. 1A, 21A.

118. Renee Beck and Sydney B. Metrick, *The Art of Ritual: A Guide to Creating and Performing Your Own Rituals for Growth and Change* (Berkeley, Calif.: Celestial Arts, 1990).

119. Grimes, *Ritual Criticism*, pp. 112–13, 123–25.

120. Bron Taylor, "Earthen Spirituality or Cultural Genocide?: Radical Environmentalism's Appropriation of Native American Spirituality," *Religion* 27, no. 2 (April 1997): 183–215.

121. Verner Bradford Phillips and Harvey Blume, *Ota Benga: The Pygmy in the Zoo* (New York: Delta, 1992), pp. 148–49.

122. On role of the media in the Olympic games, see James F. Larson and Heung-Soo Park, *Global Television and the Politics of the Seoul Olympics* (Boulder, Colo.: Westview Press, 1993).

123. Shils and Young, "The Meaning of the Coronation," pp. 70–71, 73–74, 78.

124. Katy Radford, *Elizabeth Is Queen: The Coronation of Her Majesty Queen Elizabeth II, June 2nd, 1953, Westminister Abbey*, videocassette (London: Pathe and Castle, 1992).

125. On Benjamin and this question, see Daniel Dayan and Elihu Katz, "Electronic Ceremonies: Television Performs a Royal Wedding," in Marshall Blonsky, ed., *On Signs* (Baltimore: Johns Hopkins University Press, 1985), p. 16.

126. Dayan and Katz, "Electronic Ceremonies," p. 25.

127. Dayan and Katz, "Electronic Ceremonies," p. 25–32.

128. Takashi Fujitani, "Electronic Pageantry and Japan's 'Symbolic Emperor,'" *The Journal of Asian Studies* 51, no. 4 (November 1992): 826, 828.

129. Fujitani, "Electronic Pageantry," p. 825.

130. Bradley Greenberg and Edwin B. Parker, eds., *The Kennedy Assassination and the American Public* (Stanford, Calif.: Stanford University Press, 1965); Elihu Katz and Daniel Dayan, "Media Events: On the Experience of Not Being There," *Religion* 15 (1985): 305–14; Barbie Zelizer, *Covering the Body: The Kennedy Assassination, the Media, and the Shaping of Collective Memory* (Chicago: University of Chicago Press, 1991).

131. Lawrence E, Sullivan, *Histories and Rituals: The Case of a National Rite of Mourning*, Twelfth annual university lecture in religion (Tempe: Arizona State University, 1991), p. 4.

132. Jean Cazeneuve, "Television as a Functional Alternative to Traditional Sources of Need Satisfaction," in Jay G. Blumer and Elihu Katz, eds., *The Uses of Mass Communications: Current Perspectives on Gratification Research* (Beverly Hills, Calif.: Sage Publications, 1974), pp. 216–17. Compare the different relationship between media and message analyzed by Umberto Eco in "The Myth of Superman," *Diacritics* 2 (1972): 14–22, reprinted in *Contemporary Literary Criticism*, ed. R. Davis (New York: Longman, 1986), pp. 330–44.

133. Cazeneuve, "Television as a Functional Alternative," p. 219.

134. Gregor T. Goethals, *The T.V. Affair*, pp. 6–7, 11–17, 20–21, 25–26.

135. Goethals, *The T.V. Affair*, pp. 36–56.

136. Juzo Itami, *Funeral [Ososhiki]*, [1984] (Chicago: Facets Video, 1986).

137. The film footage and recordings were condensed into the film, *Altar of Fire*, with the full documentation contained in the two-volume *Agni: The Vedic Ritual of the Fire Altar*, ed. Frits Staal (Berkeley, Calif.: Asian Humanities Press, 1983), which also contains two audiocassettes.

138. Staal, *Agni*, vol. 1, pp. xxii–xxiii, 2–3.

139. Richard Schechner, "Wrestling against Time: The Performance Aspects of Agni," *Journal of Asian Studies* 45, no. 2 (February 1989): 360; Richard Schechner, *Between Theater and Anthropology* (Philadelphia: University of Pennsylvania Press, 1985), pp. 55–65.

140. Schechner, "Wrestling against Time," p. 361.

141. Staal, *Agni*, vol. 2, p. 468; and Frits Staal, "Communications to the Editor," *Journal of Asian Studies* 46, no. 1 (February 1987): 106–7.

142. Schechner, "Wrestling against Time," pp. 361–62.

143. Gilbert Sigaux, *History of Tourism* (London: Leisure Arts, 1966); Dean MacCannell, *The Tourist: A New Theory of the Leisure Class*, rev. ed. (New York: Schocken, 1989); N. H. H. Graburn, *The Anthropology of Tourism* (New York: Pergamon Press, 1983).

144. Erik Cohen, "Pilgrimage and Tourism: Convergence and Divergence," in *Sacred Journeys: The Anthropology of Pilgrimage*, ed. Alan Morinis (Westport, Conn.: Greenwood Press, 1992), pp. 48–49, 50–52, 59. Also see Paul Post, "The Modern Pilgrim: A Study of Contemporary Pilgrims' Accounts," *Ethnologia Europea* 24, no. 2 (1994): 85–100.

145. See Valene L. Smith, ed., *Hosts and Guests: The Anthropology of Tourism* (Philadelphia: University of Pennsylvania Press, 1977).

146. James Clifford, *The Predicament of Culture: Twentieth-Century, Ethnography, Literature and Art* (Cambridge, Mass.: Harvard University Press, 1988), p. 196. Also see Regina

Bendix, "Tourism and Cultural Displays: Inventing Traditions for Whom?" *Journal of American Folklore* 102, no. 404 (1989): 131–46.

147. *The New York Times Magazine*, section 6 (March 3, 1996), p. 91, advertisement for Tova Gilead, Inc.

148. Toby Alice Volkman, "Visions and Revisions: Toraja Culture and the Tourist Gaze," *American Ethnologist* 17, no. 1 (February 1990): 101–7.

149. David J. Boyd, "The Commercialization of Ritual in the Eastern Highlands of Papua New Guinea," *Man* n.s. **20**: 325–40.

150. Ventine Tsai, "For Better or Worse? Festivals and the Media," trans. Christopher Hughes, *Sinorama* (July 1992): 98–100.

151. Xia Li, "China Heritage '94: The Year to Retrace People and Places from the Distant Past," *China Today* 43, no. 1 (January 1994): 33.

152. Exiang Zhi, "History and Tourism: Mausoleum of Emperor Yan," *China Today* 43, no. 1 (January 1994): 35–41.

153. On ritual as "restored behavior," see Schechner, *Between Theater and Anthropology*, pp. 35–116.

154. Sam D. Gill, *Native American Religions: An Introduction* (Belmont, Calif.: Wadsworth, 1982), pp. 148–49.

155. Sam D. Gill, *Beyond the Primitive: The Religions of Nonliterate Peoples* (Englewood Cliffs, N.J.: Prentice-Hall, 1982), pp. 74–77.

Chapter 8

1. Burke, "The Repudiation of Ritual," pp. 223–4.

2. For an analysis of stages in the development of a "rational" project to study "religion," see Preus, *Explaining Religion*, pp. 3–103.

3. Douglas, *Purity and Danger*, pp. 18–19.

4. Burke, "The Repudiation of Ritual," p. 223.

5. Geertz, *Intepretation of Culture*, p. 108.

6. Burke, "The Repudiation of Ritual," pp. 224–28, 236.

7. Burke,"The Repudiation of Ritual," p. 233.

8. Janet Aviad, *Return to Judaism: Religious Renewal in Israel* (Chicago: University of Chicago Press, 1983), p. ix.

9. Heilman and Friedman, "Religious Fundamentalism and Religious Jews," pp. 197–264; Heilman, *Defenders of the Faith*, pp. 14–39, 156–58.

10. M. Herbert Danzger, *Returning to Tradition: The Contemporary Revival of Orthodox Judaism* (New Haven: Yale University Press, 1989), pp. 1–2, 328.

11. Aviad, *Return to Judaism*, p. ix.

12. Danzger, *Returning to Tradition*, p. 328.

13. Danzger, *Returning to Tradition*, pp. 330–31; Peter L. Berger, *The Sacred Canopy: Elements of a Sociological Theory of Religion* (New York: Doubleday, 1967), pp. 45–51.

14. Lynn Davidman, *Tradition in a Rootless World: Women Turn to Orthodox Judaism* (Berkeley: University of California Press, 1991), pp. 26, 45, 192, 194. For a personal account, see Shira Dicker, "Mikva," *Tikkun* 7, no. 6 (1992): 62–64.

15. Peter Steinfels, "More Protestants Accept Ashes as Ritual for Lent," *New York Times* (February 24, 1993), p. B12.

16. Mary Douglas, "The Effects of Modernization," 2, 5.

17. Crapanzano, "Rite of Return: Circumcision in Morocco," 15–36; see chapter 1 in this book.

18. For a discussion of these approaches, see Richard Schechner, *The Future of Ritual: Writings on Culture and Performance* (London: Routledge, 1993), pp. 250–51, 253.

19. Tom F. Driver, *The Magic of Ritual*, pp. 8, 33, 79, 99–101.

20. Asad, *Genealogies*, pp. 56–57. The *Oxford English Dictionary* gives a more complicated picture of the evidence that Asad deduces from the *Britannica*, probably because it includes adjectival forms as well.

21. See the excerpt from Bourke's account in Sam D. Gill, *Native American Traditions*, pp. 39–41. Also see Bell, *Ritual Theory, Ritual Practice*, p. 29.

22. Stephen Greenblatt, "Filthy Rites," *Daedalus* 111, no. 3 (Summer 1982):1–3.

23. Christopher Winters, ed., *International Dictionary of Anthropologists* (New York: Garland, 1991), p. 132.

24. Sam D. Gill, "Nonliterate Traditions and Holy Books: Toward a New Model," in *The Holy Book in Comparative Perspective*, ed. Frederick M. Denny and Rodney L. Taylor (Columbia: University of South Carolina Press, 1985), p. 225.

25. Gill, "Nonliterate Traditions and Holy Books," p. 225.

26. Greenblatt, "Filthy Rites," p. 3.

27. R. David Arkush and Leo O. Lee, eds., *Land without Ghosts: Chinese Impressions of America from the Mid-Nineteenth Century to the Present* (Berkeley: University of California Press, 1989), pp. 16, 55–56.

28. Robertson Smith, *Lectures on the Religion of the Semites*, p. 338.

29. T. O. Beidelman, *W. Robertson Smith*, pp. 13–22. As Beidelman notes, the trial was technically for libel but widely understood to concern heresy (pp. 13, 17).

30. T. O. Beidelman, *W. Robertson Smith*, pp. 13–22. For another application of the myth-ritual pattern to Christianity, see E. O. James, "The Sources of Christian Ritual," in Samuel H. Hooke, ed., *The Labyrinth: Further Studies in the Relation between Myth and Ritual in the Ancient World* (New York: Macmillan, 1935), pp. 235–60.

31. Beidelman, *W. Robertson Smith*, pp. 26, 30–31.

32. See Joseph Henninger, "Ist der sogenannte Nilus-Bericht eine brauchbare religionsgeschichtliche Quelle?" *Anthropus* 50 (1955): 81–148; see Mircea Eliade, *Occultism, Witchcraft and Cultural Fashions: Essays in Comparative Religion* (Chicago: University of Chicago Press, 1976), pp. 6–7.

33. Just as some anthropologists have argued that the production of texts is integral to this process of creating "ritual" as a transcultural object of study (James Clifford and George E. Marcus, eds., *Writing Culture: The Poetics and Politics of Ethnography* [Berkeley: University of California, 1986], pp. 1–26), so is a network of scholars defined as professionals distinguished from practitioners. See Bruno Latour, *Science in Action* (Cambridge: Harvard University Press, 1987) and *We Have Never Been Modern*, trans. Catherine Porter (Cambridge: Harvard University Press, 1993).

34. Jack Goody, "Against 'Ritual': Loosely Structured Thoughts on a Loosely Defined Topic," in *Secular Ritual*, ed. Sally F. Moore and Barbara G. Myerhoff (Amsterdam: Van Gorcum, 1977), pp. 25–35.

35. Mahdi et al., eds., *Betwixt and Between*, p. ix.

36. Contested primarily on gender grounds, by Bruce Lincoln and Caroline Walker Bynum; see the discussion of the Mukanda ritual in chapter 2.

37. Beck and Metrick, *The Art of Ritual*, p. i.

38. Paul A. Holmes, "A Catechumenate for Marriage: Presacramental Preparation as Pilgrimage," *Journal of Ritual Studies* 6, no. 2 (Summer 1992): 93–113.

39. Victor Turner, Mary Douglas, Ronald Grimes—and I to a lesser extent—have all been involved in various forms of consultation as ritual experts. Grimes coined the term

"ritology" to designate this form of expertise, describing the ritologist as someone concerned with assessing the effectiveness of rituals. He argues that the ritologist is just an elaboration of an internal process of assessing a rite after its completion, a process that is a common and perhaps necessary part of the ongoing dynamics by which ritual forms are interpreted, reunderstood, and renuanced. See Grimes, *Ritual Criticism,* pp. 3–4, 9.

40. See Tom F. Driver, *The Magic of Ritual.*

41. For a critique of the ability of this perspective on ritual to understand practice in Islam, see Asad, *Genealogies,* pp. 55, 57, 79.

42. Asad, *Genealogies,* pp. 55, 57, 79.

43. Richard Schechner, *The Future of Ritual,* p. 263.

44. Bell, *Ritual, Theory, Ritual Practice,* p. 5.

References

Aberle, David. *The Peyote Religion among the Navaho*. Chicago: Aldine, 1966.

Abrahams, Roger D., and Richard Bauman. "Ranges of Festival Behavior." In Barbara A. Babcock, ed. *The Reversible World: Symbolic Inversion in Art and Society*. Ithaca, N.Y.: Cornell University Press, 1978.

Achebe, Chinua. *Things Fall Apart* [1958]. London: Heinemann, 1989.

Ackerman, Robert. "Frazer on Myth and Ritual." *Journal of the History of Ideas* 36 (1975): 115–34.

Ahern, Emily M. "The Power and Pollution of Chinese Women." In Margery Wolf and Roxane Witke, eds. *Women in Chinese Society*. Stanford, Calif.: Stanford University Press, 1975, pp. 169–90.

Allen, Douglas. *Structure and Creativity in Religion: Hermeneutics in Mircea Eliade's Phenomenology and New Directions*. The Hague: Mouton, 1978.

Amdur, Neil. "Munich 1972: Tragic Blot on Olympic Family Memory." *New York Times*, September 6, 1992, p. 25 (sports section).

Anderson, Benedict. *Imagined Communities: Reflections on the Origin and Spread of Nationalism*, rev. ed. London: Verso, 1991.

Anderson, David A. *Kwanzaa: An Everyday Resource and Instructional Guide*. New York: Gumbs and Thomas, 1992.

Aoki, Haruo, and Shigeko Okamoto. *Rules for Conversational Rituals in Japanese*. Tokyo: Taishukan Publishing Co., 1988.

Arens, W. "Professional Football: An American Symbol and Ritual." In W. Arens and Susan P. Montague, eds. *The American Dimension: Cultural Myths and Social Realities*. Port Washington, N.Y.: Alfred Publishing Co., 1976.

Arkush, R. David, and Leo O. Lee, eds. *Land without Ghosts: Chinese Impressions of America from the Mid-Nineteenth Century to the Present*. Berkeley: University of California Press, 1989.

Arlen, Shelley. *The Cambridge Ritualists: An Annotated Bibliography of the Works by and about Jane Ellen Harrison, Gilbert Murray, Francis M. Cornford, and Arthur Bernard Cook*. Mctuchcn, N.J.: Scarecrow, 1990.

Asad, Talal, *Genealogies of Religion: Discipline and Reasons of Power in Christianity and Islam*. Baltimore: Johns Hopkins Press, 1993.

Ashkenazi, Michael. *Matsuri: Festivals of a Japanese Town*. Honolulu: University of Hawaii, 1993.

Aune, Michael. *"To Move the Heart": Rhetoric and Ritual in the Theology of Philip Melanchthon*. San Francisco: Christian Universities Press, 1994.

Austin, J. L. *How to Do Things with Words*, 2d ed. Cambridge, Mass.: Harvard University Press, 1975.

Aviad, Janet. *Return to Judaism: Religious Renewal in Israel*. Chicago: University of Chicago Press, 1983.

Axtell, Roger E. *Gestures: The Do's and Taboos of Body Language around the World*. New York: John Wiley, 1991.

Aziza, Hussein. *Facts about Female Circumcision*. Cairo: Cairo Family Planning Association, 1983.

Babcock, Barbara. "Arrange Me into Disorder: Fragments and Reflections on Ritual Clowning." In John J. MacAloon, ed. *Rite, Drama, Festival, Spectacle*. Philadelphia: Institute for the Study of Human Issues, 1984, pp. 102–28.

Bakhtin, Mikhail. *Rabelias and his World*. Bloomington: University of Indiana Press, 1984.

Bascom, William. "The Myth-Ritual Theory." *Journal of American Folklore* 70 (1957): 103–14.

Baskin, Judith. "The Separation of Women in Rabbinic Judaism." In Yvonne Yazbeck Haddad and Ellison Banks Findley, eds. *Women, Religion and Social Change*. Albany: State University of New York, 1985, pp. 3–18.

Bateson, Gregory. *Steps to an Ecology of Mind*. [1955]. New York: Ballantine, 1978.

Bateson, Gregory. *Naven*, 2d ed. Stanford: Stanford University Press, 1986.

Bauman, Richard. "Verbal Art as Performance." *American Anthropologist* 77, no. 1 (1975): 290–311.

Bauman, Richard. *Let Your Words Be Few: Symbolism of Speaking and Silence among Seventeenth-Century Quakers*. Cambridge: Cambridge University Press, 1983.

Baumstark, Anton. *Comparative Liturgy*. Westminister, Md.: Newman Press, 1958.

Beane, Wendell C., and William G. Doty, eds. *Myths, Rites, Symbols: A Mircea Eliade Reader*, 2 vols. New York: Harper and Row, 1975.

Beard, Mary. "Rituel, Texts, Temps: Les *Parilia* Romains." In Anne-Marie Blondeau and Kristofer Schipper, eds. *Essais sur le rituel*. Louvain: Peeters, 1988, pp. 15–29.

Beck, Renee, and Sydney B. Metrick. *The Art of Ritual: A Guide to Creating and Performing Your Own Rituals for Growth and Change*. Berkeley, Calif.: Celestial Arts, 1990.

Becker, A. L. "Text-Building, Epistemology, and Aesthetics in Javanese Shadow Theatre." In A. L. Becker and Aram A. Yengoyan, eds. *The Imagination of Reality: Essays in Southeast Asian Coherence Systems*. Norwood, N.J.: Ablex Publishing, 1979, pp. 211–44.

Beckwith, R. T. "Thomas Cranmer and the Prayer Book." In Cheslyn Jones et al., eds. *The Study of Liturgy*, rev. ed. New York: Oxford University Press, 1992, pp. 101–5.

Beidelman, T. O. "Swazi Royal Ritual." *Africa* 36 (1966): 373–405.

Beidelman, T. O. *W. Robertson Smith and the Sociological Study of Religion*. Chicago: University of Chicago Press, 1974.

Bell, Catherine. "Ritualization of Texts and the Textualization of Ritual in the Codification of Taoist Liturgy." *History of Religions* 27, no. 4 (May 1988): 366–92.

Bell, Catherine. "Ritual, Change and Changing Rituals." *Worship* 63, no. 1 (January 1989): 31–41.

Bell, Catherine. *Ritual Theory, Ritual Practice*. New York: Oxford University Press, 1992.

Bell, Catherine. "The Authority of Ritual Experts." *Studia Liturgica* 23, no. 1 (1993): 98–120.

Bell, Catherine. "Modernism and Postmodernism in the Study of Religion." *Religious Studies Review* 22, no. 3 (July 1996): 179–90.

Bell, Catherine. "Performance." In Mark C. Taylor, ed. *Critical Terms for Religion Studies*, Chicago: University of Chicago Press, forthcoming.

Bell, Daniel. "The Return of the Sacred? An Argument on the Future of Religion." In *The Winding Passage: Essays and Sociological Journeys 1960–1980*. Cambridge, Mass.: Abt Books, 1980.

Bellah, Robert N. "Civil Religion in America." *Daedalus* 96, no. 1 (1967): 1–21.

Bellah, Robert N. *Beyond Belief: Essays on Religion in a Post-Traditional World*. New York: Harper and Row, 1970.

Bellah, Robert N., Richard Madsen, William M. Sullivan, Ann Swidler, and Steven M. Tipton. *Habits of the Heart: Individualism and Commitment in American Life*. New York: Harper and Row, 1986.

Ben-Amos, Dan, and Kenneth S. Goldstein, eds. *Folklore: Performance and Communication*. The Hague: Mouton, 1975.

Bendix, Regina. "Tourism and Cultural Displays: Inventing Traditions for Whom?" *Journal of American Folklore* 102, no. 404 (1989): 131–46.

Berger, Peter L. *The Sacred Canopy: Elements of a Sociological Theory of Religion*. New York: Doubleday, 1967.

Berger, Peter L., and Thomas Luckmann. *The Social Construction of Reality: A Treatise in the Sociology of Knowledge*. Garden City, N.Y.: Doubleday-Anchor, 1967.

Bergesen, Albert. *The Sacred and the Subversive: Political Witch-Hunts as National Rituals*. Storrs, Conn.: Society for the Study of Religion, 1984.

Berling, Judith A. "Orthopraxy." In Mircea Eliade et al., ed. *The Encyclopedia of Religion*, vol. 11, pp. 129–32.

Bernstein, Basil, H. L. Elvin, and R. S. Peters. "Ritual in Education." *Philosophical Transactions of the Royal Society of London*, series B, 251 (1966): 429–36.

Bettelheim, Bruno. *Symbolic Wounds: Puberty Rites and the Envious Male*, rev. ed. New York: Collier Books, 1971.

Biale, Rachel. *Women and Jewish Law: An Exploration of Women's Issues in Halakhic Sources*. New York: Schocken Books, 1989.

Bickers, Robert A., ed. *Ritual and Diplomacy: The Macartney Mission to China 1792–1794*. London: The British Association for Chinese Studies/Wellsweep, 1993.

Binns, Christopher A. P. "The Changing Face of Power: Revolution and Accommodation in the Development of the Societ Ceremonial System: Part I." *Man* 14, no. 4 (1979): 585–606.

Black, J. A. "The New Year Ceremonies in Ancient Babylon: 'Taking Bel By the Hand' and a Cultic Picnic." *Religion* 11 (1981): 39–59.

Blacker, Carmen. "The *Shinza* or God-seat in the *Daijōsai*—Throne, Bed, or Incubation Couch?" *Japanese Journal of Religious Studies* 17, nos. 2–3 (1990): 179–197.

Blanchard, Kendall. "The Ritual Dimensions of Play: Structure and Perspective—Introduction." In Helen B. Schwartzman, ed. *Play and Culture*. West Point, N.Y.: Leisure Press, 1980, pp. 49–50.

Blanchard, Kendall. "Sport and Ritual in Choctaw Society." In Helen B. Schwartzman, ed. *Play and Culture*. West Point, N.Y.: Leisure Press, 1980, pp. 83–90.

Bloch, Maurice. "Symbols, Song, Dance and Features of Articulation." *Archives europeénes de sociologie* 15 (1974): 55–81.

Bloch, Maurice. *Ritual, History and Power: Selected Papers in Anthropology*. London: Athlone Press, 1989.

Bly, Robert. *Iron John: A Book about Men*. New York: Random House, 1990.

Boissevain, Jeremy, ed. *Revitalizing European Rituals*. London: Routledge, 1992.

Bokser, Baruch M. *The Origins of the Seder: The Passover Rite and Early Rabbinic Judaism*. Berkeley: University of California Press, 1984.

Bokser, Baruch M. "Was the Last Supper a Passover Seder?" *Bible Review* 3, no. 2 (Summer 1987): 24–33.

Bossy, John. *Christianity in the West, 1400–1700*. New York: Oxford University Press, 1985.

Bott, Elizabeth. "Psychoanalysis and Ceremony." In J. S. La Fontaine, ed. *The Interpretation of Ritual: Essays in Honour of A. I. Richards*. London: Tavistock Publications, 1972, pp. 205–6.

Bouissac, Paul. "The Profanation of the Sacred in Circus Clown Performances." In Richard Schechner and Willa Appel, eds. *By Means of Performance: Intercultural Studies of Theatre and Ritual*. Cambridge: Cambridge University Press, 1990, pp. 194–207.

Bourdieu, Pierre. *Outline of a Theory of Practice*. Trans. Richard Nice. Cambridge: Cambridge University Press, 1977.

Bourdieu, Pierre. *In Other Words: Essays toward a Reflexive Sociology*. Trans. Matthew Adamson. Stanford, Calif.: Stanford University Press, 1990.

Bourdieu, Pierre. *The Logic of Practice*. Trans. Richard Nice. Stanford, Calif.: Stanford University Press, 1990.

Bourdieu, Pierre, and Loïc J. D. Wacquant. *An Invitation to Reflexive Sociology*. Chicago: University of Chicago, 1992.

Bouyer, Louis. *Liturgical Piety*. Indiana: University of Notre Dame Press, 1955.

Bouyer, Louis. *Rite and Man: Natural Sacredness and Christian Sacraments*. Notre Dame, Ind.: University of Notre Dame Press, 1963.

Boyd, David J. "The Commercialization of Ritual in the Eastern Highlands of Papua New Guinea." *Man* n.s. 20 (1985): 325–40.

Brandon, S. G. F. "The Myth and Ritual Position Critically Considered." In S. H. Hooke, ed. *Myth, Ritual and Kingship*. Oxford: Clarendon Press, 1958, pp. 261–91.

Broner, E. M. "Honor and Ceremony in Women's Rituals." In Charlene Spretnak, ed. *The Politics of Women's Spirituality: Essays on the Rise of Spiritual Power within the Feminist Movement*. Garden City, N.Y.: Doubleday Anchor, 1982, pp. 234–44.

Brown, Douglas. "Our Mother, Which Art in Heaven?" *History Today* 42 (November 1992): 8–10.

Brown, Karen McCarthy. "'Plenty Confidence in Myself,' The Initiation of a White Woman Scholar into Haitian Vodou." *Journal of Feminist Studies in Religion* 3, no. 1 (1987): 67–76.

Brown, Karen McCarthy. *Mama Lola: A Vodou Priestess in Brooklyn*. Berkeley: University of California Press, 1991.

Brown, Penelope, and Stephen C. Levinson. *Politeness: Some Universals in Language Usage*. Cambridge: Cambridge University Press, 1987.

Bruns, Gerald L. "Canon and Power in the Hebrew Scriptures." In Robert von Hallberg, ed. *Canons*. Chicago: University of Chicago Press, 1983, pp. 65–83.

Bugnini, A., and C. Braga, eds. *The Commentary on the Constitution and on the Instruction of the Sacred Liturgy*. Trans. V. P. Mallon. New York: Benziger Brothers, 1965.

Buitelaar, Marjo. *Fasting and Feasting in Morocco: Women's Participation in Ramadan*. Oxford: Berg Publishers, 1993.

Burke, Kenneth. *The Philosophy of Literary Form*, 3d ed. Berkeley: University of California Press, 1973.

Burke, Peter. "The Repudiation of Ritual in Early Modern Europe." In *The Historical Anthropology of Early Modern Italy: Essays on Perception and Communication*. Cambridge: Cambridge University Press, 1987.

Burkert, Walter. *Creation of the Sacred: Tracks of Biology in Early Religions*. Cambridge, Mass.: Harvard University Press, 1996.

Burnett, Jacquetta Hill. "Ceremony, Rites, and and Economy in the Student System of an American High School." *Human Organization* 28 (1969): 1–10.

Burridge, Kenelm. *New Heaven, New Earth: A Study of Millenarian Activity*. New York: Schocken Books, 1969.

Buswell, Robert E. Jr. *The Zen Monastic Experience*. Princeton, N.J.: Princeton University Press, 1992.

Bynum, Caroline Walker. "Women's Stories, Women's Symbols: A Critique of Victor Turner's Theory of Liminality." In Robert L. Moore and Frank E. Reynolds, eds. *Anthropology and the Study of Religion*. Chicago: Center for the Scientific Study of Religion, 1984, pp. 105–25.

Calder, William M., ed. *The Cambridge Ritualists Reconsidered*. Atlanta: Scholars Press, 1991.

Campbell, Joseph. *Masks of God*, 4 vols. New York: Viking, 1959.

Campbell, Joseph. *The Hero with a Thousand Faces*, 2d ed. Princeton, N.J.: Princeton University Press, 1972.

Campbell, Joseph. *Myths to Live By*. New York: Viking, 1972.

Campbell, Joseph. *The Mythic Image*. Princeton, N.J.: Princeton University Press, 1975.

Campo, Juan Eduardo. "Authority, Ritual, and Spatial in Islam: The Pilgrimage to Mecca." *Journal of Ritual Studies* 5, no. 1 (Winter 1991): 65–91.

Cannadine, David. "The Context, Performance and Meaning of Ritual: The British Monarchy and the 'Invention of Tradition.'" In Eric Hobsbawn and Terence Ranger, eds. *The Invention of Tradition*. Cambridge: Cambridge University Press, 1983, pp. 101–164.

Canon, Charlotte. *To Make and Make Again: Feminist Ritual Theology*. New York: Crossroad, 1993.

Capps, Walter H., ed. *Ways of Understanding Religion*. New York: Macmillan, 1972.

Carnes, Mark C. *Secret Ritual and Manhood in Victorian America*. New Haven: Yale University Press, 1989.

Casal, U. A. *The Five Sacred Festivals of Ancient Japan: Their Symbolism and Historical Development*. Rutland, Vt.: Charles E. Tuttle Co., 1967.

Casanova, José. *Public Religions in the Modern World*. Chicago: University of Chicago Press, 1994.

Casel, Odo. *Mystery of Christian Worship and Other Writings*. Ed. Burkhard Neunheuser, O.S.B. Westminister, Md.: Newman Press, 1962.

Caspers, Charles, and Marc Schneiders, eds. *Omnes Circumadstantes: Contributions towards a History of the Role of the People in the Liturgy*. Kampen: Uitgeversmaatschappij J. H. Kok, 1990.

Cazeneuve, Jean. "Television as a Functional Alternative to Traditional Sources of Need Satisfaction." In Jay G. Blumer and Elihu Katz, eds. *The Uses of Mass Communications: Current Perspectives on Gratification Research*. Beverly Hills, Calif.: Sage Publications, 1974, pp. 213–23.

Chaney, David. "A Symbolic Mirror of Ourselves: Civic Ritual in Mass Society." *Media, Culture and Society* 5 (1983): 119–35.

Chartier, Roger. *Cultural History: Between Practices and Representations*. Ithaca, N.Y.: Cornell University Press, 1988.

Chen-Hua. *In Search of the Dharma: Memoirs of a Modern Chinese Buddhist Pilgrimage.* Ed. Chün-fang Yü. Trans. Denis C. Mair. Albany: State University of New York, 1992.

Christian, William, Jr. *Local Religion in 16th Century Spain.* Princeton, N.J.: Princeton University Press, 1981.

Chupungco, Anscar J., O.S.B. *Cultural Adaptation of the Liturgy.* New York: Paulist Press, 1982.

Chupungco, Anscar J., O.S.B. *Liturgies of the Future: The Process and Methods of Inculturation.* New York: Paulist Press, 1989.

Clifford, James. *The Predicament of Culture: Twentieth-Century, Ethnography, Literature and Art.* Cambridge, Mass.: Harvard University Press, 1988.

Clifford, James, and George E. Marcus, eds. *Writing Culture: The Poetics and Politics of Ethnography.* Berkeley: University of California Press, 1986.

Cohen, Abner. *The Politics of Elite Cultures: Explorations in the Dramaturgy of Power in a Modern African Culture.* Berkeley: University of California Press, 1981.

Cohen, Alvin P. "Coercing the Rain Deities in Ancient China." *History of Religions* 17, nos. 3–4 (February–May 1978): 244–65.

Cohen, Erik. "Pilgrimage and Tourism: Convergence and Divergence." In Alan Morinis, ed. *Sacred Journeys: The Anthropology of Pilgrimage.* Westport, Conn.: Greenwood Press, 1992, pp. 47–61.

Cohen, Shaye J. D. "Can Converts to Judaism Say 'God of Our Fathers.'" *Judaism* 40, no. 4 (Fall 1991): 419–28.

Collins, Mary. "Liturgical Methodology and the Cultural Evolution of Worship in the United States." *Worship* 49, no. 2 (1975): 85–102.

Collins, Mary. "Critical Ritual Studies: Examining an Intersection of Theology and Culture." In John R. May, ed. *The Bent World: Essays on Religion and Culture.* Missoula, Mt.: Scholars Press, 1981, pp. 127–47.

Comaroff, Jean. *Body of Power, Spirit of Resistance: The Culture and History of a South African People.* Chicago: University of Chicago Press, 1985.

Combs-Schilling, M. E. *Sacred Performances: Islam, Sexuality, and Sacrifice.* New York: Columbia University Press, 1989.

Comstock, W. Richard, ed. *Religion and Man: An Introduction.* New York: Harper and Row, 1971.

Copage, Eric V. *Kwanzaa: An African-American Celebration of Culture and Cooking.* New York: Morrow, 1991.

Corbett, Julia Mitchell. *Religion in America.* Englewood Cliffs, N.J.: Prentice-Hall, 1990.

Crapanzano, Vincent. "Rite of Return: Circumcision in Morocco. " In Werner Muensterberger and L. Bryce Boyer, eds. *The Psychoanalytic Study of Society* 9 (1981): 15–36.

Curran, Patricia. *Grace before Meals: Food Ritual and Body Disciplines in Convent Culture.* Urbana, Ill.: University of Illinois Press, 1989.

Da Matta, Roberto. "Constraint and License: A Preliminary Study of Two Brazilian National Rituals." In Sally F. Moore and Barbara G. Myerhoff, eds. *Secular Ritual.* Amsterdam: Van Gorcum, 1977, pp. 244–64.

Da Matta, Roberto. *Carnivals, Rogues and Heroes: An Interpretation of the Brazilian Dilemma.* Trans. John Drury. Notre Dame, Ind.: Notre Dame University Press, 1979.

Danforth, Loring M. *Firewalking and Religious Healing: The Anastenaria of Greece and the American Firewalking Movement.* Princeton, N.J.: Princeton University Press, 1989.

Daniélou, Jean. *The Bible and the Liturgy.* Notre Dame, Ind.: University of Notre Dame Press, 1956.

Danzger, M. Herbert. *Returning to Tradition: The Contemporary Revival of Orthodox Judaism.* New Haven: Yale University Press, 1989.

D'Aquili, Eugene G. "Human Ceremonial Ritual and the Modulation of Aggression." *Zygon* 20, no. 1 (1985): 21–30.

D'Aquili, Eugene G., Charles D. Laughlin, and John McManus, eds. *The Spectrum of Ritual: A Biogenetic Structural Analysis*. New York: Columbia University Press, 1979.

D'Aquili, Eugene G., and Andrew B. Newberg. "Liminality, Trance and Unitary States in Ritual and Meditation." *Studia Liturgica* 23, no. 1 (1993): 2–34.

Davidman, Lynn. *Tradition in a Rootless World: Women Turn to Orthodox Judaism*. Berkeley: University of California Press, 1991.

Davies, Nigel. "Human Sacrifice in the Old World and the New." In Elizabeth H. Boone, ed. *Ritual Human Sacrifice in Mesoamerica*. Washington D.C., Dumbarton Oaks Research Library and Collection, 1984, pp. 211–24.

Davis, Natalie Z. *Society and Culture in Early Modern France: Eight Essays*. Stanford, Calif.: Stanford University Press, 1975.

Davis, Richard. *Ritual in an Oscillating Universe*. Princeton, N.J.: Princeton University Press, 1991.

Davis, Winston. "Ittōen: The Myths and Rituals of Liminality." *History of Religions* 14, no. 4 (May 1975): 282–321; and 15, no. 1 (August 1975): 1–33. Reprinted in Winston Davis. *Japanese Religion and Society: Paradigms of Structure and Change*. Albany: State University of New York, 1992, pp. 189–225.

Davis-Floyd, Robbie E. "Birth as an American Rite of Passage." In Karen L. Michaelson, ed. *Childbirth in America: Anthropological Perspectives*. South Hadley, Mass.: Bergin and Garvey, 1988, pp. 153–72.

Dayan, Daniel, and Elihu Katz. "Electronic Ceremonies: Television Performs a Royal Wedding." In Marshall Blonsky, ed. *On Signs*. Baltimore: Johns Hopkins University Press, 1985, pp. 16–32.

de Bary, William Theodore, Wing-tsit Chan, and Burton Waton, eds. *Sources of Chinese Tradition*, vol. 1. New York: Columbia University Press, 1960.

de Coubertin, Pierre. *The Olympic Idea: Discourses and Essays*. Ed. Carl-Diem-Institut. Stuttgart: Hofmann, 1967, pp. 86–87.

de Saussure, Ferdinand. *Course in General Linguistics* [1913]. Ed. C. Bally, A Sechehaye, and A. Riedlinger. Trans. Wade Baskin. New York: McGraw-Hill, 1966.

Deal, Terrence, and Allan Kennedy. *Corporate Cultures: The Rites and Ceremonials of Corporate Life*. Reading, Mass.: Addison-Wesley, 1982.

Denny, Frederick M. "Islamic Ritual: Perspectives and Theories." In Richard C. Martin, ed. *Approaches to Islam in Religious Studies*. Tucson: University of Arizona Press, 1985, pp. 63–77.

Dicker, Shira. "Mikva," *Tikkun* 7, no. 6 (1992): 62–64.

Dissanayake, Ellen. "An Ethological View of Ritual and Art in Human Evolutionary History." *Leonardo* 12, no. 1 (1979): 27–31.

Dix, Gregory, ed. and trans. *The Treatise on the Apostolic Tradition of Saint Hippolytus of Rome*. London: SPCK, 1968.

Dix, Gregory. *The Shape of the Liturgy*, rev. ed. New York: Seabury, 1983.

Dobblaere, Karel. "Secularization: A Multi-Dimensional Concept," *Current Sociology* 29, no. 2 (Summer 1981): 1–213.

Doty, William G. *Mythography: The Study of Myths and Rituals*. Tuscaloosa: University of Alabama Press, 1986.

Douglas, Mary. *Purity and Danger: An Analysis of Concepts of Pollution and Taboo*. New York: Praeger, 1966.

Douglas, Mary. "The Contempt of Ritual." *New Blackfriars* 49 (1968): 475–82 (I) and 528–35 (II).

Douglas, Mary, ed. *Witchcraft, Confessions and Accusations*. London: Tavistock, 1970.

Douglas, Mary. "Deciphering a Meal." In *Implicit Meanings: Essays in Anthropology*. London: Routledge & Kegan Paul, 1975, pp. 249–75.

Douglas, Mary. *Natural Symbols: Explorations in Cosmology*. New York: Vintage Books, 1973.

Douglas, Mary. "The Effects of Modernization on Religious Change." *Daedalus* 111, no. 1 (Winter 1982): 1–19.

Driver, Tom F. *The Magic of Ritual: Our Need for Liberating Rites That Transform Our Lives and Our Communities*. San Francisco: Harper Collins, 1991.

Duffy, Eamon. *The Stripping of the Altars: Traditional Religion in England, c. 1400–c.1580*. New Haven, Conn.:Yale University Press, 1992.

Dumont, Louis. "World Renunciation in Indian Religions." *Contributions to Indian Sociology* 4 (1960): 33–62.

Dunn, Ethel, and Stephen P. Dunn. "Religious Behavior and Socio-cultural Change in the Soviet Union." In Bohdan R. Bociurkiw and John W. Strong, eds. *Religion and Atheism in the USSR and Eastern Europe*. Toronto: University of Toronto, 1975, pp. 123–50.

Durand, Jorge, and Douglas S. Massey. *Doy Gracias: Iconografía de la Emigración México–Estados Unidos*. Guadalajara: Programa de Estudios Jaliescienses, 1990.

Durkheim, Émile. *The Elementary Forms of the Religious Life* [1915]. Trans. J. W. Swain. New York: Free Press, 1965.

Durkheim, Émile, and Marcel Mauss, *Primitive Classification*. Trans. Rodney Needham. Chicago: University of Chicago, 1963.

Ebaugh, Helen Rose. "The Revitalization Movement in the Catholic Church: The Institutional Dilemma of Power." *Sociological Analysis* 52 (1991): 1–12.

Ebrey, Patricia Buckley. *Confucianism and Family Rituals in Imperial China: A Social History of Writing about Rites*. Princeton, N.J.: Princeton University Press, 1991.

Ebrey, Patricia Buckley. *Chu Hsi's Family Rituals*. Princeton, N.J.: Princeton University Press, 1991.

Eck, Diana L. *Darsan: Seeing the Divine Image in India*. Chambersburg, Pa.: Anima Books, 1981.

Eco, Umberto. "The Myth of Superman." *Diacritics* 2 (1972): 14–22. Reprinted in R. Davis, ed. *Contemporary Literary Criticism*. New York: Longman, 1986, pp. 330–44.

Edelman, Murray. *Politics as Symbolic Action: Mass Arousal and Quiescence*. Chicago: Markham Publishing Co., 1971.

Eilberg-Schwartz, Howard. "Israel in the Mirror of Nature: Animal Metaphors in the Ritual and Narratives of Ancient Israel." *Journal of Ritual Studies* 2, no. 1 (1988): 1–30.

Eliade, Mircea. *The Myth of the Eternal Return or, Cosmos and History*. Trans. Willard R. Trask. Princeton, N.J.: Princeton University Press, 1954.

Eliade, Mircea. *The Sacred and the Profane: The Nature of Religion*. Trans. Willard R. Trask. New York: Harcourt Brace Jovanovich, 1959.

Eliade, Mircea. *Myth and Reality*. Trans. Willard R. Trask. New York: Harper and Row, 1963.

Eliade, Mircea. *Patterns in Comparative Religion*. Trans. Rosemary Sheed. New York: New American Library, 1963.

Eliade, Mircea. "Cosmogonic Myth and 'Sacred History.'" In *The Quest: History and Meaning in Religion*. Chicago: University of Chicago Press, 1969, pp. 72–87. Reprinted in Alan Dundes, ed. *Sacred Narrative: Readings in the Theory of Myth*. Berkeley: University of California Press, 1984, pp. 137–51.

Eliade, Mircea. "The Quest for the 'Origins' of Religion." In *The Quest: History and Meaning in Religion*. Chicago: University of Chicago Press, 1969, pp. 37–53.

Eliade, Mircea. *Occultism, Witchcraft and Cultural Fashions: Essays in Comparative Religion.* Chicago: University of Chicago Press, 1976.

Eliade, Mircea. *History of Religious Ideas I: From the Stone Age to the Eleusinian Mysteries.* Trans. Willard R. Trask. Chicago: University of Chicago Press, 1978.

Eliade, Mircea, and Joseph M. Kitagawa, eds. *The History of Religions: Essays in Methodology.* Chicago: University of Chicago Press, 1959.

Eliade, Mircea, et al., eds. *The Encyclopedia of Religion,* 16 vols. New York: Macmillan, 1987.

Elias, Norbert. *The Civilizing Process: The History of Manners,* 2 vols. Trans. Edmund Jephcott. New York: Urizen Books, 1978.

Ellwood, Robert S. *The Feast of Kingship: Accession Ceremonies in Ancient Japan.* Tokyo: Sophia University, 1973.

Ellwood, Robert S., and Harry B. Partin. *Religious and Spiritual Groups in Modern America,* 2d ed. Englewood Cliffs, N.J.: Prentice Hall, 1988.

Emswiler, Sharon Neufer, and Thomas Neufer Emswiler. *Women and Worship: A Guide to Nonsexist Hymns, Prayers, and Liturgies,* rev. ed. San Francisco: Harper and Row, 1984.

Engnell, Ivan. *Studies in Divine Kingship in the Ancient Near East,* 2d ed. Oxford: Basil Blackwell, 1967.

Erikson, Erik H. *Childhood And Society,* 2d rev. ed. New York: W. W. Norton, 1963.

Erikson, Erik H. "Ontogeny of Ritualization in Man." In Julian Huxley, ed. "A Discussion on Ritualization of Behavior in Animals and Man." *Philosophical Transactions of the Royal Society,* series B, 251 (1966): 37–350. Reprinted in Rudolph Loewenstein et al., eds. *Psychoanalysis—A General Psychology.* New York: International Universities Press, 1966, pp. 601–21.

Erikson, Erik H. "The Development of Ritualization." In Donald R. Cutler, ed. *The Religious Situation 1968.* Boston: Beacon, 1968, pp. 711–33.

Erikson, Erik H. *Toys and Reasons: Stages in the Ritualization of Experience.* New York: W. W. Norton, 1977.

Esposito, John L. *Islam: The Straight Path.* New York: Oxford University Press, 1991.

Evans-Pritchard, E. E. *Essays in Social Anthropology.* London: Faber and Faber, 1962.

Evans-Pritchard, E. E. *Theories of Primitive Religion.* Oxford: Clarendon Press, 1965.

Evans-Pritchard, E. E. *Witchcraft, Oracles and Magic among the Azande.* Oxford: Clarendon Press, 1965.

Evans-Pritchard, E. E. *Nuer Religion.* New York: Oxford University Press, 1974.

Farenga, Vincent. "Review of René Girard's *Violence and the Sacred.*" *Comparative Literature* 32 (1980): 419–24.

Faure, Bernard. *The Rhetoric of Immediacy: A Cultural Critique of Chan/Zen Buddhism.* Princeton: Princeton University Press, 1991.

Fenn, Richard K. "The Process of Secularization: A Post-Parsonian View." *Scientific Study of Religion* 9, no. 2 (Summer 1970): 117–36.

Fenn, Richard K. "Recent Studies of Church Decline: The Eclipse of Ritual." *Religious Studies Review* 8, no. 2 (April 1982): 124–28.

Fernandez, James W. "Symbolic Consensus in a Fang Reformative Cult." *American Anthropologist* 67 (1965): 902–29.

Fernandez, James W. "Persuasion and Performances: On the Beast in Every Body . . . And the Metaphors of Everyman." *Daedalus* 101, no. 1 (Winter 1972): 39–60.

Ferro-Luzzi, Gabriella Eichinger. "Ritual as Language: The Case of South Indian Food Offerings." *Current Anthropology* 18, no. 3 (1977): 507–14.

Feuchtwang, Stephan. *The Imperial Metaphor: Popular Religion in China.* London: Routledge, 1992.

Fingarette, Herbert. *Confucius: The Secular as Sacred.* San Francisco: Harper and Row, 1972.

Finnegan, Ruth. "How To Do Things with Words: Performative Utterances among the Limba of Sierra Leone." *Man*, n.s. 4, no. 4 (1969): 537–52.

Firth, Raymond. "Offering and Sacrifice: Problems of Organization." *Journal of the Royal Anthropological Institute* 93 (1963): 12–24.

Firth, Raymond. *The Work of the Gods in Tikopia*. New York: Athlone Press, 1967.

Firth, Raymond. "Verbal and Bodily Rituals of Greeting and Parting." In J. S. La Fontaine, ed. *The Interpretation of Ritual*. London: Tavistock Publications, 1972, pp. 1–38.

Fischer, Louis. *The Life of Mahatma Gandhi*. New York: Harper and Row, 1950.

Fletcher, George P. "Update the Pledge." *New York Times*. December 6, 1992. Section 4, p. 19.

Flexner, Stuart Berg. *I Hear America Talking*. New York: Van Nostrand Reinhold, 1976.

Fontaine, J. S. *Initiation*. Manchester: Manchester University Press, 1985.

Fontenrose, Joseph. *The Ritual Theory of Myth*. Berkeley: University of California Press, 1971.

Foucault, Michel. *Discipline and Punish: The Birth of the Prison*. Trans. Alan Sheridan. New York: Vintage Books, 1977.

Frankfort, Henri. *Kingship of the Gods* [1948]. Chicago: University of Chicago Press, 1978.

Frazer, James George. *The Golden Bough: A Study in Magic and Religion*, 3d ed. 10 vols. [1911]. London: Macmillan, 1955.

Freedman, Maurice. *The Study of Chinese Society*. Ed. G. William Skinner. Stanford: Stanford University Press, 1979.

Freud, Sigmund. *Character and Culture*. New York: Collier Books, 1963.

Freud, Sigmund. *Totem and Taboo* [1912–13]. Trans. A. A. Brill. New York: Vintage Books, 1946.

Freud, Sigmund. *Moses and Monotheism* [1939]. Trans. Katherine Jones. New York: Vintage Books, 1955.

Fried, Martha Nemes, and Morton H. Fried. *Transitions: Four Rituals in Eight Cultures*. New York: W. W. Norton, 1980.

Friedman, Menachem. "Life Tradition and Book Tradition in the Development of Ultra-orthodox Judaism." In Harvey E. Goldberg, ed. *Judaism Viewed from Within and from Without: Anthroplogical Studies*. Albany: State University of New York, 1987, pp. 235–55.

Fujitani, Takashi. "Electronic Pageantry and Japan's 'Symbolic Emperor.'" *The Journal of Asian Studies* 51, no. 4 (November 1992): 824–50.

Fustel de Coulanges, Numa Denis. *The Ancient City*. Trans. Willard Small. New York: Doubleday, 1963.

Gager, John G. *Kingdom and Community: The Social World of Early Christianity*. Englewood Cliffs, N.J.: Prentice-Hall, 1975.

Ganjei, Ayatollah Jalal. Letter to the Editor, "Islam Doesn't Sanction Rushdie Decree." *New York Times*. March 11, 1993.

Gaster, Theodor H. *Thespis: Ritual, Myth and Drama in the Ancient Near East* [1950], rev. ed. Garden City, N.Y.: Doubleday, 1961; also New York: Harper and Row, 1966.

Gay, Volney P. *Freud on Ritual: Reconstruction and Critique*. Missoula, Mont.: Scholars Press, 1979.

Gay, Volney P. *Reading Freud: Psychology, Neurosis and Religion*. Chico, Calif.: Scholars Press, 1983.

Geertz, Clifford. *The Interpretation of Culture*. New York: Basic Books, 1973.

Geertz, Clifford. *The Religion of Java*. Chicago: University of Chicago Press, 1976.

Geertz, Clifford. *Negara: The Theater State in Nineteenth Century Bali*. Princeton, N.J.: Princeton University Press, 1980.

Gelber, Steven M. "Working at Playing: The Culture of the Workplace and the Rise of Baseball." *Journal of Social History* 16, no. 4 (June 1983): 3–22.

Gelber, Steven M., and Martin L. Cook. *Saving the Earth: A History of a Middle-class Millenarian Movement*. Berkeley: University of California Press, 1990.

Gerth, H. H., and C. Wright Mills, trans. and eds. *From Max Weber: Essays in Sociology*. New York: Oxford University Press, 1946.

Gibbs, Nancy, trans. "Birth Customs." In Patricia Buckley Ebrey, ed. *Chinese Civilization and Society: A Sourcebook*. New York: Free Press, 1981, pp. 302–3.

Gilday, Edmund T. "Imperial Ritual in the Heisei Era: A Report on Research in Progress." *The Pacific World*, n.s. 10 (Fall 1994): 205–18.

Gilday, Edmund T. "Processing Tradition: The Making of an Emperor, 1989–91." Unpublished manuscript.

Gill, Sam D. "Hopi Kachina Cult Initiation: The Shocking Beginning to the Hopi's Religious Life." *Journal of the American Academy of Religion* 45, no. 2 supplement (June 1977): 447–64.

Gill, Sam D. *Beyond the Primitive: The Religions of Nonliterate Peoples*. Englewood Cliffs, N.J.: Prentice-Hall, 1982.

Gill, Sam D. *Native American Religions: An Introduction*. Belmont, Calif.: Wadsworth, 1982.

Gill, Sam D. "Nonliterate Traditions and Holy Books: Toward a New Model." In Frederick M. Denny and Rodney L. Taylor, eds. *The Holy Book in Comparative Perspective*. Columbia: University of South Carolina Press, 1985.

Gilligan, Carol. *In a Different Voice: Psychological Theory and Women's Development*. Cambridge, Mass.: Harvard University Press, 1982.

Gillis, John R. *A World of Their Own Making: Myth, Ritual, and the Quest for Family Values*. New York: Basic Books, 1996.

Gilmore, David D. *Manhood in the Making: Cultural Concepts of Masculinity*. New Haven: Yale University Press, 1990.

Girard, René. *Violence and the Sacred*. Trans. Patrick Gregory. Baltimore: Johns Hopkins University Press, 1977.

Girard, René. *The Scapegoat*. Trans. Yvonne Freccero. Baltimore: Johns Hopkins University Press, 1986.

Girard, René, with Jean-Michel Oughourlian and Guy Lefort. *Things Hidden since the Foundation of the World* [1978]. Trans. by Stephen Bann and Michael Metteer. Stanford, Calif.: Stanford University Press, 1987.

Glassberg, David. *American Historical Pageantry: The Uses of Tradition in the Early Twentieth Century*. Chapel Hill: University of North Carolina, 1990.

Glatzer, Nahum N. ed. *The Passover Haggadah*. New York: Schocken Books, 1953.

Gluckman, Mary, and Max Gluckman. "On Drama, and Games and Athletic Contests." In Sally F. Moore and Barbara G. Myerhoff, eds. *Secular Ritual*. Amsterdam: Van Gorcum, 1977, pp. 227–43.

Gluckman, Max. *Essays on the Ritual of Social Relations*. Manchester: Manchester University Press, 1962.

Gluckman, Max. *Order and Rebellion in Tribal Africa*. New York: Free Press, 1963.

Gmelch, George. "Baseball Magic." In James P. Spradley and David W. McCurdy, eds. *Conformity and Conflict: Readings in Cultural Anthropology*. Boston: Little, Brown, 1990, pp. 344–54.

Goethals, Gregor. *The TV Affair: Worship at the Video Altar*. Boston: Beacon, 1981.

Goffman, Erving. *The Presentation of Self in Everyday Life*. Garden City, N.Y.: Doubleday, 1959.

Goffman, Erving. *Interaction Ritual*. Garden City, N.Y.: Doubleday, 1967.

Goffman, Erving. "Supportive Interchanges." In *Relations in Public*. New York: Basic Books, 1971, pp. 62–74.

Goffman, Erving. *Frame Analysis: An Essay on the Organization of Experience*. New York: Harper and Row, 1974.

Goldenweiser, A. A. "Sir James Frazer's Theories." In *History, Psychology and Culture*. London: Kegan Paul, 1933. Reprinted in *Anthropology* [1937]; New York: Johnson Reprint Co., 1972.

Goldman, Irving. *The Mouth of Heaven: An Introduction to Kwakiutl Religious Thought*. New York: John Wiley, 1975.

Goldman, Ari L. "Culture and Religion Unite in a Day of Fasting by Jews." *New York Times*. July 31, 1990, section B, p. 2.

Gonda, Jan. *Viṣṇuism and Śivaism: A Comparison*. London: Athlone Press, 1970.

Goodman, Felicitas D. *How about Demons? Possession and Exorcism in the Modern World*. Bloomington: Indiana University Press, 1988.

Goody, Jack R. "Against 'Ritual': Loosely Structured Thoughts on a Loosely Defined Topic." In Sally F. Moore and Barbara G. Myerhoff, eds. *Secular Ritual*. Amsterdam: Van Gorcum, 1977, pp. 25–35.

Goody, Jack R. *The Interface between the Written and the Oral*. Cambridge: Cambridge University Press, 1987.

Goody, Jack R., and Ian Watt. "The Consequences of Literacy." In Jack R. Goody, ed. *Literacy in Traditional Societies*. Cambridge: Cambridge University Press, 1968, pp. 27–68.

Graburn, N. H. H. *The Anthropology of Tourism*. New York: Pergamon Press, 1983.

Grahn, Judy. "From Sacred Blood to the Curse and Beyond. " In Charlene Spretnak, ed. *The Politics of Women's Spirituality: Essays on the Rise of Spiritual Power within the Feminist Movement*. Garden City, N.Y.: Doubleday Anchor, 1982, pp. 219–33.

Grainger, R. *The Language of the Rite*. London: Darton, Longman and Todd, 1974.

Greenberg, Bradley, and Edwin B. Parker, eds. *The Kennedy Assassination and the American Public*. Stanford, Calif.: Stanford University Press, 1965.

Greenblatt, Stephen. "Filthy Rites." *Daedalus* 111, no. 3 (Summer 1982): 1–16.

Gregory, Peter N., and Patricia Buckley Ebrey. "The Religious and Historical Landscape." In Patricia Buckley Ebrey and Peter N. Gregory, eds. *Religion and Society in T'ang and Sung China*. Honolulu: University of Hawaii Press, 1993, pp. 1–44.

Grimes, Ronald L. *Symbol and Conquest: Public Ritual and Drama in Santa Fe, New Mexico*. Ithaca, N.Y.: Cornell University Press, 1976.

Grimes, Ronald L. *Research in Ritual Studies*. Metuchen, N.J.: Scarecrow Press, 1985.

Grimes, Ronald L. *Ritual Criticism: Case Studies in Its Practice, Essays on Its Theory*. Columbia: University of South Carolina Press, 1990.

Grimes, Ronald L. "Reinventing Rites," *Soundings* 75, no. 1 (Spring 1992): 21–41.

Grimes, Ronald L. *Beginnings in Ritual Studies* [1982], rev. ed. Columbia: University of South Carolina Press, 1995.

Gross, Rita M. "Birth." In Mircea Eliade et al., eds. *The Encyclopedia of Religion*, vol. 2. New York: Macmillan, 1987, pp. 227–31.

Guiart, J. *Les Religions de l'Océanie*. Paris: Presses Universitaires de France, 1962.

Guisso, Richard W. I., and Chai-shin Yu. *Shamanism: The Spirit World of Korea*. Berkeley, Calif.: Asian Humanities Press, 1988.

Guttman, Allen. *From Ritual to Record: The Nature of Modern Sports*. New York: Columbia University Press, 1978.

Hamerton-Kelly, Robert G., ed. *Violent Origins: Walter Burkert, Rene Girard, and Jonathan Z. Smith on Ritual Killing and Cultural Formation*. Stanford, Calif.: Stanford University Press, 1987.

Handelman, Don. "Play and Ritual: Complementary Frames of Meta-Communication." In

Anthony J. Chapman and Hugh C. Foot, eds. *It's a Funny Thing Humor*. Oxford: Pergamon Press, 1977, pp. 185–92.

Handelman, Don. *Models and Mirrors: Towards an Anthropology of Public Events*. Cambridge: Cambridge University Press, 1990.

Hannerz, Ulf. "Theory in Anthropology: Small Is Beautiful? The Problem of Complex Cultures." *Comparative Studies in Society and History* 28, no. 2 (1986): 362–67.

Hanson, F. Allan. "The Semiotics of Ritual," *Semiotica* 33, 1/2 (1981): 169–78.

Hardacre, Helen. *Shinto and the State 1868–1988*. Princeton, N.J.: Princeton University Press, 1989.

Harris, Marvin. "The Cultural Ecology of India's Sacred Cattle." *Current Anthropology* 7, no. 1 (February 1966): 51–66. Revised as "The Origin of the Sacred Cow." In *Cannibals and Kings: The Origins of Cultures*. New York: Random House, 1977, pp. 211–29.

Harris, Marvin. "The Cannibal Kingdom." In *Cannibals and Kings: The Origins of Cultures*. New York: Random House, 1977, pp. 147–66.

Harrison, Jane Ellen. *Themis: A Study of the Social Origins of Greek Religion* [1912], 2d ed. Cleveland: Meridian, 1962.

Harrison, Jane Ellen. *Prolegomena to the Study of Greek Religion* [1903], 3d ed. Cleveland: Meridian, 1966.

Harvey, Youngsook Kim. "Possession Sickness and Women Shamans in Korea." In Nancy A. Falk and Rita M. Gross, eds. *Unspoken Worlds: Women's Religious Lives in Non-Western Cultures*. San Francisco: Harper and Row, 1980, pp. 41–52.

Hebdige, Dick. *Subculture: The Meaning of Style*. London: Methuen, 1979.

Hebner, Jack, and David Osborn. *Kumbha Mela: The World's Largest Act of Faith*. La Jolla, Calif.: Entourage Publications, 1990.

Hecht, Richard D. "Studies on Sacrifice: 1970–80." *Religious Studies Review* 8, no. 3 (July 1982): 253–58.

Heilman, Samuel C. *Defenders of the Faith*. New York: Schocken, 1992.

Heilman, Samuel C., and Steven M. Cohen. "Ritual Variation among Modern Orthodox Jews in the United States." *Studies in Contemporary Jewry* 2 (1986): 164–87.

Heilman, Samuel C., and Menachem Friedman. "Religious Fundamentalism and Religious Jews: The Case of the Haredim." In Martin E. Marty and R. Scott Appleby, eds. *Fundamentalisms Observed*. Chicago: University of Chicago Press, 1991, pp. 197–264.

Hellwig, Monica K. *The Meaning of the Sacraments*. Dayton, Ohio: Pflaum/Standard, 1981.

Henderson, John B. *The Development and Decline of Chinese Cosmology*. New York: Columbia University Press, 1984.

Henisch, Bridget Ann. *Fast and Feast: Food in Medieval Society*. University Park: Pennsylvania State University, 1976.

Hevia, James L. "A Multitude of Lords: Qing Court Ritual and the Macartney Embassy of 1793." *Late Imperial China* 10, no. 2 (December 1989): 72–105.

Hobsbawn, Eric. "Introduction: Inventing Traditions." In Eric Hobsbawn and Terence Ranger, eds. *The Invention of Tradition*. Cambridge: Cambridge University Press, 1983, pp. 1–14.

Hobsbawn, Eric. "Mass-Producing Traditions: Europe, 1870–1914." In Eric Hobsbawn and Terence Ranger, eds. *The Invention of Tradition*. Cambridge: Cambridge University Press, 1983, pp. 263–307.

Hocart, A. M. [Arthur Maurice]. *The Life-Giving Myth and Other Essays* [1952]. Ed. F. R. R. S. Raglan. London: Methuen, 1970.

Hodgson, Marshall G. S. *The Venture of Islam*, vol. 1. Chicago: University of Chicago Press, 1974.

Holmberg, David. "Review Article: The Shamanic Illusion." *The Journal of Ritual Studies* 7, no. 1 (Winter 1993): 163–75.

Holmes, Paul A. "A Catechumenate for Marriage: Presacramental Preparation as Pilgrimage." *Journal of Ritual Studies* 6, no. 2 (Summer 1992): 93–113.

Holtom, Daniel C. *The Japanese Enthronement Ceremonies*, 2d ed. Tokyo: Sophia University, 1972.

Homans, George C. "Anxiety and Ritual: The Theories of Malinowski and Radcliffe-Brown." *American Anthropologist* 43 (1941): 164–72.

Hooke, S. H., ed. *Myth and Ritual*. London: Oxford University Press, 1933.

Hooke, S. H., ed. *The Labyrinth: Further Studies in the Relation between Myth and Ritual in the Ancient World*. London: Society for Promoting Christian Knowledge, 1935.

Hooke, S. H., ed. *Myth, Ritual and Kingship*. Oxford: Clarendon Press, 1958.

Hooke, S. H. "Myth and Ritual: Past and Present." In *Myth, Ritual and Kingship*. Oxford: Clarendon Press, 1958, pp. 1–21.

Hopkins, Thomas J. *The Hindu Religious Tradition*. Encino, Calif.: Dickenson Publishing Co., 1971.

Horton, Robin. "African Traditional Thought and Western Science," *Africa* 37 (1967): 50–71 and 155–87. Reprinted in *Patterns of Thought in Africa and the West*. Cambridge: Cambridge University Press, 1993, pp. 197–258.

Hou, Ching-lang. *Monnaies d'offrande et la notion de trésorerie dans la religion chinoise*. Paris: Institut des Hautes Études Chinoises, 1975.

Hubert, Henri, and Marcel Mauss. *Sacrifice: Its Nature and Functions* [1898]. Trans. W. D. Hall. Chicago: University of Chicago, 1964.

Huxley, Julian, ed. "A Discussion on Ritualization of Behavior in Animals and Man." *Philosophical Transactions of the Royal Society*, series B, 251 (1966): 247–525.

Hyman, Stanley Edgar. "The Ritual View of Myth and the Mythic." *Journal of American Folklore* 68 (1955): 463–65. Reprinted in Thomas A. Sebeok, ed. *Myth: A Symposium*. Bloomington: Indiana University Press, 1965, pp. 136–53.

Hymes, Dell. "Breakthrough into Performance." In Dan Ben-Amos and Kenneth S. Goldstein, eds. *Folklore: Performance and Communication*. The Hague: Mouton, 1975, pp. 11–74.

Iannaccone, Laurence R. "A Formal Model of Church and Sect." *American Journal of Sociology* 94, supplement (1988): S241–S268.

Iglehart, Hallie. *Womanspirit: A Guide to Women's Wisdom*. San Francisco: Harper and Row, 1983.

Imber-Black, Evan, and Janine Roberts. *Rituals for Our Times: Celebrating, Healing, and Changing Our Lives and Our Relationships*. San Francisco: Harper Perennial, 1992.

Inden, Ronald B., and Ralph W. Nicholas. *Kinship in Bengali Culture*. Chicago: University of Chicago Press, 1977, pp. 35–52.

Isenberg, Sheldon R., and Dennis E. Own. "Bodies, Natural and Contrived: The Work of Mary Douglas." *Religious Studies Review* 3, no. 1 (January 1977): 1–16.

Itami, Juzo, director. *The Funeral* [*Ososhiki*], [1984] Chicago: Facts Multimedia, 1986.

Jakobson, Roman, and M. Halle. *The Fundamentals of Language*. The Hague: Mouton, 1956.

James, E. O. "The Sources of Christian Ritual." In Samuel H. Hooke, ed. *The Labyrinth: Further Studies in the Relation between Myth and Ritual in the Ancient World*. New York: Macmillan, 1935, pp. 235–60.

Jameson, Robert. "Purity and Power at the Victorian Dinner Party." In Ian Hodder, ed. *The Archeology of Contextual Meanings*. London: Cambridge University Press, 1987, pp. 55–65.

Jay, Nancy. *Throughout Your Generations Forever: Sacrifice, Religion, and Paternity*. Chicago: University of Chicago, 1992.

Jennings, Theodore. "On Ritual Knowledge." *Journal of Religion* 62, no. 2 (1982): 111–27.

Johnson, David, ed. *Ritual Opera, Operatic Ritual*. Berkeley: Chinese Popular Culture Project, 1989.

Jonaitis, Aldona, ed. *Chiefly Feasts: The Enduring Kwakiutl Potlatch*. Seattle: University of Washington Press, 1991.

Jones, Cheslyn, Geoffrey Wainwright, Edward Yarnold S.J., and Paul Bradshaw, eds. *The Study of the Liturgy*, rev. ed. New York: Oxford University Press, 1992.

Jung, Carl. *Symbols of Transformation*. Princeton, N.J.: Princeton University Press, 1967.

Jungmann, Joseph A. *The Mass of the Roman Rite*, 2 vols. Trans. F. A. Brunner. New York: Benziger, 1951.

Jungmann, Joseph A. *The Early Liturgy to the Time of Gregory the Great*. Trans. Francis A. Brunner. Notre Dame, Ind.: University of Notre Dame Press, 1959.

Jungmann, Joseph A. "The State of Liturgical Life on the Eve of the Reformation." In J. A. Jungmann, *Pastoral Liturgy*. New York: Herder and Herder, 1962, pp. 64–80.

Kane, Cheikh Hamidou. *Ambiguous Adventure*. New York: Macmillan, 1969.

Kapferer, Bruce. "Emotion and Feeling in Sinhalese Healing Rituals." *Social Analysis* 1 (February 1979): 153–76.

Kapferer, Bruce. "Mind, Self, and Other in Demonic Illness: The Negation and Reconstruction of Self." *American Ethnologist* 6, no. 1 (February 1979): 110–33.

Kapferer, Bruce. "The Ritual Process and the Problem of Reflexivity in Sinhalese Demon Exorcisms." In John J. MacAloon, ed. *Rite, Drama, Festival, Spectacle*. Philadelphia: Institute for the Study of Human Issues, 1984, pp. 179–207.

Kapferer, Judith L. "Socialization and the Symbolic Order of the School." *Anthropology and Education Quarterly* 12, no. 4 (1981): 258–74.

Karenga, Maulana. *Kwanzaa: Origin, Concepts, Practice*. Los Angeles: Kawaida Publications, 1977.

Karenga, Maulana. *The African-American Holiday of Kwanzaa: A Celebration of Family, Community and Culture*. Los Angeles: University of Sankore Press, 1988.

Katz, Elihu, and Daniel Dayan. "Media Events: On the Experience of Not Being There." *Religion* 15 (1985): 305–14.

Kelleher, Mary Margaret O.S.U. "The Communion Rite: A Study of Roman Catholic Liturgical Performance." *Journal of Ritual Studies* 5, no. 2 (Summer 1991): 99–122.

Kelly, John D. "From Holi to Diwali in Fuji: An Essay on Ritual and History." *Man* n.s. 23 (1988): 40–55.

Kelly, John D., and Martha Kaplan. "History, Structure and Ritual." *Annual Review of Anthropology* 19 (1990): 119–50.

Kendall, Laurel. *Shamans, Housewives and Other Restless Spirits: Women in Korean Ritual Life*. Honolulu: University of Hawaii Press, 1985.

Kertzer, David I. *Ritual, Politics, and Power*. New Haven: Yale University Press, 1988.

Kilmer, Scott. "Sport as Ritual: A Theoretical Approach." In David F. Lancy and B. Allan Tindall, eds. *The Study of Play: Problems and Prospects*. Cornwall, NY: Leisure Press, 1977, pp. 44–49.

Kimball, Solon T. "Introducton" to Arnold van Gennep, 1960, *The Rites of Passage*.

Kinser, Samuel. *Carnival, American Style: Mardi Gras at New Orleans and Mobile*. Chicago: University of Chicago Press, 1990, pp. 115–17.

Kinsley, David R. *Hinduism: A Cultural Perspective*. 2d ed. Englewood Cliffs, N.J.: Prentice-Hall, 1993.

Kitagawa, Joseph M. "The History of Religions in America." In Mircea Eliade and Joseph M. Kitagawa, eds. *The History of Religions: Essays in Methodology*. Chicago: University of Chicago Press, 1959, pp. 1–30.

Kitagawa, Joseph M. "Primitive, Classical and Modern Religions: A Perspective on Understanding the History of Religions." In *The History of Religions: Essays on the Problem of Understanding*. Chicago: University of Chicago Press, 1967.

Kluckhohn, Clyde. "Myths and Rituals: A General Theory." *Harvard Theological Review* 35 (1942): 42–79.

Kokugakuin University. *Matsuri: Festival and Rite in Japanese Life*. Tokyo: Kokugakuin University, 1988.

Kuper, Adam. *Anthropology and Anthropologists: The Modern British School*. London: Routledge & Kegan Paul, 1983.

Kuper, Adam. *The Invention of Primitive Society: Transformations of an Illusion*. London: Routledge, 1988.

Kuper, Hilda. *An African Aristocracy: Rank among the Swazi*. London: Oxford University Press, 1961.

Kuykendall, Richard E. *Liturgies of the Earth*. Brea, Calif.: Educational Ministries, 1992.

La Barre, Weston. *The Peyote Cult*. Norman: University of Oklahoma Press, 1989.

La Fontaine, Jean. "Invisible Custom: Public Lectures as Ceremonials." *Anthropology Today* 2, no. 5 (1986): 3–9.

Lagerwey, John. *Taoist Ritual in Chinese Society and History*. New York: Macmillan, 1987.

Laird, Joan. "Women and Ritual in Family Therapy." In Evan Imber-Black, Janine Roberts, and Richard A. Whiting, eds. *Rituals in Families and Family Therapy*. New York: W. W. Norton, 1988, pp. 331–62.

Lamberts, J. "Active Participation as the Gateway towards an Ecclesial Liturgy." In Charles Caspers and Marc Schneiders, eds. *Omnes Circumadstantes: Contributions Towards a History of the Role of the People in the Liturgy*. Kampen: Uitgeversmaatschappij J. H. Kok, 1990, pp. 234–61.

Lambo, Thomas Adeoye. "Psychotherapy in Africa." *Human Nature* 1 (1978): 32–39.

Lancy, David F. "The Social Organization of Learning: Initiation Rituals and Public Schools." *Human Organization* 34, no. 4 (Winter 1975): 371–80.

Lane, Christel. *The Rites of Rulers: Ritual in Industrial Society—The Soviet Case*. Cambridge: Cambridge University Press, 1981.

Lang, Andrew. *The Making of Religion*. [1898]. New York: AMS Press, 1968.

Lang, Andrew. *Magic and Religion*. London: Longmans, 1901.

Langer, Susanne. *Philosophy in a New Key*. New York: Mentor Books, 1964.

Lansing, J. Stephen. *Priests and Programmers: Technologies of Power in the Engineered Landscape of Bali*. Princeton, N.J.: Princeton University Press, 1991.

Larose, Serge. "The Meaning of Africa in Haitian Vodu." In Ioan Lewis, ed. *Symbols and Sentiments: Cross-Cultural Studies in Symbolism*. New York: Academic Press, 1977, pp. 85–116.

Larson, James F., and Heung-Soo Park. *Global Television and the Politics of the Seoul Olympics*. Boulder, Colo.: Westview Press, 1993.

Latour, Bruno. *Science in Action*. Cambridge: Harvard University Press, 1987.

Latour, Bruno. *We Have Never Been Modern*. Trans. Catherine Porter. Cambridge: Harvard University Press, 1993.

Laughlin, Charles D. "Ritual and the Symbolic Function: A Summary of Biogenetic Structural Theory." *Journal of Ritual Studies* 4, no. 1 (Winter 1990): 15–39.

Laughlin, Charles D., and Eugene G. d'Aquili. *Biogenetic Structuralism*. New York: Columbia University Press, 1974.

Lawson, E. Thomas. "Ritual as Language," *Religion* 6 (1976): 123–39.

Lawson, E. Thomas, and Robert N. McCauley. "Crisis of Conscience, Riddle of Identity: Making Space for a Cognitive Approach to Religious Phenomena." *Journal of the American Academy of Religion* 61, no. 2 (Summer 1993): 201–23.

Lawson, E. Thomas, and Robert N. McCauley. *Rethinking Religion: Connecting Cognition and Culture*. Cambridge: Cambridge University Press, 1990.

Lazarus-Yafeh, Hava. *Some Religious Aspects of Islam*. Leiden: E. J. Brill, 1981.

Leach, Edmund. *Culture and Communication: The Logic by Which Symbols Are Connected*. Cambridge: Cambridge University Press, 1976.

Leach, Edmund. *The Political Systems of Highland Burma*, 2d ed. London: Athlone Press, 1945.

Leach, Edmund R. "Golden Bough or Gilded Twig?" *Daedalus* 90 no. 2 (Spring 1961): 371–87.

Leach, Edmund. "Frazer and Malinowski." *Current Anthropology* 7 (1966): 560–75.

Leach, Edmund. "Ritualization in Man in Relation to Conceptual and Social Developments." In Julian Huxley, ed. "A Discussion on Ritualization," 1966, pp. 403–8.

Leach, Edmund. "Ritual." In David L. Sills, ed. *International Encyclopedia of the Social Sciences*, vol. 13. New York: Macmillan, 1968, pp. 520–26.

Leach, Edmund. "A Poetics of Power [review of Geertz's *Negara*]." *New Republic* 184 (April 4, 1981): 30–33.

Lee, Du-Hyun. "Korean Shamans: Role Playing through Trance Possession." In Richard Schechner and Willa Appel, eds. *By Means of Performance: Intercultural Studies of Theatre and Ritual*. Cambridge: Cambridge University Press, 1990, pp. 149–66.

Legge, James, trans. *Li chi: Book of Rites*, vol. 1. New Hyde Park, N.Y.: University Books, 1967.

Lévi-Strauss, Claude. *Totemism*. Trans. Rodney Needham. Boston: Beacon Press, 1963.

Lévi-Strauss, Claude. *Structural Anthropology*. Trans. Claire Jacobsen and Brooke Grundfest Schoepf. Garden City, N.Y.: Anchor Books, 1967.

Lévi-Strauss, Claude. *The Origin of Table Manners*, vol. 3 of *Introduction to a Science of Mythology*. Trans. John and Doreen Weightman. New York: Harper and Row, 1968.

Lévi-Strauss, Claude. *The Raw and the Cooked*, vol. 1 of *Introduction to a Science of Mythology*. Trans. John and Doreen Weightman. New York: Harper and Row, 1969.

Lévi-Strauss, Claude. *The Elementary Structures of Kinship*. Trans. James Harle Bell, John Richard von Sturmer, and Rodney Needham. Boston: Beacon Press, 1969.

Lévi-Strauss, Claude. *From Honey to Ashes*, vol. 2 of *Introduction to a Science of Mythology*. Trans. John and Doreen Weightman. New York: Harper and Row, 1973.

Lévi-Strauss, Claude. *The Naked Man*, vol. 4 of *Introduction to a Science of Mythology*. Trans. John and Doreen Weightman. New York: Harper and Row, 1981.

Levy, Leonard W. *Blasphemy: Verbal Offense against the Sacred from Moses to Salman Rushdie*. New York: Knopf, 1993.

Lévy-Bruhl, Lucien. *How Natives Think*. New York: Washington Square Press, 1966.

Li, Xia. "China Heritage '94: The Year to Retrace People and Places from the Distant Past." *China Today* 43, no. 1 (January 1994): 33–34.

Lightfoot-Klein, Hanny. *Prisoners of Ritual: An Odyssey into Female Genital Circumcision in Africa*. Binghampton, N.Y.: Haworth Medical Press, 1989.

Lincoln, Bruce. *Discourse and the Construction of Society*. New York: Oxford University Press, 1989.

Lincoln, Bruce. *Emerging from the Chrysalis: Rituals of Women's Initiations*, rev. ed. New York: Oxford University Press, 1991.

Lorenz, Konrad Z. "Evolution of Ritualization in the Biological and Cultural Spheres." In Huxley, ed. "A Discussion on Ritualization," pp. 273–84.

Lowe, H. Y. *The Adventures of Wu: The Life Cycle of a Peking Man*. Princeton, N.J.: Princeton University Press, 1983.

Lowie, Robert H. *Primitive Religion*. New York: Liveright Publishing, 1952.

Lowie, Robert H. *The History of Ethnological Theory*. New York: Holt, Rinehart and Winston, 1966.

Luckmann, Thomas. *The Invisible Religion: The Problem of Religion in Modern Society*. New York: Macmillan, 1967.

Lukes, Steven. "Political Ritual and Social Integration." *Sociology: Journal of the British Sociological Association* 9, no. 2 (1975): 289–308.

Lukes, Stephen. *Émile Durkheim: His Life and Work: A Historical and Critical Study*. New York: Penguin, 1977.

MacAloon, John J. "Double Visions: Olympic Games and American Culture." *Kenyon Review*, n.s. 4 (1982): 99–112.

MacAloon, John J. "Olympic Games and the Theory of Spectacle in Modern Societies." In John J. MacAloon, ed. *Rite, Drama, Festival, Spectacle: Rehearsals towards a Theory of Cultural Performance*. Philadelphia: Institute for the Study of Human Issues, 1984, pp. 241–80.

MacAloon, John J. "*La Pintada Olímpica*: Puerto Rico, International Sport, and the Constitution of Politics." In Edward M. Bruner, ed. *Text, Play, and Story: The Construction and Recontruction of Self and Society*. Washington, D.C.: American Ethnological Society, 1984, pp. 315–55.

MacAloon, John J. *This Great Symbol: Pierre de Coubertin and the Origins of the Modern Olympic Games*. Chicago: University of Chicago , 1981.

MacCannell, Dean. "A Note on Hat Tipping." *Semiotica* 7, no. 4 (1973): 300–312.

MacCannell, Dean. *The Tourist: A New Theory of the Leisure Class*, rev. ed. New York: Schocken, 1989.

Mack, Burton. "Introduction: Religion and Ritual." In Robert G. Hamerton-Kelly, ed. *Violent Origins*, pp. 32–51.

Madhubuti, Haki R. *Kwanzaa: An African-American Holiday That Is Progressive and Uplifting*. Chicago: Third World Press, 1972.

Mahdi, Louise Carus, Steven Foster, and Meredith Little, eds. *Betwixt and Between: Patterns of Masculine and Feminine Initiation*. LaSalle, Ill.: Open Court, 1987.

Malinowski, Bronislaw. *Sex, Culture, and Myth*. New York: Harcourt, Brace and World, 1962.

Malinowski, Bronislaw. *Magic, Science and Religion and Other Essays* [1925]. Glencoe, Ill.: Free Press, 1974.

Marcus, Frances Frank. "New Orleans Weights Anti-Bias Law on Carnival." *New York Times*. December 7, 1991, p. 7.

Marcus, Frances Frank. "New Orleans Outlaws Bias by Mardi Gras Parade Clubs." *New York Times*. December 21, 1991, p. 7.

Marcus, Frances Frank. "Law Is Softened to Quell Furor over Mardi Gras." *New York Times*. February 8, 1992, p. 6;

Marcus, Frances Frank. "Behind the Fears, Mardi Gras as Usual." *New York Times*. February 25, 1992, p. 12.

Marcus, Frances Frank. "Council Eases Anti-Bias Law on Mardi Gras." *New York Times*. May 10, 1992, p. 24.

Marcus, Frances Frank. "Mardi Gras Group Quits to Protest New Law." *New York Times*. August 19, 1992, p. A18.

Markels, Alex. "A Run to Moonlight for Food and More." *New York Times*. August 21, 1994, p. 24.

Marriott, McKim. "The Feast of Love." In Milton Singer, ed. *Krishna: Myths, Rites, and Attitudes*. Chicago: University of Chicago Press, 1966, pp. 200–212.

Marriott, Michel. "New Side of Kwanzaa: Marketing." *New York Times*. December 25, 1991, p. 25.

Martin, David. *The Breaking of the Image*. New York: St. Martin's Press, 1979.

Martin, David. "Personal Identity and a Changed Church." In David Martin and Peter Mullen, eds. *No Alternative: The Prayer Book Controversy*. Oxford: Basic Blackwell, 1981, pp. 12–22.

Martin, David. "Sociology, Religion and Secularization: An Orientation." *Religion* 25, no. 4 (October 1995): 295–303.

Martin, David, and Peter Mullen, eds. *No Alternative: The Prayer Book Controversy*. Oxford: Basil Blackwell, 1981.

Martin, Richard C. *Islam: A Cultural Perspective*. Englewood Cliffs, N.J.: Prentice-Hall, 1982.

Martos, Joseph. *Doors to the Sacred: A Historical Introduction to Sacraments in the Catholic Church*. Garden City, N.Y.: Doubleday, 1981.

Marvin, Carolyn. "Theorizing the Flagbody: Symbolic Dimensions of the Flag Desecration Debate, or, Why the Bill of Rights Does Not Fly in the Ballpark." *Critical Studies in Mass Communication* 8, no. 2 (1991): 119–38.

Masur, Louis P. *Rites of Execution: Capital Punishment and the Transformation of American Culture, 1776–1865*. New York: Oxford University Press, 1989.

Masuzawa, Tomoko. *In Search of Dreamtime: The Quest for the Origin of Religion*. Chicago: University of Chicago Press, 1994.

Mauss, Marcel. "Esquisse d'une théorie générale de la magie." *Année sociologique* 7 (1902–03). Reprinted as *A General Theory of Magic*. Ed. D. Pocock. London: Routledge and Kegan Paul, 1972.

Mauss, Marcel. "Techniques of the Body" [1935]. Trans. Ben Brewster. *Economy and Society* 2, no. 1 (Feb. 1973): 70–88.

McClaren, Peter. *Schooling as a Ritual Performance*. London: Routledge and Kegan Paul, 1986.

McClester, Cedric. *Kwanzaa: Everything You Always Wanted to Know but Didn't Know Where to Ask*, rev. ed. New York: Gumbs and Thomas, 1990.

McDonough, Sheila. "Orthodoxy and Heterodoxy." In Eliade et al., eds. *The Encyclopedia of Religion*, vol. 11, pp. 124–29.

McDowell, Jennifer. "Soviet Civil Ceremonies." *Journal for the Scientific Study of Religion* 13 (1974): 265–79.

McGee, R. Jon. *Life, Ritual and Religion among the Lacandon Maya*. Belmont: Wadsworth, 1990.

McManus, John. "Ritual and Ontogenetic Development." In Eugene G. d'Aquili, Charles D. Laughlin, and John McManus, eds. *The Spectrum of Ritual: A Biogenetic Structural Analysis*. New York: Columbia University Press, 1979, pp. 183–215.

McMullen, David. "Bureaucrats and Cosmology: The Ritual Code of T'ang China." In David Cannadine and Simon Price, eds. *Rituals of Royalty: Power and Ceremonial in Traditional Societies*. Cambridge: Cambridge University Press, 1987, pp. 181–236.

Meddin, Jay. "Symbols, Anxiety, and Ritual: A Functional Interpretation." *Quantitative Sociology* 3, no. 4 (Winter 1980): 251–71.

Métraux, Alfred. *Voodoo in Haiti*. New York: Schocken Books, 1972.

Miner, Horace. "Body Ritual among the Nacirema." *American Anthropologist* 58 (1956): 503–7. Reprinted in James P. Spradley and Michael A. Rynkiewich, eds. *The Nacirema: Readings on American Culture*. Boston: Little, Brown, 1975, pp. 10–13.

Montague, Susan P., and Robert Morais. "Football Games and Rock Concerts: The Ritual Enactment of American Success Models." In W. Arens and Susan P. Montague, eds. *The American Dimension: Cultural Myths and Social Realities*. Van Nuys, Calif.: Alfred Publishing Co., 1976.

Mooney, James. *The Ghost Dance Religion and the Sioux Outbreak of 1890* [1896]. Abridged, with introduction by Anthony F. C. Wallace. Chicago: University of Chicago Press, 1965.

Moore, Robert L., Ralph Wendell Burhoe, and Philip J. Hefner, eds. "Ritual in Human Adaptation." *Zygon* 18, no. 3 (September 1983): 209–326.

Morris, Brian. "Introduction." In *Ritual Murder: Essays on Liturgical Reform*. Manchester: Carcanet Press, 1980.

Morris, Brian. *Anthropological Studies of Religion*. Cambridge: Cambridge University Press, 1987.

Morris, Desmond. *Gestures*. New York: Stein and Day, 1979.

Mote, Frederick W. *The Intellectual Foundations of China*. New York: Alfred Knopf, 1971.

Müller, F. Max. *Lectures on the Science of Language* [1861]. New York: Scribner, Armstrong and Co., 1967.

Müller, Max. *Chips from a German Workshop* [1869]. Chico, Calif.: Scholars Press, 1985.

Munn, Nancy D. "Symbolism in a Ritual Context." In John J. Honigmann, ed. *Handbook of Social and Cultural Anthropology*. Chicago: Rand McNally, 1973, pp. 579–612.

Murphy, G. Ronald, S.J. "A Ceremonial Ritual: The Mass." In Eugene G. d'Aquili, Charles D. Laughlin, Jr., and John McManus, eds. *The Spectrum of Ritual: A Biogenetic Approach*. New York: Columbia University, 1979, pp. 318–41.

Myerhoff, Barbara G. *Peyote Hunt: The Sacred Journey of the Huichol Indians*. Ithaca, N.Y.: Cornell University Press, 1974.

Myerhoff, Barbara G. "We Don't Wrap Herring in a Printed Page: Fusion, Fictions and Continuity." In Sally F. Moore and Barbara G. Myerhoff, eds. *Secular Ritual*. Amsterdam: Van Gorcum, 1977, pp. 199–224.

Myerhoff, Barbara G. "A Death in Due Time." In John J. MacAloon, ed. *Rite, Drama, Festival, Spectacle*. Philadelphia: Institute for the Study of Human Issues, 1984, pp. 149–78.

Neill, Stephen. "Liturgical Continuity and Change." In David Martin and Peter Mullen, eds. *No Alternative: The Prayer Book Controversy*. Oxford: Basic Blackwell, 1981, pp. 1–11.

Neusner, Jacob. "Ritual without Myth: The Use of Legal Materials for the Study of Religions." *Religion: Journal of Religion and Religions* 5 (Autumn 1975): 91–100.

Neusner, Jacob. *Method and Meaning in Ancient Judaism*. Atlanta: Scholars Press, 1979.

Neyrey, Jerome H. "Body Language in 1 Corinthians: The Use of Anthropological Models for Understanding Pual and His Opponents." *Semeia* 35 (1986): 129–70.

Nicholas, Ralph W. "The Effectiveness of the Hindu Sacrament (*Samskara*): Caste, Marriage, and Divorce in Bengali Culture." In Lindsey Harlan and Paul B. Courtright, eds. *From the Margins of Hindu Marriage: Essays on Gender, Religion, and Culture*. New York: Oxford University Press, 1995, pp. 137–00.

Norbeck, Edward. "The Anthropological Study of Play." *Rice University Studies* 60, no. 3 (1974): 1–8.

Norbeck, Edward. *Religion in Human Life: Anthropological Views*. Prospect Heights, Ill.: Waveland Press, 1974.

Oates, Joyce Carol. "The Cruelest Sport." *New York Review of Books*. February 19, 1992, pp. 3–6.

Obeyesekere, Gananath. *The Apotheosis of Captain Cook: European Mythmaking in the Pacific*. Chicago: University of Chicago, 1992.

Ohnuki-Tierney, Emiko. *Rice as Self: Japanese Identities through Time*. Princeton, N.J.: Princeton University Press, 1993.

Olivelle, Patrick. *The Āśrama System: The History and Hermeneutics of a Religious Institution*. New York: Oxford University Press, 1993.

Oliver, Douglas L. *Ancient Tahitian Society*, 3 vols. Honolulu: University of Hawaii Press, 1974.

Orsi, Robert Anthony. *The Madonna of 115th Street: Faith and Community in Italian Harlem, 1880–1950*. New Haven: Yale University Press, 1985.

Ortiz de Montellano, Bernard R. "Aztec Cannibalism: An Ecological Necessity?" *Science* 200, no. 4342 (May 12, 1978): 611–17.

Ortiz de Montellano, Bernard R. "Counting Skulls: Comment on the Aztec Cannibalism Theory of Harner-Harris." *American Anthropologist* 85, no. 2 (1983): 403–6.

Ortner, Sherry B. "On Key Symbols." *American Anthropologist* 75 (1973): 1338–46.

Ortner, Sherry B. *Sherpas through Their Rituals*. Cambridge: Cambridge University Press, 1978.

Ortner, Sherry B. "Theory in Anthropology since the Sixties." *Comparative Study of Society and History* 26 (1984): 126–65.

Ortner, Sherry B. *High Religion: A Cultural and Political History of Sherpa Buddhism*. Princeton, N.J.: Princeton University Press, 1989.

O'Shea, W. J. "Liturgiology." In *New Catholic Encyclopedia*, vol. 8. Washington, D. C.: Catholic University of America, 1967, pp. 919–27.

Otto, Rudolf. *The Idea of the Holy* [1917], rev. ed. Trans. John W. Harvey. New York: Oxford University Press, 1929.

Packard, Jerrold M. *Sons of Heaven: A Portrait of the Japanese Monarchy*. New York: Macmillan, 1987.

Paige, Karen Ericksen, and Jeffery M. Paige. *The Politics of Reproductive Ritual*. Berkeley: University of California Press, 1981.

Paper, Jordan. *Offering Smoke: The Sacred Pipe and Native American Religion*. Moscow: University of Idaho Press, 1988.

Peacock, James L. *Rites of Modernization: Symbolic and Social Aspects of Indonesian Proletarian Drama*. Chicago: University of Chicago Press, 1968.

Penner, Hans H. "Myth and Ritual: A Wasteland or a Forest of Symbols." *History and Theory* 8 (1968): 46–57.

Pettazzoni, Raffaele. *Essays on the History of Religions*. Leiden: Brill, 1954.

Phillips, Verner Bradford, and Harvey Blume. *Ota Benga: The Pygmy in the Zoo*. New York: Delta, 1992.

Pinault, David. *The Shiites: Ritual and Popular Piety in a Muslim Community*. New York: St. Martin's Press, 1992.

Pinker, Steven. *The Language Instinct*. New York: William Morris, 1994.

Platvoet, Jan, and Karel van der Toorn, eds. *Pluralism and Identity: Studies in Ritual Behavior*. Leiden: Brill, 1995.

Pocock, J. G. A. "Ritual, Language, Power: An Essay on the Apparent Meanings of Chinese Philosophy." *Political Science* 16 (1964): 3–31.

Poll, Solomon. *The Hasidic Community of Williamsburg: A Study in the Sociology of Religion*. New York: Schocken, 1969.

Posinsky, S. H. "Ritual, Neurotic and Social." *American Imago* 19 (1962): 375–90.

Post, Elizabeth L. *Emily Post's Etiquette*, 14th ed. New York: Harper and Row, 1984.

Post, Paul. "John Bossy and the Study of Liturgy." In Charles Caspers and Marc Schneiders, eds. *Omnes Circumadstantes*, pp. 31–50.

Post, Paul. "The Modern Pilgrim: A Study of Contemporary Pilgrims' Accounts." *Ethnologia Europea* 24, no. 2 (1994): 85–100.

Preston, David L. *The Social Organization of Zen Practice: Constructing Transcultural Reality*. Cambridge: Cambridge University Press, 1988.

Preuss, J. Samuel. *Explaining Religion: Criticism and Theory from Bodin to Freud*. New Haven: Yale University Press, 1987.

Procter-Smith, Marjorie. *In Her Own Rite: Constructing Feminist Liturgical Tradition*. Nashville: Abingdon, 1990.

Procter-Smith, Marjorie, and Janet R. Walton, eds. *Women at Worship: Interpretations of North American Diversity*. Louisville, Ky.: Westminster/John Knox Press, 1993.

Purdum, Elizabeth D., and J. Anthony Paredes. "Rituals of Death: Capital Punishment and Human Sacrifice." In Michael Radelet, ed. *Facing the Death Penalty: Essays on Cruel and Unusual Punishment*. Philadelphia: Temple University Press, 1989, pp. 139–55.

Quirk, Robert E. *An Affair of Honor: Woodrow Wilson and the Occupation of Vera Cruz*. New York: McGraw-Hill, 1964.

Radcliffe-Brown, Alfred R. "Religion and Society." *Journal of the Royal Anthropological Institute of Great Britain and Ireland* 75 (1945): 33–43.

Radcliffe-Brown, Alfred R. *The Andaman Islanders*. New York: Free Press, 1964.

Radford, Katy. *Elizabeth Is Queen: The Coronation of Her Majesty Queen Elizabeth II, June 2nd, 1953, Westminster Abbey*. London: Path and Castle, 1992.

Raglan, F. R. R. S. *The Hero: A Study in Tradition, Myth, and Drama*. New York: Oxford University Press, 1937. Reprinted in Rank, Raglan, and Dundes. *In Quest of the Hero*, pp. 89–164.

Rahula, Walpola Sri. *What the Buddha Taught*, 2d rev. ed. New York: Grove, 1974.

Rank, Otto. "The Myth of the Birth of the Hero." In Rank, Raglan, and Dundes. *In Quest of the Hero*, pp. 3–86.

Rank, Otto, Lord Raglan, and Alan Dundes. *In Quest of the Hero*. Introduction by Robert A. Segal. Princeton: Princeton University Press, 1990.

Rappaport, Roy A. "Ritual Regulation of Environmental Relations among a New Guniea People" [1967]. In *Ecology, Meaning, and Religion*, pp. 27–42.

Rappaport, Roy A. *Pigs for the Ancestors* [1968], 2d ed. (New Haven: Yale University, 1980).

Rappaport, Roy A. "Liturgies and Lies." *International Yearbook for Sociology of Knowledge and Religion* 10 (1976): 75–104.

Rappaport, Roy A. *Ecology, Meaning, and Religion*. Richmond, Calif.: North Atlantic Books, 1979.

Rappaport, Roy A. "Ecology, Adaptation, and the Ills of Functionalism." In *Ecology, Meaning, and Religion*, pp. 43–96.

Rappaport, Roy A. "The Obvious Aspects of Ritual." In *Ecology, Meaning and Religion*, pp. 173–222.

Rappaport, Roy A. "Veracity, Verity, and *Verum* in Liturgy." *Studia Liturgica* 23, no. 1 (1993): 35–50.

Ray, Benjamin C. "'Performative Utterances' in African Rituals," *History of Religions* 13, no. 1 (1973): 16–35.

Ray, Benjamin C. *African Religions: Symbol, Ritual, and Community*. Englewood Cliffs, N.J.: Prentice-Hall, 1976.

Reik, Theodor. *Ritual: Psycho-analytic Studies*. Westport, Conn.: Greenwood Publishers, 1975.

Restand, Penne L. *Christmas in America: A History*. New York: Oxford University Press, 1995.

Robertson Smith, William. *Lectures on the Religion of the Semites: The Fundamental Institutions* [1889]. New York: KTAV Publishing House, 1969.

Roff, William R. "Pilgrimage and the History of Religions: Theoretical Approaches to the Hajj." In Richard C. Martin, ed. *Approaches to Islam in Religious Studies*. Tucson: University of Arizona Press, 1985, pp. 78–86.

Rohter, Larry. "Bias Law Casts Pall over New Orleans Mardi Gras." *New York Times*. February 2, 1992, pp. 1, 18.

Rohter, Larry. "New Orleans Weakens Mardi Gras Bias Law." *New York Times*. February 7, 1992, pp. 17.

Roosevelt, Eleanor. *Book of Common Sense Etiquette*. New York: Macmillan, 1962.

Rosenthal, Elizabeth. "Struggling to Handle Bereavement as AIDS Rips Relationships Apart." *New York Times*. December 6, 1992, pp. 1A, 21A.

Ruether, Rosemary Radford. *Women-Church: Theology and Practice of Feminist Liturgical Communities*. San Francisco: Harper and Row, 1985.

Sahlins, Marshall. *Culture and Practical Reason*. Chicago: University of Chicago Press, 1976.

Sahlins, Marshall. "Culture as Protein and Profit." *New York Review of Books*. November 23, 1978, pp. 45–53.

Sahlins, Marshall. *Historical Metaphors and Mythical Realities*. Ann Arbor: University of Michigan Press, 1981.

Sahlins, Marshall. *Islands of History*. Chicago: University of Chicago Press, 1985.

Salter, Michael A. "Play in Ritual: An Ethnohistorical Overview of Native North America." *Stadion* 3, no. 2 (1977): 230–43.

Saso, Michael R. *Taoism and the Rite of Cosmic Renewal*. Pullman: Washington State University Press, 1972.

Schafer, Edward. "Ritual Exposure in Ancient China." *Harvard Journal of Asiatic Studies* 14 (1951): 130–84.

Schechner, Richard. *Essays in Performance Theory 1970–1976*. New York: Drama Book Specialists, 1977.

Schechner, Richard. *Between Theater and Anthropology*. Philadelphia: University of Pennsylvania, 1985.

Schechner, Richard. "Wrestling against Time: The Performance Aspects of Agni." *Journal of Asian Studies* 45, no. 2 (February 1989): 359–63.

Schechner, Richard. *The Future of Ritual: Writings on Culture and Performance*. London: Routledge, 1993.

Schechner, Richard, and Willa Appel, eds. *By Means of Performance: Intercultural Studies of Theater and Ritual*. Cambridge: Cambridge University Press, 1989.

Schieffelin, Edward L. "Performance and the Cultural Construction of Reality." *American Ethnologist* 12 (1985): 707–24.

Schiffrin, Deborah. "Handwork as Ceremony: The Case of the Handshake," *Semiotica* 12 (1974): 189–202.

Schipper, Kristofer. *The Taoist Body*. Trans. Karen C. Duval. Berkeley: University of California Press, 1993.

Schmidt, Leigh Eric. "From Arbor Day to the Environmental Sabbath: Nature, Liturgy, and American Protestantism." *Harvard Theological Review* 84, no. 3 (1991): 299–323.

Schmidt, Wilhelm. *Origin and Growth of Religion* [1931]. New York: Cooper Square Publishers, 1972.

Schmidt, William E. "British Courts to Doff Wig? Verdict Asked." *New York Times*, August 23, 1992, p. 4.

Schneider, Robert A. "Mortification on Parade: Penitential Processions in Sixteenth- and Seventeenth-Century France." *Renaissance and Reformation* 10, no. 1 (1986): 123–45.

Scholem, Gershom. "The Star of David: History of a Symbol." In *The Messianic Idea in Judaism*. New York: Schocken, 1971, pp. 257–81.

Scholte, Bob. "The Structural Anthropology of Claude Lévi-Strauss." In John J. Honigmann, ed. *Handbook of Social and Cultural Anthropology*. Chicago: Rand McNally, 1973, pp. 637–716.

Schwartzman, Helen B., ed. *Play and Culture: 1978 Proceedings of the Association for the Anthropological Study of Play*. West Point, N.Y.: Leisure Press, 1980.

Seaman, Gary. "The Sexual Politics of Karmic Retribution." In Emily M. Ahern and Hill Gates, eds. *The Anthropology of Taiwanese Society*. Stanford, Calif.: Stanford University Press, 1981, pp. 381–96.

Searle, John R. *Speech Acts*. Cambridge: Cambridge University Press, 1969.

Searle, Mark, ed. *Liturgy and Social Justice*. Collegeville: Liturgical Press, 1980.

Searle, Mark. "The Rites of Christian Initiation." In Louise Carus Mahdi, Steven Foster, and Meredith Little, eds. *Betwixt and Between: Patterns of Masculine and Feminine Initiation*. LaSalle, Ill.: Open Court, 1987, pp. 457–70.

Sears, John F. *Sacred Places: American Tourist Attractions in the Nineteenth Century*. New York: Oxford University Press, 1989.

Segal, Robert A. "The Myth-Ritualist Theory of Religion." *Journal for the Scientific Study of Religion* 19, no. 2 (1980): 173–185.

Segal, Robert A. *Joseph Campbell: An Introduction*, rev. ed. New York: New American Library, 1990.

Segal, Robert A. "Joseph Campbell on Jews and Judaism." *Religion* 22, no. 2 (April 1992): 151–70.

Seidel, Anna. "Buying One's Way to Heaven: The Celestial Treasury in Chinese Religions." *History of Religions* 17, nos. 3–4 (Feb.–May 1978): 419–31.

Senn, Frank. *Christian Worship and Its Cultural Setting*. Philadelphia: Fortress Press, 1983.

Shaw, G. W. *Academical Dress of British Universities*. Cambridge: W. Heffer and Sons, 1966.

Sheard, Kevin. *Academic Heraldry in America*. Marquette: Northern Michigan College Press, 1962.

Shils, Edward, and Michael Young. "The Meaning of the Coronation." *The Sociological Review* 1 (1953): 63–81.

Sigaux, Gilbert. *History of Tourism*. London: Leisure Arts, 1966.

Silber, Ilana Friedrich. "'Opting Out' in Theravada Buddhism and Medieval Christianity." *Religion* 15 (1985): 251–77.

Silver, Vernon. "Mortarboards Become Billboards for Protests." *New York Times*. June 7, 1993, p. B5.

Simons, Lewis M. "Japanese Coronation Mixes Modern Tension into Still-Sacred Rites." *San Jose Mercury News*. September 29, 1990, p. 2a.

Singer, Milton. *When a Great Tradition Modernizes*. New York: Praeger Publishers, 1972.

Sipes, Richard G. "War, Sports, and Aggression: An Empirical Test of Two Rival Theories." *American Anthropologist* 75 (January 1973): 64–86.

Smith, Brian K. "Ritual, Knowledge, and Being: Initiation and Vedic Study in Ancient India." *Numen* 33, fasc. 1 (1986): 65–89.

Smith, Brian K. *Reflections on Resemblance, Ritual and Religion*. New York: Oxford University Press, 1989.

Smith, Hugh. *Academic Dress and Insignia of the World: Gowns, Hats, Chains of Office, Hoods, Rings, Medals and Other Degree Insignia of Universities and Other Institutions of Learning*. Cape Town: A. A. Balkema, 1970.

Smith, Jonathan Z. "When the Bough Breaks." In *Map Is Not Territory: Studies in the History of Religions*. Leiden: E. J. Brill, 1978, pp. 208–39; also in *History of Religions* 12, no. 4 (1973): 342–71.

Smith, Jonathan Z. *Imagining Religion: From Babylon to Jonestown*. Chicago: University of Chicago, 1982.

Smith, Jonathan Z. *To Take Place: Toward Theory in Ritual*. Chicago: University of Chicago, 1987.

Smith, Jonathan Z. *Drudgery Divine: On the Comparison of Early Christianities and the Religions of Late Antiquity*. Chicago: University of Chicago Press, 1990.

Smith, Pierre. "Aspects.of the Organization of Rites." In Michel Izard and Pierre Smith, eds. *Between Belief and Transgression: Structuralist Essays in Religion, History and Myth*. Chicago: University of Chicago Press, 1982, pp. 103–28.

Smith, Valene L., ed. *Hosts and Guests: The Anthropology of Tourism*. Philadelphia: University of Pennsylvania Press, 1977.

Smith, Wilfred Cantwell. *Faith and Belief*. Princeton, N.J.: Princeton University Press, 1979.

Soustelle, Jacques. "Ritual Human Sacrifice in Mesoamerica: an Introduction." In Elizabeth P. Benson and Elizabeth H. Boone, eds. *Ritual Human Sacrifice in Mesoamerica*. Washington D.C.: Dumbarton Oaks Research Library and Collection, 1984, pp. 1–5.

Srinivasan, Amrit. "Reform or Conformity? Temple 'Prostitution' and the Community in the Madras Presidency." In Bina Agarwal, ed. *Structures of Patriarchy: State, Community and Household in Modernising Asia*. London: Zed Press, 1988, pp. 175–98.

Staal, Frits. "The Sound of Religion: Parts I-III," *Numen* 33, no. 1 (1968): 33–64; "The Sound of Religion: Parts IV-V," *Numen* 33, no. 2 (1968): 185–224.

Staal, Frits. "The Meaninglessness of Ritual." *Numen* 26, no. 1 (1975): 2–22.

Staal, Frits. *Agni: The Vedic Ritual of the Fire Altar*. Berkeley: Asian Humanities Press, 1983.

Staal, Frits. "Communications to the Editor." *Journal of Asian Studies* 46, no. 1 (Feb. 1987):105–108.

Staal, Frits. *Rules without Meaning: Ritual, Mantras and the Human Sciences*. Bern: Peter Lang, 1989.

Staal, Frits, and Richard Gardner. *Altar of Fire*, film. Berkeley: University of California Extension, 1976.

Starhawk [Miriam Simos]. *The Spiral Dance: A Rebirth of the Ancient Religion of the Great Goddess*, 10th anniversary ed. San Francisco: HarperCollins, 1989.

Stark, Rodney, and William Sims Bainbridge. *The Future of Religion: Secularization, Revival, and Cult Formation*. Berkeley: University of California Press, 1985.

Stein, Rolf A. *The World in Miniature: Container Gardens and Dwellings in Far Eastern Religious Thought*. Trans. Phyllis Brooks. Stanford, Calif.: Stanford University Press, 1990.

Steinfels, Peter. "More Protestants Accept Ashes as Ritual for Lent." *New York Times*. February 24, 1993, p. B12.

Steinfels, Peter. "Beliefs: Who is Jewish." *New York Times*. August 7, 1993, p. 6A.

Stewart, Charles. *Demons and the Devil: Moral Imagination in Modern Greek Culture*. Princeton, N.J.: Princeton University Press, 1991.

Stewart, Omer C. "The Ghost Dance." In W. Raymond Wood and Margot Liberty, eds. *Anthropology on the Great Plains*. Lincoln: University of Nebraska Press, 1980, pp. 179–87.

Strenski, Ivan. "Between Theory and Speciality: Sacrifice in the 90s." *Religious Studies Review* 22, no. 1 (January 1996): 10–20.

Sullivan, Lawrence E. "Sound and Senses: Toward a Hermeneutics of Performance." *History of Religions* 26, no. 1 (1986): 1–33.

Sullivan, Lawrence E. *Icanchu's Drum: An Orientation to Meaning in South American Religions.* New York: Macmillan, 1988.

Sullivan, Lawrence E. *Histories and Rituals: The Case of a National Rite of Mourning.* Twelfth annual university lecture in religion. Tempe, Az.: Arizona State University, 1991.

Swearer, Donald K. *Wat Haripunjaya: A Study of the Royal Temple of the Buddha's Relic, Lamphun, Thailand.* Missoula, Mont.: Scholars Press, 1976.

Tabory, Ephraim. "Jewish Identity, Israeli Nationalism, and Soviet Jewish Migration." *Journal of Church and State* 33, no. 2 (Spring 1991): 287–99.

Taft, Robert, S.J. *Beyond East and West: Problems in Liturgical Understanding.* Washington, D.C.: Pastoral Press, 1984.

Tambiah, S. J. "The Magical Power of Words." *Man* n.s. 3, no. 2 (1968):175–208. Reprinted in *Culture, Thought, and Social Action,* pp. 17–59.

Tambiah, Stanley J. *World Conqueror and World Renouncer.* Cambridge: Cambridge University Press, 1976.

Tambiah, S. J. "A Performative Approach to Ritual." In *Culture, Thought, and Social Action,* pp. 123–66.

Tambiah, S. J. *Culture, Thought, and Social Action: An Anthropological Perspective.* Cambridge, Mass.: Harvard University Press, 1985.

Tambiah, S. J. *Magic, Science, Religion, and the Scope of Rationality.* Cambridge: Cambridge University Press, 1990.

Taylor, Bron. "Earthen Spirituality or Cultural Genocide?: Radical Environmentalism's Appropriation of Native American Spirituality." *Religion* 27, no. 2 (1997): 183–215.

Thomas, Keith. *Religion and the Decline of Magic.* New York: Scribners, 1971.

Thompson, Bard. *Liturgies of the Western Church.* Philadelphia: Fortress Press, 1961.

Tsai, Ventine. "For Better or Worse? Festivals and the Media." Trans. Christopher Hughes. *Sinorama* (July 1992): 98–100.

Turner, Kay. "Contemporary Feminist Rituals." In Charlene Spretnak, ed. *The Politics of Women's Spirituality: Essays on the Rise of Spiritual Power within the Feminist Movement.* Garden City, N.Y.: Doubleday Anchor, 1982, pp. 219–33.

Turner, Victor. *Schism and Continuity in an African Society.* Manchester: Manchester University Press, 1957.

Turner, Victor. *The Forest of Symbols: Aspects of Ndembu Ritual.* Ithaca, N.Y.: Cornell University Press, 1967.

Turner, Victor. *The Ritual Process: Structure and Anti-Structure.* Ithaca, N.Y.: Cornell University Press, 1969.

Turner, Victor. *Dramas, Fields, and Metaphors: Symbolic Action in Human Society.* Ithaca, N.Y.: Cornell University Press, 1974.

Turner, Victor. "Ritual, Tribal and Catholic." *Worship* 50 (November 1976): 504–26.

Turner, Victor. *From Ritual to Theater: The Human Seriousness of Play.* New York: Performing Arts Journal Publications, 1982.

Turner, Victor. "Body, Brain, and Culture." *Zygon* 18, no. 3 (Sept. 1983): 221–45.

Tyler, Stephen A. *India: An Anthropological Perspective.* Prospect Heights, Ill.: Waveland Press, 1986.

Tylor, Edward B. *Anthropology* [1881], rev. ed. London: Macmillan, 1924.

Tylor, Edward B. *Primitive Culture,* 2 vols. New York: Harper, 1958.

Valeri, Valerio. *Kingship and Sacrifice: Ritual and Society in Ancient Hawaii.* Chicago: University of Chicago, 1985.

van Baaren, Theodorus P. "The Flexibility of Myth." In Alan Dundes, ed. *Sacred Narrative: Readings in the Theory of Myth.* Berkeley: University of California, 1984, pp. 217–24.

van der Hart, Onno. *Rituals in Psychotherapy: Transition and Continuity.* New York: Irvington Publishers, 1978.

van der Leeuw, Gerardus. *Religion in Essence and Manifestation*, 2 vols. New York: Harper and Row, 1963.

Van Gennep, Arnold. *The Rites of Passage*. Trans. M. B. Vizedom and G. L. Caffee. Chicago: University of Chicago Press, 1960.

Van Gennep, Arnold. "On the Method to Be Followed in the Study of Rites and Myths." In Jacques Waardenburg, ed. *Classical Approaches to the Study of Religion: Aims, Methods and Theories of Research*, vol. 1. The Hague: Mouton, 1973, pp. 287–300.

Van Kley, Dale K. *The Damiens Affair and the Unraveling of the Ancien Régime*. Princeton, N.J.: Princeton University Press, 1984.

Vanderbilt, Amy. *Amy Vanderbilt's New Complete Book of Etiquette: The Guide to Gracious Living*. Garden City, N.Y.: Doubleday, 1967.

Varam, Dev. "Ascetics Lead Millions to Holy Dip at Kumbha Mela," *India-West*. May 22, 1992, p. 27.

Vatican Council. *Constitution on the Sacred Liturgy*. Collegeville, Minn.: Liturgical Press, 1963.

Visser, Margaret. *The Rituals of Dinner: The Origins, Evolution, Eccentricities, and Meaning of Table Manners*. New York: Grove Weidenfeld, 1991.

Volkman, Toby Alice. "Visions and Revisions: Toraja Culture and the Tourist Gaze." *American Ethnologist* 17, no. 1 (Feb. 1990): 91–110.

Volosinov, V. N. *Marxism and the Philosophy of Language*. Cambridge, Mass.: Harvard University Press, 1986.

Vries, Jan de. *Perspectives in the History of Religions* [1961]. Trans. Kees W. Bölle. Berkeley: University of California Press, 1977.

Waardenburg, Jean Jacques, ed. *Classical Approaches to the Study of Religion*, 2 vols. The Hague: Mouton, 1973.

Wainwright, Geoffrey. "The Periods of Liturgical History." In Cheslyn Jones et al., eds. *The Study of Liturgy*, rev. ed. New York: Oxford University Press, 1992, pp. 61–67.

Wakeman, Jr., Frederic. "Mao's Remains." In James L. Watson and Evelyn S. Rawski, eds. *Death Ritual in Late Imperial and Modern China*. Berkeley: University of California Press, 1988, pp. 254–88.

Waley, Arthur, trans. *The Analects of Confucius*. New York: Vintage Books, 1938.

Walker, Barbara G. *Women's Rituals: A Sourcebook*. San Francisco: Harper and Row, 1990.

Walton, Janet, and Marjorie Procter-Smith, eds. *Women at Worship: Interpretations of North American Diversity*. Louisville, Ky.: Westminister/John Knox Press, 1993.

Ward, Barbara E. "Not Merely Players: Drama, Art and Ritual in Traditional China." *Man* 14, no. 1 (March 1979): 18–39.

Warner, W. Lloyd. "An American Sacred Ceremony." In *American Life*. Chicago: University of Chicago Press, 1956, pp. 5–34.

Watson, Burton, trans. *Hsün Tzu: Basic Writings*. New York: Columbia University Press, 1963.

Watson, Rubie S. "The Named and the Nameless: Gender and Person in Chinese Society." *American Ethnologist* 13 (1986): 619–31.

Watts, Richard J., Sachiko Ide, and Konrad Ehlich, eds. *Politeness in Language: Studies in Its History, Theory, and Practice*. Berlin: Mouton de Gruyter, 1992.

Weber, Max. *The Protestant Ethic and the Spirit of Capitalism*. Trans. Talcott Parsons. New York: Charles Scribner's Sons, 1958.

Weber, Max. *The Sociology of Religion*. Trans. Ephraim Fischoff. Boston: Beacon Press, 1963.

Wegner, Judith Romney. *Chattel or Person? The Status of Women in the Mishnah*. New York: Oxford University Press, 1988.

Weigle, Marta. *Brothers of Light, Brothers of Blood*. Albuquerque: University of New Mexico Press, 1976.

Weiner, Annette. "Dominant Kings and Forgotten Queens." *Oceania* 58 (1987): 157–60.

Weisinger, Herbert. "The Branch That Grew Full Straight." *Daedalus* 90, no. 2 (Spring 1961): 388–89.

Weisman, Steven R. "Tokyo Journal: Emperor's Ritual Bed Keeps Secrets." *New York Times.* October 9, 1990. Section A, p. 4.

Weisman, Steven R. "Japan Enthrones Emperor Today in Old Rite with New Twist." *New York Times.* November 12, 1990. Section A, p. 10.

Weisman, Steven R. "Akihito Performs Solitary Rite as Some Question Its Meaning." *New York Times.* November 23, 1990. Section A, p. 7.

Werblowsky, R. J., and Geoffrey Wigoder, eds. *The Encyclopedia of the Jewish Religion.* New York: Holt, Rinehart, and Winston, 1966.

Werbner, Richard P. *Ritual Passage, Sacred Journey: The Process and Organization of Religious Movement.* Washington D.C.: Smithsonian Institution Press, 1989.

Weston, Jessie L. *From Ritual to Romance.* Garden City, N.Y.: Doubleday, 1957.

Wheelock, Wade. "The Problem of Ritual Language: From Information to Situation." *Journal of the American Academy of Religion* 50, no. 1 (1982): 49–71.

Whitfield, Stephen J. *The Culture of the Cold War.* Baltimore: Johns Hopkins University Press, 1990.

Widengren, Geo. "An Introduction to Phenomenology of Religion." In Walter H. Capps, ed. *Ways of Understanding Religion.* New York: Macmillan, 1972, pp. 142–51.

Wigoder, Geoffrey, ed. *The Encyclopedia of Judaism.* New York: Macmillan, 1989.

Wijayaratna, Mohan. *Buddhist Monastic Life according to the Texts of the Theravada Tradition.* Trans. Claude Grangier and Steven Collins. Cambridge: Cambridge University Press, 1990.

Williams, James G. "The Innocent Victim: René Girard on Violence, Sacrifice, and the Sacred." *Religious Studies Review* 14, no. 4 (October 1988): 320–26.

Wilson, Bryan R. "An Analysis of Sect Development." In *Patterns of Sectarianism.* London: Heinemann, 1967, pp. 22–45.

Wilson, Edward O. *Sociobiology: The New Synthesis.* Cambridge: Harvard University Press, 1975.

Wilson, Edward O. *On Human Nature.* Cambridge: Harvard University Press, 1978.

Wilson, John F. *Public Religion in American Culture.* Philadelphia: Temple University Press, 1979.

Wilson, Samuel W. "Pilgrims' Paradox: Thanksgiving Is in the Eye of the Beholder." *Natural History* 100, no. 11 (Nov. 1991): 22–25.

Winters, Christopher, ed. *International Dictionary of Anthropologists.* New York: Garland, 1991.

Wolf, Arthur P. "Gods, Ghosts and Ancestors." In Arthur P. Wolf, ed. *Religion and Ritual in Chinese Society.* Stanford, Calif.: Stanford University Press, 1974, pp. 131–82.

Wolf, Eric R. "The Virgin of Guadalupe: A Mexican National Symbol." *Journal of American Folklore* 71 (1958): 34–39.

Wolf, Eric R. *Europe and the People without History.* Berkeley: University of California Press, 1982.

Wolf, Margery. "The Woman Who Didn't Become A Shaman." *American Ethnologist* 17 (August 1990): 419–430.

"Women Explore Drums as Means of Expression." *New York Times.* January 2, 1993. Section A, pp. 21, 27.

Wood, W. Raymond, and Margot Liberty, eds. *Anthropology on the Great Plains.* Lincoln: University of Nebraska Press, 1980.

Worsley, Peter. *The Trumpet Shall Sound: A Study of 'Cargo' Cults in Melanesia,* 2d ed. New York: Schocken, 1968.

Ya'ari, Ehud and Ina Friedman. "Curses in Verses." *Atlantic Monthly* 267, no. 2 (February 1991): 22–26.

Yocum, Glen. "Notes on an Easter Ramadan." *Journal of the American Academy of Religion* 60, no. 2 (Summer 1992): 201–30.

Zelizer, Barbie. *Covering the Body: The Kennedy Assassination, the Media, and the Shaping of Collective Memory.* Chicago: University of Chicago Press, 1991.

Zerubavel, Eviatar. *Hidden Rhythms: Schedules and Calendars in Social Life.* Berkeley: University of California Press, 1981.

Zerubavel, Eviatar. "Easter and Passover: On Calendars and Group Identity." *American Sociological Review* 47 (April 1982): 284–89.

Zhan, Kaidi. *The Strategies of Politeness in the Chinese Language.* Berkeley, Calif.: Institute of East Asian Studies, University of California, 1992.

Zhi, Exiang. "History and Tourism: Mausoleum of Emperor Yan." *China Today* 43, no. 1 (January 1994): 35–41.

Index